OECD Environmental
2050

This work is published on the responsibility of the Secretary-General of the OECD. The opinions expressed and arguments employed herein do not necessarily reflect the official views of the Organisation or of the governments of its member countries.

This document and any map included herein are without prejudice to the status of or sovereignty over any territory, to the delimitation of international frontiers and boundaries and to the name of any territory, city or area.

Please cite this publication as:
OECD (2012), *OECD Environmental Outlook to 2050*, OECD Publishing.
http://dx.doi.org/10.1787/9789264122246-en

ISBN 978-92-64-12216-1 (print)
ISBN 978-92-64-12224-6 (PDF)

OECD Environmental Outlook
ISSN 1818-7102 (print)
ISSN 1999-155X (online)

The statistical data for Israel are supplied by and under the responsibility of the relevant Israeli authorities. The use of such data by the OECD is without prejudice to the status of the Golan Heights, East Jerusalem and Israeli settlements in the West Bank under the terms of international law.

Photo credits: Cover © Subbotina Anna/Fotofolia.

Foreword

With a population of 7 billion, the world in 2012 faces highly complex economic and social challenges. While protecting the environment and conserving natural resources remain key policy priorities, many countries are also struggling with slow economic growth, stretched public finances and high levels of unemployment. Tackling these pressing challenges requires a deep cultural shift towards "greener" and more innovative sources of growth, and more sustainable consumption patterns.

The OECD Environmental Outlook to 2050 addresses the implications of demographic and economic trends over the next four decades using model based projections for four key areas of global concern: climate change, biodiversity, water and the health impacts of environmental pollution. The reality is that, if we fail to transform our policies and behaviour, the picture is rather grim.

The "Baseline" scenario projects that, unless the global energy mix changes, fossil fuels will supply about 85% of energy demand in 2050, implying a 50% increase in greenhouse gas (GHG) emissions and worsening urban air pollution. The impact on the quality of life of our citizens would be disastrous. The number of premature deaths from exposure to particulate pollutants could double from current levels to 3.6 million every year. Global water demand is projected to increase by 55% to 2050. Competition for water would intensify, resulting in up to 2.3 billion more people living in severely water-stressed river basins. By 2050, global terrestrial biodiversity is projected to decline by a further 10%.

The costs and consequences of inaction are colossal, both in economic and human terms. These projections highlight the urgent need for new thinking. Failing that, the erosion of our natural environmental capital will increase the risk of irreversible changes that could jeopardise two centuries of rising living standards. We are already witnessing the catastrophic collapse of some fisheries from overfishing, and severe water shortages damaging agriculture. However, these enormous environmental challenges cannot be addressed in isolation. They must be managed in the context of other global challenges, such as food and energy security, and poverty alleviation.

There are important dividends from integrating environmental objectives into economic and sectoral policies, such as energy, agriculture and transport. Well designed policies to tackle one environmental problem could also help alleviate others, and contribute to growth and development. Tackling local air pollution, for example, can cut GHG emissions while reducing the economic burden of chronic and costly health problems. Climate policies also help protect biodiversity, namely by reducing emissions from deforestation.

This Outlook draws on a policy framework established by the OECD's Green Growth Strategy, which countries can tailor to their level of development, their particular resource endowments and environmental pressures. But there are also several common approaches, like making pollution more costly than greener alternatives (with environmental taxes and emissions trading schemes); valuing and pricing the natural assets and ecosystem services (through water pricing, payments for ecosystem services, natural park entrance charges); removing environmentally harmful subsidies (to *fossil fuels, electricity for pumping water for irrigation); and encouraging green innovation (by making polluting production and consumption modes more expensive, public support for basic R&D).*

To make reform happen, governments will have to study the cost effectiveness of their policies in great depth. Public acceptance will depend on hard evidence that policies will successfully tackle environmental challenges, that they are affordable, and that they can deliver jobs and enable poverty alleviation.

Taken together, the OECD Environmental Outlook to 2050 and the Green Growth Strategy provide a comprehensive and practical way forward. Promoting efficient green policies will be a major contribution from the OECD to the Rio + 20 Conference, in our mission of achieving better policies for better lives.

Angel Gurría
Secretary-General

Acknowledgements

The *OECD Environmental Outlook to 2050* was prepared by a joint team from the OECD Environment Directorate and the PBL Netherlands Environmental Assessment Agency (PBL). The project was managed by Kumi Kitamori and Ton Manders (PBL), under the supervision of Simon Upton (Director), Helen Mountford (Deputy Director) and Rob Visser (former Deputy Director).

The OECD Environment Policy Committee (EPOC) was responsible for the oversight of the development of the report. In addition, the following OECD bodies reviewed and provided comments on relevant chapters of this *Outlook*: Working Party on Climate, Investment and Development (WPCID); Working Party on Biodiversity, Water and Ecosystems (WPBWE); Working Party on Integrating Environmental and Economic Policies (WPIEEP); Working Party on Environmental Information (WPEI); Joint Meeting of the Chemicals Committee and the Working Party on Chemicals, Pesticides and Biotechnology; Joint Working Party on Agriculture and Environment (JWPAE); and Committee on Fisheries (COFI).

Representatives from non-OECD countries – in particular Brazil, China, Colombia, India, Indonesia and South Africa – provided comments and input through an Expert Meeting on the Preparation of the Next *Environmental Outlook* (November 2010), and a Global Forum on Environment for the Review of the Draft *Environmental Outlook* Report (October 2011). Stakeholder representatives provided input to draft chapters, in particular environmental NGOs (co-ordinated through the European Environmental Bureau), business (co-ordinated through the Business and Industry Advisory Committee to the OECD), and trade unions (co-ordinated through the Trade Union Advisory Committee to the OECD).

The drafters of the *OECD Environmental Outlook to 2050* were:

Executive Summary	Kumi Kitamori
Chapter 1. Introduction	Kumi Kitamori, Ton Manders (PBL), Rob Dellink
Chapter 2. Socio-economic Developments	Rob Dellink, Ton Manders (PBL), Jean Chateau, Bertrand Magné, Detlef van Vuuren (PBL), Anne Gerdien Prins (PBL)
Chapter 3. Climate Change	Virginie Marchal, Rob Dellink, Detlef van Vuuren (PBL), Christa Clapp, Jean Chateau, Bertrand Magné, Elisa Lanzi, Jasper van Vliet (PBL)
Chapter 4. Biodiversity	Katia Karousakis, Mark van Oorschot (PBL), Edward Perry, Michel Jeuken (PBL), Michel Bakkenes (PBL), with contribution from Hans Meijl and Andrzej Tabeau (LEI)
Chapter 5. Water	Xavier Leflaive, Maria Witmer (PBL), Roberto Martin-Hurtado, Marloes Bakker (PBL), Tom Kram (PBL), Lex Bouwman (PBL), Hans Visser (PBL), Arno Bouwman (PBL), Henk Hilderink (PBL), Kayoung Kim
Chapter 6. Health and Environment	Richard Sigman, Henk Hilderink (PBL), Nathalie Delrue, Nils-Axel Braathen, Xavier Leflaive
Annex on Modelling Framework	Rob Dellink, Tom Kram (PBL), Jean Chateau

The socio-economic modelling for the *OECD Environmental Outlook to 2050* was undertaken by the OECD team working on the ENV-Linkages model, and the environmental modelling was undertaken by PBL using its IMAGE suite of models. Modelling work on climate change was done with both ENV-Linkages and IMAGE. PBL used IMAGE and related environmental models, including through collaboration with LEI at Wageningen University and Research Centre on agriculture-economy modelling and the UNEP World Conservation Monitoring Centre (UNEP-WCMC).

The modelling teams were:

ENV-Linkages (OECD)	IMAGE suite of models (PBL)	
Rob Dellink	*Core team:*	*Specific contributions:*
Jean Chateau	Tom Kram	Hester Biemans
Bertrand Magné	Anne Gerdien Prins	Corjan Brink
Cuauhtemoc Rebolledo-Gómez	Elke Stehfest	Frank De Leeuw (RIVM)
	Mark van Oorschot	Kathleen Neumann
	Henk Hilderink	Sebastiaan Deetman
	Detlef van Vuuren	Michel den Elzen
	Jasper van Vliet	Hans Eerens
	Rineke Oostenrijk	Jan Janse
		Angelica Mendoza Beltran
		Andrzej Tabeau (LEI)
		Hans van Meijl (LEI)

Statistical and research assistance was provided by Cuauhtemoc Rebolledo-Gómez, Rineke Oostenrijk (PBL) and Carla Bertuzzi. Pascaline Deplagne, Sarah Michelson, Elisabeth Huggard and Patricia Nilsson provided administrative and technical support to the *Outlook* project and the report preparation. Fiona Hall provided editorial services for the report. Support for the publication process was provided by Janine Treves, Stephanie Simonin-Edwards and the OECD Publishing Division. The *Outlook* team is grateful for useful comments and inputs provided, in particular, by Helen Mountford and Simon Upton, as well as Shardul Agrawala, Dale Andrew, Gérard Bonnis, Peter Börkey, Nils-Axel Braathen, Dave Brooke (Building Research Establishment Ltd), Andrea Cattaneo, Jan Corfee-Morlot, Anthony Cox, Guus de Hollander (PBL), Dimitris Diakosavvas, Jane Ellis, Christina Hood (IEA), Alistair Hunt (University of Bath), Hsin Huang, Nick Johnstone, Wilfrid Legg, Michael Mullan, Kevin Parris, Annette Prüss-Ustün (WHO), Ysé Serret, Kevin Swift (American Chemistry Council), Marie-Christine Tremblay, Frank van Tongeren, Dian Turnheim and Žiga Zarnic.

A number of OECD countries provided financial or in-kind contributions to support the modelling and *Outlook* work, including: Japan, Korea, the Netherlands and Norway.

Table of Contents

List of tables

11

This book has...

StatLinks

**A service that delivers Excel® files
from the printed page!**

Look for the *StatLinks* at the bottom right-hand corner of the tables or graphs in this book.
To download the matching Excel® spreadsheet, just type the link into your Internet browser,
starting with the *http://dx.doi.org* prefix.
If you're reading the PDF e-book edition, and your PC is connected to the Internet, simply
click on the link. You'll find *StatLinks* appearing in more OECD books.

Acronyms and Abbreviations

ADI	Acceptable daily intake
BECCS	Biomass energy with carbon capture and storage
BRIICS	Brazil, Russia, India, Indonesia, China and South Africa
CBD	Convention on Biological Diversity
CCS	Carbon capture and storage
CDM	Clean Development Mechanism
CO	Carbon monoxide
CO$_2$	Carbon dioxide
COP	Conference of the Parties
COPD	Chronic obstructive pulmonary disease
DALYs	Disability adjusted life-years
DCPP	Disease Control Priorities Project
ED	Endocrine disrupter
EEA	European Environment Agency
EFTA	European Free Trade Area
EIA	Environmental impact assessment
EPA	Environmental Protection Agency
ESD	Emission scenario document
ETS	Emissions trading scheme
FAO	Food and Agriculture Organization
FSC	Forest Stewardship Council
GDP	Gross domestic product
GEF	Global Environmental Facility
GHG	Greenhouse gas
GISMO	Global Integrated Sustainability Model
Gt	Gigatonnes
GUAM	Global Urban Air quality Model
HC	Hydrocarbon
IEA	International Energy Agency
IFIs	International financial institutions
IMAGE	Integrated Model to Assess the Global Environment
IPBES	Inter-governmental Science-Policy Platform on Biodiversity and Ecosystem Services
IPCC	Intergovernmental Panel on Climate Change
ITQ	Individual tradeable quotas
IUCN	International Union for the Conservation of Nature
JMP	Joint monitoring programme
LEDS	Low-emission development strategies

LPG	Liquid petroleum gas
LPI	Living Planet Index
LULUCF	Land use, land-use change and forestry
MAD	Mutual acceptance of data
MDG	Millennium Development Goal
MA	Millennium Ecosystem Assessment
MNs	Manufactured nanomaterials
MPA	Marine Protected Area
MSA	Mean species abundance
NBSAP	National biodiversity strategies and action plans
NEA	National ecosystem assessment
NMVOC	Non-methane volatile organic compounds
NO_x	Nitrogen oxides
ODA	Official development assistance
OECD	Organisation for Economic Co-operation and Development
PA	Protected area
PBL	PBL Netherlands Environmental Assessment Agency
PCB	Polychlorinated biphenyl
PES	Payment for ecosystem services
PFC	Perfluorocarbons
PM	Particulate matter
PPM	Parts per million
PPP	Public private partnerships
PRTRs	Pollutant release and transfer registers
PSE	Producer support estimate
(Q)SAR	(Quantitative) structure-activity relationships
R&D	Research and development
RD&D	Research, development and demonstration
REACH	Registration, Evaluation, Authorisation and Restriction of Chemicals
REDD	Reduced Emissions from Deforestation and Degradation
RoW	Rest of the world
RSPO	Roundtable on Sustainable Palm Oil
SAICM	Strategic Approach to International Chemicals Management
SEA	Strategic environmental assessments
SEEA	System of integrated environmental and economic accounting
SNA	System of national accounts
SO_x	Sulphur oxides
TNC	The Nature Conservancy
TOE	Tons of oil equivalent
TSCA	Toxic Substance Control Act
UN	United Nations
UNEP	United Nations Environment Programme
UNECE	United Nations Economic Commission for Europe
UNFCCC	United Nations Framework Convention on Climate Change
USD	United States dollars
VA	Voluntary agreement
VOCs	Volatile organic compounds

VSL	Value of statistical life
WHO	World Health Organization
WIS	Water information systems
WSS	Water supply and sanitation
WSSD	World Summit on Sustainable Development
YLL	Years of life lost

Executive Summary

1. Introduction

Over the last four decades, human endeavour has unleashed unprecedented economic growth in the pursuit of higher living standards. While the world's population has increased by over 3 billion people since 1970, the size of the world economy has more than tripled. While this growth has pulled millions out of poverty, it has been unevenly distributed and incurred significant cost to the environment. Natural assets have been and continue to be depleted, with the services they deliver already compromised by environmental pollution. Providing for a further 2 billion people by 2050 and improving the living standards for all will challenge our ability to manage and restore those natural assets on which all life depends. Failure to do so will have serious consequences, especially for the poor, and ultimately undermine the growth and human development of future generations.

OECD countries have addressed a number of environmental challenges by putting in place policies to protect human health and ecosystems from pollution, use resources more efficiently, and prevent further environmental degradation. However, the sheer scale of economic and population growth has overwhelmed the pace of progress in curbing environmental pressures. **Progress on an incremental, piecemeal, business-as-usual basis in the coming decades will not be enough.**

The *OECD Environmental Outlook to 2050* asks "What could the next four decades bring?" Based on joint modelling by the OECD and the PBL Netherlands Environmental Assessment Agency, it looks forward to the year 2050 to ascertain what demographic and economic trends might mean for the environment if humanity does not introduce more ambitious policies to manage natural assets with greater care. It then examines some of the policies that could change that picture for the better. Can the planet's resource base support ever-increasing demands for energy, food, water and other natural resources, and at the same time absorb our waste streams? Or will the growth process undermine itself? How can we balance environmental, economic and social objectives? How can we care for the environment and improve livelihoods and living conditions for the poor?

This *Outlook* focuses on four areas: climate change, biodiversity, water and the health impacts of pollution. These four key environmental challenges were identified by the previous *Environmental Outlook to 2030* as "Red light" issues requiring urgent attention (see Chapter 1). It concludes that the **prospects are more alarming than the situation described in the previous edition**, and that **urgent – and holistic – action is needed now to avoid the significant costs and consequences of inaction.** Policy makers must take decisions despite uncertainties. The *Outlook* presents achievable solutions, highlighting the linkages between different environmental issues and some of the challenges and trade-offs in the face of competing demands.

2. What could the environment look like in 2050?

By 2050, the Earth's population is expected to increase from 7 billion to over 9 billion people. Coupled with expected higher living standards across the world, global GDP is projected to almost quadruple despite the recent recession (see Chapter 2). In the coming decades, average GDP growth rates are projected to slow gradually in China and India. While

Without new policies, progress in reducing environmental pressures will continue to be overwhelmed by the sheer scale of growth.

Africa will remain the poorest continent, it is projected to see the world's highest economic growth rate between 2030 and 2050. The populations of OECD countries are expected to live longer, with over a quarter of their people projected to be over 65 years of age compared to about 15% today. China and India are also likely to see significant population ageing, with China's workforce actually shrinking by 2050. In contrast, more youthful populations in other parts of the world, especially Africa, are expected to grow rapidly. These demographic shifts and higher living standards imply evolving lifestyles, consumption patterns and dietary preferences, all of which will have significant consequences for the environment and the resources and services it provides. Cities are likely to absorb the total world population growth between 2010 and 2050. By 2050, nearly 70% of the world population is projected to be living in urban areas. This will magnify challenges such as air pollution, transport congestion, and the management of waste and water in slums, with serious consequences for human health.

Without new policy action, a world economy four times larger than today is projected to use about 80% more energy in 2050 (see Chapter 2). Furthermore, the energy mix at the global level is not projected to differ significantly from that of today. The share of fossil energy would remain at about 85%, while renewables including biofuels would make up just above 10%, with the balance being nuclear. The emerging economies of Brazil, Russia, India, Indonesia, China and South Africa (referred to here as the "BRIICS") are projected to become major energy users, increasing their reliance on fossil fuels. To feed a growing population with changing dietary preferences, agricultural land is projected to expand globally in the next decade to match the increase in food demand, but at a diminishing rate. This leads to a substantial increase in competition for scarce land. Globally, the area of agricultural land is expected to peak before 2030 and decline thereafter as population growth slows down and yield improvements continue in the OECD and the BRIICS. However, in the rest of the world (RoW), a further expansion of agricultural land area is projected. Deforestation rates are already declining – a trend that is projected to continue. In China, for example, reduced agricultural land is projected to lead to an increase in forest area, not least to meet growing global demands for wood and other forest products.

The combination of no new policies and continuing socio-economic trends constitutes this study's "*Baseline*" scenario (see Chapters 1 and 2). Under the *Baseline*, pressures on the environment from population growth and rising living standards will outpace progress in pollution abatement and resource efficiency. **As a result, continued degradation and erosion of natural environmental capital are expected to 2050 and beyond, with the risk of irreversible changes that could endanger two centuries of rising living standards.** The *Outlook Baseline* scenario suggests that the costs and consequences of inaction are significant, both in economic and human terms.

Table 0.1. **Key environmental challenges:
Trends and projections without new policies**

	Red light	Yellow light	Green light
Climate change	• Growing GHG emissions (especially energy-related CO_2); growing atmospheric concentrations. • Increasing evidence of a changing climate and its effects. • Copenhagen/Cancún pledges falling short of a cost-efficient 2 °C pathway.	• Declining GHG emissions per unit of GDP (relative decoupling) in OECD and BRIICS. • Declining CO_2 emissions from land use change (mainly deforestation) in OECD and BRIICS. • Adaptation strategies being developed in many countries but not yet widely implemented.	
Biodiversity	• Continued loss of biodiversity from growing pressures (*e.g.* land use change and climate change). • Steady decrease in primary (virgin) forest area. • Over-exploitation or depletion of fish stocks. • Invasion by alien species.	• Protected area expansion, but under-representation of certain biomes and marine protected areas. • Forest area expanding mainly due to afforestation (*e.g.* plantations); deforestation rates slowing but still high.	• Progress by the Convention on Biological Diversity in 2010 on the Strategic Plan for Biodiversity 2011-2020 and the Nagoya Protocol.
Water	• Increase in the number of people living in river basins under severe water stress. • Increase in groundwater pollution and depletion. • Deterioration of surface water quality in non-OECD countries; increase in nutrient loading globally and risk of eutrophication. • Urban dwellers increasing faster than people with connection to water services; large remaining number of people without access to safe water in both rural and urban areas; MDG on sanitation not achieved. • Increase in volume of wastewater returned to the environment untreated.	• Increase in water demand and competition among users, and need to reallocate water among users. • Increase in number of people at risk from floods.	• Decrease in point-source water pollution in OECD countries (from industry, municipalities). • MDG on access to an improved water source likely to be met in BRIICS.
Health and Environment	• Substantial increase in SO_2 and NO_x emissions in key emerging economies. • Increase in premature deaths linked to urban air pollution (particulates and ground-level ozone). • High burden of disease from exposure to hazardous chemicals, particularly in non-OECD countries.	• Decrease in child mortality from lack of access to safe water and improved sanitation. • Better, but still inadequate, information on exposure to and health impacts of hazardous chemicals in the environment, in products and from combined exposures. • Many OECD governments have changed, or are in the process of changing, legislation to expand regulatory coverage of chemicals, but enforcement still incomplete. • Decrease in premature deaths due to indoor air pollution from traditional solid fuels, but potential trade-offs if climate mitigation policies increase energy prices. • Decrease in premature mortality from malaria, despite climate change.	• Decrease in emissions of SO_2, NO_x and black carbon in OECD countries.

Notes: All trends are global, unless otherwise specified.
Green light = environmental issues which are being well managed, or for which there have been significant improvements in management in recent years but for which countries should remain vigilant.
Yellow light = environmental issues which remain a challenge but for which management is improving, or for which current state is uncertain, or which have been well managed in the past but are less so now.
Red light = environmental issues which are not well managed, are in a bad or worsening state, and which require urgent attention.

The key environmental challenges identified in this *Outlook* for the coming decades are summarised using the "traffic light" system (Table 0.1). Despite some pockets of improvements, the overall outlook for the four themes is more alarming than in the previous edition of the *Outlook*. For example, the *Outlook* does not identify any "Green light" aspects for climate change.

Without more ambitious policies, by 2050:

- **More disruptive climate change is likely to be locked in**, with global greenhouse gas (GHG) emissions projected to increase by 50%, primarily due to a 70% growth in CO_2 emissions from energy use (Figure 0.1). While the recent economic crisis did slow emission growth somewhat, the economic recovery has already reversed this temporary trend, and at current rates, the atmospheric concentration of GHGs could reach almost 685 parts per million (ppm) by 2050 (see Chapter 3). As a result, the global average temperature increase is projected to be 3 °C to 6 °C higher by the end of the century, exceeding the internationally agreed goal of limiting it to 2 °C above pre-industrial levels.

There is a notable gap between the 2 °C goal and the GHG emission reduction pledges by developed and developing countries in the Cancún Agreements. Even if the pledges are fully implemented, they will still not be enough to prevent the global average temperature from exceeding the 2 °C threshold unless very rapid and costly emission reductions are realised after 2020. A temperature increase of more than 2 °C would alter precipitation patterns; increase glacier and permafrost melt; drive sea-level rise; worsen the intensity and frequency of extreme weather events such as heat waves, floods and hurricanes; and become the greatest driver of biodiversity loss. Both the pace of change and the other environmental pressures identified in this report will hamper people's and ecosystem's abilities to adapt. The cost of inaction on climate change could equate to a permanent loss of over 14% in average world consumption per capita.

- **Biodiversity loss is projected to continue**, especially in Asia, Europe and Southern Africa. Globally, terrestrial biodiversity (measured as mean species abundance – or MSA – an indicator of the intactness of a natural ecosystem) is projected to decrease a further 10% by 2050 (see Chapter 4). Primary forests, which are rich in biodiversity, are projected to shrink in area by 13%, despite the increase in total forested area during this period. The main pressures driving biodiversity loss include land-use change and management (agriculture), the expansion of commercial forestry, infrastructure development, human encroachment and fragmentation of natural habitats, as well as pollution and climate change (Figure 0.2). Climate change is projected to become the fastest growing driver of biodiversity loss to 2050, followed by commercial forestry and bioenergy croplands.

About one-third of global freshwater biodiversity has already been lost, and further loss is projected to 2050, especially in Africa, Latin America and parts of Asia. Continued disturbances to ecosystems could pass a tipping point beyond which damage is irreversible. The current trend of declining biodiversity presents a threat to human welfare, and will be very costly. The aggregate loss of biodiversity and ecosystem service benefits associated with the global loss of forests, for example, is estimated to be between USD 2 and 5 trillion per year. Biodiversity loss will have severe implications for the rural poor and indigenous communities, whose livelihoods are often directly dependent on biodiversity and ecosystems, and the services these provide.

Figure 0.1. **GHG emissions by region: *Baseline*, 2010-2050**

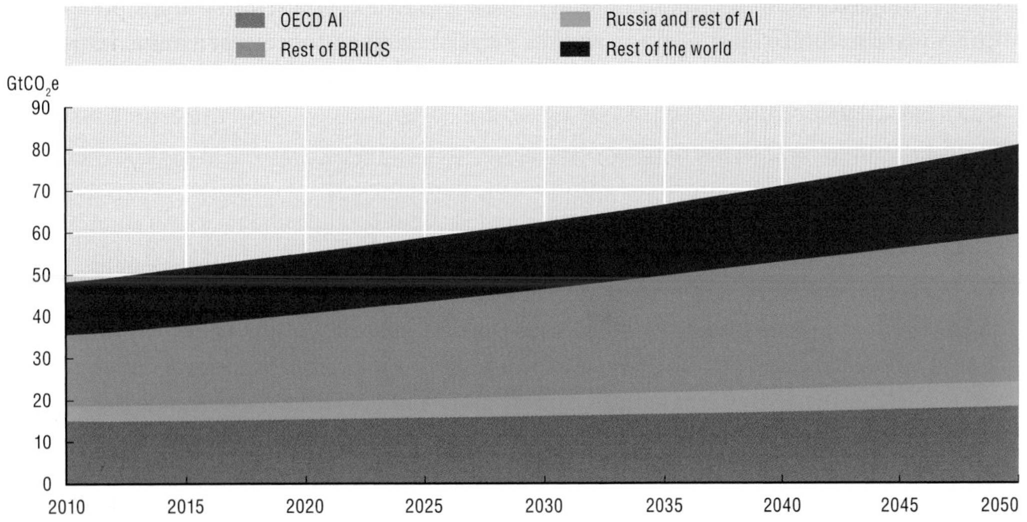

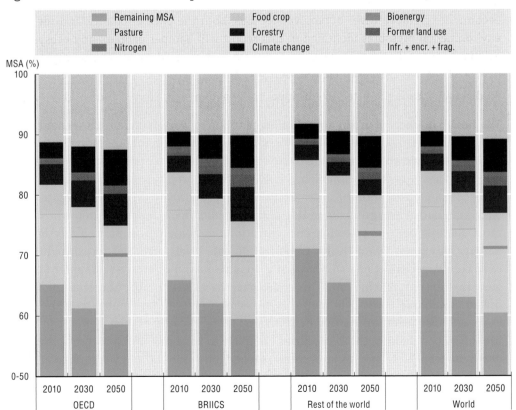

Note: "OECD AI" stands for the group of OECD countries that are also part of Annex I of the Kyoto Protocol.
GtCO$_2$e = Giga tonnes of CO$_2$ equivalent

Source: OECD Environmental Outlook Baseline; output from ENV-Linkages.

StatLink http://dx.doi.org/10.1787/888932570468

Figure 0.2. **Effects of different pressures on terrestrial MSA: *Baseline*, 2010 to 2050**

Note: MSA of 100% is equivalent to the undisturbed state; See Chapter 4, Table 4.1 for further explanations.

Source: OECD Environmental Outlook Baseline, output from IMAGE.

StatLink http://dx.doi.org/10.1787/888932570943

- **Freshwater availability will be further strained in many regions**, with 2.3 billion more people than today projected to be living in river basins experiencing severe water stress. This means in total over 40% of the world's population in water-stressed areas, especially in North and South Africa, and South and Central Asia (see Chapter 5). Overall water demand is projected to increase by some 55%, due to growing demand from manufacturing (+400%), thermal electricity generation (+140%) and domestic use (+130%) (Figure 0.3). In the face of these competing demands, there will be little scope for increasing water for irrigation under the *Baseline*. The *Baseline* shows some reduction in water for irrigation. This reflects no increase in irrigated land and significant improvements in efficiency. If these do not eventuate, competition for water will be even more acute. The combined effects of these pressures could imply water shortages that would hinder the growth of many economic activities. Environmental flows will be contested, putting ecosystems at risks, and groundwater depletion may become the greatest threat to agriculture and urban water supplies in several regions in the coming decades.

  Nutrient pollution from point sources (urban wastewater) and "diffuse sources" (mainly from agriculture) is projected to worsen in most regions, intensifying eutrophication and damaging aquatic biodiversity. Notwithstanding this, the number of people with access to an improved water source is expected to increase, essentially in the BRIICS. However, globally more than 240 million people (mostly rural residents) are expected to be without such access by 2050. Sub-Saharan Africa is unlikely to meet the Millennium Development Goal (MDG) of halving by 2015 the 1990 level of the population without access to an improved water source. Globally, more city dwellers did not have access to an improved water source in 2008 than in 1990, as urbanisation outpaced connections to water infrastructure. And access to an *improved* water source does not necessarily mean access to *safe* water fit for human consumption. It is expected that the MDG for sanitation will not be met by 2015, and by 2050 1.4 billion people are projected to be still without access to basic sanitation, mostly in developing countries.

- **The health impacts of urban air pollution** continue to worsen under this scenario, with air pollution set to become the top environmental cause of premature mortality globally (Figure 0.4). Meanwhile, premature deaths caused by indoor air pollution from the use of dirty fuels are projected to diminish, as well as child mortality from a lack of clean water and poor sanitation, with the latter decrease due primarily to an overall increase in the basic standard of living and the ageing of the population (*i.e.* fewer children who are the most susceptible). Air pollution concentrations in some cities, particularly in Asia, already far exceed World Health Organization safe levels, with deadly consequences: only very large reductions will have any positive health effects (see Chapter 6). With growing transport and industrial air emissions, the global number of premature deaths linked to airborne particulate matter is projected to more than double to 3.6 million a year, with most deaths occurring in China and India. Because of their ageing and highly urbanised populations, OECD countries are likely to have one of the highest premature death rates linked to ground-level ozone, second only to India, and worse than all other countries.

- **The burden of disease related to exposure to hazardous chemicals** is significant worldwide and falls more heavily in non-OECD countries where good chemical safety measures have not yet been put in place. Yet, non-OECD countries are projected to account for an increasing share of the world chemicals production, with the BRIICS alone accounting for a greater share of global sales than the OECD by 2050 under the *Baseline*.

Figure 0.3. **Global water demand:** *Baseline, 2000 and 2050*

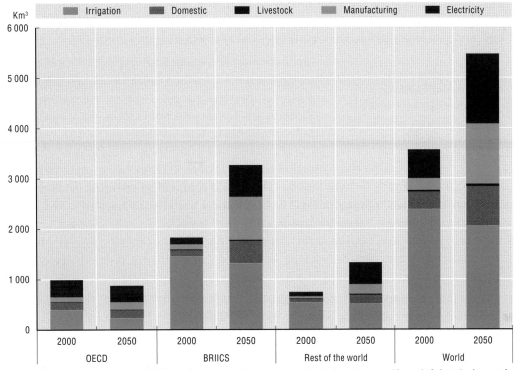

Note: This graph only measures "blue water" demand (see Box 5.1) and does not consider rainfed agriculture. The country groupings BRIICS and RoW are explained in Table 1.3 in Chapter 1.

Source: OECD Environmental Outlook Baseline; output from IMAGE.

StatLink ⬛⬛ http://dx.doi.org/10.1787/888932571171

Figure 0.4. **Global premature deaths from selected environmental risks:**
Baseline, 2010 to 2050

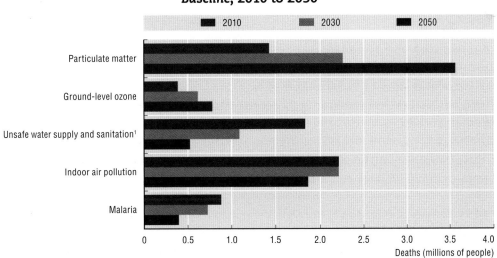

1. Child mortality only.

Source: OECD Environmental Outlook Baseline; output from IMAGE.

StatLink ⬛⬛ http://dx.doi.org/10.1787/888932571855

While governments in OECD countries are making progress collecting and assessing information on human exposure to chemicals throughout their lifecycle, knowledge of the health impacts of chemicals in products and in the environment – and in particular effects from combined exposure to mixtures of chemicals – is still limited.

Delay in tackling these environmental challenges risks potentially irreversible – and in some cases very costly or even catastrophic – changes in the future.

The *Environmental Outlook Baseline* projections highlight the urgent need for action today to change the course of our future development. Delay in alleviating these environmental pressures will impose significant costs, undermine growth and development and run the risk of irreversible and potentially catastrophic changes further into the future. Change in natural systems is not linear. **There is compelling scientific evidence that natural systems have "tipping points" or biophysical boundaries beyond which rapid and damaging change becomes irreversible** (*e.g.* for species loss, climate change, groundwater depletion, land and soil degradation). However, these tipping points or thresholds are in many cases not yet fully understood, nor are the environmental, social and economic consequences of crossing them.

The scientific community is expanding the knowledge base needed for evidence-based policy making, but in the meantime policy makers must weigh up the costs of action and inaction in the face of significant uncertainty. Nevertheless, the costs and consequences of ignoring environmental challenges are significant, even if we lack precise values. It is sensible to take precautions, as continuing to deplete natural assets and endangering the services they provide can have far-reaching economic and social consequences, especially in developing countries and for the rural poor. A key policy challenge is to

> **What if...**
>
> ... NO_x, SO_2 and black carbon emissions were cut by up to 25% by 2050? This *Air Pollution Reduction scenario* would result in an added benefit of a 5% reduction in global CO_2 emissions, but would not make much difference in preventing the expected doubling of premature deaths. Given that the pollution levels in many Asian cities in the *Baseline* scenario are far above safe levels, pollution abatement goals would have to be even more ambitious to yield positive health impacts.

strike a balance between giving clear policy signals to resource users and consumers, while leaving room for manoeuvre and adaptation given the uncertainties that surround the resilience of ecosystems and socio-economic consequences of destabilising them.

The *Outlook* highlights the linkages between the different environmental issues. For example, climate change can affect hydrological cycles, and exacerbate pressures on biodiversity and human health. Biodiversity and ecosystem services are intimately linked to water, climate and human health: marshlands purify water, mangroves protect against coastal flooding, forests contribute to climate regulation and genetic diversity provides for pharmaceutical discoveries. These cross-cutting environmental functions must be carefully considered as they have wider economic and social implications, and point to the need to improve resource efficiency and land use.

Acting now is not only environmentally rational, it is also economically rational. For example, the *Outlook* suggests that if countries act now, there is still a chance – although a receding one – of global GHG emissions peaking before 2020 and limiting the world's average temperature increase to 2 °C (see box below). To do so would make the costs of adaptation and mitigation much more affordable. But unless more ambitious decisions are taken soon, the window of opportunity will close. Investment decisions that are being made today will lock in infrastructure for years or decades to come. The environmental consequences of emissions-intensive investments today will be long-lasting. Meanwhile, other environmental investments can offer positive returns. The *Outlook* suggests, for example, that investing in further air pollution reductions in BRIICS countries could yield benefits outweighing the costs by as much as 10 to 1 (see Chapter 6). Investing in safe water and sanitation in developing countries can yield benefit-to-cost ratios as high as 7 to 1 (Chapter 5).

What if...

... we start today to limit GHG concentrations to 450 ppm using carbon pricing to meet the 2 °C goal? The *450 Core* scenario suggests the cost would be to slow economic growth by 0.2 percentage points per year on average, costing roughly 5.5% of global GDP in 2050. This pales alongside the potential cost of inaction which could be as high as 14% of average world consumption per capita according to some estimates. The *Outlook's* estimate of cost of climate action may be overestimated, as it does not reflect the benefits of climate mitigation.

Figure 0.5. **450 Core scenario: Global emissions and cost of mitigation**

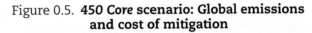

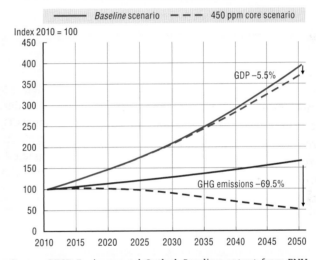

Source: OECD *Environmental Outlook Baseline*; output from ENV-Linkages.

StatLink ⟶ http://dx.doi.org/10.1787/888932570069

---

3. What policies can change this outlook?

Well-designed policies can reverse the trends projected in the *Outlook Baseline* scenario, safeguarding long-term economic growth and the well-being of future generations. Given the complexity of the environmental challenges and the inter-linkages among them, a wide array of policy instruments are needed, often in combination, to mainstream environmental considerations into economic decisions. Policy interventions also need to be able to support sustainable growth and development. The OECD's *Green Growth Strategy* provides a coherent framework for assembling the best policy mix. Drawing on this, the *Outlook* suggests the following policy priorities to tackle climate change, biodiversity loss, water challenges and the health impacts from pollution.

Make pollution an expensive business

Economic instruments such as environmental taxes and emissions trading schemes put a price on pollution and make activities that damage the environment more costly than greener alternatives (see for example, Chapter 3, Section 3). This can help to green global supply and value chains, through innovation in business practices and greener technologies. Moreover, market-based instruments can generate additional fiscal revenues to ease tight government budgets. A number of countries have embarked on green tax reforms, often using the revenues raised to reduce taxes on labour income which could help boost employment and encourage green growth.

What if...

... the emission reduction pledges that industrialised countries indicated in the Cancún Agreements were to be implemented through carbon taxes or cap-and-trade schemes with fully auctioned permits? The fiscal revenues could amount to over 0.6% of their GDP in 2020, i.e. more than USD 250 billion.

Ensure prices better reflect the true value of natural assets and ecosystem services

Valuing and properly pricing resources and the ecosystem services they provide lead to more sustainable use of these resources. For example, pricing is an effective way of allocating water, particularly where it is scarce, and to encourage more sustainable consumption. Water tariffs can also generate revenues that can help to cover the costs of water infrastructure, essential to ensuring continued and expanded access to water supply and sanitation services (see Chapter 5, Section 3). Economic instruments also show promise with respect to biodiversity and other ecosystem services. Estimating the monetary value of the services provided by ecosystems and biodiversity can make their benefits more visible, and can lead to better, more cost-effective decisions (see Chapter 4, Section 1). Creating markets to capture these values is also needed, for example through tradable water rights, payments for ecosystem services for forests and watersheds or through the use of eco-labelling certification schemes. The Convention on Biological Diversity and the OECD are together seeking to increase the use of economic instruments for biodiversity conservation and sustainable use.

Devise proactive and effective regulations and standards

Regulatory approaches are a cornerstone of environmental policy and can be used in combination with economic instruments, in particular when markets cannot deliver meaningful price signals. For example, energy efficiency opportunities may not be fully tapped through carbon pricing alone (Chapter 3, Section 3). Regulations will also be needed where strict control is warranted to safeguard human health or environmental integrity, for example through quantitative standards or limits (see for example Chapter 6, Sections 2 and 4). Examples of regulatory approaches include standards (e.g. for ambient air quality, effluent discharges, and vehicle emissions standards, plus building codes for energy efficiency); outright bans (e.g. on illegal logging and trading of endangered species, development in natural protected areas, lead in gasoline and certain toxic pesticides); and the use of planning tools (such as land use planning and environmental impact assessments).

Remove environmentally harmful subsidies

Many environmentally harmful activities are subsidised by taxpayers. Many countries, for instance, still subsidise fossil fuel production or consumption to some degree (see Chapter 3, section 3). This essentially encourages carbon emissions, undermining efforts to tackle climate change, and locking in yesterday's energy technologies. Phasing out or reforming these subsidies can reduce energy-related GHG emissions, provide incentives for increased energy efficiency and make renewable energy more competitive. This can

Support to fossil fuel production and use amounted to between USD 45-75 billion per annum in recent years in OECD countries. Developing and emerging economies provided over USD 400 billion in fossil fuel consumer subsidies in 2010.

also provide new sources of public finance to support climate action. Similarly, underpriced or subsidised water as well as some poorly-designed agricultural and fisheries subsidises have the potential to further stress land, water and ecosystems (see Chapter 4, Section 4). Removing or reforming such subsidies can send vital signals about the true cost of pollution and the value of natural assets. It can also save taxpayers or consumers money. Addressing potential adverse impacts of subsidies reform is an essential element of any move to price pollution and resources properly.

Encourage innovation

We need to significantly speed up the development and diffusion of technological improvements that will curb growing pressures on the environment, and keep the future cost of doing so manageable. For example, technologies such as bioenergy combined with carbon capture and storage (BECCS) have the potential to lower the future cost of mitigating GHG emissions (see Chapter 3, Section 4). Innovation in new business models also has a major role to play in providing solutions to key environmental challenges and promoting green growth. For instance, improved farm management techniques can help maximise water productivity or the "crop per drop" that farmers produce, reduce pollution and help protect biodiversity. The promotion of green or sustainable chemistry can lead to the design, manufacture and use of more environmentally friendly chemicals throughout their lifecycle (see Chapter 6, Section 4). Pricing and market-based instruments can provide incentives to encourage innovation in pollution-reducing and resource-saving technologies. But other measures are also needed, such as specific R&D support policies, standards, regulations and voluntary programmes to encourage innovation, as well as effective mechanisms for green technology transfer to developing countries. But innovation is not only about technologies. Policy innovation by governments, business and social organisations is also needed to spread greener production and consumption.

The economy will not decarbonise itself. Without new, more effective policies, the mix of energy technologies will not change significantly by 2050, with the share of fossil fuel-based energy remaining at 85%.

Get the policy mix right

Given the range of pressures and the complexity of interaction, a carefully designed mix of policy instruments will be needed to tackle many of the key environmental challenges. Government support for "green" behaviour such as ecological farming techniques could be part of a policy mix, but such green subsidies should be periodically reviewed and eventually phased out once the green practices have become well accepted. A policy mix can include information tools, such as eco-labelling, to raise consumer awareness and promote sustainable consumption; basic research and development; and voluntary initiatives by business to experiment with new and innovative approaches. At the same time, it will be important to ensure the policy instruments used in the mix are complementary, and do not overlap or conflict (see below). The full costs and benefits of policy mixes should be routinely assessed for environmental effectiveness, social equity and cost-efficiency. There is no "one-size-fits-all" prescription for a green growth policy mix, which needs to be adapted to specific national circumstances.

4. Making reform happen and mainstreaming green growth

Encourage policy coherence across sectors

Integrating environmental objectives in economic and sectoral policies (*e.g.* energy, agriculture, transport) is vital, as these policies have greater impacts than environmental policies alone. This lies at the heart of a greener growth path. **Environmental challenges cannot be addressed in isolation but should be assessed in the context of other global challenges such as food and energy security and poverty alleviation.** The *Environmental Outlook* highlights, for example, the increasing need for coherence among water, agriculture, environment and energy policies in the coming decades (see for example Chapter 5, Section 4). Policies to better adapt to climate change or to protect biodiversity must necessarily be part of land use, spatial planning, urban development, water and agriculture policies, and *vice versa*. It is vital to make it worthwhile for the rural poor to protect rather than destroy forests by mainstreaming biodiversity goals into poverty reduction programmes and economic development strategies, as well as forestry and agricultural policies (see for example Chapter 4, Section 4). Many countries have implemented or considered "green" fiscal reforms to reflect environmental goals into tax and national budget systems. Achieving policy coherence to effectively address cross-cutting policy agenda requires a strengthened capacity in governments to enhance co-operation between different ministries and agencies and different levels of government.

> **What if...**
>
> ... climate mitigation options avoided expansion of crop areas into natural ecosystems? The *Outlook* suggests that such a scenario would cut cumulative deforestation emissions by 12.7 GtC and contribute to 7% of the required emission reduction to 2050. At the same time, biodiversity would be protected through a reduction in the extent of cropland by some 1.2 million km^2 and 1 million km^2 less land for animal grazing by 2050 relative to the *Baseline*.

Maximise policy synergies

There are many inter-linkages among the four key environmental challenges addressed in this *Environmental Outlook*. **Policies that are designed so as to maximise synergies and co-benefits can lower the cost of meeting environmental objectives.** For example, some local air pollution abatement approaches can also reduce GHG emissions (see Chapter 6, Box 6.3, and Chapter 3, Section 4). Climate mitigation policy can include actions that can also help protect biodiversity. For example, a well-designed financing mechanism for "REDD-plus" (Reducing Emissions from Deforestation and Forest Degradation) can mitigate climate change while delivering substantial biodiversity co-benefits since avoided deforestation and degradation implies a decline in habitat destruction (Chapter 4, Box 4.9). The *Outlook* also highlights the green growth potential from tackling these environmental challenges, including poverty alleviation, fiscal consolidation and job creation.

Contradictory policies can undermine progress, and these need to be carefully monitored and addressed. For example, large-scale water infrastructure projects such as dams – intended to improve water and energy security and better regulate river flows – can disrupt wildlife habitats and ecosystem balance, with negative impacts on biodiveristy as well as compromised water quality downstream (see Chapter 5, Sections 2 and 4). Increasing the use of biofuels to meet climate goals could have negative impacts on biodiversity (Chapter 4, Box 4.9). For the poorest households in developing countries, dirty solid biofuels (*e.g.* cow dung, firewood) that cause indoor air pollution will remain attractive for cooking and heating if carbon taxes place relatively cleaner fuels beyond their reach (Chapter 6, Box 6.4).

> **What if...**
>
> ... the social impacts of climate mitigation policy were not properly addressed? The *Outlook* climate mitigation scenario suggests that, without accompanying policies to address energy access, increased energy costs could lead to an additional 300 million poor people lacking access to clean but more expensive energy sources in 2050, causing 300 000 more premature deaths from indoor air pollution than under the *Baseline* scenario. Targeted policies would be needed to provide alternative clean energy for poor households.

Work in partnerships

Governments need to work more effectively with non-government actors such as businesses, civil society organisations, the scientific research community and holders of traditional knowledge. Especially when government resources are constrained, forging strategic partnerships and capitalising on the dynamism of the larger society can help achieve green growth. **OECD experience shows that environmental policy reforms work best when high-level political leaders are committed and all stakeholders are involved.** In particular, businesses and research institutions play key roles in advancing green technology options and in developing sustainable farming practices. Further engagement by the private sector is needed in biodiversity and ecosystem management and in investing in clean energy and water infrastructure development. Innovative financing, at national and international levels, will be necessary to achieve this.

Gear up international co-operation

As many of the environmental problems are global in nature (*e.g.* biodiversity loss and climate change) or linked to the trans-boundary effects of economic globalisation (*e.g.* trade, international investment), **international co-operation at all levels (bilateral, regional, and multilateral) is indispensable to ensure an equitable sharing of the cost of action.** For example, while the world's mega-biodiverse areas are mainly located in developing countries, the burden of biodiversity conservation measures needs to be shared more broadly, given that the benefits of biodiversity accrue globally (see Chapter 4, Section 1). This calls for strategies to mobilise international financing (including REDD) to support efforts to conserve and sustainably manage biodiversity in these regions, as well as to monitor progress towards implementation. Such efforts can also contribute to alleviating poverty and promoting sustainable development. Similarly, international financing for low carbon climate-resilient growth will need to be scaled up significantly in the coming years. The *Outlook* suggests that it is possible to raise considerable additional

> **What if...**
>
> ... the global community decided to promote universal access to an improved water source and basic sanitation in two phases by 2050? The *Outlook* suggests an additional investment of USD 1.9 billion per year would be needed between 2010 and 2030, then USD 7.6 billion annually to 2050 compared to *Baseline*.

revenues from market-based climate mitigation measures; just a small part of such revenues could make a significant contribution to the finance needed for climate action (see Chapter 3, Box 3.11). International co-operation is also needed to channel financial resources and know-how for providing universal access to *safe* water and adequate sanitation, an objective that is far more ambitious than the MDGs (Chapter 5, Section 3). The *Outlook* shows that benefits will far outweigh the costs.

International agreements are instrumental in providing the legal and institutional basis for international environmental co-operation. For example, the *Outlook* highlights the recent progress by the Convention on Biological Diversity in 2010 on the Strategic Plan for Biodiversity 2011-2020 (the Aichi Biodiversity Targets, the Resource Mobilization Strategy, etc.) and the Nagoya Protocol on Access to Genetic Resources and the Fair and Equitable Sharing of Benefits Arising from their Utilization. National governments' commitment to the UN Strategic

More ambitious international co-operation on climate change needs to include the participation of all major emitting sectors and countries. Fragmented carbon markets and uneven levels of mitigation efforts may give rise to competitiveness and "carbon leakage" concerns.

Approach to International Chemicals Management (SAICM) is bringing about international co-operation for the safe management of chemicals to safeguard human health and the environment (see Chapter 6, Box 6.9). Ambitious and comprehensive international frameworks are essential to address climate change mitigation and adaptation, with the participation of all major emitters as well as those who are most vulnerable to global warming. In the absence of internationally co-ordinated action and a global carbon price, concerns regarding competitiveness impacts and carbon leakage are a barrier to the implementation of national mitigation policies. For water, strong mechanisms are required to manage river basins that cross national borders. In addition, trade, foreign direct investment and multinational enterprises can be mobilised to foster international co-operation. Other mechanisms should be systematically explored to stimulate and create larger markets for eco-innovation.

Improve our knowledge

Better information supports better policies. Assessments of policies and projects should be routinely carried out to evaluate their environmental and social impacts. Improved hydrological monitoring networks are necessary to observe long-term trends and to evaluate the effect of policy actions. Progress is also needed on data and indicators for biodiversity to enable more co-ordinated and comprehensive biodiversity policies at local, national and international levels. More information is also needed on releases

Biodiversity and ecosystems provide invaluable but largely unvalued services to people and the natural environment. For example, the economic value of pollination services provided by insects worldwide is estimated at some USD 192 billion per year.

from, and exposure to, chemicals in products and in the environment, as well as on other emerging environmental and health issues which are still poorly understood. Monitoring of climate change impacts will need to improve to identify priorities for action and inform adaptation planning. **There are many areas where economic valuation should be improved, including the benefits of biodiversity and ecosystem services, and health costs associated with exposure to chemicals.** This will help to measure those elements of improved human welfare and progress that cannot be captured by GDP alone. Better information on costs and benefits will help to improve our understanding of the costs of inaction, and make a strong case for green growth policy reforms and indicator development.

5. Conclusion

The implementation of effective green growth policy mixes will depend on political leadership and on widespread public acceptance that changes are both necessary and affordable. Not all of the solutions will be cheap, which is why seeking out the most cost-effective among them is so important. A key task is to improve understanding of the challenges and trade-offs that need to be made. This *Outlook* seeks to contribute to the need for a better-informed basis for decision making, and hopes to provide policy makers actionable policy options for today that can help to put the world on a more sustainable path.

Chapter 1

Introduction

This chapter provides background to the OECD Environmental Outlooks, explains the methodology used – including the traffic light system – and outlines the report structure. It focuses on the four "Red light" environmental challenges – climate change, biodiversity, water, and the health impacts of environmental pollution – identified as the most pressing challenges in the coming decades. The analysis in the Environmental Outlook is global, but its policy recommendations focus on OECD countries and the key emerging economies of Brazil, Russia, India, Indonesia, China and South Africa (the "BRIICS"). The Environmental Outlook makes future projections to analyse economic and environmental trends over the coming decades, by combining a general equilibrium economic modelling framework (the OECD's ENV-Linkages model) with a comprehensive environmental modelling framework (the IMAGE suite of models of the PBL Netherlands Environmental Assessment Agency). The Environmental Outlook's Baseline scenario presents stylised projections of what the world could look like in 2050 if current socio-economic and environmental trends and existing policies are maintained, but no new policies are introduced to protect the environment. To compare against the Baseline, the Outlook also presents the results of "what if…" simulations which model the potential effects of policies designed to tackle key environmental problems. This edition of the Outlook has been prepared for the Environment Ministers' Meeting at the OECD in March 2012, and as an OECD input to the United Nations Conference on Sustainable Development (Rio+20) in June 2012. It is designed to be read alongside the OECD's green growth strategy, Towards Green Growth.

1. Introduction

Since 2001, the OECD has produced a series of *Environmental Outlooks* to help policy makers understand the scale and context of the environmental challenges they face in the coming decades, as well as the economic and environmental implications of the policies that could be used to address these challenges (OECD, 2001; 2008). The *Outlooks* use models to make projections about what the world might look like in the future. They also present the results of "what if…" simulations which model the potential effects of policies designed to tackle key environmental problems.

This *Environmental Outlook* looks as far ahead as 2050, and in some cases to 2100. It focuses on the four "Red light" environmental challenges – climate change, biodiversity, water, and the health impacts of environmental pollution – identified by OECD environment ministers in 2008[1] as the most pressing and persistent challenges in the coming decades (Box 1.1).

Box 1.1. The OECD Environmental Outlook traffic lights

The *OECD Environmental Outlooks* use red, yellow and green traffic light icons to highlight the magnitude and direction of pressures on the environment as well as trends in policy development to respond to these environmental problems. The ratings were determined by the experts drafting the chapters, and then refined or confirmed by Delegates of the OECD Environment Policy Committee and its sub-groups reviewing the report. They represent the following ratings:

 Red lights indicate environmental issues or pressures that require urgent attention, either because recent trends have been negative and are expected to continue to be so in the future without new policies, or because the trends have been stable recently but are expected to worsen.

 Yellow lights indicate those pressures or environmental conditions whose impact is uncertain or changing (*e.g.* from a positive or stable trend toward a potentially negative projection); or which have been well managed in the past but are less so now; or which remain a challenge but have the potential for a more positive outlook with the right policies.

 Green lights indicate pressures that have stabilised at an acceptable level or are decreasing; environmental conditions for which the outlook to 2050 is positive; or positive policy developments to address these pressures and conditions.

The traffic light scheme is a simple, clear communication device. However, it must be remembered that it is a simplification of the often complex environmental pressures, states and responses examined in this *Outlook*.

This edition of the *Outlook* has been prepared for the Environment Ministers' Meeting at the OECD in March 2012, and as an OECD input to the United Nations Conference on Sustainable Development (Rio+20) in June 2012. It is designed to be read alongside the OECD's green growth strategy, *Towards Green Growth* (OECD, 2011), which outlines an analytical framework to underpin economic and environmental policies that are mutually supportive so as to avoid the possibility that the mismanagement of natural assets could ultimately undermine ongoing human development. While the green growth strategy provides a generic "policy toolkit" applicable to different countries and issues, the *Environmental Outlook* contains specific policy options for addressing climate change, biodiversity loss, poor water quality and quantity and the health impacts of pollution. These policy options are based on projections and analyses of the environmental and economic impacts of specific policies and the synergies and trade-offs between them (Box 1.2). Thus, the *Outlook* aims to support the international policy debates on these specific issues. The analysis in the *Environmental Outlook* is global, but its policy recommendations focus on OECD countries and the key emerging economies of Brazil, Russia, India, Indonesia, China and South Africa (the "BRIICS"). The recommendations bear in mind the need to make continuing progress towards the global goals of sustainable development and poverty alleviation.

This *Environmental Outlook* is also intended to reach beyond the environment policy community. The key environmental challenges discussed here cannot be solved by environment ministries alone. Approaches that enable green growth need to be an integral part of economic and sectoral policies. Business, the scientific community, consumers and civil society at large also have important roles to play in promoting green growth.

Box 1.2. **Coherent policies for green growth**

Many of the environmental objectives discussed in the separate chapters of this *Outlook* are inter-related – for example, climate change can damage biodiversity and human health. A key role of the *Outlook* is to highlight these inter-linkages and to draw attention to both the synergies and trade-offs in policies targeted at a specific environmental challenge. Examples show how policies which address at least two of the challenges at once in a synergistic way may lower the cost of meeting some environmental objectives (*e.g.* tackling climate change can also reduce air pollution; Chapter 3). Other examples show how contradictory policies could undermine progress, *e.g.* increasing the use of biofuels to meet climate goals could have negative impacts on biodiversity (Chapter 4). The *Outlook* also highlights the green growth potential offered from tackling these environmental challenges – including poverty alleviation, fiscal consolidation and job creation.

---

2. The Outlook methodology

Linking economic and environmental modelling

The *OECD Environmental Outlook* analyses economic and environmental trends over the coming decades. These projections are made possible by combining a general equilibrium economic modelling framework (the OECD's ENV-Linkages model) with a comprehensive environmental modelling framework (the IMAGE suite of models of the PBL Netherlands Environmental Assessment Agency). Further details of the ENV-Linkages and the IMAGE suite of models, as well as information and data sources, are provided in Annex A on the Modelling Framework at the end of this report.

■ The ENV-Linkages model developed by the OECD Environment Directorate is a global dynamic computable general equilibrium (CGE) model that describes how economic activities are linked to each other between sectors and across regions. It also links economic activity to environmental pressure, specifically to emissions of greenhouse gases (GHGs). These links between economic activities and emissions are projected several decades into the future, and thus shed light on the impacts of environmental policies for the medium- and long-term future. This model was used to make projections of key socio-economic drivers such as demographic developments, economic growth and developments in economic sectors (discussed in Chapter 2).[2]

■ The IMAGE (Integrated Model to Assess the Global Environment) suite of models run by the PBL is a dynamic integrated assessment framework to model global change. The IMAGE suite is underpinned by modelling of global land allocation and emissions, mapped onto a geospatial 0.5 x 0.5 degree[3] grid of the world (thus results for small areas or specific countries are less robust than for larger countries and regions). The IMAGE suite comprises models that also appear in the literature as models in their own right, and it has been used for other key global environmental assessments such as the *Global Environmental Outlooks* (GEOs) by the United Nations Environment Programme (UNEP). IMAGE has also been further developed and refined since the *OECD Environmental Outlook to 2030* (OECD, 2008) and is now better equipped to analyse, among other things, water-related issues, protected areas and the marine environment.

The key socio-economic trends ("Economy") to 2050 emerging from the ENV-Linkages model were fed into the IMAGE models to make projections of biophysical environmental consequences ("Environment") as depicted in Figure 1.1. In this way, the economy and the environment were connected through energy, agriculture and land use. Modelling of land and energy use provides the key connections between the economic and biophysical models. The biophysical projections from IMAGE are then used in ENV-Linkages to specify policies and assess their economic implications. The data flows between ENV-Linkages and the IMAGE suite were used to develop the *OECD Environmental Outlook Baseline* projections as well as the policy simulations which are discussed below.

Figure 1.1. **The modelling principle for the *OECD Environmental Outlook***

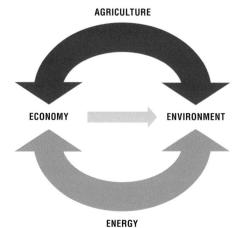

One "Baseline" – many policy simulations

The *OECD Environmental Outlook*'s *Baseline* scenario presents stylised projections of what the world could look like in 2050 if current socio-economic and environmental trends and existing policies are maintained, but no new policies are introduced to protect the environment. The *Baseline* does not reflect major future developments in policies that affect either the drivers of environmental change or environmental pressures. It should be stressed that the *Baseline* is not supposed to be a *prediction* of what the world *will* look like (as it is likely that new policies will be introduced in the coming decades), but rather a hypothetical *projection* forward of current trends without new policies (see Chapter 2, Box 2.1) against which to compare different policy scenarios.

The *Baseline* scenario does reflect current trends and existing policies, such as fossil and renewable energy policies, biofuel support programmes and agricultural support policies, to name a few. Existing trends in efficiency or productivity improvements, in some cases due to earlier policies and measures, are also assumed to continue in the *Baseline*. Selected examples of the types of trends and existing policies that are reflected in the *Baseline* scenario are summarised in Table 1.1, and discussed further in the relevant chapters.

Table 1.1. **Examples of existing policies and trends assumed under the *Baseline* scenario**

Current policies expected to continue to 2050	Indicators of existing conditions to continue to 2050
Socio-economic developments (Chapter 2, and for all chapters)	
■ All economic policies that affect economic growth, including labour policies, fiscal policies, trade policies, etc.	■ Demographics (population growth, ageing, urbanisation). ■ Factor productivity improvements. ■ Per capita GDP. ■ Land use patterns.
Climate change (Chapter 3)	
■ Fossil and renewable energy policies, biofuels support programmes. ■ Emission trading schemes.[1]	■ Emissions from industrial, energy and agricultural activities. ■ Atmospheric concentration of greenhouse gases.
Biodiversity (Chapter 4)	
■ Designation and design of protected areas. ■ Agricultural support policies.	■ Loss of species abundance. ■ Releases from industrial, energy and agricultural activities and wastewater treatment plans.
Water (Chapter 5)	
■ Investment in irrigation infrastructure and efficiency improvements. ■ Investment in water and sanitation infrastructure.	■ Hydrological cycles. ■ Releases from industrial, energy and agricultural activities and wastewater treatment plans.
Health and environment (Chapter 6)	
■ Investment in water and sanitation infrastructure.	■ Burden of disease. ■ Releases from industrial, energy and agricultural activities and wastewater treatment plans.

1. For example, the EU Emissions Trading Scheme Phase 2 (*i.e.* until 2012) is currently in force and is thus included in the *Baseline*. Phase 3, which is not yet implemented, is not included in the *Baseline*, but instead reflected in policy simulations of future mitigation action.

Because the *Baseline* reflects no new policies, it has been used in this *Outlook* as a reference scenario against which model-based simulations of new policies are compared. The differences between the *Baseline* projections and policy simulations have been analysed to shed light on their economic and environmental impacts. These simulations are meant to be illustrative rather than prescriptive. They indicate the type and magnitude of the responses that might be expected from the policies examined, but are not necessarily recommendations of specific policy actions. The policy simulations modelled for this *Outlook* are summarised in Table 1.2, and discussed further in the relevant chapters and their annexes.

Table 1.2. **Policy simulations in the *Environmental Outlook to 2050***

Policy scenario name and location	How key assumptions vary compared to the *Baseline* scenario
All chapters	
450 Core	■ Concentrations of GHGs limited to 450 parts per million (ppm) by the end of the 21st century. ■ Mitigation actions start in 2013, but with full flexibility across time, sources and gases; a global carbon market is in operation.
Chapter 3. Climate change	
450 Accelerated Action	■ As in the *450 Core* scenario, but with significant mitigation efforts undertaken before 2030 ("front-loading" of mitigation efforts).
450 Delayed Action	■ As in *450 Core*, but until 2020 mitigation action limited to the Copenhagen/Cancún pledges by countries; fragmented carbon markets in operation until 2020.
Fossil Fuel Subsidy Reform – stand alone	■ Fossil fuel subsidies are phased out of developing and emerging countries by 2020.
Fossil Fuel Subsidy Reform – plus 450	■ Combination of *450 Core* scenario and stand-alone fossil fuel subsidy reform scenario.
Chapters 3 and 4. Climate change and biodiversity	
550 Core	■ As *450 Core* scenario, but instead aiming at 550 ppm by the end of the century.
550 Low Bioenergy	■ Achieving climate stabilisation as in the *550 Core* scenario but with lower use of bioenergy in the energy mix.
450 Core + Reduced Land Use	■ Achieving climate stabilisation as in the *450 Core* scenario but adding improved land use, and including REDD in the portfolio of mitigation options.
Chapter 4. Biodiversity	
Expanded Terrestrial Protected Areas	■ Achieving the 17% protected area target for each of the 65 eco-regions for ecological representativeness.
Chapter 5. Water	
Resource Efficiency	■ As in the *450 Core* scenario, but with lower water demand for thermal electricity generation and a larger share of renewable energy. ■ Further 15% irrigation efficiency improvements in non-OECD countries. ■ Modest improvements in water efficiency in domestic and manufacturing globally.
Nutrient Recycling and Reduction	■ 20% less nitrogen (N) and phosphorus (P) surpluses in agriculture globally in 2050. ■ 35% less effluent nutrients in 2050.
Chapters 5 and 6. Water, and health and environment	
Accelerated Access	■ A two-step approach involving: *i)* halving by 2030 the population without access to improved water and basic sanitation from 2005 figures, then; *ii)* achieving universal access to improved water and basic sanitation in 2050.
Chapter 6. Health and environment	
25% Air Pollution Reduction	■ 25% reduction in Nitrogen oxides (NO_X), Sulphur dioxides (SO_2) and black carbon.

Note: Further details of the key assumptions behind the policy simulations are discussed in the relevant chapters and their annexes.

Geographical and temporal scope

While this *Environmental Outlook* is based on the analysis of long-term global trends to 2050, one goal is to identify trends and policy options for OECD countries and the BRIICS. The *Outlook* model projections are presented using different levels of regional aggregation or country groups depending on their relevance for particular topics. The three most commonly used groups throughout the report are the OECD, BRIICS, rest of the world (or RoW), and 15 regional clusters. These are shown in Table 1.3, which also shows how the country groups under the different models are equivalent to each other. Other groupings or selections of countries are also used to illustrate trends in different chapters. For example, in the Climate Change Chapter, "Annex I" countries refer to industrialised countries that are part of Annex I of the Kyoto Protocol under the UN Framework Convention on Climate Change (see Chapter 3).

Table 1.3. **Regions and country groups used
in the OECD *Environmental Outlook to 2050***

IMAGE 24 regions	ENV-Linkages 15 regions	Major regions
Canada	Canada	OECD
US	US	
Mexico	Mexico	
Japan	Japan and Korea	
Korea		
Oceania	Oceania	
OECD Europe	EU27 and EFTA	
Central Europe		
Brazil	Brazil	BRIICS
India[1]	India	
Indonesia	Indonesia	
China	China	
Southern Africa[1]	South Africa	
Russia	Russia	
Turkey	Rest of Europe	RoW
Ukraine region		
Northern Africa	Middle East and Northern Africa	
Middle East		
Western Africa	Rest of the world	
Eastern Africa		
Asia-Stan		
South East Asia		
Rest Central America		
Rest South America		

1. In the IMAGE model, India means "India region", which also includes Afghanistan, Bangladesh, Bhutan, Maldives, Nepal, Pakistan and Sri Lanka, when dealing with land use, biodiversity, water and health. For energy-related modelling, the region has been split into India (country) and the "Rest of South Asia". Similarly, the Southern Africa region includes ten other countries in this geographical area, including the Republic of South Africa, when dealing with land use, biodiversity, water and health. For energy-related modelling, the region has been split into the Republic of South Africa and "Rest of Southern Africa".

Note: For full information on regions and country groups, see *www.oecd.org/environment/outlookto2050*.

Various timeframes relevant to specific goals and objectives, *e.g.* 2015, 2020, 2030, 2050, are presented in this report. For the projections of climate change impacts and analysis of policy options, the time horizon is extended to 2100. In some of the chapters, policy actions in the medium term (*e.g.* from "today" up to 2020 or 2030) and long term (from 2020 or 2030 up to 2050) are compared to draw further insights. The base year is 2010, unless otherwise stated.

Embracing uncertainties

A good dose of humility is warranted when making any model-based projections, especially for long-term projections decades into the future. This *Environmental Outlook* is no exception. Many mechanisms that drive long-term economic growth and environmental pressure are not well understood. This means that there are uncertainties about the data input, and the relationships between drivers and environmental pressures assumed in the models (Box 1.3). There are also likely to be shocks, such as a profound or prolonged economic crises (see Chapter 2, Box 2.2) or natural disasters, which cannot be foreseen or included in these long-term projections. There are uncertainties surrounding scientific data, notably where environmental thresholds and tipping points might lie.

Box 1.3. **Important sources of model uncertainty**

Uncertainty in the model parameters: Model parameters are estimated or calibrated from empirical sources. Hence, there is statistical uncertainty in the value of the parameters. These uncertainties are often handled by examining the impact of small changes in parameters on the model's results through sensitivity analyses. They often demonstrate that while *quantitative* results from the model can change with revisions to parameters, the *qualitative* results and conclusions drawn from them are much harder to overturn.

Uncertainty in the drivers: A model requires projections of future drivers such as demographic or technological change to underpin its results. Uncertainty in the drivers translates directly into uncertainty in the model projections. When studying particular policy agendas, the range of uncertainty can be narrowed by focusing attention on key alternatives to a reference case (*i.e.* the *Baseline*) that are most important for the policy issues under consideration. A starting point for looking at those alternatives would be to examine variations in the key drivers of the *Baseline*. For example, the 2008 edition of the *OECD Environmental Outlook* explored variations in the aggregate productivity of countries. By focusing on the relative change or differences between the *Baseline* projections and policy simulations, rather than on absolute levels, outcomes are less sensitive to actual *Baseline* projections.

Uncertainty in the model structure: There are numerous theories that can be used to underpin a model's structure. A choice is made between analytical paradigms that distinguish different schools of thought. The computable general equilibrium (CGE) modelling framework (used for this *Outlook*) is a popular analytical tool for understanding economic phenomena. In practice, proper validation is a formidable task and beyond the scope of this *Outlook*. Projections are conditional on these model choices. This area of uncertainty is more likely to change qualitative results: different models will give different results.

However, these uncertainties do not need to be seen as limitations. Instead, this *Outlook* attempts to "embrace" uncertainties, as they can help to shed further light on the interactions between the economy and the environment and to identify where further work is needed to improve the knowledge base. Each of the thematic chapters of this *Outlook* outlines the uncertainties surrounding the theme, and discusses what they might mean for policy makers.

Where appropriate, the *Environmental Outlook Baseline* projections are compared with other model-based scenarios in the literature. Where the different models used for the *Outlook* were able to address the same issues (for example GHG emissions are modelled in ENV-Linkages and IMAGE), the results from the different models are compared and discussed. Comparing results from different modelling frameworks helps to understand the differences between models and to identify the ranges of estimates. Also, uncertainties surrounding the feasibility of policy options (in terms of political and public support, technological potential or costs) are addressed through simulations of a number of policy variants, as done in Chapter 3 on climate change.

3. How is the report structured?

The next chapter, Chapter 2, presents the underlying socio-economic drivers of environmental changes discussed in the later thematic environmental chapters. The first part describes the key socio-economic drivers that affect economic development and environmental change to 2050, including population dynamics and labour markets, urbanisation, and economic growth. This chapter also discusses key economic developments that most directly affect the environment, namely energy and land use.

The *Outlook* then features four chapters on the key environmental challenges: climate change (Chapter 3), biodiversity (Chapter 4), water (Chapter 5), and health and environment (Chapter 6). Each discusses key environmental trends and the *Baseline* projections to 2050, *i.e* what the future might look like without new policies. Some of these are modelled while others are addressed qualitatively. Given the availability of data and the limitations of the modelling framework, the relative coverage of quantitative *versus* qualitative analyses differs from chapter to chapter. Wherever possible, the costs of inaction in the face of these environmental challenges are discussed, drawing on available information in the literature.

Each chapter then reviews the policy options and recent policy progress for tackling the issue, before outlining further action needed and any emerging issues. The findings from the policy simulations are presented to illustrate the discussions of policy options. Where possible, specific country examples are also given. A box containing the key messages summarises the main findings and policy options at the beginning of each chapter.

Annex A on the Modelling Framework at the end of this report complements the discussion of the methodology used for this *Environmental Outlook*, and provides further technical details on the modelling framework. In-depth technical discussions of the modelling assumptions used for policy simulations are also presented in relevant chapter annexes. In addition, technical background papers accompany this *Environmental Outlook* as *OECD Environment Working Papers*.

Notes

1. The 2008 *Environmental Outlook* (OECD, 2008) projected ahead to 2030 and covered a wider range of environmental challenges and their drivers than this *Outlook*. However, OECD environment ministers asked the OECD to focus the new *Environmental Outlook* on these four key red light issues. This *Outlook* also extends projections to 2050 and takes stock of recent progress at the international and national levels in implementing policies to address the four environmental challenges. The models used for the analyses for this *Outlook* have been further refined and updated.

2. Since the 2008 edition of the *OECD Environmental Outlook* (OECD, 2008), the ENV-Linkages model was further developed and refined for analysis as published in the *Economics of Climate Change Mitigation* (OECD, 2009), which assessed the environmental effectiveness and economic costs of different policies and policy mixes to reduce global greenhouse gas emissions. More recently, ENV-Linkages has been further refined to support work requested by the 2009 G20 Pittsburgh Summit to model the impact of removing fossil fuel subsidies. For this *Environmental Outlook to 2050*, ENV-Linkages has been further developed, refined and updated (*e.g.* using more recent data for economic activity and energy use, and to reflect the economic crisis of 2008-2009, see Chapter 2).

3. Degrees in terms of latitude and longitude on the Earth's surface.

References

OECD (2001), *OECD Environmental Outlook*, OECD Publishing, doi: *10.1787/9789264188563-en*.

OECD (2008), *OECD Environmental Outlook to 2030*, OECD Publishing, doi: *10.1787/9789264040519-en*.

OECD (2009), *The Economics of Climate Change Mitigation: Policies and Options for Global Action beyond 2012*, OECD Publishing, doi: *10.1787/9789264073616-en*.

OECD (2011), *Towards Green Growth*, OECD Green Growth Studies, OECD Publishing, doi: *10.1787/9789264111318-en*.

Chapter 2

Socio-economic Developments

by

Rob Dellink, Ton Manders (PBL), Jean Chateau, Bertrand Magné,
Detlef van Vuuren (PBL), Anne Gerdien Prins (PBL)

The chapter starts by describing current demographic trends and corresponding Baseline projections (notably for population growth/composition including ageing, and urbanisation). It then outlines economic trends and projections, including economic growth (GDP, consumption, sectoral composition) and its drivers, such as labour and capital. These trends are based on a gradual conditional convergence of income levels among countries. In its final section it explores two factors which directly link economic trends to environmental pressures: energy use (energy mix such as fossil fuels, renewables and nuclear) and land use (in particular agricultural land). The projected key socio-economic developments under the Environmental Outlook Baseline scenario presented in this chapter serve as the basis for the environmental projections described in the other chapters of this Outlook. The chapter focuses on global projections for major world regions such as the group of OECD countries, emerging economies of Brazil, Russia, India, Indonesia, China and South Africa (the BRIICS) and the rest of the world.

KEY MESSAGES

This chapter explores how global and regional economic growth, population, labour force participation, urbanisation, energy and land use could develop by 2050 if no new policies are introduced. The projected key socio-economic developments under the *Environmental Outlook Baseline* scenario presented in this chapter serve as the basis for the environmental projections described in the other chapters of this *Outlook*. The overall finding is that the *Baseline* scenario (*i.e.* business as usual) is not a viable pathway for future development, as it leads to substantial environmental pressure and considerable costs.

■ **World gross domestic product (GDP)** is projected to nearly quadruple over the coming four decades, in line with the past 40 years. By 2050, the OECD's share of the global economy is projected to decline from 54% in 2010 to less than 32%, while the share of Brazil, Russia, India, Indonesia, China and South Africa (the BRIICS) is projected to grow to more than 40%. The US economy, which has been the largest in the world, as measured by GDP and expressed in purchasing power parity exchange rates (PPPs), is projected to be overtaken by China around 2012. India's GDP is projected to surpass that of the United States before 2040. Today's global "engines of growth" – China and India – could see their average GDP growth rates slow down to 2050, while remaining well above the average growth rate of the OECD region. The *Baseline* projects that Africa will experience high economic growth rates between 2030 and 2050, but will remain the poorest continent.

Projections for real gross domestic product: *Baseline*, 2010-2050

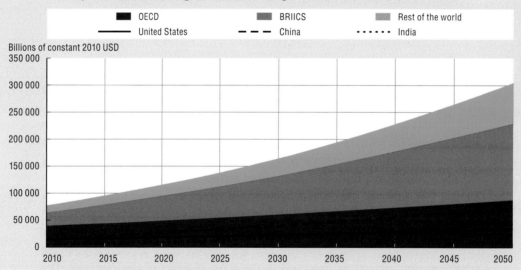

Note: Valued using constant 2010 purchasing power parity (PPP) exchange rates.
Source: OECD Environmental Outlook Baseline; output from ENV-Linkages.

StatLink ᵃᵍᵖᵍ http://dx.doi.org/10.1787/888932570183

■ There are significant differences in demographic developments across regions and countries. By 2050, the **world population** is projected to grow by another 2.2 billion people, reaching almost 9.2 billion. Most of this growth will occur in South Asia, the Middle East and especially Africa. The population profiles of all regions are ageing, especially China and the OECD countries.

■ Populations are becoming increasingly **urbanised**. By 2050, 2.8 billion more people than today are projected to be living in urban areas, which will contain nearly 70% of the world's population. The rural population is projected to decrease by 0.6 billion. This urbanisation has pros and cons – while a concentrated population might make it generally easier to supply with modern energy and water infrastructure, levels of exposure to outdoor air pollution will be higher and could worsen environmental conditions in slums, with serious consequences for human health.

- Under the *Baseline* scenario, world **energy** demand in 2050 is projected to be about 80% higher than today. The 2050 global (commercial) energy mix is not projected to differ significantly from today's, with fossil fuels still providing about 85%, renewable sources (including biofuels, but not traditional biomass) providing just above 10%, and the remainder provided by nuclear. Of fossil fuels, it is uncertain whether coal or gas will be the main source of increased energy supply.

- Globally, the area of agricultural **land** is projected to expand in the next decade to match the increase in food demand from a growing population, intensifying competition for land. Agricultural land is expected to peak before 2030 and decline thereafter, as population growth slows down and yield improvements continue. Deforestation rates are already declining, and this trend is projected to continue, especially after 2030 when demand for more agricultural land eases.

1. Introduction

This chapter describes the main socio-economic drivers of environmental change that underlie the key environmental concerns of this *Outlook*: economic growth, demographic changes, labour force participation, urbanisation, energy and land use. All these drivers have been modelled under the *Environmental Outlook* business-as-usual *Baseline* scenario to see how they might develop by 2050 if no new policies are put in place.

The chapter starts by describing current demographic trends and the *Baseline* projections (notably population growth/composition and urbanisation) (see Box 2.1). It then outlines economic trends and projections. These trends are based upon a gradual convergence of income levels among countries (Box 2.3).[1] In its final section it explores two factors which directly link economic trends to environmental pressures: energy use and land use.

Box 2.1. **Projection, not prediction**

A baseline projection is not a prediction of future developments (Chapter 1). Instead it constructs expected future trends for several key economic and environmental variables based on current trends and a number of assumptions about the future. The *Environmental Outlook Baseline* assumes no new policies for the environmental issues addressed in the *Outlook*, but implicitly includes other government policies in the projected trends for the key variables. It thus provides a benchmark against which policy scenarios aimed at improving environmental quality for the issues under investigation can be assessed.

Environmental pressure, the cost of inaction and green growth

The *Baseline* projection presented in this *Outlook* implies severe environmental pressures. As will be discussed below and in subsequent chapters, these pressures pose important risks and expected costs that could erode the natural capital base upon which economic growth is built. For this reason, the *Baseline* cannot be considered to be a viable pathway for future development.

Although the nature of these impacts is beset with uncertainty, the implications of not taking action to address the environmental pressures, and failing to account for the environmental consequences of economic activities, are potentially very large. OECD (2008a) provides an overview of the cost of inaction on key environmental challenges, including climate change, water pollution and environment-related health issues. Essential insights from that overview include the following: i) "defining and measuring the cost of inaction is complex", especially for intangible environmental impacts; and ii) "despite the measurement difficulties, existing literature suggests very strongly that the costs of policy inaction in selected environmental areas can be considerable". Each of the thematic chapters in this OECD *Environmental Outlook to 2050* highlights the impacts of a

Baseline projection when no policy action is taken and assesses costs of inaction based on insights from the literature.

If the costs of taking no action to address the key environmental challenges were fully included in this assessment, future GDP would be lower than projected under the *Environmental Outlook Baseline* discussed below. By the same token, the benefits of environmental actions may be underestimated. In terms of the physical consequences of inaction, the links between the environmental pressures and impacts for the different environmental issues have been included in the *Outlook* analysis. For example, changes in temperature and precipitation patterns induced by climate change affect agricultural productivity. This in turn increases agricultural land requirements and pressures to deforest, which may aggravate biodiversity losses. Continuing business-as-usual under the *Baseline* scenario risks exceeding biophysical limits or tipping points, and causing other non-linear large-scale (systemic) irreversible damages (see Chapter 3, Section 2; Chapter 4, Box 4.1).

Clearly, a transition is needed towards greener growth (OECD, 2011) in order to avoid the unchecked environmental consequences of the socio-economic developments presented in this chapter. The following chapters in this *Outlook* deal extensively with how such transitions towards greener growth can be made.

2. Key trends and projections

Demographic developments

Population dynamics are key drivers of local and global environmental change. Growing populations lead to increases in the consumption of natural resources and in land use, posing additional environmental pressures. Changes in wealth and age structure also modify lifestyle, consumption habits and diet, all of which can have consequences for the environment. The proportion of elderly *versus* young people in a population also affects the labour market, which is one of the main drivers of economic growth – along with technological progress, human capital improvements and physical capital accumulation. This section outlines how some of these factors are projected to develop to 2050 under the *Baseline* scenario.

Population growth and composition

The world's population has increased from less than 4 billion in 1970 to 7 billion today (Figure 2.1). By 2050, the United Nations projects global population to be almost 9.2 billion – an additional 2.2 billion people.[2]

There are significant regional and country differences in the projected demographic developments to 2050. Population growth rates are assumed to be low in the OECD countries (0.2% per year between 2010 and 2050, on average), with population even falling in Japan, Korea and some European countries. However, in countries like the United States and Canada, immigration is projected to continue to increase population levels. For the "BRIICS" countries (Brazil, Russia, India, Indonesia, China and South Africa), population is projected to grow at 0.4% per year on average, although growth rates are likely to be higher in India, while Russia's growth looks to be negative. Most of the population growth (on average +1.3% per year) in the coming decades is projected to take place in the non-BRIICS or developing countries ("Rest of the World" or RoW group). Within this group, growth rates are projected to be higher in Africa and South Asia than in Latin America.

Figure 2.1. **World population by major regions, 1970-2050**

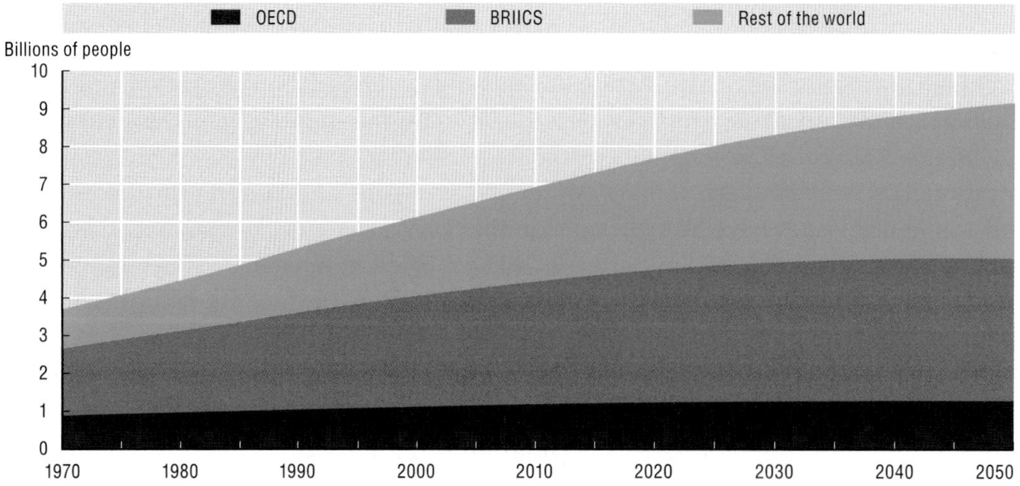

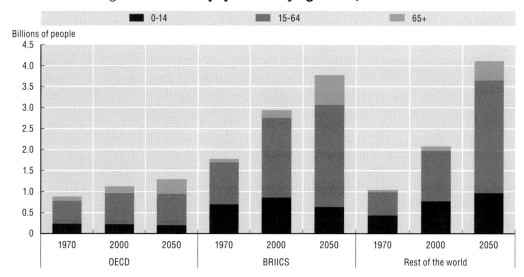

| OECD | BRIICS | Rest of the world |

Billions of people

Source: Based on UN (2009), *World Population Prospects: The 2008 Revision*, UN, New York.

StatLink http://dx.doi.org/10.1787/888932570088

Figure 2.2 illustrates how the population in OECD countries has aged since 1970: the share of children in the total population has steadily declined, while the share of elderly people has increased. Recent trends in fertility rates and life expectancy suggest that similar patterns are appearing in Russia and China. According to the UN (2009) projections, population ageing will only become prominent in the RoW group after 2030. Ageing implies changes in lifestyle and consumption patterns, and diminishes the labour force (see below, Figure 2.7). Ageing also has implications for health care and other services. In general, these trends lead to a more than proportional increase in the demand for such services (see also the section on the sectoral structure of the economy below).

Figure 2.2. **World population by age class, 1970-2050**

| 0-14 | 15-64 | 65+ |

Billions of people

| OECD | BRIICS | Rest of the world |

Source: Based on UN (2009), *World Population Prospects: The 2008 Revision*, UN, New York.

StatLink http://dx.doi.org/10.1787/888932570107

Urbanisation

The world's population is becoming increasingly urbanised (Figure 2.3). In 1970, 1.3 billion people, or 36% of the world population, lived in urban areas. By 2009 that share had reached 50%. This trend is expected to continue in the coming decades, reaching nearly 70% in 2050 (UN, 2010). The increase in absolute numbers to 2050 is 2.8 billion, which implies that the total world population growth between 2010 and 2050 (more than 2.2 billion people) would be completely absorbed by urban areas. Rural population is projected to decrease by 0.6 billion people over the same period. This growth in urban population is expected to be unevenly distributed around the world. The share of urban population in OECD countries is projected to be about 86% of total population by 2050. In Sub-Saharan Africa, one of the least urbanised regions, urban dwellers accounted for about 37% of total population in 2010 – however, their share is projected to reach 60% by 2050.

Figure 2.3. **Urban population by region, 1970-2050**

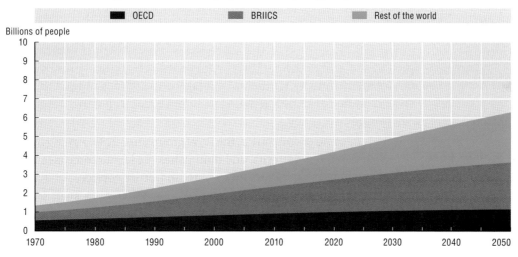

Source: Based on UN (2010), World Urbanization Prospects: The 2009 Revision, UN, New York.

StatLink 🔗 http://dx.doi.org/10.1787/888932570126

Small urban centres of less than 0.5 million inhabitants are projected to grow more rapidly than other urban areas (Figure 2.4). This would be a change from the observed trend in recent decades, when large mega-cities grew at the fastest rates (UN Habitat, 2006).

Urbanisation has both positive and negative environmental consequences. On the positive side, up to a certain level, the concentration of activities in urban areas can allow for economies of scale and easier interactions, meaning that urbanisation can lead to higher economic growth. Higher concentrations of people generally make it easier to provide access to modern and efficient infrastructure for the delivery of energy and water services. On the negative side, a greater concentration of economic activities can also cause higher levels of outdoor air pollution (Chapter 6). Urbanisation also requires adapted transportation policies to avoid major complications in the transport system, and negative environmental implications can result from traffic congestion. Furthermore, one in every three city dwellers worldwide – about one billion people – lives in a slum (UN Habitat, 2003 and 2006). Urban slums – with substandard housing and inadequate water, sanitation and waste management services – have negative consequences for human health and the environment. This could become magnified with further urbanisation unless more

Figure 2.4. **World urban population by city size, 1970-2025**

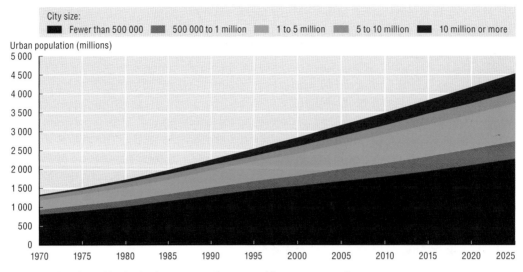

Source: UN (2010), *World Urbanization Prospects: The 2009 Revision*, UN, New York.

StatLink ⬛⬛⬛ http://dx.doi.org/10.1787/888932570145

ambitious urban development and environmental management policies are put in place. This is especially so as the number of people living in slums could well grow, despite the projected increase in average GDP levels.

Economic growth

Economic growth and rising per capita income, if based on the increased use of natural resources, may exacerbate pressures on the environment. But other sources of growth, such as technological progress (innovation) or improvements in education and human skills, can decouple environmental pressures from economic growth. This section discusses the degree to which the global economy will grow over the next four decades, the drivers of this growth and the implications.

How and where will the global economy grow to 2050?

The global economy, measured by real gross domestic product (GDP), has roughly tripled in the past four decades.[3] In the coming decades, world economic growth is likely to continue these historical trends, but the distribution of this growth across countries is projected to differ significantly. Until the end of the 20th century, OECD countries accounted for the lion's share of global economic activity (Figure 2.5) and per capita GDP levels were much higher than in the other regions. More recently, per capita GDP has increased rapidly in the BRIICS region, with an average growth rate of 5.4% between 1990 and 2008; more than three times the rate of the OECD region. The fast growth in the BRIICS has gradually shifted the relative regional weights in the global economy. By 2050, the share of global economic activity attributable to the BRIICS is projected to rise to more than 40% (Figure 2.6). By 2050, the OECD's share of the global economy is projected to decline from 54% in 2010 to less than 32%.[4] The US economy, which has been the largest in the world as measured by GDP and expressed in purchasing power parity exchange rates (PPPs), is projected to be overtaken by China around 2012. India's GDP is projected to surpass that of the United States before 2040. In nominal terms, however, GDP levels remain highest in the United States (Chateau *et al.*, 2011).

Figure 2.5. **Real gross domestic product in per capita and absolute terms, 1970-2008**

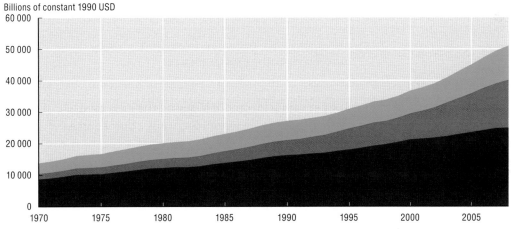

Note: Based on 1990 exchange rates.

Source: OECD calculations based on Maddison (2010), *Statistics on World Population, GDP and per Capita GDP, 1-2008 AD*, University of Groningen, *www.ggdc.net/MADDISON/oriindex.htm*.

StatLink ᴍᴤᴘ http://dx.doi.org/10.1787/888932570164

The 2008 financial crisis led to a global economic recession in 2009 and uncertain prospects for the coming years. A modest recovery in OECD countries, combined with near double-digit growth in some of the major emerging economies – especially China and India – pulled the global economy back to a growth rate of just below 5% in 2010. Box 2.2 highlights how economic shocks and environmental pressure are linked. However, the *Environmental Outlook Baseline* projections do not account for future shocks like these; they present the long-term trend rather than short-term forecasts. Short-term projections for growth remain highly uncertain.

The world real GDP (measured in constant 2010 USD) is projected to grow on average by about 3.5% per year from 2010 to 2050 (Table 2.1). This implies that world GDP would be multiplied almost fourfold over the period. This is similar to the past (1970-2008) average world GDP growth rate (expressed in 1990 USD), of close to 3.6% (Madison, 2010).

Figure 2.6. **Projections for real gross domestic product:** *Baseline,* **2010-2050**

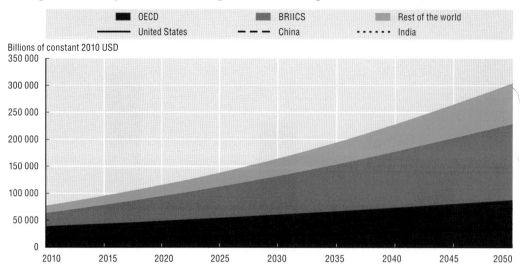

Note: Valued using constant 2010 purchasing power parity (PPP) exchange rates.

Source: *OECD Environmental Outlook Baseline;* output from ENV-Linkages.

StatLink http://dx.doi.org/10.1787/888932570183

Box 2.2. **The complex link between economic shocks and environmental pressure**

The financial and economic crisis of 2008-2009 is an example of a shock to the economy that cannot be anticipated in future projections. Scenario projections like the *Environmental Outlook Baseline* tend to focus on gradual, long-term trends. To some degree, short-term deviations from long-term trends form part of the *Baseline*. However, it should still be noted that the world economy is slowly, and unevenly, coming out of the worst crisis since World War II, making economic projections for coming years even more uncertain than in the past.

Lower output growth rates during the crisis and the potentially long recovery period may have an impact on economic output levels over the long run. It may even result in long-term growth rates that are lower than their pre-crisis levels. Long-term growth will be influenced by a handful of factors, of which the most crucial are the growth of the labour force and technical improvements. A slow process of industrial restructuring, caused for example by credit constraints, can hurt the growth of total factor productivity in the medium to long term, which in turn could also be curtailed by depressed investments in private research and development. A long and deep recession may diminish labour demand by firms due to the reduction in economic activity, as well as diminish the potential labour force by discouraging some of the unemployed from seeking jobs and by reducing migration flows. Furthermore, long unemployment spells may cause permanent damage to human capital (EU, 2009).

Environmental pressures are influenced by the economy and hence also by economic shocks. For example, greenhouse gas (GHG) emissions can be expected to be partially related to GDP. The *OECD Environmental Outlook to 2030* (OECD, 2008b), for example, modelled a high productivity scenario which showed that if global GDP was 16% higher in 2030 this would imply 10% more GHG emissions.

> Box 2.2. **The complex link between economic shocks and environmental pressure** (cont.)
>
> It is not clear at this point whether the net impacts of the current crisis on the environment will be positive or negative overall. It reduced the growth of GHG gas emissions in 2008-2009, but this was followed in 2010 by the highest emission levels ever recorded (Chapter 3). However, a prolonged period of stagnation or very low growth could once again lower emission growth. In turn, this could delay improvements in resource efficiency and technology development for a significant length of time, so the outcome might not necessarily be positive. In any case, all current policy efforts are focused on re-kindling growth, so a return to growth based on full recovery is the assumption for this *Outlook*.

China and India have been important engines of global economic growth in recent years, but their growth rates are projected to slow down in the coming decades as their underlying drivers of growth (including capital supply and human capital improvements from better education) converge towards those of OECD countries (see Annex 2.A and the section on growth drivers below). The expected slowdown is also due to underlying demographic changes – for example, ageing is a prominent factor in China. While the projected absolute size of the Chinese economy is still largest, its growth rate is projected to be surpassed by those of other Asian countries, such as India and Indonesia (Table 2.1).

Table 2.1. **Annual average real GDP growth rates:** *Baseline,* **2010-2050**

Based on constant 2010 USD

	2010-2020	2020-2030	2030-2050	2010-2050
		%		
Canada	2.5	2.3	2.1	2.2
Japan and Korea	2.1	1.6	1.0	1.4
Oceania	2.8	2.4	2.2	2.4
Russia	3.0	2.8	2.2	2.6
US	2.2	2.3	2.1	2.2
EU27 and EFTA	2.1	2.0	1.7	1.9
Rest of Europe	4.7	5.0	3.6	4.2
Brazil	3.7	4.0	3.2	3.5
China	7.2	4.2	3.0	4.3
Indonesia	5.0	4.5	4.2	4.5
India	7.3	6.2	4.8	5.7
Middle East and North Africa	4.1	4.6	4.1	4.2
Mexico	4.5	3.6	2.9	3.5
South Africa	4.2	3.8	3.3	3.6
Rest of the world	4.4	4.5	4.5	4.5
OECD	**2.3**	**2.2**	**1.9**	**2.0**
BRIICS	**6.4**	**4.5**	**3.5**	**4.5**
World	**4.1**	**3.6**	**3.1**	**3.5**

Note: See Table 1.3 in Chapter 1 for a description of the ENV-Linkages model country groupings used in this *Outlook*.

Source: OECD Environmental Outlook Baseline; output from ENV-Linkages.

StatLink http://dx.doi.org/10.1787/888932571874

The highest growth rate (of around 6% annually) between 2030 and 2050 is projected for Sub-Saharan Africa (part of the Rest of the World region), although in absolute terms it will remain the poorest continent at the end of the projection period. OECD economies are projected to grow at a much slower pace through to 2050, with most of them growing at around 2% per year on average.

In recent decades, per capita income levels have increased on average in almost all regions of the world. This increase has not been evenly spread across the different regions, with per capita GDP levels increasing twice as fast in the BRIICS (3.4% annually between 1970 and 2009) as in the other regions (1.9% in the OECD and 1.6% in the rest of the world, respectively). By 2050, however, US per capita GDP is still projected to rank first, almost double that of China. Household per capita consumption shows similar differences across regions and countries (Table 2.2).

Table 2.2. **Annual per capita GDP and household consumption:** *Baseline,*
2010-2050

Thousands constant 2010 USD/person

	GDP per capita			Consumption per capita		
	2010	2020	2050	2010	2020	2050
Canada	36.9	43.0	68.2	22.1	25.4	39.9
Japan and Korea	31.9	39.8	67.3	18.0	23.0	41.8
Oceania	27.8	32.5	50.0	17.9	20.5	31.6
Russia	15.2	21.1	49.6	9.9	15.3	35.9
US	45.7	52.3	85.3	32.3	37.1	56.6
EU27 and EFTA	30.2	36.4	63.5	18.0	21.9	39.6
Rest of Europe	10.7	16.4	53.5	7.1	10.1	31.0
Brazil	11.6	15.6	41.7	7.2	9.5	23.7
China	9.4	17.9	48.8	3.4	7.0	27.1
Indonesia	5.1	7.6	23.6	3.5	5.1	13.0
India	3.9	7.0	27.5	2.3	3.8	13.8
Middle East and North Africa	11.1	14.2	37.5	7.1	9.6	23.7
Mexico	13.2	18.9	44.3	9.5	13.1	25.8
South Africa	10.4	15.0	38.4	7.1	10.1	25.0
Rest of the world	3.9	5.0	13.3	2.6	3.4	8.3
OECD	**33.1**	**39.7**	**68.5**	**21.2**	**25.5**	**43.5**
BRIICS	**7.5**	**12.9**	**37.3**	**3.6**	**6.2**	**20.5**
World	**11.1**	**15.0**	**33.2**	**6.6**	**8.7**	**19.7**

Note: Valued using constant 2010 purchasing power parity (PPP) exchange rates.
Source: OECD Environmental Outlook Baseline; output from ENV-Linkages.

StatLink http://dx.doi.org/10.1787/888932571893

What drives economic growth?

Economic growth, or more precisely growth of GDP, is driven by i) increasing the value added of production through the increased use of capital, labour and natural resources (including land); ii) increasing the productivity of these primary production factors; and iii) reallocating production factors to those activities that yield the highest value added. Labour input (employment) is in turn driven by demographic developments, which combine population, age structure, labour market participation and unemployment scenarios.

The *OECD Environmental Outlook Baseline* projects that between 2010 and 2030, GDP growth is largely driven by the increased use of physical capital (such as buildings, machines and infrastructure), which boosts economic activity especially in the emerging economies (see Annex 2.A).[5] As physical capital and energy use mostly go together in production processes, this type of growth implies substantial increases in energy demand in the near future (see the section on energy below).

In the longer run, the *Outlook* projections foresee a slow transition towards more balanced growth in all major economies, with growth partially converging across economies and physical capital accumulation and human capital contributing more equally to GDP growth. Countries that are further behind in terms of education (which contributes to human capital) and physical capital levels are projected to experience higher growth rates during the catch-up phase, as explained in Box 2.3. Such projections are uncertain and depend on several assumptions, especially about the institutional capacity for development. The catch-up effect results in a growing contribution by human capital to long-term GDP growth, partly limiting increases in environmental pressure (decoupling environment from economic growth). However, to achieve these increases in human capital development, it will be essential that education and training policies build workers' knowledge and skills.

Box 2.3. The conditional convergence methodology: Assumptions for model-based projections

Baseline economic scenarios underlying global environmental economic projections – such as those developed for the Intergovernmental Panel on Climate Change (IPCC, 2007) – typically assume that globally, income levels will gradually converge towards those of most developed economies. This *Outlook* takes a similar approach, though placing special emphasis on the drivers of GDP growth over the projection period rather than projecting convergence only on income levels (Duval and de la Maisonneuve, 2010). Based on this, long-term projections are made for five main drivers of per capita economic growth: *i)* total factor productivity; *ii)* human capital (which drives labour productivity); *iii)* capital-to-output ratios; *iv)* population, age structure, participation and unemployment scenarios (which together drive employment levels); and *v)* natural resource availability. Gradual convergence of regions towards the best performing countries is projected within 50 to 100 years, depending on the driver. Together with population growth, these drivers are then used to project the future path of GDP.

While the labour force is ultimately constrained by population, differences between growth rates in population and employment can nevertheless persist over many years, reflecting changes in demographics, labour force participation trends and unemployment projections. The average annual growth rate of population is compared to that of employment in Figure 2.7. Continued ageing of the population is projected in many OECD countries, and also in China and some other emerging economies. This is related to lower labour participation rates. However, the much younger population profiles in many developing countries, especially in Africa and Asia, imply that the share of working-age people will increase over time, thereby boosting labour supply. This also holds for India, although this trend is combined with an increased share of elderly people.

International trade also affects economic growth, and is projected to continue to outpace GDP growth. But the existing current account imbalances seem untenable over the long run as they put pressure on exchange rates. Therefore, this *Outlook* projects a gradual reduction of current account balances over time. For most regions, the current account is projected to balance by 2050, but larger imbalances for China and the United States will require longer to fully fade.

Figure 2.7. **Average annual population and employment growth rates, 2010-2050**

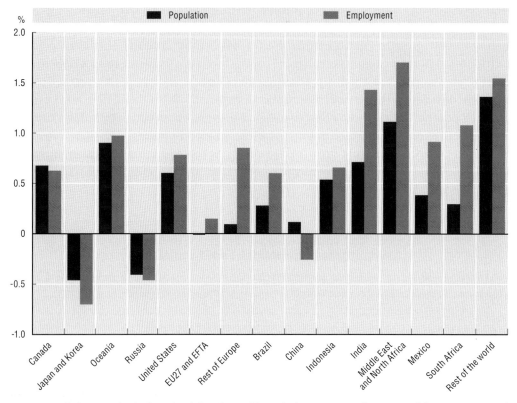

Sources: Population: UN (United Nations) (2009), *World Population Prospects: The 2008 Revision*, UN, New York. Employment: *OECD Environmental Outlook Baseline*, output from ENV-Linkages.

StatLink ⧉ http://dx.doi.org/10.1787/888932570202

How will the structure of the economy change?

The sectoral composition of the different regions has shifted over time, with the service sector contributing a growing share (Figure 2.8). This increasing share of services in value terms results from an increase in their production cost relative to other goods, but also reflects a structural shift towards a more services-oriented economy. This structural change is in part driven by the evolution of household consumption patterns. Demand for services, including health care services, increases as the average person gets older and wealthier. It is also to some extent driven by growing use of research and development (R&D) and services in industrial production. There have obviously been significant shifts within these large sectoral groupings. The types of services provided nowadays are quite distinct from those 40 years ago, for instance through the emergence of information and communications as a sector.

The *Outlook Baseline* projects that this structural shift towards a more services-oriented economy will level off in OECD countries by 2050. As indicated in Figure 2.9, sector shares in real terms (i.e. relative price effects are excluded) are more or less stable over time. According to the assumption of economic convergence, the service sectors in developing countries are projected to contribute a growing share to the global economy, while the share of the agricultural sector diminishes. These trends fit with the global shift towards more labour-driven economic growth. The declining share of agriculture does not imply that absolute levels

Figure 2.8. **Global trends in the proportion of value added by sector, 1970-2008**

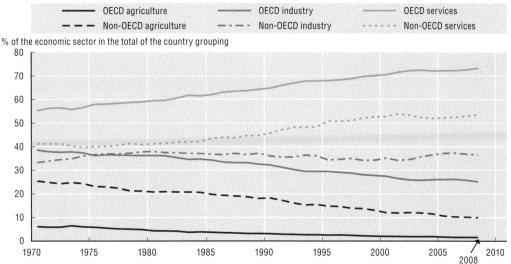

Note: The aggregate category of "industry" encompasses all manufacturing sectors.

Source: OECD calculations based on World Bank (2010), *World Development Indicators*, World Bank, Washington, DC, *http://data.worldbank.org/data-catalog/world-development-indicators*.

StatLink ⟦⟧ http://dx.doi.org/10.1787/888932570221

of food production will decrease, but merely that it grows less quickly than other sectors in the economy. To feed a growing population, global food production needs to continue to grow, thereby leading to increases in demand for agricultural land (see below).

Figure 2.9. **Share of sectors in real GDP by region:** *Baseline, 2010-2050*

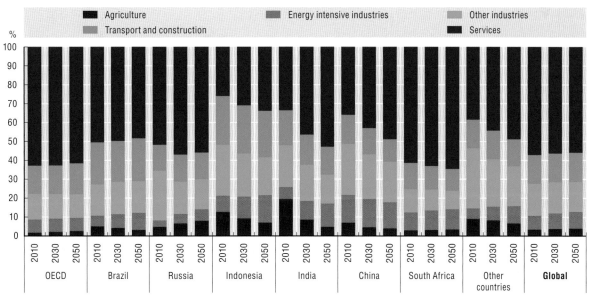

Note: The category "Energy intensive industries" encompasses chemicals, non-ferrous metals, fabricated metal products, iron and steel, pulp and paper, and non-metallic mineral products.

Source: OECD Environmental Outlook Baseline: output from ENV-Linkages.

StatLink ⟦⟧ http://dx.doi.org/10.1787/888932570240

3. The links between economic activity and environmental pressures

How do the trends outlined above link to the environment? This final section discusses trends in two drivers of environmental change – energy use and land use.

Energy use

Energy use is essentially driven by economic activity and technological developments, including energy efficiency improvements. Energy consumption patterns differ widely across the world. In OECD countries the average person consumes 3 tons of oil equivalent of energy (toe) a year, while in low-income regions, such as most of Africa and parts of Asia and Latin America, the figure is well below 1 toe (IEA, 2011). In 2009, about 1.4 billion people in low-income regions still had no access to electricity, and nearly 2.7 billion people mainly relied on traditional biomass (IEA, 2010).

As GDP is projected to almost quadruple by 2050, total commercial energy use is also projected to grow strongly over the next four decades, reaching about 900 Exajoule (EJ)[6] in 2050 – around an 80% increase over global energy consumption in 2010 (Box 2.4).[7] Continuous improvements in energy efficiency will reduce overall energy intensity (*i.e.* the ratio between energy use and GDP) to about 40% lower than current levels in 2050. Climate change (especially CO_2 emissions) and health impacts from local air pollution (Chapters 3 and 6) are strongly linked to trends in energy use and production. Figure 2.10 shows how the *Baseline* projection on total primary energy use relates to historical trends and the range found in the literature, as reviewed in van Vuuren *et al.* (2011).

Figure 2.10. **Global primary energy use: *Baseline*, 1980-2050**

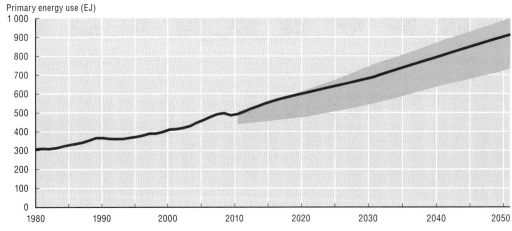

Primary energy use (EJ)

Notes: A widely accepted method for the accounting of primary energy use from different energy sources does not exist. Here, the methodology proposed by the IEA is used, which assumes a 33% efficiency for nuclear power and 100% for renewable power. Alternative methods may lead to slightly different contributions of nuclear power and renewables to the energy mix. The shaded area indicates the 10-90th percentile literature range.

Source: OECD Environmental Outlook Baseline; output from IMAGE.

StatLink 🔗 *http://dx.doi.org/10.1787/888932570259*

Figure 2.11 shows how the *Outlook Baseline* projects the different energy sources to change regionally by 2050. Despite the fact that most energy is currently consumed in industrialised countries, emerging and developing countries play a dominant role in energy production worldwide. In 2008, China supplied more than 40% of global coal production and the Middle East and Russia together accounted for almost 40% of oil production and about 35% of natural gas production (IEA, 2011). Consumption growth in the *Baseline* projection is mainly driven by increasing demand in the BRIICS and some other developing countries. Oil production in Europe, and to a lesser extent in North America,[8] decreases in the *Baseline* because of the progressive depletion of oil reserves.

Figure 2.11. **Commercial energy production by fuel:**
Baseline, 2010-2050

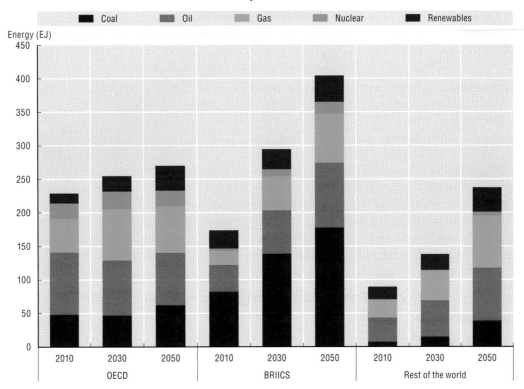

Source: OECD Environmental Outlook Baseline; output from IMAGE.

StatLink http://dx.doi.org/10.1787/888932570278

The increase in energy consumption in the *Baseline* scenario is consistent with similar projections by the International Energy Agency (IEA).[9] Assuming no change in current policies, fossil fuels retain a large market share in the *Baseline*, as their average prices remain lower than those of alternative fuels in most countries. Annual average growth rates of consumption are projected to be in the order of 0.5% for oil and 1.8% for coal and natural gas. For oil and natural gas, depletion and resulting price increases around the middle of the 21st century are projected to lead to stabilisation or even a peak in production, which is concentrated in only a few resource-rich regions. For coal, however, resource scarcity is not projected to limit production, or even lead to price increases, in the foreseeable future. With strong economic growth in coal-rich regions, it is likely that the share of coal in the energy mix will further increase. At the same time, non-fossil energy production, including nuclear, commercial biomass and other renewables, will increase steadily.[10]

Box 2.4. **Uncertainties in energy projections**

There are some key uncertainties surrounding energy projections embedded in the *Environmental Outlook Baseline* scenario:

i) The development of the energy intensity of the global economy has historically varied between 1%-2%. The assumptions made about this factor will have a major impact on projections of future emissions. The *Outlook Baseline* projects an average annual reduction in energy intensity of 1.3%, which is similar to IEA projections (IEA, 2010).

ii) A major driver of the energy mix is the relative price of different fuels. Given the complex nature of international fuel markets, and the large uncertainties surrounding resources, technology development and fuel prices in the future, this poses a major source of uncertainty in the *Baseline* projection of this *Outlook*.

Two sets of models were used for the *Environmental Outlook* (see Chapter 1 for more on the approach and methodology). Both models – ENV-Linkages and IMAGE – project that the overall share of fossil fuels in the energy mix to 2050 remains rather stable, as do the shares of nuclear and renewable energy. A key difference between the two models is whether coal or natural gas will be the main source of increased energy supply in the future. Based on IEA (2010) projections, the ENV-Linkages model projects the price of gas to increase more rapidly than that of oil and coal, thereby creating a relatively favourable environment for the build-up of coal-fired power plants in countries such as China and India. On the other hand, natural gas shows a more rapid growth rate in the next decades in IMAGE projections than in ENV-linkages projections. This is because in IMAGE, energy prices emerge from the relative availability of reserves of the different fossil fuels.

Land use

Agricultural production has increased strongly over recent decades to meet rising food demand driven by both population growth and changes in diets. About 80% of the production increase has been achieved through higher yields from existing land, and about 20% through expanding agricultural land (Bruinsma, 2003). Between 1970 and 2010, the share of agricultural land use (crop and grazing land), expanded by about 4 percentage points, largely at the expense of forest area (Figure 2.12). A somewhat lower pace of expansion has been observed over the last decade.

The *OECD Environmental Outlook Baseline* projects that competition between agricultural land use and other land uses will intensify in the coming decade under current policies (Box 2.5). This is also the conclusion of the *OECD/FAO Agricultural Outlook to 2020* (OECD/FAO, 2011). A converging GDP per capita and a growing population will both increase the demand for food, especially animal products. Moreover, policies that stimulate the use of biofuels also increase the demand for agricultural production and land area (Chapter 4). Given the limited supply of land, this means that in the short run deforestation will continue, although at slower rates than in past decades.

The population projections discussed above suggest that the global population will level off and largely stabilise around 2050. While changes in diets are expected to remain a factor in an increasing demand for agricultural production, these increases are projected to be less than the historical rates, in line with the convergence in income levels and, to some extent, consumer preferences. Based on these trends, the *Environmental Outlook Baseline* scenario projects global agricultural area to continue to

Figure 2.12. **Global land use: *Baseline*, 1970 and 2010**

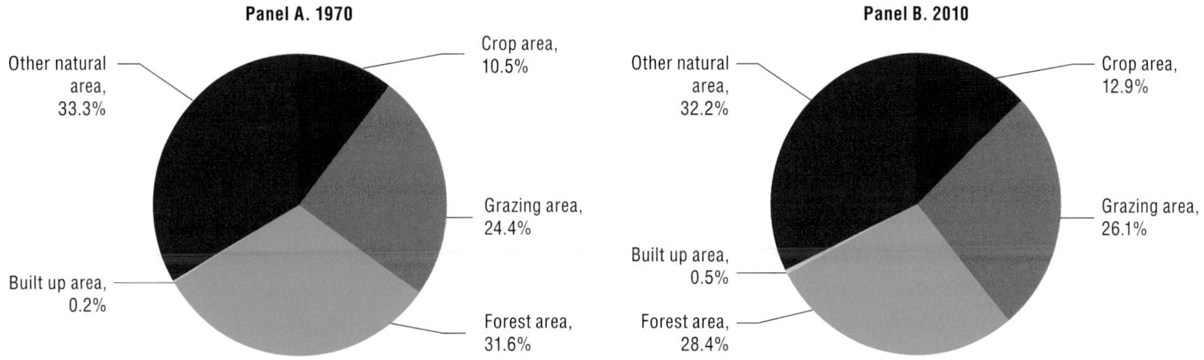

Panel A. 1970
Other natural area, 33.3%
Crop area, 10.5%
Grazing area, 24.4%
Built up area, 0.2%
Forest area, 31.6%
Panel B. 2010
Other natural area, 32.2%
Crop area, 12.9%
Grazing area, 26.1%
Built up area, 0.5%
Forest area, 28.4%

Source: OECD Environmental Outlook Baseline; output from IMAGE, calculations based on FAOStat data and additional data sources, including Klein Goldewijk, K. and G. van Drecht (2006), "HYDE 3: Current and Historical Population and Land Cover", in: Bouwman, A.F., T. Kram, K. Klein Goldewijk (eds.). Integrated Modelling of Global Environmental Change. An Overview of IMAGE 2.4. Netherlands Environmental Assessment Agency, Bilthoven.

StatLink http://dx.doi.org/10.1787/888932570297

increase to about 2030, after which it will stabilise then decline back to around today's levels by 2050. Yield improvements are assumed to be slower in the future than in past decades, but are still projected to eventually lower demand for agricultural land, even under current policies (Figure 2.13).[11]

Figure 2.13. **Global agricultural area: Various estimates, 1980-2050**

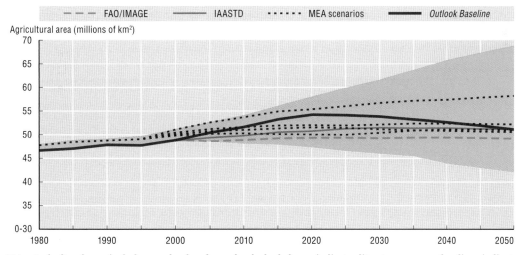

FAO/IMAGE
IAASTD
MEA scenarios
Outlook Baseline
Agricultural area (millions of km²)
70
65
60
55
50
45
40
35
0-30
1980
1990
2000
2010
2020
2030
2040
2050

Note: Agricultural area includes cropland and grassland; shaded area indicates literature range; other lines indicate specific projections.

Sources:

FAO/IMAGE = FAO (UN Food and Agriculture Organisation) (2006), *World Agriculture Towards 2030/2050*, FAO, Rome.

IAASTD = International Assessment of Agricultural Knowledge, Science and Technology for Development (2009), Global report, Island Press, Washington, DC.

MEA = Millennium Ecosystem Assessment (2005), Synthesis report, Island Press, Washington, DC.

Outlook Baseline = OECD Environmental Outlook Baseline; output from IMAGE.

StatLink http://dx.doi.org/10.1787/888932570316

Historical and projected trends in agricultural land use differ tremendously across regions. The area devoted to agriculture in OECD countries has decreased slightly since 1970, while there has been rapid expansion in other parts of the world (for instance, in Brazil, China and Indonesia, by 35%, 40% and 26% respectively). In OECD countries, a further slight decrease of 2% towards 2050 is projected (Figure 2.14). For the BRIICS as a whole, the *Baseline* projects a decrease of more than 17% to 2050, largely reflecting the declining population in China and Russia. A further expansion in agricultural area is projected for the rest of the world, at least in the coming decades, where population is still growing and the transition towards a higher calorie and more meat-based diet is likely to continue. In this region, forest areas are declining, especially where there is significant agricultural expansion. In other regions, including China, reduced demand for agricultural land is projected to lead to increases in forest area, not least to meet increased global demand for wood and other forest products.

Box 2.5. **Uncertainties in land-use projections**

As mentioned above, land-use projections are highly sensitive to the projections for climate change, population, dietary change and agricultural yield increases, and to a lesser extent urbanisation.* Yield increases have played a major role in historical land-use trends. The increase in yields in the *Baseline* projection is in line with FAO projections published in *Agriculture Towards 2030/2050* (Bruinsma, 2003). In contrast, the same assumptions on demand growth but with lower yield increases would lead to a continued expansion in land area to 2050. Both scenarios can be found in the literature: i) where agricultural area continues to grow (although more slowly); and ii) where it peaks in the next few decades, especially grazing land. Whether and when this peak might occur depends, among other things, on the extent to which yield increases continue to be driven by efficiency improvements (induced by technological progress), current policies, or by land scarcity. In comparison to the range found in the literature, the land-use projections for this *Outlook* show a rather intense competition among land uses in the short to medium term (to 2020), but a reversal of the trend in the following decades that is more optimistic than most other studies. Still, the resulting levels of land use for 2050 are well within the range found in the literature (*cf.* Figure 2.13).

* While the direct effect of urbanisation on land competition is limited, it should be noted that urbanisation often comes at the expense of highly productive agricultural land, thus stimulating further land use changes.

These agricultural developments are the main drivers of land-use change, and consequently developments in land-use related GHG emissions, changes in water stress and biodiversity pressures, as discussed in subsequent chapters.

Figure 2.14. **Projected growth of major land-use categories:** *Baseline*

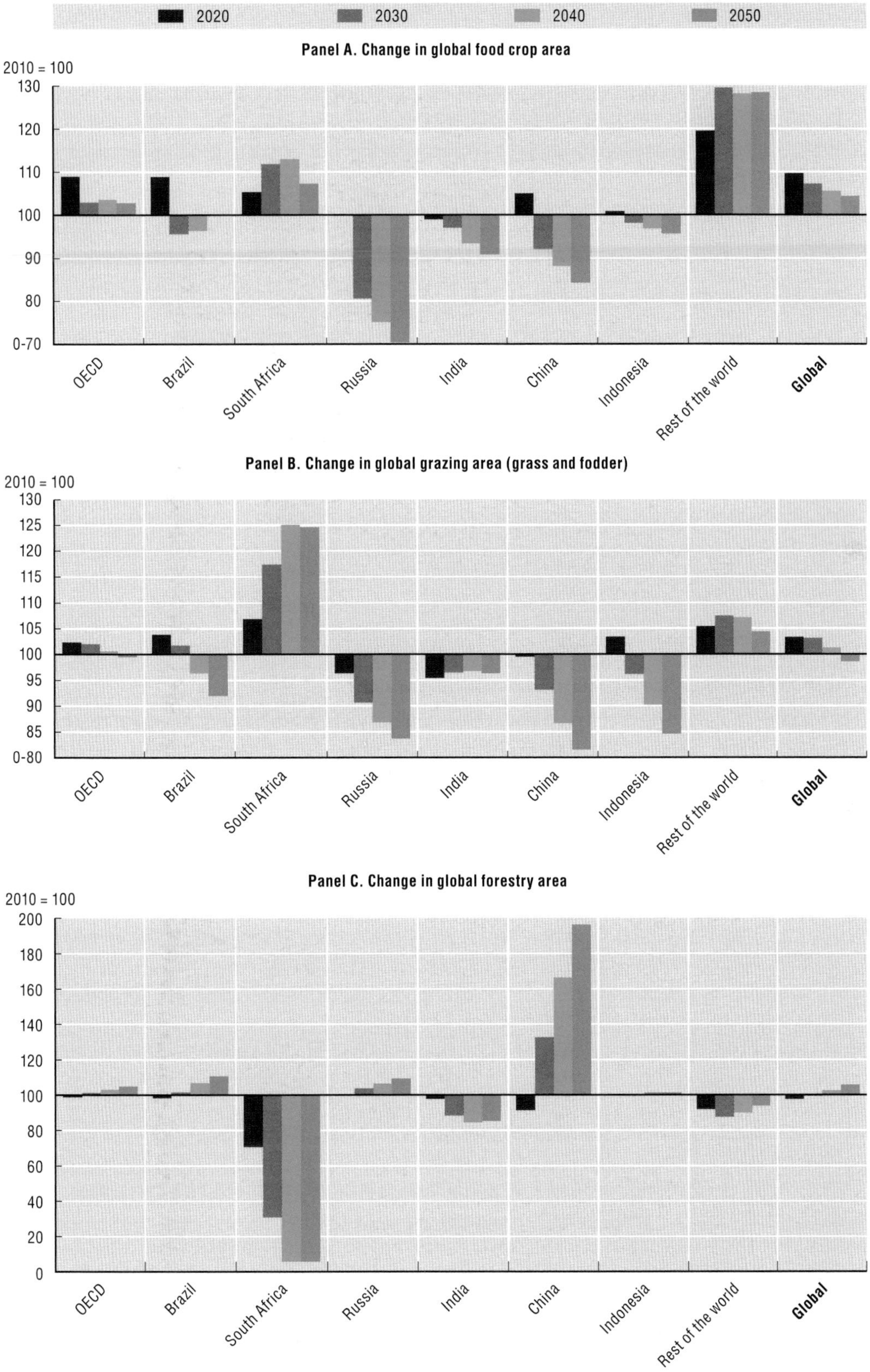

| ■ 2020 | ■ 2030 | ■ 2040 | ■ 2050 |

Panel A. Change in global food crop area

2010 = 100

OECD Brazil South Africa Russia India China Indonesia Rest of the world **Global**

Panel B. Change in global grazing area (grass and fodder)

2010 = 100

OECD Brazil South Africa Russia India China Indonesia Rest of the world **Global**

Panel C. Change in global forestry area

2010 = 100

OECD Brazil South Africa Russia India China Indonesia Rest of the world **Global**

Source: OECD *Environmental Outlook Baseline;* output from IMAGE.

StatLink ᴍᴤ▄ http://dx.doi.org/10.1787/888932570335

Notes

1. More details on the construction of the *Baseline* projection are given in Chateau *et al.* (2011).

2. This *Environmental Outlook* uses the UN's 2008 revision of medium-term population projections (UN, 2009), in which world population is projected to increase to 9.15 billion in 2050. The UN has since published revised projections for 2050 (UN, 2011) which are somewhat higher (9.3 billion), mainly due to greater projected population increase in Africa.

3. While GDP is an adequate measure of economic activity, it is not a good indicator of welfare (Stiglitz *et al.*, 2009).

4. Estimates of regional shares in global GDP depend crucially on the use of exchange rates. Here GDP aggregates are valued using constant 2010 purchasing power parity (PPP) exchange rates as presented in IMF (2010). As in recent years the US dollar has depreciated against most currencies, using older exchange rates would imply higher shares of both the US and the OECD aggregate. See Chateau *et al.* (2011) for a further discussion.

5. Although short-term cycles in economic activity are not considered in the projections presented in Figure 2.6, developments for 2010-2015 are based on short-term projections by IMF (2010), the World Bank (2010) and the OECD.

6. 1 Exajoule equals 1 billion Gigajoule, which is roughly equivalent to 23.9 million toe.

7. There is no widely accepted method for accounting for primary energy use from different energy sources. This graph uses the methodology proposed by the IEA, which assumes a 33% efficiency for nuclear power and 100% for renewable power. Alternative methods may lead to slightly different contributions of nuclear power and renewables to the energy mix.

8. The decrease in North America occurs in the United States and Mexico. In contrast, Canada is projected to increase oil production, especially from non-conventional sources such as shale oil.

9. Energy consumption patterns have been calibrated to match those of the IEA projections.

10. The projection for nuclear expansion was made before the earthquake and tsunami occurred in Japan in 2011. This emphasises that it is important to see these projections as long-term trends that do not incorporate the effects of unanticipated shocks.

11. For example, for temperate cereals the average annual yield growth rate in the *Baseline* projection is 1.0%, where it has historically been 1.5% (1970-2010; FAOStat data). Similarly, for rice the projection is +0.9% (historically +1.6%) and for maize 0.8% (historically +1.7%).

References

Bruinsma (2003), *Agriculture Towards 2015/2030*, Food and Agriculture Organization of the United Nations, Rome.

Chateau, J., C. Rebolledo and R. Dellink (2011), "The ENV-Linkages Economic Baseline Projections to 2050", *OECD Environment Working Paper*, No. 41, OECD Publishing.

Duval, R. and C. de la Maisonneuve (2010), "A Long-Run Growth Framework and Scenarios for the World Economy", *Journal of Policy Modeling* 62: 64-80.

EU (European Union) (2009), "Impact of the Current Economic and Financial Crisis on Potential Output", *Occasional Papers* 49, Directorate-General for Economic and Financial Affairs, European Commission.

FAO (2006), *World Agriculture towards 2030/2050*, Food and Agriculture Organization of the United Nations, Rome.

IAASTD (2009), *International Assessment of Agricultural Science and Technology for Development: Global Report*, Island Press, Washington, DC.

International Energy Agency (IEA) (2010), *World Energy Outlook 2010*, OECD Publishing, doi: 10.1787/weo-2010-en.

IEA (2011), *Energy Balances of non-OECD Countries 2011*, OECD Publishing, doi: 10.1787/energy_bal_non-oecd-2011-en.

IMF (International Monetary Fund) (2010), *World Economic Outlook Database*, IMF, Washington, DC, www.imf.org/external/pubs/ft/weo/2010/02/weodata/index.aspx.

IPCC (Intergovernmental Panel on Climate Change) (2007), *Fourth Assessment Report of the Intergovernmental Panel on Climate Change*, Cambridge University Press, New York.

Klein Goldewijk, K. and G. van Drecht (2006), "HYDE 3: Current and Historical Population and Land Cover", in: Bouwman, A.F., Kram, T., Klein Goldewijk, K. (eds.), *Integrated Modelling of Global Environmental Change, An Overview of IMAGE 2.4*, PBL Netherlands Environmental Assessment Agency, The Hague/Bilthoven.

MEA (2005), *Millennium Ecosystem Assessment Synthesis Report*, Island Press, Washington, DC.

Maddison (2010), *Statistics on World Population, GDP and Per Capita GDP, 1-2008 AD*, University of Groningen, *www.ggdc.net/MADDISON/oriindex.htm*.

OECD (2011), *Towards Green Growth*, OECD Green Growth Studies, OECD Publishing, doi: *10.1787/9789264111318-en*.

OECD (2008a), *Costs of Inaction on Key Environmental Challenges*, OECD Publishing, doi: *10.1787/9789264045828-en*.

OECD (2008b), *OECD Environmental Outlook to 2030*, OECD Publishing, doi: *10.1787/9789264040519-en*.

OECD/Food and Agriculture Organization of the United Nations (2011), *OECD-FAO Agricultural Outlook 2011-2020*, OECD Publishing, doi: *10.1787/agr_outlook-2011-en*.

Stiglitz, J.E., A. Sen and J. Fitoussi (2009), *Report by the Commission on the Measurement of Economic Performance and Social Progress*, available at *www.stiglitz-sen-fitoussi.fr/en/index.htm*.

UN Habitat (2003), *The Challenge of Slums: Global Report on Human Settlements 2003*, UN Habitat, New York.

UN Habitat (2006), *State of the World's Cities: 2006/2007*, UN Habitat, New York.

UN (United Nations) (2009), *World Population Prospects: The 2008 Revision*, New York.

UN (2010), *World Urbanization Prospects: The 2009 Revision*, UN Habitat, New York.

UN (2011), *World Population Prospects: The 2010 Revision*, New York.

Vuuren, van D.P., K. Riahi, R. Moss, A. Thomson, N. Nakicenovic, J. Edmonds, T. Kram, F. Berkhout, R. Swart, A. Janetos, S. Rose, A. Arnell (2011), "Developing new scenarios as a thread for future climate research", *Global Environmental Change*, in press; doi *10.1016/j.gloenvcha.2011.08.002*.

World Bank (2010), *World Development Indicators*, World Bank, Washington, DC, *http://data.worldbank.org/data-catalog/world-development-indicators*.

ANNEX 2.A

Modelling Background Information on Socio-economic Developments

Figure 2.A1. **Decomposition of the drivers of GDP growth by region, in percentage: Baseline**

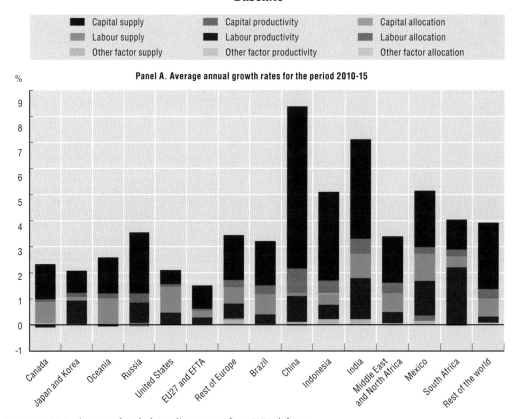

Source: *OECD Environmental Outlook Baseline; output from ENV-Linkages.*

StatLink ᴍ𝒮𝒫 *http://dx.doi.org/10.1787/888932570354*

Figure 2.A1. **Decomposition of the drivers of GDP growth by region, in percentage:**
Baseline (cont.)

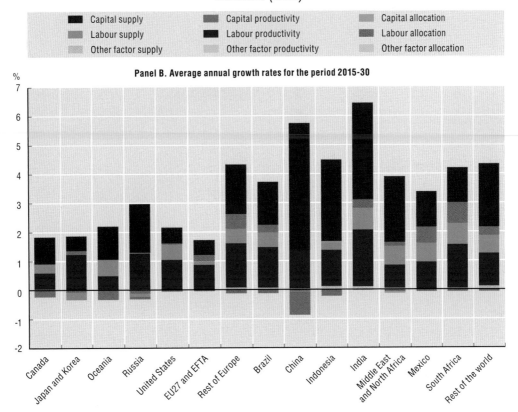

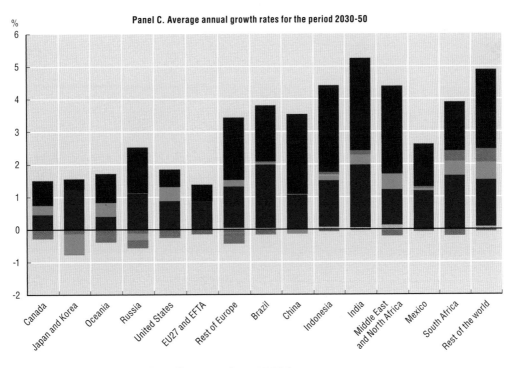

Source: *OECD Environmental Outlook Baseline; output from ENV-Linkages.*

StatLink ᵐˢ▱ http://dx.doi.org/10.1787/888932570354

Chapter 3

Climate Change

by

Virginie Marchal, Rob Dellink, Detlef van Vuuren (PBL), Christa Clapp,
Jean Chateau, Bertrand Magné, Elisa Lanzi, Jasper van Vliet (PBL)

This chapter analyses the policy implications of the climate change challenge. Are current emission reduction pledges made in Copenhagen/Cancun enough to stabilise the climate and limit global average temperature increase to 2 °C? If not, what will the consequences be? What alternative growth pathways could stabilise the global average atmospheric concentration of greenhouse gases (GHG) at 450 ppm, the level which has a 50% chance of keeping the temperature rise to 2 °C? What policies are needed, and what will be the costs and benefits to the economy? How can the world adapt to the warming that is already occurring? To shed light on these questions, this chapter first looks at trends to 2050 in GHG concentration and emissions (including from land use), temperature and precipitation under the Environmental Outlook Baseline scenario of "business-as-usual" (i.e. no new action). It then takes stock of the state of climate policy today. Most countries use a mix of policy instruments, including carbon pricing (carbon taxes, cap-and-trade emissions trading, fossil fuel subsidy reform), other energy efficiency policies, information-based approaches and innovation policies to foster clean technology. The chapter then looks at what further action is needed by comparing different mitigation scenarios against the Baseline. These include various scenarios to stabilise GHG concentrations at 450 ppm and 550 ppm using different technology options, e.g. carbon capture and storage, phasing out nuclear power, and increasing the use of biofuels; linking carbon markets; and various emissions permit allocation rules. The chapter concludes by outlining how limiting global warming will require transformative policies to reconcile short-term action with long-term climate objectives, balancing their costs and benefits. Timely adaptation policies to limit damage by the already changing climate will also be essential.

KEY MESSAGES

Climate change presents a global systemic risk to society. It threatens the basic elements of life for all people: access to water, food production, health, use of land, and physical and natural capital. Inadequate attention to climate change could have significant social consequences for human well-being, hamper economic growth and heighten the risk of abrupt and large-scale changes to our climatic and ecological systems. The significant economic damage could equate to a permanent loss in average per-capita world consumption of more than 14% (Stern, 2006). Some poor countries would be likely to suffer particularly severely. This chapter demonstrates how avoiding these economic, social and environmental costs will require effective policies to shift economies onto low-carbon and climate-resilient growth paths.

Trends and projections

Environmental state and pressures

 Global greenhouse gas (GHG) emissions continue to increase, and in 2010 global **energy-related carbon dioxide (CO_2) emissions** reached an all-time high of 30.6 gigatonnes (Gt) despite the recent economic crisis. *The Environmental Outlook Baseline* scenario envisages that without more ambitious policies than those in force today, GHG emissions will increase by another 50% by 2050, primarily driven by a projected 70% growth in CO_2 emissions from energy use. This is mainly due to a projected 80% increase in global energy demand. Transport emissions are projected to double, due to a strong increase in demand for cars in developing countries. Historically, OECD economies have been responsible for most of the emissions. In the coming decades, increasing emissions will also be caused by high economic growth in some of the major emerging economies.

GHG emissions by region: *Baseline*, 2010-2050

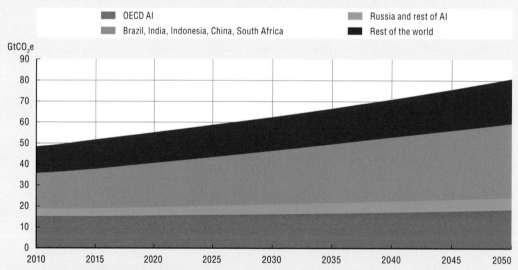

Note: "OECD AI" stands for the group of OECD countries that are also part of Annex I of the Kyoto Protocol. $GtCO_2e$ = Giga tonnes of CO_2 equivalent.

Source: OECD Environmental Outlook Baseline; output from ENV-Linkages.

StatLink ⟶ http://dx.doi.org/10.1787/888932570468

 Without more ambitious policies, the *Baseline* projects that **atmospheric concentrations of GHG** would reach almost 685 parts per million (ppm) CO_2-equivalents by 2050. This is well above the concentration level of 450 ppm required to have at least a 50% chance of stabilising the climate at a 2-degree Celsius (2 °C) global average **temperature increase**, the goal set at the 2010 United Nations Framework Convention on Climate Change (UNFCCC) Conference in Cancún. Under the *Baseline* projection, global average temperature is likely to exceed this goal by 2050, and to be 3 °C to 6 °C higher than pre-industrial levels by the end of the century. Such a high temperature increase would continue to alter precipitation patterns, melt glaciers, cause sea-level rise and intensify extreme weather events to unprecedented levels. It might also exceed some critical "tipping-points", causing dramatic natural changes that could have catastrophic or irreversible outcomes for natural systems and society.

Technological progress and structural shifts in the composition of growth are projected to improve the **energy intensity of economies** in the coming decades (*i.e.* achieving a relative decoupling of GHG emissions growth and GDP growth), especially in the OECD and the emerging economies of Brazil, Russia, India, Indonesia, China and South Africa (BRIICS). However, under current trends, these regional improvements would be outstripped by the increased energy demand worldwide.

Emissions from land use, land-use change and forestry (LULUCF) are projected to decrease in the course of the next 30 years, while carbon sequestration by forests increases. By 2045, net-CO_2 emissions from land use are projected to become negative in OECD countries. Most emerging economies also show a decreasing trend in emissions from an expected slowing of deforestation. In the rest of the world (RoW), land-use emissions are projected to increase to 2050, driven by expanding agricultural areas, particularly in Africa.

Policy responses

Pledging action to achieve national GHG emission reduction targets and actions under the UNFCCC at Copenhagen and Cancún was an important first step by countries in finding a global solution. However, **the mitigation actions** pledged by countries are not enough to be on a least-cost pathway to meet the 2 °C goal. Limiting temperature increase to 2 °C from these pledges would require substantial additional costs after 2020 to ensure that atmospheric concentrations of GHGs do not exceed 450 ppm over the long term. More ambitious action is therefore needed now and post-2020. For example, 80% of the projected emissions from the power sector in 2020 are inevitable, as they come from power plants that are already in place or are being built today. The world is locking itself into carbon-intensive systems more strongly every year. Prematurely closing plants or retrofitting with carbon capture and storage (CCS) – at significant economic cost – would be the only way to reverse this "lock-in".

Progress has been made in developing national strategies for **adapting to climate change**. These also encourage the assessment and management of climate risk in relevant sectors. However, there is still a long way to go before the right instruments and institutions are in place to explicitly incorporate climate change risk into policies and projects, increase private-sector engagement in adaptation actions and integrate climate change adaptation into development co-operation.

Policy steps to build a low-carbon, climate-resilient economy

We must act now to reverse emission trends in order to stabilise GHG concentrations at 450 ppm CO_2e and increase the chance of limiting the global average temperature rise to 2 °C. Ambitious mitigation action substantially lowers the risk of catastrophic climate change. The cost of reaching the 2 °C goal would slow global GDP growth from 3.5 to 3.3% per year (or by 0.2 percentage-points) on average, costing roughly 5.5% of global GDP in 2050. This cost should be compared with the potential cost of inaction, which could be as high as 14% of average world consumption per capita according to some estimates (Stern, 2006).

Delaying action is costly. Delayed or only moderate action up to 2020 (such as implementing the Copenhagen/Cancún pledges only, or waiting for better technologies to come on stream) would increase the pace and scale of efforts needed after 2020. It would lead to 50% higher costs in 2050 compared to timely action, and potentially entail higher environmental risk.

A prudent response to climate change calls for both an ambitious mitigation policy to reduce further climate change, and timely adaptation policies to limit damage from the impacts that are already inevitable. In the context of tight government budgets, finding least-cost solutions and engaging the private sector will be critical to finance the transition. Costly overlaps between policies must also be avoided. The following actions are a priority:

■ **Adapt to inevitable climate change.** The level of GHG already in the atmosphere means that some changes in the climate are now inevitable. The impact on people and ecosystems will depend on how the world adapts to those changes. Adaptation policies will need to be implemented to safeguard the well-being of current and future generations worldwide.

■ **Integrate adaptation into development co-operation.** The management of climate change risks is closely intertwined with economic development – impacts will be felt more by the poorest and most vulnerable populations. National governments and donor agencies have a key role to play and integrating climate change adaptation strategies into all development planning is now critical. This will involve assessing climate risks and opportunities within national government processes, at sectoral and project levels, and in both urban and rural contexts. The uncertainty surrounding climate impacts means that flexibility is important.

■ **Set clear, credible, more stringent and economy-wide GHG-mitigation targets** to guide policy and investment decisions. Participation of all major emission sources, sectors and countries would reduce the costs of mitigation and help to address potential leakage and competitiveness concerns.

■ **Put a price on carbon.** This *Outlook* models a *450 ppm Core* scenario which suggests that achieving the 2 °C goal would require establishing clear carbon prices that are increased over time. This could be done using market-based instruments like carbon taxes or emission trading schemes. These can provide a dynamic incentive for innovation, technological change and driving private finance towards low-carbon, climate-resilient investments. These can also generate revenues to ease tight government budgets and potentially provide new sources of public funds. For example, if the Copenhagen Accord pledges and actions for Annex I countries were to be implemented as a carbon tax or a cap-and-trade scheme with fully auctioned permits, in 2020 the fiscal revenues would amount to more than USD 250 billion, i.e 0.6% of their GDP.

■ **Reform fossil fuel support policies.** Support to fossil fuel production and use in OECD countries is estimated to have been about USD 45-75 billion a year in recent years; developing and emerging economies provided USD 409 billion in 2010 (IEA data). OECD *Outlook* simulation shows that phasing out fossil fuels subsidies in developing countries could reduce by 6% global energy-related GHG emissions, provide incentives for increased energy efficiency and renewable energy and also increase public finance for climate action. However, fossil fuel subsidy reforms should be implemented carefully while addressing potential negative impacts on households through appropriate measures.

■ **Foster innovation and support new clean technologies.** The cost of mitigation could be significantly reduced if R&D could come up with new breakthrough technologies. For example, emerging technologies – such as bioenergy from waste biomass and CCS – have the potential to absorb carbon from the atmosphere. Perfecting these technologies, and finding new ones, will require a clear price on carbon, targeted government-funded R&D, and policies to reduce the financial risks.

■ **Complement carbon pricing with well-designed regulations.** Carbon pricing and support for innovation may not be enough to ensure all energy-efficiency options are adopted or accessible. Additional targeted regulatory instruments (such as fuel, vehicle and building-efficiency standards) may also be required. If designed to overcome market barriers and avoid costly overlap with market-based instruments, they can accelerate the uptake of clean technologies, encourage innovation and reduce emissions cost-effectively. The net contribution of the instrument "mix" to social welfare, environmental effectiveness and economic efficiency should be regularly reviewed.

1. Introduction

Climate change is a serious global systemic risk that threatens life and the economy. Observations of increases in global average temperatures, widespread melting of snow and ice, and a rising global average sea level indicate that the climate is already warming (IPCC, 2007a). If greenhouse gas (GHG) emissions continue to grow, this could result in a wide range of adverse impacts and potentially trigger large-scale, irreversible and catastrophic changes (IPCC, 2007b) that will exceed the adaptive capacity of natural and social systems. The environmental, social and economic costs of inaction are likely to be significant. Agreements reached in Cancún, Mexico, at the 2010 United Nations Climate Change Conference recognised the need for deep cuts in global GHG emissions in order to limit the global average temperature increase to 2 degrees Celsius (2 °C) above pre-industrial levels (UNFCCC, 2011a). A temperature increase of more than 2 °C is likely to push components of the Earth's climate system past critical thresholds, or "tipping points" (EEA, 2010).

This chapter seeks to analyse the policy implications of the climate change challenge. Are current emission reduction pledges enough to stabilise climate change and limit global average temperature increase to 2 °C? If not, what will the consequences be? What alternative growth pathways could achieve this goal? What policies are needed, and what will be the costs and benefits to the economy? And last, but not least, how can the world adapt to the changes that are already occurring?

To shed light on these questions, this chapter first looks at the "business-as-usual" situation, using projections from the *Environmental Outlook Baseline* scenario, to see what the climate would be like in 2050 if no new action is taken.[1] It then compares different policy scenarios against this "no-new-policy" *Baseline* scenario to understand how the situation could be improved. Section 3 ("Climate Change: The state of policy today") describes how a prudent response to climate change involves a two-pronged approach: ambitious mitigation policies[2] to reduce further climate change, as well as timely adaptation[3] policies to limit damage by climate change impacts that are inevitable. Mitigation and adaptation policies are essential, and they are complementary. Most countries have begun to respond through actions at the international, national and local levels, drawing on a mix of policy instruments that include carbon pricing, other energy-efficiency policies, information-based approaches and innovation. Some progress can be noted, but much more needs to be done to achieve the 2 °C goal.

The chapter concludes by outlining how limiting global warming will require transformative policies to reconcile short-term action with long-term climate objectives, balancing their costs and benefits. The transition to a low-carbon, climate-resilient development path requires financing, innovation and strategies that also address potential negative competitiveness and employment impacts. Such a path can also create new opportunities as part of a green growth strategy. Thus, the work presented here shows that through appropriate policies and international co-operation, climate change can be tackled in a way that will not cap countries' aspirations for growth and prosperity.

2. Trends and projections

Greenhouse gas emissions and concentrations

Historical and recent trends

Several gases contribute to climate change. The Kyoto Protocol[4] intends to limit emissions of the six gases which are responsible for the bulk of global warming. Of these, the three most potent are carbon dioxide (CO_2), methane (CH_4), and nitrous oxide (N_2O), currently accounting for 98% of the GHG emissions covered by the Kyoto Protocol (Figure 3.1). The other gases, hydrofluorocarbons (HFCs), perfluorocarbons (PFCs) and sulphur hexafluoride (SF_6) account for less than 2%, but their total emissions are growing. These gases differ in terms of their warming effect and their longevity in the atmosphere. Apart from these six GHGs, there are several other atmospheric substances that lead to warming (*e.g.* chlorofluorocarbons or CFCs, and black carbon – see Box 3.14) or to cooling (*e.g.* sulphate aerosols). Unless otherwise mentioned, in this chapter the term "emissions" refers to the Kyoto gases only, while the climate impacts described are based on a consideration of all the climate forcing gases (the term "climate forcer" is used for any gas or particle that alters the Earth's energy balance by absorbing or reflecting radiation).

Figure 3.1. **GHG emissions, 1970-2005**

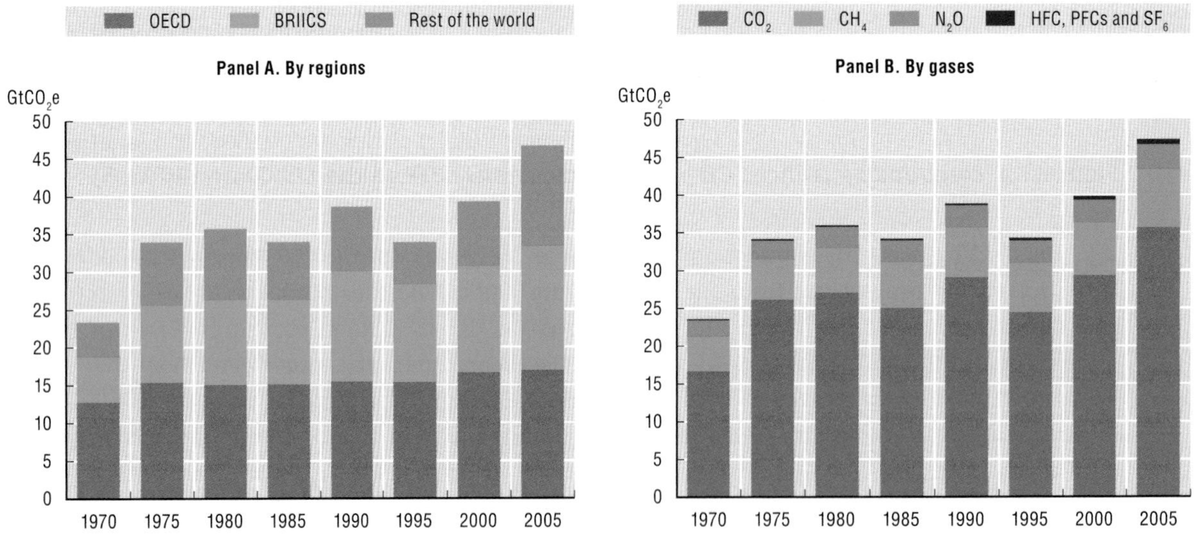

Note: BRIICS excludes the Republic of South Africa which is aggregated in the rest of the world (RoW) category. The emissions of fluor gases are not included in the totals by region.

Source: OECD Environmental Outlook Baseline; output from IMAGE.

StatLink http://dx.doi.org/10.1787/888932570373

Global GHG emissions have doubled since the early 1970s (Figure 3.1), driven mainly by economic growth and increasing fossil-energy use in developing countries. Historically, OECD countries emitted the bulk of GHG emissions, but the share of Brazil, Russia, India, Indonesia, China and South Africa (the BRIICS countries) in global GHG emissions has increased to 40%, from 30% in the 1970s.

Overall, the global average concentrations of various GHGs in the atmosphere have been continuously increasing since records began. In 2008, the concentration of all GHGs regulated in the Kyoto Protocol was 438 parts per million (ppm) CO_2-equivalent (CO_2e). This was 58% higher than the pre-industrial level (EEA, 2010a). It is coming very close to the 450 ppm threshold, the level associated with a 50% chance of exceeding the 2 °C global average temperature change goal (see Section 4).

Carbon dioxide emissions.   Today CO_2 emissions account for around 75% of global GHG emissions. While global CO_2 emissions decreased in 2009 – by 1.5% – due to the economic slowdown, trends varied depending on the country context: developing countries (non-Annex I, see Section 3.3) emissions continued to grow by 3%, led by China and India, while emissions from developed countries fell sharply – by 6.5% (IEA, 2011a). Most CO_2 emissions come from energy production, with fossil fuel combustion representing two-thirds of global CO_2 emissions. Indications of trends for 2010 suggest that energy-related CO_2 emissions will rebound to reach their highest ever level at 30.6 gigatonnes (GtCO₂), a 5% increase from the previous record year of 2008.[5] A slow-down in OECD emissions has been more than compensated for by increased emissions in non-OECD countries, mainly China – the country with the largest energy-related GHG emissions since 2007 (IEA, 2011a).

In 2009, CO_2 emissions from fossil fuel combustions were based on coal (43%), followed by oil (37%) and gas (20%). Today's rapid economic growth, especially in the BRIICS, is largely dependent on increased use of carbon-intensive coal-fired power, driven by the existence of large coal reserves with limited reserves of other energy sources. While emission intensities in economic terms (defined as the ratio of energy use to GDP) vary greatly around the world, CO_2 emissions are growing at a slower rate than GDP in most OECD and emerging economies (Figure 3.2). In other words, CO_2 emissions are becoming relatively "decoupled" from economic growth.

Figure 3.2. **Decoupling trends: CO_2 emissions *versus* GDP in the OECD and BRIICS, 1990-2010**

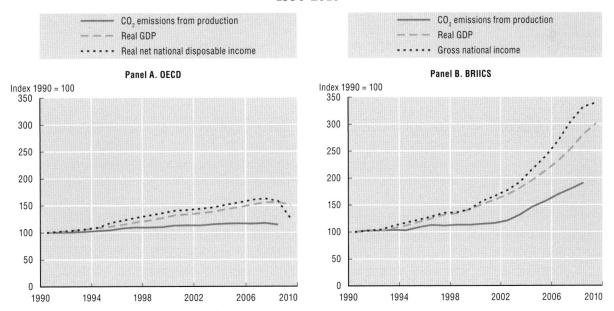

Note: CO_2 data refer to emissions from energy use (fossil fuel combustion).

Source: Adapted from OECD (2011e), *Towards Green Growth: Monitoring Progress*, OECD Green Growth Studies, OECD, Paris, based on OECD, IEA and UNFCCC data.

StatLink ᵃˢᵖ http://dx.doi.org/10.1787/888932570392

On a per-capita basis, OECD countries still emit far more CO_2 than most other world regions, with 10.6 tonnes of CO_2 emitted per capita on average in OECD countries in 2008, compared with 4.9 tonnes in China, and 1.2 tonnes in India (Figure 3.3). However, rapidly expanding economies are significantly increasing their emissions per capita. China for instance doubled its emissions per capita between 2000 and 2008. These calculations are based on the usual definition that emissions are attributed to the place where they occur, sometimes labelled the "production-based emissions accounting approach". If one allocates emissions according to their end-use, i.e. using a consumption-based approach, part of the emission increases in the BRIICS regions would be attributed to the OECD countries, as these emissions are "embedded" in exports from the BRIICS to the OECD (see Box 3.1).

Figure 3.3. **Energy-related CO_2 emissions per capita, OECD/BRIICS: 2000 and 2008**

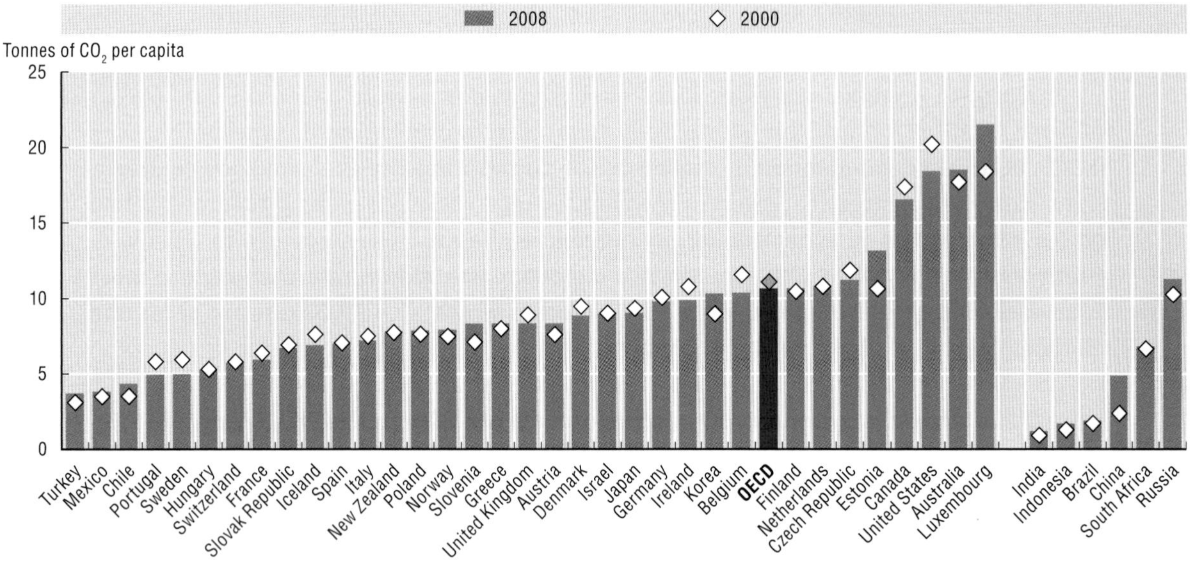

Note: Production-based emissions, in tonnes of CO_2 per capita.

Source: Based on OECD (2011e), *Towards Green Growth: Monitoring Progress*, OECD Green Growth Studies, from IEA data.

StatLink ᵐˢ᷄ʳ http://dx.doi.org/10.1787/888932570411

Other gases. Methane is the second largest contributor to human-induced global warming, and is 25 times more potent than CO_2 over a 100-year period. Methane emissions contribute to over one-third of today's human-induced warming. As a short-lived climate forcer, limiting methane emissions will be a critical strategy for reducing the near-term rate of global warming and avoiding exceeding climatic tipping points (see below). Methane is emitted from both anthropogenic and natural sources; over 50% of global methane emissions are from human activities,[6] such as fossil fuel production, animal husbandry (enteric fermentation in livestock and manure management), rice cultivation, biomass burning and waste management. Natural sources of methane include wetlands, gas hydrates, permafrost, termites, oceans, freshwater bodies, non-wetland soils, and other sources such as wildfires.

Nitrous oxide (N_2O) lasts a long time in the atmosphere (approximately 120 years) and has powerful heat trapping effects – about 310 times more powerful than CO_2. It therefore has a large global warming potential. Around 40% of N_2O emissions are anthropogenic, and come mainly from soil management, mobile and stationary combustion of fossil fuel,

Box 3.1. **Production *versus* demand-based emissions**

Production-based accounting of CO_2 emissions allocates emissions to the country where production occurs – it does not account for emissions caused by final domestic demand. Alternatively, consumption-based accounting differs from traditional, production-based inventories because of imports and exports of goods and services that, either directly or indirectly, involve CO_2 emissions. Emissions embedded in imported goods are added to direct emissions from domestic production, while emissions related to exported goods are deducted. A comparison between the two approaches shows that total emissions generated to meet demand in OECD countries have increased faster than emissions from production in these countries (Figure 3.4).

However, international comparisons should be interpreted with caution as country differences are due to a host of factors – including climate change mitigation efforts, trends in international specialisation, and countries' relative competitive advantages. While the fast growth of production-based emissions in the BRIICS may partly reflect the worldwide shift of heavy industry and manufacturing to emerging economies, these figures should not be confused with carbon leakage[*] effects as they are based on observed trends in production, consumption and trade patterns.

Figure 3.4. **Change in production-based and demand-based CO_2 emissions: 1995-2005**

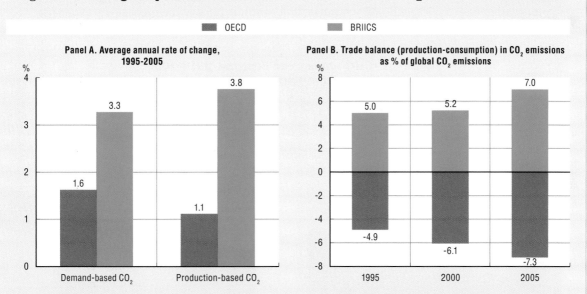

Source: OECD (2011e), *Towards Green Growth: Monitoring Progress*, OECD Green Growth Studies, based on IEA data.

StatLink http://dx.doi.org/10.1787/888932570430

[*] Carbon leakage occurs when a mitigation policy in one country leads to increased emissions in other countries, thereby eroding the overall environmental effectiveness of the policy. Leakage can occur through a shift in economic activity towards unregulated countries, or through increased fossil-energy use induced by lower pre-tax fuel prices resulting from the mitigation action.

adipic acid production (used in the production of nylon), and nitric acid production (for fertilisers and the mining industry).

CFCs and HCFCs are powerful GHGs that are purely man-made and used in a variety of applications. As they also deplete the ozone layer, they have been progressively phased out under the Montreal Protocol on Substances That Deplete the Ozone Layer. HFCs and PFCs are being used as replacements for CFCs. While their contribution to global warming is still relatively small, it is growing rapidly. They are produced from chemical processes involved in the production of metals, refrigeration, foam blowing and semiconductor manufacturing.

Future emission projections

This section presents the key findings of the *Environmental Outlook Baseline* scenario, which looks forward to 2050 and is based on business as usual in terms of policies and on the socio-economic projections described in Chapter 2 (see Annex 3.A for more detail on the assumptions underlying the *Baseline*). Any projection of future emissions is subject to fundamentally uncertain factors, such as demographic growth, productivity gains, fossil fuels prices and energy efficiency gains. The scenario suggests that GHG emissions will continue to grow to 2050. Despite sizeable energy-efficiency gains, energy and industry-related emissions are projected to more than double to 2050 compared to 1990 levels. Meanwhile, net emissions from land-use change are projected to decrease rapidly (Box 3.2). Emissions from BRIICS countries are projected to account for most of the increase (Figure 3.5). This is driven by growth in population and GDP per capita, leading to growing per-capita GHG emissions. In the OECD, emissions are projected to grow at a slower pace, partly reflecting demographic decline and slower economic growth, as well as existing climate policies. Overall, the contribution of OECD countries to global GHG emissions is projected to drop to 23%, but OECD countries will continue to have the highest emissions per capita (Figure 3.6).

Figure 3.5. **GHG emissions: *Baseline*, 2010-2050**

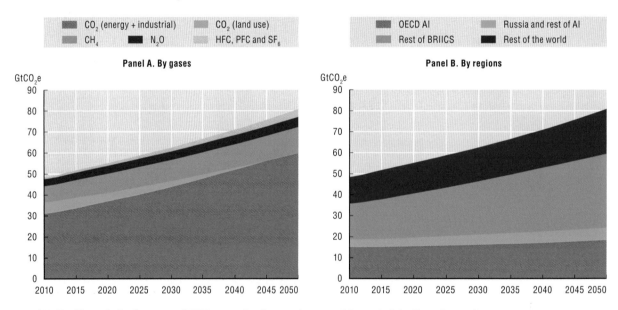

Note: "OECD AI" stands for the group of OECD countries that are also part of Annex I of the Kyoto Protocol.
GtCO$_2$e = Giga tonnes of CO$_2$ equivalent.
Source: OECD Environmental Outlook Baseline; output from IMAGE/ENV Linkages.

StatLink ⬛⬛⬛ http://dx.doi.org/10.1787/888932570468

Carbon dioxide emissions. CO$_2$ emissions are projected to remain the largest contributor to global GHG emissions, driven by economic growth based on fossil fuel use in the energy and industrial sectors. The International Energy Agency (IEA) estimates that unless policies prematurely close existing facilities, 80% of projected 2020 emissions from

Figure 3.6. **GHG emissions per capita:** *Baseline, 2010-2050*

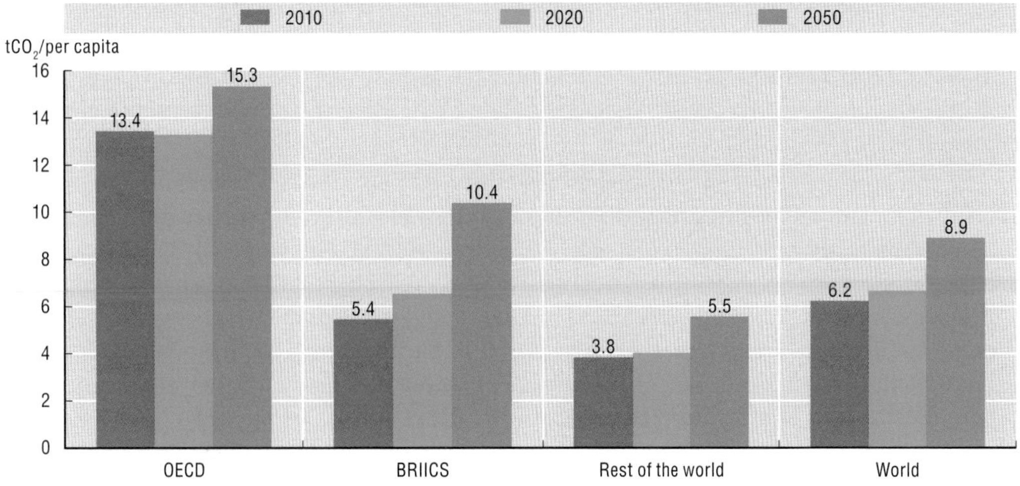

| 2010 | 2020 | 2050 |

tCO$_2$/per capita

[Bar chart showing GHG emissions per capita for OECD, BRIICS, Rest of the world, and World. OECD: 13.4 (2010), 15.3 (2050). BRIICS: 5.4 (2010), 10.4 (2050). Rest of the world: 3.8 (2010), 5.5 (2050). World: 6.2 (2010), 8.9 (2050).]

Source: OECD Environmental Outlook Baseline; output from IMAGE/ENV-Linkages.

StatLink http://dx.doi.org/10.1787/888932570487

the power sector are already locked in, as they will come from power plants that are currently in place or under construction (IEA, 2011b). Under the *Environmental Outlook Baseline*, demand for energy is projected to increase by 80% between 2010 and 2050. Transport emissions are projected to double between 2010 and 2050, due in part to a strong increase in demand for cars in developing countries, and growth in aviation (Figure 3.7). However, CO$_2$ emissions from land use, land-use change and forestry (LULUCF), driven in the last 20 years by the rapid conversion of forests to grassland and cropland in tropical regions, are expected to decline over time and even become a net sink of emissions in the 2040-2050 timeframe in OECD countries (Figure 3.5 and 3.8 and Box 3.2).

Figure 3.7. **Global CO$_2$ emissions by source:** *Baseline, 1980-2050*

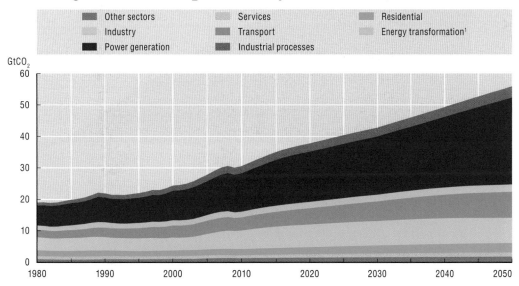

1. The category "energy transformation" includes emissions from oil refineries, coal and gas liquefaction.
Source: OECD Environmental Outlook Baseline; output from IMAGE.

StatLink http://dx.doi.org/10.1787/888932570506

Box 3.2. **Land-use emissions of CO_2 – past trends and future projections**

Historically, global net-CO_2 emissions from land-use change (mainly deforestation driven by the expansion of agricultural land) have been in the order of 4-8 $GtCO_2$ a year. Other factors also contribute to land-use related emissions, *e.g.* forest degradation and urbanisation.

In the *Baseline* scenario, the global agricultural land area is projected to expand until 2030, and to decline thereafter, due to a number of underlying factors such as demographics and agricultural yield improvements (see Chapter 2 for detailed discussions). However, the projected trends in agricultural land area differ tremendously across regions. In OECD countries, a slight decrease (2%) to 2050 is projected. For the BRIICS as a whole, the projected decrease is more than 17%, reflecting in particular the declining population in Russia and China (from 2035). At least for the coming decades, a further expansion in agricultural area is still projected in the rest of the world, where population is still growing and the transition towards a higher calorie and more meat-based diet is likely to continue. These agricultural developments are among the main drivers of land-use change, and consequently of developments in GHG emissions from land use (Figure 3.8). From about 2045 onwards, a net reforestation trend is projected – with CO_2 emissions from land use becoming negative.

However, there is large uncertainty over these projections, because of annual variations and data limitations on land-use trends and the exact size of various carbon stocks.[*] To date, the key driver of agricultural production has been yield increases (80%), while only 20% of the increase has come from an expansion in agricultural area (Smith *et al.*, 2011). If agricultural yield improvements turn out to be less than anticipated, global agricultural land area might not decline, but could stabilise or grow slowly instead.

Figure 3.8. **CO_2 emissions from land use: *Baseline*, 1990-2050**

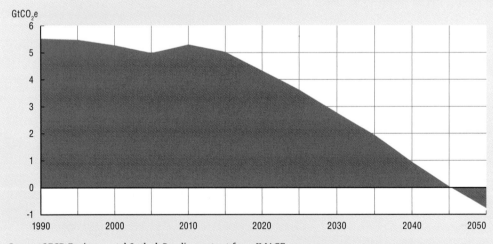

Source: OECD Environmental Outlook Baseline; output from IMAGE.

StatLink 🔗 http://dx.doi.org/10.1787/888932570525

[*] Land-use related emissions can be more volatile than energy emissions. For instance, emissions are not only influenced by land-use changes but also by land management. Furthermore, there is considerably more uncertainty in methodologies for evaluating land-use related emissions, as these are less well-established.

Other gases. Methane and nitrous oxide emissions are projected to increase to 2050. Although agricultural land is expected to expand only slowly, the intensification of agricultural practices (especially the use of fertilisers) in developing countries and the change of dietary patterns (increasing consumption of meat) are projected to drive up these emissions. At the same time, emissions of HFCs and PFCs, driven by increasing demand for coolants and use in semiconductor manufacturing, will continue growing rapidly.

Impacts of climate change

Temperature and precipitation

Global warming is underway. The global mean temperature has risen about 0.7 °C to 0.8 °C on average above pre-industrial levels. These observed changes in climate have already had an influence on human and natural systems (IPCC, 2007b). The greatest warming over the past century occurred at high latitudes, with a large portion of the Arctic having experienced warming of more than 2 °C.

The projected large increase in global GHG emissions in the *Baseline* is expected to have a significant impact on the global mean temperature and the global climate. The Intergovernmental Panel on Climate Change's Fourth Assessment Report (IPCC, 2007a) concluded that a doubling of CO_2 concentrations from pre-industrial levels (when they were approximately 280 ppm) would likely lead to an increase of temperature somewhere between 2.0 °C and 4.5 °C[7] (the so-called climate sensitivity[8]). Climate sensitivity values above 5 °C, such as 8 °C or more, cannot be ruled out, which would shift the estimated temperature increases for existing emission levels even higher (Meinshausen *et al.* 2006; Weitzman, 2009).

Under the *Outlook Baseline* scenario, the global concentration of GHGs is expected to reach approximately 685 ppm CO_2-equivalent (CO_2e) by mid-century and more than 1 000 ppm CO_2e by 2100. The concentration of CO_2 alone is projected to be around 530 ppm in 2050 and 780 ppm in 2100 (Figure 3.9). As a result, global mean temperature is expected to increase,

Figure 3.9. **Long-run CO_2-concentrations and temperature increase: *Baseline*, 1970-2100**[1]

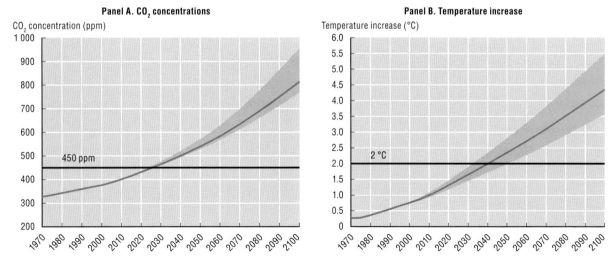

1. Uncertainty range (orange shading) is based on calculations of the MAGICC-5.3 model as reported by van Vuuren *et al.*, 2008.
Source: OECD Environmental Outlook Baseline, output from IMAGE.

StatLink ⓘ http://dx.doi.org/10.1787/888932570544

though there is still uncertainty surrounding the climate sensitivity. The *Outlook Baseline* scenario suggests that these GHG-concentration levels would lead to an increase in global mean temperature at the middle of the century of 2.0 °C-2.8 °C, and 3.7 °C-5.6 °C at the end of the century (compared to pre-industrial times). These estimates are roughly in the middle ranges of temperature changes found in the peer-reviewed literature (IPCC, 2007b).

Regions will be affected differently by these changes, and climate change patterns across regions are even more uncertain than the changes in the mean values. Figures 3.10

Figure 3.10. **Change in annual temperature:** *Baseline* **and** *450 ppm scenarios,* **1990-2050**

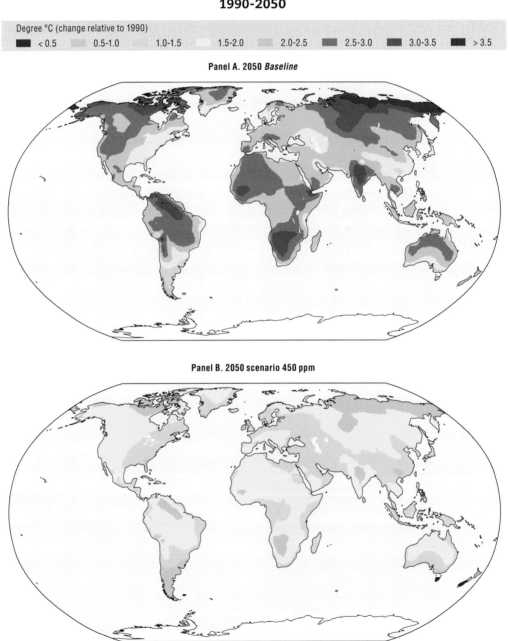

Source: OECD Environmental Outlook projections, output from IMAGE.

and 3.11 map the projected temperature and precipitation changes by region, both for the *Baseline* scenario and for the 450 ppm scenarios modeled as part of this *Outlook,* which would limit global average temperature increase to 2 °C above pre-industrial levels (see Section 4). For temperature, most climate models agree that changes at high-latitude areas will be larger than at low latitudes. For precipitation, while changes differ strongly across models, they all show that some areas will experience an increase in precipitation, while others will experience a decrease.

Figure 3.11. **Change in annual precipitation:** *Baseline,* **1990-2050**

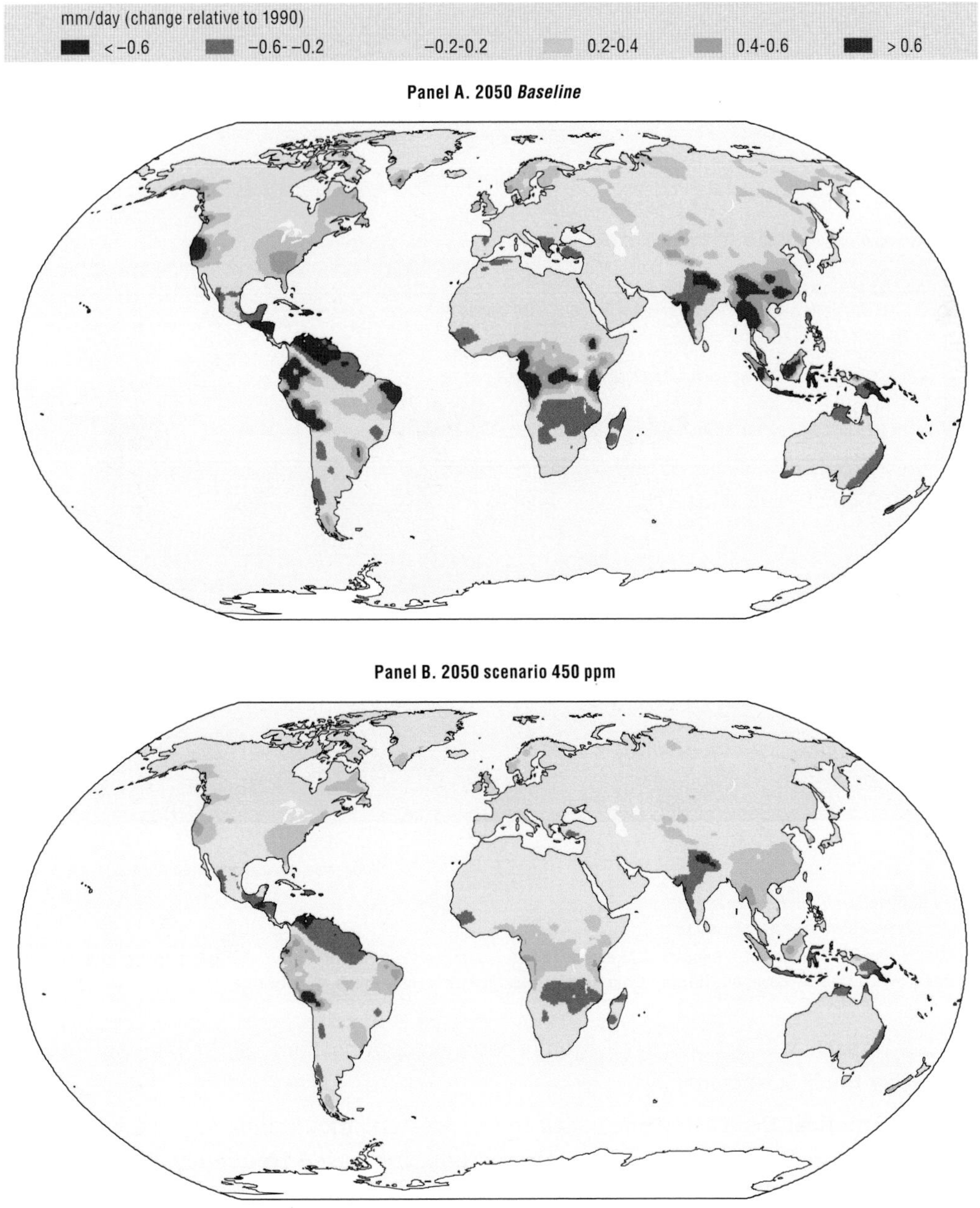

Panel A. 2050 *Baseline*

Panel B. 2050 scenario 450 ppm

Source: OECD Environmental Outlook projections, output from IMAGE.

Natural and economic impacts of climate change

In its Fourth Assessment Report, the IPCC concludes that global climate change has already had observable and wide-ranging effects on the environment in the last 30 years (Figure 3.12). Given the expected increase in temperature, the IPCC expects more impacts in the future.

Figure 3.12. **Key impacts of increasing global temperature**

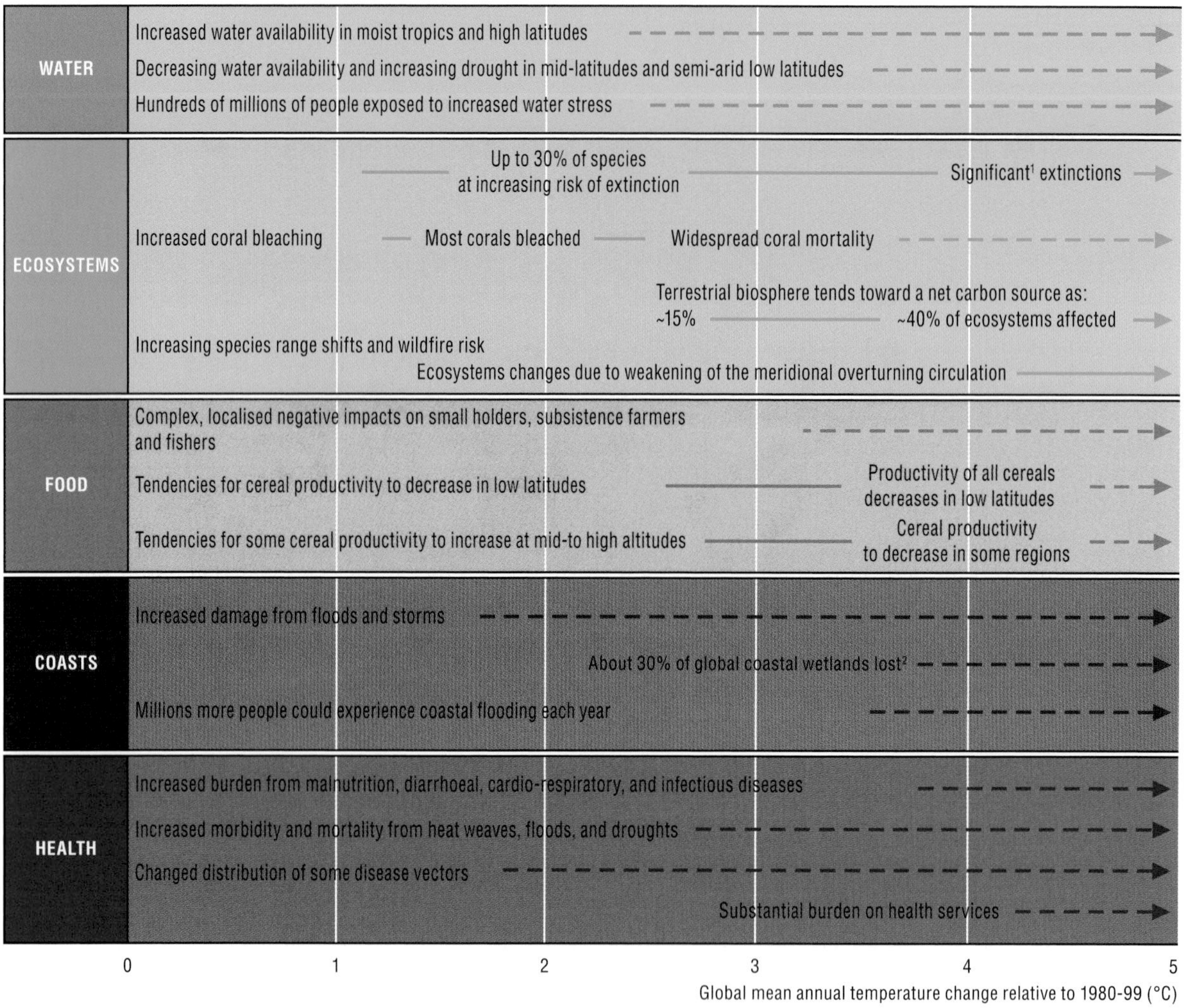

		0	1	2	3	4	5

Global mean annual temperature change relative to 1980-99 (°C)

1. Significant is defined here as more than 40%.
2. Based on average sea level rise of 4.2mm/year

Source: IPCC (2007b), *Climate Change 2007: Impacts, Adaptation and Vulnerability*, Contribution of Working Group II to the Fourth Assessment Report of the Intergovernmental Panel on Climate Change, Cambridge University Press, Cambridge.

The impacts will not be spread equally between regions. Some of the regional impacts forecast by the IPCC include:

■ **North America:** Decreasing snowpack in the western mountains; 5%-20% increase in yields of rain-fed agriculture in some regions; increased frequency, intensity and duration of heat waves in cities that already experience them.

■ **Latin America:** Gradual replacement of tropical forest by savannah in eastern Amazonia; risk of significant biodiversity loss through species extinction in many tropical areas;

significant changes in water availability for human consumption, agriculture and energy generation.

■ **Europe:** Increased risk of inland flash floods; more frequent coastal flooding and increased erosion from storms and sea-level rise; glacial retreat in mountainous areas; reduced snow cover and winter tourism; extensive species losses; reductions of crop productivity in southern Europe.

■ **Africa:** By 2020, between 75 and 250 million people are projected to be exposed to increased water stress; yields from rain-fed agriculture could be reduced by up to 50% in some regions by 2020; agricultural production, including access to food, may be severely compromised.

■ **Asia:** Freshwater availability projected to decrease in Central, South, East and Southeast Asia by the 2050s; coastal areas will be at risk due to increased flooding; the death rate from diseases associated with floods and droughts is expected to rise in some regions.

Overall, all regions are expected to suffer significant net damage from unabated climate change, but the most significant impacts are likely to be felt in developing countries because of already challenging climatic conditions, the sectoral composition of their economy and their more limited adaptive capacities. The costs of damages are expected to be much more important in Africa and Southeast Asia than in OECD or Eastern European countries (see Nordhaus and Boyer, 2000; Mendelsohn *et al.*, 2006 and OECD, 2009a for a compilation of results). Coastal areas would be particularly exposed as well (Box 3.3).

Recent research suggests that the impacts of unabated climate change may be more dramatic than estimated by the IPCC. For example, the extent of sea-level rise could be greater (Oppenheimer *et al.*, 2007; Rahmstorf, 2007). Accelerated loss of mass in the Greenland ice sheet, mountain glaciers and ice caps could, according to the Arctic Monitoring Assessment Programme (AMAP, 2009), lead to an increase of global sea levels in 2100 of 0.9m-1.6 m. In addition, researchers investigating climate feedbacks in more detail have found that rising Arctic temperatures could lead to extra methane emissions from melting permafrost (Shaefer *et al.*, 2011). They also conclude that the climate sensitivity could be higher than anticipated, meaning that a given temperature change could result from lower global emissions than those suggested in the Fourth IPCC Assessment Report.

Climate change might also lead to so-called "tipping-points", *i.e* dramatic changes in the system that could have catastrophic and irreversible outcomes for natural systems and society. A variety of tipping points have been identified (EEA, 2010), such as a 1 °C-2 °C and 3 °C-5 °C temperature increase which would respectively result in the melting of the West Antarctic Ice Sheet (WAIS) and the Greenland Ice Sheet (GIS). The potential decrease of Atlantic overturning circulation[9] could have unknown but potentially dangerous effects on the climate. Other examples of potential non-linear irreversible changes include increases in ocean acidity which would affect marine biodiversity and fish stocks, accelerated methane emissions from permafrost melting, and rapid climate-driven transitions from one ecosystem to another. The level of scientific understanding – as well as the understanding of possible impacts of most of these events – is low, and their economic implications are therefore difficult to estimate. Some transitions are expected to occur over shorter timeframes than others – the shorter the timeframe, the less opportunity to adapt (EEA, 2010).

Box 3.3. **Example of assets exposed to climate change: Coastal cities**

Coastal zones are particularly exposed to climate change impacts, especially low-lying urban coastal areas and atolls. Coastal cities are especially vulnerable to rising sea levels and storm surges. For example, by 2070, in the absence of adaptation policies such as land-use planning or coastal defence systems, the total population exposed to a 50cm sea-level rise could grow more than threefold to around 150 million people. This would be due to the combined effects of climate change (sea-level rise and increased storminess), land subsidence, population growth and urbanisation. The total asset exposure could grow even more dramatically, reaching USD 35 000 billion by the 2070s, more than 10 times current levels (Figure 3.13).

Figure 3.13. **Assets exposed to sea-level rise in coastal cities by 2070**

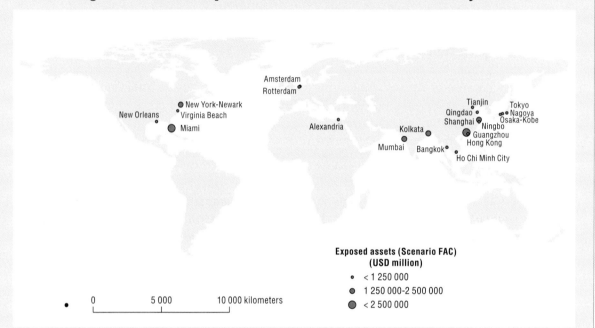

Note: Scenario FAC refers to the "Future City All Changes" scenario in Nicholls *et al.*, 2010, which assumes 2070s economy and population and 2070s climate change, natural subsidence/uplift and human-induced subsidence.

Source: OECD (2010a), *Cities and Climate Change*, OECD, Paris; Nicholls, R J. *et al.* (2008), "Ranking Port Cities with High Exposure and Vulnerability to Climate Extremes: Exposure Estimates", *OECD Environment Working Papers*, No. 1.

Climate change impacts are closely linked to other environmental issues. For example, the *Environmental Outlook Baseline* scenario projects negative impacts of climate change on biodiversity and water resources. Without new policies, climate change would become the greatest driver of future biodiversity loss (see Chapter 4 on biodiversity). The cost of biodiversity loss is particularly high in developing countries, where ecosystems and natural resources account for a significant share of income. Climate change can also affect human health; either directly through heat stress or indirectly through its effects on water and food quality and on the geographical and seasonal ranges of vector-borne diseases (see Chapter 6). Climate change will also have an impact on the availability of freshwater (see Chapter 5).

The costs of taking no further action on climate change are likely to be significant, though estimating them is challenging. The types of costs range from those that can easily be valued in economic terms – such as losses in the agricultural and forestry sectors – to those that are more intangible – such as the cost of biodiversity loss and catastrophic events like the potential shutdown of the Atlantic overturning circulation. Cost estimates vary due to the inclusion of different categories of cost and incomplete information. Most studies do not include non-market impacts, such as the impacts on biodiversity. A few include impacts associated with extreme weather events (*e.g.* Alberth and Hope, 2006) and low-probability catastrophic events (*e.g* Nordhaus, 2007). Depending on the scale of impacts covered in the models and the discount rate used, the discounted value of the costs of taking no further action to tackle climate change could equate to a permanent loss of world per-capita consumption of between 2% to more than 14% (Stern, 2006; OECD, 2008a).

These considerations must also be weighed against the potential of extreme and sudden changes to natural and human systems. The impacts of these low-probability but high-impact changes could have very significant or even catastrophic economic consequences (Weitzman, 2009). Some argue that in such contexts standard cost-benefit analyses may not be appropriate. It may be better to approach the issue in terms of risk management, using for example "safe minimum standards" (Dietz *et al.*, 2006) and "more explicit contingency planning for bad outcomes" (Weitzman, 2009; 2011).[10] In this context, assessments need to take into account the uncertainties involved; and decision making should be informed as much through sensitivity analysis which includes the extreme numbers as through central estimates. From a political perspective, the Cancún agreement to focus (at least partly) on the so-called 2 °C goal (see Section 1) has already established a political goal based on scientific evidence. This suggests that the world's governments find that the costs of allowing the temperature increase to go beyond 2 °C outweigh the costs of transitioning to a low-carbon economy.

3. Climate change: The state of policy today

This section first outlines the international framework for climate change mitigation and adaptation, before dealing with the current policies and challenges facing these two areas of action at the national level.

The international challenge: Overcoming inertia

Tackling climate change presents nations with an international policy dilemma of an unprecedented scale. Climate change mitigation is an example of a global public good (Harding, 1968): each country is being asked to incur costs – sometimes significant – to reduce GHG emissions, but the benefits of such efforts are shared globally. Other factors which complicate the policy challenge include the delay between the GHG being emitted and the impacts on the climate, with some of the most severe impacts not projected to materialise until the last half of this century. Climate impacts and the largest benefits of mitigation action are also likely to be distributed unevenly across a range of countries, with developing countries likely to suffer most from unabated climate change, in addition to having the least capacity to adapt. This means that although at the global level benefits of climate action are significant, country incentives to mitigate climate change are not sufficient to trigger the deep and urgent levels of mitigation required (OECD, 2009a).

Concerted international co-operation will be needed to overcome these strong free-rider effects that are causing individual regions and countries to delay action (Barrett, 1994; Stern, 2006). This will need to be underpinned by international agreements and include the use of financial transfers to encourage broad engagement by all economies. Creating an international architecture to advance climate mitigation also requires even stronger co-operation for low-carbon technology transfer and institutional capacity building to support action in developing countries. To be successful and widely accepted, international co-operation on climate change will also need to address equity and fairness concerns, issues which are often referred to as the "burden sharing" elements of the international regime.

Signature of the UNFCCC in 1992 was a first step towards achieving a global policy response to the climate change problem. Countries who signed the convention (the "Parties") have agreed to work collectively to achieve its ultimate objective: "stabilization of GHG-concentrations in the atmosphere at a level that would prevent dangerous anthropogenic interference of the climate system" (Article 2, UNFCCC[11]). By signing this convention, OECD and other industrialised economies (known as the Annex I Parties)[12] agreed to take the lead to achieve this objective, and to provide financial and technical assistance to other countries (non-Annex I[13] Parties) to help them address climate change. In 2005, the Kyoto Protocol entered into force and this created a legal obligation for Annex I Parties[14] to limit or reduce their GHG emissions between 2008 and 2012 to within agreed emission levels. By 2009, CO_2-emission levels for the group of countries participating in the Kyoto protocol were 14.7% below their 1990 level (IEA, 2011a), although with significant differences among countries.

Recent scientific evidence of climate change, including that provided in IPCC work, has led to agreement about the specific details of Article 2 of the Convention. This resulted in a statement in the 2010 Cancún Agreements that:

> "… recognizes that deep cuts in global GHG emissions are required (…), with a view to reducing global GHG emissions so as to hold the increase in global average temperature below 2 °C above preindustrial levels, (…) also recognizes the need to consider, in the context of the first review, strengthening the long-term global goal on the basis of the best available scientific knowledge, including in relation to a global average temperature rise of 1.5 °C" (UNFCCC, 2011a).

Another step forward has been the mitigation pledges made by many countries – both developed and developing – first in the 2009 Copenhagen Accord and later in the Cancún Agreements, to reduce emissions by 2020 (see Table 3.6 in Section 4; UNFCCC, 2009; and UNFCCC, 2011a).[15] Our analysis of all these pledges and commitments, however, shows that without significant further action post-2020, they are unlikely to be sufficient to stay within the 2 °C goal (see Section 4 and UNEP, 2010).

In order to share equitably the burden of action needed to meet the 2 °C goal, the Cancún Agreements reiterated the commitment by developed countries to provide new and additional financial resources to developing countries for climate action. This will include "Fast Start Finance" of USD 30 billion between 2010 and 2012, with a longer-term goal of raising USD 100 billion per year by 2020 from public and private sources.[16] Countries also agreed in Cancún to establish a Green Climate Fund that will support projects, programmes, policies and other activities in developing countries.[17] Nevertheless, significant challenges remain in the international climate negotiations regarding the future of the Kyoto Protocol and its instruments after it expires in 2012, and on the ability for governments to unlock additional finance and to monitor, report and verify those flows.

Until the 7th Conference of the Parties (COP7) in Marrakech in 2001, adaptation had received less attention in the international negotiation process, though it was mentioned in both the UNFCCC and the Kyoto Protocol. Parties at COP7 established three funds dealing with adaptation, the Least Developed Countries Fund, the Special Climate Change Fund and the Adaptation Fund. Adaptation has received more attention since then. The Cancún Agreements stressed the importance of adaptation and established a Cancún Adaptation Framework with an associated Adaptation Committee. The Green Climate Fund also recognises the need for balanced treatment of adaptation and mitigation.

National action to mitigate climate change

Despite some progress and the media attention focused on the global summits, only decisive policy action at the national level will limit local and global climate risks. To achieve the 2 °C goal, economies worldwide will have to go through unprecedented transformations in terms of energy production, consumption, transport and agriculture patterns. The transition to a low-carbon, climate resilient economy will require significant investments in mitigation and adaptation, and a shift of investment from fossil fuels and conventional technologies to newer, cleaner technologies and less carbon-intensive infrastructure. In the context of tight government budgets, finding least-cost solutions and engaging the private sector will be critical to finance the transition (OECD, 2012), and costly overlaps between policies must be avoided (OECD, 2011b). Government intervention will be needed to overcome existing barriers and create the appropriate market conditions for green investments.

The multiple market failures presented by climate change call for a mix of policy instruments to cut GHG emissions effectively. While there is no single recipe for a successful climate policy mix, there are certainly some important common ingredients, as noted by the OECD Green Growth Strategy (OECD, 2011e) and earlier OECD work (OECD, 2011a; OECD, 2009a; Duval, 2008). Key elements of a least-cost policy mix include (Table 3.1):

- national climate change strategies;
- price-based instruments, *e.g.* cap and trade, carbon taxes and removing fossil fuels subsidies;
- command and control instruments and regulations;
- technology support policies, including R&D;
- voluntary approaches, public awareness campaigns and information tools.

Each of these is discussed in turn below.

National climate change strategies and legislation

The Cancún Agreements state that industrialised countries should develop low-carbon development plans and strategies and also assess how best to meet them, including through market mechanisms. Developing countries are encouraged to do the same. Many industrialised countries have already developed national laws or strategies to address climate change. The objective of these tends to be centred on achieving Kyoto commitments and/or medium- to long-term emissions reduction targets. These targets,

Table 3.1. **Examples of policy tools for climate change mitigation**

Price-based instruments	Taxes on CO_2 emissions.
	Taxes on inputs or outputs of process (energy or vehicles).
	Removal of environmentally harmful subsidies (*e.g* for fossil fuels).
	Subsidies for emissions-reducing activities.
	Emissions trading systems (cap-and-trade or Baseline-and-credit).
Command and control regulations	Technology standards.
	Performance standards.
	Prohibition or mandating of certain products or practices.
	Reporting requirements.
	Requirements for operating certification.
	Land-use planning, zoning.
Technology support policies	A robust intellectual property rights system.
	Public and private R&D funding.
	Public procurement of low-carbon products and services.
	Green certificates (*e.g.* renewable portfolio standard).
	Feed-in tariffs for electricity from renewables.
	Public investment in infrastructure for new low-carbon technologies.
	Policies to remove financial barriers to green technology (loans, revolving funds, direct financial transfers, preferential tax treatment).
	Capacity building for the workforce, infrastructure development.
Information and voluntary approaches	Rating and labelling programmes.
	Public information campaigns.
	Education and training.
	Product certification and labelling.
	Award schemes.

Source: Adapted from de Serres A., F. Murtin and G. Nicoletti (2010), "A Framework for Assessing Green Growth Policies", *OECD Economics Department Working Papers*, No. 774, OECD, Paris.

plans or strategies are essential within a policy framework to encourage and steer investment to low-carbon, climate resilient outcomes; they also provide a long-term, stable investment signal to the private sector (Clapp *et al.*, 2010; Buchner, 2007; Bowen and Rydge, 2011).

National climate policy frameworks are emerging in Annex I countries, some of which establish legally binding, economy-wide emission constraints and/or long-term emission goals (Table 3.2). These aim to implement, reinforce or – in some cases – go beyond the country's international obligations. For example, the United Kingdom has a legally binding absolute emissions reduction target of at least 34% below 1990 levels by 2020 and at least 80% below 1990 levels by 2050 in its Low Carbon Transition Plan (LCTP). It introduces the concept of five-year carbon budget periods with binding milestones, beginning in 2008. The European Union's "20-20-20 Energy and Climate Package", adopted in January 2008, is an example of a comprehensive and legally binding climate strategy with three different objectives:

i) A reduction of GHG emissions by at least 20% compared to 1990 by 2020, with a commitment to increase it to 30% if a satisfactory international agreement is reached.

ii) A target of 20% of energy coming from renewable sources by 2020, supplemented by 10% of renewable transport fuel.

iii) A commitment to reduce the European Union's energy consumption by 20% compared to the *Baseline* in 2020.

In the United States, there is no federal law or economy-wide commitment to reduce GHG emissions, but the United States is bound by law to achieve reductions as a result of a Supreme Court case (Massachusetts v. EPA[18]). Fuel-efficiency standards for transport and stationary power plants have been finalised for 2012-2016 and regulations for 2017-2025 are in the process of being proposed. Also, following another two court cases and settlement agreements, the Environmental Protection Agency (EPA) will regulate GHGs from oil refineries and electric utilities by mid-2012.

Table 3.2 shows the emerging range of national climate policy and legislative frameworks, based on the *Climate Legislation Study* conducted by the Global Legislators Organisation (GLOBE). The study considers various areas of mitigation: specific energy-efficiency policies, carbon pricing, renewable energy and transport, as well as activities that can help both in adaptation and mitigation, such as forestry and land use. The authors analyse "flagship" legislation – a key piece of legislation on climate change policy – and consider the different sectoral priorities of the countries. Table 3.2 only considers activities implemented at national level, and not at local or regional level.

Table 3.2. **National climate change legislation: Coverage and scope, selected countries**

| | Coverage of legislation | | | | | | | Examples of flagship national legislation |
	Pricing carbon	Energy efficiency	Renewable energy	Forestry	Other land use	Transport	Adaptation	
Australia	M	X	X	X	X		X	Clean Energy Act (2011)
Brazil	X	X	X	M	X	X	O	National Policy on Climate Change (NPCC) (2009)
Canada		M	O	X	X	X		Canadian Environmental Protection Act, 1999 (CEPA 1999) and the Energy Efficiency Act (EEA)
Chile		X	X				M	National Climate Change Action Plan (2008)
China		M	X	X	X	X	X	12th Five Year Plan (2011)
EU	M	X	X	O	O	X	O	Climate and Energy Package (2008)
France	X	M	X		O	X	X	Grenelle I et II (2009 et 2010)
Germany	X	M	M			X		Integrated Climate and Energy Programme (2007, updated 2008) and 2010 Energy Concept
India		M	X	X	X	X	X	National Action Plan on Climate Change (NAPCC) (2008)
Indonesia	X	X	X	M	X	X	X	Presidential Regulation on the National Council for Climate Change (NCCC) (2008)
Italy	X	M	X	O		X		Climate Change Action Plan (CCAP) (2007)
Japan	X	M	X	X	X	X	X	Law Concerning the Promotion of Measures to Cope with Global Warming (1998, amended in 2005)
Mexico	X	X	M	X	X	O	O	Inter Secretariat Commission on Climate Change; LUREFET[1] (2005 and 2008)
Russia		M	O	O			X	Climate Doctrine (2009)
Portugal	O	M	M	X	X	X		National Climate Change Programme (PNAC), last revised in 2008
South Africa	X	X	M			X	X	Vision, Strategic Direction and Framework for Climate Policy (2008)
Korea	M	X	X	X	X	X	X	Framework Act on Low Carbon Green Growth (2009)
UK	M	X	X			X	X	Climate Change Act (2008)
US		X	M	O	O	X		No integrated federal climate change legislation[2]

Notes: M main focus; X detailed coverage; O some coverage.
1. Law for the Use of Renewable Energies and for the Finance of the Energy Transition.
2. Key environmental legislations include the Executive Order 13514; federal leadership in environmental energy and economic performance; and American Recovery and Re-investment Act. This table only considers activities implemented at national level, and not at local or regional level.
Source: Adapted from Townshend, T., S. Fankhauser, A. Matthews, C. Feger, J. Liu and T. Narciso (2011), The 2nd *GLOBE Climate Legislation Study*, GLOBE International, London.

Countries have also devised a variety of planning and strategy tools to meet specific targets, building on collection and analysis of historical trend data and often using model-based projections. France is undertaking a projection exercise to forecast energy consumption and GHG emissions to 2030 and to inform policy makers and stakeholders about progress to date and the need for further action. Japan has used model-based projections to prepare a roadmap for policy and measures to achieve a reduction of GHG emissions by 25% below 1990 levels by 2020 and 80% by 2050. Japan has developed the Asia-Pacific Integrated Model (AIM) and jointly used it in collaboration with institutes in other Asian countries to assess climate policy options through the low carbon scenario exercises. It is also using the modelling tool to work with sub-national stakeholders in regions and cities, as well as at the national level, to inform dialogue and decision making about climate policy. Experiences from all these collaborative activities are shared among researchers and policy makers through the International Research Network for Low Carbon Societies (LCS-RNet), a platform to link policies and researchers in the field of low-carbon strategies.

Price-based instruments

Putting a clear, credible and long-term price on carbon emissions across the economy through market-based instruments such as emission trading schemes or carbon taxes is necessary to drive investments in low-carbon technologies. It penalises carbon-intensive technologies and processes, creates markets for low-carbon technologies (*e.g.* for energy efficiency, solar, wind energy and carbon capture and storage [CCS][19]) and stimulates action in the energy, industry, transport and agriculture sectors. Putting a price on carbon can also help trigger green innovations and enhance energy efficiency (OECD, 2010b).

Emission trading schemes. Under emission trading systems (ETS) – often referred to as "cap and trade" – a central authority (usually a government body) sets a limit or cap on the amount of a pollutant that can be emitted. The limit or cap is allocated or sold to firms in the form of emissions permits which represent the right to emit or discharge a specific volume of the specified pollutant. Firms are required to hold a number of permits (or carbon credits) equivalent to their emissions. The total number of permits cannot exceed the cap, limiting total emissions to that level. Firms that need to increase their emission permits must buy permits from those who require fewer permits. In effect, the buyer is paying a charge for polluting, while the seller is being rewarded for having reduced emissions. Thus, in theory, those who can reduce emissions most cheaply will do so, achieving the pollution reduction at the lowest cost to society.

Emission trading schemes are becoming increasingly important in the climate policy portfolio. In the last 10 years, almost all Annex I Parties have either established or strengthened existing trading schemes and are in some way participating in either national or international carbon markets (UNFCCC, 2011b; Hood 2010). As of March 2011, there were seven active GHG-emissions trading schemes in OECD countries (some of which are sub-national), and several more under discussion, including in developing countries (Table 3.3). Nevertheless, there are several issues that need to be considered in order to increase the environmental effectiveness and economic efficiency of permit trading (*e.g.* the choice between a cap-and-trade system *versus* a Baseline-and-credit system;[20] the initial allocation of the emission allowances; and ways of limiting the transaction costs associated with the permit trading system) (OECD, 2008b).

Table 3.3. **Status of emission trading schemes**

Existing	Planned
The New South Wales Greenhouse Abatement Scheme (2003)	The Western Climate Initiative (WCI) (US)
European Union Emission Trading Scheme (2005)	California cap-and-trade programme
The New Zealand Emissions Trading Scheme (2008)	The Australian Clean Energy Future plan[2]
The Swiss Emission Trading Scheme and CO_2 Tax (2008)	The Midwestern Greenhouse Gas Reduction Accord (US)
The Regional Greenhouse Gas Initiative (RGGI) in the northeast of the US (2009)	The Japanese National Trading System
The United Kingdom Carbon Reduction Commitment (CRC) Energy Efficiency Scheme (2010)	Schemes are being discussed and implemented in Brazil, the State of California, Chile, China, Korea, Mexico, Turkey
The Tokyo Cap and Trade Programme	India is scheduled to launch an industrial sector energy-efficiency, or "white" certificate, trading programme in 2011
Alberta, Canada, Climate Change and Emissions Management Act (2007)[1]	

1. This is an emissions intensity reduction programme, not a cap-and-trade system. Facilities can purchase offset credits to meet their intensity reduction goals or purchase emissions performance credits, but there is no cap.
2. See *www.cleanenergyfuture.gov.au*.
Source: Based on data in UNFCCC (2011b), *Compilation and Synthesis of Fifth National Communications*, UNFCCC, Montreal.

The EU-Emission Trading Scheme (EU-ETS) is the world's largest emissions trading system and has led the way in building an international carbon market (Box 3.4). Outside the European Union, the New Zealand emissions trading scheme is the most developed. It is more comprehensive than any other trading schemes, covering all six Kyoto Protocol gases (CO_2, CH_4, N_2O, HFCs, PFCs and SF_6) from energy, transport, industry, waste, synthetic gases, and forestry sectors. It began operating in 2008 in the forestry sector, adding energy, industry and transportation in 2010. A recent independent review of the scheme has recommended that it should continue beyond 2012, although with changes to aspects of its design (Emissions Trading Scheme Review Panel, 2011).

To promote green electricity, several countries use quotas and certificates which allow sectors a certain level of emissions. They are tradable and are thus in effect market-based instruments. The certificates are usually not accounted for in tonnes of CO_2, but in amounts of energy produced from different sources (*e.g.* green certificates for energy from renewable sources, white certificates for energy savings, blue certificates for electricity production from combined heat and power). Such national trading schemes are in use in Poland, Sweden, the United Kingdom, Italy, Belgium, and some US states. Energy savings programmes (white certificates) are used in France, Demark, Italy, the United Kingdom, Australia, Belgium and around 30 US States. The Australian Renewable Energy Target (RET) of 20% by 2020 is implemented through a system of tradable green certificates known as renewable energy certificates. Quotas and feed-in tariffs have been used extensively in the energy sector in the European Union under the "20-20-20 Energy and Climate Package" (see above). Most EU member states use feed-in tariffs to meet their renewable energy target, while others – such as Poland, Romania and Sweden – use green certificates. Belgium, Italy and the United Kingdom use both feed-in tariffs and certificates.

In the absence of national regulation in a number of countries, sub-national governments, states and cities have initiated mandatory emission trading schemes. For example, the Regional Greenhouse Gas Initiative (RGGI) began operating in 2009 as a CO_2 cap-and-trade programme for electricity generators in 10 of the northeastern US States; and Tokyo in Japan has implemented the first local government-level CO_2 ETS. Offset market mechanisms[21] (such as the Clean Development Mechanism – see below – and Joint

Implementation[22]) could be designed to provide better carbon market access to urban mitigation projects so as to tap the potential for cost-effective mitigation in this area, (Clapp *et al.*, 2010).

Box 3.4. **The EU-Emissions Trading Scheme: Recent developments**

Launched in January 2005, the EU-Emissions Trading Scheme is the world's largest trading scheme, operating in 30 countries[*] and covering more than 10 900 large installations in Europe, such as power stations, combustion plants, oil refineries, iron and steel works, and factories making cement, glass, lime, bricks, ceramics, pulp and paper. The installations currently covered account for half of the European Union's CO_2 emissions (40% of GHG emissions). The EU-ETS faced significant challenges in its first two phases (2005-2007 and 2008-2012), such as over-allocation of permits, windfall profits for electricity generators due to free allocation systems, and price volatility, all of which reduced the efficiency of the scheme. However, it has shown that the price signal has been effective in promoting low carbon pathways.

For Phase III (2013-20), European Union heads of state and government and the European Parliament have revised legislation to include the following changes:

■ a single EU-wide cap instead of 27 national caps;

■ more allowances auctioned (50% or more by 2013, rising to 100% over time) to avoid windfall profits;

■ harmonisation of rules governing free allocation of emissions and extending coverage to petrochemicals, aluminium, ammonia, and new gases, including N_2O and PFCs;

■ higher rate of free allocation (based on benchmarks) for sectors and sub-sectors considered at risk of carbon leakage, in the absence of a comprehensive international agreement;

■ coverage of domestic and international aviation emissions from 2012.

[*] This includes EU27 and Norway, Iceland and Lichtenstein.

Source: Ellerman, A. and B. Buchner (2008), "Over-Allocation or Abatement? A Preliminary Analysis of the EU-ETS Based on the 2005-06 Emissions Data", *Environmental and Resource Economics*, Vol. 41, No. 2, pp. 267-287; Ellerman, A. *et al.* (2010), *Pricing Carbon: The European Union Emissions Trading Scheme*, Cambridge University Press.

Carbon taxes. Carbon taxes are a cost effective way to reduce emissions. These taxes provide incentives for polluters and resource users to change their behaviour today. They also provide long-term incentives to innovate. Although carbon taxes are not strongly supported by the public in all contexts, there are various ways in which this support can be increased over time (*e.g.* through measures to limit negative impacts on the competitiveness of certain sectors and/or on income distribution) (OECD, 2008a).

Countries are increasingly considering ETSs and carbon taxes as complementary measures, with the former targeting energy-intensive sectors and the latter targeting the residential and commercial sector (UNFCCC, 2011b). Where carbon taxes are in place, they are usually applied to fuels and electricity so that prices reflect their CO_2-emission factors. It is, however, important to note that if electricity generation is covered by a trading scheme (as for example in the EU ETS), taxes on electricity use will not affect total CO_2 emissions (OECD, 2011f).

Carbon taxes are currently used in 10 OECD countries, with Denmark, Finland, the Netherlands, Norway, Sweden and the United Kingdom leading these efforts since the early 1990s (OECD, 2009a). Sweden was one of the first countries to introduce a carbon tax in 1991, with the general level of the tax increasing over the years to reach EUR 111 per tonne in 2010. A positive side effect of the UK's Climate Change Levy, which taxes industrial and commercial GHG-emitting power production, has been to stimulate innovation (OECD, 2010b). Those companies that pay a lower-than-normal tax rate under negotiated Climate Change Agreements (which entitle them to an 80% discount off the tax liability, provided they adopt a binding target on their energy use)[23] have registered fewer patents for inventions to tackle climate change than those that pay the full levy. In Canada, British Colombia (BC) has had a carbon tax in place since 2008.[24] The carbon tax is a critical component of BC's *Climate Action Plan* to reduce GHG emissions by 33% by 2020.

The state of play in developing countries. Emerging economies and developing countries are already participating in carbon markets through the Clean Development Mechanism (CDM) implemented under the Kyoto Protocol.[25] A further deepening and extension of carbon markets could enable substantial transfers of private funds from developed to developing countries. In the near term, the main channel for such transfers may be based on scaled-up versions of existing crediting mechanisms such as the CDM. Improving the CDM framework, supporting institutions, and addressing barriers to investments through this mechanism could increase the potential for attracting financial flows for mitigation in developing countries (Ellis and Kamel, 2007). Well-functioning crediting mechanisms also reduce the global cost of mitigation (OECD, 2009a).

Some developing countries are also investigating domestic market-based instruments to mitigate GHG emissions. For example, in July 2010 India introduced a national clean energy tax on both imported and domestically produced coal to fund R&D in renewable energy technologies. In April 2011 it implemented a scheme called "Perform Achieve Trade", to improve the energy efficiency of large energy-intensive industries (GoI, 2010). In September 2010 South Africa introduced a carbon related rate differentiation on taxes for new vehicles. It also plans carbon taxes to meet its national long-term mitigation scenarios (South Africa Revenue Service, 2010). In China, 10 areas have been selected to draft plans to reduce their carbon emissions under a low-carbon pilot programme researching the use of market mechanisms to promote emissions reductions. Announcements have been made on the launch of a domestic ETS in 2015 (Reuters, 2011). In 2009, Brazil launched a National Climate Change policy outlining its commitments to reduce GHG emissions by 36%-40% of projected emissions by 2020. It plans to draft specific legislation for tax measures to stimulate emission reductions (Government of Brazil, 2008). Indonesia released its climate change green paper in December 2009, which suggested carbon pricing initially through a carbon tax, indicating that later transition to emissions trading is a possibility. While the emergence of all these trading schemes is encouraging, fragmented markets are less efficient and effective than one global market (see Section 4 for a discussion).

Removing environmentally harmful subsidies. Removing or reforming inefficient and environmentally harmful support to fossil fuel production and consumption is an important step in "getting the prices right" on GHG emissions. Reforming fossil fuel support can help to shift the economy away from activities that emit CO_2, can encourage energy efficiency, and can promote the development and diffusion of low-carbon technologies and renewable energy sources (Section 4 presents a model simulation of reforming fossil fuel subsidies). Furthermore, removing fossil fuel subsidies and other support will save money for governments and taxpayers. An inventory of 24 OECD countries indicates that fossil fuel production and use in these countries was supported by about USD 45-75 billion per year between 2005 and 2010 (OECD, 2011b). The inventory is a first step towards increased transparency on fossil fuel support, but further analysis of the merits of the individual measures is needed to understand which might be harmful or inefficient. Fossil fuel consumption subsidies in developing and emerging economies amounted to more than USD 300 billion in 2009, increasing to just over USD 400 billion in 2010 (IEA, 2011b).

Removing those subsidies that are inefficient can however be politically challenging, and may also lead to more use of traditional bioenergy in developing countries with potentially negative health effects (see Chapter 6 on health and environment). The combustion of traditional bioenergy is associated with high black carbon emissions, and these can also contribute to climate change. As a result, reform of fossil fuel support should be implemented carefully, in particular to ensure that potential negative impacts on household affordability and well-being are mitigated through appropriate measures (*e.g.* means-tested social safety net programmes).

Regulations and command-and-control instruments

Regulations are needed in a policy mix along with market-based instruments, and can be most appropriate where markets cannot provide price signals to individuals or organisations that reflect the costs of polluting behaviour. This can be the case where, for example, pollution cannot be adequately monitored at source or there is no good proxy that could be subject to taxation. Regulatory approaches may also be more politically feasible where certain sectors are strongly against tax increases. The design of regulations is important. They should be:

- closely targeted to the policy goal;
- stringent enough so that the benefits outweigh the cost;
- stable enough to give investors confidence;
- flexible enough to foster genuinely novel solution;
- updated regularly to provide incentives for continuous innovation.

In the transport sector, fuel-economy and CO_2-emission standards are increasingly mandatory, and have been widely implemented in many countries. Fleet renewal schemes have also been introduced, but they have shown mixed results. They are often put in place as a way of stimulating consumer spending and/or assisting car manufacturers in times of economic recession. During the economic crisis of 2008-2009, several countries implemented fleet renewal schemes as part of economic stimulus plans, claiming that they would also deliver significant CO_2 and pollution reduction benefits as new cars are more fuel efficient than the old fleet. However, an analysis of such programmes in France, Germany and the United States suggests that they are not cost effective (OECD/ITF, 2011). There is also a risk of significant rebound effects (see below) if fuel prices are not increased at the same time (as the cost per kilometre of driving decreases with higher fuel efficiency).

Regulations are also used to reduce emissions of gases that are subject to the Montreal Protocol on Substances that Deplete the Ozone Layer. For example, Australia has the Ozone Protection and Synthetic Greenhouse Gas Management regulation; the European Union has directives on fluorinated gases, mobile air conditioning and integrated pollution prevention and control; and the United States has a Significant New Alternatives Programme.[26] Regulations have also long contributed to landfill methane emissions reductions as well as industrial N_2O and HFC reduction in industrialised countries. For example, France's industrial N_2O emissions were cut by 90% in the 1990s through those schemes.

Energy-efficiency measures can be encouraged by carbon pricing (see above), but might require additional targeted regulatory instruments (such as fuel, vehicle and building-efficiency standards). If well designed to target market barriers[27] and avoid costly overlap with market-based instruments, these measures can accelerate the uptake of clean technologies, promote innovation and support cost-effective mitigation. Policy makers should pay attention also to the "rebound effects": higher efficiency without proper pricing will lower the costs of using the equipment in question, hence providing a potential incentive to use it more intensively. Mixing energy-efficiency measures and carbon pricing is therefore critical (OECD, 2009a).

Fostering innovation and supporting green technologies

Technological innovation is key for the transition to a low-carbon economy. For example, OECD work shows that the cost of mitigation in 2050 could be halved, from about 4% to 2% of GDP, if R&D could come up with two carbon-free backstop technologies in the electricity and non-electricity sectors (OECD, 2011c). However, fostering innovation faces a number of challenges. First, it is difficult for firms to appropriate the returns to their investments in innovation (see Box 3.5). Second, specific barriers to entry exist for new technologies and competitors due to the prevalence of dominant designs in energy and transport markets.

The following three factors are necessary to foster innovation in low-carbon technologies. Each is discussed further in the sections which follow:

i)   Public investment in basic research: this area is often too risky or uncertain for private-sector investments. International co-operation could help to share the cost of public investment, improve access to knowledge and foster international transfer of technologies.

ii) Carbon pricing: without this, potential users will have few incentives to take up any low-carbon technologies that are invented – this significantly reduces the incentives to develop such innovations. However, carbon pricing alone is unlikely to be sufficient to drive short-term investments in costly technologies that have long-term CO_2 reduction impact.

iii) Public policy framework, tools and instruments: these can help to overcome the dominance of existing technologies, systems and firms, again through the establishment of competitive market conditions, as well as public support for R&D and in the commercialisation of green innovations.

Public investment in basic research. More investment in low-carbon energy technology research, development and demonstration (RD&D) is needed, including direct government funding, grants and private-sector investment. After years of stagnation, government spending on low-carbon energy technologies has risen. But current levels still fall well short of what is needed to deliver green growth (Figure 3.14). The current tight fiscal situations faced by many governments may further limit public spending on energy-related R&D.

Figure 3.14. **Government RD&D expenditures in energy in IEA member countries: 1974-2009**

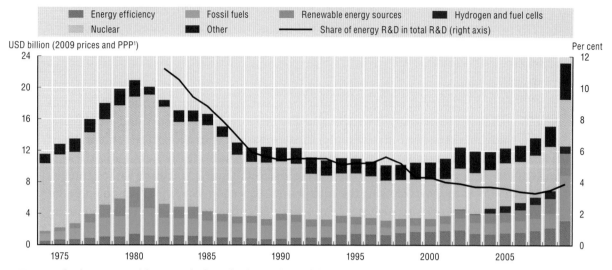

1. PPP = Purchasing Power Parities. RD&D budgets for the Czech Republic, Poland and Slovak Republic have not been included for lack of availability.

Source: IEA (2010), "Global Gaps in Clean Energy RD&D Update and Recommendations for International Collaboration", *IEA Report* for the Clean Energy Ministerial OECD/IEA, Paris.

StatLink ⁀⁀⁀ http://dx.doi.org/10.1787/888932570582

In 2009, governments of both the Major Economies Forum[28] and the IEA intervened directly in energy markets in order to promote investment in low-carbon technologies, such as renewable energy power plants, with a view to doubling investments in low-carbon RD&D by 2015. Such measures appear to have had some success (Box 3.5).

However, simply increasing funding will not be enough to deliver the necessary low-carbon technologies. Current government RD&D programmes and policies need to be improved by adopting best practices in design and implementation. This includes the design of strategic programmes to fit national policy priorities and resource availability; the rigorous evaluation of results and adjusting support if needed; and the increase of linkages between government and industry, and between the basic science and applied energy research communities to accelerate innovation. Examples of public support for RD&D in low-carbon technology include the European Technology Platform Programme[29] (2007-2013) and the Innovation and New Technology[30] programme support in Germany.

Using carbon pricing to spur innovation. Spurring innovation in low-carbon technologies would require a higher price of carbon than the price set by current initiatives. Governments can intervene with additional targeted policies to raise the carbon price and create a market for low-carbon alternatives (Box 3.5). OECD work demonstrates that carbon pricing provides much broader innovation incentives than technology adoption subsidies (OECD, 2010b). Subsidies can encourage the adoption of low-carbon technologies and market transformations, but are an expensive option, especially when public budgets are strained.

Technology deployment subsidies. Most new technologies will require, at some stage, both the "push" of RD&D and the "pull" of market deployment (IEA, 2009b). The over-riding objectives of public policy should be to reduce some of the financial and policy risk of

Box 3.5. **The growth in renewable energy power plants**

Figure 3.15 gives an overview of the total plant entry capacities (measured in megawatts electric) for major renewable energy sources – wind, solar, biomass and geothermal – built between 1978 and 2008. The increasing trend for investment in renewable energy power facilities in all regions since 1997 coincides with the agreement and implementation of the Kyoto Protocol. In this period, developed-country governments have provided targeted support for renewable energy investment, which can be justified by the relative immaturity of these technologies. This immaturity makes it more difficult for lenders to accurately price relative risk of investments in "clean" energy, and thus for investors in the sector to obtain financing at reasonable cost. Moreover, in some cases there can be important learning and demonstration effects, which will not be realised without initial support (Kalamova *et al.*, 2011). At the same time, the rate of entry of coal and oil-based plants plummeted in these countries.

Figure 3.15. **New plant entry by type of renewable energy in North America, Pacific and EU15 regions, 1978-2008**

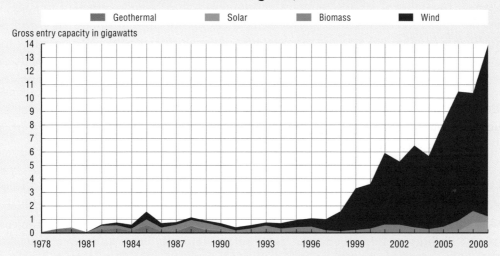

Source: Kalamova, M., C. Kaminker and N. Johnstone (2011), "Sources of Finance, Investment Policies and Plant Entry in the Renewable Energy Sector", *OECD Environment Working Papers*, No. 37.

StatLink http://dx.doi.org/10.1787/888932570601

investing in new, low-carbon technologies, stimulate uptake and bring down costs. Evidence suggests that a large proportion of breakthrough innovations tend to come from new firms that challenge existing business models. Thus, government measures to remove barriers to entry and to support growth of new firms have an important part to play in low carbon energy technology development.

Government-support policies need to be appropriately tailored to different stages of technology development and should be based on assessments of *expected* costs and *expected* benefits – taking any interactions with other instruments into account. Examples of technology support policies include minimum feed-in tariffs for electricity production from renewable sources, differentiated purchase taxes on automobiles based on fuel economy, and grants, loans and guarantees for emission mitigation projects. However, technology-specific policies risk "locking in" outdated technology and can dampen incentives to innovate and search for cheaper and better abatement options. It is also important to consider carefully how these policies interact with any caps on total emissions that might be in place (OECD, 2011b). The policies should be carefully designed to avoid capture by vested interests and regularly evaluated to make sure they are efficient and directed towards policy objectives. While predictability and long-term policy signals are necessary if investors are to invest in low-carbon energy technologies, predictability should not be equated with permanence. It is important to phase out technology support policies.

OECD work on innovation suggests that general factors beyond technology support policies may also play a key role in inducing clean technology innovation and diffusion (OECD, 2011g). General market conditions such as competition policy, intellectual property regimes, and education policy are important complements to direct technology support policies. Also, the stringency of the environmental policy framework matters (*e.g.* level of emission caps or carbon price) as well as the predictability and the flexibility of policy regimes. Governments could be tempted to "pick winners", but it is more efficient to be technology neutral. The use of "flexible" environmental policy instruments is one means of ensuring neutrality. If targeted support is required, it may be more efficient to support general infrastructure or technologies which benefit a wide range of applications, such as improved energy storage and grid management in the electricity sector. The design of the schemes plays a critical role, to ensure competitive selection processes, focus on performance, avoid vested interests and ensure evaluation of policies (Johnstone and Haščič 2009; Haščič *et al.,* 2010)

Voluntary approaches, public awareness campaigns and information tools

Information instruments, education and public awareness programmes encourage consumer and investor behavioural changes by improving the availability and accuracy of information. They include labels indicating the energy and emissions profile for appliances and automobiles, audits for buildings and plants, and dissemination of best practices. Many energy-efficiency improvements, such as phasing-out incandescent lamps, can cost little or nothing to implement, but can bring potentially large and rapid emission reductions. However, people need to be persuaded to take them up. Well-designed information-based instruments, such as energy-efficiency labels on household appliances, combined with market-based and regulatory tools, can be an effective approach (OECD, 2007a, b; OECD, 2011d; Box 3.6).

Labelling the environmental characteristics of products – such as their carbon footprint – is becoming increasingly popular. In the United States, the retailer Wal-Mart obliges some of its suppliers to use carbon indicators. In the United Kingdom, highlighting the carbon footprint of different goods and services is also becoming common. The EU Energy Label or Energy Star labels (used in Canada, the European Union, Japan, New Zealand, Taiwan and the United States) have been in place for several years. Currently none of these schemes is mandatory, although under France's Grenelle Law for the environment, the government plans to make labelling of a number of environmental indicators on certain products a legal requirement from 2012.

The use of voluntary approaches has declined in recent years in Annex I countries to the benefit of binding instruments and regulations (UNFCCC, 2011b). Although voluntary arrangements should not be viewed as a replacement for mandatory mitigation policies, carbon prices and other climate policies, they can strengthen domestic climate policies.

> ## Box 3.6. **Greening household behaviour: The role of public policies**
>
> As consumers account for 60% of final consumption in the OECD area, their purchasing decisions have a major impact on the extent to which markets can work to promote green products. However, their decisions to buy "green" depends on the financial cost of green options and the infrastructure to support such choices; the quality and reliability of information on the products; and the knowledge consumers have of environmental issues. Industry, government and civil society can play an important role in creating the enabling environment for consumers to make greener purchasing choices.
>
> Recent OECD work on environmental policy and household behaviour is exploring the factors driving households' environment-related decisions in order to inform policy design and implementation. A survey of over 10 000 households across 10 OECD countries (Australia, Canada, Czech Republic, France, Italy, Korea, Mexico, the Netherlands, Norway and Sweden) confirms the impact of economic incentives on household behaviour and the important complementary role played by information-based measures such as energy-efficiency labelling of appliances and housing.
>
> The findings confirm the importance of providing the right economic incentive to spur behavioural changes, in particular in energy and water savings. The evidence also indicates that pricing consumption by volume is partially useful – the mere act of metering and introducing a price on the use of natural resources has an effect on people's decision making. The survey indicates that "softer" instruments, such as information to consumers and public education, can play a substantial complementary role. Eco labels are particularly useful, as long as they are clear and comprehensible, and that they identify both "public" and "private" benefits. These "soft" instruments need to be given close attention in developing more comprehensive strategies for influencing consumer and household environmental behaviour.
>
> *Sources:* OECD (2011d), *Greening Household Behaviour*, OECD Publishing.

Their adoption is often much easier than mandatory instruments, and helps raise awareness of climate change issues. In Japan, voluntary measures such as the Keidanren's Voluntary Action Plan played a role in reducing industrial GHG emissions. Voluntary enterprise partnerships are particularly important in the United States to improve the energy performance of buildings (Save Energy Now and Energy Star for Industry Programmes) and in the transport sector (SmartWayTransport Partnership). There are also active programmes in the waste sector, such as the Landfill Methane Outreach Programme in the United States aimed at reducing GHGs from landfills by supporting the recovery and use of landfill gas for energy.

Getting the policy mix right

The previous sections have shown that there is no single instrument available to policy makers for achieving a cost-effective reduction of GHG emissions. Instead, a mix of policies is needed. However, poorly designed policy mixes can result in undesirable overlaps, can undermine cost-effectiveness and, in some cases, can themselves be environmentally damaging (Duval, 2009; OECD, 2011b; Hood, 2011). The wide range of GHG emissions-reducing policies available and the many possible interactions among them, raise the issue of whether and how they can be integrated into a coherent framework.

For instance, a great advantage of cap-and-trade systems compared to most other policy instruments is that they give all sources covered an equal incentive to abate emissions, enhancing the cost-effectiveness of emission abatement. It is, however, important to keep in mind that with the use of a cap-and-trade system, other policy instruments addressing the same emission sources will only affect total emissions if they allow for setting a stricter emissions cap in the future. As long as the cap remains unchanged, overlapping instruments will not influence total emissions, and will only increase the overall cost of mitigation (OECD, 2011b).

Thus policies have to be designed as a package, taking these interactions into account. In addition, interactions can happen beyond specific climate change policies. The cost-effectiveness of global emission cuts can be further enhanced by reforming a number of policies that either increase GHG emissions or distort the incentives – and, therefore, raise the cost – of mitigation instruments. These include fuel tax rebates, energy price regulations and lack of property rights to forests in a number of developing countries, as well as import barriers to emissions-reducing technologies and agricultural support in a number of developed countries.

National action to adapt to climate change

The existing stock of GHG in the atmosphere means that the world is now committed to several decades of climate change. Although changes in the climate are now inevitable, the effects they will have on people and ecosystems will depend on the actions taken in response to those changes (adaptation). Adaptation can also involve harnessing any beneficial opportunities that may arise.

Adaptation encompasses a multitude of behavioural, structural and technology adjustments. As a result, there are many possible typologies of adaptation strategies and instruments. These include structural and technological measures; legislative and regulatory instruments; institutional and administrative measures; market-based instruments; and on-site operations (Table 3.4). This section summarises the state of play of many of these, focusing especially on:

■ national adaptation strategies and risk assessments;

■ innovative insurance systems to reduce climate risks;

■ price signals and environmental markets to improve natural resource management;

■ the role of the private sector;

■ integrating adaptation into development co-operation.

For regions affected by particularly extreme events or climate conditions, many adaptation measures may not be sufficient to offset the impacts. In these cases, the role of early warnings and disaster risk management are particularly important.

National adaptation strategies and risk assessments

Establishing national adaptation strategies is particularly important to identify the main climate vulnerabilities and to prioritise among them. Progress has been made in implementing national strategies for adaptation, which also encourage the management of climate risks in all relevant sectors. However, in a preliminary review of adaptation actions undertaken by OECD countries, Gagnon-Lebrun and Agrawala (OECD, 2006) found that climate change impacts and adaptation received much less attention within the

Table 3.4. **Adaptation options and potential policy instruments**

Sector	Adaptation options	Potential policy instruments
Agriculture	Crop insurance; investment in new technologies; removal of market distortions; change crops and planting dates; yield-development of yield-improving crops (*e.g.* heat and drought resistant crops).	Price signals/markets; insurance instruments; microfinance; R&D incentives and other forms of public support.
Fisheries	Installations to prevent storm damage; techniques to deal with temperature stress; breeding technology innovations; improved food sourcing away from reliance on fish; reduced antibiotic use; ecosystem approach to fisheries; aquaculture.	R&D incentives and other forms of public support; regulatory incentives, marine spatial planning.
Coastal zones	Coastal defences/sea walls; surge barriers; sediment management; beach nourishment; habitat protection; land-use planning; relocation.	Coastal zone planning; differentiated insurance; PPPs for coastal defence schemes.
Health	Air conditioning, building standards; improvements in public health; vector control programmes; disease eradication programmes; R&D on vector control, vaccines, disease eradication.	R&D incentives and other forms of public support; regulatory incentives (*e.g.* building codes); insurance; heat alert and response systems; air quality health indices.
Water resources	Leakage control; reservoirs; desalination; risk management to deal with rainfall variability; water permits, water pricing; rational water use, rainwater collection.	Price signals/markets; regulatory incentives; financing schemes; R&D incentives and other forms of public support.
Ecosystems	Reduce *Baseline* stress; habitat protection; change in natural resource management; market for ecological services; facilitate species migration; breeding and genetic modification for managed systems.	Ecosystem markets; land-use planning; environmental standards; microfinance schemes; R&D incentives and other forms of public support.
Settlements and economic activity	Insurance, weather derivatives; climate-proofing of housing stock and infrastructure; zone planning, location decisions.	Building standards; insurance schemes; adjustments to infrastructure PPPs, direct public support.
Extreme weather events	Insurance; flood barriers; storm/flood-proof infrastructure, housing stock; early warning systems; enhanced disaster management; land-use planning, location decisions; green infrastructure or ecosystems based adaptation.	Building codes, land-use planning; private finance or PPPs for defence structures.

Source: Adapted from OECD (2008c), *Economic Aspects of Adaptation to Climate Change: Costs, Benefits and Policy Instruments,* OECD, Paris.

National Communications (NCs)[31] than discussions on GHG emissions and mitigation policies. Any discussion on impacts and adaptation in the NCs was dominated by the assessment of future climatic changes and impacts. The discussion on adaptation is often limited to identifying generic options rather than specific action plans or policies. However, more recently, Bauer *et al.,* (2011) show that adaptation and information on climate risks is becoming more integrated into the national policies of the countries they reviewed.[32] Other studies similarly find that most countries do mention adaptation in their national policies, but in most cases not as prominently as mitigation (Townshend *et al., 2011*; and see Table 3.2). However if one includes forestry and land-use measures as a part of adaptation (both have adaptation benefits), the coverage increases significantly.

Assessing climate risks and vulnerabilities is fundamental for evaluating different adaptation options at the national, local and project levels. Governments have invested considerable effort in recent years in developing methodologies and tools to screen the risks posed by climate change and to conduct vulnerability assessments. The OECD proposes the use of environmental impact assessment (EIA) or Strategic Environmental Assessment (SEA) to incorporate climate change impacts and adaptation within existing approaches for project design, approval and implementation in both developed and developing countries (Agrawala *et al.,* 2010a). Using an integrated framework to address climate change in the context of other environmental impacts would also diminish the risks of maladaptation, as an integrated assessment would ensure that a project does not affect the vulnerability of natural and human systems. Although countries have shown progress in examining the possibility of incorporating climate change impacts and adaptation measures within EIA, much less has been done in adjusting current policy frameworks, creating guidance and actually incorporating climate change into EIA. A recent assessment could only find examples from three countries – Australia, Canada, and the Netherlands (Agrawala *et al.*, 2010b). Some progress has been made in the use of SEA (Agrawala *et al.*, 2010a). For instance, Spain's National Climate Change Adaptation Plan includes the objective of mainstreaming climate change adaptation into sectoral legislation.

There are significant gaps in the available evidence on the costs and benefits of adaptation. A review of this literature shows that there is a relatively large amount of information available about adaptation options and their costs at the sectoral level, although it is unevenly distributed across sectors and by applicable geographic coverage (OECD , 2008c; Agrawala *et al.*, 2011). In particular, there is a significant body of literature on assessing adaptation in coastal zones and agriculture. By contrast, the information on costs of adaptation is much less diffused for the water resources, energy, infrastructure, tourism and public health sectors and limited largely to developed country contexts. A notable exception is Chile – between 2008 and 2010 it carried out the first ever quantification of the impacts of climate change in eight river basins throughout its central valley. Such information is also very context-specific, making broader generalisations difficult.

Innovative insurance systems to reduce climate risks

There is a long track record of insurance provision to deal with weather risks. Insurance schemes will need to consider the effects of increasing climate damage. Insurance companies see climate adaptation insurance mechanism as a business opportunity (NBS, 2009), and are developing new ways of spreading risk away from affected communities while encouraging adaptation actions by exposed populations. They have already developed specific insurance products to mitigate climate risks, such as risk transfer mechanisms; weather related insurance and catastrophe bonds; and weather index-based insurance, which are especially relevant for developing countries. Swiss Re, through its Climate Adaptation Development Programme, has developed financial risk transfer markets to tackle the effects of adverse weather in non-OECD countries through partnerships with local insurers, banks, micro-finance institutions, government and NGOs (PwC, 2011). It has already designed and implemented index-based weather risk transfer instruments in India, Kenya, Mali and Ethiopia.

Despite the encouraging developments in this area, the application of insurance to climate change adaptation faces some challenges. These mainly concern the lack of available data and information on climate change. Government intervention is critical to support the private sector through gathering information, or through public private partnerships to share risk. Nevertheless, care should be taken, as in some cases insurance may not be viable[33] and subsidising it may be more costly and more likely to delay adaptation (OECD, 2008c). Another critical role for governments is therefore to evaluate whether the level of insurance cover is adequate and whether risk-sharing systems are fair. They also might have to develop publicly funded adaptation measures that bring down risks, or share the most extreme layer of risks with commercial insurers.

Price signals and environmental markets to improve natural resource management

Policies to price natural resources create incentives for owners to preserve natural assets and for consumers to use them carefully. From an adaptation point of view, environmental markets and pricing, such as for ecosystem services, help to reduce stress and make systems more resilient to climate change. They also help to monetise the adaptation services provided by ecosystems or other natural resources (see Chapter 4). Examples of such policies include water prices and water markets, and payments for ecosystems services (*e.g.* watershed protection, carbon sequestration, biodiversity protection and landscape and cultural preservation; see Chapter 4). Governments need to ensure that the trade-offs among the financial sustainability of schemes, efficiency of allocation and social impacts are appropriately dealt with.

The role of the private sector

In a context of tight government budgets in both developed and developing countries, the private sector will have to play an important role in financing adaptation and can help to overcome operational constraints and accelerate investment in infrastructure (Agrawala *et al.*, 2011). This is particularly relevant for expensive infrastructure investments, such as the construction and operation of dedicated defence structures (flood barriers), or the climate proofing of existing infrastructure (road, water systems and electric power networks), which constitute the majority of the required adaptation funding.

Some adaptation by private actors will take place out of self interest, as it will reduce vulnerability and improve resilience to climate change. Business opportunities may also arise from designing new products or entering new markets when implementing adaptation actions (OECD, 2008c). Reducing or managing climate change risks can translate into competitive advantage, cost savings (though perhaps not in the short-term), reduced liabilities, and investor confidence. In addition to internalising climate change adaptation into their own decision-making processes, businesses can support local-level adaptation by providing economic opportunities and growth, delivering services, providing financial, technical and human resources, and influencing policy making.

However, in some of the potentially worst affected areas, such as low-lying island states, the challenge is great and the necessary capacity for the private sector to reduce vulnerability may be lacking. Private action may be insufficient because of external effects or other market or information failures. Governments have to implement the right mix of policy instruments to ensure the engagement of private actors in making timely, well-informed, and efficient adaptation decisions. Setting up the right incentive and partnership structures to promote adaptation will be a daunting task.

Public private partnerships (PPPs) are one means for governments to enhance the adaptive capacity of industries. They can also play a significant role in many sectors, especially by stimulating investments in R&D. Indeed, technological innovation is key to reducing the cost of adapting to climate change. However, the public good nature of this type of innovation may cause the private sector to underinvest in R&D. In such cases, policy instruments need to be put in place to give the private-sector incentives to engage. PPPs can help to realign research incentives, along with fiscal incentives and intellectual protection provided by appropriate policy frameworks (OECD, 2008c).

Integrating adaptation into development co-operation

The management of climate risks is closely intertwined with development activities as climate change has a particularly strong impact on the poor and most vulnerable populations. International donor agencies are playing an important role in scaling up the financing for adaptation and integrating climate change into development co-operation. Donor agencies can support a variety of activities ranging from R&D and technological development, to information gathering and diffusion, co-ordination or development of adaptive capacity. In order to support donors and partner countries, the OECD has developed guidance on *Integrating Climate Change Adaptation into Development Co-operation*, which advocates a "whole-of-government" approach (OECD, 2009b). It proposes assessing and addressing climate risks and opportunities within centralised national government processes, at sectoral and project levels, as well as in urban and rural contexts.

The integration of adaptation at each of these levels requires an analysis of the governance architecture and the different stages of the policy cycle to identify entry points where climate change adaptation could be incorporated. At the national level, typical entry points include various stages in the formulation of national policies, long-term and multi-year development plans, sectoral budgetary allocation processes, as well as regulatory processes. On the other hand, the entry points would be very different for on-the-ground projects, where climate change adaptation considerations might need to be factored within specific elements of the project cycle.

Information, monitoring and evaluation

It is necessary to collect and provide information on climate hazards, vulnerability, resilience and adaptive capacity. The establishment of international organisations that encourage information sharing and exchange is also very important. One example is the Asia Pacific Adaptation Network (APAN) launched in October 2009 in response to an urgent need for immediate and adequate actions to adapt to climate change. It is a regional hub of the Global Climate Change Adaptation Network (GAN). The GAN aims to support countries to build the climate resilience of vulnerable human systems, ecosystems and economies through the mobilisation and sharing of knowledge and technologies to support adaptation capacity building, policy setting, planning and practices.

With increasing investment in adaptation, one important challenge for the future will be to establish the right sets of indicators for identifying priorities, as well as monitoring and evaluation frameworks for adaptation. While progress on mitigation can be interpreted from trends in national GHG emissions, comparable measurable outcomes do not yet exist for adaptation. The difficulties in monitoring and evaluating adaptation range from the ambiguous definition of adaptation to the identification of targets and the choice of indicators used to monitor performance. Consequently, while international discussions on adaptation have focused on implementation of adaptation and the associated costs, systematic evaluation of how much progress is being made in this direction is generally lacking and needs further development (Lamhauge *et al.*, 2011).

Getting the policy mix right: Interactions between adaptation and mitigation

In recent years progress has been made in recognising the importance of adapting to climate change, in understanding climate projections and in assessing climate impacts and adaptation options. However, there is still a long way to go before the right instruments and institutions are in place for adaptation. In particular, improvements are needed in establishing institutional mechanisms and explicitly incorporating climate change risks in projects and policies. At the national level it is also necessary to increase the understanding of climate change in order to be able to set priorities. Progress is also needed in increasing private-sector engagement and integrating climate change in development co-operation.

Both mitigation and adaptation policies are essential and complementary: the near-term impacts of climate change are already locked-in, thus making adaptation inevitable; and over the longer term, without mitigation, the magnitude and rate of climate change will exceed the capacity of natural and social systems to adapt. OECD and other analysis show that the total costs of climate change will be lowest when both mitigation and adaptation occur together (Agrawala *et al.*, 2010b; de Bruin *et al.*, 2009; IPCC, 2007b).

However, there is a need to find an appropriate balance between short- and long-term action, both for mitigation and adaptation. Taking early action implies a degree of irreversibility and opportunity cost, as, at least hypothetically, there is some value in waiting for better information about the severity of climate impacts or availability of new abatement technologies and many of the investments undertaken are "sunk", embodied in long-lived capital stocks and infrastructure. The optimal means and timing of interventions remains unknown and there is a difficult trade-off between avoiding irreversible policy cost and avoiding irreversible, and possibly extreme, damages. However, policies can influence this trade-off (Jamet and Corfee-Morlot, 2009; Weitzman, 2009).

The sector emphasis of national climate strategies, the balance between mitigation and adaptation and the mix of policy instruments used to address climate change will vary among countries according to national circumstances, economic and demographic profiles, cultural (and regulatory) preferences, energy mix, the nature and size of the market failures and differences in institutional capacities. Adaptation and mitigation policy strategies may compete for resources in some contexts. However, investing heavily in one option will undoubtedly reduce the need for investments in the other. Yet unlimited investments in adaptation do not replace the need for mitigation.

Multilevel governance is increasingly a feature of national climate mitigation and adaptation strategies and plans, where regional and local/city level actions contribute to overall national climate policy strategies (OECD, 2010a). Given their concentration of population, economic activities and GHG emissions, cities and local governments have an important role to play in mitigating and adapting to climate change (OECD, 2010a). However, aligning incentives and effective co-ordination among different levels of government will help to avoid duplicative or costly policy measures. For example, there is a danger that measures taken by one city automatically will be counteracted by another city failing to reduce emissions, especially if total emissions across a certain area are "capped" (OECD, 2011b).

4. Policy steps for tomorrow: Building a low-carbon, climate-resilient economy

Having looked at the international and national policy instruments that are currently in place, this final section outlines what further policies are required for achieving the 2 °C goal. To do so, the section draws on a number of different OECD *Outlook* modelling scenarios to highlight the feasibility, cost and emission implications of different emission pathways. It also looks at the implications of less stringent targets and of phasing out fossil fuel subsidies. The section ends with a discussion of synergies between climate change policies and other goals.

The Cancún Agreements also indicate the necessity of considering strengthening the long-term global goal, for example to limit the global average temperature rise to 1.5 °C. Achieving this more stringent target would require even more significant and urgent mitigation action. The UNEP overview (Box 3.7 and UNEP, 2010) could find virtually no integrated assessment model able to identify cost-effective pathways that would have a medium chance, let alone a likely chance, of reaching this more ambitious goal by the end of the century. The models used in this *Outlook* are also not able to simulate the pathways that would have at least a medium chance of achieving this more ambitious goal.

Box 3.7. **The UNEP Emissions Gap Report**

The Copenhagen Accord declared that deep cuts in global emissions are required "so as to hold the increase in global temperature below 2 °C". The Accord called for an assessment that would consider strengthening the long-term goal including "temperature rises of 1.5 °C". Since December 2009, many countries have pledged to reduce their emissions or constrain their growth up to 2020. Some of the pledges have conditions attached, such as the provision of finance and technology or ambitious action from other countries. For these reasons, it is not easy to tell what the outcomes will be from these various pledges. UNEP (2010) reviewed the literature on the assessment of the pledges.

The review shows that emission levels of approximately 44 gigatonnes of CO_2 equivalent ($GtCO_2e$) (with a range of 39-44 $GtCO_2e$) in 2020 would be consistent with a "likely" chance of limiting global warming to 2 °C (*i.e.* greater than 66% probability), and for a medium (at least 50%) chance of staying below 2 °C temperature increase, the range is 41-48. The corridor for emissions for the medium chance is represented in Figure 3.16. Under business-as-usual projections, *i.e.* if no pledges were to be implemented, the studies reviewed indicated global emissions could reach 56 $GtCO_2e$ (within a range of 54-60 $GtCO_2e$) in 2020, leaving a gap of 12 $GtCO_2e$ for the likely chance (with a range of 10-21).

The report suggests this gap could be reduced substantially by:

■ Countries implementing more ambitious, conditional pledges, such as the provision of adequate climate finance and ambitious action from other countries.

■ The negotiations adopting rules that avoid a net increase in emissions from *i)* "lenient" accounting rules which allow credit to be given for land use, land-use change and forestry (LULUCF) activities that would have happened in any case without further policy intervention; and *ii)* the use of surplus emission units, particularly those that could be carried over from the current commitment period of the Kyoto Protocol, to meet industrialised country targets.

■ Avoiding "double counting" of offsets.

If the above policy options were to be implemented, the size of the gap could be reduced to 5 $GtCO_2e$. This is approximately equal to the annual global emissions from all the world's cars, buses and transport in 2005 and is also more than half the way towards reaching the 2 °C goal. More ambitious domestic actions, some of which could be supported by international climate finance, could close the gap further.

The review has been updated in UNEP (2011c), which revealed that the emissions gap has somewhat increased, not because the pledges themselves have changed, but because business-as-usual emissions projections for 2020 have been revised upwards.

Source: UNEP (2010), *The Emissions Gap Report*, UNEP, Nairobi.

What if ...? Three scenarios for stabilising emissions at 450 ppm

Research shows that if the world could stabilise GHG concentrations[34] at 450 ppm CO_2e, the chance of keeping the global temperature increase under 2 $^\circ$C would be between 40% and 60% (Meinshausen *et al.*, 2006; 2009).[35] To explore the feasibility and implications of achieving this target, three different scenarios for stabilising concentrations at 450 ppm by the end of the 21st century have been modelled. Table 3.5 summarises the main characteristics of the three scenarios, as well as a less ambitious 550 ppm scenario for comparative purposes. Annex 3.A contains further details of the assumptions underlying these scenarios, while Chapter 1 provides background information on the models used for the analysis.

Table 3.5. **Overview of the *Environmental Outlook* mitigation scenarios**

Scenario	Assumptions	Average GHG emissions per decade (GtCO₂e)			
		2010-2020	2020-2030	2030-2050	2050-2100
450 Core	Concentrations of GHGs limited to 450 ppm by the end of the 21st century; policy starts in 2013; full flexibility across time, sources and gases; global carbon market	485	450	315	80
450 Accelerated Action	As *450 Core*, plus additional mitigation efforts between 2013 and 2030	480	435	280	85
450 Delayed Action	As *450 Core*, but until 2020 no mitigation action beyond Cancún and Copenhagen pledges and fragmented regional carbon markets	505	495	325	65
550 Core	As *450 Core*, but aiming at 550 ppm by the end of the century	505	525	490	280

Source: OECD Environmental Outlook projections; output from IMAGE.

The **450 Core** pathway assumes full flexibility in the timing of emission reductions and the use of mitigation options, including biomass energy with CCS known as "BECCS"[36] (see also Box 3.13). It further assumes that global co-operation is achieved for tackling climate change, and thus the pathway is implemented through a fully harmonised carbon market that encompasses all regions, sectors and gases. Achieving this pathway thus depends on: i) acting now to put a price on carbon, and immediately tapping into the cheap mitigation options in all sectors, regions and gases; ii) gradually transforming the energy system to become a low-carbon sector; and iii) using the large opportunities for low-cost advanced technologies – including BECCS – that are stimulated by the carbon price. As all least-cost mitigation options are included in the analysis, this scenario acts as the cost-effective reference point against which to compare the other scenarios.

The 450 *Core* scenario assumes that there can be negative emissions in some regions in the latter half of the century by using BECCS. This allows this pathway to be achieved despite relatively high emission levels in the first half of the century. However, experience with bioenergy and CCS technologies is currently limited. Both face challenges related to climate policy uncertainty, public acceptance, first-of-a-kind technology risks, and high costs relative to other technologies (especially CCS). Bioenergy can also have harmful side-effects through indirect land-use change, potentially leading to higher emissions and biodiversity losses. Thus, uncertainty about the costs and effectiveness of the BECCS technology remains considerable (Box 3.13). If BECCS turns out not to fulfill its promise of negative emissions, the world runs the risk of being locked into higher temperature increases. Thus, an optimal pathway for the coming decade should balance the long-term climate risks, short-term costs and mitigation potentials and expectations about technology development.

By contrast, the **450 Accelerated Action** scenario assumes greater mitigation effort in the first half of the century, and less reliance on unproven emissions technologies (like BECCS) in later decades. Additionally, this scenario would offer greater potential for achieving more ambitious long-term temperature stabilisation targets, such as 1.5 °C, although opportunities are limited to speed up emission reductions beyond the pathway shown here.

On the other hand, the **450 Delayed Action** scenario starts from the premise that it may not be realistic to expect large emission reductions in the coming decade.[37] It reflects the current situation in that it models the high end of the pledges made in the Copenhagen Accord and Cancún Agreements (with strict land-use accounting rules and no use of surplus emission credits from the current Kyoto Protocol commitment period). It also assumes that the various domestic carbon markets are not linked to each other until 2020. If this scenario comes to pass, by 2020, emissions would be outside the 41-48 $GtCO_2e$ range that UNEP (2010) suggests is necessary for least-cost pathways to have at least a medium chance of limiting average global temperature to 2 °C. The 450 Delayed Action scenario assumes that significant additional efforts will have to be made after 2020 to "catch up" and very rapid rates of emission reduction will be required to give a 50% chance of meeting the 2 °C goal. Postponing compensation for the higher short-term emissions until after 2050 would increase the chance of exceeding the temperature limit and increase the risks of negative environmental consequences caused by a 10% higher annual temperature increase in the coming decades than under the 450 Core scenario. Moreover, it relies heavily on i) unlocking the global energy system from its current high-carbon reliance; and ii) the ability to rapidly transform the energy system later in the century. This goes against the current trend, in which the world is in fact locking itself into high-carbon systems more strongly every year (IEA, 2011b).

Finally, the 550 Core scenario explores what is needed to limit GHG concentrations at the higher level of 550 ppm by the end of the century. Under this scenario the chance of the average global temperature increasing beyond 2 °C is much higher, and there is only a medium chance of limiting temperature increase to 2.5 °C-3 °C. Other climate change impacts are also more severe than in the 450 ppm scenarios.

Figure 3.16 shows how these different pathways affect the growth of global emission levels over time and compares it to the range of pathways presented in UNEP (2010) (see Box 3.7). All three 450 ppm scenarios show emissions peaking before 2020. The 450 Delayed Action scenario shows a short delay before global emission levels start reducing, implying that after 2025 there would need to be a rapid reversal of current trends to still achieve the 2 °C target. Note that until 2020, the 450 Delayed Action pathway is almost identical to the 550 ppm scenario.

The 2 °C pathways presented in this OECD Environmental Outlook assume an optimal allocation of mitigation efforts across different sources and gases. These stylised optimisation scenarios temporarily allow the targeted concentration level (450 ppm) to be exceeded or overshot in the middle of the century, before falling to reach the target concentration by the end of the century (Figure 3.17). However, overshooting may have serious environmental impacts by causing higher rates of temperature change in the coming decades than if action was taken earlier. A more rapidly changing climate and a

Figure 3.16. **Alternative emission pathways, 2010-2100**

Annual net emissions of all Kyoto gases in $GtCO_2e$

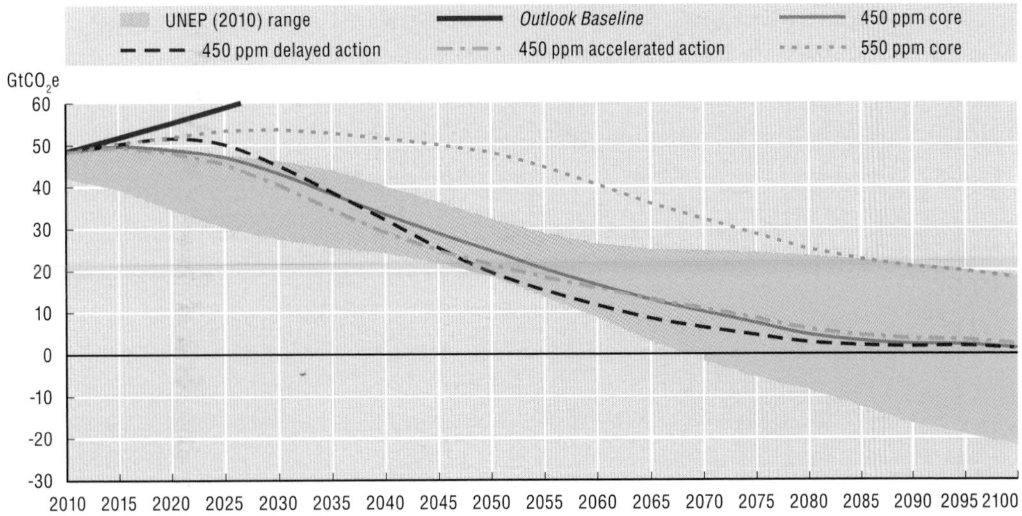

Source: OECD Environmental Outlook projections; output from ENV-Linkages.

StatLink ⬛️≡📊 http://dx.doi.org/10.1787/888932570620

greater overshoot of concentration targets could have serious consequences for some systems that are already under threat at lower levels of change (*e.g.* coral reefs and possibly ocean marine systems more broadly; IPCC, 2007a and b; Hoegh-Guldberg *et al.*, 2007). In principle, the delay in temperature response from changes in concentrations implies that for small changes in emissions – if compensated for within two to three decades – changes in global climate parameters will be very small (den Elzen and van Vuuren, 2007) and the scenarios presented here do not result in overshooting the 2 °C goal.

Figure 3.17 illustrates the projected concentration pathways of the various scenarios, including all climate forcers.[38] It shows that the pathway of the 450 *Delayed Action* scenario reflects a larger degree of overshoot than the other two 450 ppm scenarios. The catch-up in mitigation efforts in the middle of the century implies that concentration levels gradually fall back to the pathway of the 450 *Core* scenario and are nearly identical from 2080 onwards. In contrast, the 450 *Accelerated Action* scenario prevents some of the overshoot and has concentration levels peaking at less than 470 ppm. In all three 450 scenarios concentration levels decline after 2050 to ensure that temperature increases do not overshoot. Finally, note that the lower mitigation efforts in the coming decade under the 450 *Delayed Action* and 550 ppm scenarios lead to higher emission levels of aerosols, especially sulphur. This is because energy use is generally reduced less. The cooling effect of these gases would reduce temperatures in the short run compared to the 450 *Core* scenario, which explains the very similar concentration levels until 2030.

Compared with the "no new policies" *Baseline* projection, all three 450 ppm scenarios would have significantly lower climate impacts, and offer at least a medium chance of limiting global average temperature increase in 2100 to 2 °C.[39] Precipitation patterns would also change less in the 450 scenarios than in the *Baseline* (see Figures 3.10 and 3.11). However, the mitigation efforts undertaken in the 450 ppm scenarios will not avoid all climate impacts. Thus, adaptation to remaining impacts will still be required.

Figure 3.17. **Concentration pathways for the four *Outlook* scenarios including all climate forcers, 2010-2100**

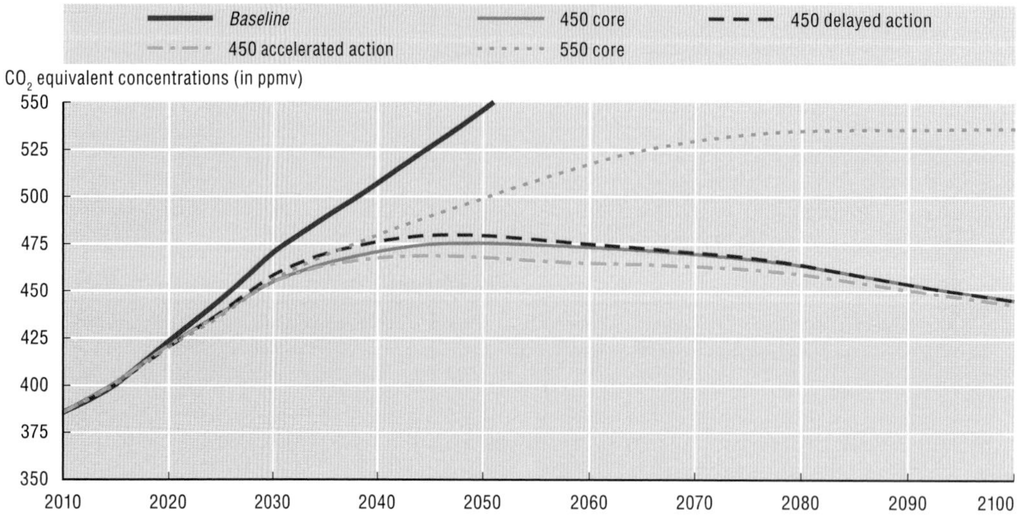

Source: OECD Environmental Outlook projections; output from IMAGE.

StatLink ᵃᶜᵐˢ🔗 http://dx.doi.org/10.1787/888932570639

The implications of achieving the 450 Core scenario

Figure 3.18 indicates that to achieve the 450 ppm stabilisation target, global emission reductions of 12% will be needed by 2020 and 70% by 2050 compared to the *Baseline* (for 2050 this means 52% below 2005 levels, and 42% below 1990 levels). Emissions would therefore have to decrease at an average rate of 1.7% per year between 2010 and 2050, compared to the increase of +1.3% projected under the *Baseline*. Reduced CO_2 emissions from fossil fuel combustion would account for 75% of the global reduction by 2050. For emissions from land-use change the situation is reversed: the *450 Core* scenario would require additional land for growing bioenergy crops. Thus there would be a less rapid reduction of emissions from land-use change compared to the *Baseline*, and lower levels of net CO_2 uptake in the later decades (the difference is 1.2 $GtCO_2e$ in 2050). In order to achieve the 450 ppm target these additional emissions (and reduced uptake) would have to be compensated for by greater emission reductions by energy and industry.

The scenario assumes that carbon pricing is used to give incentives for mitigation efforts in all parts of the economy. A relatively large portion of emission reductions could be achieved relatively cheaply and quickly by limiting emissions of non-CO_2 gases from industries (*e.g.* coal mining, oil and gas processing and shipping, acid production) and the agricultural sector (*e.g.* changing rice cultivation patterns and nutrient management); and improving waste handling (waste recycling and methane capture from landfills). Curbing global emissions beyond 2020 would require a rapidly increasing carbon price (to USD 325/tCO_2e in 2050) to discourage intensive reliance on carbon-based energy sources. Only a strong and lasting carbon price signal will achieve the major transition required in carbon-intensive sectors, and those with large-scale infrastructural investments.

This scenario implies that world GDP growth would slow down between 2010 and 2050 as a result of lower energy consumption and the shift in supply options driven by higher energy prices. The average growth rate decreases from 3.5% per year in the *Baseline* to 3.3% per year in the *450 ppm Core* scenario, giving a world GDP that is 5.5% lower in 2050 than under the *Baseline*

Figure 3.18. **450 *Core* scenario: emissions and cost of mitigation, 2010-2050**

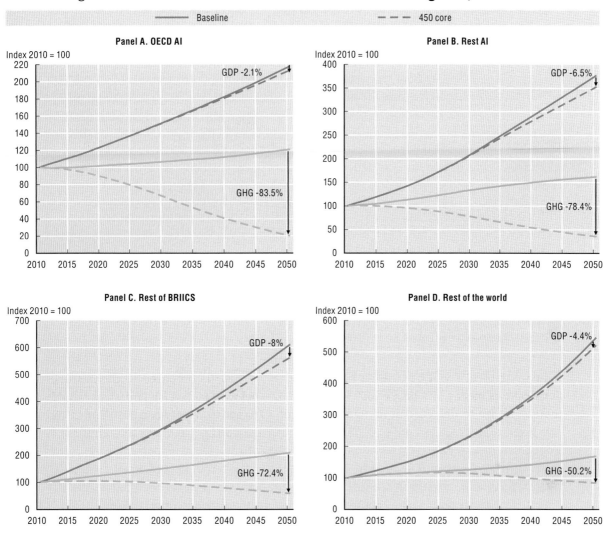

Notes: Emission projections are before permit trading, *i.e.* they reflect emission allowances.

"OECD AI" stands for the group of OECD countries that are also part of Annex I of the Kyoto Protocol; "Rest AI" stands for the other Annex I parties, including Russia; "Rest of BRIICS" are the BRIICS countries excluding Russia, and "Rest of the World" represent all other regions distinguished in the ENV-Linkages model.

GDP figures do not include the costs of inaction.

Source: OECD Environmental Outlook projections; output from ENV-Linkages.

StatLink ᵃᵗˢᵖ *http://dx.doi.org/10.1787/888932570658*

scenario. However, it should be stressed that a major limitation of all the results presented here (Box 3.8) is that they do not factor in any benefits of the mitigation action (see Chapter 2 on the cost of inaction and Chapter 3, Section 4 for synergies with other environmental issues). The economic impacts therefore reflect purely the cost of action, not the net costs or benefits.

Energy use grows between 2010 and 2020 in both the *Baseline* projection and the 450 *Core* scenario (although at a slower pace in the latter). After 2020, emissions would be reduced primarily by energy-efficiency improvements and strong supply changes. The ENV-Linkages simulations find that energy-efficiency improvements are the main driver (especially producers substituting more expensive energy with labour and capital, such as more expensive but energy-efficient machines), leading to a sharp drop in emissions by 2050.[40] A vast decarbonisation is required in the power generation and transport sector, as well as replacing existing dirty energy use by consumers (*e.g.* use of cooking fuels) with more efficient electricity-based technologies. This all involves a drastic restructuring of the energy sector.

Box 3.8. **Cost uncertainties and modelling frameworks**

Apart from uncertainties about climate and emission reduction timing, there are also significant uncertainties surrounding the costs of implementing climate change policies. The variations in the cost estimates across different modelling frameworks reflect fundamental uncertainties about the availability of technological options and their costs and development over time, as well as assumptions about economic growth, treatment of options that could have negative net costs (such as energy savings) and other model characteristics. For example, the ENV-Linkages model assumes a higher mitigation potential for non-CO_2 GHGs at moderate cost than the IMAGE model suite. Consequently, the 450 *Core* scenario in ENV-Linkages leads to substantially lower carbon prices by 2020 than IMAGE (USD 10/tCO_2e *versus* USD 50/tCO_2e).

While results presented here only come from the ENV-Linkages and IMAGE models, these belong to a large family of models designed to study climate change policy. Modelling comparison exercises have been conducted to better understand the influence of modelling frameworks on the results, as well as to identify the range of cost estimates (see Edenhofer *et al.*, 2009 and 2010; Clarke *et al.*, 2009; and van Vuuren *et al.*, 2009). A 450 ppm pathway would lead to a reduction of GDP in 2050 of either 5%-6% (ENV-Linkages) or 4% (IMAGE). These results fall within the range of estimates found in Luderer *et al.* (2009), which vary from about –0.5% to 6.5% (in 2060), and are similar to cost estimates for 2050 cited in IPCC (2007c). As emphasised by Tavoni and Tol (2010) such ranges should be assessed with care, because they usually exclude models which are unable to meet the target. Within the range, larger mitigation costs can for instance be caused by more conservative assumptions on substitution across production factors and energy technologies or by the limited availability of advanced technologies in the models (Edenhofer *et al.*, 2010). The low end of the range usually corresponds to models with a wide technology portfolio and optimistic assumptions about technological advances.

The costs shown in Figure 3.18 result from a regional permit allocation rule where regional emission allowances evolve over time towards equal per-capita allowances (Box 3.9). This so-called "contraction and convergence" allocation rule is not meant as a policy recommendation, but is used here purely for illustrative purposes. Alternative permit allocation rules lead to similar global costs, at least when full permit trading is allowed, but the allocation of these costs across the regions can vary significantly.

When allowing full emission permit trading, GHG emission reduction pathways are similar across all regions (ranging from 67% to 71% reduction by 2050 compared to the *Baseline*), as the stringency of the 450 *Core* target calls for action in all regions. Nonetheless, mitigation strategies will differ depending on the level of economic development and growth perspectives. Switching rapidly to low-carbon technologies allows OECD economies to be partially decarbonised, while energy-efficiency measures are the main mitigation option in BRIICS countries.[41] Energy intensity, defined as the ratio of energy use to GDP, is projected to decrease by 3.2% annually in OECD countries (close to the world average), while this ratio will reach 3.9% and 4.5% per year in BRIICS and RoW countries respectively.

Box 3.9. **What if... the mitigation burden was shared differently? How permit allocation rules matter**

In a global cap-and-trade system (as assumed in the 450 *Core* scenario), emission allowances are allocated to individual countries. As illustrated in Figure 3.19, determining regional emission allowances could be an effective step in shifting part of the burden of mitigation costs from developing economies to OECD countries. All the cases presented here assume that countries can auction their domestically allocated permits, with the revenues redistributed to households as a lump sum. The international burden sharing regime is thus primarily aimed at distributing costs among countries, not between individual polluters. Also, it is assumed that full international trading of permits is allowed. Essentially, this separates the place where mitigation action takes place from where the economic burden falls. Unless transaction costs are prohibitive, these permit allocation rules are a very powerful mechanism for ensuring that least-cost options are taken.

The following different permit allocation rules, which all have the same global emission pathway as the 450 *Core* scenario, are considered here:[1]

■ The 450 *Core* scenario: assumes a "contraction and convergence" rule, where the allocation of emission permits across regions is based on a gradual convergence from actual (2010) levels of emissions to equal emission allowances per capita by 2050 in all countries; this is effectively a transition from a grandfathering rule to a per-capita rule. Alternative convergence criteria or convergence dates are also conceivable.

■ The *Grandfathering*[2] scenario: assumes that every year countries will receive the same share in global allowances, based on actual (2010) emissions.

■ The *Per-capita* scenario: assumes that countries will receive a share in global allowances based on the projected levels of population, *i.e.* per-capita emission allowances are equal across countries.

■ The *Global carbon tax* scenario: assumes a carbon tax is implemented globally; this is equivalent to a permit allocation where emission allowances are allocated such that marginal costs are equal across regions, and so there is no permit trading.

As GDP is a poor indicator of the welfare impacts of policies when large volumes of emission permit trading occur, these allocation schemes should be compared using equivalent variation in real income.[3]

Figure 3.19. **Impact of permit allocation schemes on emission allowances and real income in 2050**

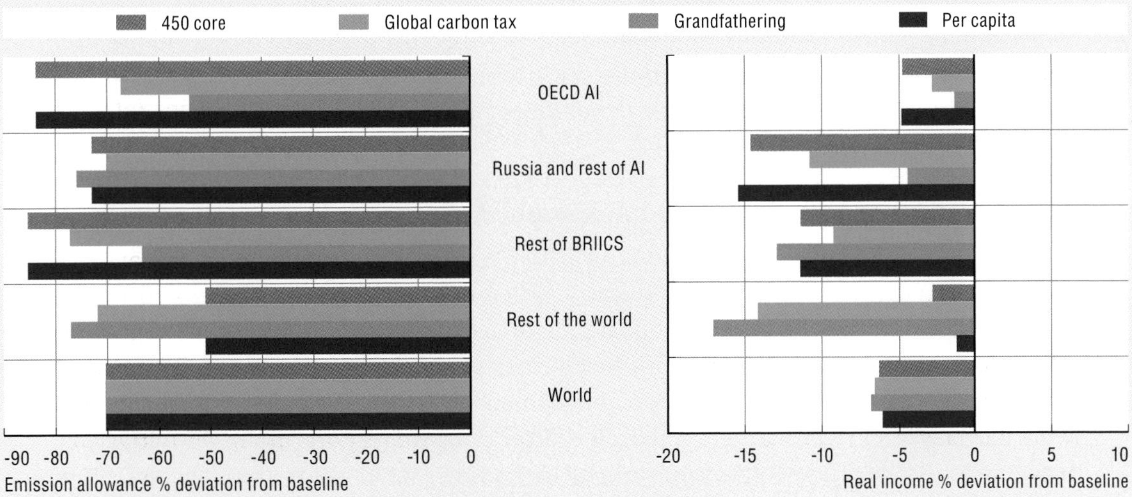

Source: OECD Environmental Outlook projections, output from ENV-Linkages.

StatLink http://dx.doi.org/10.1787/888932570677

> Box 3.9. **What if... the mitigation burden was shared differently?**
> **How permit allocation rules matter** *(cont.)*
>
> Globally, the allocation schemes do not matter much for income levels, as they all constrain global emissions at identical levels (Figure 3.19) and allow emissions trading. Regional differences are quite pronounced, however, largely mimicking the differences in emission allowances. Under the *Per-capita* scenario, poor and populated regions like India and developing countries (rest of the world group or RoW) would become large permit exporters, and the trade in allocations would reduce costs in these regions. Most OECD countries have the lowest income losses under the *Grandfathering* scenario. Russia and China would also be better off in a grandfathering allocation scheme (given their high current emission intensities), although income losses in these regions would be above global levels in all schemes.
>
> 1. More details on the shares of regions in the permit allocation scheme are given in Annex 3.A.
> 2. "Grandfathering" uses a company, sector or country's historical emissions levels to set their future permit allowances.
> 3. The equivalent real income variation is defined as the change in real income (in %) necessary to ensure the same level of utility to consumers as in the *Baseline* projection. One problem with using real GDP changes is that permit trades are not valued (see OECD, 2009b for more details). It is also important to note that permit transfers across countries would change international trade patterns and put pressure on exchange rates, *i.e.* the terms of trade across countries would be affected. For this reason real household income could be more affected by the allocation than GDP levels (OECD, 2009b).

There is more potential for improvement in energy efficiency in these regions as their carbon intensity is on average higher than in OECD countries (IEA, 2009b).[42]

Given the "contraction and convergence" distribution of emission permits under the *450 Core* scenario, the OECD region is the main buyer of permits, implying that they achieve part of their required emission reductions abroad. The developing countries in the RoW group are the main suppliers of permits. The related costs to the economies vary more widely among regions. The relatively high GDP losses in the BRIICS are largely concentrated in i) Russia – which is negatively affected by the reduced demand for fossil fuels; and ii) China, where emission growth is much more rapid than population growth, implying that in the later decades China would have to buy substantial amounts of emission permits on the international market.

Using an appropriate system for allocating revenues from market-based mitigation policies domestically could reduce the economic costs of mitigation. For example, using carbon tax or permit revenues to lower labour taxes could stimulate employment and would reduce the cost of mitigation in the short term (*e.g.* see Chateau *et al.*, 2011). In the long run, however, when labour markets are more flexible, the scope for such a "double dividend" would be less.

The implications of achieving the 450 Accelerated Action scenario

Both the *450 Accelerated Action* and the *450 Core* scenarios reduce the projected *Baseline* emissions by more than 75% by 2050. The main difference between the two scenarios is the timing of global mitigation efforts in the next two decades. These result in differences in which gases are reduced most (or which fuel in the case of energy-related CO_2 emissions), as well as different regional and sectoral mitigation choices. These elements are illustrated in the four panels of Figure 3.20. Of course, the larger mitigation efforts in the *450 Accelerated Action* scenario imply lower environmental risks but higher costs than the *450 Core* scenario. By 2030 carbon prices would be about 50% higher in the *450 Accelerated Action* scenario than in the *450 Core*.

Figure 3.20. **GHG abatements in the *450 Core Accelerated Action* and *450 Core* scenarios compared to the *Baseline*, 2020 and 2030**

(a) by GHG, (b) by aggregate region, (c) by economic activity and (d) by fossil fuel

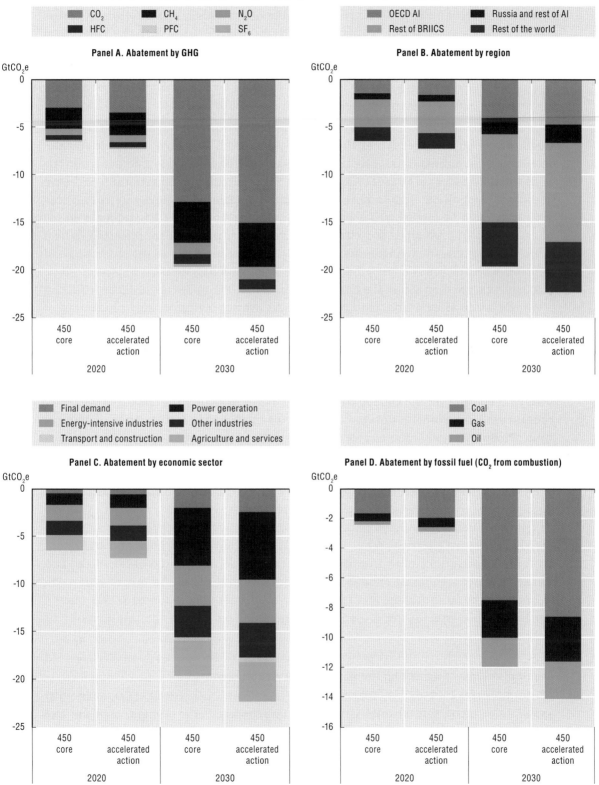

In aggregate terms, both scenarios lead to very similar emission reduction patterns across regions, given the shared permit allocation rule. BRIICS countries account for about half of the total mitigation effort, the other half being split evenly between OECD and RoW countries. However, the analysis of country details reveals larger differences across scenarios: China and the Middle East account respectively for about one-third and 7% of total mitigation in the *450 Accelerated Action* scenario, and are more sensitive to the targeted emission level in 2020. In other countries, such as India, mitigation efforts depend less on the scenario architecture because the mitigation potentials in these countries are less sensitive to the carbon price level around the years 2020 and 2030.

In both simulations, the lowest cost mitigation options are mobilised in the early stages of action, irrespective of the carbon price level. The level of ambition then determines the optimal mix of reduction measures. Non-CO_2 GHGs (methane, nitrous oxide and fluorinated or "F gases", such as HFCs, PFCs and sulphur hexafluoride – SF_6) have sizeable mitigation potential and reductions can be achieved at moderate cost. These potentials could be tapped into even under modest carbon prices. For example, easily adjusted industrial activities and changes in agricultural practices are projected to help reduce large volumes of methane efficiently (*e.g.* in coal mining, oil and gas processing and shipping; waste recycling and methane capture from landfills). Methane mitigation alone accounts for more than 60% of the total reduction of non-CO_2 gases by 2020. The reduction of nitrous oxide arising from changes in rice cultivation patterns, acid production or nutrient management, covers another 20%.

Accelerated action would require a quicker decarbonisation of electricity production, while a more gradual response to climate change would require relatively more effort from energy intensive industries, services and agriculture. In both scenarios, oil is the fossil fuel affected the most over the coming decade. Coal use is particularly discouraged for power generation and even moderate carbon prices are enough to trigger efficiency improvements in coal-based electricity generation and to favour a switch towards gas-based production capacity that is less carbon-intensive, notably in China and India. Natural gas is affected evenly in both scenarios and represents about 20% of total reduction in 2020 and 2030. In both scenarios, gas acts as a bridging fuel until lower carbon technologies become available on a large scale. Nuclear energy is projected to supply almost two-thirds of low-carbon electricity in 2020 and only half of it by 2030 in both cases. The share of hydro electricity tends to diminish over time as wind, solar and other non-hydro renewables take over. However, the carbon price differential between the two scenarios is not significant enough to drive notable changes in the mix of renewable technologies by 2030. Finally, fossil fuel based electricity generation with CCS plays a significant role later in the projection period (see Box 3.10 on the implications of technology options).

The implications of achieving the 450 Delayed Action scenario

As discussed above, the *450 Delayed Action* scenario assumes that until 2020 mitigation efforts will aim to achieve the high end of the pledges made in the Copenhagen Accord and Cancún Agreements (Table 3.6). A large number of countries have submitted reduction targets or national mitigation plans as part of the 2009 Copenhagen Accord – these were subsequently incorporated into the 2010 UNFCCC Cancún Agreements. Almost all developed countries have pledged to meet quantified

Box 3.10. **Implications of technology options**

Many different pathways are possible for achieving a given mitigation target. The policy scenarios investigated in this *Outlook* model different technology pathways to reduce emissions. In the *Baseline* scenario the power sector globally accounts for more than 40% of CO_2 emissions in 2050, and therefore plays a key role in the decarbonisation of the economy. To explore the role of energy technologies under the *450 Accelerated Action* scenario, three alternative simulations were conducted using the ENV-Linkages model (for more details see Annex 3.A). These scenarios all aim at achieving the same 450 ppm emission pathway, with the same timing of emission reductions but assume different patterns of technological developments to achieve it:

i) *Low efficiency and renewables*: assumes lower efficiency improvements in energy use compared to the default assumptions in the *450 Accelerated* Action scenario, through less improvement of energy inputs in production, and slower increases in production of renewables.

ii) *Progressive nuclear phase-out*: assumes that nuclear capacity currently under construction and planned until 2020 will be built and connected to the grid. However, after 2020, no new nuclear unit will be built so that the world total capacity by 2050 will be reduced because of the natural retirement of existing plants.

iii) *No CCS*: assumes no greater use of CCS technologies beyond the levels projected in the *Baseline*.

In the short run – to 2020 – altering the set of mitigation technologies results in only limited changes in the electricity generation mix and level because the carbon penalty is too low to overcome the inertia in the energy system. In all simulations the bulk of emission reduction over this timeframe is therefore achieved by decreasing emissions of methane, nitrous oxide and F gases, although there is also some reduction in energy consumption induced by the carbon price.

However, the role of these energy technologies in the longer run – to 2050 – is more pronounced as low-carbon technologies are projected to have taken over in all regions of the world (Figure 3.21). Panel A illustrates GDP impacts and carbon prices for each scenario, while Panel B shows the electricity generation mix and the overall production level for each of the three macro-regions. What becomes clear from Panel A is that having sufficient flexibility in the energy system will protect regions against large, sudden, unexpected increases in cost, or reduced availability of a specific technology at the scale originally anticipated.[*]

By 2050, when all technologies are assumed to be available, renewable electricity is assumed to supply about half of the needs in OECD and BRIICS, which will also rely on capital-intensive nuclear and fossil fuel plants with CCS. The results reveal strong complementarities between nuclear and fossil fuels (with or without CCS) in most regions. Phasing out nuclear facilities in the BRIICS countries, where most new capacity is expected to be built in the coming decades, causes a substantial reduction in electricity generation. Power plants with CCS become competitive around 2030 and increasingly so by the end of the time horizon in both OECD and BRIICS. In the absence of CCS power plants by 2050, switching to more expensive technologies increases electricity prices and alters consumption patterns. Fossil fuel power plants without CCS are projected to decline to about 10% of total power supply worldwide, due to the high carbon price, unless nuclear is phased out, in which case such a steep decline is not feasible.

The RoW region is projected to follow a different mitigation strategy, predominantly relying on increasing renewable energy sources. This region is therefore very sensitive to the assumptions about energy efficiency and productivity of renewable energy technologies, but less affected by the exclusion of nuclear and CCS. Given this projected strategy, substituting away from renewable energy sources is more difficult and costly. In turn, corresponding income losses in the RoW region are more than doubled in the *low efficiency and renewables* scenario compared to the *450 Accelerated Action* scenario.

---

[*] The 2011 incident at the Fukushima nuclear plant in Japan and the following reconsideration of nuclear energy use in other countries was a harsh reminder that possible large-scale disruptions to the energy system cannot be ignored.

Box 3.10.   **Implications of technology options** (*cont.*)

Figure 3.21.   **Technology choices for the *450 Accelerated Action* scenario**

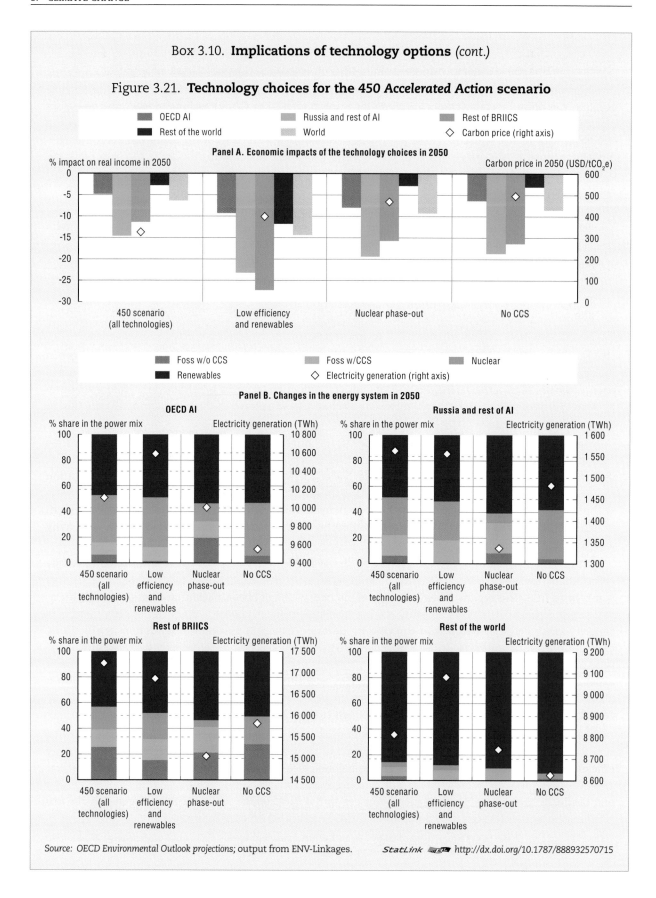

Source: OECD Environmental Outlook projections; output from ENV-Linkages.   StatLink http://dx.doi.org/10.1787/888932570715

economy-wide emission targets by 2020, and 44 developing countries have pledged mitigation actions.[43] Table 3.6 summarises the quantitative targets and actions, and also translates these pledges into quantified GHG emission reductions compared with 1990 (for Annex I Parties) and 2020 *Baseline* (for non-Annex I) emission levels in the modelling simulations.[44] Many Annex I Parties have not detailed their policies on the use of offsets; therefore, this information is only added for a few regions, and a default assumption that a maximum of 20% of the reduction targets is used in all other cases. Annex I Parties could potentially use land use, land-use change and forestry (LULUCF) credits to meet their pledged target; the extent to which this is assumed in the simulation is provided in the last column (see Annex 3.A for further details).

Table 3.6. **How targets and actions pledged under the Copenhagen Accord and Cancún Agreements are interpreted as emission changes under the 450 *Delayed Action* scenario: 2020 compared to 1990**

Region	Declared country emissions targets and actions	Emissions under *450 Delayed Action* scenario
Canada	−17% from 2005; no credits from international offsets currently assumed	+2.5% from 1990 (5 MtCO$_2$e LULUCF credits)
Japan and Korea	Japan −25% from 1990; Korea −30% from business as usual (BAU)	−16% from 1990 (35 MtCO$_2$e LULUCF credits)
Oceania	Australia −5% to −25% from 2000; New Zealand −10% to −20% from 1990	−12% from 1990 (0 MtCO$_2$e LULUCF credits)
Russia	−15% to −25% from 1990	−25% from 1990 (0 MtCO$_2$e LULUCF credits)
United States	−17% from 2005	−3.5% from 1990 (150 MtCO$_2$e LULUCF credits)
EU27 and EFTA	EU27, Liechtenstein and Switzerland −20% to −30% from 1990; Norway −30% to −40% from 1990; Iceland and Monaco −30% from 1990; max. 4 percentage-points credits from international offsets; no LULUCF credits for low pledge	−30% from 1990 (195 MtCO$_2$e LULUCF credits)
Rest of Europe	Ukraine −20% from 1990; Belarus −5% to −10% from 1990; Croatia −5% from 1990; emissions for other countries in this group without a pledge (incl. Turkey) are assumed to remain at BAU level.	−19.5% from 1990 (25 MtCO$_2$e LULUCF credits)
Brazil	−36% to −39% from BAU	−39% from BAU (incl. 775 MtCO$_2$e REDD)
China	Carbon intensity −40% to −45% from 2005; share of non-fossil fuels in primary energy consumption 15%; forest coverage +40 mln ha and volume +1.3 bln m^3	−4% from BAU
Indonesia	Indonesia −26% from BAU	−26% from BAU (incl. 200 MtCO$_2$e REDD)
India	Carbon intensity −20% to −25% from 2005	−2% from BAU
Middle East and Northern Africa	Israel −20% from BAU; no pledge for other countries in this group	No restriction on emissions
Mexico	Mexico −30% from BAU	−30% from BAU (incl. 115 MtCO$_2$e REDD)
South Africa	South Africa −34% from BAU	−25% from BAU[1]
Rest of the world	Pledges have been made by some countries in this group (incl. Costa Rica, Maldives, Marshall Islands) but not by the major emitters in this group.	No restriction on emissions

1. The domestic BAU projection used by South Africa has substantially higher emissions than the OECD *Baseline* projection; therefore the target for South Africa has been adjusted for this difference.

Note: The pledges presented here are an interpretation of their main quantitative aspects for the purpose of establishing a stylised modelling scenario. Many countries have provided additional details and nuances in their submissions to the UNFCCC, and often conditions are stated. For full details on the pledges see FCCC/SB/2011/INF.1/ Rev. 1 and FCCC/AWGLA/2011/INF.1 at *www.unfccc.int*.

Although up until 2020 the emission reductions in the *450 Delayed Action* scenario are smaller than in the *450 Core* scenario, real income losses are larger for most regions, because of the fragmentation of the carbon market (Figure 3.22). Carbon prices vary between regions in *Delayed Action*, ranging from zero for regions that do not have a binding pledge (including the Middle East and North Africa and rest of the world countries) to more than USD 50/tCO$_2$e for the combined Japan and Korea region. These results depend on a number of crucial but uncertain assumptions about the interpretation of the pledges (Box 3.11).

Figure 3.22. **Regional real income impacts, *450 Core* versus *450 Delayed Action* scenarios**

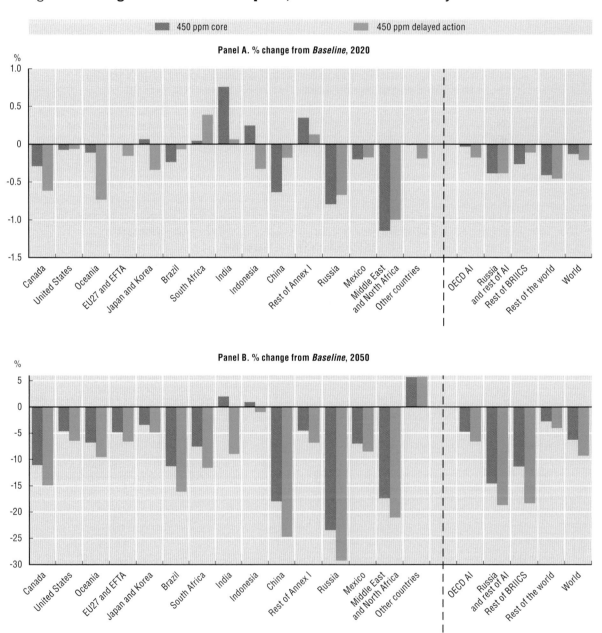

Source: OECD Environmental Outlook projections; output from ENV-Linkages.

StatLink http://dx.doi.org/10.1787/888932570753

Box 3.11. **Mind the gap: Will the Copenhagen pledges deliver enough?**

The Copenhagen pledges reflected in the 450 *Delayed Action* scenario would not be enough to achieve the 450 ppm pathway in a cost-effective way. This is confirmed by other analysis, which shows that these pledges fall short of UNEP's (2010) cost-effective range of 41-48 GtCO$_2$e for global GHG emissions in 2020 (see Box 3.8 above). These are the maximum emissions allowed to give the world a medium to likely chance of meeting the 2 °C target at least cost (Dellink *et al.*, 2010; UNEP, 2010). Table 3.7 confirms this: global emissions in 2020 would amount to 51.6 GtCO$_2$e for the high pledges and above 52 GtCO$_2$e for the low pledges (but including the conditional pledges).[1] The gap between the emission reductions in the 450 *Delayed Action* scenario and the pathway consistent with 2 °C is thus between 3 and 11 GtCO$_2$e (whereas total mitigation efforts in 450 *Delayed Action* in 2020 amount to less than 4 GtCO$_2$e).[2] As argued in UNEP (2010) and confirmed by our analysis (see next section), it is virtually impossible to identify what temperature increases these pledges to 2020 would lead to, as the assumptions about the pathway after 2020 will largely affect the resulting temperature changes.

Combining the lower end of the pledges with LULUCF accounting rules[3] that result in credits that are not induced by a change in management activities and use of surplus Assigned Amounts Units (AAUs)[4] from the current Kyoto commitment period (2008-2012) could widen this gap even further. There are other uncertainties that have less effect on environmental effectiveness, but do affect costs. They include limitations on the use of offsets, international financing of mitigation action in developing countries and linking of carbon markets in Annex I countries. Table 3.7 shows how these uncertainties affect global emissions (in GtCO$_2$e) and regional costs (in real income deviation from *Baseline*).

Table 3.7. **How different factors will affect emissions and real income from the Cancún Agreements/Copenhagen Accord pledges: 450 *Delayed Action* scenario (deviation from *Baseline*)**

Based on individual variations in key assumptions (deviation from baseline in %)

Scenario	Global emissions of GHG incl. LULUCF (GtCO2e)	Income equivalent variation impact			
		OECD members of Annex I	Russia and rest of Annex I	Rest of BRIICS	Rest of the World
...the pledge level (high vs. low pledges)	51.6 vs. 52.2	−0.2 vs. −0.1	−0.4 vs. −0.3	−0.1 vs. −0.1	−0.5 vs. −0.4
... the use of surplus AAUs (0%-100%)	51.6 vs. 51.6	−0.2 vs. −0.2	−0.4 vs. −0.4	−0.1 vs. −0.1	−0.5 vs. −0.5
... land use accounting (net-net vs. no LU credits)	51.6 vs. 50.8	−0.2 vs. −0.3	−0.4 vs. −0.6	−0.1 vs. −0.2	−0.5 vs. −0.6
... international financing (100% vs. 0%)	51.6 vs. 51.6	−0.2 vs. −0.2	−0.4 vs. −0.4	−0.1 vs. −0.1	−0.4 vs. −0.5
... use of offsets (50% vs. 0%)	51.6 vs. 51.6	−0.1 vs. −0.3	−0.3 vs. −0.5	−0.1 vs. 0	−0.3 vs. −0.5
... linking carbon markets (none vs. Annex I)	51.6 vs. 51.8	−0.2 vs. −0.1	−0.4 vs. 0	−0.1 vs. 0	−0.4 vs. −0.2
... linking combined with surplus AAUs	53.6	0	−0.2	0	−0.1

Source: OECD Environmental Outlook projections; output from ENV-Linkages.   *StatLink* 🔗 http://dx.doi.org/10.1787/888932571912

Both the high and low pledge levels show limited overall costs, although for some regions and sectors the costs are somewhat higher (see Figure 3.22). Costs increase in the OECD Annex I countries especially when they abstain from using land-use credits and/or offsets. Costs can be reduced in these countries by adopting lower pledges, linking carbon markets or allowing surplus AAUs; however, in all cases these reductions come at the cost of higher global emissions. International financing above and beyond participation in the offset mechanism can reduce the costs for developing countries. However, the effect is limited as the simulations assume that only Brazil, Mexico and South Africa qualify for these international funds (see Annex 3.A; and note that the other non-Annex I countries are eligible as offset hosts). Russia and the Rest

Box 3.11. **Mind the gap: Will the Copenhagen pledges deliver enough?** (*cont.*)

of Europe region (incl. Ukraine) benefit most from linking carbon markets, as they have large amounts of permits to sell. Finally, note that for the "rest of the world" countries costs can be limited by either allowing more offsets or linking carbon markets in the Annex I countries. Both options lead to price harmonisation across the Annex I countries and limit negative spill-over effects through a global contraction of international trade.

The use of market-based instruments, such as carbon taxes or cap-and-trade with auctioned emission permits, can provide a source of fiscal revenue. If the Cancún Agreements/Copenhagen Accord pledges and actions for Annex I countries as described above were to be implemented as a carbon tax or a cap-and-trade with fully auctioned permits, in 2020 the fiscal revenues would amount to more than USD 250 billion, i.e. 0.6% of their GDP.[5] Although there would be many competing uses of such revenue, just a fraction of this amount would make a significant contribution to climate change financing specified in the Cancún Agreements.[6]

1. Some countries made both unconditional (less ambitious) and conditional (more ambitious) pledges. These latter would be honoured if the conditions they attached to the pledges were fulfilled, for example providing adequate climate finance and ambitious action from other countries.
2. These numbers differ from Dellink et al. (2010) because the analysis here is based on the methodology of Den Elzen et al. (2011) and includes emissions from land use, land-use change and forestry, not because the pledges themselves have substantially changed.
3. Accounting rules for land use, land-use change and forestry (LULUCF) can potentially weaken the mitigation targets of industrialised countries. This could occur if credit is given for LULUCF activities that would have happened in any case without further policy intervention.
4. An Assigned Amount Unit (AAU) is a tradable "Kyoto unit" or carbon credit representing an allowance to emit one tonne of GHGs. Assigned Amount Units are issued up to the level of the initial "assigned amount" of an *Annex* I Party to the Kyoto Protocol. See Annex 3.A for more.
5. These numbers are lower than in Dellink et al. (2010) primarily because the use of LULUCF credits lowers the carbon price and because costs are expressed here in constant 2010 USD, not because the pledges themselves have changed.
6. In the simulations presented here the revenues are redistributed to households in a lump sum manner and alternative destinations would affect this lump sum transfer and, indirectly, the economy.

As the 450 *Delayed Action* scenario assumes that until 2020 international permit trading is not allowed, many low-cost mitigation options remain unexploited until 2020, driving up global costs. Figure 3.22 clearly illustrates that domestic policies are not the only, and sometimes not even the main, determinant of the macroeconomic costs of the policies. Fossil fuel exporters, such as Russia and the Middle East region, are projected to have higher income losses, despite having hardly or no costs from domestic mitigation efforts. Panel A of Figure 3.22 also shows how international financing of mitigation action (assumed to take place in South Africa, Brazil and Mexico, see Annex 3.A) can help to limit the costs of domestic action. Combined with the opportunity to sell credits on the offset market, the "Rest of BRIICS" group have only very small income losses in the 450 *Delayed Action* scenario.

In the longer run (2050), the 450 *Delayed Action* scenario requires more ambitious mitigation efforts to bring concentration levels back down to the 450 ppm target before the end of the century. As these efforts occur later than in the 450 *Core* scenario, it is not surprising that income losses are again higher in the 450 *Delayed Action* scenario (Figure 3.22, Panel B). By 2050 in both the 450 *Core* and *Delayed Action* scenarios a global carbon market has formed with permit allocations based on population; thus the larger income losses reflect the additional costs resulting from inadequate mitigation efforts in the earlier decades. There is both a direct effect – stemming from the increased mitigation efforts required in 2050 to limit concentrations – and an indirect effect from the lack of structural reform in the energy sector in the earlier decades.

Table 3.8 shows how competitiveness is likely to be affected by the *450 Delayed Action* mitigation policy. Not surprisingly, energy producers including power plants are projected to reduce their output and export levels following reduced demand due to carbon pricing. Given the low trade exposure of power plants, however, the energy sector is less vulnerable from a competitiveness perspective than energy-intensive industries. The relatively low emission-intensity of energy-intensive industry in OECD countries implies that while they would be faced with substantial cost increases due to the mitigation policy, in the long run, they can gain market share at the expense of less efficient competitors in the BRIICS and RoW, and thereby even increase their output levels compared to the *Baseline* scenario. More detailed analysis at the sub-sectoral level could identify more precisely where the largest effects are.

Table 3.8. **Competitiveness impacts of the 450 *Delayed Action* scenario, 2020 and 2050: % change from *Baseline***

	2020					2050				
	OECD Annex I	Rest of BRIICS	Russia and rest of Annex I	Rest of the world	GLOBAL	OECD Annex I	Rest of BRIICS	Russia and rest of Annex I	Rest of the world	GLOBAL
					%					
Panel I: macroeconomic indicators										
Terms of trade (% change from *Baseline*)	0.3	0.6	−0.6	−0.7	0.0	2.9	23.4	−4.4	−14.4	3.5
Share of EII in GDP	7.2	15.0	6.8	6.8	8.5	7.2	4.3	6.7	8.1	3.9
Panel II: volume of output in selected sectors (% change from *Baseline*)										
Agriculture	−1.1	−0.2	0.3	0.2	−0.4	−14.8	−11.6	−16.2	−19.7	−15.4
Energy-intensive industries (EII)	−0.9	0.3	1.4	1.0	−0.2	5.2	−30.1	4.1	−12.0	−14.1
Energy producers	−3.9	−1.0	0.1	−0.4	−2.0	−36.0	−44.5	−43.3	−45.2	−42.1
Services	0.0	−0.1	−0.2	−0.2	0.0	−2.3	−6.3	−6.7	−1.1	−3.2
Rest of the economy	−0.1	−0.3	0.0	0.0	−0.1	−1.0	−17.9	−4.4	−8.4	−8.2
Panel III: volume of exports by selected sectors (% change from *Baseline*)										
Agriculture	−2.4	−2.3	1.3	1.0	−1.4	−27.2	−34.1	−19.0	−41.4	−29.7
Energy-intensive industries	−1.4	0.8	2.1	1.9	−0.4	9.7	−28.1	14.1	−11.3	−3.8
Energy producers	−4.0	−4.1	−1.0	−1.3	−2.0	−43.6	−30.6	−55.0	−52.0	−49.1
Services	−0.1	−0.5	−0.6	0.0	−0.2	−5.2	12.2	2.8	−4.0	−0.3
Rest of the economy	−0.2	−0.6	−0.3	0.1	−0.3	0.2	−17.0	0.8	−15.0	−7.8

Source: OECD *Environmental Outlook projections*; output from ENV-Linkages.

StatLink ⎘ http://dx.doi.org/10.1787/888932571931

The fragmented carbon markets in the *450 Delayed Action* scenario also lead to some carbon leakage. Table 3.6 shows that as all the largest emitting countries have pledged reductions that effectively cap their emission levels, leakage rates will be rather low. In 2020, global leakage is projected to be around 50 MtCO$_2$e, or 1% of total mitigation action by the countries with pledges. The leakage rates found in the literature for the high end of the Copenhagen pledges vary widely, from no or very low leakage (*e.g.* McKibbin *et al.*, 2011) to 13% (547 MtCO$_2$e) in Peterson *et al.* (2011) and 16% in Bollen *et al.* (2011). Two key differences appear to influence the leakage assessment: *i)* to what extent binding targets are included for non-Annex I countries (as these limit the scope for leakage to occur); and *ii)* price responsiveness of fossil fuel supply. A price-elastic fuel supply implies that the reduced fuel price leads to smaller global supply and hence less leakage through the fossil fuel channel (see Burniaux and Oliveira-Martins, 2000).

To counter negative leakage and competitiveness impacts, governments have considered exempting firms or industries at risk, or providing financial compensation, *e.g.* through free distribution of permits or output-based rebates, or border tax adjustments. However, while temporary use of some target measures may be a way to ease the transition to a low-carbon economy, these measures should be carefully reviewed in terms of their economic efficiency, the (dis)incentives they create for GHG reductions and their impacts on developing countries (OECD, 2010d; Agrawala *et al.*, 2010a). In addition, they have also been shown to reduce the rate of innovation among firms (OECD, 2010e), and the benefits of these schemes will decline with the increase in the number of countries implementing mitigation policies (OECD, 2009b; Burniaux *et al.*, 2010). Instead, multilateral policy co-ordination would be an efficient alternative to unilateral measures. This was demonstrated by the UNECE Convention on long-range transboundary air pollution, where the transfer of knowledge and technologies was greater among signatories (OECD, 2011e).

Less stringent climate mitigation (550 ppm) scenarios

Achieving the 450 ppm scenarios requires global emission levels to peak before or around 2020. This is only possible if emissions can be reduced in nearly all global regions and if action starts now. If not, as suggested by the *450 Delayed Action* scenario, emissions in 2020 may be too high to achieve the 2 °C/450 ppm goal cost-effectively. If the 450 ppm target is to be reached, unprecedented rates of emission reductions will be required after 2020. The only way to do this will be to drastically transform the high-carbon energy system into which the world is becoming more tightly locked every year (IEA, 2011b). Given the uncertainties surrounding our ability to achieve this, less stringent long-run targets should also be investigated. Up until 2020, the *450 Delayed Action* scenario is very close to a *550 Core* scenario, which would require less mitigation in the rest of the century (see Figure 3.17 above). However, the 550 ppm *Core* scenario represents a much greater likelihood of a global average temperature rise above 2 °C. This implies that unless the required rapid transformation occurs after 2020, the Copenhagen pledges are more likely to lead to a 2.5 °C to 3 °C increase in global average temperature than 2 °C.

If the *550 Core* pathway is followed this would imply a trade-off between lower short-term mitigation costs and higher long-term costs from more serious climate impacts and the need for higher levels of adaptation than the *450 Delayed Action* scenario.[45] Once the "low-hanging fruit" (cheap mitigation options) have been exhausted, the marginal abatement cost of mitigation actions rises significantly.[46] The *550 Core* scenario requires that emissions in 2050 are down to 2010 levels (Figure 3.23). It leads to a decline in global real income of 1.3% as shown in Figure 3.24. Achieving the additional 28 $GtCO_2e$ reduction necessary to reach the *450 Delayed Action* pathway would lead to an additional real income decline of about 8 percentage-points, and global emissions would be 60% below 2010 levels.[47]

Actions needed for an ambitious, global climate policy framework

The first and best solution to address the competitiveness concerns described above would be a global, comprehensive and ambitious climate policy framework that creates a level playing field, covering all sectors and all GHGs (Agrawala *et al.*, 2010a). Broadening the scope of mitigation action also reduces the related problem of carbon leakage – when mitigation policy in one country leads to increased emissions in other countries, thereby eroding the environmental effectiveness of the policy. Leakage can occur through a shift in economic activity towards unregulated countries, or through increased fossil energy use in unregulated

Figure 3.23. **Change in global GHG emissions in 2050 compared to 2010: 450 Delayed Action and 550 ppm scenarios**

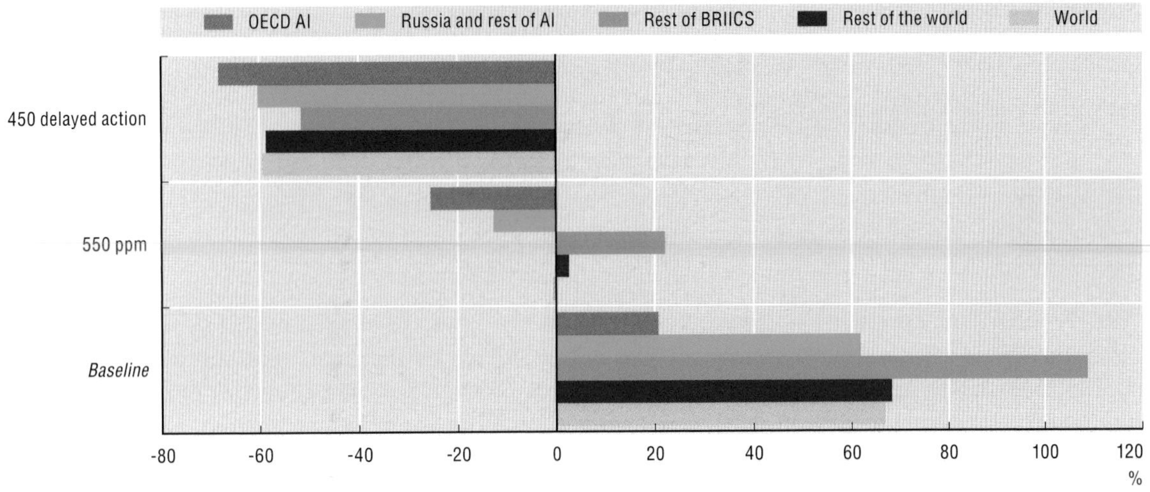

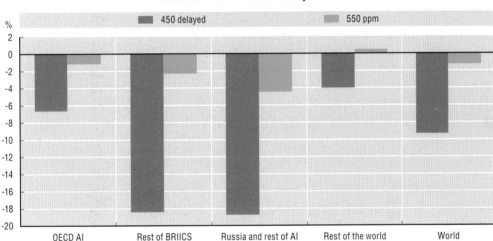

Source: OECD Environmental Outlook projections, output from ENV-Linkages.
StatLink http://dx.doi.org/10.1787/888932570772

Figure 3.24. **Change in real income from the Baseline for the 450 Delayed Action and 550 Core scenarios, 2050**

Source: OECD Environmental Outlook projections, output from ENV-Linkages.
StatLink http://dx.doi.org/10.1787/888932570791

countries as a result of lower international fuel prices in response to the reduced energy demand in mitigating countries.

As long as countries take such varied approaches to carbon markets, concerns about leakage and international competitiveness will remain a significant stumbling block to ambitious climate change action in many OECD countries (Box 3.12). In evaluating the potential competitiveness impacts, governments may be most concerned about emission leakage and conserving output and employment, whereas energy-intensive industries are more likely to be concerned about profits and market share. In fact, competitiveness impacts of climate policies are likely to be limited to a small number of sectors representing a small share of total economic activity, i.e. trade-exposed, energy-intensive industries (including

Box 3.12. **What if... a global carbon market does not emerge?**

Since reaching the 450 ppm target would require the combined effort of all countries, this box analyses the impact of market fragmentation under the 550 *Core* scenario. Linking carbon markets in only some regions will have a number of inefficiencies. These are illustrated in Figure 3.25 using alternative scenarios. The different variations modelled are as follows:

- 550 *No linking*: unilateral actions only and no linking at all;
- 550 *OECD linking*: regional linking within subsets of OECD countries;
- 550 *Annex I linking*: linking within Annex I countries only;
- 550 *OECD-BRIICS linking*: linking within OECD and BRIICS countries only;
- 550 Full linking: this is the 550 Core scenario.

The overarching conclusion from these simulations is that linking markets can help limit the costs of mitigation policies for participating countries, but it matters drastically which countries link their ETS systems. Countries that rely mostly on renewable energy sources for electricity generation, and that are therefore more difficult to decarbonise, tend to benefit most from market linking. Linking has only minor effects on countries that are not directly involved in the linked schemes, although they do benefit from the more efficient carbon market through increases in international trade.

OECD countries are projected to be the main permit buyers. Mitigation in OECD countries represents about a third of global efforts when permit exchange is restricted to Annex I countries and has very limited effects on macroeconomic costs. Opening trade further to include the rest of the BRIICS implies that China and India become the major suppliers of permits (similar to the current CDM), decreasing the OECD contribution by 8 percentage-points of global mitigation levels. Full trading further reduces the contribution of the OECD countries to 22% of the global effort.

By 2050, mitigation in the RoW countries would represent 25% of total emission reductions in the 550 *Core* (*Full linking*) scenario. This falls to about 10% if their carbon market is not internationally linked. Allowing the RoW countries to sell large volumes of emission permits would be a significant and low-cost mitigation option, and would also earn them sizeable revenues from internationally sold permits. For a detailed discussion of the potential and risks of linking ETSs, see OECD (2009b).

Figure 3.25. **Income impact of fragmented emission trading schemes for reaching concentrations of 550 *ppm* compared to the *Baseline*, 2050**

% change in real income

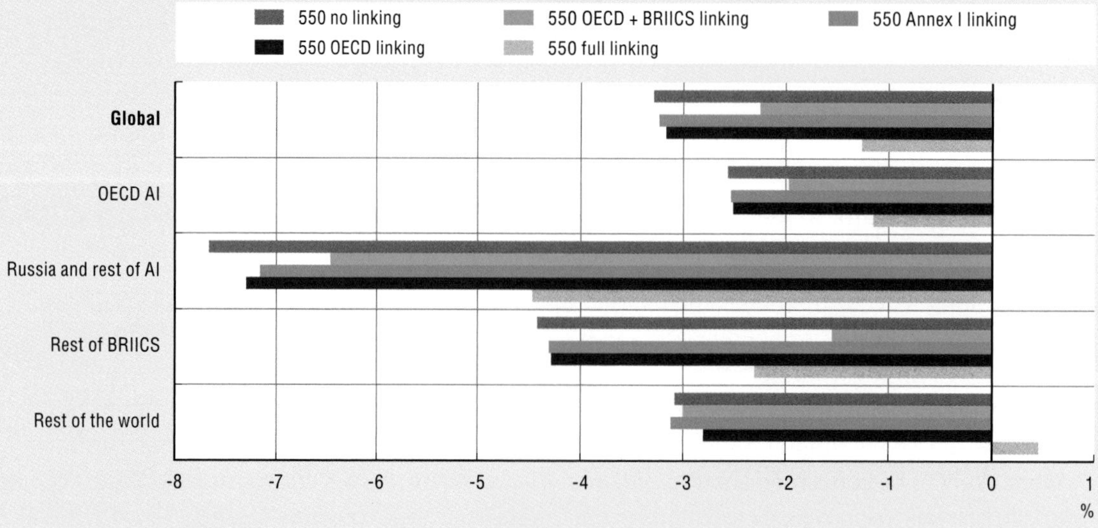

Source: OECD Environmental Outlook projections; output from ENV-Linkages..   StatLink 🔗 http://dx.doi.org/10.1787/888932570810

chemicals, non-ferrous metals, fabricated metal products, iron and steel, pulp and paper, and non-metallic mineral products).

The patchwork of climate policies across the globe today entails higher compliance costs in some countries than others, and raises concerns in some countries about the competitiveness of their energy- and/or carbon-intensive industries at the international level. These in turn often delay action or discourage more ambitious action. The cheapest policy response to climate change would be to set a global carbon price – this would require linking the various ETSs that are emerging locally. Linking generally allows polluters to purchase credits from a larger set of suppliers. Access to cheaper mitigation options lowers costs by reducing domestic efforts for permit buyers; polluters with relatively cheap mitigation options can gain from increasing domestic reduction efforts and selling these on the international market.

Reforming fossil fuels support

Reforming environmentally harmful subsidies, and specifically fossil fuel subsidies, is an important step in "getting the prices right" to reduce GHG emissions. An inventory of 24 OECD countries finds that fossil fuel production and use was supported by USD 45-75 billion per year between 2005 and 2010 (OECD, 2011f). Fossil fuel consumption subsidies in 37 developing and emerging economies amounted to an estimated USD 554 billion in 2008, USD 300 billion in 2009 and USD 409 billion in 2010 (IEA/OECD/OPEC/WB, 2010; IEA, 2011b and see Annex 3.A at the end of this chapter).[48]

Removing these subsidies would lower the global cost of stabilising GHG concentrations, saving money for governments and taxpayers. It helps to shift the economy away from activities that emit CO_2, encourages energy efficiency, and promotes the development and diffusion of low-carbon technologies and renewable energy sources. OECD *Outlook* simulations using IEA data (2008 estimates) indicate that phasing-out fossil fuel consumption subsidies in emerging and developing countries could reduce global GHG emissions (excluding land-use change emissions) by 6% globally by 2050, compared with business as usual, and by over 20% in Russia and Middle East and North Africa countries (Figure 3.26). As subsidies artificially reduce the price paid by final consumers, removing this price-wedge would influence behaviour and reduce final energy demand. This could increase global real income by 0.3% in 2050, and would be especially beneficial for the BRIICS countries (+1.1% for the Rest of BRIICS category).

However, some trade effects offset the pure economic efficiency gains of these subsidy reforms for the main fossil fuel exporting countries (*e.g.* Russia and the Middle East). This is because a lower demand for fossil fuels in the reforming countries will cause a decrease in global energy prices. Moreover, unless OECD countries cap their total emission levels, this decrease in international prices could create an increase in emissions in some OECD countries (relative to *Baseline*), leading to a partial offset of the original reduction of demand and GHG emissions. Despite this leakage effect, the net effect on global emissions is, however, projected to be positive.

If fossil fuel subsidy phase-out is included in the *450 Core* scenario, the cost of mitigation would be lower than in the *450 Core* scenario without the subsidy reform. These lower costs would occur first and foremost in the countries undertaking the subsidy reform, but also at the global level (Table 3.9). Note that the high costs for the rest of world in 2020 – both for fossil fuel subsidy reform on its own and a *450 Core* scenario that includes fossil fuel subsidy reform – are

Figure 3.26. **Impact on GHG emissions* of phasing out fossil fuels subsidies, 2050**

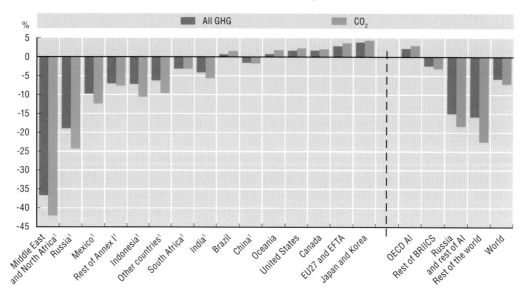

* Excludes emissions from land-use change.
1. Regions for which fossil fuel subsidies reform is simulated.
Source: OECD ENV-Linkages model using IEA fossil fuel subsidies data (IEA, 2009b).

StatLink http://dx.doi.org/10.1787/888932570829

due to the impacts on oil-exporting countries in the Middle East. The income gains of the reform are smaller in the *450 Core* scenario than under a framework involving only fossil fuels subsidy reform. This is because fossil-energy use is lower in the *450 Core* scenario and thus the savings from removing fuel subsidies are also lower.

Table 3.9. **Income impacts of a fossil fuel subsidy reform with and without the 450 Core scenario, 2020 and 2050**

% real income deviation from the *Baseline*

Region	2020			2050		
	Only FFS reform	*450 Core* no reform	*450 Core* with FFS reform	Only FFS reform	*450 Core* no reform	*450 Core* with FFS reform
World	**0.1**	**−0.1**	**−0.1**	**0.3**	**−6.3**	**−6.0**
OECD Annex I	0.2	0.0	0.2	0.2	−4.8	−4.5
Rest of BRIICS	0.6	−0.3	0.3	1.1	−11.4	−10.7
Russia and rest of Annex I	−0.6	−0.4	−1.0	0.2	−14.6	−13.8
Rest of the World	−1.2	−0.4	−1.4	−0.3	−2.8	−2.6

Source: OECD ENV-Linkages model using IEA fossil fuel subsidies data (IEA, 2009b).

StatLink http://dx.doi.org/10.1787/888932571950

However, removing these subsidies can be politically challenging, and may also lead to more use of traditional bioenergy (*e.g.* cooking using wood or animal manure) in developing countries, with potentially negative health effects (see Chapter 6). The combustion of traditional bioenergy is also associated with high black carbon emissions that also contribute to climate change (see Box 3.14 below). As a result, fossil fuel subsidy reforms should be implemented carefully to ensure that potential negative impacts on household affordability and well-being are reduced through appropriate measures (*e.g.* means-tested social safety net programmes).

Finding synergies among climate change strategies and other goals

Designing policies which address two or more goals at once (environmental, social and economic) can help to multiply the benefits of policy action. This final section explores some opportunities for maximising the benefits of combining climate change action with biodiversity protection, health and green growth.

Climate change, biodiversity and bioenergy

Climate change is projected to play the driving role in further biodiversity loss in the future (Chapter 4). The right strategies for mitigating climate change will therefore also have benefits for biodiversity, slowing down the pace of species loss. However, some climate mitigation policies can have negative impacts on biodiversity. For example, the use of bioenergy can be an attractive option – its use can reduce GHG emissions and it can be easily applied as an alternative to liquid fuels in transport (especially for specific purposes such as aviation and freight transport), in power generation or even to create negative emissions (if combined with CCS). But it also may have negative impacts on direct and indirect GHG emissions, and on biodiversity via the need for additional land for biofuel crops (Box 3.13). On the other hand, other mitigation strategies, such as REDD-plus measures, avoided emissions from land-use changes in forested areas, or the use of second generation bioenergy would result in additional biodiversity co-benefits (Chapter 4 on biodiversity presents some more policy simulations on this issue).

Box 3.13. **Bioenergy: Panacea or Pandora's Box?**

Bioenergy is energy generated from food crops such as grains, sugar cane and vegetable oils (first generation bioenergy) or from cellulose, hemicellulose or lignin sourced from non-food crops or inedible waste products (second generation bioenergy). Bioenergy may play an important role in mitigating climate change. It can be used as liquid fuel in the transport sector to replace fossil-energy based fuels, leading to lower CO_2 emissions. It can also be used in the power sector as a replacement for coal or natural gas. In power and in hydrogen production, bioenergy can also be combined with CCS to create a technology which could actually remove emissions from the atmosphere (known as BECCS). Through this approach, CO_2 is absorbed during the growth phase of the biomass, and then captured and stored when the biomass is converted to power or hydrogen (Azar et al., 2010; Read and Lermit, 2005).

The downsides of bioenergy

However, the use of bioenergy may also have serious disadvantages. First, the production of bioenergy crops requires land, putting it into competition with other activities (such as food production) (Azar, 2005; Bringezu et al., 2009; Searchinger et al., 2008). Some studies have reported that considerable food price increases may occur as a result of the direct and indirect land-use impacts of bioenergy (indeed, price rises in 2008 and 2011 have also partly been attributed to the rapid rise in bioenergy use). Secondly, bioenergy may have considerable GHG emissions associated with its production. These include the emissions from nitrogen fertilisers and fuel used during the growth and conversion phase, as well as the CO_2 emissions from land-use change either directly (conversion of natural ecosystems) or indirectly (competition with other forms of land use may cause more natural ecosystems to be converted to farmland; Searchinger et al., 2008; Smeets et al., 2009). In some cases, the emissions associated with bioenergy may be as much as fossil fuels or even higher. These impacts may be partly mitigated by: i) using second generation bioenergy (e.g. producing fuels

---

Box 3.13. **Bioenergy: Panacea or Pandora's Box?** *(cont.)*

from grasses, woody biomass or even biologically derived waste which does not require additional cropland to produce); *ii)* the application of sustainability criteria; *iii)* careful choices for high-yield crops which limit land-use requirements or using extensive bioenergy production systems; or *iv)* the use of biomass both in material and energy applications (so-called cascading). Finally, experience with bioenergy and CCS technologies is still limited. Both face challenges related to climate policy uncertainty, public acceptance and first-of-a-kind technology risks. CCS is currently much more expensive than other technologies.

The impacts of bioenergy on biodiversity, land use, and food prices and availability thus depend on rather complex interactions in the agricultural and energy system. The calculations for the *OECD Environmental Outlook* assume that bioenergy use occurs mostly in the power sector and that fuel production is mostly based on second-generation bioenergy (mainly from residues). The 450 *Core* scenario in the IMAGE model simulations assumes that by around 2050 about 20% of primary energy use is supplied from bioenergy. While this substantially reduces emissions from the combustion of fossil fuels, it also implies some increased emissions from land use. The implications for biodiversity are discussed in Chapter 4. As the exact trade-offs are rather uncertain at this stage, more careful monitoring of the use and impacts of bioenergy is needed.

Can we get by without bioenergy?

The 550 *Core* scenario using the IMAGE model assumes a lower reliance on bioenergy. In the 550 *Core* scenario, about 13% of total primary energy use is supplied by bioenergy, while in the 550 *Low bioenergy* scenario this is reduced to 6.5%. An important question is whether easily substitutable alternatives exist in the transport sector. In these calculations, hydrogen produced from fossil fuels with CCS would be an alternative with only limited additional costs; however, if this alternative cannot come about, relying less on bioenergy may substantially increase climate policy costs. Achieving lower concentration targets (450 ppm) depends significantly on the use of BECCS. Achieving ambitious climate policy scenarios with less reliance on bioenergy is likely to concentrate its use in the power sector (in combination with BECCS). However, the complete exclusion of bioenergy use might make very low concentration targets unachievable. Given these uncertainties, further work will be important to explore options for sustainable bioenergy use, and several models will be needed to better understand the impacts of different shares of bioenergy in mitigation option portfolios.

Climate change mitigation and health co-benefits

Some climate warming gases – such as black carbon (Box 3.14), methane, sulphur dioxide (SO_2) and nitrogen oxides (NO_x) – are also air pollutants which have negative health impacts. Well-designed climate mitigation policies can therefore also help to meet air pollution reduction objectives. Mitigation policies affect climate in the long run, while the health benefits of reducing local air pollution will be felt in the short to medium run (Bollen *et al.*, 2009; UNEP, 2011b). In these cases, cost-benefits analyses should take account of those additional co-benefits (see Chapter 6 for further discussion). While it is important to stress that targeting short-lived climate forcers or GHGs should not detract from broader GHG-mitigation policies and the need to achieve lasting decarbonisation of the economy, these policies can be a complement to a full range of climate change action.

The existence of any health-related co-benefits can also to some extent depend on the policy instruments being applied. If a cap-and-trade system is used to limit CO_2 emissions, any additional policy instruments applied to the same emission sources would (as mentioned above) not lead to further CO_2-emission reductions – or any reductions in SO_2 or NO_x emissions, due to interactions with the CO_2 cap (OECD, 2011b).

Box 3.14. **The case of black carbon**

Black carbon is produced from the incomplete combustion of solid or liquid fuels such as fossil fuels, biofuels, and biomass. It is not a single substance, but is the fraction of particulate matter that most efficiently absorbs visible light (Bond et al., 2004; UNEP, 2011b). The sources of black carbon emissions are numerous and include mobile diesel engines without particulate traps, cooking stoves, savanna and forest burning, agricultural waste combustion, and small-scale industry such as brick kilns and coke production (Bond and Sun, 2005). Although black carbon is not a GHG, it is an important short-lived climate forcer and directly affects the Earth's climate by absorbing solar radiation in the upper atmosphere, where it remains for days or weeks (Molina et al., 2009). Additionally, deposits of black carbon on snow or ice change a region's "albedo" – the proportion of incident light reflected – leading to more absorbed solar radiation.

It is difficult to measure the total net effect of black carbon, but limiting black carbon emissions is one important element in a climate protection strategy (UNEP, 2011a). For example, some CO_2 mitigation measures result in short-term warming by also limiting co-emitted sulphur (UNEP, 2011a). In addition to climate benefits, reducing black carbon can have significant health and agricultural productivity benefits. The full implementation of measures to jointly curtail black carbon and tropospheric (i.e. ground-level) ozone precursors would jointly prevent 2.4 million premature deaths, and the loss of between 1% and 4% of the total annual production of wheat, rice, maize and soybeans (UNEP, 2011a). Mitigation approaches vary widely by country due to differing emitting activities. Emissions from OECD countries come largely from diesel vehicles (EPA, 2011). In other countries such as China and India, sources include cookstoves, brick kilns and coke ovens – these also cause indoor air pollution.

Marginal abatement costs for black carbon vary across regions and are higher in North America and Europe where relatively low cost abatement measures for particulate matter have already been implemented (Rypdal et al., 2009). Given black carbon's regional variance, more work is needed to develop the best policy approach for reducing it. Further analysis and comparison of cost-effective black carbon mitigation strategies could integrate multiple criteria including i) local atmospheric conditions; ii) the proportion of black carbon to other co-emitted particulate matter; iii) impact on sensitive regions where snow/albedo effect is important; and iv) impact of black carbon emitting activities on non-climate outcomes such as health and agricultural effects.

Climate change, green growth and green jobs

Green growth means fostering economic growth and development while ensuring that natural assets continue to provide the resources and environmental services on which our well-being relies. To do that, it must catalyse innovation and investment that will underpin sustained growth and give rise to new economic activities. The financing and investment requirements of shifting the traditional carbon intensive energy sector to a low-carbon sector would require an additional USD 1.6 trillion per year of investment between 2030 and 2050

(USD 750 billion from 2010 to 2030) over and above existing investment (IEA, 2009b). However, the IEA also estimates that the 17% (USD 46 trillion) increase in global energy investment required to deliver low-carbon energy systems could yield cumulative fuel savings equal to USD 112 trillion between 2010 and 2050 (IEA, 2009b). Domestic policies are necessary to provide the adequate risk-return profile to make green investment more profitable than business-as-usual options, with some authors calling for "investment-grade" climate policies (Hamilton, 2009; OECD, 2012). The transition to a low-carbon economy will require the development of new sectors and activities, requiring a new set of skills in both new jobs and existing jobs (OECD, 2011a). Key sectors would include transport, directed towards more efficient and alternative vehicles; building refurbishment and solar installation; and the decarbonisation of the power sector, mainly involving investments in renewable energy technologies. If public policy frameworks manage to shift private-sector investments to low-carbon, climate-resilient alternatives, those investments will create new businesses and jobs and offset losses from the "brown" economy model (IEA, forthcoming).

Labour market and skills development policies can make an important contribution to greener growth. By minimising skill bottlenecks and preventing a rise in structural unemployment, these policies can make the transition to green growth quicker and more beneficial. The OECD report *Towards Green Growth* (OECD, 2011e) underlines how an increasing number of studies are showing the potential for net job creation associated with the restructuring of the energy sector towards a cleaner energy mix.[49] This means that through shifting sources of energy towards renewable sources and emphasising non-energy intensive sectors, climate policies could create more jobs than would be lost in the long run. By causing important changes in relative prices, GHG-mitigation policy will affect the composition of both final and intermediate demand and hence composition of labour demand. In particular, the relative price of energy and energy-intensive goods and services will increase.[50] The macroeconomic impacts of climate policies on employment are various and the global effect is not easy to establish; however, certain policy mixes can improve both environmental and labour market performance (see Box 3.15 for an illustration).

Box 3.15. **What if... reducing GHGs could increase employment?**

The OECD has investigated the labour market impacts of GHG-mitigation policies (Chateau *et al.*, 2011; OECD, 2011e). This analysis uses a specifically revised version of the ENV-linkages model with labour market rigidities, *i.e.* frictions in the adjustment of wages to differences between supply and demand of labour, to simulate an illustrative climate policy scenario where the OECD area as a whole reduces emissions by 50% in 2050 compared to their 1990 levels (through implementing a joint ETS). Non-OECD countries are assumed to each reduce their emissions by 25% in 2050 relative to business as-usual levels.

Table 3.10 indicates that this mitigation policy has a limited impact on economic growth (real GDP levels are reduced by 0.8% for low labour market rigidity and by 2.1% for high rigidity) and job creation (employment levels are reduced by 0.3 to 2.2%). When permit revenues are redistributed in the form of uniform lump-sum transfers, mitigation costs increase with the degree of labour market rigidity. Yet, even in the worst-case scenario, under very strong labour market rigidities, economic growth is only slightly affected by the introduction of carbon permits: on average in the OECD area, real GDP increases by almost 41% over the period 2013-2030, as compared to 44% in the absence of mitigation actions. The resulting slowdown in job creation is more pronounced, but still limited.

Box 3.15. **What if... reducing GHGs could increase employment?** *(cont.)*

Table 3.10. **Economic impact of an OECD-wide emissions trading scheme where labour markets are rigid, assuming lump-sum redistribution, 2015-2030**

% deviation from the business-as-usual scenario

	Real GDP		Employment		Real wage		Real income	
	Low rigidity	Strong rigidity	Low rigidity	Strong rigidity	Low rigidity	Strong rigidity	Low rigidity	Strong rigidity
2015	−0.04	−0.10	−0.03	−0.12	−0.11	−0.03	−0.04	−0.13
2020	−0.23	−0.62	−0.13	−0.70	−0.53	−0.18	−0.25	−0.80
2030	−0.78	−2.09	−0.32	−2.19	−1.30	−0.56	−0.83	−2.68

Source: OECD ENV-linkages model (based on Chateau et al., 2011).

However, for a medium level of labour market rigidity (between the two extremes presented in Table 3.10), and if the lump-sum redistribution is replaced by a policy where permit revenues are used to reduce taxation on labour, employment growth is boosted (Table 3.11). OECD employment would increase by 0.8% in 2030 compared to the *Baseline* projection, resulting in an increase of 7.5% between 2013 and 2030, compared with 6.5% in the absence of mitigation actions. Moreover, there is no loss of purchasing power for workers.

Table 3.11. **Economic impact of an OECD-wide ETS for different revenue recycling options, assuming medium labour market rigidity, 2015-2030**

% deviation from the business-as-usual scenario

	Real GDP		Employment		Real wage		Real income	
	Lump sum transfers	Lower labour taxes	Lump sum transfers	Lower labour taxes	Lump sum transfers	Lower labour taxes	Lump sum transfers	Lower labour taxes
2015	−0.06	0.06	−0.05	0.12	−0.08	0.11	−0.07	0.09
2020	−0.34	0.26	−0.29	0.59	−0.44	0.54	−0.40	0.44
2030	−1.08	−0.03	−0.75	0.80	−1.14	0.76	−1.26	0.24

Source: OECD ENV-linkages model (based on Chateau et al., 2011).

These estimates illustrate how certain policy mixes can improve both environmental and labour market performance. They also show that both the quality of labour market institutions and the redistribution of permit revenues need to be jointly addressed in order to reap the full potential benefit of climate change policies in terms of job creation. However, empirical estimates on the degree of labour market imperfections are scarce, and therefore the numbers presented here are purely illustrative.

These conclusions are in line with many other studies analysing the employment impact of mitigation actions within the framework of a general equilibrium model. Such models, including ENV-Linkages, allow an evaluation of the transition costs, but over a longer time horizon. Certain employment gains induced by mitigation policies (or job losses avoided) are not captured. Indeed, as innovation is intrinsically difficult to predict, the potential effects of environmental policies in stimulating the innovation of new green technologies are not fully captured.

Source: Chateau, J., T. Manfredi, A. Saint-Martin and P. Swaim (2011), "Employment Impacts of Climate Change Mitigation Policies in OECD: A General-Equilibrium perspective", OECD Environment Working Paper, No. 32, OECD, Paris.

There are several limitations to the potential positive impact on jobs of greening growth. Firstly, the direct effect of energy sector composition of employment is limited, since intensely polluting industries account for only a small share of the total workforce. Secondly, these "first-round" net employment impacts do not fully account for the "second-round" effects of a change in energy mix: they do not fully capture the full macroeconomic impact of climate policies. Barriers to industrial restructuring could hinder the reallocation process consecutive to mitigation policies and, ultimately, reduce the pace of employment growth. Thirdly, as these policies would generally reduce GDP (see Section 3), this could have negative impacts on aggregate employment.

Public revenues raised by carbon pricing mechanisms could be used to reduce other taxes and fiscal distortion in the economies. These revenue-neutral mitigation policies are sometimes advocated on the basis that they can generate a "double-dividend": reducing GHGs emissions and improving efficiency by reducing distortive taxes, such as labour taxes.

Notes

1. See Chapter 1 for the methodology used for the *Environmental Outlook*, and Chapter 2 for the key socio-economic assumptions behind the *Baseline* scenario. See Chapter 3, Section 2 on trends and projections for further discussion of the existing policies that are included in the *Baseline*.

2. Mitigation consists of activities that aim to reduce GHGs, directly or indirectly, by avoiding or capturing GHGs before they are emitted to the atmosphere or sequestering those already in the atmosphere by enhancing "sinks" such as forests. Such activities may entail, for example, changes to behavioural patterns or technology development and diffusion (IPCC, 2007).

3. Adaptation is defined as adjustments in human and natural systems, in response to actual or expected climate stimuli or their effects, to moderate harm or exploit beneficial opportunities (IPCC, 2001).

4. The Kyoto Protocol is an international agreement linked to the United Nations Framework Convention on Climate Change (UNFCCC). It was adopted in Kyoto, Japan, on 11 December 1997 and entered into force on 16 February 2005. The major feature of the Kyoto Protocol is that it sets binding targets for 37 industrialised countries and the European Community for reducing greenhouse gas (GHG) emissions. These amount to an average of 5% reduction from 1990 levels between 2008 and 2012.

5. See *www.iea.org/index_info.asp?id=1959*.

6. See *www.epa.gov/methane/scientific.html*.

7. In the IPCC report, the median value is 3 °C and 2 °C-4.5 °C represents the 66% confidence interval. This is the assumption used in the projections outlined in this *Outlook*.

8. Climate sensitivity is a measure of how responsive the climate system is to a change in the radiative forcing. It is usually expressed as the temperature change associated with a doubling of the concentration of carbon dioxide in Earth's atmosphere.

9. The term overturning or thermoaline circulation refers to the part of the large-scale ocean circulation that is driven by global density gradients created by surface heat and freshwater fluxes. Computer models predict that more freshwater flowing into a few crucial places in the North Atlantic could slow, or even stop, dense water forming and sinking. This could shut down the return flow in this current.

10. Other economists (*e.g.* Nordhaus, 2011 and Pindyck, 2011) suggest that Weitzman's Dismal Theory, which says that cost-benefit analysis breaks down due to potential catastrophes, only holds under very specific circumstances.

11. See *http://unfccc.int/resource/docs/convkp/conveng.pdf*.

12. The Annex I Parties to the 1992 UNFCCC are: Australia, Austria, Belarus, Belgium, Bulgaria, Canada, Croatia, the Czech Republic, Denmark, Estonia, European Economic Community, Finland, France, Germany, Greece, Hungary, Iceland, Ireland, Italy, Japan, Latvia, Lichtenstein, Lithuania, Luxembourg, Malta, Monaco, the Netherlands, New Zealand, Norway, Poland, Portugal, Romania, Russia, the Slovak Republic, Slovenia, Spain, Sweden, Switzerland, Turkey, Ukraine, United

Kingdom and United States. See *www.unfccc.int*. Annex II countries, a sub-group of the Annex I countries, are those that committed to give financial support to action in developing countries. Annex II countries include the OECD members in 1992, excluding those that were *economies in transition* (EIT countries).

13. For the list of Non-Annex I parties, see *http://unfccc.int/parties_and_observers/parties/non_annex_i/ items/2833.php*.

14. Note that the United States has not ratified the Kyoto Protocol, and that Turkey had not ratified the UNFCCC at the time that the Kyoto Protocol was negotiated. Both these Annex I countries do not therefore have emission commitments under the Protocol.

15. For a full list of pledges made, see *http://unfccc.int/resource/docs/2011/sb/eng/inf01r01.pdf* (developed countries) and *http://unfccc.int/resource/docs/2011/awglca14/eng/inf01.pdf* (developing countries).

16. The High Level Advisory Group on climate financing suggests that 85% of the funds may need to come from the private sector by 2020 (AGF, 2010).

17. The new Green Climate Fund will be governed by a board of 24 members, with an equal number from developing and developed countries, and will be administered by the World Bank for the first three years (Cancún Agreements 2010, *http://unfccc.int/resource/docs/2010/cop16/eng/ 07a01.pdf#page=2* § 102-112).

18. Massachusetts v. Environmental Protection Agency, 549 US 497 (2007), is a US Supreme Court case decided 5-4 in which twelve states and several cities of the United States brought suit against the United States Environmental Protection Agency (EPA) to force that federal agency to regulate carbon dioxide and other GHGs as pollutants. See *www.supremecourt.gov/opinions/06pdf/05-1120.pdf*.

19. Carbon capture and storage (CCS) is a means of reducing the contribution of fossil fuel emissions to global warming. The process is based on capturing carbon dioxide (CO_2) from large point sources, such as fossil fuel power plants, and storing it in such a way that it does not enter the atmosphere.

20. In these baseline-and-credit plans there is no explicit cap on aggregate emissions. Instead, each firm has the right to emit a certain baseline level of emissions. This baseline may be derived from historical emissions or from a performance standard that specifies the permitted ratio of emissions to output. Firms create emission reduction credits by emitting fewer than their baseline emissions.

21. "Offsets" are a general term referring to credits that offset the need to reduce emissions elsewhere.

22. Joint implementation is one of three flexibility mechanisms set forth in the Kyoto Protocol to help countries with binding GHG emissions targets (Annex I Parties) meet their obligations. Under Article 6, any Annex I country can invest in emission reduction projects (referred to as "Joint Implementation Projects") in any other Annex I country as an alternative to reducing emissions domestically.

23. The discount was reduced to 65% in April 2011.

24. See *www.fin.gov.bc.ca/tbs/tp/climate/carbon_tax.htm*, accessed September 2011.

25. The purpose of the CDM is to promote clean development in developing countries. The CDM allows industrialised countries to invest in emission-reduction projects wherever it is cheapest globally. The emission-reduction projects in developing countries can earn certified emission reduction (CER) credits, each equivalent to one tonne of CO_2. These CERs can be traded and sold, and used by industrialised countries to meet a part of their emission reduction targets under the Kyoto Protocol.

26. This limits the manufacture of, or improves the manufacturing, handling, use and end-of-life recovery of fluorine-containing gases used as substitutes for ozone-depleting substances.

27. Energy efficiency measures face complex barriers: market and financial barriers with split incentives problems when investors cannot capture the benefits; transaction costs; price distortions; informational barriers on the part of the consumers to make rational consumption and investment decisions; incentive structures that encourage energy providers to sell energy rather than invest in energy efficiency; and technical barriers (see IEA, 2009a).

28. The Major Economies Forum on Energy and Climate (MEF) was launched on 28 March, 2009 to facilitate a candid dialogue among major developed and developing economies, help generate the political leadership necessary to achieve a successful outcome at the December UN climate change conference in Copenhagen, and advance the exploration of concrete initiatives and joint ventures that increase the supply of clean energy while cutting GHG emissions. The 17 major economies participating in the MEF are: Australia, Brazil, Canada, China, the European Union, France, Germany, India, Indonesia, Italy, Japan, Korea, Mexico, Russia, South Africa, the United

139

Kingdom, and the United States. Denmark, in its capacity as the President of the December 2009 Conference of the Parties to the UN Framework Convention on Climate Change, and the United Nations have also been invited to participate in this dialogue. See *www.majoreconomiesforum.org*.

29. See *www.cordis.europa.eu/technology-platforms*.

30. See *www.fp7.org.tr/tubitak_content_files/270/ETP/PV/energyresearchprogramme.pdf*.

31. Parties to the UNFCCC must submit national reports on their implementation of the Convention to the Conference of the Parties (COP). The core elements of the national communications for both Annex I and non-Annex I Parties are information on emissions and removals of GHGs and details of the activities a Party has undertaken to implement the Convention.

32. The countries included in the study are: Australia, Austria, Canada, Denmark, Finland, Germany, Norway, Spain, the Netherlands, and the United Kingdom.

33. Many climate change risks are not monotonic, which makes identification of trends difficult. In these cases weather-based insurance is not viable.

34. The different GHGs have been aggregated using CO_2-equivalents (CO_2e).

35. Rogelj *et al.* (forthcoming) estimate that a 450 ppm pathway will have around a 60% chance of exceeding 2 °C in the long-term (in equilibrium), with a 15% chance of exceeding 3 °C and a 5% chance of exceeding 4 °C.

36. BECCS combine bioenergy in power and in hydrogen production with carbon capture and storage (CCS) to create a technology which could actually remove emissions from the atmosphere: CO_2 is absorbed during the growth phase of the biomass, and then captured and stored when the biomass is converted to power or hydrogen (Azar *et al.*, 2010; Read and Lermit, 2005). Several studies have identified BECCS as an attractive mitigation option later in the century (van Vuuren and Riahi, 2011).

37. The label "delayed action" does not imply that all action is delayed, but rather that in the coming decades less mitigation takes place than in the other scenarios.

38. Due to the cooling effect of the aerosols, these concentration levels are lower than the corresponding concentration levels of the Kyoto gases only.

39. The long-term equilibrium temperature increase will be lower than 2 °C, as by the end of the century the declining concentrations of GHGs are already projected to lead to less radiative forcing.

40. The IMAGE suite of models assume that a larger share would come from fuel switching, and have more conservative estimates on energy efficiency improvements.

41. However, energy efficiency also plays a role in the OECD region – energy efficiency improvements are an essential part of a cost-effective mix of mitigation options.

42. Average energy intensity also differs across regions due to national circumstances, including climate.

43. Information from UNFCCC website (*www.unfccc.int*), accessed August 2011.

44. The calculations are based on the methodology described in Den Elzen *et al.* (2011), but revised to reflect the *Environmental Outlook Baseline* projections. More information on the assumptions behind the assessment of the pledges is given in Annex 3.A.

45. Remember that the benefits of mitigation action are not represented in the cost figures calculated using the ENV-Linkages model.

46. Clearly, these cost estimates depend crucially on the assumptions that are made about the availability and cost-effectiveness of the major mitigation options shown in Box 3.10 on key energy technologies.

47. Regional income losses depend on the permit allocation scheme, which is based on equal per-capita emission allowances in both mitigation scenarios.

48. This annual level fluctuates widely with changes in international energy prices but it also indicates that some recent reform has been undertaken in some major countries (China and India).

49. For example see the recent report by UNEP, ILO, IOE and ITUC, "*Green Jobs: Towards Decent Work in a Sustainable, Low-Carbon World*" (UNEP/ILO/IOE/ITUC, 2008).

50. Eco-innovation is also likely to have important relative price effects, while also directly affecting labour input and job skill requirements in sectors making use of the new technologies. As a result, new jobs will be created while many existing jobs will need to be "greened" even as others will have to be reallocated from downsizing to expanding sectors or firms.

References

Agrawala, S., *et al.* (2010a), "Incorporating Climate Change Impacts and Adaptation in Environmental Impact Assessments: Opportunities and Challenges", *OECD Environment Working Papers*, No. 24, OECD Publishing, doi: *10.1787/5km959r3jcmw-en*.

Agrawala, S., *et al.* (2010b), "Plan or React? Analysis of Adaptation Costs and Benefits Using Integrated Assessment Models", *OECD Environment Working Papers*, No. 23, OECD Publishing, doi: *10.1787/5km975m3d5hb-en*.

Agrawala, S., *et al.* (2011), "Private Sector Engagement in Adaptation to Climate Change: Approaches to Managing Climate Risks", *OECD Environment Working Papers*, No. 39, OECD Publishing, doi: *10.1787/5kg221jkf1g7-en*.

Agrawala. S., F. Bosello, C. Carraro, E. de Cian and E. Lanzi (2011), "Adapting to Climate Change: Costs, Benefits, and Modelling Approaches", *International Review of Environmental and Resource Economics*: Vol. 5, No. 3, pp. 245-284. *http:/dx.doi.org/10.1561/101.00000043*.

Alberth, S. and C. Hope (2006), *Policy Implications of Stochastic Learning Using a Modified PAGE2002 Model*, Cambridge Working Papers in Economics, Faculty of Economics, University of Cambridge, Cambridge, UK.

AMAP (Arctic Monitoring and Assessment Programme) (2009), *The Greenland Ice Sheet in a Changing Climate: Snow, Water, Ice and Permafrost in the Arctic (SWIPA) 2009*, AMAP, Oslo.

Azar, C. (2005), "Emerging Scarcities: Bioenergy-Food Competition in a Carbon Constrained World", in D. Simpson, M. Toman and R. Ayres (eds.), *Scarcity and Growth in the New Millennium*, John Hopkins University Press, Baltimore.

Azar, C. *et al.* (2010), "The Feasibility of Low CO_2 Concentration Targets and the Role of Bioenergy with Carbon Capture and Storage (BECCS)", *Climatic Change*, 100: 195-202.

Barrett, S. (1994), "Self-Enforcing International Environmental Agreements", *Oxford Economic Papers* 46, 878-894.

Bauer, A., J. Feichtinger, and R. Steurer (2011), *The Governance of Climate Change Adaptation in Ten OECD Countries: Challenges and Approaches*, Discussion Paper 1-2011, Institute of Forest, Environmental, and Natural Resource Policy, University of Natural Resources and Applied Life Sciences, Vienna.

Bollen, J. *et al.* (2009), "Co-Benefits of Climate Change Mitigation Policies: Literature Review and New Results", *OECD Economics Department Working Papers*, No. 693, OECD Publishing. doi: *10.1787/224388684356*.

Bollen, J., P. Koutstaal, and P. Veenendaal (2011), *Trade and climate change*, CPB, The Hague.

Bond, T.C. and H. Sun (2005), "Can Reducing Black Carbon Emissions Counteract Global Warming?", *Environmental Science and Technology*, 39(16), 5921-5926.

Bond, T.C. *et al.* (2004), "A Technology-Based Global Inventory of Black and Organic Carbon Emissions from Combustion", *Journal of Geophysical Research*, 109(D14), D14203.

Bowen, A. and J. Rydge (2011), "Climate-Change Policy in the United Kingdom", *OECD Economics Department Working Papers*, No. 886, OECD Publishing, doi: *10.1787/5kg6qdx6b5q6-en*.

Bringezu, S., *et al.* (2009), *Towards Sustainable Production and Use of Resources: Assessing Biofuels*, International Panel for Sustainable Resource Management, UNEP (United Nations Environment Programme), Nairobi.

Bruin, K. de, R. Dellink, and S. Agrawala (2009), "Economic Aspects of Adaptation to Climate Change: Integrated Assessment Modelling of Adaptation Costs and Benefits", *OECD Environment Working Papers*, No. 6, OECD Publishing, doi: *10.1787/225282538105*.

Buchner, B. (2007), "Policy Uncertainty, Investment and Commitment Periods", OECD/IEA, Paris. *www.oecd.org/dataoecd/1/39/39745122.pdf*.

Burniaux, J., J. Chateau, and R. Duval (2010), "Is there a Case for Carbon-Based Border Tax Adjustment?: An Applied General Equilibrium Analysis", *OECD Economics Department Working Papers*, No. 794, OECD Publishing, doi: *10.1787/5kmbjhcqqk0r-en*.

Burniaux, J. and J. Chateau (2011), "Mitigation Potential of Removing Fossil Fuel Subsidies: A General Equilibrium Assessment", *OECD Economics Department Working Papers*, No. 853, OECD Publishing, doi: *10.1787/5kgdx1jr2plp-en*.

Burniaux, J. and J. Oliveira Martins (2000), "Carbon Emission Leakages: A General Equilibrium View", *OECD Economics Department Working Papers*, No. 242, OECD Publishing, doi: 10.1787/410535403555.

Chateau, J., T. Manfredi, A. Saint-Martin and P. Swaim (2011), "Employment Impacts of Climate Change Mitigation Policies in OECD: A General-Equilibrium Perspective", *OECD Environment Working Paper*, No. 32, OECD, Paris, forthcoming.

Clapp, C., G. Briner and K. Karousakis (2010), "Low-Emission Development Strategies (LEDS): Technical, Institutional and Policy Lessons", OECD/IEA, Paris.

Clarke, L. *et al.* (2009), "International Climate Policy Architectures: Overview of the EMF22 International Scenarios", *Energy Economics* 31, S64-S81.

Dellink, R., G. Briner and C. Clapp (2010), "Costs, Revenues, and Effectiveness of the Copenhagen Accord Emission Pledges for 2020", *OECD Environment Working Papers*, No. 22, OECD Publishing, doi: 10.1787/5km975plmzg6-en.

Dietz, S. *et al.* (2006), "On Discounting Non-Marginal Policy Decisions and Cost-Benefit Analysis of Climate-Change Policy", paper presented at the *ISEE 2006: Ninth Biennial Conference of the International Society for Ecological Economics*, 15-19 December 2006, India Habitat Centre, Delhi, India.

Duval, R. (2008), "A Taxonomy of Instruments to Reduce Greenhouse Gas Emissions and their Interactions", *OECD Economics Department Working Papers*, No. 636, OECD Publishing. doi: 10.1787/236846121450.

EEA (European Environment Agency) (2010a), "Atmospheric Greenhouse Gas Concentrations (CSI 013): Assessment published Nov 2010", EEA website, *www.eea.europa.eu/data-and-maps/indicators/ atmospheric-greenhouse-gas-concentrations/atmospheric-greenhouse-gas-concentrations-assessment-3*, accessed 27 September 2011.

EEA (2010b), *The European Environment: State and Outlook 2010*, EEA, Publications Office of the European Union, Luxembourg.

Edenhofer, O. *et al.* (2009), *The Economics of Decarbonization: Report of the RECIPE Project*, Potsdam-Institute for Climate Impact Research, Potsdam.

Edenhofer, O. *et al.* (2010), "The Economics of Low Stabilization: Model Comparison of Mitigation Strategies and Costs", *The Energy Journal*, Volume 31 (Special Issue 1).

Ellerman, A. and B. Buchner (2008), "Over-Allocation or Abatement? A Preliminary Analysis of the EU-ETS Based on the 2005-06 Emissions Data", *Environmental and Resource Economics*, Vol. 41, No. 2, pp. 267-287.

Ellerman, A., F. Convery, and C. de Perthuis (2010), *Pricing Carbon: The European Union Emissions Trading Scheme*, Cambridge University Press, Cambridge, UK.

Ellis, J. and S. Kamel (2007), "Overcoming Barriers to Clean Development Mechanism Projects", *OECD Papers*, Vol. 7/1, doi: 10.1787/oecd_papers-v7-art3-en.

Elzen, M. den, and D.P. van Vuuren (2007), "PeakiNg Profiles for Achieving Long-term Temperature Targets with More Likelihood at Lower Costs", PNAS 104(46):17931-17936.

Elzen, M. den, A.F. Hof, and M. Roelfsema (2011), "The Emissions Gap Between the Copenhagen Pledges and the 2 °C climate Goal: Options for Closing and Risks that Could Widen the Gap", *Global Environmental Change* 21, 733-743.

EPA (Environmental Protection Agency) (2011), "Report to Congress on Black Carbon", EPA, Washington, DC.

Government of Brazil (2008), "National Climate Change Plan, 2008", Government of Brazil, Brasília.

Government of India (2010), *Notification No. 01 /2010-Clean Energy Cess*, 22 June 2010 Ministry of Finance, Government of India, New Delhi, *www.coal.nic.in/cbec140710.pdf*.

Hamilton, K. (2009), *Unlocking Finance for Clean Energy: The Need for "Investment Grade" Policy*. Chatham House Briefing Paper, The Royal Institute of International Affairs, London.

Hardin, G. (1968), "The Tragedy of the Commons", *Science*, Vol. 162, No. 3859, pp. 1243-1248.

Hoegh-Guldberg, O. *et al.* (2007), "Coral Reefs Under Rapid Climate Change and Ocean Acidification", *Science*, 318: 1737-1742.

Hood, C. (2010), "Reviewing Existing and Proposed Emissions Trading Systems", *IEA Energy Papers*, No. 2010/13, OECD Publishing, doi: 10.1787/5km4hv3mlg5c-en.

Hood, C. (2011), "Summing Up the Parts: Combining Policy Instruments for Least-Cost Climate Mitigation Strategies", *IEA Information Paper*, OECD/IEA, Paris.

IEA (International Energy Agency) (2009a), *Implementing Energy Efficiency Policies: are IEA Member Countries on Track?*, OECD Publishing, doi: 10.1787/9789264075696-en.

IEA (2009b), *Energy Technology Perspectives 2010: Scenarios and Strategies to 2050*, OECD Publishing. doi: 10.1787/energy_tech-2010-en.

IEA (2010), "Global Gaps in Clean Energy RD&D Update and Recommendations for International Collaboration", *IEA Report for the Clean Energy Ministerial*, OECD/IEA, Paris.

IEA (2011a), "CO_2 Emissions from Fuel Combustion: Highlights", OECD/IEA, Paris.

IEA (2011b), *World Energy Outlook 2011*, OECD Publishing, doi: 10.1787/weo-2011-en.

IEA, OECD, OPEC, World Bank (2010), "Analysis of the Scope of Energy Subsidies and Suggestions for the G-20 Initiative", Joint report prepared for submission to the *G-20 Summit Meeting, Toronto, 26-27 June 2010*, IEA/OPEC/OECD Publishing/World Bank.

IPCC (2007a), "Summary for Policymakers", in M.L. Parry, O.F. Canziani, J.P. Palutikof, P.J. van der Linden and C.E. Hanson (eds.), *Climate Change 2007: Impacts, Adaptation and Vulnerability. Contribution of Working Group II to the Fourth Assessment Report of the Intergovernmental Panel on Climate Change*, Cambridge University Press, Cambridge.

IPCC (2007b), *Climate Change 2007: Impacts, Adaptation and Vulnerability. Contribution of Working Group II to the Fourth Assessment Report of the Intergovernmental Panel on Climate Change*, Cambridge University Press, Cambridge.

IPCC (2007c), *Climate Change 2007: Mitigation of climate change. Contribution of Working Group II to the Fourth Assessment Report of the Intergovernmental Panel on Climate Change*, Cambridge University Press, Cambridge.

Jamet, S. and J. Corfee-Morlot (2009), "Assessing the Impacts of Climate Change: A Literature Review", *OECD Economics Department Working Papers*, No. 691, OECD Publishing, doi: 10.1787/224864018517.

Johnstone, N. and I. Haščič (2009), *Environmental Policy Framework Conditions, Innovation and Technology Transfer*, OECD, Paris.

Haščič, I., N. Johnstone, F. Watson, C. Kaminker (2010), "Climate Policy and Technological Innovation and Transfer: An Overview of Trends and Recent Empirical Results", *OECD Environment Working Papers*, No. 30, OECD Publishing, doi: 10.1787/5km33bnggcd0-en.

Kalamova, M., C. Kaminker and N. Johnstone (2011), "Sources of Finance, Investment Policies and Plant Entry in the Renewable Energy Sector", *OECD Environment Working Papers*, No. 37, OECD Publishing, doi: 10.1787/5kg7068011hb-en.

Lamhauge, N., E. Lanzi and S. Agrawala (2011), "Monitoring and Evaluation for Adaptation: Lessons from Development Co-operation Agencies", *OECD Environment Working Papers*, No. 38, OECD Publishing, doi: 10.1787/5kg20mj6c2bw-en.

Luderer, G. *et al.* (2009), "The Economics of Decarbonization: – Results from the RECIPE Model Intercomparison", RECIPE Background Paper, Potsdam-Institute for Climate Impact Research, Potsdam, *www.pik-potsdam.de/recipe*.

McKibbin, W., A. Morris and P. Wilcoxen (2011), "Comparing climate commitments: a model-based analysis of the Copenhagen Accord", *Climate Change Economics* 2(2), 79-103.

Meinshausen, M. *et al.* (2006), "Multi-Gas Emission Pathways to Meet Climate Targets", *Climatic Change*, 75, 151-194.

Meinshausen, M., *et al.* (2009), "Greenhouse Gas Emission Targets for Limiting Global Warming to 2 °C", *Nature*, 458, 1158-1162.

Mendelsohn, R., A. Dina and L. Williams (2006), "The Distributional Impact of Climate Change on Rich and Poor Countries", *Environment and Development Economics*, Vol. 11, pp. 159-178.

Molina, M. *et al.* (2009), "Reducing Abrupt Climate Change Risk using the Montreal Protocol and Other Regulatory Actions to Complement Cuts in CO_2 Emissions", *Proceedings of the National Academy of Sciences*, 106(49), 20616.

NBS (Network for Business Sustainability) (2009), *Concepts and Theories: Business Adaptation to Climate Change*, NBS, Canada.

Nicholls, R. J. et al. (2008), "Ranking Port Cities with High Exposure and Vulnerability to Climate Extremes: Exposure Estimates", *OECD Environment Working Papers*, No. 1, OECD Publishing. doi: *10.1787/011766488208*.

Nordhaus, W.D. (2007), *The Challenge of Global Warming: Economic Models and Environmental Policy*, Yale University, New Haven.

Nordhaus, W.D. (2011), "The Economics of Tail Events with an Application to Climate Change", *Review of Environmental Economics and Policy*, 5(2): 240-257.

Nordhaus, W.D. and J. Boyer (2000), "Warming the World: Economic Models of Global Warming", The MIT Press.Nordhaus

OECD (2006), "Progress on Adaptation to Climate Change in Developed Countries: An Analysis of Broad Trends", *OECD Papers*, Vol. 6/2, doi: *10.1787/oecd_papers-v6-art8-en*.

OECD (2007a), *OECD Principles for Private Sector Participation in Infrastructure*, OECD Publishing. doi: *10.1787/9789264034105-en*.

OECD (2007b), *Instrument Mixes for Environmental Policy*, OECD Publishing, doi: *10.1787/9789264018419-en*.

OECD (2008a), *Costs of Inaction on Key Environmental Challenges*, OECD Publishing. doi: *10.1787/9789264045828-en*.

OECD (2008b), "An OECD Framework for Effective and Efficient Environmental Policies: Overview", *Meeting of the Environment Policy Committee (EPOC) at Ministerial Level, Environment and Global Competitiveness*, 28-29 April 2008, *www.oecd.org/dataoecd/8/44/40501159.pdf*.

OECD (2008c), *Economic Aspects of Adaptation to Climate Change: Costs, Benefits and Policy Instruments*, OECD Publishing, doi: *10.1787/9789264046214-en*.

OECD (2009a), *The Economics of Climate Change Mitigation: Policies and Options for Global Action beyond 2012*, OECD Publishing, doi: *10.1787/9789264073616-en*.

OECD (2009b), *Integrating Climate Change Adaptation into Development Co-operation: Policy Guidance*, OECD Publishing, doi: *10.1787/9789264054950-en*.

OECD (2010a), *Cities and Climate Change*, OECD Publishing, doi: *10.1787/9789264091375-en*.

OECD (2010b), *Taxation, Innovation and the Environment*, OECD Publishing, doi: *10.1787/9789264087637-en*.

OECD (2010d), *Globalisation, Transport and the Environment*, OECD Publishing, doi: *10.1787/9789264072916-en*.

OECD (2010e), *Measuring and Monitoring Innovation*, OECD, Paris.

OECD (2011a), Delivering on Green Growth, in OECD, *Towards Green Growth*, OECD Publishing. doi: *10.1787/9789264111318-7-en*.

OECD (2011b), "Interactions Between Emission Trading Systems and Other Overlapping Policy Instruments", *General Distribution Document*, Environment Directorate, OECD, Paris.

OECD (2011c), *Fostering Innovation for Green Growth*, OECD Green Growth Studies, OECD Publishing. doi: *10.1787/9789264119925-en*.

OECD (2011d), *Greening Household Behaviour: The Role of Public Policy*, OECD Publishing, doi: *10.1787/9789264096875-en*.

OECD (2011e), *Towards Green Growth*, OECD Green Growth Studies, OECD Publishing, doi: *10.1787/9789264111318-en*.

OECD (2011f), *Inventory of Estimated Budgetary Support and Tax Expenditures for Fossil Fuels*, OECD, Paris.

OECD (2011g), *Invention and Transfer of Environmental Technologies*, OECD Studies on Environmental Innovation, OECD Publishing, doi: *10.1787/9789264115620-en*.

OECD (2012), "Policy Framework for Low-carbon, Carbon-resilient Investment: The Case of Infrastructure Development", OECD, Paris.

OECD/ITF (International Transport Forum) (2011), *Car Fleet Renewal Schemes: Environmental and Safety Impacts*, ITF, OECD, Paris, *www.internationaltransportforum.org/Pub/pdf/11Fleet.pdf*.

Oppenheimer, M., B.C. O'Neill, M. Webster, and S. Agrawala (2007), "The limits of consensus", *Science* 317: 1505-1506.

PwC (PricewaterhouseCoopers) (2011), *Business Leadership on Climate Change Adaptation: Encouraging Engagement and Action*, PwC, London, *www.pwc.co.uk/eng/publications/adapting-to-climate-change.html*.

Peterson, E.B., J. Schleich and V. Duscha (2011), "Environmental and economic effects of the Copenhagen pledges and more ambitious emission reduction targets", *Energy Policy* 39, 3697-3708.

Pindyck, R.S. (2011), "Fat Tails, Thin Tails, and Climate Change Policy", *Review of Environmental Economics and Policy*, 5(2): 258-274.

Rahmstorf, S. (2007), "A Semi-Empirical Approach to Projecting Future Sea-Level Rise", *Science*, 315, 368-370.

Read, P. and J. Lermit (2005), "Bioenergy with Carbon Storage (BECS): A Sequential Decision Approach to the Threat of Abrupt Climate Change", *Energy*, 30(14): 2654-2671.

Reuters (2011), "China to Launch Energy Cap-and-Trade Trials in Green Push", Reuters website, 5 March 2011, *www.reuters.com/article/2011/03/05/us-china-npc-energy-idUSTRE7240VX20110305*.

Rypdal, K. *et al.* (2009), "Costs and Global Impacts of Black Carbon Abatement Strategies", *Tellus B*, 61(4): 625-641.

Searchinger, T. *et al.* (2008), "Use of US Croplands for Biofuels Increases Greenhouse Gases through Emissions from Land-Use Change", *Science*, 319(5867): 1238-1240.

Serres, A. de, F. Murtin and G. Nicoletti (2010), "A Framework for Assessing Green Growth Policies", *OECD Economics Department Working Papers*, No. 774, OECD Publishing, doi: 10.1787/5kmfj2xvcmkf-en.

Shaefer, K. *et al.* (2011), "Amount and Timing of Permafrost Carbon Release in Response to Climate Warming", *Tellus B*, 63(2): 165-180.

Smeets, E.M.W. *et al.* (2009), "Contribution of N_2O to the Greenhouse Gas Balance of First-Generation Biofuels", *Global Change Biology*, 15(1): 1-23.

Smith P. *et al.* (2010), "Competition for land", Phil. Trans. R. Soc. B (2010) 365, 2941-2957 doi:10.1098/rstb.2010.0127

South African Revenue Service (2010), "Customs and Excise Act, 1964", Amendment of Rules (DAR/74), *Government Gazette*, No. 33514, available at *www.info.gov.za/view/DownloadFileAction?id=131016*.

Stern, N., (2006), *The Economics of Climate Change: The Stern Review*, HM Treasury, Cambridge University Press, Cambridge, UK.

Tavoni, M. and R.S.J. Tol (2010), "Counting Only the Hits? The Risk of Underestimating the Costs of a Stringent Climate Policy", *Climatic Change*, Vol. 100, No. 3-4, pp. 769-778.

Townshend, T. *et al.* (2011), *The 2nd GLOBE Climate Legislation Study: a review of climate change legislation in 17 countries*, GLOBE International, London.

UNEP (United Nations Environment Programme (2010), *The Emissions Gap Report: Are the Copenhagen Accord Pledges Sufficient to Limit Global Warming to 2 °C or 1.5 °C?*, UNEP, Nairobi.

UNEP (2011a), *Integrated Assessment of Black Carbon and Tropospheric Ozone: Summary for Decision Makers*, UNEP and WMO (World Meteorological Organization), Nairobi.

UNEP (2011b), *Towards an Action Plan for Near-Term Climate Protection and Clean Air Benefits*, UNEP Science-Policy Brief, UNEP, Nairobi.

UNEP (2011c), *Bridging the Emissions Gap: A UNEP synthesis report*, UNEP, Nairobi.

UNEP/ILO/IOE/ITUC (2008), *Green Jobs: Towards Decent Work in a Sustainable, Low-Carbon World*, UNEP, Nairobi.

United Nations AGF (November 2010), Report of the Secretary General's High Level Advisory Group on Climate Change Financing, UN.

UNFCCC (2009), *Copenhagen Accord*, UNFCCC, Bonn, Germany, *http://unfccc.int/resource/docs/2009/cop15/eng/l07.pdf*.

UNFCCC (2011a), *Report of the Conference of the Parties on its Sixteenth Session, held in Cancún from 29 November to 10 December 2010*, UNFCCC, Bonn, Germany, *http://unfccc.int/resource/docs/2010/cop16/eng/07a01.pdf#page=2*.

UNFCCC (2011b), *Compilation and Synthesis of Fifth National Communications*, UNFCCC, Bonn, Germany.

Vuuren, D.P. van et al. (2008), "Temperature Increase for 21st Century Mitigation Scenarios", *Proceedings of the National Academy of Sciences of the United States of America*, 105:40, 15258-15262.

Vuuren, D.P. van et al. (2009), "Comparison of Top-Down and Bottom-Up Estimates of Sectoral and Regional Greenhouse Gas Emission Reduction Potentials", *Energy Policy*, vol 37(12), 5125-5139.

Vuuren, D.P. van, Riahi, K. (2011), "The Relationship between Short-term Emissions and Long-term Concentration Targets – A letter", *Climatic Change* 104, 793-801.

Weitzman, M.L. (2009), "On Modelling and Interpreting the Economics of Catastrophic Climate Change", *Review of Economics and Statistics*, 91(1): 1-19.

Weitzman, M.L. (2011), "Fat-Tailed Uncertainty in the Economics of Catastrophic Climate Change", *Review of Environmental Economics and Policy* 5(2):275-92.

ANNEX 3.A

Modelling Background Information on Climate Change

This annex provides further descriptions of some of the assumptions behind the model-based policy simulations used in this chapter.

The *Baseline* scenario

The *OECD Environmental Outlook Baseline* scenario makes projections of a number of socio-economic developments (summarised in Chapters 1 and 2):

- Based on assumptions governing a conditional convergence of the drivers of economic growth across countries, world GDP is projected to nearly quadruple over the coming four decades, in line with the past 40 years and based on detailed projections on the main drivers of economic growth. By 2050, the OECD's share of the global economy is assumed to decline from 54% in 2010 to less than 32%, while the share of Brazil, Russia, India, Indonesia, China and South Africa (BRIICS) is assumed to grow to more than 40%.

- By 2050, the world is assumed to add over 2.2 billion people to the current 7 billion. All world regions are assumed to be facing population ageing but will be at different stages of this demographic transition.

- By 2050, nearly 70% of the world's population is assumed to be living in urban areas.

- World energy demand is assumed to be 80% higher in 2050 under current policies. The 2050 global energy mix is assumed to be fairly similar to today's, with the share of fossil energy still at about 85% (of commercial energy), renewables including biofuels (but excluding traditional biomass) just above 10%, with the balance being nuclear. Among fossil fuels, it is uncertain whether coal or gas will be the main source of increased energy supply.

- Globally, the area of agricultural land is assumed to expand in the next decade, but at a slower rate. It is assumed to peak before 2030 to match the increase in food demand from a growing population, and decline thereafter, as population growth slows down and yield improvements continue (Box 3.2). Deforestation rates are already declining, and this trend is assumed to continue, especially after 2030 with demand for more agricultural land easing.

- No new climate policies are assumed to be introduced, but policies in existence in 2010 are assumed to still be in operation. For instance, the EU Emission Trading Scheme (ETS, see Section 4) is included in the *Baseline* until 2012 (as these policies are already in place). Additional (new) legislated policies in the European Union are not reflected in the *Baseline*, but the European Union's energy and climate package is assumed to be implemented in all policy simulations carried out in the analysis. Energy-efficiency measures already in place (in the European Union and other countries) are also included in the *Baseline*.

While there are substantial uncertainties around the assumptions, the *Baseline* projected global trend in GHG emissions is within the range of plausible trends identified in a number of model comparison exercises (*e.g* those done by the United Nations Environment Programme – UNEP, 2010; the Intergovernmental Panel on Climate Change – IPCC, 2007a, b&c; and the Energy Modelling Forum – Clark *et al., 2009).

The 450 ppm climate stabilisation scenarios

The *450 Core* scenario pathway is modelled by the IMAGE model, and allows for temporary overshooting of the concentration levels in the middle of the century. The associated emissions pathway is chosen such that total costs of achieving the target are minimised according to the mitigation technologies available in IMAGE. The ENV-Linkages model harmonises with the corresponding emissions pathway. In the *450 Accelerated Action* pathway, higher mitigation efforts are imposed for the first few decades, implying less negative emissions in the second half of the century stemming from the BECCS (bioenergy with CCS) technology. Finally, the *450 Delayed Action* pathway is based on fragmented carbon markets until 2020 with targets based on the high end of the pledges in the Copenhagen Accord/Cancún Agreements (see below for more details), and a global carbon market from 2021 onwards.

These scenarios all assume a burden sharing regime based on contraction and convergence: global emissions contract over time according to the global pathway, and regional emission allowances (*i.e.* regional permit allocation) as a share of the global budget converge from shares in current emission levels to equal per-capita emissions by 2050 (see also simulation 2 below). Note that in the *450 Delayed Action* scenario the burden sharing regime only applies after 2020.

Fossil fuel subsidy reform is not included in these scenarios, but investigated separately (see below).

Alternative permit allocation schemes

The regional shares of permits used for the permit allocation schemes presented in Box 3.9 are reported in Figure 3.A1 below. In the *Global carbon tax* scenario (called "450 carbon tax" in the figure) allocation of permits is an endogenous result of the model. It corresponds to the rule where there is no gain from permit trading among countries. For the other rules, when the share of permits received is greater than the share in the global carbon tax case, the country will export permits (and *vice versa*).

Technology options in the 450 ppm scenario

These policy scenarios incorporate alternative assumptions about advanced technologies to explore how dependant the energy systems in the different regions are on these energy technologies (Box 3.10 in main text). The technology specifications are based on the concurrent Energy Modelling Forum exercise (EMF24) in which both ENV-Linkages and IMAGE are participating. These scenarios are variants of the *450 Accelerated Action*

Figure 3.A1. **Permit allocation schemes, 2020 and 2050**

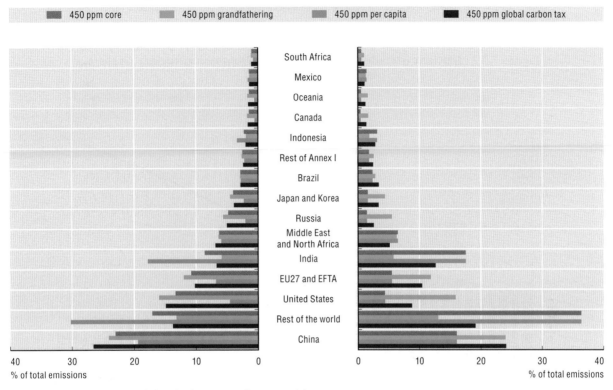

Source: *OECD Environmental Outlook projections*, output from ENV-Linkages.

StatLink http://dx.doi.org/10.1787/888932570848

scenario, with all major mitigation technologies available, using the following technology assumptions:

- **No CCS:** in the alternative setting CCS is restricted to levels as they are projected in the *Baseline*, and cannot expand further. CCS in the *Baseline* is not directed at avoiding emissions to the atmosphere, but for use of CO_2 in the enhanced oil recovery (EOR) technology.

- The ***progressive nuclear phase-out*** scenario is constructed assuming that nuclear capacity currently under construction and planned until 2020 will be built and connected to the grid (data sourced from IAEA Power Reactor Information System database). These mid-term nuclear capacities are consistent with the projections from the IEA Current Policies Scenario (IEA, 2009b). After 2020, no new nuclear unit is allowed, so that the world total capacity by 2050 will be reduced because of the natural retirement of existing plants that come at the end of their technical lifetime. By 2020, cumulative nuclear capacity additions in OECD represent one-third of the total 105 GW. Remaining additions are built in the BRIICS countries, with China alone representing almost half of total new capacity. The expansion of the nuclear fleet in the RoW countries is negligible. The estimated world nuclear capacity in this scenario reaches about 460 GW in 2020, starting from current 390 GW, and falls down to about 240 GW by 2050, a four-fold reduction compared to the 450 scenario (Figure 3.A2).

- ***Low efficiency and renewables*** scenario: Efficiency improvements embedded in energy production together with productivity gains in renewable technologies are assumed to develop more slowly over time than in the *450 Accelerated Action* scenario. Both are 20% lower than the base by 2050, leading to slower adoption of efficiency measures and slower deployment of renewable technologies.

Figure 3.A2. **Nuclear installed capacity in the *Progressive nuclear phase-out* scenario, 2010-2050**

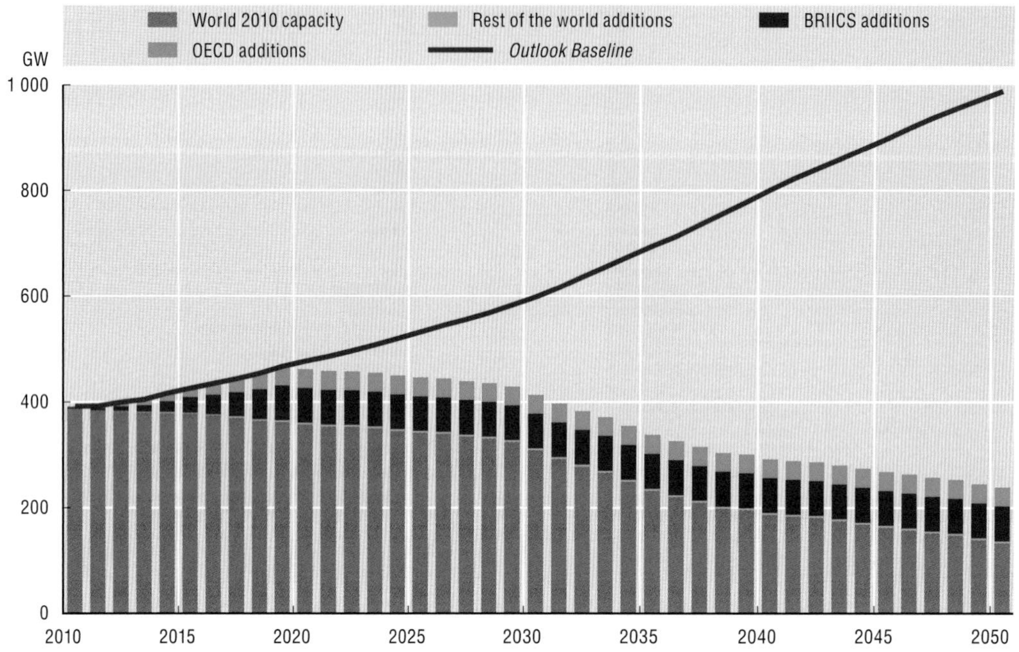

Source: OECD Environmental Outlook projections, output from ENV-Linkages.

StatLink http://dx.doi.org/10.1787/888932570867

Cancún Agreements/Copenhagen Accord pledges

Some interpretation of the Cancún Agreements/Copenhagen Accord pledges and targets is necessary for the specification of the *450 Delayed Action* scenario, because some pledges are provided in the form of a range, which is dependent on the action or financing of other countries. Due to limited specific information on how countries plan to meet their targets or actions, uncertainty remains about how the emissions reductions will affect different sectors, how much financing will be received from international sources, and how emission reductions are counted towards pledges or offsets. The most important assumptions for interpretation are:

- The methodology for assessing the pledges is based on Den Elzen *et al.* (2011), but the evaluation has been revised to reflect the *OECD Environmental Outlook Baseline* projections.

- In order to estimate costs and effectiveness in a consistent manner, all Annex I emission reduction targets are translated into reductions from the same base year (1990) and all non-Annex I mitigation actions, including the emission intensity targets of China and India, are expressed as emission reductions from business as usual (BAU) in 2020.[1] The ENV-Linkages *Baseline* projections are used for this evaluation, rather than the national baselines used by countries in their submission; this may cause substantial differences (this especially holds for South Africa, and therefore the target for South Africa has been revised to reflect the differences in baselines). In line with the general modelling framework, countries are assumed to implement their policies through the introduction of an economy-wide Emission Trading Scheme (ETS), with full auction of permits.

■ Due to the limited information available on what offset policies might be in the future, and to what extent countries intend to meet their pledge through the use of offsets, this analysis requires *ad hoc* assumptions about the level of offsets. For Annex I countries, an assumption of 20% of the total required emission reductions[2] is assumed to be achieved through international offsets, with two exceptions: *i)* Canada has currently no government policy on international offset purchases (which is interpreted in the simulations as no use of offsets for Canada); and *ii)* the European Union is assumed to limit offsets to 4 percentage-points (for the 20% reduction targets this is equivalent to the default assumption of 20%, but for the higher pledge of 30% reduction this constitutes an offset percentage of 13% of the mitigation requirements). The offsets are assumed to be entirely international and flexible across non-Annex I countries. Further, emission reductions in non-Annex I countries cannot be double-counted towards both domestic pledges and for sale in the international offset market. The default of 20% is varied in sensitivity analysis.

■ With respect to credits from land use, land-use change and forestry (LULUCF), the assumption is made that Annex I countries will use a net-net accounting rule for credits from this sector using 2020 as base year.[3] The *OECD Environmental Outlook Baseline* projection for LULUCF emissions is used to calculate the volume of credits. This leads to additional credits for most Annex I countries. Note that the current Kyoto Protocol rules for LULUCF accounting are more lenient and would therefore imply more credits from this sector, less emission reductions in the other sectors and lower short term costs. Non-Annex I countries use REDD activities to reach their pledge, but REDD activities are excluded from the international offset system.

■ International financing of mitigation actions in non-Annex I countries is assumed to be limited to Brazil, Mexico and South Africa. China, India and Indonesia have explicitly stated that their actions are unilateral, whereas no commitments are assumed for the Middle East and rest of the world regions. By default, 50% of domestic costs are assumed to be compensated by Annex I countries, but this is varied in a sensitivity analysis.

■ Some countries are likely to have emission levels that are below their targets for the current commitment period of the Kyoto Protocol (2008-2012); this creates so-called surplus Assigned Amount Units (AAUs). Based on the *Baseline* projection, the amount of surplus AAUs is estimated to be 6.5 $GtCO_2e$ for Russia, 1.9 $GtCO_2e$ for the Rest of Europe group of countries (primarily Ukraine), and 0.7 $GtCO_2e$ for the European Union and European Free Trade Area (EFTA). The existence of surplus AAUs in the post-2012 period would effectively allow for higher emissions in that period than would occur otherwise (see den Elzen *et al.*, 2011, for further discussion) and thus would reduce the costs of action. The impact of potential surplus AAUs depends in part on the assumptions about use of the units across accounting periods. As a default, no use of these surplus AAUs in the period 2013-2020 is assumed. For Russia and Rest of Europe this is varied in a sensitivity analysis, but the surplus for the European Union and EFTA is not used in any simulation as the European Union has stated it will not use its surplus.[4]

■ Note that the non-binding targets for Russia and Rest of Europe in the period 2013-2020 also imply that they have some scope to sell permits without undertaking additional mitigation actions when international permit trading is allowed in the simulations.

Phasing out fossil fuel subsidies

This policy scenario (discussed in Section 4 of the main text) is based on the analysis for the G20 on reform of fossil fuel subsidies. The ENV-Linkages model *Baseline* scenario has been updated using the latest IEA fossil fuel based consumer subsidies for the year 2009 (for developing economies). The IEA energy price gaps calculated by the IEA (2010) have been introduced in the ENV-Linkages model as percentage price-wedges between consumer prices and reference or world prices. A negative wedge is then considered as a subsidy rate. Since 2010 this IEA database covers 37 countries, of which 35 are non-OECD and 2 OECD, for the years 2007-2009 (IEA, 2009b).[5] These prices gaps only fall on fossil fuel based energy consumption but distinguish both VAT tax rates from subsidy rates. In the ENV-Linkages *Baseline* projection it is assumed that after 2009 the subsidy and VAT tax rates remain constant in percentage terms up to 2050. Since 2009 subsidy rates are lower than 2008 rates used in Burniaux and Chateau (2011) one could consider that the new *Baseline* takes into account the latest fossil fuel subsidy reforms undertaken during 2009.

In the policy simulations of generic subsidy reforms the subsidy rates are gradually phased-out over the period 2013 to 2020. Two experiments are undertaken. In the first simulation there is a stand-alone multilateral fossil fuel reform in all the 37 countries of the IEA database with no mitigation policies elsewhere (and no EU-ETS after 2012); this is an update of the G20 report simulation. The second simulation assesses the case where these fossil fuel reforms are associated with the *450 Core* mitigation scenario. This second simulation allows an assessment of the importance of fossil fuel subsidy reform in a context where carbon leakages are partly frozen by overall mitigation action.

Notes

1. Given the expected relatively small impact of the policies on GDP in China and India, the intensity target can be approximated by an absolute cap on emissions.

2. The 20% limit on offsets in most Annex I regions is in line with the assumption in OECD (2009a).

3. An exception is the assumption that when the low ends of the pledges are implemented, no LULUCF credits are assumed for the European Union and European Free Trade Area.

4. In the alternative specification, the surplus is progressively used over the years, as reduction targets become more strict; thus 22% of the surplus enters the market in 2020. This is in contrast with other models that assume the same amount of surplus AAUs will be used yearly between 2013 and 2020 (see UNEP, 2010).

5. Iran, Russia, Saudi Arabia, India, China, Egypt, Venezuela, Indonesia, Uzbekistan, UAE, Iraq, Kuwait, Argentina, Pakistan, Ukraine, Algeria, Thailand, Malaysia, Turkmenistan, Bangladesh, Mexico, South Africa, Qatar, Libya, Ecuador, Kazakhstan, Vietnam, Chinese Taipei, Azerbaijan, Nigeria, Angola, Colombia, Brunei, Rep. of Korea, Philippines, Sri Lanka, Peru.

Chapter 4

Biodiversity

by

Katia Karousakis, Mark van Oorschot (PBL), Edward Perry, Michel Jeuken (PBL),
Michel Bakkenes (PBL), with contribution from Hans Meijl and Andrzej Tabeau (LEI)

Biodiversity loss is a major environmental challenge facing humankind. Despite some local successes, biodiversity is on the decline globally and this loss is projected to continue. Continuing with business as usual may have far-reaching adverse implications for human well-being, security and economic growth. This chapter summarises the considerable benefits and often hidden values of biodiversity and the ecosystems of which it is a part. It then looks at trends in several indicators of biodiversity – species abundance (e.g. mean species abundance or MSA), threatened species, forest area (deforestation) and marine fish stocks – and the implications of business-as-usual trends continuing to the year 2050 under the OECD Environmental Outlook Baseline scenario. The chapter provides an overview of the different policy instruments available for biodiversity conservation and sustainable use, ranging from regulations to market-driven approaches, such as payments for ecosystem services (PES). Some more ambitious policy scenarios are examined – such as the implications of meeting the Aichi Biodiversity Target under the Convention on Biological Diversity (CBD) to expand the global protected area network to at least 17% of terrestrial land by 2020. Possible synergies and trade-offs of meeting climate mitigation goals (through different bioenergy and land use scenarios, for example) and the impacts on biodiversity are also examined. The chapter concludes with a discussion of key needs for further policy action in the context of biodiversity and how this links to the broader green growth agenda.

KEY MESSAGES

Biodiversity – the diversity of living organisms – is declining at the global level. Loss of biodiversity and the degradation of ecosystems and the services they provide are one of the major environmental challenges facing humankind. Continuing with business as usual will have adverse and costly impacts on human well-being, security and economic growth. Reversing these trends will require a more consistent, co-ordinated and strategic response, driven by a high level of political commitment and broader stakeholder involvement. A coherent and comprehensive policy mix will be needed to foster economic growth and development while ensuring that biodiversity continues to provide the resources and ecosystem services upon which our well-being relies.

Trends and projections

Biodiversity and natural ecosystems

 The *Environmental Outlook Baseline* or business-as-usual scenario projects **biodiversity** (measured as terrestrial mean species abundance) to decline by about 10% between 2010 and 2050 globally, with especially high losses in parts of Asia, Europe and Southern Africa. These losses will be driven mainly by land-use change and management (*e.g.* for pasture, food crops and bioenergy), commercial forestry, infrastructure development, habitat encroachment and fragmentation, pollution (*e.g.* nitrogen deposition) and climate change.

Effects of different pressures on terrestrial MSA: *Baseline*, 2010 to 2050

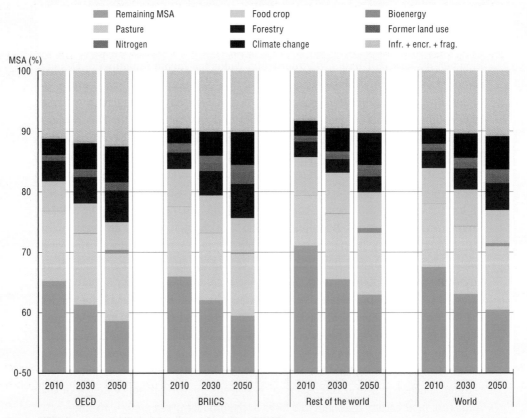

Source: *OECD Environmental Outlook Baseline*; output from IMAGE.

StatLink ⬛⬛⬛ http://dx.doi.org/10.1787/888932570943

Disturbance can damage ecosystems irreversibly, with negative social, environmental and economic impacts. The lack of understanding of the **complex non-linear dynamics of ecosystems** and the **uncertainties** surrounding these thresholds means that continued loss of biodiversity poses significant risks and calls for a precautionary approach.

Invasive alien species are considered to be an important driver of biodiversity loss across the globe. This pressure is likely to increase over the next few decades.

After 2030 the **area of natural land converted to agriculture** is projected to decrease under the *Baseline* as a result of improved productivity, stabilising populations and dietary changes, thus reducing pressure on biodiversity and ecosystems. Nevertheless, the impacts on biodiversity will continue for decades after land has ceased to be cultivated.

Globally, the number and size of **protected areas** have increased and now account for nearly 13% of the global terrestrial area. However, temperate grasslands, savannas, shrublands and marine ecosystems are poorly represented and only 7.2% of territorial seas are designated as Marine Protected Areas.

A new policy package for biodiversity was agreed by the 10th Conference of the Parties to the **Convention on Biological Diversity** (CBD) in 2010. Parties successfully agreed on the Strategic Plan for Biodiversity 2011-2020, the Aichi Biodiversity Targets for 2020, a Resource Mobilisation Strategy, and the Nagoya Protocol on Access to Genetic Resources and the Fair and Equitable Sharing of Benefits Arising from their Utilisation.

Forests

Primary forests, which tend to be most rich in biodiversity, have been on the decline and are projected to decrease steadily to 2050 in all regions under the *Baseline* scenario.

The rate of **global deforestation** has recently slowed. The *Baseline* projects no net forest loss after 2020, and an expansion in forest cover to 2050 due to regeneration, restoration, reforestation and afforestation (including plantations), mainly in OECD and large emerging economies. However, an increase in the forested area does not necessarily mean a reduction in biodiversity loss as there will be more commercial and plantation forestry which supports less biodiversity.

Fisheries

The proportion of fish stocks that are over-exploited or depleted has increased over the past few decades. Today, over 30% of marine fish stocks are over-exploited or depleted, around 50% are fully exploited and fewer than 20% have the potential for increased harvests.

Policy options and needs

■ **Adopt more ambitious policy measures** to achieve internationally agreed plans, targets and strategies, such as the Aichi protected area targets of 17% of the world's terrestrial and inland water areas and 10% of coastal and marine areas by 2020, agreed under the CBD. *Outlook* simulations suggest that in order to reach the 17% terrestrial target in a way that is also ecologically representative, a further 9.8 million km^2 of land would need to be protected.

■ **Mainstream and integrate biodiversity conservation and sustainable use into other policy areas** (*e.g.* economic affairs, agriculture, fisheries, forestry, land-use and urban planning, development co-operation, climate change, national accounting and R&D) to enhance synergies and prevent trade-offs. For example, some greenhouse gas mitigation strategies provide greater benefits to biodiversity than others. A mitigation strategy involving heavy reliance on bioenergy could require an expansion of agricultural land, reducing the net benefits to biodiversity. Conversely, the financial mechanism for reducing emissions from deforestation and forest degradation (REDD) in developing countries could also have benefits for biodiversity.

■ **Remove and reform environmentally harmful subsidies,** including those that promote, without any environmental considerations, the intensification or geographic expansion of economic sectors such as agriculture, bioenergy, fishing, forestry and transport. Subsidy reform can also increase economic efficiency and reduce the fiscal pressures confronting governments.

■ **Scale up private-sector engagement in biodiversity** conservation and sustainable use, including through innovative financing mechanisms at the local, national and international level. Clear price signals for natural resource use and pollution are needed that provide certainty yet offer the private sector flexibility in determining how they can most cost-effectively reduce their impacts on ecosystems.

■ **Improve the quantity and quality of data** available to inform biodiversity policy (at local, regional and global levels) and make further progress on the economic valuation of biodiversity and ecosystem services.

1. Introduction

Biodiversity loss is a major environmental challenge facing humankind today. Despite some local successes, biodiversity is on the decline globally and this loss is projected to continue. Continuing with business as usual may have far-reaching adverse implications for human well-being, security and economic growth.

This chapter summarises the considerable benefits and often hidden values of biodiversity and the ecosystems of which it is a part. It then looks at the current trends in several aspects of biodiversity – species abundance, threatened species, forest area and marine stocks – and the implications of business-as-usual biodiversity trends continuing to the year 2050. The chapter then provides an overview of the different policy options available for biodiversity conservation and sustainable use, ranging from regulations to market-driven approaches. Some more ambitious policy scenarios are examined – such as the implications of meeting the new internationally agreed target of 17% of terrestrial land as protected areas. The chapter concludes with a discussion of key needs for further policy action in the context of biodiversity, and how this links to the broader green growth agenda (see Chapter 1).

Biodiversity: An invisible life support system

Biodiversity is defined as the "variability among living organisms from all sources, including, *inter alia*, terrestrial, marine, and other aquatic ecosystems, and the ecological complexes of which they are a part: this includes diversity within species, between species and of ecosystems" (Article 2 of the Convention on Biological Diversity). Biodiversity and ecosystems provide invaluable (but largely unvalued) services to people and the natural environment, locally, regionally and globally. The 2005 Millennium Ecosystem Assessment (MA) identified four types of ecosystem services: regulating, supporting, provisioning, and cultural services, which together maintain critical life-support functions (Figure 4.1).

The benefits generated by these services are captured in the notion of total economic value (TEV), which aggregates direct and indirect use values and non-use values (Box 4.1). The total economic value of biodiversity and ecosystem services is large. For example, the worldwide economic value of pollination services provided by insect pollinators was estimated at USD 192 billion per year in 2005 (Gallai *et al.*, 2009). First sale value of global capture fisheries is almost USD 94 billion per year (FAO, 2010a) and the global net value of coral reefs for fisheries, coastal protection, tourism and biodiversity is estimated at USD 30 billion per year (UNEP, 2007). Moreover, every year wildlife trade generates an estimated USD 15 billion worldwide, excluding large-scale commercial trade in fish and timber (OECD, 2008a). Estimates suggest that the aggregate loss of biodiversity and ecosystem service benefits associated with the global loss of forests is between USD 2 and 5 trillion per year (TEEB, 2009).

Figure 4.1. **The four components of biodiversity and ecosystem services**

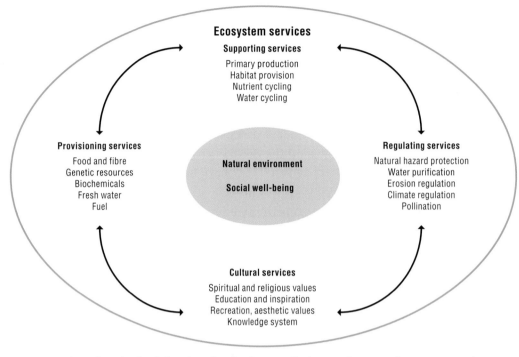

Source: OECD (2010a), Paying for Biodiversity: Enhancing the Cost-Effectiveness of Payments for Ecosystem Services, OECD, Publishing.

Box 4.1. **Valuing biodiversity: The components of total economic value**

The notion of total economic value (TEV) is composed of use and non-use values:

■ Use values: derived directly from biodiversity in the form of consumables (e.g. food and wood) and indirectly through non-consumable services (e.g. climate regulation).

■ Non-use values: existence, bequest and option values.

❖ Existence values are the benefits individuals derive from the knowledge that biodiversity exists.

❖ Bequest values are the benefits individuals derive knowing that these will be available to future generations.

❖ Option values reflect the value people place on the potential for future use, and how future advances in information can reveal new use or non-use values (e.g. for pharmaceutical purposes).

Source: OECD (2002), Handbook of Biodiversity Valuation: A Guide for Policiy Makers, OECD, Publishing.

The biodiversity financing gap

These values (or benefits) of biodiversity and ecosystem services provide a compelling case for investing in conservation and sustainable use. While it is difficult to estimate both the financing needs for optimal biodiversity and ecosystem service provision, and the existing financing flows, it is clear that the financing gap is large. Current levels of financial flows for biodiversity have been estimated at USD 36-38 billion per year, about half of which is delivered domestically in the European Union, the United States and China (Parker and Cranford, 2010).

Financing needs will vary according to the level of ambition. One estimate suggests that an additional USD 18-27.5 billion per year is required to establish a comprehensive protected area (PA) network covering 10-15% of the global terrestrial area, with an additional USD 290 billion required for conservation outside PAs (James *et al.*, 2001). Pursuing a more ambitious PA target of 15% of terrestrial area and 30% of oceans is estimated to cost USD 45 billion per year over 30 years (Balmford *et al.*, 2002). Building on these studies, Berry (2007) estimates that a total of between USD 355 and 385 billion per year is needed for financing additional climate change adaptation in terrestrial and marine PAs and the wider landscape matrix. While these estimates may seem large, the costs of inaction in many areas are considerable.

The large biodiversity financing gap is exacerbated by the fact that most biodiversity-rich areas are located in developing countries, which are least able to afford conservation measures and where pressures to convert land to other uses tend to be high (Figure 4.2).

Figure 4.2. **Overlay of biodiverse areas with human development**[1]

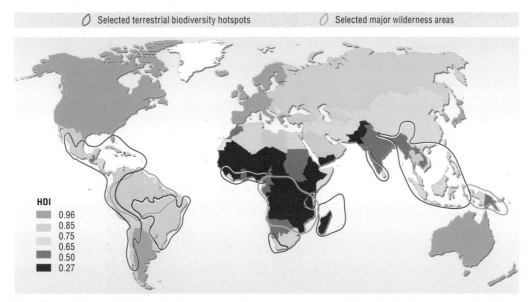

Notes: To qualify as a biodiversity hotspot, a region must meet two strict criteria: it must contain at least 1 500 species of endemic vascular plants (> 0.5% of the world's total), and have lost at least 70% of its original habitat. A major wilderness area is identified as biodiverse if it has 75% of the original vegetation remaining in pristine condition and a low human population density (< 5 people/km²). Wilderness areas are based largely on the world's terrestrial ecoregions (see Olson *et al.*, 2001).

1. Measured as the Human Development Index (HDI), which is a composite indicator used to rank countries by their level of human development. It includes life expectancy, literacy, education and standards of living for countries worldwide. The lower the index, the less developed the country.

Source: Ahlenius, H. (2004), *Global Development and Biodiversity*, UNEP/GRID-Arendal Maps and Graphics Library, based on data from UNDP 2004 and Conservation International 2004 *http://maps.grida.no/go/graphic/global-development-and-biodiversity*.

The year 2010 was politically important for biodiversity. It marked the culmination of the 2010 biodiversity target to "significantly reduce the rate of biodiversity loss" agreed by Parties to the Convention on Biological Diversity (CBD) in 2002. However, it is widely acknowledged that this target has not been met. Recognising the challenges ahead and the need for further action, the UN General Assembly declared 2010 as the International Year of Biodiversity, and 2011-2020 as the UN Decade of Biodiversity. The United Nations Conference on Sustainable Development in 2012, known as Rio+20, also provides an opportunity to secure renewed commitment to the conservation and sustainable use of biodiversity, to highlight its role in human well-being and development in the context of green growth, and to leverage synergies between the three Rio Conventions.[1]

2. Key trends and projections

Biodiversity trends: Past and present

Although there is no single, comprehensive metric to monitor and assess the state of biodiversity, the Parties to the CBD agreed on 17 headline indicators to evaluate progress towards the 2010 targets and to communicate trends in biodiversity.[2] These indicators include the extent and types of forest area, coverage of protected areas, change in status of threatened species, areas under sustainable management, invasive alien species, and a marine trophic index.[3] Data on species abundance, threatened species, forest area, and marine stocks – some of the few indicators which are available both globally and over time – are examined below.

Species abundance

Species abundance refers to the population sizes of species. Two indicators that can be used to assess changes in species abundance are mean species abundance (MSA) and the Living Planet Index (LPI). The MSA provides a measure of the change in populations of species relative to intact or pristine ecosystems. MSA is determined by the intensity of human pressure, according to established dose-response relations between these pressures and MSA (Alkemade et al., 2009).[4] The LPI is based on observed trends in almost 8 000 populations of over 2 500 vertebrate species (mammals, birds, reptiles, amphibians and fish). The index is the aggregated score of changes in the population size of each species since 1970, which is given a value of 1 (WWF, ZSL and GFN, 2010).

As depicted in Figures 4.3 and 4.4, both indicators suggest a decline in global species abundance. More specifically, global MSA declined by nearly 11% between 1970 and 2010. Of course, changes in species abundance are not distributed equally across biomes[5] (Figure 4.3), and MSA loss has been most pronounced in temperate forests (a 24% decline), followed by tropical forests (13%) and scrubland and savannah (16%).[6] According to the LPI, the period 1970-2007 witnessed a 30% decline in global abundance of vertebrate species (Figure 4.4).[7]

Threatened species

The International Union for the Conservation of Nature (IUCN) maintains a Red List of Threatened Species, categorising them as of least concern, near threatened, vulnerable, endangered, critically endangered, and extinct. It has also devised a Red List Index to measure changes in the risk of extinction for four sets of species – corals, birds, mammals, amphibians (Figure 4.5). This indicates the proportion of species expected to still be present in the near future if no additional conservation action is taken. The index is calculated from the number of species in each Red List category and the number of species that moved between categories as a result of genuine changes in threat status.[8] The status of all four sets of species has deteriorated since 1980. Amphibians are currently the most threatened group of species, while the status of corals is deteriorating fastest.

Figure 4.3. **Global mean species abundance per biome: 1970-2010**

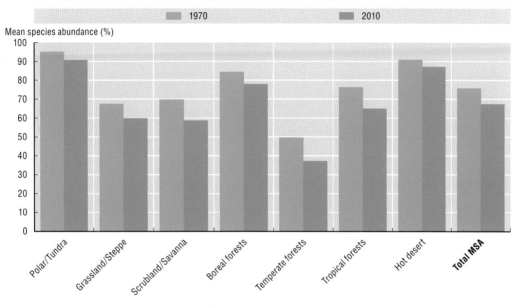

Note: If the MSA is 100%, this implies an undisturbed state. A decreasing MSA value reflects increasing human pressure on ecosystems and a decline in intactness or naturalness.

Source: OECD Environmental Outlook Baseline; output from IMAGE.

StatLink http://dx.doi.org/10.1787/888932570886

Figure 4.4. **Global Living Planet Index, 1970-2007**

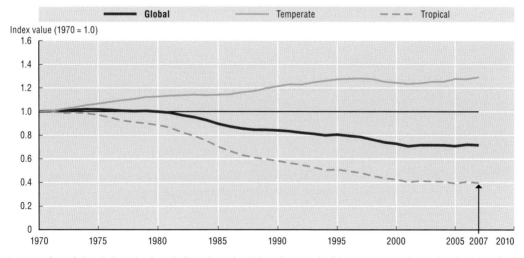

Source: Loh *et al.* (2010), "Monitoring Biodiversity – the Living Planet Index" in WWF, ZSL and GFN (2010), *Living Planet Report 2010.* WWF, Gland, Switzerland.

Figure 4.5. **Red List Index of Threatened Species**

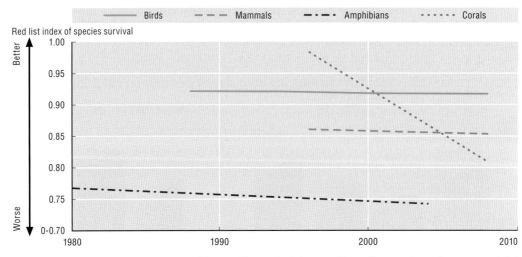

Source: Hilton-Taylor *et al.* (2008), "Status of the World's Species", in J.-C. Vié, C. Hilton-Taylor and S.N. Stuart (eds.), *The 2008 Review of the IUCN Red List of Threatened Species,* IUCN, Gland, Switzerland.

Forest area

Forests tend to be highly diverse and provide multiple ecosystem services including habitat provision, carbon sequestration, water regulation and erosion prevention. Information on the extent of forest cover[9] is therefore an important indicator of global biodiversity. Between 1990 and 2010, global forest cover decreased from 41.7 million km^2 to 40.3 million km^2 (Figure 4.6). However, while deforestation remains a cause of concern, annual deforestation rates are slowing down: in the 1990s, an average of approximately 160 000 km^2 of forest were either converted for human use or lost to natural causes each year. Between 2000 and 2010 this figure was 130 000 km^2 a year (FAO, 2010b). Primary forest

Figure 4.6. **Global trends in extent of forest cover, 1990-2010**

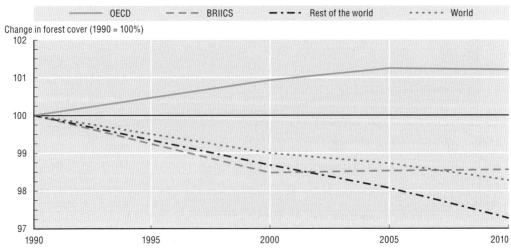

Note: BRIICS = Brazil, Russia, India, Indonesia, China, South Africa.

Sources: FAO (2010b), *The Global Forests Resource Assessment: 2010,* FAO, Rome; data from Global Tables: *www.fao.org/ forestry/fra/fra2010/en.*

loss decreased from 60 000 km^2 per year between 1990 and 2000 to 40 000 km^2 per year between 2000 and 2010 (FAO, 2006; 2010b).

Today, primary forests account for 36% of global forest cover, whereas 57% is "other naturally regenerated forest" and 7% is planted forests (FAO, 2010b). The global area for planted forests has increased by about 50 000 km^2 a year over the past five years, mainly due to afforestation (establishment of forests through planting and/or seeding on land that is not classified as forest). A number of countries are witnessing a net increase in forest cover partly as a result of natural expansion, but largely from an increase in planted forests (FAO, 2010b). This, however, does not necessarily represent a reduction or reversal in the loss of forest biodiversity, as plantation forests are often monocultures with exotic species, supporting less biodiversity than natural forests. They may also replace more biodiverse habitats such as natural grasslands.

Marine fish stocks

Trends in world marine stocks provide an indication of marine biodiversity. The status of marine fish stocks exploited by commercial capture fisheries gives cause for concern. Since 1974, when monitoring of global fish stocks began, the proportion of fully exploited fish stocks[10] appears to have remained fairly constant, while the proportion of overexploited and depleted stocks has increased (Figure 4.7). Today over 30% of stocks are over-exploited, depleted, or recovering; around 50% are fully exploited; and less than 20% have the potential for further development (FAO, 2010a). Depletion of commercial fish stocks threatens livelihoods and may affect entire ecosystems by altering food webs and population dynamics.

Figure 4.7. **State of world marine stocks, 1974-2008**

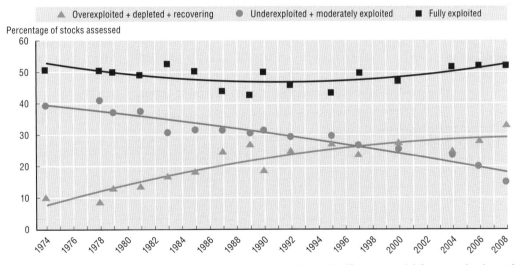

Notes: Underexploited = undeveloped or new fishery. Believed to have a significant potential for expansion in total production.

Moderately exploited = exploited with a low level of fishing effort. Believed to have some limited potential for expansion in total production.

Fully exploited = the fishery is operating at or close to an optimal yield level, with no expected room for further expansion.

Overexploited = the fishery is being exploited at above a level which is believed to be sustainable in the long term, with no potential room for further expansion and a higher risk of stock depletion/collapse.

Depleted = catches are well below historical levels, irrespective of the amount of fishing effort exerted.

Recovering = catches are again increasing after having been depleted.

Source: FAO (2010a), The State of the World's Fisheries and Aquaculture: 2010, FAO, Rome.

According to the Marine Living Planet Index,[11] global marine biodiversity declined by 24% from 1970 to 2007 (WWF, ZSL and GFN, 2010). In addition to over-exploitation, the drivers of this loss include fishing by-catch, habitat loss (*e.g.* due to coastal development), pollution and climate change.

Biodiversity is in decline across each of the indicators described above. A broader, more comprehensive assessment of state indicators for biodiversity is difficult as global time series data are not readily available. Though indicator development has progressed since the 2010 CBD biodiversity target was set in 2002, significant data gaps remain (especially in developing countries – see Butchart *et al.*, 2010 for an overview). Further work is needed to identify data priorities and address them (see Section 4 for further discussion).

Biodiversity trends: Future projections

The *Environmental Outlook Baseline* scenario models the likely status (measured as MSA) of terrestrial biodiversity in 2050 in the absence of new policy interventions. It assumes the economic, sectoral and social trends described in Chapter 2 (and summarised in Annex 4.A). The *Baseline* scenario also serves as a reference against which future progress and policy impacts can be assessed. Under the *Baseline*, total terrestrial MSA is projected to further decline by approximately 10% between 2010 and 2050, with the majority of loss occurring before 2030 (Figure 4.8). Looking across projections in specific biomes, the steepest decline in MSA is projected in scrubland and savannah (19%), temperate forests (19%) and tropical forests (14%). However, these projections are probably optimistic as they do not take into consideration all the drivers of biodiversity loss (*e.g.* invasive alien species) or ecosystem thresholds.

Figure 4.8. **Terrestrial mean species abundance per biome: *Baseline*, 2000-2050**

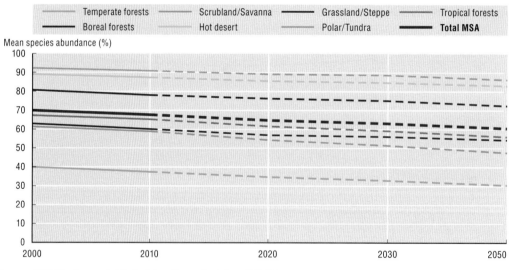

Source: *OECD Environmental Outlook Baseline*; output from IMAGE.

StatLink ⬛⬛ *http://dx.doi.org/10.1787/888932570905*

At the country group level (Figure 4.9), highest losses are projected for the rest of the world (RoW) category (11%), although losses are similar for all the other groups of countries (10%). However, as these groups are very different in total area, their relative share in global loss differs much more. OECD countries (35 million km^2) account for a relative share of 25%

of total MSA loss; Brazil, Russia, India, Indonesia, China and South Africa (BRIICS) (50 million km^2) for 36% and the RoW (45 million km^2) for 39%. The projected MSA loss to 2050 in individual regions is particularly high in Japan and Korea (36% decline); Europe (24%); Southern Africa (20%) and Indonesia (17%).

Figure 4.9. **Terrestrial mean species abundance per region:** *Baseline,* **2010-2050**

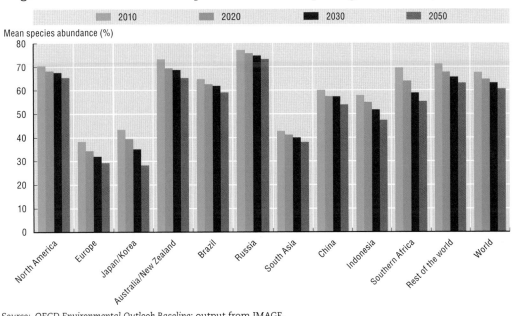

Source: *OECD Environmental Outlook Baseline;* output from IMAGE.

StatLink ⬛⬛ http://dx.doi.org/10.1787/888932570924

In the *Baseline,* global terrestrial biodiversity loss is driven by land-use change and management; forestry; infrastructure, encroachment and fragmentation; climate change; and pollution (*e.g.* nitrogen deposition). Table 4.1 describes these categories as modelled in this *Outlook* (see Alkemade *et al.,* 2009). Indirect drivers include population growth as well as increases in GDP per capita, which leads to dietary changes and rising consumption. These socio-economic drivers are discussed in detail in Chapter 2 and summarised in Annex 4.A.

To date, the main drivers of global terrestrial biodiversity loss have been land-use change and management (*i.e.* conversion of natural ecosystems for producing food and bioenergy crops and livestock). This has accounted for a 16% decline in MSA to date (relative to the pristine state). Infrastructure, encroachment and fragmentation account for a 10% decline. According to the *Baseline* projections, these will remain key pressures on biodiversity up to 2050 (Figure 4.10).

However, the *relative* contribution of pressures to further (additional) biodiversity loss between 2010 and 2050 deviates from past trends (Figure 4.11). Overall, the relative impact of land-use change and management on MSA loss is projected to decrease. While expansion of food crop production and live-stock farming is projected to cause about half of the further MSA loss in the RoW between 2010 and 2030, it is not projected to be a major driver of further loss in the OECD countries or the BRIICS. Instead of agricultural land expansion, land abandonment is projected to occur in several regions, allowing considerable area for ecosystem recovery and regeneration to take place. These areas will however bear the effects of "former land use" for several decades after land abandonment.

Table 4.1. **Biodiversity pressures modelled for the *Environmental Outlook to 2050***

Driver of terrestrial MSA loss	Definition
Land-use change and management (pasture, food crop, bioenergy)	Pressures on biodiversity due to land conversion and production attributed to: ■ Livestock farming on pastures (semi-natural grasslands). ■ Food crop farming. ■ Bioenergy crop farming.
Former land use	This pressure concerns effects on biodiversity that remain after land is abandoned from agricultural production. It is the consequence of slow recovery, and can be interpreted as biodiversity loss due to inertia effects.
Forestry	The use of (semi-)natural and planted forests for wood production. Together these are referred to as forestry (but not deforestation, as that is included under land-use change). It encompasses different forest use/management types, *i.e.* selective logging or clear-cutting of semi-natural or natural forest systems; and production from plantations (planted forests with introduced species).
Infrastructure, encroachment and fragmentation	The following pressures have been aggregated: ■ Infrastructure: direct infrastructure effects due to noise, road kill, etc. Includes the effects of urbanisation. ■ Encroachment: loss due to poaching, wood gathering and other small-scale exploitation by people from settlements around infrastructure. ■ Fragmentation: the effects of cutting up natural areas into smaller areas by roads and by land-use change (conversion), thus affecting ecosystem connectivity and health.
Nitrogen deposition	Changes in biodiversity resulting from deposition of atmospheric nitrogen (*e.g.* eutrophication and acidification).
Climate change	Pressure on biodiversity resulting from changes in climatic conditions, (*e.g.* temperature and rainfall), which can alter species distribution and ecosystem composition.

Figure 4.10. **Effects of different pressures on terrestrial MSA:
Baseline, 2010 to 2050**

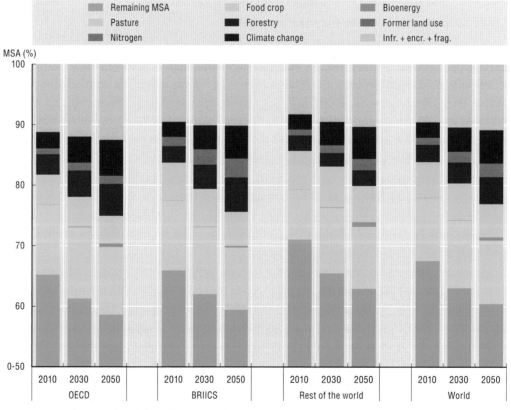

Source: *OECD Environmental Outlook Baseline*; output from IMAGE.

StatLink ᴍᴤᴾ http://dx.doi.org/10.1787/888932570943

Figure 4.11. **Relative share of each pressure to additional terrestrial MSA loss:** *Baseline,* **2010-2030 and 2030-2050**

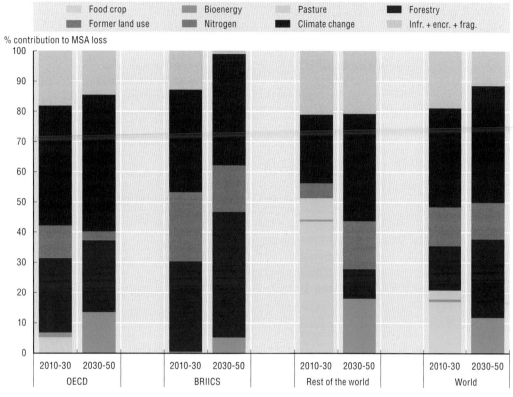

Source: *OECD Environmental Outlook Baseline;* output from IMAGE.

StatLink ⟨⟨⟨ http://dx.doi.org/10.1787/888932570962

Forestry is projected to exert increasing pressure on biodiversity across all three country groups, accounting for close to 15% of global MSA loss between 2010 and 2030 and 30% of loss between 2030 and 2050. Bioenergy crops will also become an increasingly important pressure worldwide, particularly in the RoW. However, in the *Baseline,* the worldwide effect of bioenergy production is still modest in the absence of ambitious climate change policy in OECD and BRIICS regions (see Section 4).

Climate change is projected to become an increasingly important pressure in the *Baseline,* driving just over 40% of additional global MSA loss between 2010 and 2050.[12] The relative contribution to future biodiversity loss of infrastructure, encroachment and fragmentation is projected to diminish in the OECD and BRIICS countries between 2030 and 2050, whereas it will increase in the RoW. Nitrogen deposition is projected to add marginally to further MSA loss in the BRIICS to 2030 and in the RoW to 2050.

Looking more closely at projections in land cover and land-use change shows that global forest cover is projected to decline by almost 1 million km[2] between 2010 and 2020 (mainly due to conversion of land to agricultural production). However, it is projected to then increase to 2050 as a result of natural forest regeneration, reforestation and afforestation (*i.e.* following land abandonment) (Figure 4.12). By 2050 forest cover is projected to reach almost 40 million km[2]. However, this will not necessarily mean more favourable conditions for forest biodiversity in every region, as increasing demand for wood and paper is projected to result in the expansion of forestry activities including wood production from plantations. Primary forest (*i.e.* native forests where ecological processes are not significantly disturbed) is projected to keep steadily decreasing (Figure 4.12). As a consequence, the average biodiversity of forests will also diminish.

Figure 4.12. **Global forest area change:** *Baseline,* **2010-2050**

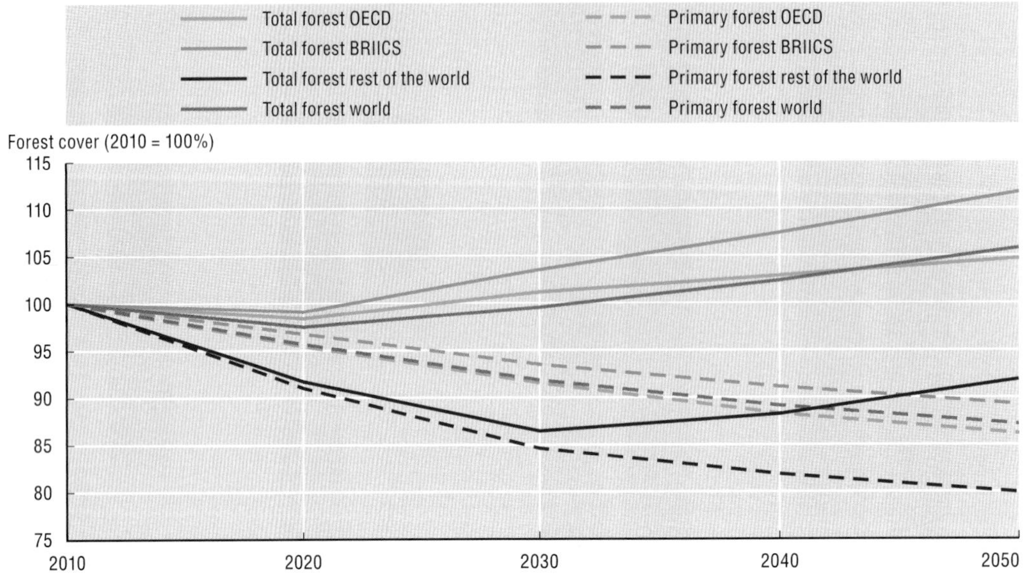

Source: OECD Environmental Outlook Baseline; output from IMAGE.

StatLink 🔗 http://dx.doi.org/10.1787/888932570981

Of course, forest cover trends will differ between regions. Projected total forest area declines to 2020 by nearly 200 000 km^2 in both the OECD countries and the BRIICS, and then expands to 2050 to reach a greater extent than in 2010, mainly on abandoned agricultural land. In the RoW, decline in forest area is projected to continue until 2030 with a total loss of around 1 million km^2 due to expansion of agriculture. After that, forest area expands, but does not regain the 2010 level.

Under the *Baseline* scenario, the global area of production forests (forests managed for the production of timber, pulp and paper, and fuelwood) is projected to increase by close to 60% between 2010 and 2050, to a total of 15 million km^2.[13] Increases in the area of production forests are projected to occur in all regions, except for the RoW (Figure 4.13), as a result of steady increases in demands for timber, paper and fuelwood (although fuelwood is projected to slowly be replaced by other energy sources).

Under the *Environmental Outlook Baseline* scenario, the land area in use for agricultural crop production worldwide is projected to expand between 2010 and 2030 by about 1 million km^2 (Figure 4.14). Most of the expansion is projected in the RoW group, in particular Sub-Saharan Africa. After peaking (before 2030), global food crop area is projected to decline, particularly in North America, Brazil, Russia, South Asia and China. This is based on the assumptions of slowly growing populations in the OECD and a shrinking population in Russia and China, stabilising diets (*i.e.* maximum caloric intake being reached) in most OECD and BRIICS countries, and increasing crop yields due to technological improvements (for a further discussion of the agricultural land projections under the *Baseline* scenario, see Chapter 2).

Figure 4.13. **Change in production forest area:** *Baseline,* **2010-2050**

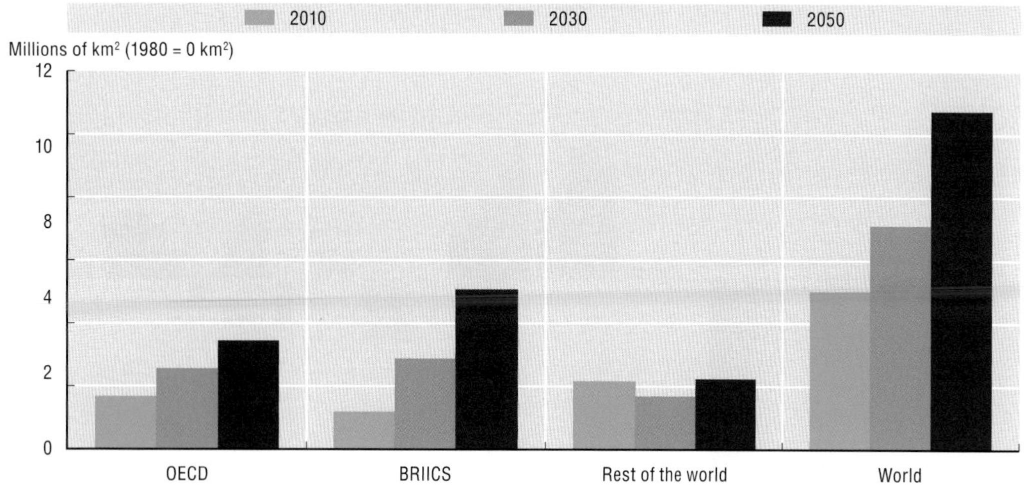

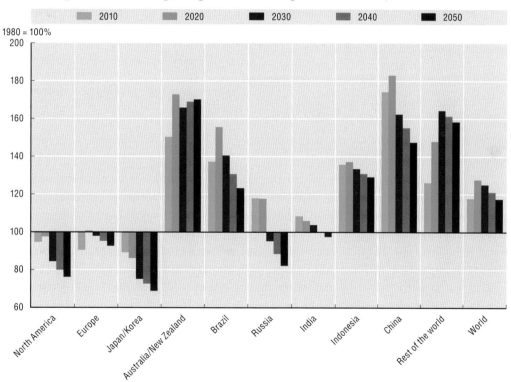

Source: OECD Environmental Outlook Baseline; output from IMAGE.

StatLink ⟨⟨⟨⟨ http://dx.doi.org/10.1787/888932571000

Figure 4.14. **Change in global food crop area:** *Baseline,* **2010-2050**

Source: OECD Environmental Outlook Baseline; output from IMAGE.

StatLink ⟨⟨⟨⟨ http://dx.doi.org/10.1787/888932571019

A similar trend is projected in the *Baseline* for areas designated for grazing and fodder production (Figure 4.15). Between 1980 and 2010 global grazing and fodder areas expanded considerably (2.5 million km^2), mainly in the BRIICS. It is projected that global expansion will continue until 2030 by another 1 million km^2, after which time the total area is projected to

Figure 4.15. **Change in global grazing area (grass and fodder):**
Baseline, 2010-2050

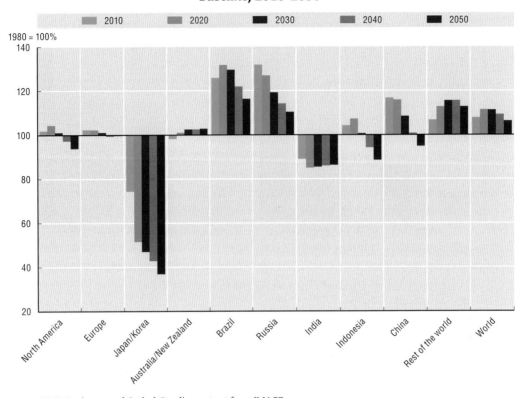

Source: OECD Environmental Outlook Baseline; output from IMAGE.

StatLink 🖏 http://dx.doi.org/10.1787/888932571038

decrease. In Russia and China, a considerable decline in grazing area is projected to commence from 2010 onwards.

There are other important drivers of biodiversity loss which have not been modelled here. These include invasive alien species, forest fires, other forms of pollution (such as phosphorous) and over-exploitation of natural resources.[14] The number of alien species in Europe has increased by 76% since 1970, and similar trends are likely in the rest of the world (Butchart et al., 2010). Invasive alien species[15] can contribute to the loss of natural resources, reduction in food production, poor human health and increased costs for agriculture, forestry, fisheries and water management (OECD, 2008b; SCBD, 2009a). This increase is likely to continue over the next few decades, posing further risk to biodiversity. For example, transport connected to trade and travel is expected to grow strongly in the future – these have been the predominant agents for moving species outside their natural ranges (e.g. ballast water used by ships, and seeds or animals carried on vehicles).

Over-harvesting, for example of trees (particularly in South America and Asia), marine species, and bushmeat (e.g. in Central Africa), has already caused extinctions in the past and remains a threat to biodiversity today. Given the growth in global population and in demand for fish and wood products, as well as the jobs that depend on these resources, managing them sustainably, and transforming those jobs into green jobs, are critical for conservation of biodiversity in coming decades.

Impacts of biodiversity loss and linkages with climate change, water and health

Biodiversity loss can have severe impacts on human well-being, security and economic growth (MA, 2005; SCBD, 2010a; TEEB, 2010a; OECD, 2011a). In Canada, for example, over-exploitation led to the collapse of the North Atlantic cod fishery, resulting in estimated short-term costs of USD 235 million in foregone income. In the long term, the potential annual income foregone by not managing the cod fishery sustainably reached an estimated USD 0.94 billion (cited in OECD, 2008a). Invasive alien species are estimated to cost the US USD 120 billion per year in environmental damage and losses, and the global economy more than USD 1.4 trillion (Pimentel et al., 2005; SCBD, 2010a).

Developing countries tend to bear the majority of the costs of biodiversity loss as they are often more directly dependent on natural resources for economic development than developed countries. Natural capital accounts for an estimated 26% of total wealth in low-income countries compared to only 2% in OECD countries (World Bank, 2006). In developing countries, natural resources play a key role in the economy including for exports, employment and public revenues. Fisheries, for example, provide employment for 47 million fishermen (95% of the world's fishermen) in developing countries and account for between 10 and 30% of government budgets in several countries. In developing countries forestry provides formal employment for another 10 million people and informal employment for 30-50 million, and can account for more than 10% of GDP (OECD, 2009a). Eco-tourism is another important source of revenue in biodiversity-rich developing countries. In Namibia, for example, protected areas contribute 6% of GDP in tourism alone, and in Rwanda, tourism in national parks protecting mountain gorillas is one of the largest sources of foreign exchange, mobilising USD 42 million in 2007 (SCBD, 2009b).

Moreover, biodiversity loss and ecosystem degradation have particularly severe implications for the rural poor. About 70% of the world's poor live in rural areas and are directly dependent on agriculture for their survival (World Bank, 2008). Forest resources underpin the livelihoods of about 90% of the 1.2 billion people living in extreme poverty (World Bank, 2004). Indigenous people are also often disproportionally adversely affected by biodiversity loss and degradation. While richer groups of people may be able to respond to loss of biodiversity and ecosystem services by purchasing alternatives, the poor may be less able to do so.

The need for appropriate policies for biodiversity conservation and sustainable use is even more important given the uncertainty surrounding the impacts of biodiversity and ecosystem service loss, and the fact that damage to ecosystems can often be irreversible (Box 4.2).

Biodiversity loss and ecosystem degradation have other impacts, including on climate change, water quantity and quality, and human health. Understanding these inter-linkages and interactions can help policy makers identify potential policy synergies and trade-offs, and thus enable more co-ordinated and strategic decision making.

Climate change

Biodiversity plays an important role in both climate change mitigation and adaptation. Together, terrestrial and marine ecosystems are estimated to store 1 500-2 500 gigatonnes (Gt) of carbon (Cao and Woodward, 1998; IPCC, 2001), and to provide a net yearly sink for 3.55 Gt of carbon dioxide (Dalal and Allen, 2008). On the other hand, deforestation and other land-use changes account for up to 20% of global anthropogenic greenhouse gas

> **Box 4.2. Ecosystem thresholds: Avoiding irreversible decline through a precautionary approach**
>
> Most environmental policy decisions are made in a context of irreversibility and uncertainty. Ecosystems can only absorb pressure up to a certain threshold, beyond which the basic integrity of the system is undermined. Where thresholds are crossed, a change in the structure and function of an ecosystem may occur (SCBD, 2010a).
>
> These changes are typically costly to reverse – if not impossible – and may have negative environmental, economic and social consequences. Eutrophication of marine and freshwater ecosystems, for example, has created "dead zones", where decomposing algae use up the oxygen in the water rendering it uninhabitable. This can be seen in the Baltic Sea and Gulf of Mexico, and in Lake Erie (Larsen, 2005; Dybas, 2005). Marine trophic cascades, where changes in the population of top predators have knock-down effects on lower trophic levels, have also been documented. Over-fishing of predatory sharks at the apex of the food chain in the Northwest Atlantic, for instance, is thought to have led to a rise in the number of Cownose Ray, increasing predation on bay scallops and causing the collapse of the scallop fishery (Myers et al., 2007).
>
> The capacity of an ecosystem to absorb disturbance and re-organise itself so as to retain essentially the same function, structure, identity and feedbacks is known as ecosystem resilience (Walker et al., 2004). The combined and often synergistic effects of different perturbations can reduce ecosystem resilience, increasing the risk that thresholds will be crossed. For example, biodiversity loss from overfishing, pollution or physical damage can reduce the capacity of coral reefs to absorb changes in climate and ocean acidity. Conversely, conserving biodiversity insures ecosystems against functional decline: more species with the same functional roles provide greater guarantees that some will maintain the function even when others fail (Yachi and Loreau, 1999).
>
> Thresholds are expected to be crossed more frequently in the coming decades as a result of increased human pressure (SCBD, 2010a). The complex non-linear dynamics of ecosystems and their interactions with human systems make it difficult to predict where thresholds lie, when they will be crossed and what the scale of impact will be (Groffman et al., 2006; Rockström et al., 2009). Given this uncertainty, it is prudent to take a precautionary approach and keep disturbance well below likely thresholds. Some science-based limits do exist (e.g. maximum sustainable yields in fisheries) and work is underway to develop monitoring strategies and indicators to warn environmental managers and policy makers when ecosystems may be approaching a threshold (e.g. the Indicator of Coastal Eutrophication Potential; Billen and Garnier, 2007). However, further efforts are needed (ten Brink et al., 2008; Paerl et al., 2003; Scheffer et al., 2009).

(GHG) emissions (IPCC, 2007). Maintaining and restoring ecosystems (e.g. through reforestation) can therefore help mitigate GHG emissions and increase carbon sequestration. It is estimated that the contribution of marine biodiversity alone to climate regulation may be as much as USD 12.9 billion annually (Beaumont et al., 2006). Biodiversity and ecosystems can also play an integral role in climate change adaptation. Examples of "ecosystem-based adaptation" include maintaining and restoring "natural infrastructure" such as mangroves, coral reefs and watershed vegetation that provide a cost-effective buffer against storm surge, rising sea levels and changing precipitation patterns (SCBD, 2009c).

Changes in temperature and precipitation regimes influence the distribution of species and ecosystems. As temperatures increase, ecosystems and species' ranges tend to shift towards the poles or to higher altitudes (Beckage *et al.*, 2007; Salazar *et al.*, 2007). This migration causes some ecosystems to shrink and others to expand. Climate change also alters ecosystem composition, structure and functioning, leading to an overall decline in biodiversity, and disrupting ecosystem services such as water regulation, carbon sequestration and provisioning. Moreover, certain climate change adaptation and mitigation policies may exacerbate the adverse impacts on biodiversity. For example, agricultural adaptation approaches such as draining wetlands during times of flooding and the use of dykes may cause habitat loss, soil erosion and eutrophication (Olsen, 2006). Renewable energy sources such as biofuel, hydro-electric dams and wind turbines have also been observed to have negative impacts on biodiversity (OECD, 2008c; The Royal Society, 2008; New and Xie, 2008; Everaert and Stienen, 2006). In addition to maximising synergies and reducing trade-offs between climate change policies and biodiversity, efforts should be made to enhance the adaptive capacity of ecosystems by, for example, increasing ecosystem connectivity (see Section 3).

Water

The hydrological services provided by ecosystems include water purification, flow regulation, erosion and sedimentation control (Emerton and Bos, 2004). Wetlands and forest soils are particularly effective at removing bacteria, microbes, excess nutrients, and sediments. Forest soils and wetlands generally have a good capacity to absorb water, releasing water gradually and reducing peak flows. In this way, peat bogs in Sri Lanka provide a flood-buffering service estimated at USD 5 million per year (Sudmeier-Rieux, 2006). Forest soils and wetlands also serve as reservoirs of water during drought and release water gradually, maintaining its flow.

Conversely, impaired water quality and quantity negatively affects biodiversity. Eutrophication, habitat loss through land drainage, river flow regulation and sediment load from soil erosion can cause declines in freshwater and marine biodiversity and changes in ecosystem structure and functioning. Chapter 5 explains the impact of dams on the balance between silicon (sediments), nitrogen and phosphate, which results in deteriorating water quality in coastal zones. Regional assessments in the United States, the Mediterranean Basin and elsewhere indicate that freshwater species are, in general, at much greater risk of extinction than terrestrial species (Smith and Darwall, 2006, Stein *et al.*, 2000). Indeed, the *Environmental Outlook Baseline* projections for MSA in freshwater biomes show continuing declines to 2050, particularly in Africa, Latin America and some Asian regions (Figure 4.16). This is likely to be an underestimation because the effects of future river dams, wetland reclamation and climate change are not included in the projections.

Human health

Biodiversity and ecosystems provide services which are critical to human health. These include basic human needs; preventing disease through biological control; medical and genetic resources; and opportunities for recreational, creative and therapeutic activities for improved mental health (Zaghi *et al.*, 2010) (see also Chapter 6).

Food provision is an essential service that is both delivered by and dependent on biodiversity. A biodiverse agricultural crop base is more resilient to drought, flood, pests

Figure 4.16. **Projections of aquatic MSA in freshwater:** *Baseline, 2000-2050*

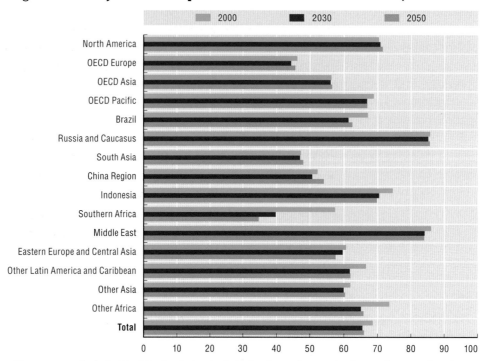

Note: The pressures included in this simulation include: land use changes in the catchment, phosphorus and nitrogen pollution, and flow changes due to water abstraction or river damming. Climate change, over-exploitation and invasive alien species are not included.

Source: OECD Environmental Outlook Baseline; output from IMAGE.

StatLink ᐅᐸᒐᐦ http://dx.doi.org/10.1787/888932571057

and disease, and reduces dependence on any one crop (COHAB Initiative, 2010; MA, 2005; SCBD, 2009b). Reliable and diverse food sources reduce the risk of famine and also the likelihood of micronutrient and vitamin deficiencies, which weaken the immune system. Other provisioning services include clean air and water, and building materials.

Demand for these services, however, places considerable pressure on biodiversity. An emphasis on increasing the output and standardisation of agriculture and livestock farming systems, for instance, has tended to drive down genetic diversity (Heal *et al.*, 2002). In China, for example, the number of local rice varieties declined from 46 000 in the 1950s to slightly more than 1 000 in 2006. In an estimated 60%-70% of areas where wild relatives of rice used to grow, they are no longer found or the area where they are cultivated has been dramatically reduced (SCBD, 2010a). Over-exploitation (*e.g.* of bushmeat for protein) is also a significant concern.

Ecosystems with high biodiversity also ensure the regulation of interactions between predators, prey, hosts, vectors and parasites and thus provide a mechanism for controlling the emergence and spread of infectious diseases. Outbreaks of malaria, yellow fever, lyme disease, avian influenza, and tick-borne encephalitis have all been attributed, among other causes, to ecosystem degradation (Box 4.3).

Biodiversity is an important source of raw materials for pharmaceuticals and biotechnology, and it provides medical models which can further understanding of human physiology and mechanisms of disease. However, the demands of the health sector place considerable pressure on biodiversity. It is estimated, for example, that more than two-

> ## Box 4.3. **Biodiversity and human health**
>
> ■ Urban trees in the United States remove an estimated 711 000 metric tonnes of air pollutants every year, a service valued at USD 3.8 billion (Nowak *et al.*, 2006).
>
> ■ Globally, more than 50% of prescription drugs contain natural compounds derived from plant or animal species or synthesised compounds based on naturally occurring compounds (Newman and Cragg, 2007). While 25% of modern drugs are derived from tropical rainforest species, less than 5% have been studied for their pharmaceutical potential, suggesting a great potential for new drug discovery (McDonald, 2009).
>
> ■ There is an increasing demand for traditional medicines (which rely on wild and cultivated plants) on all continents; up to 80% of the population of many developing countries rely upon traditional medicine for the treatment of disease (Zaghi *et al.*, 2010; WHO, 2002).
>
> ■ Denning bears have provided valuable insights into osteoporosis, renal disease, diabetes and cardio-vascular disorders in humans (Chivian, 2002).
>
> ■ The incidence of malaria is linked to climate change, deforestation, and changes in aquatic ecosystems (Zaghi *et al.*, 2010). In heavily deforested areas of the Amazon for example, the human-biting rate of the primary malaria vector, *Anopheles darlingi*, may be close to 300 times higher than in intact forests, even after controlling for human population density (Vittor *et al.*, 2006).

thirds of the medicinal plants in use today are harvested from the wild and that 4 000-10 000 of these may now be endangered (Hamilton, 2003). While international and national laws have gone some way to reduce unsustainable harvesting, illegal markets for medicinal plant and animal species continue to encourage over-exploitation (Alves and Rosa, 2007).

3. Biodiversity: The state of policy today

Policy frameworks for biodiversity conservation and sustainable use

Renewed efforts will be needed to conserve biodiversity and use natural resources sustainably to reverse current and projected trends for biodiversity loss. As biodiversity provides public benefits at local, regional and global scale, governments have a role to play at all these levels. The policy instruments available for biodiversity conservation and sustainable use can be categorised as: regulatory (*i.e.* command-and-control) approaches, economic instruments, and information and other instruments (Table 4.2). Each of these is discussed in turn.

Regulatory approaches

Regulatory approaches for biodiversity conservation and sustainable use are common in most countries. The Convention on International Trade in Endangered Species of Wild Fauna and Flora (CITES) regulates international trade in around 5 000 species of animals and 28 000 species of plants to ensure that trade does not threaten their survival. Species are subject to different trade restrictions according to the degree of protection they need (CITES, 2011).

A cornerstone of most national biodiversity conservation policies and strategies is protected areas (PAs). In the European Union for example, Natura 2000 sites protect

Table 4.2. **Policy instruments for biodiversity conservation and sustainable use**

Regulatory (command-and-control) approaches	Economic instruments	Information and other instruments
Restrictions or prohibitions on use (*e.g.* trade in endangered species and CITES).[1]	Price-based instruments: ■ Taxes (*e.g.* groundwater, pesticide and fertiliser use). ■ Charges/fees (*e.g.* for natural resource use, access to national parks, hunting or fishing license fees). ■ Subsidies.	Eco-labelling and certification (*e.g.* organic agriculture labelling schemes; labels for sustainably harvested fish or timber).
Access restrictions or prohibitions (*e.g.* protected areas; legislated buffer zones along waterways).	Reform of environmentally harmful subsidies.	Green public procurement (*e.g.* of sustainably harvested timber).
Permits and quotas (*e.g.* for logging and fishing).	Payment for ecosystem services.	Voluntary agreements (*e.g.* between businesses and government for nature protection or voluntary offset schemes).
Quality, quantity and design standards (*e.g.* commercial fishing net mesh-size specifications).	Biodiversity offsets/biobanking.	Corporate environmental accounting.
Spatial planning (*e.g.* ecological corridors).	Tradable permits (*e.g.* individual transferable quotas for fisheries, tradable development credits).	
Planning tools and requirements (*e.g.* environmental impact assessments [EIAs] and strategic environmental assessments [SEA].	■ Liability instruments. ■ Non-compliance fines. ■ Performance bonds.	

1. Convention on International Trade in Endangered Species.

Source: Adapted from OECD, (2010a), *Paying for Biodiversity: Enhancing the Cost-Effectiveness of Payments for Ecosystem Services*, OECD Publishing.

approximately 18% of European territory and 130 000 km^2 of its seas (Natura 2000, 2011). Globally, terrestrial PAs cover about 12.7% of the Earth's area, excluding Antarctica (c. 17 million km^2) (IUCN and UNEP, 2011a) (Figure 4.17). Some biomes are better represented than others however. For example, just under 30% of montane grasslands and shrublands and more than 40% of flooded grasslands and savannas are protected, compared to less than just 5% of temperate grasslands, savannas and shrublands (Coad *et al.*, 2009).

In contrast, there are still very few marine protected areas (MPAs) in place worldwide – 7.2% of territorial seas are currently covered (up to 12 nautical miles from coastline) (IUCN and UNEP, 2011a), despite studies that show that MPAs can increase the density, diversity and size of species (Halpern, 2003; Gaines *et al.*, 2010). For example, within two years of establishing no-take marine reserves in Australia's Great Barrier Reef, there was a 57%-75% increase in Coral Trout density in six of eight regions assessed (Russ *et al.*, 2008). One shortcoming of existing MPAs is that they are often not big enough to protect adequate habitat to support the target species; as a result their net benefit to marine ecosystems may be minimal (Gaines *et al.*, 2010). Increasing the size of MPAs and establishing networks would help to address this.

Designing networks of PAs connected by natural corridors is also important for restoring, maintaining or enhancing ecological coherence and the natural adaptive capacity of ecosystems. This is particularly important where PAs are small or under pressure, and in the context of climate change (Bennett and Mulongoy, 2006). Where ecosystems span political boundaries, maintaining connectivity may require co-ordination among managers and scientists from neighbouring countries. As of 2007, 227 transboundary

Figure 4.17. **Global trend in protected area cover, 1990-2010**

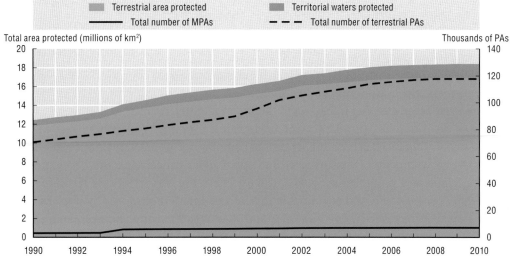

Source: IUCN and WCMC (2011), *The World Database on Protected Areas* (WDPA), UNEP-WCMC, Cambridge, UK.

PAs had been established globally, combining more than 3 000 individual PAs or internationally designated sites (UNEP-WCMC, 2008).[16]

Often, however, protected areas do not receive the level of protection intended,[17] due to poor management, inadequate monitoring and enforcement, and lack of funds. The term "paper parks" has been used to describe PAs that have protective legislation but are in fact open access. A global assessment of management effectiveness of 3 080 PAs indicated an average management effectiveness score of 0.53, on a scale from zero (extremely ineffective management) to one (highly effective management). Approximately 14% of PAs were considered to be lacking basic management requirements (Leverington *et al.*, 2008).

In establishing and managing PAs, governments should ensure that the legal and customary rights of indigenous people, local communities and other stakeholders are fully respected, and consider the important role local and indigenous communities can play in the management of PAs and as a source of local and traditional knowledge.

Environmental standards are another widely adopted regulatory instrument for biodiversity. Standards come in a variety of forms, including quality standards (*e.g.* upper limits on heavy metal concentrations in agricultural soils or water); quantity standards (*e.g.* upper limits on number of daily grazing animals per hectare; maximum emissions of pollutants); and design standards (*e.g.* commercial fishing net specifications). An advantage of quantity-based standards is that they are broadly applicable and specify biodiversity conservation and sustainable use goals explicitly. However, due to information deficiencies and variations in abatement costs, standards may not always be cost-effective. Furthermore, they may "lock-in" specific technologies.

In some cases a standard may not be sufficient and it may be necessary to ban an activity completely (*e.g.* DDT[18] use). Bans can also be implemented temporarily to relieve pressure and provide an opportunity for ecosystem restoration. China, for example, has introduced an annual two-month fishing ban on the entire Pearl River system, corresponding to the start of the peak spawning season. The purpose of the ban is to restore fish numbers and improve water quality (Quanlin, 2011). Bans have also been introduced where ecosystems are still intact but poorly understood, as a precaution. The FAO's General Fisheries Commission for the Mediterranean, for instance, introduced a ban in 2005 on bottom trawling at depths beyond 1 000m (GFCM, 2005).

Other types of commonly used regulatory instruments include land-use planning, environmental impact assessments (EIA) and strategic environmental assessments (SEA). The implementation of an EIA is a planning requirement in many countries. While legislation and implementation vary from country-to-country, the procedural framework is the same. EIAs are used by private and public-sector actors to identify, predict, evaluate and mitigate effects of development projects prior to decision making (IAIA, 1999). The SEA is a complementary approach used in higher tiers of planning and decision making to identify and assess the environmental consequences and stakeholder concerns in the development of policies, plans and programmes (OECD, 2006). There are opportunities to mainstream biodiversity conservation and sustainable use into planning procedures by improving and building upon the biodiversity criteria of EIAs and SEAs, which are often quite limited. The CBD and OECD have established guidelines for achieving this (CBD, 2005; OECD, 2006).

Economic instruments

Environmental taxes, charges and fees are some of the more commonly used economic instruments for managing biodiversity across OECD countries. Examples of taxes which help prevent biodiversity loss include those on logging (*e.g.* British Columbia, Canada), waste water discharge (*e.g.* Germany), groundwater extraction (*e.g.* Netherlands), as well as pesticide and fertiliser taxes (*e.g.* Denmark) (OECD, 2008d; Larsen, 2005). Applications of fees and charges include fishing and hunting (*e.g.* fees for commercial marine fishing licenses in Canada and hunting licenses in Finland); development of natural areas (*e.g.* charges for development of coastal areas in Korea); water supply and use (*e.g.* charges on water supply and consumption in France); and admission fees to national parks (*e.g.* in Israel).

Subsidies are one of the most commonly used economic instruments for biodiversity conservation and sustainable use in OECD countries (OECD, 2008d). They come in several forms, including monetary payments, tax exemptions or reductions, soft loans or the provision of infrastructure. They can be used to reward landowners for environmental work (*e.g.* for restoring degraded forest ecosystems in Korea); for removing land from production (*e.g.* Austria); for promoting eco-friendly improvements in fishing gear and practices (*e.g.* Mexico and the European Union); for compensating farmers for bans on fertiliser use in areas of conservation importance (*e.g.* Czech Republic); for supporting farmers in maintaining biodiverse farming systems (*e.g.* the European Union); and for supporting the development of conservation parks and nature trails (*e.g.* Japan) (OECD, 2008d). However, while subsidies can encourage biodiversity-friendly behaviour, the downside is they may place a heavy burden on government coffers and taxpayers and can stifle, rather than encourage, innovation. Where subsidy programmes are introduced, they should be time-bound and closely monitored.

Payments for ecosystem services (PES) are a rapidly emerging instrument used to reduce the loss or enhance the provision of ecosystem services. They are defined as "a voluntary, conditional agreement between at least one 'seller' and one 'buyer' over a well-defined environmental service – or a land use presumed to produce that service" (Wunder, 2005). For instance, downstream hydroelectric utilities that use clean water as an input to production pay upstream forest managers to ensure a sustainable flow of this service. PES can be potentially much more cost-effective than indirect payments or other regulatory approaches used for environmental objectives. Examples include the Tasmanian Forest Conservation Fund programme in Australia, and the Sumberjaya Watershed programme in Indonesia. PES schemes can also mobilise finance from the private sector – examples include the national PES programme in Costa Rica and Vittell's (Nestle Water) PES scheme in France (see OECD, 2010a). There are also international PES-like schemes emerging that can benefit biodiversity, including REDD-plus,[19] and payments for Access and Benefits Sharing.[20]

Another emerging instrument is biodiversity offsets, which are conservation activities designed to deliver measurable biodiversity benefits to compensate for losses caused by project development, after appropriate prevention and mitigation measures have been taken. Biodiversity offsets can operate in either a regulatory or voluntary framework. Brazil, Canada, China, France, Mexico and South Africa, among others, have developed guidelines or incorporated biodiversity offsets into their legal framework, while several industry leaders have voluntarily incorporated offset policies into their corporate strategy. These include Rio Tinto, BHP Billiton, Anglo Platinum, and Shell (ten Kate *et al.*, 2004; Treweek, 2009).

Biodiversity offsets may be carried out by the developer or contracted out to a third party. This can be done as an *ad hoc* arrangement or within a biodiversity banking or "biobanking" scheme. Biobanks serve as a repository of biodiversity credits representing beneficial biodiversity outcomes beyond business as usual. The credits can be stored over time and eventually purchased by developers to offset biodiversity loss at development sites. Examples include the US Conservation Banking and the New South Wales Biobanking programme in Australia.

Tradable permits are another instrument for creating biodiversity conservation and sustainable use markets. In tradable permit schemes, the government sets a limit or cap on user access to a resource. Access rights are then allocated to individual users who are able to transfer or bank these permits according to their needs. Users who exceed the limits imposed by their permit allocation are penalised. Tradable permit schemes relevant to biodiversity include those for hunting and fishing – the latter are often referred to as individual transferable quotas (ITQs). At least 120 fisheries worldwide have adopted ITQs. Studies show that under a well-designed ITQ programme, fish stocks, and the profits from harvesting them, have the potential to recover substantially (Costello *et al.*, 2008).

Information and other instruments

Information instruments can be an effective way of addressing informational asymmetries that often exist between business, government and society. Eco-labels, for example, inform consumers of the environmental impact of their purchasing decisions, enabling them to make environmentally friendly choices. Eco-labelling and certification have become popular in a number of sectors, particularly agriculture (*e.g.* Roundtable on Sustainable Palm Oil certification), fisheries (*e.g.* Marine Stewardship Council certification), forestry (*e.g.* the Programme for the Endorsement of Forest Certification Schemes), and tourism (*e.g.* Green Globe Company Standard). It is important to note that there are limitations in inducing change in consumer behaviour via information instruments alone. For example, a recent OECD study of 10 000 households across 10 OECD countries indicated that consumers are generally not willing to pay a premium of more than 15% for organic-certified food relative to conventional food products, whatever the food category (OECD, 2011b).

Voluntary agreements are voluntary commitments to pursue actions that improve the environment. They include unilateral commitments, which are programmes for improved environmental performance set up by firms and communicated to their stakeholders (*e.g.* the International Council for Metals and the Environment); public voluntary schemes, where participating firms agree to standards that have been developed by public bodies (*e.g.* the European Eco-Management and Auditing Scheme); and negotiated agreements, which are contracts resulting from negotiations between public authorities and industry (*e.g* "The Voluntary Initiative" which promotes responsible pesticide use in the United Kingdom) (OECD, 2000). Green public procurement is another type of voluntary agreement whereby public authorities use their purchasing power to choose environmentally friendly goods, services and works, thereby contributing to sustainable consumption and production. Voluntary agreements may be used in advance of and in supplement to legislation. They can be used to experiment with new and innovative approaches, to promote awareness about biodiversity issues, and to collect information and data. While generally the environmental targets of most – but not all – voluntary programmes seem to have been met, care needs to be taken to set goals that are sufficiently ambitious (OECD, 2003).

Selecting the appropriate policy mix: key considerations

A combination of command-and-control, economic and information instruments will be required to address biodiversity loss and sustainable use. Selecting the appropriate mix of policy instruments to address biodiversity conservation and sustainable use is not necessarily straightforward. It will require taking into account local and regional priorities as well as international commitments under the CBD and other agreements. The policy mix will depend not only on the nature of the environmental problem, but also the social, cultural, political and economic context. Indeed, biodiversity policy may affect broader national priorities, such as poverty alleviation, sustainable development and economic growth, and these need to be considered in a coherent way so as to maximise synergies and address any trade-offs. Policy coherence will also be required across countries in order to avoid "leakage" effects – where increased conservation efforts in one country shift pressures on biodiversity to another.

Under certain circumstances, regulatory approaches will be most appropriate. For example, if an over-exploited fish stock is on the verge of collapse, a (temporary) ban on fishing may be most effective. Economic instruments, however, are often able to achieve policy objectives at a lower total cost than regulatory approaches, allowing greater flexibility for the economic actor, and provide continuous incentives for improvement, thereby fostering innovation. They also have the ability to generate revenues for government (OECD, 2011a).

While some policy instruments may interact synergistically resulting in more environmentally and cost-effective outcomes, other combinations may be counter-productive or simply redundant, serving only to increase the administrative costs. For instance, regulatory standards combined with voluntary schemes such as Forest Stewardship Council certification for sustainably-sourced timber can interact synergistically by enforcing a minimum level of performance while encouraging industry leaders to go above and beyond compliance. However, the flexibility of economic instruments such as taxes may be hampered by prescriptive regulatory instruments addressing the same behaviour. Whether instruments interact synergistically or in conflict will also depend largely on how they are designed (*i.e.* what and whom they are targeted to address and at what regulatory scale) (OECD, 2007).

It is also important to consider the distribution of social costs and benefits ("distributional impacts") associated with each policy option, and to ensure that appropriate measures are put in place to address any negative effects (OECD, 2008e). Distributional impacts occur at different scales, including between countries, regions, sectors and groups in society. The costs of policies to maintain and enhance biodiversity are generally borne by the populations living in the area where these policies are implemented. At the same time, many of the benefits generated by policies to maintain and enhance biodiversity are delivered elsewhere. This mismatch between costs and benefits also occurs at a global scale. As the majority of biodiversity is found in developing countries, they are often burdened with the costs of biodiversity policies while a significant proportion of the benefits accrue worldwide. International financing mechanisms for biodiversity can help to address this (see Section 4).

Finally, biodiversity policies have a temporal dimension. Policies not only affect individuals today; they also affect future generations. The policy-making process therefore needs to compare costs and benefits of biodiversity-related policies that may arise at different points in time and justify them against some measure of intergenerational equity.

Recent progress

Although the 2010 Biodiversity Target to "significantly reduce the rate of biodiversity loss" agreed by CBD Parties in 2002 has not been met, there have been some areas of progress since the last *OECD Environmental Outlook* (OECD, 2008b). At the international level, there have been two important political achievements:

■ In October 2010 the 10th Conference of the Parties to the CBD (COP10) was held in Nagoya, Aichi Prefecture, Japan. The Parties agreed on a new package, which includes the *Strategic Plan for Biodiversity, 2011–2020*, the *Aichi Biodiversity Targets* (Boxes 4.4 and 4.5 and a *Strategy for Resource Mobilization*. They also adopted the Nagoya Protocol on Access to Genetic Resources and the Fair and Equitable Sharing of Benefits Arising from their Utilization.[21]

■ The approval of an Intergovernmental Science-Policy Platform on Biodiversity and Ecosystem Services (IPBES) by the United Nations General Assembly in 2010 is intended to provide an interface between the scientific community and policy makers. Governments have agreed that the four main functions of the IPBES will be to i) identify and prioritise key scientific information needed for policy makers and to catalyse efforts to generate new knowledge; ii) perform regular and timely assessments of knowledge on biodiversity and ecosystem services and their inter-linkages; iii) support policy formulation and implementation by identifying policy-relevant tools and methodologies; and iv) prioritise key capacity-building needs to improve the science-policy interface, as well as to provide and call for financial and other support for the highest-priority needs related directly to its activities (IPBES, 2011).

At the national level, a number of countries have made progress in establishing National Biodiversity Strategies and Action Plans (NBSAPs) as requested in Article 6 of the CBD. Between 2008 and 2010, an additional 14 countries established NBSAPs (raising the total to 171 countries or 89% of the CBD Parties) and 10 countries updated their existing NBSAPs (2nd or 3rd versions) (Prip *et al.*, 2010). CBD Parties will now need to consider revising and updating their NBSAPs to reflect the Aichi Biodiversity Targets (Target 17, Box 4.4).

Box 4.4. **The Strategic Plan for Biodiversity 2011-2020 and the 20 Aichi Biodiversity Targets**

The strategic plan envisages that, "By 2050, biodiversity is valued, conserved, restored and wisely used, maintaining ecosystem services, sustaining a healthy planet and delivering benefits essential for all people".

The mission of the new plan is to:

"… take effective and urgent action to halt the loss of biodiversity in order to ensure that by 2020 ecosystems are resilient and continue to provide essential services, thereby securing the planet's variety of life, and contributing to human well-being, and poverty eradication. To ensure this, pressures on biodiversity are reduced, ecosystems are restored, biological resources are sustainably used and benefits arising out of utilization of genetic resources are shared in a fair and equitable manner; adequate financial resources are provided, capacities are enhanced, biodiversity issues and values mainstreamed, appropriate policies are effectively implemented, and decision-making is based on sound science and the precautionary approach."

The new plan consists of five strategic goals:

- Strategic Goal A: Address the underlying causes of biodiversity loss by mainstreaming biodiversity across government and society.

- Strategic Goal B: Reduce the direct pressures on biodiversity and promote sustainable use.

- Strategic Goal C: Improve the status of biodiversity by safeguarding ecosystems, species and genetic diversity.

- Strategic Goal D: Enhance the benefits to all from biodiversity and ecosystem services.

- Strategic Goal E: Enhance implementation through participatory planning, knowledge management and capacity building.

Some examples of the Aichi Biodiversity Targets most relevant to this chapter are:

- Target 2. By 2020, at the latest, biodiversity values have been integrated into national and local development and poverty reduction strategies and planning processes are being incorporated into national accounting, as appropriate, and reporting systems.

- Target 3. By 2020, at the latest, incentives, including subsidies, harmful to biodiversity are eliminated, phased out or reformed in order to minimize or avoid negative impacts, and positive incentives for the conservation and sustainable use of biodiversity are developed and applied, consistent and in harmony with the convention and other relevant international obligations, taking into account national socio economic conditions.

- Target 5. By 2020, the rate of loss of all natural habitats, including forests, is at least halved and where feasible brought close to zero, and degradation and fragmentation is significantly reduced.

- Target 16. By 2015, the Nagoya Protocol on Access to Genetic Resources and the Fair and Equitable Sharing of Benefits Arising from their Utilization is in force and operational, consistent with national legislation.

- Target 17. By 2015 each Party has developed, adopted as a policy instrument, and has commenced implementing an effective, participatory and updated national biodiversity strategy and action plan.

- Target 20. By 2020, at the latest, the mobilisation of financial resources for effectively implementing the Strategic Plan for Biodiversity 2011-2020 from all sources, and in accordance with the consolidated and agreed process in the *Strategy for Resource Mobilization*, should increase substantially from the current levels. This target will be subject to changes contingent to resource needs assessments to be developed and reported by Parties.

Source: CBD (2010), *Strategic Plan for Biodiversity 2011-2020, including Aichi Biodiversity Targets*, CBD, Montreal, available at *www.cbd.int/sp/targets/*.

Recent years have also witnessed an increase in the cover of terrestrial and marine PAs (see also Figure 4.17). Today, 12.7% of terrestrial area and 7.2% of territorial waters are designated as protected (IUCN and UNEP, 2011a). Further progress will be required if CBD Parties are to meet the Aichi Biodiversity Targets for PAs agreed upon at COP10 in Nagoya (Box 4.5).

Box 4.5. **What if... terrestrial protected area coverage expanded to 17% globally?**

The Aichi Biodiversity Target 11 is to expand the global protected area network to at least 17% of terrestrial areas by 2020. It specifies that the network should cover "areas of particular importance for biodiversity and ecosystem services" and be "ecologically representative" (Decision X/2, CBD, 2010). One way of achieving ecological representativeness is to apply a 17% target to each of the major 65 ecoregions,[1] rather than simply in terms of terrestrial area. A model-based simulation was run to implement this representation (known as the *Expanded Terrestrial Protected Areas* scenario, see Annex 4.A at the end of this chapter). This shows that the amount of additional land that each country would need to set aside varies greatly (Figure 4.18). The largest effort would be required from the BRIICS, both in terms of absolute area and as a percentage of the regional area, especially Russia (14%) and India (10%). A substantial effort would also be required by OECD Europe (10%).[2] Relatively lower amounts are required in Southern Africa, Japan/Korea and Brazil.[3] According to this "17% PA" scenario projection, establishing 17% of each ecoregion as PAs would result in only a 1% decline in global land area in production (0.5 million km^2 of around 40 million km^2 for crops and grazing).

Figure 4.18. **Additional protected areas needed worldwide to achieve the Aichi 17% target**

■ Situation 2010   ■ Expansion to 17% of each eco-region

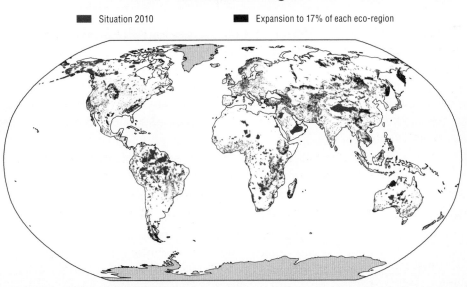

Source: OECD Environmental Outlook Baseline; output from IMAGE.
1. Ecoregions are a combination of biogeographic realms and major biome types (Olson *et al.* 2001).
2. The EU member states have 18% of their terrestrial area already covered by Natura 2000 protected areas. However, an additional 10% would be required if 17% of all representative ecoregions are to be protected.
3. In Brazil and Southern Africa especially, a large part of the territory already has protected status, although with different degrees of enforcement.

There has also been some progress in securing public finance for biodiversity. Official development assistance (ODA) or aid for biodiversity-related activities[22] given to developing countries by donor countries (the members of the OECD's Development Assistance Committee) increased from about USD 3 billion in 2005 to USD 6.9 billion in 2010 (Figure 4.19). As a percentage of total ODA, this has increased from about 2.5% in 2005 to over 5% in 2010. Biodiversity-related aid with the principal objective[23] of biodiversity increased from about USD 1.7 billion to 2.6 billion over the same period (OECD, 2010b).

Figure 4.19. **Biodiversity-related ODA, 2005-2010**

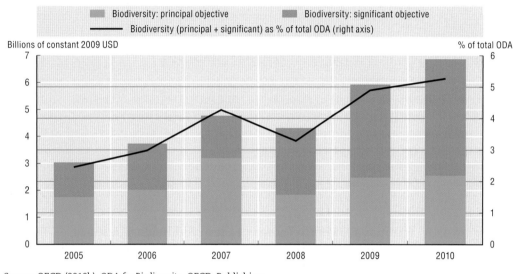

Source: OECD (2010b), *ODA for Biodiversity*, OECD, Publishing.

StatLink ᴹˢᴾ *http://dx.doi.org/10.1787/888932571076*

Recent years have witnessed a substantial increase in climate change finance with large opportunities to harness synergies between climate change mitigation and adaptation, and biodiversity. A well-designed mechanism for REDD-plus, in the context of climate change mitigation, for example, could deliver substantial biodiversity co-benefits since avoiding deforestation and degradation should protect habitat and therefore biodiversity (Karousakis, 2009). Commitments to REDD-plus for the "fast start" climate finance period (*i.e.* 2010-2012) totalled around USD 4.3 billion in December 2010.[24]

Recent annual financial flows for climate change adaptation are estimated to be in the order of USD 100 to USD 200 million per year (Haites, 2011; Corfee-Morlot *et al.*, 2009), and provide opportunities for biodiversity conservation in the context of ecosystem-based adaptation. Colombia, for example, received a grant from the Global Environment Facility and additional co-financing totalling close to USD 15 million to implement an Integrated National Adaptation Plan in which ecosystem-based adaptation measures play an integral role. These measures include restoring natural ecosystems in upper watersheds, along riversides and in landslide areas. These have been developed at the local level (27 completed as of 2010) and are incorporated into local and national policy making and spatial planning (Andrade Pérez *et al.*, 2011; World Bank, 2011).

4. Need for further action

Despite the progress reviewed above, the scale of the biodiversity challenge means that significant further efforts are needed at the local, national and international level. Four overarching priorities for further action are:

i)   Remove or reform environmentally harmful subsidies.

ii) Significantly scale-up private-sector engagement in biodiversity conservation and sustainable use, including via innovative financing mechanisms and the creation of markets.

iii) Improve data, metrics and indicators, including on the economic valuation of biodiversity.

iv) Mainstream and integrate biodiversity conservation and sustainable use into other policy areas and sectors of the economy.

Removing or reforming environmentally harmful subsidies

One of the 20 Aichi Targets agreed at CBD COP10 is that, by 2020 at the latest, subsidies harmful to biodiversity should be eliminated, phased out or reformed in order to minimise or avoid negative impacts. Subsidies that can be harmful to biodiversity are those that promote, without any environmental considerations, the intensification or geographic expansion of economic sectors such as agriculture, bioenergy, fishing, forestry and transport.

Support to agricultural producers in OECD countries, for example, measured through the producer support estimate (PSE), was estimated at USD 265 billion in 2008 (OECD, 2009b). Though global trade liberalisation and domestic budgetary pressures have led to a move to de-couple support from direct production (this type of support tends to be particularly environmentally harmful), further progress is required to switch it towards supporting environmental objectives for which there is a notional demand *e.g.* subsidising environmental "public goods" and penalising damaging externalities. A recent example of subsidy reform that reduces pressure on biodiversity is the abolition of subsidies for fertiliser in Korea (OECD, 2008d).

Subsidies to fisheries also merit further attention. Apart from natural cycles, fish stocks are vulnerable to intensified fishing pressure as well as excessive fishing capacity caused in large part by growing demand for food products and subsidies in a number of countries. The accelerating depletion of stocks, the use of various forms of damaging fishing gear, as well as emissions and pollution from fishing activities are undermining marine biodiversity and ecosystem goods and services (which are much less understood and quantified than terrestrial biodiversity). Overall, world capture fishery resources are yielding negligible resource rents, with continuing investment in non-performing capital assets (Arnason, 2008). Low yields are partly explained by substantial overcapacity in many parts of the global fishing fleet and lack of firmly-established user/property rights in fisheries in both national and international waters; overcapacity has been fuelled by subsidies to fishing. The reversal of this common resource management failure thus offers a potential win-win, in terms of biodiversity recovery, as well as potentially large financial savings on sub-optimal investment decisions (see ten Brink *et al.*, 2010).

There is considerable debate over the full direct and indirect impacts of switching to bioenergy. In many countries, the use of "first-generation" bioenergy (produced primarily from food crops such as grains, sugar cane and vegetable oils) has had perverse outcomes in terms of increased GHG emissions as a result of land conversion and soil disturbance. In addition, there is currently little data on the ancillary costs and benefits for biodiversity. The UK House of Commons Committee (2008) notes that the ambiguous savings arising from the implementation of EU bioenergy support policies in the United Kingdom highlight the potential risks of replacing one harmful subsidy with another. Doornbosch and Steenblik (2007) suggest that the rush to energy crops threatens to cause food shortages and damage biodiversity with limited benefits. Moreover, there is some evidence to suggest that domestic support to bioenergy may not be cost-effective (OECD, 2008c). Further research into second-generation bioenergy (produced from cellulose, hemicelluloses or lignin)[25] might obviate some of the inherent trade-offs between energy, food (productivity) and biodiversity, if such technologies can use bio-wastes arising for example from agriculture or forestry (see also Chapter 3).

Scaling up private-sector engagement in biodiversity

Given the trends in biodiversity loss and the large levels of financing needed (see Section 1), there is an urgent need to better engage the private sector in biodiversity conservation and sustainable use. Although voluntary private-sector initiatives for biodiversity are beginning to emerge (Box 4.6), governments will need to do more to provide the right incentives for the private sector to take action. These include clear price signals for encouraging sustainable natural resource use and preventing pollution – they must provide certainty while offering the private sector the flexibility to determine how they can adhere to them most cost effectively. Though economic instruments are being increasingly applied worldwide (*e.g.* biodiversity offsets and payments for ecosystem services; see Section 3), in most cases these are neither sufficiently stringent nor sufficiently comprehensive to address the scale of the biodiversity challenge. Governments will also need to do more to show that there are both significant business risks and

---

Box 4.6. **Private-sector initiatives for biodiversity**

World Business Council for Sustainable Development (WBCSD): this global partnership has a membership of around 200 companies from more than 30 countries and 20 major industrial sectors. The WBCSD provides a platform for companies to explore sustainable development; share knowledge, experiences and best practices; and to advocate business positions on these issues. Biodiversity is one of the key themes addressed by the WBSCD. Recent work includes: i) the Ecosystem Evaluation Initiative, which aims to promote ecosystem valuation as a tool to inform and improve corporate decision making; and ii) the Corporate Ecosystem Services Review, which provides guidelines for identifying business risks and opportunities arising from ecosystem change.

Dow Chemicals and The Nature Conservancy: this USD 10 million partnership was announced in early 2011. Scientists from both organisations will apply a range of scientific models, maps and analysis for biodiversity and ecosystem services to help Dow recognise, value and incorporate nature into its business decisions and strategies. The collaboration intends to share the tools, lessons learned and results publicly and through peer review so that other companies, scientists and interested parties can test and apply them. An additional objective of the partnership is to help stimulate the emergence of biodiversity markets and the adoption of market mechanisms for biodiversity conservation.

Sources: www.wbcsd.org; The Nature Conservancy (2011), Working with Companies: Dow Announces Business Strategy for Conservation, Nature Conservancy website, www.nature.org/aboutus/ourpartners/workingwithcompanies/explore/dow-announces-business-strategy-for-conservation.xml.

---

opportunities associated with biodiversity and ecosystem services and to encourage and facilitate innovation (see *e.g.* OECD, 2009c; TEEB, 2010b).

Public finance will need to be complemented by and used to leverage private-sector finance. For example, under the Green Investment Funds scheme in the Netherlands, government provides beneficial financial arrangements and tax reductions to private investors to facilitate the implementation of green projects such as nature restoration in drinking water production areas. Since 1995, around EUR 10 billion has been invested in green projects through this scheme.

As biodiversity provides local, regional and global public good benefits, innovative financing is needed at all these levels.[26] Local and national policies need to be scaled up, and instruments for international financing of biodiversity need to be developed – this is a key policy gap. For example, opportunities for international co-financing of existing, effective domestic biodiversity programmes could be explored. One example of where this has been undertaken is in a recently established PES programme in the Los Negros Valley in Bolivia. The programme involves payments for two ecosystem services simultaneously: watershed protection and bird habitat. While downstream irrigators are paying local farmers for watershed services (with mainly local benefits), the US Fish and Wildlife Service is paying them for the protection of habitat for migratory bird species (Asquith *et al.*, 2008, cited in OECD, 2010a), which will have global benefits.

It is important to note that the development and scaling up of instruments to help address biodiversity loss and degradation need to be supplemented by more comprehensive and transparent systems to measure, report and verify financial flows towards biodiversity. The OECD data on biodiversity-related bilateral ODA is a good starting point (see Section 3), but similar information is required for national, multilateral and private-sector finance. This would help to better identify where the largest financial gaps are, and thus to help target biodiversity finance more effectively.

Improving knowledge and data for more effective biodiversity policy

Better biodiversity metrics and indicators are an essential pre-requisite for policy interventions that are effective both environmentally and in terms of cost. Metrics and indicators are critical to establish business-as-usual baselines, quantify benefits and target biodiversity expenditures. They also enable the assessment of biodiversity performance and hence the effectiveness of policy interventions over time. There is an urgent need to further develop and improve biodiversity metrics and indicators for local, national and international use. The methodologies applied for the collection and reporting of data should be as consistent as possible, so as to allow for the comparison of information both within and between countries.

At the international level, one of the key applications of indicators is the assessment of global biodiversity trends and progress towards the CBD biodiversity targets. However, as indicated in Section 2, few of the headline indicators used to assess progress towards the CBD targets are available at global level and over time. An extended framework of indicators is currently under consideration to assess progress towards the 2020 Aichi Biodiversity Targets. At the regional level, one of the more developed indicator initiatives is the European Initiative Streamlining European Biodiversity Indicators (SEBI) for 2010, which was established to assess and inform on progress towards the EU 2010 biodiversity targets. A number of countries have developed, or are in the process of developing, complementary national indicator sets. The United Kingdom, for example, has published a list of 18 indicators grouped under six focal areas that are aligned with those used in the CBD and European biodiversity indicators (DEFRA, 2010). However, many countries will need to build scientific and technical capacity, including for information sharing,[27] in order to better assess global biodiversity trends over time.

Metrics and indicators are also needed for the application of national, regional and local biodiversity policies. As the benefits of biodiversity are not constant across space, applying metrics that account for geographic variations (*e.g.* to enable targeting of biodiversity areas with highest benefits), can increase the cost-effectiveness of a policy. In addition to targeting areas with high biodiversity benefits, cost-effectiveness is enhanced by targeting those areas where there is a high risk of biodiversity or ecosystem service loss, or where its provision can be substantially enhanced. Finally, another consideration for cost-effective policy outcomes is to target first those ecosystem service providers with lowest opportunity costs. A number of methods as well as tools (such as spatial mapping) are increasingly being developed and applied to do this. Though the use of more sophisticated targeting approaches can increase the costs of administering a programme, the overall cost-effectiveness gains can increase substantially (see OECD, 2010a).

Another area where data could be improved is in the context of environmental-economic accounting (or green accounting). The purpose is to establish accounts that reflect the depletion and degradation of natural assets, and that integrate information on the economy and the environment by using concepts, definitions and classifications consistent with the System of National Accounts (SNA). Environmental-economic accounts (EEA) can provide policy makers with coherent indicators and statistics to support strategic planning and policy analysis. Several countries have explored or adopted elements of EEA, including Australia, Botswana, Canada, Germany, Namibia, the Netherlands, Norway, and the Philippines (World Bank, 2006). Practical applications generally focus on areas where the demand for accounting tools is clearly identified and linked to specific policy questions – such as the management and planning of natural resources and materials use (*e.g.* water, energy, material flows) or pollution control (emission accounts) – and the associated indicator development. Only a few countries have established comprehensive accounts. Recent developments include:

- work on ecosystem accounts and on the valuation of environmental services, including the World Bank's project on Wealth Accounting and the Valuation of Ecosystem Services (WAVES) that will support the implementation of natural capital accounting and its integration in the national economic accounting framework;

- work by the European Environment Agency (EEA) on ecosystem accounts;

- work in the United Kingdom to integrate natural capital into the UK economic accounts and planning.

A globally recognised framework is the System of Integrated Environmental and Economic Accounting (Box 4.7).

Despite providing essential direct and indirect services to all societies, biodiversity is often given a low priority by decision makers. This is because its value is predominantly implicit rather than explicit, and what cannot be quantified or is difficult to monitor and evaluate is easy to ignore. The recent study on The Economics of Ecosystems and Biodiversity (TEEB, 2010a and 2010b) made a strong case for integrating economics of biodiversity and ecosystem services into decision making by national and local policy makers as well as by

---

Box 4.7. **Environmental-economic accounting: The SEEA**

The System of Integrated Environmental and Economic Accounting (SEEA) was developed in 1993 as a satellite to the System of National Accounts (SNA) and revised in 2003. It aims to address the deficiencies of SNA in dealing with the stocks and flows of natural resources. The SEEA comprises four categories of accounts: i) flow accounts for pollution, energy and materials; ii) environmental protection and resource management expenditure; iii) physical and monetary accounting of environmental assets; and iv) valuation of non-market flow and environmentally adjusted aggregates. The SEEA is currently being revised and comprises three volumes: i) the central framework consisting of agreed concepts, definitions classifications, accounting rules and tables; ii) experimental accounts for ecosystems; and iii) extensions and applications of the SEEA (forthcoming 2012/2013).

Source: UN, EC, IMF, World Bank and OECD (2003), Integrated Environmental and Economic Accounting (SEEA2003), UN Statistical Division, New York and http://unstats.un.org/unsd/envaccounting/seea.asp.

---

businesses. Proper economic valuation of biodiversity and its loss will lead to better, more cost-effective decisions and can help avoid inappropriate trade-offs (OECD, 2002).

There are many applications of biodiversity and ecosystem service valuation. They include the cost-benefit analyses of policies (e.g. those of US federal environmental regulations); determining environmental externality costs of an activity for use in investment decisions or for taxation (e.g. the EC's ExternE Project); undertaking green national accounting (e.g. The European Framework for Integrated Environmental and Economic Accounting for Forests (IEEAF); and determining compensation payments for natural resource damage (e.g. Natural Resource Damage Assessment in the United States) (OECD, 2002). More generally, valuation is essential for raising awareness about the importance of biodiversity conservation and sustainable use.

A number of initiatives to value biodiversity and ecosystem services emerged following the Millennium Ecosystem Assessment (MA, 2005). The UK National Ecosystem Assessment (NEA) is the first national scale assessment to be completed (Box 4.8) with other countries – including Spain, Israel and the United States – at different stages of developing similar assessments.

Box 4.8. **Improving economic decision making for ecosystem goods**

The UK's National Ecosystem Assessment

In 2011, the United Kingdom completed an ambitious National Ecosystem Assessment of how terrestrial, freshwater and marine ecosystems across the United Kingdom have changed over the past 60 years and how they might continue to change in the future. The NEA quantifies the state and value of the natural environment and the services it provides to society. It assesses policy and management options to ensure the integrity of natural systems in the future, and help raise awareness of their central importance to human well-being and economic prosperity. It provides a better basis for linking ecosystems to growth objectives and will be used by the government to direct policy in the future.

Source: UNEP-WCMC (2011), UK National Ecosystem Assessment: Synthesis of Key Findings, UNEP-WCMC, Cambridge, http://uknea.unep-wcmc.org/.

Mainstreaming biodiversity into other policy areas

Related to each of the three priorities identified above is the need to better mainstream and integrate biodiversity into broader national and international policy objectives in other sectors. Policies need to be aligned to ensure that synergies are harnessed and potential trade-offs minimised. One example in the context of environmental policy is the need to account for the inter-linkages between biodiversity and climate change. As noted in Section 2, climate change is projected to play an increasing role in biodiversity loss in the future. Mitigating climate change can therefore also lead to significant biodiversity co-benefits (Box 4.9).

Box 4.9. **What if... ambitious climate change mitigation is done in a way that also reduces biodiversity loss?**

Under the *Environmental Outlook Baseline*, the concentration of greenhouse gases (GHG) in the atmosphere is projected to continue to rise. The corresponding expected temperature increase of 2.4 °C above pre-industrial levels by 2050 (uncertainty range 2.0 °C-2.8 °C) will result in an additional MSA loss of 2.9 percentage points by 2050 (see Figure 4.10 above). The *Environmental Outlook* modelling work has explored a *450 Core* scenario, in which GHG concentrations are stabilised at 450 ppm CO_2eq in order to limit the global average temperature increase to 2 °C above pre-industrial levels by the end of the 21st century with a 50% chance. According to the models, this would reduce MSA loss from climate change between 2010 and 2050 to 1.4 percentage points (see Chapter 3 on climate change and its annex for further information).

There are, however, a number of climate change mitigation options that can be adopted to reach this target, some of which are more biodiversity-friendly than others:

■ In the *450 Core* scenario, about 20% of total primary energy supply by 2050 is assumed to come from the use of bioenergy, requiring a total of 3.1 million km^2 of bioenergy cropland (compared to only 0.9 million km^2 in the *Baseline*). This increased land-use change would drive an additional 1.2 percentage points of MSA loss, although the reduction in global average temperature increase would have positive benefits for biodiversity. The net benefits for biodiversity from the combination of reduced climate change *versus* increased land use and other pressures would be a net gain of 0.1 percentage points by 2050 compared to the *Baseline* (Figure 4.20). The gain would grow over time because of inertia in the climate system, and also simply because the number of harvested bioenergy crops from a dedicated area would increase over time, avoiding even more emissions (see Annex 4.A for more details).

■ Another way of achieving the 450 ppm target, while also preventing the expansion of agricultural areas into natural ecosystems like forests, is explored in the *450 ppm + Reduced Land Use* policy simulation (see Annex 4.A for more details). This involved combining the *450 Core* scenario with projections that assume reduced agricultural expansion. Under this simulation, crop area is projected to decline by 1.2 million km^2 and pastures by 1 million km^2 by 2050 relative to the *Baseline* as a result of increases in agricultural productivity. Under this approach, deforestation due to the level of agricultural expansion projected in the *Baseline* could be completely avoided, reducing forest-related GHG emissions by 12.7GtC in 2050, and delivering 7% of the required emission reduction effort by 2050. The combined biodiversity benefit of climate change mitigation, reduced agricultural land use and other pressures is projected to be an MSA gain of 1.2 percentage points relative to the *Baseline* by 2050. About one-third of the net biodiversity gain would be realised in tropical and temperate forest biomes, and may thus be potentially realised as a co-benefit from climate change mitigation, including REDD incentives.

Chapter 3 also describes a less ambitious 550 ppm mitigation scenario. Under the *550 Core* scenario, bioenergy is assumed to account for 13% of total primary energy supply by 2050. This corresponds to 2.2 million km^2 of bioenergy cropland. The net impact of all changed pressures on biodiversity under the *550 Core* scenario would

---

Box 4.9. **What if... ambitious climate change mitigation is done in a way that also reduces biodiversity loss?** *(cont.)*

now result in a gain of 0.2 percentage points in MSA by 2050 compared to the *Baseline*. However, the long-term improvement would be much less after 2050 and there would be a much higher global average temperature than in the *450 Core* scenario. Reducing bioenergy use even further in this scenario – to only 6.5% of total energy use (the *550 Low Bioenergy* scenario) – would lead to much greater net biodiversity benefits (1.3 percentage points in MSA compared to the *Baseline*). Limiting the contribution from bioenergy will probably lead to additional mitigation costs, strongly depending on the availability of alternatives (*e.g.* in transport).

These simulations (all depicted in Figure 4.20) emphasise the important trade-offs between climate policy, the use of bioenergy, and land use and biodiversity policy. The exact values of the trade-offs are uncertain. First, the negative impacts of bioenergy on biodiversity could potentially be minimised by reducing the extent of land-use change. This might be achieved by implementing higher-yield bioenergy production systems and by concentrating on bioenergy sources that do not require additional land (*e.g.* non-edible residues from agriculture and the forest industry, and the organic parts of municipal solid waste). Further, bioenergy production could be done on land with low biodiversity values (*e.g.* degraded soils), although this is likely to cost more. Finally, it should be noted that the exact future climate change impacts on biodiversity are very uncertain (due to uncertainty in climate responses to increased CO_2 levels, the relationship between climate change and biodiversity, and the indirect GHG emissions that can be attributed to bioenergy use). The results suggest a need to closely monitor the impacts of increased bioenergy use on land-use changes and impacts on biodiversity so as to improve the coherence between climate change and biodiversity policy.

This examination of alternative climate change mitigation portfolios shows the need to evaluate environmental policies using integrated approaches that can highlight potential trade-offs and the delivery of co-benefits between different policy objectives.

Figure 4.20. **Impacts on biodiversity of different *Outlook* climate change mitigation scenarios**

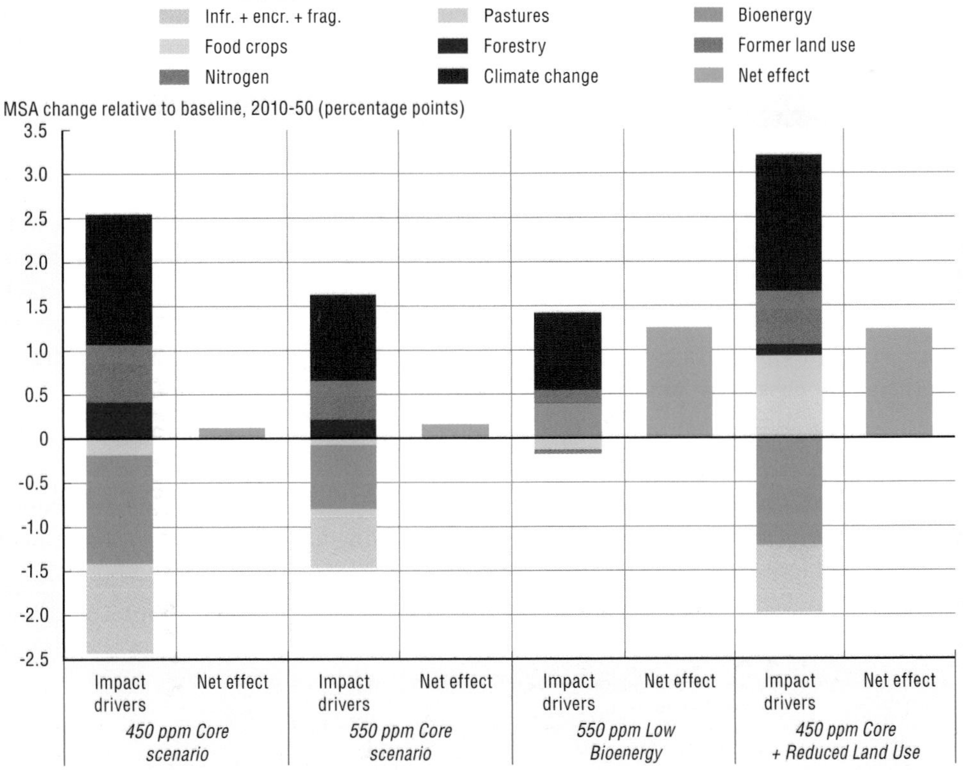

Source: *OECD Environmental Outlook projections; output from IMAGE.*   StatLink ᴍᴮᴸ http://dx.doi.org/10.1787/888932571095

In addition to promoting synergies among different environmental objectives, it is critical to also identify synergies and trade-offs that exist beyond the environmental agenda. In terms of biodiversity conservation and employment synergies for example, investment in the protection of biodiversity in a Mayan reserve in Guatemala generated annual earnings of close to USD 50 million, creating 7 000 jobs and increasing the earning of local families (UNEP, 2010). Many of the drivers of biodiversity and ecosystem service loss and degradation stem from policies outside the auspices of environmental ministries. Mainstreaming and integrating biodiversity objectives more broadly across national economic objectives is one element in the broader pursuit of an effective green growth strategy (OECD, 2012); it is also fundamental to the success of the *CBD Strategic Plan 2011-2020* (CBD, 2010; see Strategic Goal A and Target 2 in Box 4.4).

Mainstreaming of biodiversity will be realised through changes in policies, strategies, plans, programmes and budgets. It will require a more consistent, co-ordinated and strategic response to the multiple priorities faced by national governments, along with high-level political commitment and stakeholder involvement. Core policy areas of relevance include agriculture, urban development practices, transport, energy for biofuels, forestry and climate change. A framework for developing a more comprehensive, integrated approach to tackling the challenge of biodiversity and ecosystem service loss is summarised in Box 4.10 (OECD, 2011c).

Box 4.10. **A strategy for green growth and biodiversity**

Key elements of a proposed green growth strategy for biodiversity entail the following:

i)   Assess business-as-usual projections for biodiversity trends (taking into account population growth, economic growth, and demand for agriculture in particular). This would help to determine the reference point (or *Baseline*) against which future progress could be assessed. This process would serve to identify the key drivers of biodiversity loss and degradation and where change is projected to occur most rapidly.

ii) Develop a long-term vision for green growth and biodiversity (*e.g.* developed by a joint high-level task force and based on cost-benefit analysis). This would need to be undertaken in co-ordination (and in tandem) with similar green growth efforts across other areas and sectors of the economy, including agriculture, energy, climate change, and development. To foster better co-ordination and collaboration between different ministries (environment, economics, agriculture, energy, treasury, etc.), joint high-level task forces could be created to develop the long-term vision in such a way as to capture available synergies and to address potential trade-offs. To the extent possible, a long-term vision would be based on cost-benefit analysis.

iii) Identify least-cost policy options and areas for intervention (to identify policy priorities and sequencing).

iv) Implement the strategy. This would involve selecting the appropriate instruments (regulatory, economic and voluntary) from the policy toolbox and putting in place the policy instrument mix needed to achieve the interim and long-term goals.

v)   Monitor and review the strategy: track progress towards the goals, and revise approaches over time to improve them, based on new information and lessons learned.

Source: Based on OECD (2012), "Green Growth and Biodiversity", OECD, Publishing.

Notes

1. The United Nations Framework Convention on Climate Change (UNFCCC), the Convention on Biological Diversity (CBD) and the United Nations Convention to Combat Desertification (UNCCD).

2. See *www.bipindicators.net/indicators*. Additional indicators are being considered for the 2020 biodiversity targets.

3. The marine trophic index is based on data of global catch composition and indicates the mean trophic level (position on the food chain) of fisheries catches.

4. For a description of the GLOBIO model used for the computation of mean species abundance, see Annex A, Modelling Framework, at the end of this *Environmental Outlook* report.

5. Biomes are a generalised natural ecosystem type. They are defined by soil types and climate conditions (Prentice *et al.*, 1992).

6. This does not imply that there has been greater species loss in, for example, temperate forests as tropical forests tend to be more species rich.

7. Several factors may account for the differences in species abundance estimated by the MSA and LPI: The LPI only considers vertebrate species, whereas MSA comprises all species; in contrast to the MSA, the LPI definition of a temperate zone includes the arctic polar and tundra regions; the MSA indicator covers terrestrial systems, while the LPI covers terrestrial, marine and freshwater biodiversity; the LPI uses the geometric mean, which makes it difficult to deal with extinctions since the geometric mean can only be applied to positive values.

8. The index can be calculated for any set of species that has been assessed at least twice for the IUCN Red List.

9. Forest cover, as defined by the FAO (FAO, 2010b), is forest land spanning more than 0.5 hectares with trees higher than 5 metres and a canopy cover of more than 10%. It does not include land that is predominantly under agricultural or urban land use.

10. Fully exploited means the fishery is operating at or close to an optimal yield level, with no expected room for further expansion.

11. This index tracks changes in 2 023 populations of 636 species of fish, seabirds, marine turtles and marine mammals found in temperate and tropical marine ecosystems.

12. See Alkemade *et al.*, 2009 and Annex A to this *Environmental Outlook* on the Modelling Framework.

13. The rate of increase is probably an overestimation, due to data limitations on historical forest use. In 2010, the total reported forest area in use for wood production was about one-third of the global forest area according to the FAO (2010b). However, in the *Baseline* projections this level is only reached by 2050. This difference is most probably caused by the fact that most of the projected forest use increase will in reality be re-use of forest that has already been logged in previous decades (pre-1970). There are however no long-term trends on forest use reported in FAO census statistics (consecutive Forest Resource Assessments) that cover this historical period.

14. Invasive alien species and other forms of pollution are not included in the GLOBIO model used for the *Environmental Outlook*, nor is marine over-exploitation. Terrestrial over-exploitation of natural resources is partially and indirectly addressed under land-use and encroachment.

15. Invasive alien species are defined by the IUCN as "animals, plants or other organisms introduced by man into places out of their natural range of distribution, where they become established and disperse, generating a negative impact on the local ecosystem and species" (IUCN, 2011). An example is the arrival of the Brown Tree Snake (*Boiga irregularis*) in Guam, which caused the near-total extinction of native forest birds (ISSG, 2000).

16. The Global Transboundary Conservation Network was launched at the Vth IUCN World Parks Congress to provide expertise and guidance on all aspects of transboundary conservation planning, management and governance. See *www.tbpa.net/page.php?ndx=78*.

17. The IUCN recognises seven categories of protected areas ranging from those where human activity is severely restricted, to those where only certain aspects of the natural environment are prohibited from being altered. These categories recognise that protection and sustainable use are complex objectives that have to be achieved in different ways to serve various social goals.

18. DDT (Dichlorodiphenyltrichloroethane) is a synthetic pesticide that was banned for agricultural use worldwide, under the Stockholm Convention. DDT has been linked to poor human health and declines in a number of bird species including the Bald Eagle and the Brown Pelican.

19. Reducing emissions from deforestation and forest degradation (REDD) is a new financial mechanism proposed for the post-2012 climate change regime under the auspices of the United Nations Framework Convention on Climate Change (UNFCCC). REDD was expanded to include conservation, sustainable forest management, and enhancement of carbon stocks, as listed in the Bali Action Plan (Decision 1/CP. 13), and is collectively referred to as REDD-plus.

20. One role of the Convention on Biological Diversity (CBD) is to provide countries with a set of principles, obligations and responsibilities on how access to genetic resources can be provided and benefits arising from use of such resources be shared.

21. The Nagoya Protocol is a commitment to attain prior-informed consent from the country of origin before accessing genetic resources and to share both monetary and non-monetary benefits derived from genetic resource use, based on mutually agreed terms.

22. "Biodiversity-related aid" refers to activities that contribute to at least one of the three objectives of the CBD: i) conservation of biodiversity; ii) sustainable use of its components; and iii) fair and equitable sharing of the benefits from the use of genetic resources.

23. Activities that are considered to be biodiversity-related aid can be scored as significant or principal. The activity will score "principal objective" only if it *directly* and *explicitly aims* to achieve one of the three objectives of the CBD.

24. Norway and the United States will provide almost 50% of this. Six countries – Norway, United States, Japan, Germany, United Kingdom, France – account for 88% of the total commitments, while the remaining 12% is shared by 8 other sources (Simula, 2010).

25. Definition from IEA Bioenergy Task 39 (2009).

26. Innovative finance for biodiversity refers to new and emerging instruments, such as payments for ecosystem services (PES) and international PES (IPES), biodiversity offsets and banking, and the auctioning of tradable permits, among others (see Section 3).

27. An example of an information sharing initiative is the Global Biological Information Facility.

References

Ahlenius, H. (2004), *Global Development and Biodiversity*, UNEP/GRID-Arendal Maps and Graphics Library, *http://maps.grida.no/go/graphic/global-development-and-biodiversity*.

Alkemade, R. *et al.* (2009), "GLOBIO3: A Framework to Investigate Options for Reducing Global Terrestrial Biodiversity Loss", *Ecosystems* 12: 374-390.

Alves, R. and I. Rosa (2007), "Biodiversity, Traditional Medicine and Public Health: Where Do they Meet?", *Journal of Ethnobiology and Ethnomedicine*, 3(14).

Andrade Pérez, A., B. Herrera Fernandez and R. Cazzolla Gatti (eds.) (2010), *Building Resilience to Climate Change: Ecosystem-based adaptation and lessons from the field.* Gland, Switzerland: IUCN.

Arnason, R. (2008), *Rents and Rent Drain in the Icelandic Cod Fishery, Revised Draft*, prepared for the World Bank PROFISH Program, Washington, DC.

Balmford, A. *et al.* (2002), "Economic Reasons for Conserving Wild Nature", *Science*, 297(5583): 950-953.

Beaumont, N., M. Austen, S. Mangi and M. Townsend (2006), "Marine Biodiversity: An Economic Valuation", DEFRA, London.

Beckage, B. *et al.* (2007), "A Rapid Upward Shift of a Forest Ecotone During 40 Years of Warming in the Green Mountains of Vermont", *PNAS* (Proceedings of the National Academy of Sciences of the United States of America), 105: 4197-4202.

Bennett, G. and K.J. Mulongoy (2006), "Review of Experience with Ecological Networks, Corridors and Buffer Zones", Technical Series No. 23, SCBD (Secretariat of the Convention on Biological Diversity), Montreal.

Berry, P., (2007), *Adaptation Options on Natural Ecosystems. A Report to the UNFCCC Secretariat Financial and Technical Support Division*, UNFCCC (United Nations Framework Convention on Climate Change), Bonn.

Billen, G. and J. Garnier (2007), "River Basin Nutrient Delivery to the Coastal Sea: Assessing its Potential to Sustain New Production of Non-Siliceous Algae", *Marine Chemistry*, Vol. 106(1-2): 148-160.

Brink, P. ten *et al.* (2008), "Critical Thresholds, Evaluation and Regional Development", *European Environment*, Vol. 18: 81-95.

Brink, B. ten *et al.* (2010), *Rethinking Global Biodiversity Strategies: Exploring Structural Changes in Production and Consumption to Reduce Biodiversity Loss*, PBL Netherlands Environment Assessment Agency, The Hague/Bilthoven.

Brooks, T.M. *et al.* (2006), "Global Biodiversity Conservation Priorities", *Science*, 313(5783): 58-61.

Butchart, S. *et al.* (2010), "Global Biodiversity: Indicators of Recent Declines", *Science*, 348(5982): 1164-1168.

Cao, M. and I. Woodward (1998), "Net Primary and Ecosystem Production and Carbon Stocks of Terrestrial Ecosystems and their Responses to Climate Change", *Global Change Biology*, 4: 185-198.

CBD (Convention on Biological Diversity) (2005), *Biodiversity-Inclusive Impact Assessment: Information Document in Support of the CBD Guidelines on Biodiversity in EIA and SEA*, Conference of the Parties to the CBD, Montreal.

CBD (2010), *Strategic Plan for Biodiversity 2011-2020, Including Aichi Biodiversity Targets* CBD, Montreal.

Chivian, E. (ed.) (2002), *Biodiversity: Its Importance to Human Health, Interim Executive Summary*, Center for Health and the Global Environment, Harvard Medical School, Boston, MA.

CITES (Convention on International Trade in Endangered Species) (2011), Convention on International Trade in Endangered Species of Wild Fauna and Flora, *www.cites.org*.

Coad, L., N. Burgess, B. Bomhard and C. Besançon (2009), "Progress Towards the Convention on Biological Diversity's 2010 and 2012 Targets for Protected Area Coverage", A technical report for the IUCN international workshop, *Looking to the Future of the CBD Programme of the CBD Programme of Work on Protected Areas*, Jeju Island, Republic of Korea, 14-17 September 2009, IUCN, Gland.

COHAB (Co-operation on Health and Biodiversity) Initiative (2010), "The Importance of Biodiversity to Human Health", *UN CBD COP 10 Policy Brief 10*, COHAB Initiative Secretariat, Galway, Ireland.

Conservation International (2004), Biodiversity Hotspots Revisited (Data Basin Dataset) *www.arcgis.com/home/item.html?id=bc755b56fce8492d9817a9de49255f99*.

Corfee-Morlot, J., B. Guay and K.M. Larsen (2009), *Financing Climate Change Mitigation: Towards a Framework for Measurement, Reporting and Verification*, OECD/IEA (International Energy Agency), Paris.

Costello, C., S. Gaines and J. Lynhams (2008), "Can Catch Shares Prevent Fisheries Collapse?", *Science*, 321 (1678).

Dalal, R. and D. Allen (2008), "Greenhouse Gas Fluxes from Natural Ecosystems", *Australian Journal of Botany*, Vol. 56: 369-407.

DEFRA (Department for the Environment Food and Rural Affairs) (2010), *UK Biodiversity Indicators in Your Pocket 2010: Measuring Progress Towards Halting Biodiversity Loss*, DEFRA, London.

Doornbosch, R. and R. Steenblik (2007), "Biofuels – Is the Cure Worse than the Disease?" Official report by the OECD presented at the *Round Table on Sustainable Development*, Paris, 11-12 September 2007.

Dybas, C.L. (2005), "Dead Zones Spreading in World Oceans", *Bioscience*, 55, 552-557.

Eickhout, B. *et al.* (2006), "Modelling Agricultural Trade and Food Production under Different Trade Policies", in A.F. Bouwman, T. Kram and K. Klein Goldewijk (eds.), *Integrated Modelling of Global Environmental Change: An Overview of IMAGE 2.4*, PBL Netherlands Environmental Assessment Agency, The Hague/Bilthoven.

Emerton, L. and E. Bos (2004), *Value: Counting Ecosystems as Water Infrastructure*, IUCN (International Union for Conservation of Nature and Natural Resources), Gland, Switzerland and Cambridge, UK.

Everaert, J. and E. Stienen (2006), "Impact of Wind Turbines in Zeebrugge (Belgium): Significant Effect on Breeding Tern Colony Due to Collisions", *Biodiversity and Conservation*, 16: 3345-3359.

FAO (Food and Agriculture Organization of the United Nations) (2006), *The Global Forests Resource Assessment: 2005*, FAO, Rome.

FAO (2010a), *The State of the World's Fisheries and Aquaculture: 2010*, FAO, Rome.

FAO (2010b), *The Global Forests Resource Assessment: 2010*, FAO, Rome.

Gaines, S., C. White, M. Carr and S. Palumbi (2010), "Designing Marine Reserve Networks for Both Conservation and Fisheries Management", PNAS (Proceedings of the National Academy of Sciences of the United States of America), 107 (43): 18286-18293.

Gallai N., J.M. Salles, J. Settele and B.E. Vaissière (2009), "Economic Valuation of the Vulnerability of World Agriculture Confronted with Pollinator Decline", *Ecological Economics*, 68, 810-821.

GFCM (General Fisheries Commission for the Mediterranean) (2005), "Recommendation GFCM/2005/1: On The Management of Certain Fisheries Exploiting Demersal and Deepwater Species", *2005 GFCM Recommendations on Mediterranean Fisheries Management*, GFCM, Rome.

Groffman, P. *et al.* (2006), "Ecological Thresholds: The Key to Successful Environmental Management or an Important Concept with No Practical Application?", *Ecosystems* 9: 1-13.

Haites, E. (2011), "Climate Change Finance", *Climate Policy*, 11(3): 963-969.

Halpern, B. (2003), "The Impact of Marine Reserves: Do Reserves Work and Does Reserve Size Matter?", *Ecological Society of America*, Vol. 13(1): 117-137.

Hamilton, A. (2003), *Medicinal Plants and Conservation: Issues and Approaches*, International Plants Conservation Unit, WWF-UK, Godalming, UK.

Heal G. *et al.* (2002), "Genetic Diversity and Interdependent Crop Choices in Agriculture", *Beijer Discussion Paper* 170, The Beijer Institute of Ecological Economics, The Royal Swedish Academy of Sciences, Stockholm.

Hilton-Taylor, C. *et al.* (2008), "Status of the World's Species", in J.-C. Vié, C. Hilton-Taylor and S.N. Stuart (eds.), *The 2008 Review of the IUCN Red List of Threatened Species*, IUCN, Gland, Switzerland.

House of Commons Environmental Audit Committee (2008), *Are Biofuels Sustainable? First Report of Session 2007-08*, Vol. 1, The Stationery Office, by order of the House of Commons, London.

IAIA (International Association for Impact Assessment) (1999), *Principles of Environmental Impact Assessment Best Practice*, IAIA, Fargo, North Dakota.

IEA Bioenergy Task 39 (2009), Commercializing 1st- and 2nd-generation Liquid Biofuels: Definitions, *www.task39.org/About/Definitions/tabid/1761/language/en-US/Default.aspx*.

IPBES (2011), Intergovernmental Platform on Biodiversity and Ecosystem Services, website *http://ipbes.net*.

IPCC (Intergovernmental Panel on Climate Change) (2001), *Climate Change 2001: Synthesis Report. A Contribution of Working Groups I, II, and III to the Third Assessment Report of the Intergovernmental Panel on Climate Change*, Cambridge University Press, Cambridge.

IPCC (2007), *Climate Change 2007: Synthesis Report. Contribution of Working Groups I, II, III to the Fourth Assessment. Report of the Intergovernmental Panel on Climate Change*, IPCC, Geneva, Switzerland.

ISSG (Invasive Species Specialist Group)(2000), *Aliens 12*, IUCN, Gland, Switzerland.

IUCN (International Union for Conservation of Nature and Natural Resources) (2011), *Invasive Species*, IUCN website, *www.iucn.org/about/union/secretariat/offices/iucnmed/iucn_med_programme/species/invasive_species/*.

IUCN and UNEP (United Nations Environment Programme) (2011a), *The World Database on Protected Areas (WDPA)*,UNEP-WCMC (World Conservation Monitoring Centre), Cambridge, UK, data accessed January 2011.

IUCN and UNEP (2011b), *The World Database on Protected Areas (WDPA)*, UNEP-WCMC (World Conservation Monitoring Centre), Cambridge, UK, data accessed April 2011.

James, A., K. Gaston and A. Balmford (2001), "Can We Afford to Conserve Biodiversity?", *BioScience*, 5(1): 43-52.

Kapos, V. *et al.* (eds.) (2008), *Carbon and Biodiversity: a Demonstration Atlas,* UNEP-WCMC, Cambridge, UK.

Karousakis, K. (2009), "Promoting Biodiversity Co-Benefits in REDD", *OECD Environment Working Papers*, No. 11, OECD Publishing, doi: *10.1787/220188577008*.

Kate, K. ten, J. Bishop and R. Bayon (2004), *Biodiversity Offsets: Views, Experience, and the Business Case*, IUCN Gland, Switzerland, Cambridge and Insight Investment London.

Kindermann, G. *et al.* (2008), "Global Cost Estimates of Reducing Carbon Emissions through Avoided Deforestation", PNAS (Proceedings of the National Academy of Sciences of the United States of America) 105(30): 10302-10307.

Larsen, H. (2006), "The Use of Green Taxes in Denmark for the Control of the Aquatic Environment", in OECD, *Evaluating Agri-Environmental Policies: Design, Practice and Results*, OECD Publishing. doi: *10.1787/9789264010116-20-en*.

Leverington, F., M. Hockings and K. Costa (2008), *Management Effectiveness Evaluation in Protected Areas: Report for the Project "Global Study into Management Effectiveness Evaluation of Protected Areas"*, The University of Queensland, Gatton, IUCN, WCPA, TNC, WWF, Australia.

Loh, J. *et al.* (2010), "Monitoring Biodiversity – the Living Planet Index", in: WWF (World Wide Fund for Nature), ZSL (Zoological Society of London) and GFN (Global Footprint Network), *Living Planet Report 2010 Biodiversity, Biocapacity and Development*, WWF, Gland, Switzerland.

MA (Millennium Ecosystem Assessment) (2005), *Millennium Ecosystem Assessment – Ecosystems and Human Well-being: Biodiversity Synthesis*, World Resources Institute, Washington, DC.

McDonald, I. (2009), "Current Trends in Ethnobotany", *Tropical Journal of Pharmaceutical Research*, 8(4): 295-296

Myers, R., J. Baum T. Shepherd S. Powers and C. Peterson (2007), "Cascading Effects of the Loss of Apex Predatory Sharks from a Coastal Ocean", *Science*, 315(5820): 1846-1850.

Natura 2000 (2010), *Natura 2000 Good Practice Exchange* website, *www.natura2000exchange.eu*, accessed 10 May 2010.

Nature Conservancy, The (2011), "Working with Companies: Dow Announces Business Strategy for Conservation", Nature Conservancy website, *www.nature.org/aboutus/ourpartners/workingwithcompanies/explore/dow-announces-business-strategic-for-conservation.xml*.

New, T. and Z. Xie (2008), "Impacts of Large Dams on Riparian Vegetation: Applying Global Experience to the Case of China's Three Gorges Dam", *Biodiversity and Conservation*, 17: 3149-3163.

Newman, D. and G. Cragg (2007), "Natural Products as Sources of New Drugs over the Last 25 Years", *Journal of Natural Products*, 70(3): 461-477.

Nowak, D., D. Crane and J. Stevens (2006), "Air Pollution Removal by Urban Trees and Shrubs in the United States", *Urban Forestry and Urban Greening*, 4: 115-123.

OECD (2000), *Voluntary Approaches for Environmental Policy: An Assessment*, OECD Publishing. doi: 10.1787/9789264180260-en.

OECD (2002), *Handbook of Biodiversity Valuation: A Guide for Policy Makers*, OECD Publishing. doi: 10.1787/9789264175792-en.

OECD (2003), *Voluntary Approaches for Environmental Policy: Effectiveness, Efficiency and Usage in Policy Mixes*, OECD Publishing, doi: 10.1787/9789264101784-en.

OECD (2006), *Applying Strategic Environmental Assessment: Good Practice Guidance for Development Co-operation*, DAC Guidelines and Reference Series, OECD Publishing, doi: 10.1787/9789264026582-en.

OECD (2007), *Instrument Mixes for Environmental Policy*, OECD Publishing, doi: 10.1787/9789264018419-en.

OECD (2008a), *Costs of Inaction on Key Environmental Challenges*, OECD Publishing. doi: 10.1787/9789264045828-en.

OECD (2008b), *OECD Environmental Outlook to 2030*, OECD Publishing, doi: 10.1787/9789264040519-en.

OECD (2008c), *Biofuel Support Policies: An Economic Assessment*, OECD Publishing. doi: 10.1787/9789264050112-en.

OECD (2008d), *Report on Implementation of the 2004 Council Recommendation on the Use of Economic Instruments in Promoting the Conservation and Sustainable Use of Biodiversity*, Working Group on Economic Aspects of Biodiversity, OECD, Paris.

OECD (2008e), *People and Biodiversity Policies: Impacts, Issues and Strategies for Policy Action*, OECD Publishing, doi: 10.1787/9789264034341-en.

OECD (2009a), *Natural Resources and Pro-Poor Growth: The Economics and Politics*, DAC Guidelines and Reference Series, OECD Publishing, doi: 10.1787/9789264060258-en.

OECD (2009b), *Agricultural Policies in OECD Countries 2009: Monitoring and Evaluation*, OECD Publishing, doi: 10.1787/agr_oecd-2009-en.

OECD (2009c), *The Bioeconomy to 2030: Designing a Policy Agenda*, OECD Publishing. doi: 10.1787/9789264056886-en.

OECD (2010a), *Paying for Biodiversity: Enhancing the Cost-Effectiveness of Payments for Ecosystem Services*, OECD Publishing, doi: 10.1787/9789264090279-en.

OECD (2010b), *ODA for Biodiversity*, OECD Creditor Reporting System online, OECD Publishing, *http://stats.oecd.org/* (Development).

OECD (2011a), *Towards Green Growth*, OECD Green Growth Studies, OECD Publishing. doi: 10.1787/9789264111318-en.

OECD (2011b), *Greening Household Behaviour: The Role of Public Policy*, OECD Publishing. doi: 10.1787/9789264096875-en.

OECD (2012), "Green Growth and Biodiversity", OECD Publishing.

Olsen, R. (2006), "Climate Change and Floodplain Management in the United States", *Climatic Change*, 76(3-4): 407-426.

Olsen, D.M., E. Dinerstein *et al.* (2001), "Terrestrial Ecoregions of the World: A New Map of Life on Earth", *Bioscience* 51(11): 933-938.

Paerl, H. *et al.* (2003), "Phytoplankton Photopigments as Indicators of Estuarine and Coastal Eutrophication", *BioScience*, 53(10): 953-964.

Parker, C. and M. Cranford (2010), *The Little Biodiversity Finance Book*, Global Canopy Programme, Oxford.

Peréz, A., R. Gatti and B. Fernández (2011), "Building Resilience to Climate Change: Ecosystem Based Adaptation and Lessons from the Field", *Ecosystem Management Series*, No. 9, IUCN, Gland, Switzerland.

Pimental, D., R. Zuniga, D. Morrison (2005), "Update on the Environmental and Economic Costs Associated with Alien-Invasive Species in the United States", *Ecological Economics* 52: 273-288.

Prentice, I. *et al.* (1992), "A Global Biome Model Based on Plant Physiology and Dominance, Soil Properties and Climate", *Journal of Biogeography*, 19, 117-134.

Prip, C., T. Gross, S. Johnston and M. Vlerros (2010), "Biodiversity Planning: An Assessment of National Biodiversity Strategies and Action Plans", United Nations University Institute of Advanced Studies, Yokohama, Japan.

Quanlin, Q. (2011), "Pearl River Fishing Ban May Reduce Net Loss", *China Daily*, 14/04/2011 *www.chinadaily.com.cn/cndy/2011-04/14/content_12322894.htm*.

Rockström, J. *et al.* (2009), "Planetary Boundaries: Exploring the Safe Operating Space for Humanity", *Ecology and Society*, 14, No. 2, 32.

Royal Society, The (2008), *Sustainable Bioenergy: Prospects and Challenges*, The Royal Society, London.

Russ, G. *et al.* (2008), "Rapid Increase in Fish Numbers Follows Creation of World's Largest Marine Reserve Network", *Current Biology*, 18(12): 514-515.

Sala, O.E. *et al.* (2000), "Global Biodiversity Scenarios for the Year 2100", *Science*, 287: 1770-1774.

Salazar, L.F., C.A. Nobre and M.D. Oyama (2007), "Climate Change Consequences on the Biome Distribution in Tropical South America", *Geophysical Research Letters*, 34, L09708.

SCBD (Secretariat of the Convention on Biological Diversity) (2009a), *Invasive Alien Species: A Threat to Biodiversity*, SCBD, Montreal.

SCBD (2009b), *Biodiversity, Development and Poverty Alleviation: Recognizing the Role of Biodiversity for Human Well-Being*, SCBD, Montreal.

SCBD (2009c), "Review of the Literature on the Links Between Biodiversity and Climate Change: Impacts, Adaptation and Mitigation", *CBD Technical Series*, No. 42, SCBD, Montreal.

SCBD (2010a), *Global Biodiversity Outlook 3*, SCBD, Montreal.

SCBD (2010b), *Updating and Revision of the Strategic Plan for the Post-2010 Period*, SCBD, Montreal.

Scheffer, M. *et al.* (2009), "Early Warning Signals for Critical Transitions", *Nature*, 461 53-59.

Simula, M. (1999), *Trade and Environmental Issues in Forest Production. Environment Division Working Paper*, Inter-American Development Bank.

Simula, M. (2010), "Analysis of REDD+ Financing Gaps and Overlaps", REDD+ Partnership, *www.reddpartnership.org*.

Smith, K. and W. Darwall (2006), *The Status and Distribution of Freshwater Fish Endemic to the Mediterranean Basin*, IUCN, Gland, Switzerland and Cambridge, UK.

Stein, B., L. Kutner and J. Adams (2000), *Precious Heritage. The Status of Biodiversity in the United States*, Oxford University Press, New York.

Sudmeier-Rieux, K. (2006), *Ecosystems, Livelihoods and Disasters: an Integrated Approach to Disaster Risk Management*, IUCN, Gland, Switzerland and Cambridge, UK.

TEEB (The Economics of Ecosystems and Biodiversity) (2009), *The Economics of Ecosystems and Biodiversity for National and International Policy Makers – Summary: Responding to the Value of Nature*, TEEB, United Nations Environment Programme, Geneva.

TEEB (2010a), *The Economics of Ecosystems and Biodiversity: Mainstreaming the Economics of Nature: A Synthesis of the Approach, Conclusions and Recommendations of TEEB*, TEEB, United Nations Environment Programme, Geneva.

TEEB (2010b), *The Economics of Ecosystems and Biodiversity: Report for Business*, TEEB, United Nations Environment Programme, Geneva.

Treweek, J. (2009), *Scoping Study for the Design and Use of Biodiversity Offsets in an English Context: Final Report to Defra*, DEFRA (Department for the Environment Farming and Rural Affairs), UK.

UN, EC (European Commission), IMF (International Monetary Fund), World Bank, OECD, (2003), *Integrated Environmental and Economic Accounting (SEEA 2003)*, UN Statistical Division, New York.

UNDP (United Nations Development Programme) (2004), *Human Development Report 2004: Cultural Liberty in Today's Diverse World*, United Nations Development Programme. New York

UNEP (United Nations Environment Programme) (2007), *Global Environmental Outlook 4: Environment for Development*, UNEP, Nairobi.

UNEP (2010), *Our Planet: Biodiversity – Our Life*. Nairobi, Kenya. *www.unep.org/ourplanet*.

UNEP-WCMC (World Conservation Monitoring Centre) (2008), *State of the World's Protected Areas 2007: an Annual Review of Global Conservation Progress*, UNEP-WCMC, Cambridge, *www.unep-wcmc.org/medialibrary/2010/09/17/f3a52175/stateOfTheWorldsProtectedAreas.pdf*.

UNEP-WCMC (2011), *UK National Ecosystem Assessment: Synthesis of Key Findings*, UNEP-WCMC, Cambridge, *http://uknea.unep-wcmc.org/*.

Vinodhini, R., M. Narayanan (2008), "Bioaccumulation of Heavy Metals in Organs of Fresh Water Fish Cyprinus carpio (Common Carp)", *International Journal of Environmental Science Technology* 5 (2): 179-182.

Vittor, A. *et al.* (2006), "The Effect of Deforestation on the Human-Biting Rate of *Anopheles darlingi*, the Primary Vector of Falciparum Malaria in the Peruvian Amazon", *American Journal of Tropical Medicine and Hygiene*, 74: 3-11.

Vuuren, D. van, E. Bellevrat, A. Kitous, and M. Isaac (2010), "Bioenergy Use and Low Stabilization Scenarios", *The Energy Journal*, Vol. 31: 192-222.

Walker, B., C. Holling, S. Carpenter and A. Knizig (2004), "Resilience, Adaptability and Transformability in Social-Ecological Systems", *Ecology and Society*, 9(2): 5.

WHO (World Health Organization) (2002), *Traditional Medicine Strategy (2002-2005)*,WHO, Geneva.

World Bank (2004), *Sustaining Forests: A Development Strategy*, World Bank, Washington, DC.

World Bank (2006), *Where is the Wealth of Nations? Measuring Capital for the 21st Century*, World Bank, Washington, DC.

World Bank (2008), *World Development Report 2008: Agriculture for Development*, World Bank, Washington, DC.

World Bank (2011), *Implementation Status and Results. Colombia: Integrated National Adaptation Program (P083075)*, Report Number ISR2733, World Bank, Washington, DC.

Wunder, S. (2005), "Payments for Environmental Services: Some Nuts and Bolts", *CIFOR Occasional Paper*, No. 42, Center for International Forestry Research, Bogor, Indonesia.

WWF (World Wildlife Fund), ZSL (Zoological Society London) and GFN (Global Footprint Network) (2010), *Living Planet Report 2010: Biodiversity, Biocapacity and Development*, WWF, Gland, Switzerland.

Yachi, S. and M. Loreau (1999), "Biodiversity and Ecosystem Productivity in a Fluctuating Environment: The Insurance Hypothesis", *PNAS* 96: 1463-1468.

Zaghi, D. *et al.* (2010), *Literature Study on the Impact of Biodiversity Changes on Human Health*, Comunità Ambient Srl, Report for the European Commission (Directorate General Environment), EC, Brussels.

ANNEX 4.A

Modelling Background Information on Biodiversity

This annex provides further detail on the following modelling aspects:

■ a summary of the projected socio-economic developments behind the *Baseline* scenario;

■ the Expanded Terrestrial Protected Areas scenario;

■ the biodiversity impacts of different climate change mitigation scenarios.

Socio-economic developments in the Baseline scenario

The *Environmental Outlook Baseline* scenario makes projections of a number of socio-economic developments outlined below (and further discussed in Chapters 1 and 2), and these in turn were used to construct the *Baseline* projections on biodiversity-related issues discussed in this chapter:

■ World GDP is projected to nearly quadruple over the coming four decades, in line with the past 40 years and based on detailed projections on the main drivers of economic growth. By 2050, the OECD's share of the global economy is assumed to decline from 54% in 2010 to less than 32%, while the share of Brazil, Russia, India, Indonesia, China and South Africa (BRIICS) is assumed to grow to more than 40%.

■ By 2050, the world is assumed to add over 2.2 billion people to the current 7 billion. All world regions are assumed to be facing population ageing but will be at different stages of this demographic transition.

■ By 2050, nearly 70% of the world's population is assumed to be living in urban areas.

■ World energy demand is assumed to be 80% higher in 2050 under current policies. The 2050 global energy mix is assumed to be fairly similar to that of today, with the share of fossil energy still at about 85% (of commercial energy), renewables including biofuels (but excluding traditional biomass) just above 10%, and the balance being nuclear. Among fossil fuels, it is uncertain whether coal or gas will be the main source of increased energy supply.

■ Globally, the area of agricultural land is assumed to expand in the next decade, but at a slower rate. It is assumed to peak before 2030 to match the increase in food demand from a growing population, and decline thereafter, as population growth slows down and yield improvements continue. Deforestation rates are already declining, and this trend is assumed to continue, especially after 2030 with demand for more agricultural land easing (Section 3, Chapter 2).

The Expanded Terrestrial Protected Areas scenario

For the Expanded Terrestrial Protected Areas scenario (Box 4.5 in main text), a geo-explicit network of protected areas (PAs) was designed, consistent with the new CBD target of 17% PAs by 2020, with a representative cover of global ecosystem types (ecoregions).

A map with current PAs served as a starting point (IUCN and UNEP, 2011b). To date, a total of about 19 million km^2 of terrestrial area is reported to have protected status (IUCN and UNEP, 2011; Coad *et al.*, 2009). However, due to spatial inaccuracies, only 15.6 million km^2 could be taken into account for this simulation (12%).

Newly protected areas were selected, based on the following criteria:

■ Ecoregions are implemented as a combination of bio-geographic realms and major biome types (Olsen *et al.*, 2001), giving a total of 65. The assumption is that the 65 ecoregions sufficiently distinguish between the different ecosystem and species types found globally to attain a representative situation. A further spatial disaggregation (for instance using the 200 WWF ecoregions) could not be performed due to (spatial) data limitations. New areas were added until the 17% area criterion was reached for each ecoregion.

■ Preference was given to those parts of an ecoregion that present "hotspot" areas for biodiversity. Selection of biodiversity-rich areas can be done for different species groups and purposes, and therefore such selection always involves some degree of subjectivity (Brooks *et al.*, 2006). A UNEP-WCMC map was used that combines several indicators to select biodiversity-rich areas (Kapos *et al.*, 2008). The following biodiversity indicators are included in the UNEP-WCMC overlay (see Figure 4.A1): Birdlife International's endemic bird areas; amphibian diversity areas, WWF's Global 200 terrestrial ecoregions, Conservation International's biodiversity hotspots and WWF/IUCN's centres of plant diversity.

■ When necessary, preference was given to those cells that are nearest to agricultural land. These areas probably receive the largest threat from agricultural expansion.

Figure 4.A1. **Overlapping global biodiversity priority schemes**

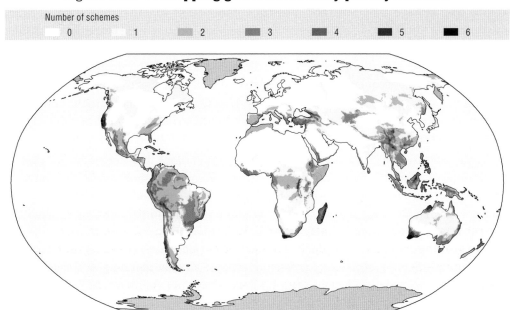

Note: The higher the number of overlapping schemes, the higher the consensus on the globally important areas for biodiversity conservation (Kapos *et al.*, 2008).

Representativeness of global ecosystem types (ecoregions) and hotspots is the prime criterion for this gap analysis, and not the absolute number of species, or species richness. This is in accordance with the CBD target, and indicators reported in the Global Biodiversity Outlook 3 (SCBD, 2010a).

With the 17% maps, the land-supply curves for LEITAP were adapted to account for the restrictions on the amount of land available for agriculture given the increase in PA cover (Eickhout *et al.*, 2006). The LEITAP outcomes for regional agricultural production were fed into IMAGE-GLOBIO to calculate the effects of introducing a 17% PA-map on the pressures that influence MSA (mostly changed land use for this simulation).

The biodiversity impacts of climate change mitigation under the 450 and 550 *Core* scenarios and the 550 *Low Bioenergy* scenario

Climate change is projected to play an increasingly important role in biodiversity loss in the future. Climate change mitigation could help achieve the goals of both the climate change and biodiversity conventions. Climate change is related to biodiversity in several ways. It affects ecosystems through changed meteorological conditions (precipitation and temperatures) that alter the living environment of species. As a consequence, species abundances will change, and species may even disappear from certain regions. In analysing potential synergies and trade-offs between these policy areas, it is important to take possible land-use changes from climate change mitigation efforts into account, as land-use change has been the most important driver for historical biodiversity loss. The most relevant land-use changes in climate policy measures may come from bioenergy, (avoiding) deforestation (REDD) and reforestation.

The role of bioenergy

Most mitigation scenarios identify bioenergy as an important element of the climate policy portfolio. Bioenergy can be an attractive alternative for oil in transport, can be used as feedstock in power and hydrogen production and can also be combined with carbon capture and storage in power and hydrogen production in order to create negative emissions (van Vuuren *et al.*, 2010). Several studies have indicated the potential downsides and risks of bioenergy use because of the vast areas of land required for bioenergy production (either directly or indirectly), that may lead to considerable loss of natural ecosystems with consequences for biodiversity and carbon (Sala *et al.*, 2009; ten Brink *et al.*, 2010). It may also lead to increased food prices. Quantitative assessment of negative and positive effects of bioenergy could shed more light on the exact trade-offs of different bioenergy policies.

In each of the core climate change mitigation simulations, bioenergy use is based on constructing a cost-effective portfolio of mitigation options that meets the targeted concentration pathway (see the Annex to Chapter 3). In the biodiversity chapter, these scenarios are used to examine the effects of climate change mitigation on biodiversity (Box 4.9). The scenarios used are the 450 and 550 *Core* scenarios. These scenarios use mostly woody bioenergy and residues. The total use of bioenergy is respectively 20% and 13% of total primary energy supply (TPES). In addition, a sensitivity analysis was carried out on the 550 *Core* portfolio, which assumes lower levels of bioenergy use (low-bioenergy case). In all calculations, it is assumed that bioenergy is produced on abandoned agricultural land and, to some extent, on natural grasslands. Protected areas are excluded from bioenergy production.

In the 550 ppm low-bioenergy case, the use of bioenergy on natural grasslands has been excluded altogether. Moreover, more strict sustainability criteria have been introduced that do not allow for bioenergy production in water scarce areas and severely degraded areas. Finally, compared to the 550 *Core* simulation, short-term bioenergy targets that stimulate technology development for bioenergy technologies have been removed. These restrictions lead to a bioenergy use of 6.5% of TPES.

The biodiversity impacts of climate change mitigation under a *450 ppm + Reduced Land Use* scenario

In IMAGE, the most important driver of deforestation and loss of natural grasslands is the expansion of agricultural land use. The model projects for the 2010-2030 period, globally, a net loss of natural area, including forests, as a result of the increased land use for food and bioenergy production. Clearly, avoiding expansion of agricultural areas into natural ecosystems like forests reduces greenhouse gas emissions and biodiversity loss. The option of Reduced Emissions from Deforestation and Degradation (REDD) provides an example of a policy that aims to use this potential. Studies show that avoiding CO_2 emissions through REDD is a relatively low-cost option (Kindermann *et al.*, 2008), especially in developing countries. Given the high carbon price in ambitious climate scenarios considered in this report, the implementation of REDD measures is very attractive.

As a sensitivity study, to explore the potential of a *Reduced Land Use* scenario, the *450 Core* climate mitigation scenario was combined with projections on improving agricultural yields with the aim to avoid further expansion of agricultural area (food, feed and fuel) beyond 2020 (Box 4.9). The level of agricultural yield improvement depends on the expansion of agricultural area in the *Baseline* scenario and thus differs per region and crop (the highest improvements occur in the African region). The global average yield in the 2020-2030 period is 3-18% higher (than the *Baseline*) depending on the crop (highest numbers for crops grown mostly in the African region). Under this *450 ppm + Reduced Land Use* policy simulation, crop area is projected to decline by 1.2 million km^2 and pastures by 1 million km^2 by 2050 compared to the *Baseline* as a result of increases in agricultural productivity. This totally avoids the loss of forests and other natural ecosystems through expansion of natural areas. For forests, studies suggest that this could be implemented and financed through policies like REDD. For other ecosystems, this is less straightforward – although studies indicate that some of these ecosystems might also store considerable amounts of carbon and/or have high biodiversity value.

Chapter 5

Water

by

Xavier Leflaive, Maria Witmer (PBL), Roberto Martin-Hurtado, Marloes Bakker (PBL), Tom Kram (PBL), Lex Bouwman (PBL), Hans Visser (PBL), Arno Bouwman (PBL), Henk Hilderink (PBL), Kayoung Kim

Around the world, cities, farmers, industries, energy suppliers, and ecosystems are increasingly competing for their daily water needs. Without proper water management, the costs of this situation can be high – not just financially, but also in terms of lost opportunities, compromised health and environmental damage. Without major policy changes and considerable improvements in water management, by 2050 the situation is likely to deteriorate, increasing uncertainty about water availability. This chapter summarises the key pressures on water, as well as the main policy responses. It starts by looking at current water challenges and trends and how they could affect the water outlook in 2050. It considers competing demands for water (from agriculture/irrigation, industry, electricity, domestic/urban supply, environment flows) and over-exploitation (both surface and groundwater), water stress, water-related disasters (e.g. floods), water pollution (in particular nutrient effluents – nitrogen and phosphorus – from agriculture and wastewater) and discharge into the seas, and lack of access to water supply and sanitation (as defined by the Millennium Development Goals or MDGs). It reviews the existing policy tools to manage water (such as water rights, water pricing), and explores how the water outlook could be improved by more ambitious policies. The chapter discusses emerging issues in water policy; it pays particular attention to water as a driver of green growth, the water-energy-food nexus, allocating water for healthy ecosystems, and alternative sources of water (reuse). For all these, governance, the use of economic instruments, investment and infrastructure development are important dimensions. They all contribute to and facilitate water policy reforms in OECD countries and globally.

KEY MESSAGES

Access to clean water is fundamental to human well-being. Managing water to meet that need is a major – and growing – challenge in many parts of the world. Many people are suffering from inadequate quantity and quality of water, as well as stress from floods and droughts. This has implications for health, the environment and economic development. **Without major policy changes and considerable improvements in water management processes and techniques, by 2050 the situation is likely to deteriorate, and will be compounded by increasing competition for water and increasing uncertainty about water availability.**

Trends and projections

Water quantity

- The *Outlook Baseline* scenario projects that by 2050, 3.9 billion people, over 40% of the world's population, are likely to be living in river basins under **severe water stress**.

- **Water demand** is projected to increase by 55% globally between 2000 and 2050. The increase in demand will come mainly from manufacturing (+400%), electricity (+140%) and domestic use (+130%). In the face of these competing demands, there will be little scope for increasing water for irrigation.

Global water demand: *Baseline scenario, 2000 and 2050*

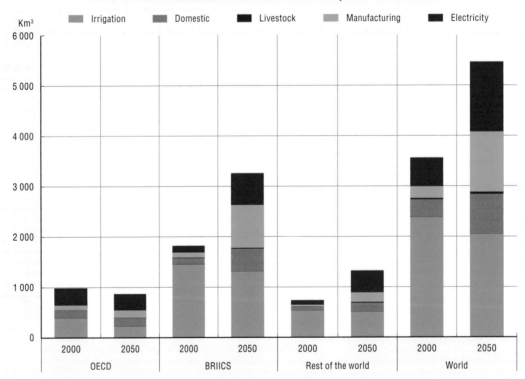

Notes: This graph only measures "blue water" demand (see Box 5.1) and does not consider rainfed agriculture. The country groupings BRIICS and RoW are explained in Table 1.3 in Chapter 1.

Source: *Environmental Outlook Baseline*; output from IMAGE.

StatLink ⬛⬛⬛ http://dx.doi.org/10.1787/888932571171

In many regions of the world, **groundwater** is being exploited faster than it can be replenished and is also becoming increasingly polluted. The rate of groundwater depletion more than doubled between 1960 and 2000, reaching over 280 km^3 per year.

Water quality

 Continued efficiency improvements in agriculture and investments in wastewater treatment in developed countries are expected to stabilise and restore **surface water and groundwater quality in most OECD** countries by 2050.

 The **quality of surface water outside the OECD** is expected to deteriorate in the coming decades, through nutrient flows from agriculture and poor wastewater treatment. The consequences will be increased eutrophication, biodiversity loss and disease. For example, the number of lakes at risk of harmful algal blooms will increase by 20% in the first half of this century.

 Micro-pollutants (medicines, cosmetics, cleaning agents, and biocide residues) are an emerging concern in many countries.

Water supply and sanitation

 The number of people with **access to an improved water source** increased by 1.8 billion between 1990 and 2008, mostly in the BRIICS group (Brazil, Russia, India, Indonesia, China and South Africa), and especially in China.

 More than 240 million people (most of them in rural areas) are expected to be without **access to an improved water source** by 2050. The Millennium Development Goal for improved water supply is unlikely to be met in Sub-Saharan Africa. Globally, more city dwellers did not have access to an improved water source in 2008 than in 1990, as urbanisation is currently outpacing connections to water infrastructure. The situation is even more daunting given that access to an *improved* water source does not always mean access to *safe* water.

 Almost 1.4 billion people are projected to still be without **access to basic sanitation** in 2050, mostly in developing countries. The Millennium Development Goal on sanitation will not be met.

Water-related disasters

 Today, 100-200 million people per year are **victims of floods, droughts and other water-related disasters** (affected or killed); almost two-thirds are attributed to floods. The number of people **at risk from floods** is projected to rise from 1.2 billion today to around 1.6 billion in 2050 (nearly 20% of the world's population). The economic value of assets at risk is expected to be around USD 45 trillion by 2050, a growth of over 340% from 2010.

Policy options and needs

Create incentives for water efficiency

■ **Improve water pricing** to signal scarcity and to create incentives for efficient water use in all sectors (*e.g.* agriculture, industry, domestic); address social consequences through well-designed tariff structures or targeted measures. Combine multiple policy instruments to curb water demand and make alternative water sources (such as reusing treated wastewater) competitive.

■ **Implement flexible water allocation mechanisms** (*e.g.* by combining water rights reform and pricing policies).

Improve water quality

■ **Better co-ordinate the expansion of wastewater collection (sewerage systems) with wastewater treatment** to avoid wastewater being discharged untreated. Innovative techniques and business models will be needed; the private sector is an important player.

■ Improve and increase the use of appropriate wastewater treatment equipment and techniques, and the efficient management of nutrients and agricultural run-off. Encourage further R&D to **speed up and disseminate innovation** in developed and developing countries. Build capacity in target economies (essentially farmers), through training and education.

Invest in green infrastructure

■ **Invest in innovative water storage capacities** which do not conflict with other environmental policy objectives (*e.g.* preservation of ecosystem services, forests or biodiversity).

■ **Reduce the impact and occurrence of water–related disasters** by restoring the ecosystem functions of floodplains and wetlands, paying attention to hydromorphology and removing incentives which encourage people to settle or invest in risk-prone areas.

■ **Accelerate the deployment of water supply and sanitation infrastructure** in developing countries. Explore innovative options which consume less water, energy or capital. This can be funded partially by OECD member states, *e.g.* by increasing the portion of official aid to these areas, and the private sector can also play an essential role.

Ensure policy coherence

■ **Improve water governance** to ensure coherence with other policy areas such as energy, agriculture and urban planning. Engage all relevant stakeholders (different levels of government, water user groups, private companies). Ensure appropriate governance to prevent tensions over transboundary waters.

■ **Assess and reform subsidies that encourage unsustainable water use**, and ensure coherence between water policy objectives and initiatives in other sectors (including energy and agriculture).

Fill in information gaps

■ **Invest in better water-related information** (*e.g.* on consumption, irrigation, and the impact of climate change on water resources).

1. Introduction

Around the world, individuals, farmers, industries, and ecosystems are increasingly competing for their daily water needs. Without proper management, the costs of this situation can be high – not just financially, but also in terms of lost opportunities, compromised health and environmental damage.

This chapter summarises the key pressures on water, as well as the main policy responses. The chapter starts by looking at current water challenges and trends – how competing demands and over-exploitation, water-related disasters, poor water quality and lack of access to water supply and sanitation services could affect the water outlook in 2050. It then reviews the existing policy toolbox, and presents a few more ambitious policy scenarios[1] building on OECD data (where available) and models to explore how the water outlook could be improved. This leads to a discussion of the actions that need to be taken now by national governments, the international community and the private sector.

Key drivers of water health

What processes are affecting the quantity and quality of our water systems? This section briefly outlines the main drivers, followed by summarising the key policy responses (developed more fully in Section 4). The state of water systems is affected by both human activities and environmental change. Today the key human drivers include population, income growth and economic activities (see Chapter 2, on socio-economic developments). To date, economic growth and population dynamics have affected water more than climate. However, after 2050, climate change is expected to become a major driver (see Box 5.3 for an illustration, and Annex 5.A).[2]

Population growth and lifestyle changes drive household water demand and the release of pollutants into water bodies. Projections discussed in Chapter 2 anticipate that global population will continue to grow until 2050, albeit at a slower pace, mainly in developing countries and particularly in West Africa.

Growth in gross domestic product (GDP) drives agricultural and industrial water demand and water pollution discharges, as well as water demand for electricity generation. Agriculture deserves particular attention: production will need to increase significantly by 2050 to meet the growing demand for food. Agriculture has an impact on both water availability (by altering run-off and competing with other uses for surface and groundwater) and quality (through the release of nutrients and micro-pollutants into surface water and groundwater). Different types of energy sources also affect the quality and quantity of water available for other uses. Increasing energy demand and shifting energy mixes have to be factored into water management.

Urbanisation drives water supply and sanitation needs. On the one hand, urbanisation lowers the per-capita costs of connection to water infrastructure. On the other hand, as city dwellers become more numerous, they require more investment to connect to water and wastewater infrastructure. The situation is particularly complex in slums. Urbanisation also drives the need for flood control infrastructure: sealed surfaces alter run-offs from rain and storm water, impair the recharge of underground aquifers and increase flood risks.

Policy responses: A summary

Governments and the private sector must co-ordinate and act urgently to address the water-related challenges we are already facing. Additional action will be needed to address future water stress and the emerging challenges described in the next sections.

The *Environmental Outlook* models show that incremental improvements in water use efficiency will not be enough (see Section 3 Policy: current and future scenarios). Even radical changes in the efficiency of current uses may not be enough to avoid a more fundamental appraisal of the allocation of water. Rapidly growing water demands for electricity production, industry and urban supply are likely to come into increasingly acute competition with agriculture for available water in the coming decades. As described below, OECD governments are gaining experience with innovative approaches to water allocation (such as tradable water rights, smart metering), water reuse, or sustainable water pricing (which includes abstraction charges or licences that reflect scarcity). More needs to be done to properly assess and scale up the use of some of these instruments, to secure environmental values while meeting social and economic needs.

Some of the required policy responses will make claims on public spending. But in the current context of fiscal consolidation, the extent of such claims need to be backed by robust valuation of benefits, the exploration of alternative financing schemes, and a search for low-cost options.

Innovation has a major role to play in promoting sustainable water resource management. This includes (but is not limited to) technologies. Examples include efficient irrigation systems and ecological farming techniques to reduce fertiliser run-off, crop research, water treatment technologies such as membranes and filtration techniques, and advanced wastewater treatment. Technologies need to be supported by innovative business models and corresponding regulatory regimes to improve water management, and to integrate water priorities into other policy areas such as energy, food, and spatial planning. Developing an inventory and improving the valuation of hydrological ecosystems services can pave the way to greater use of innovative, ecologically-based and low-cost approaches to address some of the challenges identified here. Water purification, flow regulation, erosion and sedimentation control, and restoration of hydromorphology all have a role to play, together with new techniques being developed to improve the collection, processing and presentation of data that support both policy-making and water operations.

In the search for innovative technologies and business models, the private sector has a pivotal role to play. This includes the water industry, the financial sector (which may realise water-related investment opportunities) and water users in the fields of energy production, industry, farming and their suppliers (which will develop and diffuse water efficient practices).

Water governance is also key, as water policies intersect with a wide array of sectors at different geographical scales, from local to transboundary levels. Analysis of water governance arrangements in OECD countries has highlighted that a lack of finance for water resource management is a primary concern for most countries, followed by the fragmentation of roles and responsibilities at central and sub-national levels, and the lack of capacity (infrastructure and knowledge) at the territorial level (OECD, 2011g). In the case of transboundary rivers, lakes or aquifers, governance is essential to prevent diplomatic and social tensions. Generic instruments, such as the UNECE Convention on the Protection and Use of Transboundary Watercourses and International Lakes (Water Convention) and specific ones (such as the International Fund for Saving the Aral Sea, IFAS) have a role to play.

2. Key trends and projections

This section reviews trends and long-term projections for water demand, exploitation and availability (including groundwater and water stress), water-related disasters, water quality and access to water supply and sanitation services. It also provides definitions of the terms used (Box 5.1). More detail on the assumptions made and analysis underpinning this section can be found in Chapter 1 (Introduction) and in Annex 5.A at the end of this chapter.

Box 5.1. **Key definitions**

The chapter refers to several concepts which need to be carefully defined.

Water demand: the demand for water by different water users. Water demand can be met from freshwater withdrawn from the environment (a river, lake or aquifer) or from other sources of water (*e.g.* recycled water).

Water abstraction (or withdrawal) is water physically withdrawn from the environment. Part of that water may return to the environment. Typically, a number of industries abstract water for cooling purposes – then return the water to the environment in a suitable condition for use by other purposes. However, a significant part of the water abstracted from the environment is lost. For instance, in some cities, up to 40% of the water treated for domestic uses leaks from pipes.

Water consumption: water use that reduces either the quantity or quality of water that is returned to the environment. Consumed water is not necessarily abstracted from the environment (it can be generated from other sources, *e.g.* recycled water). A variety of water uses do not consume water (*e.g.* shipping, swimming, the environment). These uses should however be taken into account in water resource management (*e.g.* through environmental flow and quality requirements for environmental purposes). In the case of agriculture, water consumption occurs through evapotranspiration and harvesting of crops. In the case of hydropower, water consumption includes the additional evaporation that results from the increased surface of the water body impounded by the dam. The impacts of domestic and industry uses on water quality depend on treatment before discharge into the environment.

Groundwater depletion: when groundwater is abstracted at a greater rate than natural recharge.

Blue water: freshwater in aquifers, rivers, lakes, that can be withdrawn to serve people, for example as water for irrigation, manufacturing, human consumption, livestock, generation of electricity.

Green water: precipitation that naturally infiltrates into the soil and leaves the drainage basin through evapotranspiration into the atmosphere.

Box 5.1. **Key definitions** (cont.)

Water stress: a measure of the total, annual average water demand of "blue water" (see above) in a river basin (or sub-basin) compared with the annual average water available (precipitation minus evapotranspiration) in that basin. The green water flow is thus taken into account in the volume of available water. Often the resulting ratios are grouped into four categories: less than 10% = no stress; 10-20% = low stress; 20-40% = medium stress; and more than 40% = severe stress. Given seasonal and inter-annual variability of demand and supply, and the wish to maintain an environmental flow level, high ratios imply a high risk that water supply will be inadequate.

Sources: Adapted from FAO publications, including FAO (1996), *Land Quality Indicators and Their Use in Sustainable Agriculture and Rural Development*, Rome; see in particular the section on indicators for sustainable water resources development (*www.fao.org/docrep/W4745E/w4745e0d.htm*); FAO (2010), *Disambiguation of Water Use Statistics*, FAO, Rome.

Freshwater demand and exploitation

Recent trends in OECD countries

Globally, it is estimated that water demand rose twice as fast as population growth in the last century. Agriculture was the largest user of water, accounting for about 70% of total global freshwater demand (OECD, 2008c). The largest global water demand after irrigated agriculture in 2000 was for electricity generation, primarily for cooling of thermal (steam cycle-based) power generation.

In the OECD area, total surface water abstraction has not changed since the 1980s (Figure 5.1). This is despite increases in abstractions for public water supply and, to a lesser extent, irrigation. This stability can be explained by more efficient irrigation techniques; the decline of water intensive industries (*e.g.* mining, steel); more efficient use of water for

Figure 5.1. **OECD freshwater abstraction by major use and GDP, 1990-2009**

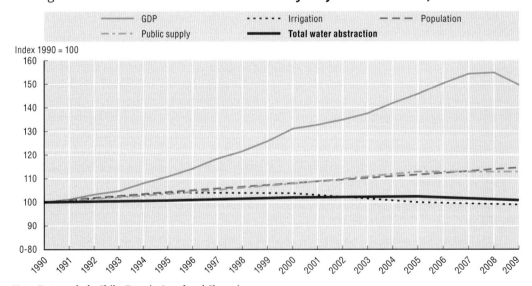

Note: Data exclude Chile, Estonia, Israel and Slovenia.

Source: OECD Environment Directorate.

StatLink ⟲ http://dx.doi.org/10.1787/888932571114

thermoelectric power generation; the increased use of cleaner production technologies; and reduced leaks from piped networks. More recently, this stabilisation also partly reflects droughts, *i.e.* that water was physically not available for abstraction in some regions.

OECD agricultural water use rose by 2% between 1990 and 2003, but has declined since then. Irrigation accounted for 43% of total OECD water use in 2006. Much of the growth in OECD agricultural water use occurred in Australia, Greece, Portugal and Turkey – countries where farming is a major water user (more than 60% of total freshwater abstractions) and/ or irrigation plays a key role in the agricultural sector (on more than 20% of cultivated land).

Although at the national level, most OECD-country water use is sustainable overall, most still face at least seasonal or local water shortages and several have extensive arid or semi-arid regions where lack of water constrains sustainable development and agriculture.

Figures 5.2 and 5.3 display the intensity of use of freshwater resources (both surface and groundwater) expressed as gross abstractions per capita and as a percentage of renewable resources. Indicators of water-use intensity show large variations among individual OECD countries. European countries tend to be less water intensive in per-capita terms. Water use is more sustainable in some countries than in others. For example, Canadians withdrew roughly 1.2% of the country's total average water yield in 2005, while Korea abstracted more than 40%, putting its water balance at risk. The situation is also a concern in some OECD European countries such as Belgium and Spain, where abstraction as a share of renewable water resources is higher than 20% (Figure 5.3).

However, the situation is more complex than is implied by aggregate indicators. National indicators may conceal unsustainable use in some regions and periods, and high dependence on water from neighbouring countries (in the case of transboundary basins). In arid regions, freshwater resources may at times be so limited that demand, so far, is only met by exploiting it unsustainably.

Figure 5.2. **Annual freshwater abstraction per capita, OECD countries**

2009 or latest year available

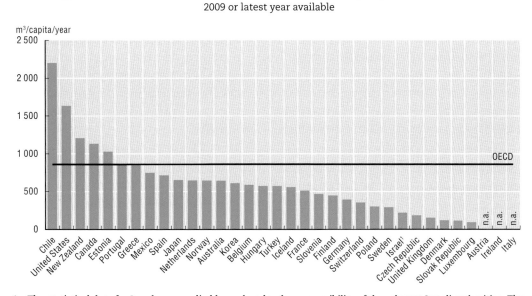

1. The statistical data for Israel are supplied by and under the responsibility of the relevant Israeli authorities. The use of such data by the OECD is without prejudice to the status of the Golan Heights, East Jerusalem and Israeli settlements in the West Bank under the terms of international law.

Source: OECD Environment Directorate.   *StatLink* ⌐╦╦╦ *http://dx.doi.org/10.1787/888932571133*

Figure 5.3. **Water stress, OECD countries**

2009 or latest year available; water abstractions as a % of renewable resource

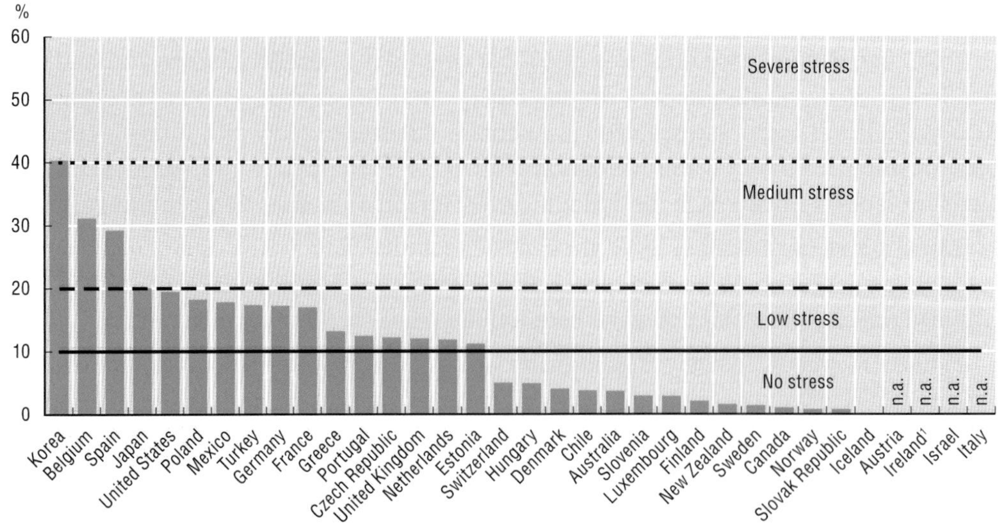

1. The statistical data for Israel are supplied by and under the responsibility of the relevant Israeli authorities. The use of such data by the OECD is without prejudice to the status of the Golan Heights, East Jerusalem and Israeli settlements in the West Bank under the terms of international law.

Source: OECD Environment Directorate.

StatLink ⬛⬛ *http://dx.doi.org/10.1787/888932571152*

In OECD countries, principal concerns are the inefficient use of water (including waste, for instance through leaks from urban supply systems) and its environmental and socio-economic consequences: low river flows, water shortages, salinisation of freshwater bodies in coastal areas, human health problems, loss of wetlands and biodiversity, desertification and reduced food production.

Global water demand by 2050

The *Environmental Outlook Baseline* scenario projects future global water demand to increase significantly – from about 3 500 km^3 in 2000 to nearly 5 500 m^3 in 2050 (Figure 5.4), or a 55% increase. This increase is primarily due to growing demand from manufacturing (+400%, about 1 000 km^3), electricity (+140%, about 600 km^3) and domestic use (+130%, about 300 km^3). However, demand does not automatically translate into consumption, as a significant share of water is discharged back into water bodies after use, remaining available for use downstream, depending on water quality.

Without new policies, the relative importance of uses which drive water demand is also projected to shift significantly by 2050. Sharp rises in water demand are expected in South Asia and China as well as other emerging economies of the BRIICS (Brazil, Russia, India, Indonesia, China and South Africa), with much higher shares for manufacturing, electricity and domestic supply in 2050. Developing countries (rest of the world or the RoW) are also projected to see significant water demand for electricity generation. In all parts of the world, the growing demand for these uses will compete with demand for irrigation water. As a result, the share of water available for irrigation is expected to decline (Box 5.2). If the model projections were to factor in the additional water needed to ensure enough flows to maintain ecosystem health, the competition among different water users would intensify even further.

Figure 5.4. **Global water demand:** *Baseline*, **2000 and 2050**

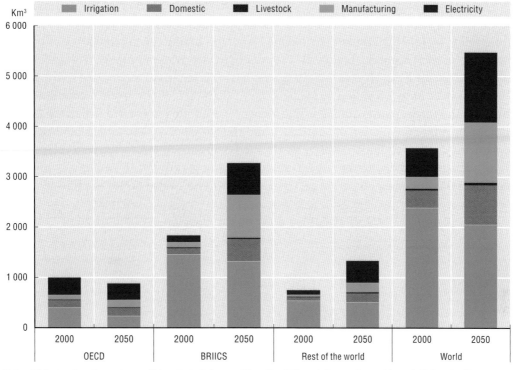

Notes: This graph only measures "blue water" demand (see Box 5.1) and does not consider rainfed agriculture.
Source: *OECD Environmental Outlook Baseline;* output from IMAGE.

StatLink *http://dx.doi.org/10.1787/888932571171*

Box 5.2. **Uncertainties about agricultural water demand**

The projections for irrigation water use in this *Environmental Outlook* assume that the area of irrigated land will stay constant to 2050 for several reasons:

■ Most analysts observe that massive extension of irrigation will not be possible in the coming decades because available land for irrigation is scarce in most regions; where it is available, the land is unlikely to be irrigated soon because of lack of infrastructure and limited public budgets.

■ Irrigation is expected to compete increasingly with other water uses, and experience indicates that domestic uses usually receive priority over irrigation in water allocation.

■ There is significant uncertainty about the current extent and future extension of irrigated land and irrigation water use. A review of scenario projections in the literature with similar assumptions to the OECD's *Outlook Baseline* indicates that projections range from the current uncertain level to plus 10%-20% until the middle of the century (see Annex 5.A).

Given the uncertainty regarding this issue and the limited potential for expansion, this *Outlook* takes a conservative approach and assumes no expansion of irrigated land. This may underestimate future water stress in some regions. Further discussion of the methods used to estimate water demands for the *Environmental Outlook* is provided in Annex 5.A.

Water stress: A growing problem

Increased water demand will exacerbate water stress (see Box 5.1 for definition) in many river basins, in particular in densely populated areas in rapidly developing economies. More river basins are projected to come under severe water stress by 2050 under the *Baseline* scenario, mainly as a result of growing water demands (Figure 5.5). The number of people living in these stressed river basins is expected to increase sharply, from 1.6 billion in 2000 to 3.9 billion by 2050, or more than 40% of the world's population. By then, around three-quarters of all people facing severe water stress will live in the BRIICS. Almost the entire population of South Asia and the Middle East, and large shares of China and North Africa's population, will be located in river basins under severe water stress. The consequences for daily life are uncertain, depending greatly on the adequacy of water management strategies put in place. On the other hand, water stress is projected to be

Figure 5.5. **Water stress by river basin: *Baseline*, 2000 and 2050**

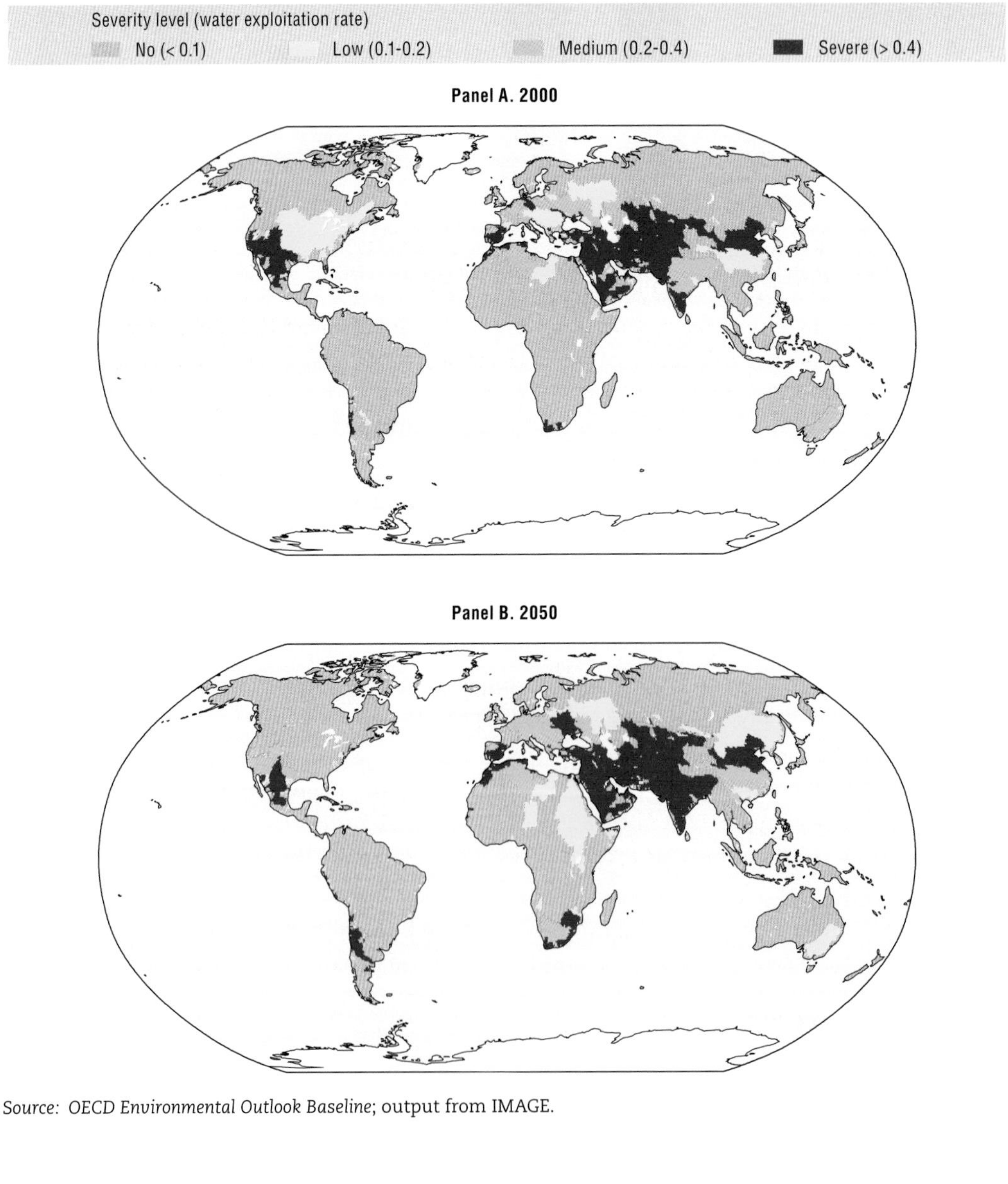

Source: OECD Environmental Outlook Baseline; output from IMAGE.

somewhat reduced in some OECD countries, *e.g.* the United States. This results from a projected decrease in demand (driven by efficiency gains, and a structural shift towards service sectors that are less water intensive) and higher precipitation caused by climate change (Box 5.3).

Box 5.3. **The impact of climate change on freshwater: An example from Chile**

Climate change will affect freshwater resources through shifts in the hydrological cycle. The Intergovernmental Panel on Climate Change (IPCC) projects that the impact of climate change on freshwater systems and their management will be felt primarily through temperature increases, sea-level rise and precipitation variability. There will be shifts in the quantity, variability, timing, form, and intensity of precipitation and annual average run-off; the frequency and intensity of extreme events such as floods and droughts will increase; water temperature and the rate of evapotranspiration will increase; and water quality will deteriorate (Bates *et al.*, 2008). The nature and magnitude of these projected impacts are highly context specific, with some regions projected to have too much or too little water and many regions suffering unsustainable levels of water pollution driven by higher variability in precipitation and river discharge. These problems will become more severe in the second half of the century (IPCC, 2008).

To date, economic growth and population dynamics have affected water more than climate. A more immediate consequence of climate change is a call for resilience and flexibility in water allocation mechanisms and water infrastructures (including hydropower, structural flood defences, drainage and irrigation systems, wastewater treatment), as future water regimes are less certain.

For example, in recent years, various national studies conducted in Chile have allowed for the preliminary quantification of the impacts of climate change on water resources. In particular, studies have analysed the impact of the changes in temperature, evapotranspiration and precipitation on hydrologic resources in eight river basins located along the central valley of Chile.

The analysis projects water flow to decrease on average in all river basins by 35% between 2041 and 2070. The most northern and southern regions analysed (the Limarí and Cautín basins) will be more severely affected in the short term. The results also show variations in the timing of increased flow levels produced by melting snow in some river basins, which in some cases would shift from spring and summer to winter months. Practically all of the river basins analysed show a major increase in the number of months with hydrological deficits. This will greatly affect the availability of water resources for different productive sectors in Chile. At the same time, the predicted rise in temperatures is expected to produce an upward shift in the altitude of the snow line and lead to an increase in hydrologic flows generated during the winter in the Andes Mountains.

Sources: See for instance Vicuña, S., R.D. Garreaud, J. McPhee (2010), "Climate Change Impacts on the Hydrology of a Snowmelt Driven Basin in Semiarid Chile", *Climate Change*, doi: 10.1007/s10584-010-9888-4; Bates, B.C., Z.W. Kundzewicz, S. Wu and J.P. Palutikof (eds.) (2008), *Climate Change and Water*, Technical Paper of the Intergovernmental Panel on Climate Change, IPCC Secretariat, Geneva.

Groundwater depletion

Groundwater is by far the largest freshwater resource on Earth (not counting water stored as ice). It represents over 90% of the world's readily available freshwater resource (UNEP, 2008; Boswinkel, 2000). The total amount is difficult to assess, but one estimate suggests that, worldwide, groundwater resources amount to some 10.5 million km^3 (Shiklomanov and Rodda, 2003). Especially in areas with limited surface water supply, such as parts of Africa, and where there is no other alternative, it is a relatively clean, reliable and cost-effective resource. Groundwater also plays a significant role in maintaining surface water systems through flows into lakes and rivers.

However, the rate of groundwater exploitation is becoming unsustainable in a number of regions. The role of groundwater as a water source is becoming increasingly prominent as modern extraction technologies become commonplace and more accessible surface water resources are gradually over-exploited. The fraction of global freshwater use currently drawn from groundwater is estimated globally at 50% of domestic water supply, 40% of water withdrawals for self-supplied industry and 20% of irrigation water supply (Zektser and Everett, 2004). In the European Union, the fraction of groundwater supply for domestic water use is approximately 70%; in France, groundwater accounts for 63% of withdrawals for domestic uses, 41% for industry, and 20% for irrigation.

In the last half of the 20th century, the boom in agricultural groundwater use has improved livelihoods and food security for billions of farmers and consumers. But groundwater depletion may be the single largest threat to irrigated agriculture, exceeding even the build-up of salts in soils. Rapid groundwater depletion is a consequence of the explosive spread of small pump irrigation throughout the developing world. The volume of groundwater used by irrigators is substantially above recharge rates in some regions of Australia, Greece, Italy, Mexico and the United States, undermining the economic viability of farming. In countries with significant semi-arid areas such as Australia, India, Mexico and the United States, more than one-third of irrigation water is pumped from the ground (Zektser and Everett, 2004). Over-exploited aquifers, especially in semi-arid and arid regions, lead to environmental problems (poor water quality, reduced stream flows, drying up of wetlands), higher pumping costs and the loss of a resource for future generations (Shah *et al.*, 2007).

Although we use only a relatively small fraction of the Earth's known groundwater reserves, the rate at which global groundwater stocks are shrinking ("groundwater depletion" – see Box 5.1) has more than doubled between 1960 and 2000, from 130 (± 30) to 280 (± 40) km^3 of water per year (Wada *et al.*, 2010). During the past 50 years, groundwater depletion has spread from isolated pockets to large areas in many countries. One assessment shows that the highest rates of depletion are in some of the world's major agricultural centres, including northwest India, northeast China, northeast Pakistan, California's central valley, and the Midwest of the United States (Wada *et al.*, 2010). It found, furthermore, that the rate of depletion increased almost linearly from the 1960s to the early 1990s, linked to rapid economic growth and population increase, mainly in India and China.

The depletion of even a small portion of the total volume of groundwater (in some cases only a few percent) has a substantial effect on water resources. For example, it can cause land subsidence, which permanently reduces aquifer storage capacity and increases susceptibility to flood damage. And where groundwater discharges to streams and lakes, even a small amount of groundwater depletion reduces stream flow and lowers lake water levels, reducing the amount of surface water available for use by humans or riparian and aquatic ecosystems. These external effects can in turn become limiting factors to the further development of the groundwater resource (Alley, 2007).

Although it is essential to balance exploitation of groundwater resources with supplementation, many dry countries subsidise groundwater exploitation either directly or indirectly (for instance, some policies relieve farmers of the need to pay the price of energy for pumping water from aquifers), and do not have policies to replenish the exploited groundwater. Energy subsidies to agriculture have significantly lowered the costs of extracting groundwater in a number of OECD countries and India.

Water-related disasters

Many people already have to use water that is inadequate in both quantity and quality. The stress from droughts and floods threatens their security even further. Flood, storm and drought disasters have implications for health, the environment and economic development. For example, in 1983, drought in Ethiopia and Sudan led to over 400 000 deaths through famine. Drought in India, and floods and storms in China affected 450 million people in 2002. In the United States in 2005, Hurricane Katrina and the flooding it caused led to damage valued at USD 140 billion.

Recent trends

The number of weather-related disasters has increased worldwide over the last three decades, particularly floods, droughts and storms (Figure 5.6). Trends in water and weather-related disasters between 1980 and 2009 have been analysed using information from the Emergency Events database (EM-DAT), maintained by the Centre for Research on the Epidemiology of Disasters (CRED).[3] The database compiles information on the human and economic impacts of water-related disasters and indicators monitor direct economic losses and the number of victims (people affected or killed). Disasters are categorised according to their causes (floods, droughts and storms).

Figures 5.6 shows historic trends in the number of weather-related "severe" disasters (Panel A), in terms of number of victims (Panel B) and economic losses (Panel C). The main drivers of this increase are a growing world population, increasing wealth and expansion of built-up areas. Although there is a tight relation between extremes in climate variables and weather-related disasters (IPCC, 2011), there is not enough data to confirm a link between frequencies of disasters and climate change. Studies where economic losses have been corrected for population growth and economic growth generally show stabilised or even decreasing trends in losses due to severe water events (Neumayer and Barthel, 2011; Bouwer, 2011; and see Annex 5.A).

Floods made up well over 40% of all weather-related disasters between 1980 and 2009, storms nearly 45% and droughts 15%. The number of victims ranges between about 100 million and 200 million per year, with peaks of 300 million or more. Almost two-thirds of the victims can be attributed to floods. Droughts and other temperature extremes account for 25% and storms the remaining 10%.

Economic losses are estimated to range between USD 50-100 billion per year between 1980 and 2009. A peak of USD 220 billion reflects the Katrina disaster in the United States in 2005. Storms account for half of all losses, floods one-third and droughts almost 15%.

The number of disasters has been spread quite equally over the regions: almost 40% in the OECD, 30% in the BRIICS and 30% in the RoW. But there is a striking difference in impacts between these three groups of countries. Well over 80% of victims (people affected

Figure 5.6. **Global weather-related disasters, 1980-2009**

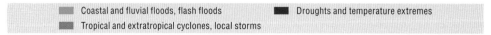

Coastal and fluvial floods, flash floods   Droughts and temperature extremes
Tropical and extratropical cyclones, local storms

Panel A

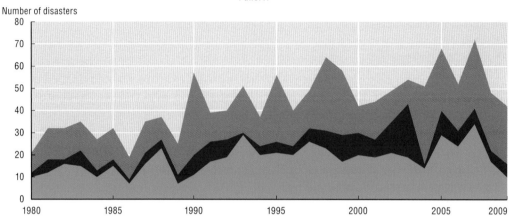

Number of disasters

Panel B

Number of victims (millions)

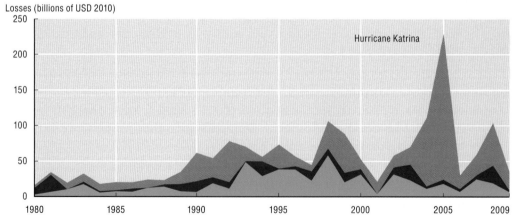

Drought India

Drought India, flood China

Flood China

Panel C

Losses (billions of USD 2010)

Hurricane Katrina

Note: Losses are in USD 2010, for comparison purposes.

Source: Visser, H., A.A. Bouwman, P. Cleij, W. Ligtvoet and A.C. Petersen (forthcoming), *Trends in Weather-related Disaster Burden: A global and regional study*, PBL Netherlands Environmental Assessment Agency, The Hague/Bilthoven.

StatLink ᴍ⤳ http://dx.doi.org/10.1787/888932571190

or killed) were in the BRIICS countries, nearly 15% in the RoW and only about 5% in OECD countries. OECD countries suffered almost two-thirds of the economic losses, BRIICS one quarter and RoW over 10%. These figures reflect differences in adaptive capacity and the economic value of real estate and other property in the three groups of countries.

Floods: The picture to 2050

The *Environmental Outlook Baseline* projects the world's population to increase by one-third to over 9 billion in 2050 (Chapter 2). In flood plains and deltas – those areas most affected by floods – the population is projected to increase even more rapidly, by nearly 40% over the same period. Changes in exposure of people and economic assets, and in some cases changes in vulnerability, have been the major drivers of the observed increase in disaster losses in the past (IPCC, 2011). This trend may continue in the coming decades. Leaving aside climate change as a likely key driver of floods by 2050, the number of people and value of assets at risk will still be significantly higher than today: more than 1.6 billion people (or nearly 20% of the world's population) and economic assets worth some USD 45 trillion (340% more than in 2010). By region, the increase in economic value at risk is almost 130% for the OECD, over 640% for the BRIICS and nearly 440% for developing countries (see Annex 5.A for more detail on these calculations).

Vulnerability to floods is not evenly distributed within countries and often the poorest suffer disproportionally. For example, Dhaka, Kolkata, Shanghai, Mumbai, Jakarta, Bangkok, and Ho Chi Minh City represent the cities with most people at risk to flooding and all are also situated in countries with low national GDPs per capita in both 2010 and 2050 (see Annex 5.A). This list of cities agrees with an earlier OECD study on coastal cities referred to in Chapter 3 on climate change (Nicholls *et al.*, 2008).

Water quality

Good quality water is essential for human well-being, to support healthy aquatic ecosystems and for use in primary industries such as agriculture and aquaculture. Eutrophication (discussed below), acidification, toxic contamination and micro-pollutants all place pressures on human health, the cost of treating drinking water, irrigation and the maintenance of aquatic ecosystems. Water quality that is too poor for use exacerbates the problem of water scarcity.

Recent trends in OECD countries

Despite significant progress in OECD countries in reducing pollution loads from municipal and industrial point sources by installing wastewater treatment plants and reducing chemical use, improvements in freshwater quality are not always easy to discern,[4] except for organic pollution. Pollution loads from diffuse agricultural and urban sources (fertilisers and pesticides, run-off from sealed surfaces and roads, and pharmaceuticals in animal and human waste) are continuing challenges in many countries.

The share of nutrient water pollution from farming has risen as absolute levels of industrial and urban pollution have decreased more rapidly than those from agriculture. The pressure from agriculture on water quality in rivers, lakes, groundwater and coastal waters in most OECD countries eased between 1990 and the mid-2000s due to a decline in nutrient surpluses and pesticide use. Despite this improvement, absolute levels of nutrient and pesticide pollution remain significant in many OECD countries and regions. In nearly half of OECD countries, nutrient and pesticide concentrations in surface and groundwater in agricultural areas exceed national recommended limits for drinking water standards. Another concern is agricultural pollution of deep aquifers, where natural recovery from pollution can take several decades. In some cases, a reduction of agricultural pollution has not helped to improve water quality due to legacy pollution from slow-moving older groundwater.

The economic costs of treating water to remove nutrients and pesticides to meet drinking water standards are significant in some OECD countries. Eutrophication of marine waters also imposes high economic costs on commercial fisheries for some countries (*e.g.* Korea and the United States). Persistent micro-pollutants in water bodies also add to the costs of treating water for potable use (Box 5.4).

Box 5.4. **Addressing the risks from micro-pollutants**

A growing source of concern is micro-pollutants and their effects on aquatic ecosystems and human health. Micro-pollutants include medicines, cosmetics, cleaning agents, or biocide residues (herbicides, fungicides). They enter water bodies from urban drainage, agriculture, rainwater runoff from transport routes and sealed surfaces. They can have negative effects on organisms, including humans, typically by interfering with endocrine (hormone) systems leading to cancers, birth defects, and other developmental disorders (see Chapter 6, Section 4 on chemicals). The risks are compounded by the combination of multiple pollutants in water bodies, which can together create additional pressures on organisms. Moreover, micro-pollutants tend to be persistent: they are not adequately removed by regular treatment technologies. This allows them to accumulate in water bodies and sediments, leading to higher concentrations. The expected increase in the frequency and intensity of extreme weather events and high flow rates caused by climate change may cause re-suspension of pollutants stored in sediments.

Addressing this issue requires complementary approaches: reducing contamination at source; retrofitting of existing wastewater treatment plants with additional treatment facilities such as ozonation, and powdered active carbon;[*] setting up decentralised treatment plants for places where large volumes of micro-pollutants are likely to be generated (*e.g.* hospitals, nursing homes); and developing and disseminating new treatment technologies such as sensors, nanotechnologies, and hybrid treatments.

[*] The Swiss authorities plan to retrofit 100 out of 700 operating wastewater treatment plants.

Eutrophication of surface water and coastal zones

Eutrophication occurs when water bodies receive excess nutrients that stimulate too much plant growth, leading to oxygen depletion and harmful algal blooms. It is a serious concern, causing aquatic biodiversity loss in rivers, lakes and wetlands, hampering human use of the water (*e.g.* drinking water, recreation, fishing, swimming) and it can also affect human health (see below and Chapter 4 on biodiversity). Eutrophicating pollution originates from point sources (urban wastewater systems) and diffuse sources (mainly run-off from agricultural land). Each issue is discussed below.

Under the *Baseline* scenario, eutrophication is expected to increase globally in the coming two decades, then stabilise in some regions (the OECD, Russia and Ukraine). In Japan and Korea nutrient surpluses per hectare of agricultural land have already reached high levels. In China, India, Indonesia and developing countries, eutrophication is projected to increase after 2030; in

China, this is driven by nutrients from wastewater – surpluses in agriculture are projected to stabilise. In Brazil, eutrophication is expected to increase, driven by growing phosphorus surpluses from agriculture, while phosphorus from wastewater effluents and nitrogen is projected to stabilise or decrease after 2030.

Nutrient effluents from wastewater

In the *Baseline*, nutrient effluents from wastewater are projected to increase rapidly. Nitrogen (N) effluents are projected to grow by 180% (from about 6 to 17 million tonnes per year between 2000 and 2050 globally); and phosphorus (P) effluents by over 150% (from 1.3 to 3.3 million tonnes per year in the same period) (Figure 5.7). This is primarily due to population growth, rapid urbanisation, an increasing number of households with improved sanitation and connections to sewage systems, and lagging nutrient removal in wastewater treatment systems. The nutrient removal in wastewater treatment systems is also expected to improve rapidly, but not fast enough to counterbalance the large projected increase in nutrient inflows.

Nutrient effluents from agriculture

Nutrient surpluses in agriculture occur if more nutrients are added to the soil than are withdrawn. If there is a surplus of nitrogen, it is likely to be leached into the groundwater, run off the fields into watercourses, or be lost to the atmosphere through conversion to ammonia (volatilisation). Nitrogen enters the soil through biological fixation, atmospheric deposition, application of synthetic nitrogen fertiliser and animal manure. Nitrogen is withdrawn from the soil through crop harvesting and livestock grazing. Phosphorus comes from animal manure and fertiliser. It follows the same routes as nitrogen, except that it accumulates in the soil and is not leached to the groundwater or lost to the atmosphere (see Annex 5.A for more detail).

Surpluses of nitrogen in agriculture are projected to decrease in the *Baseline* in most OECD countries by 2050 (Figure 5.8, Pannel A). This is because the efficiency of fertiliser use is likely to improve more rapidly than increases in productivity. In China, India and most developing countries, the trend goes in the opposite direction: nitrogen surplus per hectare is likely to increase as production grows more rapidly than efficiency. In China and India, crop production is expected to grow by more than 50% between 2000 and 2030 and 10% to 20% between 2030 and 2050. In Brazil, crop production is expected to grow by 65% between 2000 and 2030 and another 10% by 2050. The production of soybeans and other pulses in Brazil is projected to grow by over 75% between 2000 and 2030, stabilising by 2050. The efficiency of nitrogen fertiliser use in Brazil is projected to be high and nearly stable by 2030, because soybeans fix atmospheric nitrogen and require little nitrogen fertiliser input.[5]

The growth in fertiliser surpluses in Africa (excepting Southern Africa) is dominated by North Africa, which is projected to contribute 20% of Africa's total nitrogen surplus and 40% of its phosphorus surplus by 2050. Surpluses in Sub-Saharan Africa are smaller than in many other developing countries. As soils are often deficient in phosphorus, increased fertilisers are needed to restore and improve soil fertility and sustain crop production. Overall, total crop production in Africa is projected to increase in the *Baseline* scenario between 2000 and 2050 (North Africa by 150%; West Africa, 375%; East Africa, 265%). This is assumed to be achieved through a considerable expansion in agricultural land and increased yields. If this production increase is to be sustained without expanding agricultural land any further, restoration and improvement of soil fertility, technological improvements and higher fertiliser application rates – especially phosphorus – are likely to be needed. More ecological farming techniques will be needed as well.

Figure 5.7. **Nutrient effluents from wastewater:** *Baseline, 1970-2050*

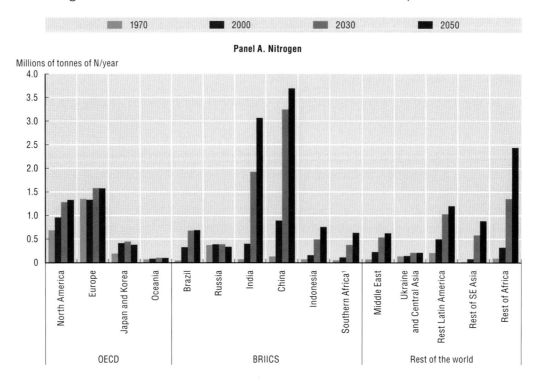

Panel A. Nitrogen

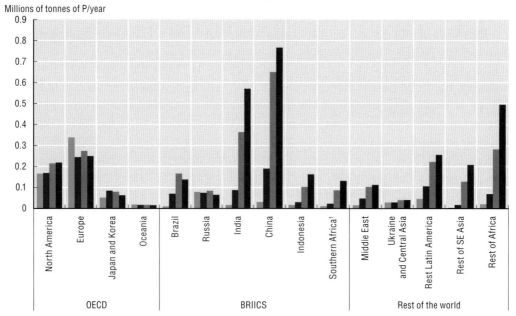

Panel B. Phosphorus

1. In the IMAGE model the *Southern Africa* region includes ten other countries in this geographical area including the Republic of South Africa, when dealing with land use, biodiversity, water and health. For energy-related modelling the region has been split into the Republic of South Africa and "Rest of Southern Africa".

Source: OECD Environmental Outlook Baseline; output from IMAGE.

StatLink 🔗 http://dx.doi.org/10.1787/888932571209

Figure 5.8. **Nutrient surpluses per hectare from agriculture:** *Baseline,* **1970-2050**

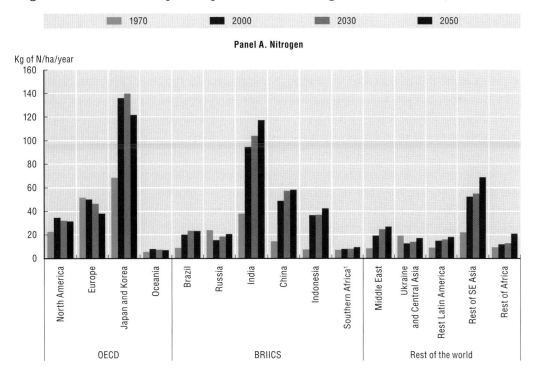

Panel A. Nitrogen

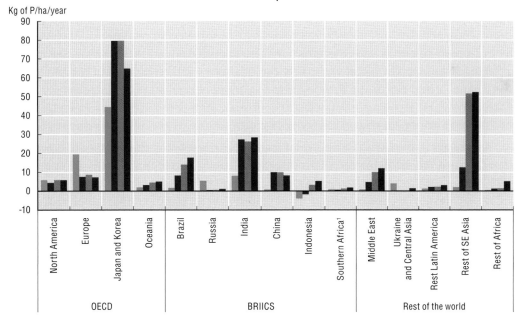

Panel B. Phosphorus

1. In the IMAGE model the *Southern Africa* region includes ten other countries in this geographical area including the Republic of South Africa, when dealing with land use, biodiversity, water and health. For energy-related modelling the region has been split into the Republic of South Africa and "Rest of Southern Africa".

Source: OECD Environmental Outlook Baseline; output from IMAGE.

StatLink ᴀᴍˢᴾ *http://dx.doi.org/10.1787/888932571247*

In most OECD countries, phosphorus surpluses per hectare are projected to increase slightly in the coming two decades, but to decrease thereafter (Figure 5.8, Pannel B). In China and India, phosphorus surpluses are also expected to decrease or stabilise, while in most developing countries and Brazil, they are projected to increase. Phosphorus is fixed in the soil and builds up until the soil is saturated. It is necessary to add a surplus of phosphorus to compensate for this fixation and leave enough phosphorus for the crop. These surpluses cause extra run-off. If the soil is saturated, fixation stops, and fertiliser inputs can approximately equal crop withdrawal to produce crops. In that situation surpluses may tend to be zero. This is the case in many agricultural regions in Europe, for example. China and India's soils are rapidly becoming saturated –hence surpluses are projected to stabilise or slightly decrease.

Brazil currently has a much lower fertiliser use per unit of production than most OECD countries – this is projected to change slowly until it reaches similar levels to OECD countries, allowing for a large increase in crop production. Another important factor is that soybeans and other pulses require large amounts of phosphorus. These two factors explain the increase in phosphorus surpluses in Brazil.

Environmental consequences

The deterioration in water quality is estimated to have already reduced biodiversity in rivers, lakes and wetlands by about one-third globally, with the largest losses in China, Europe, Japan, South Asia and Southern Africa (model calculations, see Chapter 4 on biodiversity). In the *Baseline* scenario, a further decrease in aquatic biodiversity is expected in the BRIICS and developing countries up until 2030, followed by stabilisation (see Chapter 4 on biodiversity for further discussion). However, this modelled decrease is an underestimation because the effects of future river dams, wetland reclamation and climate change have not been included. Over-exploitation of some water resources and changes in the hydromorphology of water systems have also damaged aquatic ecosystems. Setting and enforcing minimum ecological water flow rates in rivers and restoration of morphology of river channels and banks and flow regimes to a more natural state are increasingly a part of environmental planning in some OECD countries, stimulated in the European Union by the European Water Framework Directive (Box 5.9).

As a result of the increasing nutrient loads in surface water, the number of lakes with harmful algal blooms is projected to increase globally under the *Baseline* by some 20% in 2050 compared to 2000, mostly in Asia, Africa and Brazil. It is expected that these effects will be aggravated by climate change and increased water temperatures (Mooij *et al.*, 2005; Jeppesen *et al.*, 2009).

The occurrence, frequency, duration and extent of oxygen depletion and harmful algal blooms in coastal zones are projected to increase under the *Baseline* to 2050, as rivers discharge rapidly growing amounts of nutrients into the sea, especially the Pacific (Figure 5.9). Phosphorus discharges are projected to increase more rapidly than those of nitrogen and silicon (Figure 5.9, Panel B), leading to deterioration in the natural balance of coastal marine ecosystems. Another driver exacerbating this trend is the rapid growth in the number of dams worldwide. Dams cause sediment with silicon to settle down in the reservoir and lower the sediment loading in rivers downstream, thereby reducing the level of silicon. This imbalance increases the risk of harmful algal blooms.

Figure 5.9. **River discharges of nutrients into the sea:** *Baseline, 1950-2050*

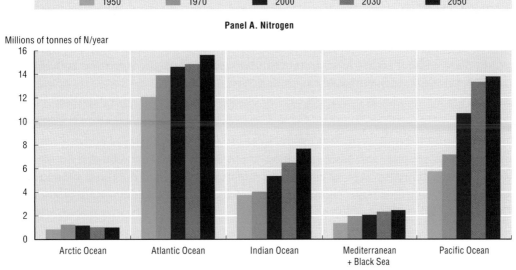

Panel A. Nitrogen

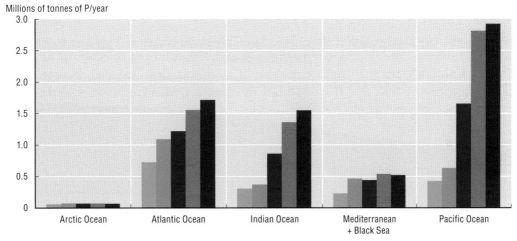

Panel B. Phosphorus

Source: OECD *Environmental Outlook Baseline*; output from IMAGE.

StatLink http://dx.doi.org/10.1787/888932571285

Besides wastewater and agriculture, aquaculture is a growing source of nutrient discharges. As these are not included in the model calculations, the projected nutrient discharges to rivers and the sea may be underestimated.

Access to water supply and sanitation services

Current trends

The Millennium Development Goal (MDG) Target 7C is "to halve, by 2015, the proportion of people without sustainable access to safe drinking water and basic sanitation". This section measures the number of people without access to *improved water sources* and to basic sanitation, as reported by the Joint Monitoring Programme. However, access to an improved water source does not guarantee access to *safe water*.

The official monitoring of the MDG Target 7C shows that worldwide between 1990 and 2008, the number of people with access to an improved drinking water source grew by an estimated 1.1 billion people in urban areas and 723 million people in rural areas (UN, 2011). Most of them live in the BRIICS. Nevertheless, in 2008, 141 million city dwellers and 743 million rural dwellers still relied on unimproved sources of drinking water (UN, 2011). The number of city dwellers without access to an improved water source actually increased between 1990 and 2008, as urbanisation outpaced connection (Figure 5.12).

The official monitoring also indicates that in 2008, 2.6 billion people still did not have access to basic sanitation. According to the Global Annual Assessment of Sanitation and Drinking-Water (GLAAS; WHO, 2010),[6] the greatest numbers of people without improved drinking water supplies and basic sanitation are in South Asia, East Asia and Sub-Saharan Africa. To date, efforts to increase connection rates have benefitted the better-off more than the poor (UN, 2011). This poses enormous health risks, especially to the poorest, who are the most vulnerable.

In OECD countries, the share of the population connected to a municipal wastewater treatment plant rose from nearly 50% in the early 1980s to about 70% today (Figures 5.10 and 5.11). For the OECD as a whole, almost half of public pollution abatement and control expenditure relates to water (sewerage and wastewater treatment). When expenditures from the private sector are factored in, this domain represents up to 1% of GDP in some countries.

Figure 5.10. **OECD population connected to wastewater treatment plants, 1990-2009**

% of total population

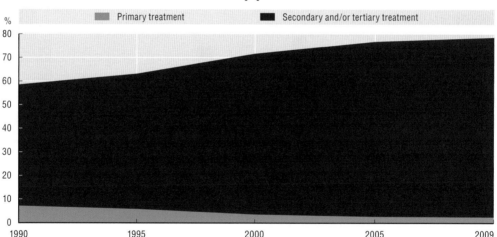

Note: This indicator shows the percentage of national population connected to public wastewater treatment plants, and the degree of treatment (primary treatment only, secondary treatment and tertiary treatment – defined below). "Connected" here means actually connected to a wastewater treatment plant through a public sewage network. Non-public treatment plants, i.e. industrial wastewater plants, or individual private treatment facilities such as septic tanks are not covered. The optimal connection rate is not necessarily 100%; it may vary among countries and depends on geographical features and on the spatial distribution of habitats. Primary treatment refers to treatment of (urban) wastewater by a physical and/or chemical process involving settlement of suspended solids, or other processes in which the biological oxygen demand (BOD) of the incoming wastewater is reduced by at least 20% before discharge and the total suspended solids of the incoming wastewater are reduced by at least 50%. Secondary treatment refers to treatment of (urban) wastewater by a process generally involving biological treatment with a secondary settlement or other process, resulting in a BOD removal of at least 70% and a chemical oxygen demand (COD) removal of at least 75%. Tertiary treatment refers to treatment (additional to secondary treatment) of nitrogen and/or phosphorous and/or any other pollutant affecting the quality or a specific use of water: microbiological pollution, colour, etc. The different possible treatment efficiencies cannot be added and are exclusive.

Data exclude: Australia, Chile, Mexico, Slovak Republic and Slovenia.

Source: OECD Environment Directorate.   *StatLink* 〰 *http://dx.doi.org/10.1787/888932571323*

Figure 5.11. **OECD population connected to public wastewater treatment plants by country**

2009 or latest year available, in % of total population

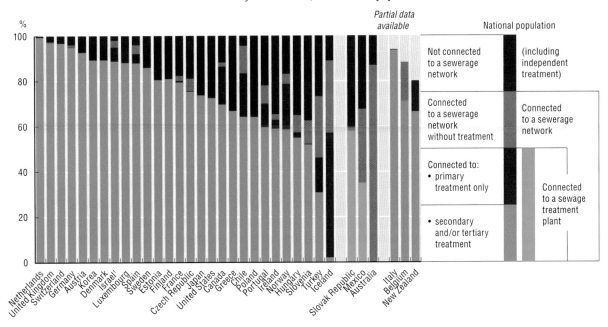

Note: See note for the previous figure.

1. The statistical data for Israel are supplied by and under the responsibility of the relevant Israeli authorities. The use of such data by the OECD is without prejudice to the status of the Golan Heights, East Jerusalem and Israeli settlements in the West Bank under the terms of international law.

Source: OECD Environment Directorate.

StatLink ⛭ http://dx.doi.org/10.1787/888932571342

The share of population connected to wastewater treatment plants and the level of treatment vary significantly among OECD countries (Figure 5.11): secondary and tertiary treatment has progressed in some, while others are still completing sewerage networks or the installation of first generation treatment plants. In the future, additional treatments will be required to eliminate micro-pollutants (Box 5.4). Additional points of concern are the management of and pollution in storm water and surface water run-off. Some countries have reached the economic limit in terms of sewerage connection, and use other, non-collective ways of treating wastewater, mainly from small, isolated settlements (Box 5.5).

Box 5.5. **The Iberoamerican Water Programme**

Spain is promoting the Iberoamerican Water Programme, endorsed by the Iberoamerican Summit of Heads of State in 2007. This programme is devoted to achieving the MDGs on water supply and sanitation in Latin America and involves four activities: capacity building, technical transfer, institutional strengthening and supporting the Ibero-American Water Director's Conference (CODIA). One notable development is the establishment of a Research and Testing Centre for non-conventional water treatment technologies in Uruguay, fostering technological research and transfer through dialogue among stakeholders and countries. This sort of technology park tests new unconventional sanitation techniques for small and isolated communities and identifies the best option according to climatic conditions and the specific pollutants involved.

Future trends

Under the *Baseline* scenario, access to improved water supply in the BRIICS is projected to be universal before 2050 (Figure 5.12).[7] Connection rates are likely to improve because of higher income levels and continuing urbanisation, which makes water supply and sanitation (WSS) coverage easier to achieve. However, far slower progress is expected in developing countries (RoW). The United Nations estimates that by 2015, 89% of the population in developing regions are likely to have access to improved sources of drinking water, compared with 70% in 1990 (UN, 2011). The MDG of halving by 2015 the 1990 level of population without improved water supply is expected to be met in most regions, but not in Sub-Saharan Africa.

However, this apparent success can be misleading. This is so for three reasons. Firstly, progress has been rapid in rural areas – a trend which is projected to continue under the *Environmental Outlook Baseline* – but the absolute number of people in rural areas without access is still a concern (Figure 5.12). Secondly, as noted above, the number of city dwellers without access to improved water supply worldwide has actually increased between 1990 and 2008, as service extension fails to keep pace with city growth. Thirdly, the MDG target indicator – the "proportion of population using an improved drinking water source" – does not necessarily reflect access to *safe* water, which was defined as a fundamental human right by the UN in 2010 (see Section 3 for more on this). OECD work has shown ample evidence of this, in particular in Eastern Europe, the Caucasus and Central Asia (EECCA; see OECD, 2011d).

Figure 5.12. **Population lacking access to an improved water source: Baseline, 1990-2050**

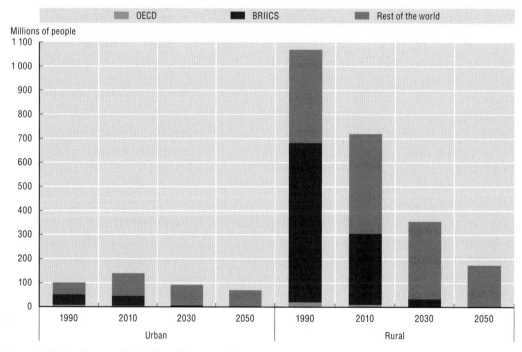

Source: OECD Environmental Outlook Baseline; output from IMAGE.

StatLink ⟶ http://dx.doi.org/10.1787/888932571361

Under the *Baseline*, the number of people without access to basic sanitation is expected to remain at 2.5 billion in 2015 and to be almost 1.4 billion in 2050, with 60% of them living outside the OECD and the BRIICS (Figure 5.13). This means that Sub-Saharan Africa and a number of Asian countries are unlikely to meet the MDG target for sanitation.

As can be seen in Figures 5.12 and 5.13, the vast majority of those without access to water supply and sanitation today live in rural areas. This trend is projected to continue to 2050, when the number of people in rural areas who lack access to sanitation is likely to become comparable with urban areas.

Figure 5.13. **Population lacking access to basic sanitation facilities:**
Baseline, 1990-2050

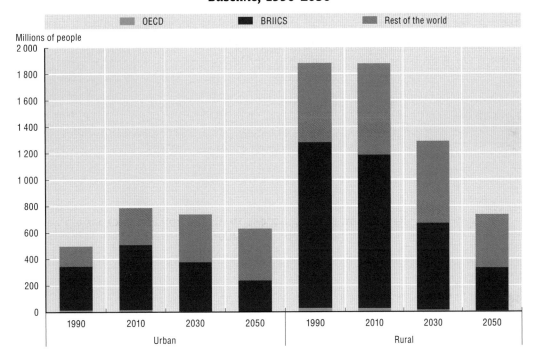

Source: *OECD Environmental Outlook Baseline;* output from IMAGE.

StatLink http://dx.doi.org/10.1787/888932571380

These figures are daunting, and the serious consequences of failing to speed up progress cannot be overemphasised. The health consequences are well documented. Worldwide every year unsafe water, inadequate sanitation and poor hygiene claim the lives of an estimated 2.2 million children under the age of 5. Of these deaths, 1.5 million are due to diarrhoea, the second leading contributor to the global burden of disease. The death (mortality) impact of diarrhoeal disease in children under 15 is greater than the combined impact of HIV and AIDS, malaria, and tuberculosis (see Chapter 6 on health and the environment).

The implications for water quality of the failure to meet the sanitation target are also severe. With progress in wastewater treatment lagging behind that of wastewater collection, new sources of nutrients and pathogens are being deposited untreated into the environment. The environmental consequences of this situation have been discussed in the section on water quality above.

3. Policy: Current and future scenarios

This section first reviews the policy instruments currently available to manage water resources and develop water and sanitation services, illustrated by examples of recent progress in OECD countries in applying these policy approaches. It then explores three model-based policy simulations to discuss alternative futures for water use efficiency, nutrient reduction and improved access to safe water and sanitation.

An inventory of water policy instruments

OECD countries have adopted a range of policy approaches to address the water challenges they face, including regulatory approaches, economic instruments, information-based and other policy tools (Table 5.1).

Table 5.1. **Selected policy instruments for water resource management**

Regulatory (command-and-control) approaches	Economic instruments	Information and other instruments
Norms and standards for water quality (*e.g.* drinking water quality, ambient water quality for recreational water bodies, industrial discharges).	Charges (*e.g.* abstraction, pollution). User tariffs (*e.g.* for water services). Payment for watershed services (*e.g.* for protection of catchment upstream).	Metering of water usage. Eco-labelling and certification (*e.g.* for agriculture, water-saving household appliances).
Performance-based standards.	Reform of environmentally harmful subsidies (*e.g.* production-linked agricultural support; energy subsidies for pumping water).	Voluntary agreements between businesses and government for water efficiency.
Restrictions or bans on activities which have an impact on water resources (*e.g.* polluting activities in catchment areas; ban on phosphorus detergents).	Subsidies (*e.g.* public investment in infrastructure, social pricing of water).	Promotion of, awareness raising and training in ecological farming practices or improved irrigation technologies.
Abstraction and discharge permits Water rights.	Tradable water rights and quotas.	Stakeholder initiatives and co-operative arrangements seeking to improve water systems, *e.g.* between farmers and water utilities.
Land use regulation and zoning (*e.g.* buffer zone requirements for pesticides application).	Insurance schemes.	Planning tools (*e.g.* integrated river basin management plans). Cost-benefit analysis of water management policies.

Regulatory approaches

To protect human health, most countries set ambient water quality standards for different uses, such as drinking water supplies, recreation use or bathing. Quality standards are regulated for discharges from municipal sewage systems and wastewater treatment plants, industries and power generation facilities.

For example, Australia has non-mandatory national guidance (The National Water Quality Management Strategy) that may be taken up in state or territory legislation and regulated at that level. The levels of phosphorus and nitrates in the EU's freshwater have declined in recent years (1992-2008) according to long-term data from monitoring stations (Eionet), primarily due to improved wastewater treatment and bans on phosphorous detergents.

Water rights[8]

Modern water rights specify the volume of water that may be abstracted by right owners from a water body. The volume can be a fixed amount, or a proportion of available water. In most countries, when explicitly defined, water rights are attached to land ownership. Countries are gaining experience with unbundling water rights from land ownership and managing them separately. This opens opportunities for flexible reallocation of water rights. Indeed, water rights are potentially an effective policy instrument to re-allocate water to higher-value uses (be it valuable crops, or selected industrial uses).

Water rights come with a range of conditions, including the payment of water fees or charges. In practice, however, right holders may consider high water prices as depriving them of their entitlement. In a number of jurisdictions, water rights may be traded. Water rights tend to have a limited duration. This generates trade-offs between the security of right holders and the flexibility of water allocation.

In most cases, before water rights can be used as a policy tool, they need to be reformed to place water under state ownership and control. This can generate opposition from right holders and rent seekers. Appropriate processes and compensation measures need to be considered.

Recent developments illustrate important policy issues related to water rights. Firstly, fast-growing economies that need to secure food supplies are increasingly making land-lease deals with poorer nations that have fertile land with water availability (WEF, 2011); unbundling water rights from land ownership in these countries would ensure that water benefits domestic needs, but this may generate tensions with the new owners of the land. Secondly, there is a risk that some water rights may be purchased for speculative purposes. To mitigate this risk, several states in Australia prohibit or cap the ownership of water rights by people not owning or occupying land, or restrict the proportion of entitlements in a given catchment that can be held by non-farm users. As a result, water markets are often inaccessible to urban users (Ekins and Salmons, 2010). Thirdly, potential negative impacts of water re-allocation on third parties should be minimised. In particular, the needs of the environment have to be factored in, for instance through ensuring minimum ecological reserves.

A variant of tradable water rights is tradable nutrient rights to mitigate nutrient pollution. The case of Lake Taupo in New Zealand is an interesting example of a tradable rights mechanism that reduces nutrient run-offs to lakes and helps restore water quality (see Box 5.6).

Water pricing

Putting the right price on water and water-related services encourages people to waste less, pollute less, invest more in water infrastructure and value watershed services. Pricing water can help serve four objectives:

■ Along with tax incentives and transfers, tariffs on water-related services generate finance to cover investment and operation and maintenance costs.

■ It helps to allocate water among competing uses.

■ It can manage demand and discourage depletion of water resources.

■ Appropriate tariffs ensure adequate and equitable access to affordable water and water-related services.

Box 5.6. **Tradable nutrient rights to mitigate nutrient flows: The case of Lake Taupo, New Zealand**

Lake Taupo is the largest freshwater lake in New Zealand, and supports an important fishery. The regional government has decided to reduce nutrient inputs to Lake Taupo in order to maintain or improve water quality. This is to be done through a "cap-and-trade" scheme, which involves the following steps:

1. Define the "cap" – the nutrient load that maintains lake water quality.

2. Define the players in the market – those who release the most nutrients into the lake's catchment.

3. Allocate nutrient polluting allowances to the key players.

4. Trade allowances – this involves having a market place and setting a price.

5. Monitor compliance.

This system ensures that any increases in nitrogen leaching are offset by corresponding and equivalent reductions in nitrogen leaching within the Lake Taupo catchment. The target is to reduce the nitrogen load by 20%. Farms contribute more than 90% of the manageable nitrogen input to the lake, so farmers are key parties to the scheme. Another party is the Lake Taupo Protection Trust, which administers a fund to protect lake water quality, and will be able to purchase nitrogen discharge allowances (NDA) and/or farmland.

The initial allowances are being allocated based on documented stocking rates, meat and wool production, fertiliser use, and other parameters, during a five-year window and using Overseer® (a computer model that calculates and estimates the nutrient flows in a productive farming system) to predict nitrogen exports. When this process is completed, each farmer will have a consent which details their NDA – a fixed amount expressed as tonnes of nitrogen per year.

From year to year, farmers can alter how they farm, provided their nitrogen export (as predicted by Overseer®) does not exceed their NDA. If a farmer wants to increase production, they must purchase NDA from another farmer who wants to decrease production. Once a trade has been agreed between two farmers, each of their consents is adjusted to increase or decrease their NDA.

Source: Adapted from Rutherford K., T. Cox (2009), "Nutrient Trading to Improve and Preserve Water Quality", *Water and Atmosphere*, 17(1).

Efforts are being made in OECD countries to better account for the costs and externalities of water use by households and industrial users (OECD, 2010a). This is reflected in the level of prices (which have increased, at times substantially, over the last decade) and in the structure of tariffs (which better reflect consumption and treatment costs).

OECD countries are also gaining experience with abstraction, pollution/effluent charges and other economic instruments – such as tradable water rights or payment for watershed services – to achieve more economically efficient, socially equitable and environmentally sustainable abstraction and allocation among competing uses:

■ Abstraction charges are often designed to provide funding for water resources management or for watershed protection activities. However, they seldom reflect water scarcity and tend to be relatively low. Abstraction taxes imposed on groundwater tend to be higher than on surface water. In most cases, charges are collected and retained locally.

■ Pollution charges can be linked to different characteristics of the polluter, the effluents or the recipient water body. In most cases, they are collected at the local level – only rarely at the river basin level – and earmarked to finance environmental activities. In some countries, revenues collected from downstream beneficiaries are used to compensate upstream residents for restrictions put on their land use. This is an important step towards truly integrated water and land management across a river basin.

The level of prices for water supplied to farms has risen in OECD countries. Frequently, however, farmers are only paying the operation and maintenance costs for water supplied, with little or no recovery of capital costs of irrigation infrastructure. Water scarcity and environmental costs are rarely reflected in water prices. This often results from claims that higher water prices will undercut farmers' competitiveness on global markets. However, where countries have raised water charges for farmers, the available evidence indicates no reduction in agricultural output (OECD, 2010c). Pricing policies for farmers are often combined with other (regulatory) instruments, such as abstraction thresholds and permits.

Tariff levels charged to households for water supply and sanitation services vary greatly among OECD countries (Figure 5.14), reflecting contrasted efforts to recover the costs of the services through prices. The data show that in half of the countries, wastewater services can be more expensive than drinking water supply. They also confirm that prices have risen over the last decade (although in some cases more slowly in the most recent years), primarily driven by wastewater charges, which were brought in line with the costs of investment needed for environmental compliance (e.g. tertiary treatment). Value added tax (VAT) and other taxes also explain part of the increase.

Tariff structures for water supply vary within and across OECD countries, reflecting the degree of decentralisation of the tariff-setting process. Several OECD surveys note that fewer countries over the years are reporting the use of flat fees and decreasing block tariff structures. An emerging trend in some OECD countries is the combination of fixed charges alongside a

Figure 5.14. **Unit price of water and wastewater services to OECD households (including taxes), 2007/08**

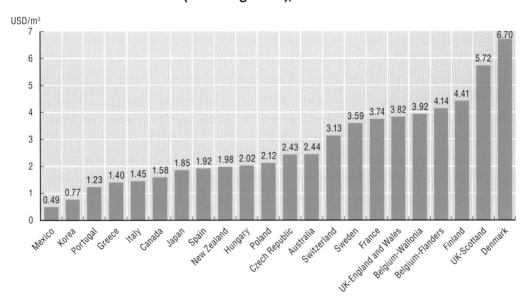

Source: OECD estimates based on country replies to the 2007/08 survey or on public sources validated by the countries; see OECD (2010a), *Pricing Water Resources and Water and Sanitation Services*, OECD Publishing.

StatLink ⬛⬛⬛ http://dx.doi.org/10.1787/888932571399

component based on the volume of water used, or the progressive increase in the weight of fixed charges in the overall bill.

Increasingly, wastewater charges are being introduced to cover wastewater management costs. Most countries levy separate charges for sewerage and for wastewater treatment, although in most cases the basis for charging remains water consumption. Only the size of the volumetric rate differs.

Lessons have been learned on the social consequences of water tariff policies. Low water prices hurt the poor most, as they deprive utilities from revenues to expand coverage, forcing the poor to procure poor quality water from private vendors. Water tariffs can be structured to account for the basic needs of all segments of the population. However, social policy objectives are better attained through socially targeted measures such as income support. Targeting and keeping the transaction costs low are essential criteria in designing such measures.

The pricing of water supply and sanitation services to industry is a little different to household tariff structures. For example, more countries and regions use decreasing block water tariffs for industry, particularly for large users. The desire to keep large customers that provide substantial local and stable revenues seems to inhibit the use of tariff structures that would encourage less water use. With regard to wastewater management, there is a growing use of separate charges for wastewater collection and for wastewater treatment, with the latter increasingly based on the pollution load of industrial effluents, thus better reflecting actual treatment costs.

Policy mix: Towards a coherent policy framework

Effective water management requires a coherent mix of policy instruments combining regulatory and market-based tools, often within comprehensive management plans with specific goals and targets. The boxes below (5.7-5.9) give examples from OECD countries of various combinations of policy instruments, including economic instruments (pricing, trading) and institutional reforms:

- Australia's National Water Initiative which places a strong emphasis on water planning, pricing and trading;
- Israel's water policy which combines improved technologies with water pricing and metering; and
- the EU Water Framework Directive, which places an emphasis on River Basin Management Plans and cost-effectiveness.

Australia's National Water Initiative includes a comprehensive mix of policy instruments addressing different aspects of water management. This initiative is being assessed and adjusted periodically since its implementation in 2004.

In Israel, the intensity of freshwater use is extremely high by OECD standards. Israel already consumes more water than supplied from the environment (essentially rainfall). Water scarcity has been exacerbated in recent years by several multiyear cycles of drought and consequent over-pumping of water to meet growing water demands. Rainfall has decreased by 9% since 1993, on average, and could drop by a further 10% between 2015 and 2035, according to climate change models. Israel's water outlook to 2050 (Figure 5.15) anticipates that increasing population and agricultural growth will place additional pressures on the country's limited water resources, in terms of both quantity and quality (OECD, 2011c). In this context, the water policy mix in Israel has emphasised targets to reduce freshwater use, and the diffusion of economic instruments to manage demand and to allocate water.

Box 5.7. **Australia's National Water Initiative**

The Intergovernmental Agreement on a National Water Initiative (NWI) was established in Australia in 2004. It is Australia's blueprint for water reform. The overall objective of the NWI is to achieve a nationwide market, regulatory and planning based system for managing surface and groundwater resources for rural and urban use that optimises economic, social and environmental outcomes at the national level. The NWI agreement includes objectives, outcomes and commitments across eight inter-related elements of water management: water access entitlements and planning, water markets and trading, best practice water pricing, integrated management of water for the environment, water resource accounting, urban water reform, knowledge and capacity building, community partnerships and adjustment.

The Australian government publishes biennial assessment reports on the implementation of the NWI. These national assessments cover all groundwater and surface water systems across the states and territories, rural and urban. The 2011 assessment noted that progress has been made since the initiation of the NWI in 2004, particularly in improving planning frameworks, water markets and trading. The major criticisms tended to be over the pace of reform, which was considered too slow and unequal across jurisdictions.

To address these and other issues, the Australian government has passed Commonwealth legislation: *the Water Act 2007, the Water Amendment Act 2008* and relevant water regulations. This regulatory framework established the Murray-Darling Basin Authority and required it to prepare a strategic plan for the integrated and sustainable management of water resources in the basin. The *Water Act 2007* also established a Commonwealth Environmental Water Holder to manage the Commonwealth's environmental water to protect and restore the environmental assets of the Murray-Darling Basin (Australia's most important agriculture region, producing one third of Australia's food supply), and outside the basin where the Commonwealth owns water.

The Australian government is also funding the Water for the Future initiative (Box 5.13). This is a long-term initiative to secure the water supply of all Australians (AUD 12.9 billion investment over 10 years); it builds on the NWI and the Water Act 2007.

Sources: National Water Commission website *www.nwc.gov.au/www/html/117-national-water-initiative.asp*; Australian National Water Commission (2011), *The National Water Initiative – Securing Australia's Water Future: 2011 Assessment*, NWC, Canberra.

The European Water Framework Directive (WFD) was adopted in 2000. It takes a holistic approach to water policy for the European Union. Its overarching objective is to restore the status of European water bodies (surface waters, transitional waters, coastal waters and ground waters) to good ecological and chemical condition by 2015. It is a flexible policy framework for the EU member states to implement according to national legislation, but sets a number of principles and ambitious targets and makes the case for the use of economic instruments.

Box 5.8. **Policy response to water stress in Israel**

Israel's national goal is to supply water to all consumers sustainably, based on approved requirements for quality, quantity, efficiency, and economic feasibility. To this end, Israel has set specific targets to gradually reduce its reliance on natural potable water by 2050. The key policy initiatives aim to reduce demand by i) requiring by law that all water supplies are metered; ii) monitoring water reuse and the use of brackish water in agriculture; and iii) promoting drip irrigation and reuse of treated domestic wastewater in agriculture. The government also aims to increase potable water supply by constructing large-scale desalination facilities.

Efforts are also being made to use economic instruments. Significant increases in water tariffs have taken place or are planned in all sectors, and lower prices for effluent and brackish water encourage their use for irrigation. A quota of potable water is allocated to the agricultural sector each year; farmers who opt to exchange part of this quota for alternative sources can secure the volume of wastewater they will procure at a fixed price.

Figure 5.15. **Israel's water consumption outlook to 2050**
Per type of water

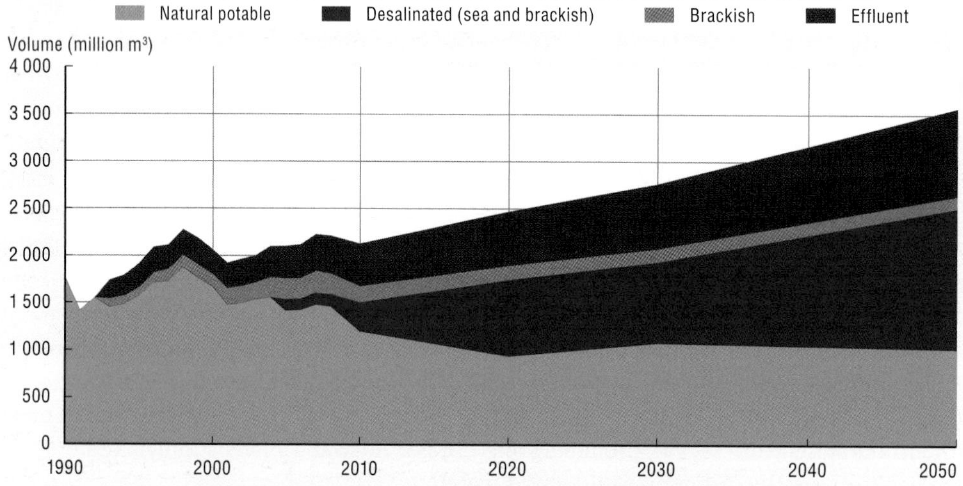

Note: The statistical data for Israel are supplied by and under the responsibility of the relevant Israeli authorities. The use of such data by the OECD is without prejudice to the status of the Golan Heights, East Jerusalem and Israeli settlements in the West Bank under the terms of international law.

Source: Water Authority, quoted in OECD (2011c), *OECD Environmental Performance Review: Israel 2011*, OECD, Publishing. StatLink http://dx.doi.org/10.1787/888932571418

The case of agricultural water

For the world to feed its growing population, world agricultural production would need to increase by some 70% between 2005 and 2050 (FAO, 2006; Bruinsma, 2009). According to the *Environmental Outlook Baseline*, this will probably have to be achieved with less water, mainly because of pressure from growing urbanisation, industrialisation and possibly climate change.

This implies an urgent need to adopt water-efficient irrigation technologies, such as drip emitters, and better maintenance of irrigation infrastructure. OECD work on the transfer of environment friendly technologies has found that the most positive environmental effects materialise when transfer mechanisms develop the absorptive capabilities of the target economy (see OECD, 2011f); education and training are therefore essential.

Box 5.9. **The EU Water Framework Directive: A river basin approach**

The WFD considers all pressures and impacts on the aquatic environment and integrates requirements from other pieces of EU water legislation. The directive has a number of objectives. The key ones are general protection of aquatic ecology, specific protection of unique and valuable habitats, protection of drinking water resources, and protection of bathing water. All these objectives must be integrated for each river basin.

The WFD is ambitious but flexible, as it does not prescribe one single policy package. Member states can implement it according to their own legislation, and are free to set their own targets for the share of water bodies which will be restored by 2015.

One core principle of the WFD is that the best model for water management is by river basin – the natural geographical and hydrological unit – instead of according to administrative or political boundaries. Therefore, member states are requested to develop river basin management plans (RBMPs). Economic instruments, including water pricing, play a prominent role in the WFD. The aim is to lead to the recovery of the financial and environmental costs of water services (the cost recovery principle).

The EU WFD comes with a suite of water-related directives (*e.g.* Directive 2007/60/EC on the assessment and management of flood risks entered into force on 26 November 2007), and this requires co-ordination. In the case of the Flood Directive, co-ordination is required between flood risk management plans and river basin management plans, and between public participation procedures.

The first phase of a recent assessment concluded that, although the right measures may be in place, they are sometimes difficult to enforce and vulnerable to political pressure at national level (Deloitte, IEEP, 2011). Moreover, many plans appeared to delay action until the final stages of EU law implementation. Member states have made only sluggish progress with introducing economic instruments such as water pricing, while the principle of cost recovery remains controversial (see Deloitte and IEEP, 2011).

In parts of the OECD water use has become more efficient and there are fewer leakages – overall the average water application rate per hectare irrigated declined by 9% between 1990 and 2003 (OECD, 2010c). Reductions have been most notable in Australia, and to a lesser extent in Mexico, Spain and the United States. However, in other countries – including Greece, Portugal and Turkey – water application rates are increasing (OECD, 2008b).

Steps must be taken to move towards more efficient management of water resources in agriculture, while responding to the growing global food demand and the impacts of climate change (OECD, 2010c):

■ Institutions and water rights need to be strengthened.

■ Water supplied to agriculture needs to be subject to tariffs which take into account the cost of supply, scarcity, social values and environmental costs and benefits. The latter are usually addressed by other policy measures, including agri-environmental payments, pollution taxes and water allocation mechanisms (Box 5.10). Some countries are using the principle of full cost recovery to guide their water policy frameworks (defined as using tariffs to recover the financial and environmental costs of water services). Trading water entitlements places a price on scarcity and can promote the highest value use of water resources. However, such a policy may interfere with food security issues, and requires a well-informed and transparent debate to be successfully implemented. Trade must be factored in, as freer trade in agricultural commodities can enhance food security and protect environmental values.

■ Agriculture's resilience to climate change needs to be enhanced, using strategies to adapt agricultural production systems. These are likely to be more effective if they are embedded in longer-term strategies closely linked to agricultural policy reform and risk management policy.

Box 5.10. Reform of agricultural support and water: The case of the European Union

Until 2005, EU agricultural policy (the Common Agricultural Policy or CAP) was based on direct aid payments to farmers to promote production. These payments were accompanied by optional agri-environmental payments to protect and improve the environment. A common view is that this policy has traditionally promoted a large expansion in agricultural production. At the same time it has allowed farmers to use unecological ways of increasing production, such as the indiscriminate use of fertilisers and pesticides, with serious environmental consequences. A total re-focusing of the payment scheme in 2004 now puts the environment at the centre of farming policy. By linking farmers' payments to a number of strict environmental standards (among others) in the so-called cross-compliance scheme, farmers now have to face cuts in their subsidy levels if they don't meet the strict environmental requirements.

Across the European Union, there are numerous examples of crops with high water requirements that were nevertheless encouraged by the CAP. For example, maize is considered a water-demanding crop in temperate countries, but until 2003 EU maize growers were entitled to a direct subsidy of EUR 54/tonne. With the new decoupling policy, this inconsistency has been eliminated, and farmers' use of water will not be driven by subsidy differences across crops. Garrido and Varela-Ortega (2008) have reported the gradual but steady changes of irrigated land allocation that have occurred in Spain since the CAP reform. The major and most significant changes are that drier areas are being allocated to vineyards, olive trees and citrus (especially in Andalusia), while higher rainfall areas have been allocated to water-consuming crops such as maize and other reformed crops, including sugar beet, cotton and tobacco.

When EU farm subsidies become completely decoupled from production in 2012, the economics of irrigation will be more guided by the productivity of crops and their water requirements, than by the agricultural support available.

Sources: Adapted from OECD (2010c), *Sustainable Management of Water Resources in Agriculture*, OECD, Publishing; Calatrava J. and Garrido, A. (2010), *Agricultural Water Pricing: EU and Mexico*, OECD consultant report available at *www.oecd.org/water*.

"Virtual water": A limited concept for policy making

The concepts of "virtual water" and "water footprints" have gained broad appeal for raising awareness of water scarcity, global impacts of consumption and production on water resources, and allocation issues. However, these indicators have limits as policy or management tools, as they do not take into account the opportunity cost of water in production, other inputs used in production (*e.g.* labour), or distinguish between the management of water resources and water quality. They should be used in combination with other indicators to discuss broader policy goals, such as reducing poverty, stimulating economic development and ensuring high employment while preserving natural resources (Box 5.11). Moreover, they would certainly benefit from more work to refine the calculations of water footprints.

Box 5.11. **Economic analysis of the virtual water and water footprint concepts for water policies**

Virtual water: The term "virtual water" began appearing in the water resources literature in the mid-1990s. Professor Tony Allan of London University chose the term to describe the water used to produce crops traded in international markets. During the 15 years since its inception, the virtual water concept has been very helpful in gaining the attention of public officials and policy makers responsible for encouraging wise use of limited water resources.

However, the fundamental shortcoming of the virtual water concept as a valid policy prescriptive tool is the lack of an underlying conceptual framework. Some researchers have incorrectly described virtual water as analogous to, or consistent with the economic theory of comparative advantage. The virtual water concept is applied most often when discussing or comparing water-short and water-abundant countries. By focusing on the water resource endowment alone, virtual water represents an application of absolute advantage, rather than comparative advantage. For this reason, policy prescriptions that arise from virtual water discussions will not maximise the net benefits of engaging in international trade. Comparative advantage is the pertinent economic concept, and virtual water considers only absolute advantage.

A number of authors have begun describing the important role of non-water factors such as population densities, historical production trends, national food security goals, poverty reduction targets, and the availability of complementary inputs when determining whether to transfer water from one region to another, or to achieve desired outcomes alternatively by transporting or trading agricultural commodities.

Water footprints: The notion of water footprints describes the volume of water required to support production and consumption in selected regions or countries. It is used to assess whether a region or country is consuming resources in a sustainable or unsustainable fashion from a global perspective. However, estimated water footprints are somewhat one-dimensional, as they depict the use of only one resource. In addition, water footprints do not describe the implications of water use. Instead they consider only the amounts of water used in production and consumption activities. Hence, ecological water footprint analysis is not sufficient for determining optimal policy alternatives, as it does not account for the opportunity (scarcity) costs of water resources and the ways in which water is combined with other inputs in production and consumption. Water footprints enable one to compare estimated water use per person or in aggregate across countries, but they are inadequate for evaluating the incremental costs, benefits, or environmental impacts of water use.

Farmers, traders, and public officials must consider many economic and social issues when determining optimal strategies. Virtual water and water footprint concepts will be helpful in policy discussions in many settings, in combination with other environmental, economic, and social indicators. But they will not be sufficient for determining the optimal outcomes of those discussions and establishing economically efficient and environmentally effective policy alternatives.

Source: Adapted from OECD (2010c), *Sustainable Management of Water Resources in Agriculture*, OECD Publishing.

A recent analysis confirms that "virtual water transfers are highly unequal but represent a small volume of water relative to total water needs" (Seekel *et al.*, 2011). It concluded that "virtual water transfer is not sufficient to equalise water use among nations primarily because internal agricultural water use, the main contributor to inequality, dominates national water needs and cannot be completely compensated by current volumes of virtual water transfers".

What if...? Three model-based simulations of alternative water futures

So far this chapter has described the situation for water in 2050 under a "business-as-usual" policy context of the *Baseline* scenario. But could the situation be improved in the future with more ambitious policies? This section presents the *Outlook* modelling work which explores the implications of three hypothetical scenarios:

■ a *Resource Efficiency* scenario;

■ a *Nutrient Recycling and Reduction* scenario;

■ an *Accelerated Access* scenario for water and sanitation.

Resource Efficiency scenario

The *Resource Efficiency* scenario models how the water-stress picture would change if more ambitious policies reduced water demand and enhanced water-use efficiency. This policy simulation is based on the *450 Core* scenario explored in Chapter 3, climate change. That scenario assumes lower water demand for thermal electricity generation and a greater share of electricity produced through solar and wind generation. In addition, the *Resource Efficiency* scenario assumes further efficiency improvements of 15% for irrigation in non-OECD countries, as well as 30% improvements in domestic and manufacturing uses globally. Further details on the assumptions used for this policy simulation are given in Annex 5.A.

Under the *Resource Efficiency* scenario, the rate of increase in global water demand is expected to slow down. Total demand in 2050 would be around 4 100 km^3, 15% above the demand in 2000, but 25% below the *Baseline* scenario. In the *Resource Efficiency* scenario, water demand in OECD countries would be 35% lower in 2050 than in 2000 (compared to 10% lower in the *Baseline* scenario).

Water stress would also improve under the *Resource Efficiency* scenario in many river basins in China, the United States, Southern Europe and Eastern Europe and Russia. However, the number of people globally living under severe water stress would be reduced only slightly compared to the *Baseline*, from 3.9 to 3.7 billion (Figure 5.16), suggesting that this scenario can only tame the severity of stress in a number of regions. The number of people facing no stress would increase, but many would still face severe water stress, especially in North Africa and Middle East, the India region and Central Asia.

This simulation suggests that, in a number of regions, efficiency gains alone will not be sufficient to reduce water stress. More ambitious and radical approaches are needed to further reduce demand and mitigate competition across water users. Allocation of water across users (including for ecosystems) will be an important challenge.

Nutrient Recycling and Reduction scenario

This second model-based policy simulation reflects the need for aggressive policies to further reduce nutrient discharges in order to decrease eutrophication of lakes and oceans. The *Nutrient Recycling and Reduction* scenario assesses the impact of measures to reuse nutrients in agriculture and reduce both domestic and agricultural discharges of nitrogen (N) and phosphorus (P). As supplies in phosphorus rock dwindle,[9] P recovery from wastewater may help to fill the gap. The assumptions used are described in Annex 5.A.

Figure 5.16. **Number of people living in water-stressed river basins in 2000
and in 2050**

Baseline (BL) and Resource Efficiency scenario (RE)

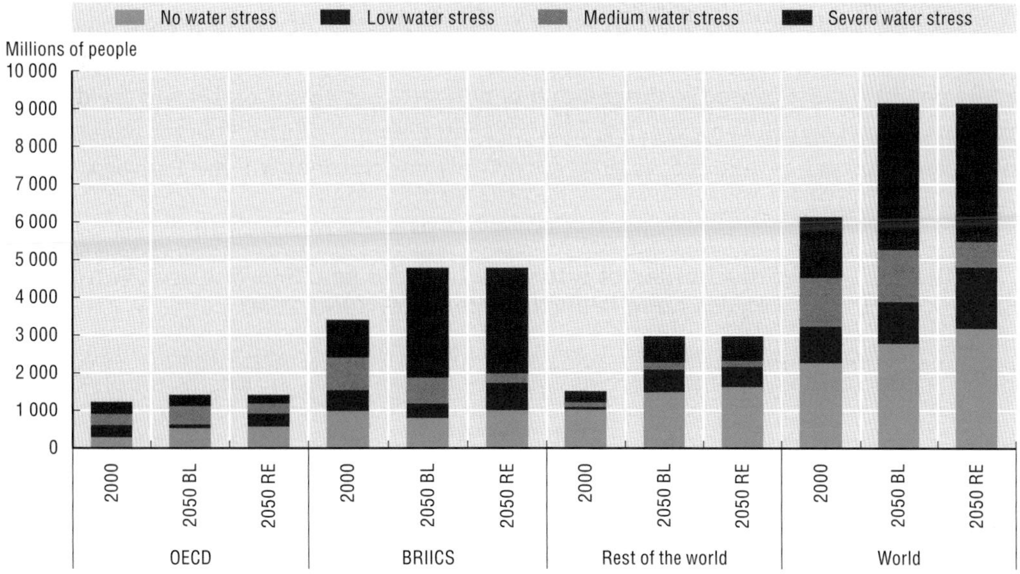

Source: OECD Environmental Outlook projections; output from IMAGE.

StatLink http://dx.doi.org/10.1787/888932571437

New measures that could bring about these improvements would include an increase in fertiliser use efficiency, higher nutrient efficiencies in livestock production and using animal manure instead of synthetic N and P fertilisers in countries with a fertiliser-dominated arable system. The scenario assumes investments in sewage systems that separately collect urine from other wastewater in households (see Table 5.A1 in Annex 5.A) – recycling treated wastewater back into agriculture would significantly reduce wastewater nutrient flows *and* fertiliser use.

Under this scenario, by 2050 the global N and P surpluses in agriculture could be almost 20% less than in the *Baseline* scenario, and the effluent of nutrients in wastewater could fall by nearly 35%. Total nutrient loads to rivers would be reduced by nearly 40% for nitrogen and 15% for phosphorus compared to *Baseline*. Such reductions could help to prevent further biodiversity loss in rivers, lakes and wetlands in the long term, and even allow some recovery locally. As for coastal zones, the measures to reduce nutrient flows would be most effective in the Pacific Ocean. For the Atlantic and Indian Oceans, the opportunities to reduce nutrient losses from agriculture are limited due to the projected rapid growth in production (Figure 5.17). Phosphorus emissions to the Indian Ocean would even increase in the *Nutrient Recycling and Reduction* scenario. This is because of the following developments in the world regions that discharge into this ocean:

■ A small fraction of the population would have a sewage connection.

■ Current fertiliser use is low, and would have to increase to achieve the higher yields that are assumed in this scenario; consequently run-off of N and P would increase.

■ As the use of fertilisers is low, opportunities to substitute fertiliser by manure would be limited.

■ Manure that in the *Baseline* would end up outside the agricultural system (fuel or building material, especially in India), would be used in agriculture in the *Nutrient Recycling and Reduction* scenario.

However, even if N and P loadings are reduced, the risk of harmful algal blooms in coastal zones would stay high as the imbalance between nitrogen, phosphorus and silicon would persist. This is caused by different reduction rates between P and N and the growing number of dams, which decrease river loads of sediment and silicon. This suggests that an integrated approach is required, as progress on only one nutrient will have adverse effects in the long term.

Figure 5.17. **River discharges of nutrients into the sea: *Baseline* and *Nutrient Recycling and Reduction* scenario, 1950-2050**

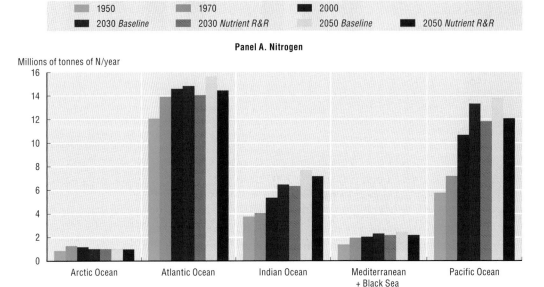

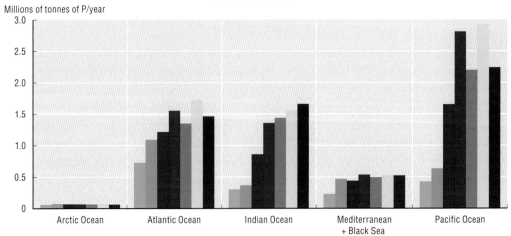

Source: *OECD Environmental Outlook projections; output from IMAGE.*

StatLink ⬛ᵐ⬛ *http://dx.doi.org/10.1787/888932571456*

Accelerated Access to water and sanitation scenario

In June 2010, the United Nations General Assembly adopted a resolution recognising access to clean water and sanitation as a human right. The resolution calls on states and international organisations to provide financial resources, build capacity and transfer technology, particularly to developing countries, in scaling up efforts to provide safe, clean, accessible and affordable drinking water and sanitation for all. In May 2011, the Special Rapporteur on the human right to safe drinking water and sanitation noted that these rights should be described in terms of availability, quality, acceptability, accessibility and affordability.[10]

These depart significantly from the definitions encapsulated in the MDGs. The MDGs originally refer to "*safe* drinking water" and "*adequate* sanitation", but actually monitor access to "an *improved* water source" and "*improved* sanitation". This potentially leads to a radical re-evaluation of how many people (and what kind of people) do not have "access to *safe* drinking water and sanitation". The WHO/UNICEF Joint Monitoring Programme for Water Supply and Sanitation, the official UN mechanism tasked with monitoring progress towards the MDG on drinking water and sanitation, is considering additional criteria to better monitor some of these dimensions.

The *Environmental Outlook's Accelerated Access* scenario explores the additional annual costs and health benefits of meeting more ambitious targets than the MDGs. The targets would occur in two steps as follows:

i) By 2030 the population without access to an *improved* water source and to basic sanitation is halved again from the 2005 base year, building on the progress already achieved under the current MDG.

ii) Universal access to a water source and to basic sanitation is achieved by 2050.

Under this scenario, by 2030 almost 100 million additional people would have access to an improved water source and around 470 million more people would have access to basic sanitation facilities than under the *Baseline* (Figure 5.18). Almost all of these people would be living outside OECD and BRIICS countries (*i.e.* in the rest of the world – RoW). By 2050, an additional 242 million would have access to an improved water source, with the RoW accounting for most of this gain. Over 1.36 billion additional people would have access to basic sanitation facilities (nearly 800 million in the RoW, and more than 560 million in the BRIICS).

What would the benefits be from this scenario? The consequences for health are discussed in Chapter 6. The estimated number of avoided deaths per year would be about 76 000 by 2030 and 81 000 by 2050, essentially in the RoW group of countries. The benefits for the environment and certain economic sectors, such as fisheries or tourism, are substantial. Actual benefits are even greater, given that some significant positive consequences (such as pride and dignity, or amenity value) are more difficult to quantify in monetary terms.

In least developed countries in particular, the benefits are massive and far outstrip the costs. The World Health Organization estimates that benefit-to-cost ratios can be as high as 7 to 1 for basic water and sanitation services in developing countries (quoted in OECD, 2011b). According to the GLAAS report, improved access to water and sanitation produces economic benefits that range from USD 3 to USD 34 for every dollar invested, increasing a country's GDP by an estimated 2% to 7% (WHO, 2010).

Figure 5.18. **Number of additional people with access to water supply and sanitation in the *Accelerated Access* scenario, compared to the *Baseline*, 2030 and 2050**

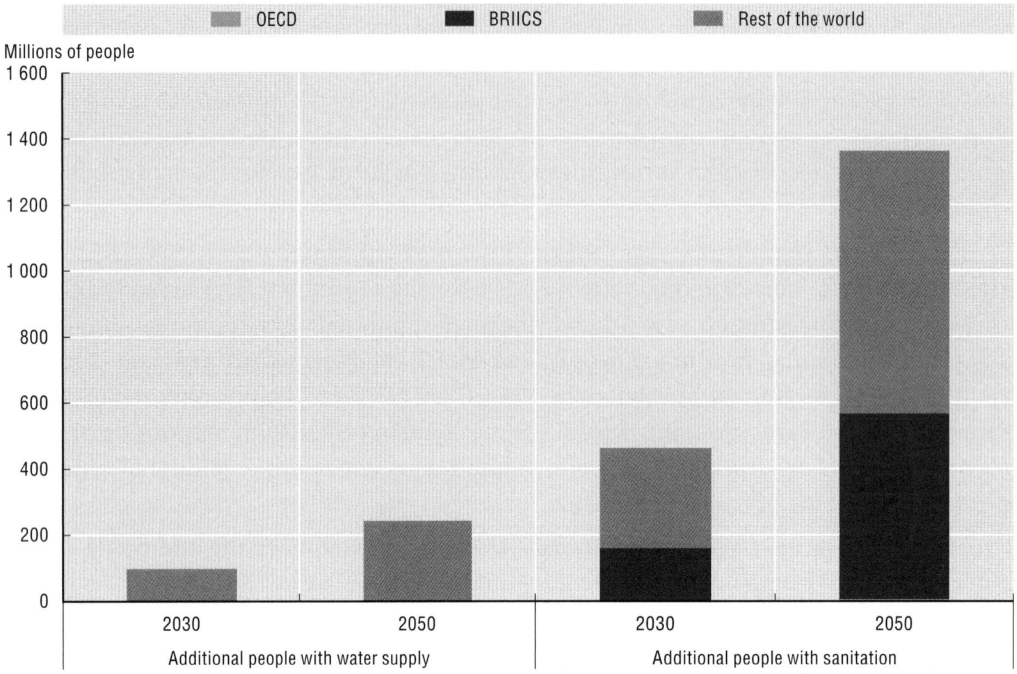

Source: OECD Environmental Outlook projections; output from IMAGE.

StatLink http://dx.doi.org/10.1787/888932571494

The valuation of the benefits for any single country must take account of national circumstances, such as the stage of infrastructure development and GDP per capita. In addition, benefit values are highly location specific, depending, for example, on the prevalence of water-related diseases or the condition of receiving water bodies. Some benefits are likely to tail away as there tends to be diminishing returns from further investments in improving quality of water related services. Benefits are more likely to materialise if investments are appropriately sequenced, thereby lowering costs and ensuring that collected wastewater is properly treated.

OECD experience indicates that increasing access to water supply and sanitation requires large investments to retrofit poorly adapted infrastructure and to build new facilities. The *Accelerated Access* scenario indicates that globally an average of USD 1.9 billion would need to be invested each year between 2010 and 2030 to achieve the 2030 target in addition to what would be invested under the *Baseline* scenario; and an additional USD 7.6 billion beyond the *Baseline* would be needed annually between 2031 and 2050 to achieve the 2050 target. The difference between the two figures reflects the fact that the last step is more costly than the previous ones. In Sub-Saharan Africa these additional costs would make up 0.09% of the GDP in 2030 and 0.08% in 2050.

In addition, significant and stable financial flows will be needed to maintain and operate this infrastructure. This will require well-developed and realistic strategies which tap three main sources of finance: revenues from tariffs for water services, taxes channelled through public budgets, and transfers from the international community (OECD, 2010a). The private sector (the water industry and financial institutions) can also play a key role in developing and channelling innovations and enhancing efficiency. They can also harness private savings and facilitate investment when appropriate framework conditions are in place (OECD, 2009; 2010e). Increasing competition to access scarce public financial resources may be an incentive to revisit past experience with private sector finance in the water sector, which has been disappointing in developing countries (Annez, 2006). Public funds to achieve universal access are expected to increase when the UN Resolution on water as a human right is translated into action. In addition, all OECD member states are committed to raising their official development assistance to reach 0.7% of their GDP; some of this increase could help fund these much-needed developments.

4. Need for further action: Emerging issues in water policy

The previous sections have shown that more ambitious policies and new ways of looking at the water challenge are urgently needed. This final section highlights some of the most important emerging directions for water policy and its reform. These include:

■ seeing water as an essential driver of green growth;

■ allocating enough water for healthy ecosystems;

■ fostering greater coherence among water, energy, environment and food policies;

■ finding alternative sources of water (*e.g.* water reuse);

■ filling information gaps;

■ designing reforms that are realistic and politically acceptable.

Seeing water as an essential driver of green growth

The OECD is working to reconcile the demand for continued economic growth and development with the need to ensure that natural assets continue to provide the resources and environmental services on which all human well-being relies. This underpins the concept of "green growth", which sees sustainable water use as an essential driver, since a lack of water of appropriate quality can significantly hinder growth (OECD, 2011a). As discussed above, water management can generate huge benefits for health, agricultural and industrial production. Water management can preserve ecosystems and the watershed services they provide, thereby avoiding the enormous costs that can be imposed by flooding, drought, or the collapse of watershed services.

Similarly, UNEP (2011) confirms that investments in infrastructure and operation of water-related services can provide high returns for both the economy and the environment. It highlights the need for more private and public investment in green technologies and infrastructure to boost water (and energy) efficiency and sees such investments as critical to building the green economy of the future.

Thus, water efficiency and water demand management are essential ingredients for green growth, along with water reuse and recycling. The Four Rivers Project in Korea (Box 5.12) is an example of a green growth policy factoring in investment in water-related infrastructure.

The following specific policy approaches can more systematically harness water management for green growth:

■ Invest in ecologically sensitive water storage and water distribution systems in water scarce regions. Reliable resources are essential for green growth. However, water storage

---

Box 5.12. **Korea's Four Rivers Restoration Project (4RR)**

The Four Rivers Project is a good illustration of an holistic approach to water resource management that also aims to drive green growth. Following the economic crisis, Korea decided to allocate 2% of its GDP every year between 2009 and 2013 (totalling USD 86 billion) to green investment to solve short-term economic problems and create jobs. Twenty per cent of this green budget (USD 17.6 billion) is to be invested in the water sector through the Four Rivers Restoration Project (4RR).

This project brings five ministries together in a holistic approach (Environment; Food, Agriculture, Forestry and Fisheries; Culture, Sports and Tourism; and Public Administration and Security; Ministry of Land, Transport and Maritime Affairs). Its aims are to secure enough water to respond to future water scarcity and severe drought due to climate change (target: water supply of 1.3 billion m^3); to take preemptive measures against floods due to climate change, as well as 200-year floods, by dredging sediment, strengthening old levees, and building small multipurpose dams (target: secure 920 million m^3 of flood control capacity); to improve water quality by expanding sewage treatment facilities and establishing green algae reduction facilities (target: BOD 3 mg/L); to restore ecological rivers, create wetlands, and readjust farmland to rehabilitate the ecosystem (223 restoration projects planned); to develop river banks to ensure space for leisure; and to develop the regions around rivers. The deadline for implementation of the plan is 2012.

The government expects the 4RR to generate USD 32.8 billion in economic benefits, and to create 340 000 jobs. Ultimately, the government expects the experiences and technologies developed in the 4RR project to make Korea one of the leading countries in the water management sector.

Source: Korea Environmental Policy Bulletin (2009), "Four Major River Restoration Project of Republic of Korea", *Korea Environmental Policy Bulletin*, Issue 3, Volume VII.

---

technologies and infrastructure such as large dams can disturb ecosystem balances. Soft infrastructure (*e.g.* wetlands, flood plains, groundwater recharge), small-scale dams, rainwater harvesting, or appropriately designed infrastructure are more ecologically sensitive and cost-effective.

■ Put a sustainable price on water and water-related services as an effective way to signal the scarcity of the resource and to manage demand. This will require identifying the beneficiaries and implementing mechanisms to ensure beneficiaries contribute to cover the costs of the benefits they enjoy.

■ Be prepared to allocate water across sectors and across water uses where it adds most value. This difficult policy challenge – diverting water to value-adding activities (including environmental services, see below) may require reallocation between water users (*e.g.* from farmers to cities). Some OECD countries are gaining experience with socially fair and politically acceptable approaches for achieving this. These include water abstraction licences which reflect scarcity; market mechanisms, *e.g.* tradable water rights; and information-based instruments (smart metering). How best to allocate water is still the subject of widespread debate. More needs to be done to properly assess and scale up the use of some of these instruments, to secure environmental values while meeting social and economic needs. Experience from OECD and non-OECD countries indicates that building a strong constituency and aligning incentives are two major requisites (see the discussion below on the political economy of water policy reforms).

■ Invest in water supply and sanitation infrastructure, in particular in urban slums where unsafe water and lack of sanitation generate huge health costs and lost opportunities to the economy.

■ Catalyse investment and innovation which will underpin sustained growth and give rise to new economic opportunities.

Allocating enough water for healthy ecosystems

The need to restore environmental flows and to allocate more water to watershed services is already generating interesting initiatives in several countries (Box 5.13). Well-designed regulations (on environmental flows) and market mechanisms (such as payment for watershed services) still need to disseminate more widely. They all benefit from more thorough assessments of the benefits of watershed services.

However, shifting water allocation – especially for environmental flows, but also among other users – can be challenging, as it requires difficult policy reforms that overturn expectations about "rights" to existing uses by different stakeholders. Gaining support for such reforms is a major challenge for policy makers. Experience from OECD and non-OECD countries indicates that building a strong constituency and aligning incentives are two major requisites (see the discussion below on the political economy of water policy reforms).

Fostering greater coherence among water, energy, environment and food policies

Water policies intersect with a wide array of sectors at different geographical scales, from local to international; coherent water governance is therefore pivotal. Analysis of water governance arrangements in OECD countries has highlighted that along with a lack of finance for water resource management for most countries, the fragmentation of roles and responsibilities at central and sub-national levels and the lack of capacity (infrastructure and knowledge) in local administrations are both limitations and drivers for future water policy reforms (OECD, 2011g).

The nexus among water, energy, environment and agriculture is close, complex, and challenging. Policy coherence among water policies and other sectoral policies – particularly energy and agriculture – is thus a key component of a co-ordinated approach to water resource management (OECD, forthcoming). Water is an essential element in energy production (*e.g.* for biofuels, hydropower, and cooling techniques for thermal and nuclear power plants). Energy is a critical input for transferring water and tapping alternative sources of water (*e.g.* desalinisation). In an increasing number of locations, there is competition between food and energy commodities for limited water resources. Under current trends, water for the environment and for food production will conflict in several regions (see Rosegrant *et al.*, 2002).

Tensions may arise from real or perceived trade-offs, for instance between food security (and the willingness to secure domestic production) and water productivity (and the allocation of water to activities which add more value). Inefficiencies may result from harmful subsidies (*e.g.* subsidising energy for groundwater abstraction by farmers).

Resolving such tensions requires a global perspective. For instance, freer trade in agricultural commodities and the reform of farm support policies in OECD countries can alleviate some of the tensions between food security and water productivity (Box 5.10). The linkages between the policy areas also have to be considered early on. For instance, when

---

Box 5.13. **Prioritising the environmental health of water courses: OECD case studies**

Australia

The Australian Commonwealth Government is funding the Water for the Future initiative – a long-term initiative to secure the water supply of all Australians. Under this programme, which involves an AUD 12.9 billion investment over 10 years, the government is acquiring tradable water entitlements with the objective of returning more water to the environment. The water is acquired through direct buybacks of water entitlements from irrigators as well as savings from infrastructure upgrades. These entitlements become part of the Commonwealth environmental water holdings and are managed so that increased flows are provided to rivers and wetlands, particularly within the Murray-Darling Basin (see also Box 5.7). Between June 2009 and July 2011, the Commonwealth government's environmental water holdings rose from 65 to 1 001 gigalitres. By 30 June 2011, over 550 gigalitres of Commonwealth environmental water had been delivered back to rivers, wetlands and floodplains of the Murray-Darling Basin. A strategic Basin Plan is also being developed in consultation with stakeholders from across the Murray-Darling to ensure the integrated and sustainable management of the basin in the longer term. A key part of the plan will be to set limits for water consumption in order to return sufficient water to the environment.

Switzerland

In December 2009, the Swiss Parliament decided that all rivers and lakes should be revitalised to restore their natural functions and to enhance the benefits they provide to society. At the same time the major negative environmental impacts of hydropower generation (surge and flow, reduced connectivity and impaired bed load regimes) are to be mitigated. This is considered a new step in the restoration of river quality in the country.

The following considerations were therefore added to the Water Code:

■ River bank space for waters: the ordinance sets minimal width requirements and defines which extensive agricultural practices are allowed. The code requires that space be made available for waters and that this is integrated into a management plan in the next five years.

■ Revitalisation: the ordinance defines the process which will be followed to plan the revitalisation. Highest priority will be given to revitalisations with the greatest impacts.

■ Reduction of the negative impacts of hydropower generation: the ordinance sets the impacts considered as significant and defines equipments for which remediation actions will be required. It also defines the process for planning and implementing such actions. Recommendations on prioritising small hydropower station projects are being developed to assist local authorities to implement cost-covering remuneration for feeding-in to the electricity grid (Confédération Suisse, 2011).

Sources: Australian Government Commonwealth Environmental Water website: *www.environment.gov.au/ ewater/about/index.html*; Confédération Suisse (2011), *Renaturation des Eaux: Modifications d'Ordonnances en Consultation*, Environment Switzerland, Bern/Neuchâtel, available at *www.news.admin.ch/message/ index.html?lang=fr&msg-id=33269.*

---

countries set biofuel production targets, there is a need to factor in potential consequences for water withdrawal in the future.[11]

Policy co-ordination requires institutions to support discussion among different communities. This is more difficult where responsibility is fragmented among various ministries, and where decision making needs to be co-ordinated at different territorial levels (national, regional, state, municipal, river basin, etc.). Institutions' capacity needs to be strengthened through better information and data exchange, sector integration and joint planning.

More coherent policy approaches are beginning to take shape in a growing number of OECD countries. This is particularly evident around climate change, with many countries starting to co-ordinate previously separate policy domains such as energy, water, flood and drought control, and agri-environment (Box 5.14). For example, the restoration of agricultural land in floodplains by planting trees has helped to reduce flood impacts, improve water quality, restore biodiversity and sequester greenhouse gases (OECD, 2010c). While some progress has been made, there is clearly much more to be done to achieve greater policy coherence.

Box 5.14. **Combining hydropower, river restoration and private investment in Bavaria, Germany**

Within the context of the European Water Framework Directive, in 2006 the Bavarian Ministry for Environment, Health and Consumer Protection, the Bavarian Ministry of Economic Affairs, Infrastructure, Transport and Technology and major electric supply companies in Bavaria agreed on a master plan on the future of hydropower in Bavaria, which aims to combine increased use of hydropower with restoring the ecological status of the region's main water bodies.

The implementation of the measures recommended in the plan would result in an increase in climate-friendly hydropower production in Bavaria, and in private sector investments. The plan envisages an increase in the production of hydropower by almost 14% through a combination of new plants at new sites, new plants at existing weirs or steps, modernisation and retrofitting.

Once implemented, the plan will be a good example of how economic development and ecological performance can be mutually reinforcing in Bavaria.

Source: Adapted from Haselbauer, M. and C. Göhl (2010), *Evaluation of Feasible Additional Hydro Potential in Bavaria/Germany*, RMD-Consult GmbH, Berlin, *www.rmd-consult.de/fileadmin/rmd-consult/news/ 2010_Hydro_paper_HA.pdf*.

Developing alternative sources of water

Tapping alternative water sources – rain and storm water, used water, and desalinated sea or brackish water – or encouraging successive uses of water can help to alleviate scarcity and can be a low-cost response to the water challenge. Additional benefits can include saving energy (depending on the technologies and on contextual features) and cutting investment, operation and maintenance costs. However, there are also risks attached to these technologies (see Box 6.6 in Chapter 6 on Environment and Health for a discussion).

Countries are already accumulating experience with these approaches. For example Israel is using wastewater to recharge groundwater or for irrigation. Pollutant discharges have been reduced by 20% (total nitrogen), 40% (organic matter) and 70% (total phosphorus) since 2000, largely due to the construction of new wastewater treatment plants and increasing reuse of effluent in agriculture. Windhoek in Namibia and Singapore are paving the way in recycling wastewater for urban water supply. Rainwater harvesting is increasingly considered as a complement to piped water supply (*e.g.* it is mandatory in Calcutta).

A wide array of technologies, equipment and systems is available for different uses: wastewater reuse for groundwater recharge, irrigation, gardening, or non-potable domestic uses; rainwater harvesting to increase the yields of rain fed agriculture, or to supply water for non-potable domestic uses, etc. Markets for technologies related to water reuse are booming, contributing to green growth.

Governments and local authorities would benefit from considering installing these alternative water sources and their support infrastructure. Wastewater reuse for irrigation is being adopted in different contexts. Reuse for domestic uses is gaining traction as well, sometimes combined with small-scale, distributed systems. This combination is particularly appropriate in new urban areas where there is no existing central infrastructure; in city centres with decaying water infrastructure or with infrastructure facing diseconomies of scale or capacity constraints; in urban renewal projects; in unstable contexts, where flexibility, resilience and adaptation are valuable (*i.e.* because of climate change impacts); and in projects where property developers operate the buildings they invest in (to recoup investment costs).

The technologies involved are often simple, and future research and development will make alternative water sources (such as sea water desalination) even more competitive. To realise the full benefits of alternative water systems and to mitigate the risks they generate (such as pollution of agricultural land, or health risks), the following steps will be important:

■ Involve and inform the public through effective communication and sound evidence; people are usually sceptical about reusing water.

■ Provide regulations that allow for alternative options for supplying water to be explored. In particular, water quality standards need to be adjusted to specific uses and potential reuse. Typically, urban wastewater can only be reused if it is not heavily polluted. Such regulations need to factor in several dimensions, including life-cycle costs and benefits, and the risks and uncertainties attached to the various water sources and technologies.

■ Ensure that water sector regulators monitor the quality of a variety of water sources.

■ Ensure that the price of water reflects its scarcity in order to stimulate markets for alternative water sources.

■ Plan the development of several water sources and infrastructure (*e.g.* central and distributed systems) thoroughly, as tapping alternative water sources can challenge the business model of existing operators (either public or private).

Filling information gaps

Reforms and new policies are most successful when: i) they rely on robust data and information (on water availability, water use, the costs and benefits of water-related services); ii) they are backed by realistic and enforceable action and investment plans; and iii) they are designed by a community of stakeholders with a clear understanding of their own needs and priorities.

There is a crucial need to develop water information systems (WIS) to support more efficient and effective delivery of sustainable water resource management and policies (OECD, 2010d). In particular, the rapid development in water policy reforms has created an information imbalance in many countries, with implementation of water policy initiatives often supported by little data and information.

There are also uncertainties when analysing the kinds of trends and model-based projections presented in this chapter because of data gaps and uncertainties surrounding future scientific developments or policy outcomes. Examples of uncertainties include the impact of climate change (patterns of precipitation and temperature change) on water resources at a disaggregated level; the development and diffusion of new technologies in the water sector (*e.g.* desalinisation, leakage control, etc.), in agriculture (*e.g.* new crop varieties, improved agricultural practices, irrigation efficiency, etc.), and in the energy sector (*e.g.* cooling towers, waterless biofuels, water efficiency in energy production operations); the impact of policy measures on economic behaviour (*e.g.* water pricing elasticity); and the responses of water ecosystems to policy and management interventions (*e.g.* as outlined in preparation of river basin management plans in Europe or in the design of "payment for environmental services" schemes).

In addition to these genuine sources of uncertainty, many international and national water information systems are maintained without sufficiently addressing the policy relevance of the data and information that is regularly being collected. Data concerning the economic and institutional aspects of water systems are much less developed than physical data and are only partially covered in the regular updates of most national and international WIS.

To address these issues, there is a need to:

■ Assess existing WIS at local, regional, national and international levels to determine how current water information and data are collected (or not collected) and used (or not used) by policy makers, and the costs and benefits of collecting, analysing and communicating this information.

■ Implement a System of Environmental and Economic Accounts for Water[12] (SEEAW) that is flexible enough to respond to varying water basin, country and international policy needs.

■ Improve the understanding of hydrological systems to better guide WIS data collection efforts, for example improving knowledge of the connections between groundwater and surface water, and determining environmental flows in the context of climate change.

■ Encourage innovations in water data collection, such as using new technologies or voluntary initiatives to collect data; or public agencies may regulate, finance or charge for data collection, maintenance and analysis.

■ Strengthen economic and financial information including improving the understanding and measurement of the value of water.

Designing reforms that are realistic and politically acceptable

The OECD has gained extensive experience in water policy reforms, learning from successful reforms in member countries, and accompanying water policy reforms in countries of Eastern Europe, the Caucasus and Central Asia (EECCA). Valuable lessons have been learned from this experience in making water reform happen.

A general lesson is that reform is a process that takes time, it is continuous and planning is key. Specific recommendations include:

Build a broad constituency

■ Solutions to the water challenges cannot be expected to come from water policies alone, as discussed above. Water authorities need to work with other constituencies, including the agriculture and energy sectors, while taking the environment into account; they also need to work at different levels of government (local, basin, municipal, state and federal levels).

■ For river basins which cross international boundaries, international co-operation can help – not only to share information and best practices – but also to share costs and benefits. For example, there has been long-standing co-operation between Canada and the United States through the Canada-US Boundary Waters Treaty and the Canada-US Great Lakes Water Quality Agreement. The United Nations Economic Commission for Europe operates the Convention on the Protection and Use of Transboundary Watercourses and International Lakes, providing an important framework for international co-operation.

Explore a mix of policy options and build capacity

■ As noted above, there is a range of policy approaches available to address water challenges (Table 5.1). An optimal policy mix combines a variety of these approaches (for example, Israel's water policy combines improved technologies with water pricing and metering; see Box 5.8).

■ Institutions and capabilities have to be adjusted to ensure there is the expertise to make complex technical and non-technical choices and to undertake comprehensive options assessments (including economic, social and environmental impact assessments).

Factor in financial sustainability from the start

■ The financial dimension should be factored in early in the process (to avoid designing a plan that is not financially affordable); cost reduction potentials have to be systematically considered; and financial realism needs to be brought to Water Resource Management (WRM) plans.

■ There are only three ultimate sources of finance for water-related investment and services, the 3Ts: tariffs, taxes, transfers from the international community (e.g. EU funds, or official development assistance). All other sources of finance, which have a role to play, have to be paid back.

■ Strategic financial planning can help in defining and prioritising water policies within the practical constraints of available financial resources.[13]

■ Financial incentives from other sectors should be aligned with water policy objectives (e.g. subsidies for energy or agriculture).

Manage the political process and improve the knowledge base

■ Hard facts on the economic dimension of water policies can facilitate water policy reforms, demystify taboos and advance debates. This requires information on water demand and availability, and on the economic dimension and distributional impacts of the reform of water policies.

■ Sharing international experience on water policy reforms can substantiate such a process.

Notes

1. Future projections are global, with a particular emphasis on policy actions needed in OECD countries and the emerging economies of Brazil, Russia, India, Indonesia, China and South Africa (BRIICS).

2. See Alcamo et al., 2007 for a detailed assessment and review of existing literature on the processes driving water health.

3. More details are given by Visser et al. (forthcoming). The disaster database gives information on "weather-related" rather than "water-related" disasters. These terms largely overlap but are not identical. The main difference is the category "storms", which comprises both storm-induced floods, such as due to hurricane Katrina, and the direct impact of wind. The category "floods" comprises coastal, fluvial and flash floods, along with landslides and avalanches.

4. This is because of poor data and because quality may not have systematically improved despite these changes. Over time, improvements in monitoring of physico-chemical pollutants and biological indicators can partly help to address this.

5. The soy is grown in a system of crop rotation, e.g. with maize that uses up nitrogen that has built up in the soil; soy grown under these conditions does not leak activated nitrogen into groundwater.

6. The Global Annual Assessment of Sanitation and Drinking-Water (GLAAS) is a UN-Water initiative implemented by the World Health Organization (WHO). The objective of UN-Water GLAAS is to provide policy makers at all levels with a reliable, easily accessible, comprehensive and global analysis of the evidence to make informed decisions in sanitation and drinking water.

7. See Annex 5.A for some assumptions underlying this analysis.

8. This section is based on FAO (2007).

9. Predictions for how long the world's rock phosphorus supply will last are very uncertain. They vary from 50 to over 100 years, but depend on estimates of available resources (van Vuuren et al., 2010).

10. See for instance the Keynote by Catarina de Albuquerque (www.ohchr.org/EN/NewsEvents/Pages/DisplayNews.aspx?NewsID=11017&LangID=E).

11. van Lienden et al., (2010) calculate that by 2030, water use for first generation biofuels such as sugar cane, maize and soy beans may have increased more than tenfold compared to today, enhancing the competition for freshwater resources in many countries. A breakthrough in producing second generation biofuels that do not require expansion of croplands (e.g. using residues from agriculture or forestry) will greatly reduce these impacts on environment and water resources. See further discussions on bioenergy in Chapters 3 and 4.

12. To support implementation of environmental-economic accounts, the System of Environmental-Economic Accounts for Water (SEEA-Water), a SEEA sub-system, provides compilers and analysts with agreed concepts, definitions, classifications, tables, and accounts for water and water-related emission accounts (see http://unstats.un.org/unsd/envaccounting/seeaw/).

13. See OECD (2011e) for more information on how strategic financial planning can help in practice.

References

Alcamo, J., M. Flörke and M. Märker (2007), "Future Long-Term Changes in Global Water Resources Driven by Socio-Economic and Climatic Changes", Hydrological Sciences Journal, 52:2, 247-275.

Alley, W.M. (2007), "Another Water Budget Myth: The Significance of Recoverable Ground Water in Storage", Ground Water, 45, No. 3, p. 251.

Annez, P.C. (2006), "Urban Infrastructure Finance from Private Operators: What Have We Learned from Recent Experience?", World Bank Policy Research Working Paper, No. 4045, The World Bank, Washington, DC.

Australian Government (2011), About Commonwealth Environmental Water, Commonwealth Environmental Water website, www.environment.gov.au/ewater/about/index.html.

Bates, B.C., Z.W. Kundzewicz, S. Wu and J.P. Palutikof (eds.) (2008), Climate Change and Water, Technical Paper of the Intergovernmental Panel on Climate Change, IPCC Secretariat, Geneva.

Berg, M. van den, Maurits van den Berg, J. Bakkes, L.Bouwman, M. Jeuken, T. Kram, K. Neumann, D.P. van Vuuren, H. Wilting (2011), "EU Resource Efficiency Perspectives in a Global Context",

Policies Studies, PBL publications 555085001, PBL Netherlands Environmental Assessment Agency, The Hague/Bilthoven.

Boswinkel, J.A. (2000), *Information Note*, International Groundwater Resources Assessment Centre (IGRAC), Netherlands Institute of Applied Geoscience, Netherlands.

Bouwer, L. (2011), "Have Disaster Losses Increased Due to Anthropogenic Climate Change?", *Bulletin of the American Meteorological Society*, January 2011, 39-46.

Bouwman A.F., A.H.W. Beusen and G. Billen (2009), "Human Alteration of the Global Nitrogen and Phosphorus Soil Balances for the Period 1970-2050", *Global Biogeochemical Cycles*, 23, doi: 10.1029/2009GB003576.

Bouwman, A.F. *et al.* (2011), "Exploring Global Changes in Nitrogen and Phosphorus Cycles in Agriculture, Induced by Livestock Production, Over the 1900-2050 Period", *Proceedings of the National Academy of Sciences of the United States* (PNAS), doi: 10.1073/pnas.1012878108.

Bouwman, A.F., T. Kra, K. Klein Goldewijk (eds.) (2006), *Integrated modelling of global environmental change. An overview of IMAGE 2.4.* Publication 500110002/2006, PBL Netherlands Environmental Assessment Agency, The Hague/Bilthoven.

Bruinsma, J. (ed.) (2003), *World Agriculture: Towards 2015/2030. An FAO Perspective*, Earthscan Publications, London.

Bruinsma J. (2009), "The Resource Outlook to 2050: By How Much do Land, Water and Crop Yields Need to Increase by 2050?", Paper presented at the *FAO Expert Meeting on "How to Feed the World in 2050"*, 24-26 June 2009, Rome.

Calatrava, J. and A. Garrido (2010), "Agricultural Water Pricing: EU and Mexico", in OECD, *Sustainable Management of Water Resources in Agriculture*, OECD Publishing, doi: 10.1787/9789264083578-12-en.

Confédération Suisse (2011), *Renaturation des Eaux: Modifications d'Ordonnances en Consultation*, Environment Switzerland, Bern/Neuchâtel, available at *www.news.admin.ch/message/index.html?lang=fr&msg-id=33269*.

Conley, D. (2002), "Terrestrial Ecosystems and the Global Biogeochemical Silica Cycle", *Global Biogeochemical Cycles* 16, 68-1 to 68-8 (1121, doi: 10.1029/2002GB001894)

Deloitte, IEEP (Institute for European Environmental Policy) (2011), *European Commission General Directorate Environment: Support to Fitness Check Water Policy*, report commissioned by the European Commission, DG Environment, IEEP, *www.ieep.eu/assets/826/Water_Policy_Fitness_Check.pdf*.

Dobermann, A. and K.G. Cassman (2004), "Environmental Dimensions of Fertilizer Nitrogen: What Can be Done to Increase Nitrogen Use Efficiency and Ensure Global Food Security", in A.R. Mosier, J.K. Syers and J.R. Freney (eds.), *Agriculture and the Nitrogen Cycle*, Island Press, Washington, DC.

Dobermann, A. and K.G. Cassman (2005), "Cereal Area and Nitrogen Use Efficiency are Drivers of Future Nitrogen Fertilizer Consumption", *Science in China Series C, Life Sciences*, 48, Supp 1-14.

Drecht, G. van, A.F. Bouwman, J. Harrison and J.M. Knoop (2009), "Global Nitrogen and Phosphate in Urban Waste Water for the Period 1970-2050", *Global Biogeochemical Cycles*, 23, GB0A03, doi: 10.1029/2009GB003458.

Edwards, R., D. Mulligan and L. Marelli (2010), *Indirect Land Use Change from Increased Biofuels Demand. Comparison of models and results for marginal biofuels production from different feedstocks*, Joint Research Centre, Institute for Energy, Italy.

EEA, (European Environment Agency) 2001, *Eutrophication in Europe's Coastal Waters*, EEA Copenhagen, p. 86.

Ekins, P. and R. Salmons (2010), "Making Reform Happen in Environmental Policy", in OECD, *Making Reform Happen: Lessons from OECD Countries*, OECD Publishing, doi: 10.1787/9789264086296-6-en.

Ensign, S.H., M.W. Doyle (2006), "Nutrient Spiraling in Streams and River Networks", *J. Geophys. Res.* 111, G04009.

Fader, M. *et al.* (2010), "Virtual Water Content of Temperate Cereals and Maize: Present and Potential Future Patterns", *Journal of Hydrology*, 384 (2010) 218-231.

FAO (Food and Agriculture Organization) (1996), *Land Quality Indicators and Their Use in Sustainable Agriculture and Rural Development*, FAO, Rome.

FAO (2006), *World Agriculture: Towards 2030/2050 – Interim Report*, Global Perspective Studies Unit, FAO, Rome.

FAO (2007), "Modern Water Rights: Theory and Practice", *FAO Legislative Study*, 92, November 2007, FAO, Rome.

FAO (2010), *Disambiguation of Water Use Statistics*, FAO, Rome.

Fischer, G., F.N. Tubiello, H. van Velthuizen and D.A. Wiberg (2007), "Climate Change Impacts on Irrigation Water Requirements: Effects of Mitigation, 1990-2080", *Technological Forecasting and Social Change* 74 (2007) 1083-1107.

FOEN (Federal Office for the Environment)/FSO (Federal Statistics Office) (2011), *Environment Switzerland 2011*, FOEN/FSO, Bern/Neuchâtel.

Fraiture, C. de et al. (2007), "Looking Ahead to 2050: Scenarios of Alternative Investment Approaches", in D. Molden (ed.), *Water for Food, Water for Life: A Comprehensive Assessment of Water Management in Agriculture*, IWMI (International Water Management Institute), Earthscan Publications, London.

Freydank, K. and S. Siebert (2008), "Towards Mapping the Extent of Irrigation in the Last Century: Time Series of Irrigated Area Per Country", *Frankfurt Hydrology Papers*, 08, Institute of Physical Geography, University of Frankfurt.

Garrido, A. and C. Varela-Ortega (2008), *Economía del Agua en la Agricultura e Integración de Políticas Sectoriales*, Panel Científico técnico de seguimiento de la política de aguas, University of Seville and Ministry of the Environment, Seville.

Hallegraeff, G.M. (1993), "A Review of Harmful Algal Blooms and their Apparent Global Increase". *Phycologia* 32, 79-99.

Haselbauer, M. and C. Göhl (2010), *Evaluation of Feasible Additional Hydro Potential in Bavaria/Germany*, RMD-Consult GmbH, Berlin, *www.rmd-consult.de/fileadmin/rmd-consult/news/2010_Hydro_paper_HA.pdf*.

Human Rights Council (2010), *Report of the Independent Expert on the Issue of Human Rights Obligations Related to Access to Safe Drinking Water and Sanitation*, Catarina de Albuquerque, Human Rights Council, UN, New York.

Hutton, G. and L. Haller (2004), *Evaluation of the Costs and Benefits of Water and Sanitation Improvements at the Global Level*, Water, Sanitation and Health Protection of the Human Environment, WHO (World Health Organization), Geneva.

IPCC (Intergovernmental Panel on Climate Change) (2011), *Managing the Risks of Extreme Events and Disasters to Advance Climate Change Adaptation*, IPCC Special Report of Working Groups I and II, IPCC, Geneva. (*http://ipcc-wg2.gov/SREX/images/uploads/SREX-SPM_Approved-HiRes_opt.pdf*).

Jeppesen E., B. Kronvang, M. Meerhoff, M. Søndergaard, K.M. Hansen, H.E. Andersen, T.L. Lauridsen, M. Beklioglu, A. Ozen, J.E. Olesen (2009), "Climate Change Effects on Runoff, Catchment Phosphorus Loading and Lake Ecological State, and Potential Adaptations", *Journal of Environmental Quality*, 38: 1930-1941.

Kim, I.J. and H. Kim (2009), "Four Major River Restoration Project of Republic of Korea", *Korea Environmental Policy Bulletin*, Issue 3, Volume VII, Ministry of Environment/Korea Environment Institute.

Klijn, F., J. Kwadijk et al. (2010), Overstromingsrisico's en droogterisico's in een veranderend klimaat; verkenning van wegen naar een klimaatveranderingsbestendig Nederland. Delft, Deltares (in Dutch).

Ladha, J.K. et al. (2005), "Efficiency of Fertilizer Nitrogen in Cereal Production: Retrospects and Prospects", *Advances in Agronomy*, 87, 85-156.

Lehner, B. and P. Döll (2004), "Development and Validation of a Global Database of Lakes, Reservoirs and Wetlands", *Journal of Hydrology*, 296/1-4: 1-22.

Lienden van, A.R., P.W. Gerbens-Leenes, A.Y. Hoekstra and T.H. van der Meer (2010), "Biofuel Scenarios in a Water Perspective: The Global Blue and Green Water Footprint of Road Transport in 2030", *Value of Water Research Report Series*, No. 34, UNESCO-IHE Institute for Water Education, Delft, The Netherlands.

Mooij, W.M., S. Hülsmann, L.N. De Senerpont Domis, B.A. Nolet, P.L.E. Bodelier, P.C.M. Boers, L.M.D. Pires, H.J. Gons, B.W. Ibelings, R. Noordhuis (2005), "The Impact of Climate Change on Lakes in the Netherlands: A review", *Aquatic Ecology*, 39:381-400

National Land and Water Resources Audit (2002), *Australian Catchment, River and Estuary Assessment 2002*, National Land and Water Resources Audit, Canberra.

National Water Commission (n.d.), *National Water Initiative*, National Water Council website, Government of Australia, *www.nwc.gov.au/www/html/117-national-water-initiative.asp*.

Neumann, K. (2010), *Explaining Agricultural Intensity at the European and Global Scale*, PhD Thesis, Wageningen University.

Neumayer, E. and F. Barthel (2011), "Normalizing Economic Loss from Natural Disasters: a Global Analysis", *Global Environmental Change* 21, 13-24.

Nicholls, R.J. et al. (2008), "Ranking Port Cities with High Exposure and Vulnerability to Climate Extremes: Exposure Estimates", *OECD Environment Working Papers*, No. 1, OECD Publishing. doi: 10.1787/011766488208.

Nocker, L. de, S. Broekx, I. Liekens, B. Görlach, J. Jantzen and P. Campling (2007), *Costs and Benefits Associated with the Implementation of the Water Framework Directive, with a Special Focus on Agriculture: Final Report*, Study for DG Environment, 2007/IMS/N91B4/WFD, 2007/IMS/R/0261 (available at *www.i-etme.nl/pdf/framework_directive_economic_benefits_implementation_report_sept12.pdf*).

OECD (2006), "Keeping Water Safe to Drink", *OECD Policy Brief*, OECD, Paris.

OECD (2008a), *OECD Environmental Outlook to 2030*, OECD Publishing, doi: 10.1787/9789264040519-en.

OECD (2008b), *Environmental Performance of Agriculture in OECD Countries Since 1990*, OECD Publishing, doi: 10.1787/9789264040854-en.

OECD (2008c), *Environmental Data Compendium*, OECD, Paris.

OECD (2009), *Private Sector Participation in Water Infrastructure: OECD Checklist for Public Action*, OECD Publishing, doi: 10.1787/9789264059221-en.

OECD (2010a), *Pricing Water Resources and Water and Sanitation Services*, OECD Publishing, doi: 10.1787/9789264083608-en.

OECD (2010b), *Water Resources in Agriculture: Outlook and Policy Issues*, OECD website, *www.oecd.org/document/20/0,3746,en_21571361_43893445_44353044_1_1_1_1,00.html*.

OECD (2010c), *Sustainable Management of Water Resources in Agriculture*, OECD Publishing, doi: 10.1787/9789264083578-en.

OECD (2010d), *OECD Workshop on Improving the Information Base to Better Guide Water Resource Management Decision Making*, Zaragoza, Spain, 4-7 May 2010. *www.oecd.org/document/43/0,3746,en_2649_37425_43685739_1_1_1_37425,00.html*

OECD (2010e), *Innovative Financing Mechanisms for the Water Sector*, OECD Publishing, doi: 10.1787/9789264083660-en.

OECD (2011a), *Towards Green Growth*, OECD Green Growth Studies, OECD Publishing, doi: 10.1787/9789264111318-en.

OECD (2011b), *Benefits of Investing in Water and Sanitation: An OECD Perspective*, OECD Publishing, doi: 10.1787/9789264100817-en.

OECD (2011c), *OECD Environmental Performance Reviews: Israel 2011*, OECD Publishing, doi: 10.1787/9789264117563-en.

OECD (2011d), *Ten Years of Water Sector Reform in Eastern Europe, Caucasus and Central Asia*, OECD Publishing, doi: 10.1787/9789264118430-en.

OECD (2011e), *Meeting the Challenge of Financing Water and Sanitation: Tools and Approaches*, OECD Studies on Water, OECD Publishing, doi: 10.1787/9789264120525-en.

OECD (2011f), *Better Policies to Support Eco-innovation*, OECD Studies on Environmental Innovation, OECD Publishing, doi: 10.1787/9789264096684-en.

OECD (2011g), *Water Governance in OECD Countries: A Multi-level Approach*, OECD Studies on Water, OECD Publishing, doi: 10.1787/9789264119284-en.

OECD (forthcoming), *Policy Coherence between Water Energy and Food*, OECD, Paris.

Prins, A.G., E. Stehfest, K. Overmars and J. Ros (2010), Are Models Suitable for Determining ILUC Factors?, Publication number 500143006, BPL Netherlands Environmental Assessment Agency, The Hauge/Bilthoven.

Rockström, J. et al. (2009), "Planetary Boundaries: Exploring the Safe Operating Space for Humanity", *Ecology and Society* 14(2): 32, *www.ecologyandsociety.org/vol14/iss2/art32/*

Rosegrant, M.W., X. Cai and S.A. Cline (2002), *World Water and Food to 2025: Dealing with Scarcity*, International Food Policy Research Institute, Washington, DC.

Rost, S. *et al.* (2008), "Agricultural Green and Blue Water Consumption and its Influence on the Global Water System", *Water Resources Research*, 44, W09405, doi: *10.1029/2007WR006331*

Rutherford, K. and T. Cox (2009), "Nutrient Trading to Improve and Preserve Water Quality", *Water and Atmosphere*, 17(1).

Seekell, D.A., P. D'Odorico and M.L. Peace (2011), "Virtual Water Transfers Unlikely to Redress Inequality in Global Water Use", *Environmental Research Letters*, 6(2).

Shah, T. *et al.* (2007), "Groundwater: A Global Assessment of Scale and Significance", in D. Molden (ed.), *Water for Food, Water for Life: A Comprehensive Assessment of Water Management in Agriculture*, IWMI, Earthscan Publications, London.

Shen, Y. *et al.* (2008), "Projection of Future World Water Resources Under SRES Scenarios: Water Withdrawal", *Hydrological Sciences*, 53(1) February 2008.

Shiklomanov, I.A. and J.C. Rodda (2003), *World Water Resources at the Beginning of the 21st Century*, Cambridge University Press, Cambridge, UK.

Smith, S.V., D.P. Swaney, L. Talaue-McManus, D.D. Bartley, P.T. Sandhei, C.J. McLaughlin, V.C. Dupra, C.J. Crossland, R.W. Buddemeier, B.A. Maxwell, F. Wulff (2003), "Humans, Hydrology, and the Distribution of Inorganic Nutrient Loading to the Ocean", *BioScience* 53, 235-245.

Statistics Canada (2010), "Study: Freshwater Supply and Demand in Canada", Statistics Canada Website, 13 September 2010, *www.statcan.gc.ca/daily-quotidien/100913/dq100913b-eng.htm*.

UN (United Nations) (2011), *The Millennium Development Goals Report 2011*, UN, New York.

UNEP (United Nations Environment Programme) (2008), *Vital Water Graphics – An Overview of the State of the World's Fresh and Marine Waters* 2nd Ed, UNEP, Nairobi, Kenya, *www.unep.org/dewa/vitalwater/index.html*.

UNEP (2011), *Decoupling, Water Efficiency and Water Productivity*, International Panel for Sustainable Resource Management, UNEP, Nairobi, Kenya.

Veeren, R. van der (2010), "Different Cost-benefit Analyses in The Netherlands for the European Water Framework Directive", in *Water Policy*, Vol. 12, No. 5, pp. 746-760.

Vicuña S., R.D. Garreaud, J. McPhee (2010), "Climate Change Impacts on the Hydrology of a Snowmelt Driven Basin in Semiarid Chile", *Climate Change*, doi: *10.1007/s10584-010-9888-4*.

Visser, H., A.A. Bouwman, P. Cleij, W. Ligtvoet and A.C. Petersen (forthcoming), *Trends in Weather-related Disaster Burden: A global and regional study*, PBL Netherlands Environmental Assessment Agency, The Hague/Bilthoven.

Vuuren, D.P. van, A.F. Bouwman and A.H.W. Beusen (2010), "Phosphorus Demand for the 1970 – 2100 Period: A Scenario Analysis of Resource Depletion", *Global Environmental Change*, 20(3), 428-439, *www.sciencedirect.com/science/article/pii/S0959378010000312#sec3.2*.

Wada, Y. *et al.* (2010), "A Worldwide View of Groundwater Depletion", *Geophysical Research Letters*, 37, L20402, doi: *10.1029/2010GL044571*

2030 Water Resources Group (2009), "Charting Our Water Future Economic Frameworks to Inform Decision-making", McKinsay website, *www.mckinsey.com/App_Media/Reports/Water/Charting_Our_Water_Future_Exec%20Summary_001.pdf*.

WEF (World Economic Forum) (2011), *Water Security, the Water-Food-Energy-Climate Nexus*, WEF Water Initiative, Island Press, Washington, Covelo, London.

WHO (World Health Organisation) (2010), *GLAAS 2010 UN-Water Global Annual Assessment of Sanitation and Drinking-Water: Targeting Resources for Better Results*, WHO, Geneva.

WHO/UNICEF (United Nations Children's Fund) (2008), *Progress on Drinking Water and Sanitation: Special Focus on Sanitation*, WHO/UNICEF Joint Monitoring Programme (JMP), World Health Organization, Geneva and UNICEF, New York.

World Water Council (2000), *World Water Vision*, London.

Zektser, I. S. and L.G. Everett (eds.) (2004), *Groundwater Resources of the World and Their Use*, UNESCO IHP-VI Series on Groundwater, No. 6, UNESCO (United Nations Education, Scientific and Cultural Organization), Paris, *http://unesdoc.unesco.org/images/0013/001344/134433e.pdf*.

ANNEX 5.A

Modelling Background Information on Water

This annex contains further background detail for the following modelling aspects:

■ a summary of the projected socio-economic developments behind the *Baseline* scenario;

■ freshwater demand, especially irrigation;

■ the *Resource Efficiency* scenario;

■ water quality, especially nutrient effluents;

■ the *Nutrient Recycling and Reduction* scenario;

■ people and assets at risk from water-related disasters;

■ water supply and sanitation.

More general information on the modelling context for the *Environmental Outlook* is provided in Chapter 1, and further details on the models used are in the Annex on the Modelling Framework at the end of the report.

Socio-economic developments under the *Baseline* scenario

The *Environmental Outlook Baseline* scenario makes projections of a number of socio-economic developments as outlined below (and further discussed in Chapters 1 and 2), and these in turn were used to construct the *Baseline* projections on water-related issues discussed in this chapter (except water-related disasters):

■ World GDP is projected to nearly quadruple over the coming four decades, in line with the past 40 years and based on detailed projections on the main drivers of economic growth. By 2050, the OECD's share of the global economy is assumed to decline from 54% in 2010 to less than 32%, while the share of Brazil, Russia, India, Indonesia, China and South Africa (BRIICS) is assumed to grow to more than 40%.

■ By 2050, the world is assumed to add over 2.2 billion people to the current 7 billion. All world regions are assumed to be facing population ageing but will be at different stages of this demographic transition.

■ By 2050, nearly 70% of the world's population is assumed to be living in urban areas.

■ World energy demand is assumed to be 80% higher in 2050 under current policies. The 2050 global energy mix is assumed to be fairly similar to today's, with the share of fossil energy still at about 85% (of commercial energy), renewables including biofuels (but excluding traditional biomass) just above 10%, with the balance being nuclear. Among fossil fuels, it is uncertain whether coal or gas will be the main source of increased energy supply.

■ Globally, the area of agricultural land is assumed to expand in the next decade, but at a slower rate. It is assumed to peak before 2030 to match the increase in food demand from a growing population, and decline thereafter, as population growth slows down and yield improvements continue. Deforestation rates are already declining, and this trend is assumed to continue, especially after 2030 with demand for more agricultural land easing (Section 3, Chapter 2).

Water demand

Demands for irrigation are calculated by the process-based LPJmL model (Box 5.A1). LPJmL stands for "Lund – Potsdam – Jena managed Land Dynamic Global Vegetation and Water Balance Model" (Rost *et al.*, 2008). Abstractions for domestic uses are estimated using a relatively simple equation, which takes into account the number of people, their income level, climate and cultural influences and whether or not they are connected to tap water supply. Geographical distribution is modelled from downscaled population projections, corrected for urban/rural splits and income dependent connection rates to tap water systems. Industrial water for processing and cooling purposes is based on the value added of the output produced, corrected by efficiency improvements in processes and applications. A relatively small share of water, though vital at the place of consumption, is used for livestock (see below). Finally, a large and growing volume is assumed to be used in electricity production for cooling purposes. Electricity produced from thermal (steam) cycle plants is the main driver. The model takes into account the change over time in efficiency, the cooling mode and the share of new technologies with reduced cooling water demand, such as combined cycle installations.

Not all demands lead one-on-one to consumptive use. Varying shares are lost to the atmosphere or embedded in products carried off to other locations. The remainder returns to the same water basin, with some delay and changes in heat and pollution load. For water stress calculations, the total demands are compared with the renewable supply, on an average annual basis and aggregated per major water (sub-) basin.

Estimation of historical, current and future water demand is characterised by many uncertainties. Water is often freely available to users, and can be withdrawn from surface waters (rivers, natural lakes, reservoirs), but also from groundwater reservoirs and wells without any formal metering or monitoring taking place. There is very little published monitoring data on the global area equipped for irrigation, and even less for the areas actually irrigated, the water volumes applied to the fields and extracted from river systems. Existing data sources show substantial differences, even for OECD countries, which are relatively well monitored compared to other world regions.

Estimate of water demands in 2000

The global demand for irrigation water estimated with the LPJmL model is estimated at $2\,400\,\text{m}^3$ for the year 2000, though estimating this is fraught with uncertainty (see section below). On the global scale as much as 50% of the water extracted is estimated to be lost for effective supply to crops, and does not contribute to soil moisture for plant growth. Other estimates in the literature end up around the same level: *e.g.* 51% (Fischer *et al.*, 2007) to 60% (Fraiture *et al.*, 2007).

Based on an estimate made for the previous OECD *Environmental Outlook* (OECD, 2008a), corrected for population, the estimated global domestic water use for the year 2000 is around 350 km^3, while the demand by the manufacturing sector is estimated to be around 230 km^3. For the manufacturing sector and for electricity production, OECD 2008 calculations were used as the starting point. While water use in different industrial sectors can vary significantly, an overall average relationship with total industrial value added was assumed per geographical region, according to assumed regional structure of the sector and technological level. Over time this relationship was adapted according to assumed structural sector shifts and technological progress.

Box 5.A1. **The LPJmL model: Calculating water demand, especially irrigation**

The LPJmL model describes how water flows are influenced by precipitation, evaporation from soil and water surfaces, and transpiration of plants, both natural and managed by humans. A water balance can be established for each grid cell (see Chapter 1), taking account of land-use patterns, natural vegetation, crop distribution and management, climate parameters (temperature, precipitation and CO_2 concentration), and soil parameters. This shows the resulting run-off per grid cell, i.e. the amount that ends up in river systems, lakes and dams, and the volumes available for downstream extraction. The demand for non-agricultural use of water is calculated at the world region level and down-scaled to grid-cell level using the spatial distribution of people and GDP as a measure of human activity. Together with demands for irrigation per grid-cell (see below), the run-off is then corrected for the total withdrawals in the cell. The resulting run-off is passed on to the next downstream cell and so on until the entire water basin is covered.

The irrigation water requirement is calculated by comparing the amount of water needed for unrestrained growth with the supply from precipitation. The gap is filled by irrigation, using surface water and groundwater available in the same or neighbouring grid cells.

Depending on the irrigation system in place and its management, the ratio can vary between the water effectively contributing to soil moisture for plant growth and the volume extracted from river systems. Open canal systems evaporate water and lose water through canal walls, cracks, etc. Piped systems do not lose water through evaporation, but by leaking through faults in joints and pipes. Another variation in efficiency is the method of application on the field, for example sprinklers lose water via evaporation, interception by leaves and drift; surface irrigation loses it to evaporation, surface run-off, non-uniform soil wetting, etc. Drip irrigation close to the roots is the most efficient. In the LPJmL model, estimates are made of the dominant systems in use in countries and regions, and their typical efficiencies (Fader *et al.*, 2010).

The largest global water demand after irrigated agriculture in 2000 was for electricity generation, primarily for cooling of thermal (steam cycle-based) power generation. Based on rough estimates, the global water use for electricity was around 540 km^3 in 2000. Differences of water use per unit of electricity produced between individual thermal power plants can be significant, according to their overall efficiency (from less than 30% to around 60%), the type of plant (steam cycle or combined gas/steam cycle) and the cooling system in place (once-through or closed-loop). Hydropower plants are assumed to return withdrawn water back to the river after use, so except for relatively small evaporative losses from reservoirs they do not contribute to the water demand.

Finally, relatively small amounts of water are needed for livestock globally, estimated at around 25 km^3 in 2000. However, this can sometimes represent a large share of water use locally. Breed varieties, diets and climate all influence water demand from this sector.

Uncertainties in calculating future irrigation demand

Future water demand for irrigation is driven by the change in irrigated area and by the change in water use per area. Future projections on irrigation demand differ widely in the literature. Irrigation is not only driven by biophysical and technical factors, but also by socio-economic and governance factors (Neumann, 2010). For instance, low political stability and low economic strength may reduce the options for irrigation, whereas a strong tradition and government support may stimulate it. These factors are hard to model. Projections published in the literature for future irrigation demand therefore range from the current (uncertain) level to plus 10%-20% until the middle of the century (Alcamo et al., 2007; Bruinsma, 2003; Bruinsma, 2009; Fischer et al., 2007; Fraiture et al., 2007; Shen et al., 2008). For example, Alcamo et al. (2007) computed several scenarios of future increase of irrigated land which between 1995 and 2050 ranged between 0.4% and 9.7%. The resulting changes in global irrigation water withdrawals are computed to range between –15.3% and +43.3% over the same period.

The *Environmental Outlook Baseline* projection assumes constant irrigated area and constant water efficiency outside the OECD to 2050. The first assumption will probably underestimate irrigation water demand in 2030 and 2050 and the second assumption may overestimate the demand outside the OECD.

There is a practical reason why the model framework used for the *Outlook* keeps the future irrigated area at its current level. Changing the area would require the model to be able to allocate water demand for irrigation according to different crops and actual locations; this facility is currently not available. Even if the *Environmental Outlook Baseline* projection were to consider a modest expansion of irrigation,[1] the associated growth in irrigation water demands would not alter the total demands decisively. These are increasingly determined by much faster growing demands for domestic and industrial use and electricity production. Other projections of total water demands show a comparable picture (Shen, 2008).

Data from Freydank (2008; also used for FAO projections) show that the area of arable land equipped for irrigation grew between 1900 and 2008 at variable growth rates (Figure 5.A1). However, despite being equipped, the area is often not irrigated for various reasons such as lack of water, absence of farmers, land degradation, damage and organisational problems. No long-term data are available on trends of the area actually irrigated on which to base future projections.

FAO projections made in 2003 assumed an increase in the area equipped for irrigation from 287 to 328 million hectares (Mha) by 2030 (Bruinsma, 2003). A more recent FAO projection (Bruinsma, 2009) reduced the expansion expected to 2030 to 310 Mha (+ 8%), and practically no further increase through to 2050 (Figure 5.A1). All expansion is projected to take place in emerging economies and developing countries.

Methods for projecting future demand range from using a simple rule of constant area per person so the area grows with population (Shen, 2008), to more sophisticated approaches combining potential demand (the ratio of precipitation to evapotranspiration) with local availability of water resources to supply irrigation water (Fischer, 2007). Still others assume investment strategies to meet future food demands through improvements in rainfed and/or irrigated agriculture by targeting either area expansion, or yield and water productivity improvements (Fraiture *et al.*, 2007). A mixed scenario spreads investments over the various measures, resulting in fairly limited expansion of irrigated land (+16%) and water withdrawals (+13%).

Figure 5.A1. **Global area of arable land equipped for irrigation, 1900-2050**

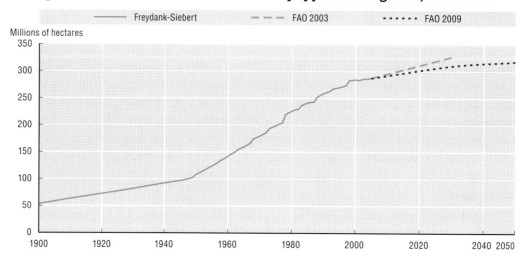

Sources: Bruinsma, J.E. (2003), *World Agriculture: Towards 2015/2030. An FAO Perspective*, Earthscan, London; Bruinsma, J.E. (2009), "The Resource Outlook to 2050: By How Much do Land, Water and Crop Yields Need to Increase by 2050?", paper presented at the *FAO Expert Meeting on "How to Feed the World in 2050"*, 24-26 June 2009, Rome; Freydank, K. and Siebert, S. (2008), "Towards Mapping the Extent of Irrigation in the Last Century: Time Series of Irrigated Area per Country", *Frankfurt Hydrology Paper* 08, Institute of Physical Geography, University of Frankfurt, Frankfurt am Main, Germany.

All the strategies explored by Fraiture *et al.* (2007) assume significant efforts and hundreds of billion dollars of investments. Expanding irrigation is relatively expensive and less cost-effective than other investment strategies for increasing agricultural production explored. The cheapest option is enhanced trade in agricultural commodities, so that production in regions with potential for rainfed agriculture increases at the expense of irrigated agriculture. In their assessment this is the cheapest option, and would mean no change in irrigated area and only a minor change in water withdrawals compared with today.

In addition to the extent, the current and projected amount of water withdrawn per hectare of irrigated land is important for calculating total irrigation water demand. This depends on crop water consumption, the gap between water required to sustain crop growth and precipitation, and the irrigation and water transport system.

In the *Outlook* projection, efficiency improvements are assumed in OECD countries, based on observed trends under current policies. In other regions it is unclear if and to what extent similar improvements can be expected in the absence of specific policies, hence the efficiency is kept constant per region, estimated on the basis of an analysis of prevailing technology and management practices per region (LPJmL model, Fader, 2010).

Crop requirements can be influenced by climate change: a higher temperature induces more evapotranspiration, and changes in (seasonal) precipitation can either decrease or increase the irrigation demand. A related phenomenon is the water-use efficiency of plants, which increases in principle with more elevated atmospheric CO_2 concentration. The LPJ model assumes a relatively strong effect, but the strength of this mechanism is under discussion among experts.

Transporting water for irrigation can result in a range of losses, such as over-watering, leakage from canals or pipe systems, evaporation from uncovered canals and soil, spray losses, etc. Estimates of global average losses range from 40% to over 50%.

Projections in other sectors

In the *Outlook Baseline*, demand for domestic water use increases by a factor of 2.3 between 2000 and 2050. This is a faster growth rate than for the population, caused by rising per capita disposable income and a larger share of the population being connected to tap water supply systems. Industrial use grows by a factor of five over the same period, following a more than sevenfold increase in value added. Finally, water for electricity production is projected to increase by a factor of 2.5 through to 2050.

Water-specific hypotheses under the Resource Efficiency scenario

A simple "what-if" scenario approach was modelled to explore the potential to reduce the water stress observed in the *Outlook Baseline* by reducing demand (van den Berg *et al.*, 2011).

The assumptions made are as follows:

- For irrigation, all non-OECD countries are assumed to improve their efficiency by 15% more than in the *Baseline*. This is based on Fischer *et al.* (2007), who extended an FAO assumption (Bruinsma, 2003) of a 10% improvement by 2030 to reach 20% by 2080. Considering that the annual rate of improvement declines over time, this is consistent with our assumption of a 15% efficiency improvement by 2050. Further efficiencies than those assumed in the *Baseline* are considered less likely for OECD countries and therefore this remains unchanged in this scenario; it is assumed that irrigation in the OECD in the *Baseline* has reached an upper limit of efficiency as risks of salinisation and pollution problems are associated with more than 70% evapotranspiration of irrigation water (Fraiture *et al.*, 2007).

- For domestic and manufacturing uses, it is assumed that water savings can be achieved that are comparable to savings in energy consumption. Hence, compared to the *Baseline*, the water demands in each region are reduced in proportion with the energy savings rate in the *Resource Efficiency* scenario (van den Berg *et al.*, 2011).

- This scenario makes the same assumptions as the *450 Core* scenario explored in the Climate Change chapter, (for details, see Chapter 3, Section 4). Larger shares for solar and wind-based power generation *versus* thermal are assumed, but until 2050 an assumed shift to (thermal) bio-energy and nuclear power plants limits the overall reduction in this sector. The assumed reduction in energy demand described in the point above translates directly into less water demand for cooling.

- No adjustment was made for the livestock sector. Demand may well be reduced from dietary and conversion efficiency improvements. But no attempt was made to quantify the effect as the *Baseline* demand is already so small that any adjustment will be negligible compared to the large uncertainties surrounding each of the much larger demand categories.

■ Finally, in the (global) *Resource Efficiency* scenario, climate change is well below the *Baseline,* implying lower temperatures and atmospheric carbon dioxide levels compared to the Baseline. Given the net response of the LPJmL model, this may result in slightly higher demand for irrigation water. Differences up to 2050 are relatively limited however, and are not quantified here.

As a result, total water demands in 2050 could be reduced by some 25% under this scenario, from 5 465 km^3 in the *Baseline* to 4 140 km^3. The largest difference between the *Baseline* and this scenario is brought about by reducing water demand from electricity generation (down by 37% in 2050), followed by domestic and manufacturing demands (each down by nearly 30%).

Water quality

Baseline

Nutrient effluents from wastewater

Nutrient flows in urban wastewater were calculated using the approach presented by van Drecht *et al.* (2009). Human nitrogen (N) emission is the N emitted in wastewater by households and industries that are connected to the same sewerage system. The overall approach for calculating human N emission that is actually discharged into surface water is as follows:

$$E_{sw}^{N} = E_{hum}^{N} D(1 - R^{N}) \tag{1}$$

where E_{sw}^{N} is the N emission to surface water (kg person^{-1} yr^{-1}), E_{hum}^{N} is the human N emission (kg person^{-1} yr^{-1}), D is the fraction of the total population that is connected to public sewerage systems (no dimension), and R^{N} is the overall removal of N through wastewater treatment (no dimension). The total P emission to surface water is calculated as:

$$E_{sw}^{P} = (E_{hum}^{P} + E_{Ldet}^{P} + \frac{E_{Ddet}^{P}}{D}) D(1 - R^{P}) \tag{2}$$

where E_{sw}^{P} is the P emission to surface water (kg person^{-1} yr^{-1}), E_{hum}^{P} is the human P emission (kg person^{-1} yr^{-1}), E_{Ldet}^{P} is the P emission from laundry detergents (kg person^{-1} yr^{-1}), and E_{Ddet}^{P} the P emission from dishwasher detergents (kg person^{-1} yr^{-1}), and R^{P} is the overall removal of P through wastewater treatment (no dimension). E_{Ddet}^{P} is calculated for the population connected to sewerage systems. Dividing by D results in a value that applies to the total population.

The assumptions for the population with access to improved sanitation, population with a sewage connection, detergent use and nutrient removal in wastewater treatment plants are provided in Table 5.A1.

Nutrient effluents from agriculture

Data on fertiliser use, animal manure distributions and fertiliser use efficiency were obtained from trends described in the FAO study *Agriculture Towards 2030* (Bruinsma, 2003), combined with data on crop and livestock production from the IMAGE model.

Generally, in the *Baseline,* farmers in countries with a nutrient surplus are assumed to be motivated to be increasingly efficient in their use of fertiliser. Especially for China a

Table 5.A1. **Scenario assumptions for** *Baseline* **and point source reduction in the** *Nutrient Recycling and Reduction* **scenario**

Scenario driver	*Baseline* scenario	Reduction of point sources in *Nutrient Recycling and Reduction* scenario
Population	*Baseline* data	As in *Baseline*
Per capita GDP	*Baseline* data	As in *Baseline*
Urbanisation	*Baseline* data	As in *Baseline*
Fraction of population with access to improved sanitation	2030: reduce 50% of the gap between Su(2000)[1] and 100% improved sanitation. 2050: reduce 50% of the gap between Su (2030) and 100% improved sanitation.	As in *Baseline*
Fraction of population connected to public sewerage	50% of the gap between the situation in 2000 and 100% is closed in the period 2000-2030 and constant afterwards.	As in *Baseline*; in 2030 25% of the urine from connected households is collected and recycled in agriculture; in 2050 this is 50%.
Detergent use	Laundry detergent use and fraction of P-free laundry detergents, and automatic dishwasher detergent use and fraction P-free dishwasher detergents are entirely based on GDP.	In 2030 25% of P-based detergents are replaced by P-free detergents; in 2050 this is 50%.
Removal of N and P through wastewater treatment plants	Removal of N and P through wastewater treatment plants will increase by a gradual shift to a higher technological treatment classes. The removal efficiency per class remains constant; 50% of each treatment class shifts toward the next in line in the period 2000-2030 and another 50% in 2030-2050 (50% of "no treatment" is replaced by mechanical; 50% of mechanical treatment is replaced by biological; 50% of biological is replaced by advanced treatment).	As in *Baseline*

1. Su(2000) = Percentage of urban population with improved sanitation in the year 2000.

rapid decrease in the use of P fertiliser to levels comparable to Europe and North America is assumed, thus reducing emissions to surface water. In countries with nutrient deficits, it is assumed that nutrient discharges to surface water will gradually increase due to increasing fertiliser use.

Total surpluses are calculated on the basis of all inputs. N inputs include biological N fixation (N_{fix}), atmospheric N deposition (N_{dep}), application of synthetic N fertiliser (N_{fert}) and animal manure (N_{man}). Outputs in the soil N budget include N withdrawal from the field through crop harvesting, hay and grass cutting, and grass consumed by grazing animals (N_{withdr}). The soil N budget (N_{budget}) was calculated as follows:

$$N_{budget} = N_{fix} + N_{dep} + N_{fert} + N_{man} - N_{withdr} \tag{1}$$

A positive value for the budget indicates a surplus, and a negative value indicates a deficit. For P the same approach was used, P inputs being animal manure and fertiliser. A surplus represents a potential loss to the environment; for N, this includes NH_3 volatilisation, denitrification, surface run off and leaching; for P, it refers to run off and accumulation of nutrients in the soil. Negative budgets indicate soil N or P depletion. Details on the various terms in equation (1) and the uncertainties can be found in recent peer-reviewed articles (Bouwman *et al.*, 2009; 2011).

Livestock production plays a major role in the nutrient budgets for cropland. An increase in livestock production will cause an increase of manure storage and availability for spreading in croplands, and is therefore an important driver of the increases of N and P budgets in croplands. Production of animal manure is a result of livestock production increase, intensification and productivity increase. The contribution of animal manure to total N budget of croplands is only 6%-14% in OECD countries, while it is up to 50% in some African countries. In India, animals contribute 38% to total N supply, and in China 18%. Similar to croplands, the uses of grasslands by ruminants also involves the development of surpluses. This is because losses of N by NH_3 volatilisation, denitrification and leaching are inevitable. For P, the build up of residual soil P by adsorption to soil material causes the development of surpluses.

In the FAO study (Bruinsma, 2003) assumptions of the fertiliser use efficiency were based on economic and agronomic considerations, and the soil and climatic conditions of the country considered. The use of fertiliser may change as a result of production increase and efficiency changes.

Various ways to analyse efficiency of nutrient use are available (Ladha *et al.*, 2005). This *Environmental Outlook* uses the concept of apparent fertiliser N and P use efficiency (NUE and PUE, respectively), which represents the production in kg dry matter per kg of fertiliser N or P (Dobermann and Cassman, 2004 and 2005; Bouwman *et al.*, 2009). This is the broadest measure of N and P use efficiency, also called the "partial factor productivity" of the applied fertiliser N (Dobermann and Cassman, 2004 and 2005). NUE and PUE incorporate the contributions of indigenous soil N, fertiliser uptake efficiency and the efficiency of conversion of uptake to harvested product. NUE and PUE vary among countries because of differences in the crop mix, their attainable yield potential, soil quality, amount and form of N and P application and management. For example, very high values in many African and Latin American countries reflect current low fertiliser application rates; NUE and PUE values are much lower in many industrialised countries with intensive, high-input agricultural systems. In contrast, countries in Eastern Europe and the former Soviet Union had a rapid decrease in fertiliser use after 1990, causing a strong apparent increase in the fertiliser use efficiency.

In the *Baseline* scenario, generally farmers in countries with nutrient surplus are motivated to use fertiliser increasingly efficiently. For China it is assumed that there will be a rapid decrease of the use of P fertilisers to PUE levels comparable to Europe and North America, and in both China and India further decreases up until 2050, thus reducing emissions to surface water. In countries with nutrient deficits, it is assumed that nutrient discharges to surface water will gradually increase due to increasing fertiliser use.

See Section 3 of Chapter 2 on socio-economic developments, and Box 3.2 in Chapter 3 on climate change for assumptions on developments in agriculture.

Nutrient Recycling and Reduction scenario

Nutrient effluents from wastewater

It is assumed that the urine from 25% of the population with a sewage connection in 2030 and 50% in 2050 will be collected and recycled in agriculture. A gradual replacement of P-based detergents to P-free ones between 2030 and 2050 is also assumed (Table 5.A1).

The potential for P recycling is much larger. Total P removal in wastewater treatment amounted to 0.7 million tonnes a year in 2000, which was assumed to increase to 1.7 million tonnes a year in 2030 and 3.3 million tonnes in 2050. Using this removed P to produce fertiliser could provide 15% of the projected P needed in agriculture (22 million tonnes a year in 2050). However, this would imply considerable efforts to remove heavy metals, pharmaceuticals and other chemicals from sewage sludge.

Nutrient effluents from agriculture

This scenario involves combining different strategies in the crop and livestock production system to improve both productivity and nutrient use efficiency, as follows:

■ In crop production systems the yield increase is assumed to be 40% higher than in the *Baseline*. A larger production per unit area is assumed, and thus a smaller harvested area than in the *Baseline*. This could be achieved if fertiliser use as well as fertiliser use efficiencies were higher than in the *Baseline*; it is assumed that half of the yield increase originates from increased fertiliser use and half from improved crop varieties and better management practices, leading to higher efficiencies.

■ Major changes are also assumed in the livestock sector. Compared to the *Baseline* the following modifications were made:

  ❖ Production in mixed and intensive production systems is 10% larger, and thus production in pastoral systems 10% smaller.

  ❖ Feed conversion rates (feed use in kg per kg of product) in mixed and industrial production systems are 10% lower.

  ❖ Productivity in mixed and industrial systems is 10% higher (milk production per animal per year, and carcass weight of ruminants).

  ❖ Off-take rates (fraction of animal stock that is slaughtered) is 10% higher.

  ❖ The fraction of concentrates in feed rations is 18% higher (3% to 10% in industrialised countries, and up to 65% increase in developing countries where use of concentrates is currently limited).

  All these modifications have an effect on the use of different feedstuffs, including feed crops. This is accounted for in the IMAGE model. The result of this set of strategies is an improved N and P efficiency, and on top of the improvement in the *Baseline*, N and P excretion rates are assumed to be 90% of those in the *Baseline*.

■ A final strategy is to better integrate animal manure in crop production, leading to a reduction in the use of fertiliser.

People and assets value at risk of water-related disasters

The *Environmental Outlook Baseline* assumes that climate change will (still) not be a dominant driver of the occurrence of flood disasters in 2050. This is based on the IPCC *Special Report Managing the Risks of Extreme Events and Disasters to Advance Climate Change Adaptation* (IPCC, 2011). Laurens Bouwer also shows that in the next 40 years, increases in population and GDP by far prevail over climate change as causes of increased risk of flood disasters (Bouwer, 2011).

For the *Outlook* analysis presented in Section 2 on water-related disasters, a static flood map has been combined with dynamic maps of the population and GDP for 2010 and 2050. The following data were used to map potential inundated areas:

■ the detailed Dartmouth Flood Database (satellite images): *http://floodobservatory.colorado.edu/*;

■ floodplains from the Global Lakes and Wetlands Database (Lehner and Döll, 2004);

■ Spaceshuttle Radar Topographic Mission Digital Elevation Map for low coastal zones which might be inundated by the sea (coastal zones were selected at an elevation of maximum 5 metres above sea level): *www2.jpl.nasa.gov/srtm/*.

These three maps were aggregated into one map. The main uncertainty in this map is that it has no return period and no inundation depth in it. The theoretical return period is the inverse of the probability that the event will be *exceeded* in any one year. For example, a 10-year flood (return period) has a 1 in 10 = 0.1 or 10% chance of being exceeded in any one year and a 50-year flood has a 1 in 50 = 0.02 or 2% chance of being exceeded in any one year.[2]

Data on population and GDP were derived from PBL's GISMO model (see Annex 6.A in Chapter 6 on health and environment). The urban and rural population data based on GRUMP are available for 2010 and 2050. The GDP is based on the purchasing power parity (PPP) per capita on a national level. The PPP is used as an approximation of the value of goods at a certain location in order to estimate value of losses from flood risks.

In order to combine the population with the more detailed flooding data, the GISMO results were downscaled from 0.5 by 0.5 degrees to 30 by 30 arcseconds. The GRUMP[3] urban and rural extent dataset, in combination with Landscan 2007 population data, were used to allocate the urban and rural population in the downscaling process. The GDP was downscaled and regionalised using the downscaled population data and the PPP per capita. Concerning the downscaling from cells of 0.5 degrees to cells of 30 arcseconds, the greatest uncertainty is in assigning population to grid cells using GRUMP and fractions based on the Landscan population 2007. Hence, population growth is projected to be within current urban areas; expansion of urban areas is not included, and neither is the development of new cities. Using the GDP based on PPP per nation is just an approximation of the real value of buildings, infrastructure and goods at certain locations within a country.

To calculate the most vulnerable cities the results of population and value at risk were combined with a world cities map. All cells were ranked from 0 to 1 based on the absolute number of people at risk (highest risk is ranked as 1) and the absolute GDP at risk as a proxy for adaptive capacity (lowest GDP is ranked as 1). Both ranking results were summed. This resulted in a list of the cities most vulnerable to floods, *i.e.* those with a high score on both the ranking of population and value at risk.

Water supply and sanitation

Levels of water supply and sanitation were modelled separately for urban and rural populations by applying regressions based on available data for 1990 and 2000 (WHO/UNICEF, 2008). The explanatory variables include GDP per capita, urbanisation rate and population density. Region-specific parameters are included using calibration.

The associated costs for the projected connection rates are based on Hutton and Haller (2004), who estimated annual costs for various levels of connection rates. Their annualised cost assumptions are based on investment and recurrent costs, using values from the literature. For example, the annual costs for in-house piped water are USD 10-15 per person, while other improved water supply connections range from USD 1-4 per person. It is important to note that the costs in this simulation are approximate since the categories and regions do not fully match those of Hutton and Haller. In addition, translating initial investment costs to annual costs might underestimate the costs when using them over time.

Notes

1. Applying the simple rule of a region-weighted population growth factor for irrigation (Shen, 2008) to the Outlook *Baseline* projection would end up 25% above the current level.

2. *http://en.wikipedia.org/wiki/Return_period*

3. Global Rural-Urban Mapping Project, Version 1 (GRUMPv1). Center for International Earth Science Information Network (CIESIN), Columbia University; International Food Policy Research Institute (IFPRI); The World Bank; and Centro Internacional de Agricultura Tropical (CIAT). 2004. Global Rural-Urban Mapping Project, Version 1 (GRUMPv1). Palisades, NY: Socio-economic Data and Applications Center (SEDAC), Columbia University. Available at *http://sedac.ciesin.columbia.edu/gpw*.

Chapter 6

Health and Environment

by

Richard Sigman, Henk Hilderink (PBL), Nathalie Delrue,
Nils-Axel Braathen, Xavier Leflaive

This chapter examines the current and projected impacts on human health of four key environmental factors – air pollution (focusing on premature deaths from exposure to outdoor airborne particulate matter, or PM, and ground-level ozone as well as indoor air pollution), unsafe water supply and poor sanitation (including in the context of the relevant Millennium Development Goals or MDGs), chemicals (chemical hazards, exposure) and climate change (focusing on the incidence of malaria). For each issue the chapter first describes the current trends, then how the picture could look in 2050 without new policies (the Environmental Outlook's Baseline scenario), and finally the policy actions required. Air pollution, unsafe water supply, poor sanitation and hazardous chemicals exert significant pressures on human health, particularly for the elderly and the young. While some global trends (e.g. access to improved water sources) are getting better, others – such as urban air pollution and lack of access to basic sanitation – continue to pose a serious risk to human health. In addition, the incremental effects of climate change are contributing to the global burden of disease. Ambitious and flexible abatement policies (e.g. standards, fuel taxes, chemical testing and assessment, green procurement, cap-and-trade emissions trading, transport policies) as well as further investment in water and sanitation services are needed to address these risks. Identified hazards need to be assessed and tackled, and there is also a need to be vigilant and react quickly to new and emerging risks to human health that are not well understood (e.g. endocrine disrupters, manufactured nanomaterials).

KEY MESSAGES

Air pollution, unsafe water supply, poor sanitation and hazardous chemicals exert significant pressures on human health, particularly the elderly and the young. While some global trends (e.g. access to improved water sources) are getting better, others – such as urban air pollution and lack of access to basic sanitation – continue to pose a serious risk to human health. In addition, the incremental effects of climate change are contributing to the global burden of disease. Ambitious and flexible abatement policies are needed to address these risks. Identified hazards need to be assessed and tackled, and there is also a need to be vigilant and react quickly to new and emerging risks to human health that are not well understood (e.g. electromagnetic fields, endocrine disrupters and manufactured nanomaterials).

Trends and projections

Air pollution

 If no new policies are implemented, the *OECD Environmental Outlook Baseline* scenario projects that **urban air quality** will continue to deteriorate globally. By 2050, outdoor air pollution is projected to become the top cause of environmentally related deaths worldwide (see figure below).

Global premature deaths from selected environmental risks: *Baseline*, 2010 to 2050

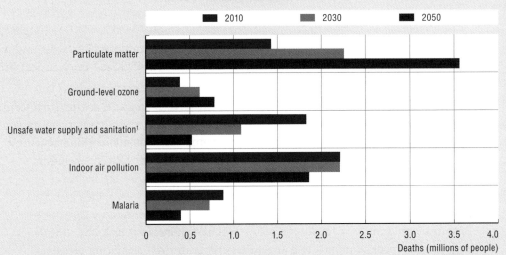

1. Child mortality only.

Source: OECD Environmental Outlook Baseline; output from IMAGE.

StatLink http://dx.doi.org/10.1787/888932571855

 Air pollution concentrations in some cities, particularly in Asia, are already far above acceptable health standards. This situation is likely to continue and significant reduction efforts will be needed to reduce their effects on health.

The **number of premature deaths from exposure to particulate matter** (PM) worldwide is likely to more than double to 3.6 million in 2050 under the Baseline, mostly in China and India, with increasing urbanisation and population ageing (leading to more susceptible people) likely to outstrip the benefits of any emission reductions. The absolute number of **premature deaths linked to ground-level ozone** in 2050 is also likely to be highest in China and India. However, OECD countries are likely to have one of the highest ozone-related mortality rates in terms of number of deaths per million inhabitants – second only after India – due to the much greater ageing of the population in the region.

Substantial increases **in sulphur dioxide (SO_2) and nitrogen oxides (NO_x) emissions** are likely to occur **in the key emerging economies** in the coming decades. Compared to the year 2000, emission levels of SO_2 are projected to be 90% higher and NO_x 50% higher in 2050.

With rising income and living standards, the number of people using traditional (and more polluting) solid fuels for cooking and heating is projected to decline after 2020, implying a reduction in **premature deaths from indoor air pollution**. However, it might become more difficult for poor households to move away from these polluting traditional energy sources, (*e.g.* firewood) if climate change policies increase energy prices. Targeted measures to provide alternative clean energy (*e.g.* efficient cook stoves) for poor households will therefore be needed.

OECD air emissions of SO_2, NO_x and black carbon (precursors to PM and ozone pollution) are expected to continue to fall in the coming decades.

Unsafe water supply and poor sanitation

Child mortality from diarrhoea – caused by unsafe water supply and poor sanitation – is projected to decrease to 2050. However, Sub-Saharan Africa will lag behind most other regions, particularly due to lack of access to adequate sanitation.

Hazardous chemicals

The **global burden of disease attributable to exposure to hazardous chemicals** is already significant and is likely to be more serious than the available data indicate. This burden falls more heavily on non-OECD countries, where people are at greater risk of exposure to hazardous chemicals and waste and where the *OECD Environmental Outlook Baseline* projects a six-fold increase in chemical production by 2050.

While OECD governments continue to make good progress collecting and assessing **information on human exposure to individual chemicals** throughout their lifecycle, knowledge gaps still exist concerning the health effects from thousands of chemicals present in the environment. More information on potential exposures to chemicals in products and in the environment, as well as the adverse effects of combined human exposure to multiple chemicals is needed.

Many OECD governments have changed, or are in the process of changing, national legislation to expand their **regulatory coverage of chemicals**, but enforcement is still incomplete.

Incidence of malaria from climate change

Climate change will mean that a greater number of people will be living in malaria risk areas in 2050. Despite this, **global premature mortality from malaria** is projected to decrease to 2050 under the *Baseline* scenario, due to greater urbanisation and increased per-capita income. Even so, it is projected that Africa will suffer around 400 000 premature deaths in 2050 from malaria.

Policy options and needs

- **Curb the growing health impacts of air pollution** through more ambitious and targeted regulatory standards and economic instruments, such as taxes on polluting activities. An urgent policy priority is to reduce the sources of particulate air pollutants in non-OECD countries, especially emissions from transportation.

- **Reduce motor vehicle emissions** through policy mixes which include taxes and regulations, and promoting cleaner public transport. Encourage behavioural changes in business models and lifestyle (*e.g.* car sharing, teleconferencing, teleworking).

■ **Maximise synergies between local air pollution abatement and climate change mitigation policies.** *Outlook* modelling suggests that measures to cut conventional air pollution (NO_x, SO_2 and black carbon) by up to 25% could also reduce CO_2 emissions by 5% in 2030 compared to the *Baseline*. Air pollution abatement through structural measures (*e.g.* shifts in energy sources and demand) will have more co-benefits for climate-related emissions than end-of-pipe measures.

■ **Scale up investment in water supply and sanitation.** The benefit-to-cost ratios can be as high as 7 to 1 in developing countries.

■ **Improve the knowledge base.** This includes doing more to harmonise data; improving methodologies for determining environmental burdens of disease and the cost and benefits of policies to address risks to human health; improving our understanding of chemical hazards; collecting more data on exposures to chemicals from production to use and final disposal; and keeping the public informed by making chemical information widely available through the Internet and other sources.

■ **Intensify international co-operation in the management of chemicals.** This includes work sharing on the assessment of chemicals and development of methodologies for assessing existing, emerging or poorly-understood issues (*e.g.* endocrine disrupters, nanomaterials and chemical mixtures); increasing the sustainable use of chemicals and green chemistry; and implementing policies to protect the most vulnerable human life stages (*i.e.* early life).

1. Introduction

This chapter examines the current and projected impacts on human health of four key environmental factors – air pollution, unsafe water supply and poor sanitation, chemicals and climate change. It begins with an overview of the combined impacts of these challenges, and then each of the four environmental health issues is discussed in turn – first to describe the current trends, then how the picture could look in 2050 without new policies (the *Environmental Outlook's Baseline* scenario – see Chapter 1), and finally the policy actions required.

The World Health Organization (WHO) estimates that today, outdoor and indoor air pollution, unsafe water supply and poor sanitation, and the effects of climate change are responsible for around 8%-9% of global premature deaths and "burden of disease" (Box 6.1), and almost 25% of global premature deaths and burden of disease in children under five years of age (WHO, 2009a). Most of the deaths occur in low-and middle-income countries, while for higher income countries the main environmental risk is local air pollution (Table 6.1).

Table 6.1. **Percentage of deaths attributable to four environmental risks by region, 2004**

Risk	% Deaths		
	World	Low- and middle-income countries	High-income countries
Indoor smoke from solid fuels	3.3	3.9	0.0
Unsafe water, sanitation and hygiene	3.2	3.8	0.1
Urban outdoor air pollution	2.0	1.9	2.5
Global climate change	0.2	0.3	0.0
All four risks	**8.7**	**9.9**	**2.6**

Source: World Health Organization (WHO) (2009a) *Global Health Risks: Mortality and Burden of Disease Attributable to Selected Major Risks*, WHO, Geneva.

Other environmental risks also affect health. Radon, a naturally occurring gas which is released from the ground, causes between 6% and 15% of all lung cancers (WHO, 2005). Loss of biodiversity (discussed in Chapter 4) reduces opportunities for developing new medicines and drugs, many of which are based on, or come directly from, natural compounds found in plants and animals. Micropollutants – industrial compounds detected in aquatic systems in low concentrations (*e.g.* antibiotics) – are a growing source of concern (see Box 5.4 in Chapter 5). Noise also affects human health, while public concern has been expressed about possible impacts from exposure to electromagnetic fields. Environmental pollution affects human health in a variety of ways, from contaminating food crops to exposing wildlife such as fish to harmful substances which accumulate in the food chain.

Public health is influenced not only by environmental hazards but also – particularly in developing countries – by social and economic factors including high population densities, poor education, inadequate health care systems, low per-capita income, increasing urbanisation, inadequate living and working standards and access to health care, and displaced and disadvantaged populations. Environmental health threats may be felt more acutely in some countries (and some communities within countries) which lack the political and economic resources to combat such threats.

Average health care costs in OECD countries rose from 7.7% in 1999 to 9.6% in 2009 as a percentage of GDP (OECD, 2011a). Total public and private pollution abatement and control expenditures in OECD countries range from about 1 to 2.5% of GDP (OECD, 2007). While it is difficult to estimate what portion of heath care expenditures are associated with exposure to environmental pollutants, it is reasonable to assume that the health care costs of addressing impacts from environmental exposure have also risen. It is important to note that it is often cost-efficient to improve environmental conditions in order to prevent negative environmental health impacts.

Populations most susceptible to the effects of pollution

The elderly and children – from *in utero* through adolescence – are particularly susceptible to environmental pollution. Worldwide, the per-capita number of healthy life years lost to environmental risk factors is about five times greater in children under five years of age than in the total population (Prüss-Üstün and Corvalàn, 2006). In addition, an increasing number of epidemiological studies suggest that prenatal exposure to food contaminants, air pollutants and chemicals in consumer products are associated with non-genetically transmitted adverse health effects which appear after birth (Schoeters et al., 2011).

Children are more susceptible to air pollution owing to their different physiological, metabolic factors and activity levels compared to adults. Children breathe more per unit of body weight than adults, have smaller airways and lungs and immature host defence mechanisms. Children also have different rates of toxification and detoxification, and have greater exposure to air pollutants as they spend more time outdoors and ventilate more, due to play and exercise. The elderly are also at high risk due to the deterioration of biochemical and physiological processes that make them more susceptible to lung infections in particular.

Demographic shifts

Globally, the proportion of elderly people in the population is expected to increase due to declining birth rates and health improvements (see Chapter 2 for more information). The proportion of people aged 65 years and older is projected to increase from 7.6% in 2010 to 16.3% in 2050, and of those aged 75 years and older from 3% in 2020 to 7.5% in 2050. In absolute terms this implies an increase of almost 1 billion people over the age of 65. Most of the increase in the number of elderly is expected to take place in India and China. Over the same period, globally the proportion of children (0-14 years) is projected to decrease from 26.9% to 19.6%, which equates to around 1.8 billion people; however, even by 2050, the number of children in Sub-Saharan Africa will still make up 28.4% of the population.

Identifying and predicting environmental impacts on public health

Recent years have seen increasing sophistication in the systematic collection, integration, analysis and evaluation of data collected from public health surveillance and environmental hazard monitoring. Many countries are conducting large and comprehensive epidemiology studies, focusing in particular on early life stage exposure, to better characterise links between exposure and human health effects. In addition, testing and assessment of chemicals is moving towards an integrated approach including the use of predictive models such as Quantitative Structure-Activity Relationship – or (Q)SARs models. New technologies and promising alternatives to traditional chemical testing are also being developed, such as in vitro high-throughput tests and toxicogenomics (the study of gene activity using bioinformatic techniques). These new techniques may allow better, cheaper and quicker identification of potential environmental hazards from chemicals.

Current approaches for determining the environmental burden of disease and evaluating policy options to address identified hazards (e.g. cost-benefit analysis) are important tools used by many governments and international organisations. However, such approaches suffer from large uncertainties about environmental impacts on health – more research is needed into methodologies for quantifying and comparing these impacts (Box 6.1).

Box 6.1. **Measurement challenges**

Disease burden is the impact of a health problem in an area. It is usually measured by indicators such as mortality (death) and morbidity (disease, disability, or poor health). It is often quantified in terms of quality-adjusted life years (QALYs) or disability-adjusted life years (DALYs). The DALY is a measure of overall disease burden, expressed as the number of years lost due to ill-health, disability or early death. This combines the burden due to both mortality and morbidity into one index, allowing for the comparison of the disease burden due to various risk factors or diseases. It also makes it possible to predict the possible impact of health interventions. However, estimates of disease burden involve uncertainty. For instance, estimates of cancer may be based on simple assumptions, and the effects of chemicals on the endocrine system may not be considered in burden estimates. Further, certain methods for estimating disease burden (e.g. disability weighting and age discounting) are subject to debate, as is the comparability of some data collected across countries. In addition, DALYs figures have only been calculated for substances for which there are known dose-response functions and measurable endpoints. Thus, it is important to account for model uncertainty when reviewing disease burden estimations.

While economic valuation studies of health impacts from pollution tend to focus more on the number of deaths (mortality), the frequency of illness linked to pollution (morbidity) is typically much greater and should be an important element of assessments.

---

2. Air pollution

Impacts on human health

This section looks at both outdoor and indoor air pollution, both of which can have significant impacts on human health. The most serious types of outdoor air pollution for human health are airborne particulate matter[1] (PM) and ground-level ozone.

Particulate matter

PM can be divided into two types: i) primary particulates: matter emitted directly to the atmosphere, such as black carbon (see Box 6.3); and ii) secondary particulates: particulates formed in the atmosphere from a reaction involving precursor gases, primarily ammonia, nitrogen oxides (NO_x), sulphur dioxide (SO_2) and, to some degree, volatile organic compounds (VOCs).

The effects of particulate matter can range from eye and respiratory irritation to cardiovascular disease, lung cancer and consequent premature death. The particles of most concern are in the finer fractions, PM_{10} and especially $PM_{2.5}$, as these particles are small enough to be able to penetrate deeply into the lungs. Globally, 8% of lung cancer deaths, 5% of cardiopulmonary deaths and around 3% of respiratory infection deaths can be attributed to exposure to fine particulate matter only (WHO, 2009a). There are an estimated 299 400 premature deaths in China and 119 900 in India each year from exposure to PM_{10} (WHO, 2009c; 2009d).

The WHO has set air quality guidelines and three interim targets to help countries with high PM concentrations to gradually improve their air quality (Table 6.2). However, at the levels of the "Interim Target 1", there would be an estimated 15% higher long-term mortality than at the WHO Air Quality Guideline level.

Table 6.2. **WHO air quality guidelines and interim targets for annual PM concentrations**

Target	PM_{10} ($\mu g/m^3$)	$PM_{2.5}$ ($\mu g/m^3$)
Interim Target 1	70	35
Interim Target 2	50	25
Interim Target 3	30	15
WHO Air Quality Guideline	**20**	**10**

Note: $\mu g/m^3$ = microgram per cubic metre.
Source: World Health Organization (WHO) (2006), *Air Quality Guidelines for Particulate Matter, Ozone, Nitrogen Dioxide and Sulfur Dioxide: Global Update 2005*, WHO, Geneva.

Ground-level ozone

Ground-level or tropospheric ozone is formed in the atmosphere by a chemical reaction between precursor gases such as NO_x, VOCs and methane, and sunlight. Ozone occurs in significant quantities as both a pollutant and a natural component of the atmosphere. At higher elevations, ozone screens out harmful ultraviolet radiation. However, close to the ground ozone is harmful to human health, vegetation and some materials. There is a complex relationship between ozone and nitrogen oxides; under some conditions, emissions of NO_x will lead to ozone formation, while under others they will lead to a reduction in local ozone levels.

Exposure to high levels of ozone can damage lung function, inflame airways and cause cardiovascular health problems. In Europe, exposure to ozone concentrations is linked to more than 20 000 premature deaths each year (EEA, 2010). While the European Union, the United States, and other OECD countries have been regulating emissions of ozone precursors, higher ground-level ozone formation from precursor emissions in Asia and Africa in the future will likely increase these regions' mortality and morbidity rates in the absence of abatement policies (The Royal Society, 2008).

The precursors of ozone, such as VOCs, can also affect health directly, for example from exposure to solvents and benzene. Human exposure to precursors of PM and ozone depends on specific local conditions and thus is not modelled on a global scale or quantified in this report.

The main sources of ground-level ozone and PM pollutants and their precursors are:

■ the energy sector: black carbon, NO_x and sulphur oxides;

■ transportation: black carbon, NO_x, VOCs, $PM_{2.5}$;

■ household burning of coal and wood: black carbon and $PM_{2.5}$;

■ animal husbandry, waste and wastewater treatment and emissions from rice paddies: methane.

The concentrations of ozone and particulate matter are influenced both by long-range transport of air pollutants and their precursors, as well as local emissions of these pollutants. Air pollutants emitted from one location can have an impact elsewhere on the globe, depending on their travel distances and residence times. Particulate matter can travel as far as 1 000 km, while the precursors of ozone show an even wider range. Nitrogen oxides can travel up to 10 km, while carbon monoxide and methane can travel over 10 000 km and 1 million km respectively and can remain in the atmosphere for 3 months and 8-10 years respectively. These features make these pollutants a global problem.

The UNECE (United Nations Economic Commission for Europe) has found an increasing trend in ozone concentrations measured in remote sites in the Northern Hemisphere which suggests that hemispheric baseline ozone concentrations have increased by a factor of two during the latter half of the twentieth century, most likely due to increases in anthropogenic emissions of ozone precursors (UNECE, 2010). Model calculations demonstrate that a reduction of 20% in anthropogenic emissions in North America, East Asia and South Asia would reduce the background ozone level in Europe by 0.6 parts per billion (ppb), which is similar to the 0.8 ppb reduction that would be achieved from a 20% fall in European emissions. Reducing anthropogenic methane emissions globally by 50% would nearly halve the incidence of high-ozone events in the United States (Fiore *et al.*, 2002).

Indoor air pollution

Human health is also affected by exposure to indoor air pollution (Box 6.4). The most significant source is burning of traditional solid fuels such as coal and biomass (*e.g.* cow dung and wood) for indoor cooking and heating by households which cannot afford cleaner fuels. Each year an estimated 2 million people die prematurely from indoor air pollution, almost half of them are children affected by lower respiratory infections or pneumonia; the other million are due to chronic obstructive pulmonary disease (COPD), primarily in the elderly. These deaths are most prevalent in low- and medium-income countries (about 64%) – particularly in Southeast Asia and Africa. About 28% of them occur in China (WHO, 2009a). But indoor air pollution is also a concern in developed countries, mainly from releases of chemicals from carpets, furniture and household cleaning products, as well as radon (see above) and pesticides.

Key trends and projections in air pollution

This section presents results from the *OECD Environmental Outlook Baseline* scenario, which models the likely trend in mortality rates from exposure to particulate matter (PM_{10} and $PM_{2.5}$) and ground-level ozone up until 2050, assuming that there will be no new policy interventions put in place. These estimates are based on:

■ regional emissions and urban concentrations of PM for 3 245 "major cities", *i.e* cities with populations of over 100 000 or national capitals (World Bank, 2001);[2]

■ ground-level ozone concentrations derived at the global level and then downscaled to regions using the geographical-specific ozone projections of the European Commission's Ispra Joint Research Centre (van Aardenne *et al.*, 2010).

The modelling of urban air pollution (PM) is based on several assumptions which may lead to uncertainty in the results (see Box 6.A1 in the annex to this chapter for more information).

Emissions of SO_2, NO_x and black carbon

Under the *OECD Environmental Outlook Baseline*, OECD emissions of SO_2, NO_x and black carbon are expected to continue a downward trend to 2050 (Figure 6.1), with the exception of OECD emissions of black carbon, where a slight increase is expected until 2015. Substantial increases in emissions of SO_2 and NO_x are projected in the key emerging economies of Brazil, Russia, India, Indonesia, China and South Africa (the BRIICS) driven by a growth in economic activity in the next two decades, especially in the energy sector. Emissions will then stabilise at around two times the 2000 level by 2050 (for SO_2) and one and a half times (for NO_x) due to increasing uptake of cleaner fuels and combustion technologies driven by rising income levels. In the rest of the world group (RoW), a significant increase in SO_2 and NO_x is expected and this is unlikely to level off by 2050. Emissions of black carbon are projected to drop significantly in the BRIICS and to stabilise in the RoW over the next four decades.

Figure 6.1. **SO_2, NO_x, and black carbon (BC) emissions by region: *Baseline*, 2010-2050**

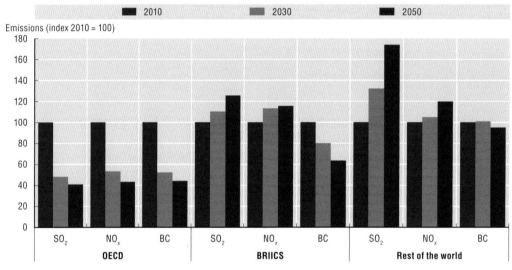

Source: *OECD Environmental Outlook Baseline*; output from IMAGE. *StatLink* http://dx.doi.org/10.1787/888932571513

PM and ozone concentrations

The *OECD Environmental Outlook Baseline* has projected the annual average atmospheric concentrations of PM_{10} for cities with populations over 100 000 between 2010 and 2050 (Figure 6.2). Overall, the average concentrations in all regions are already higher than the WHO Air Quality Guideline of 20 µg/m^3 (Table 6.2), and this will still be the case in 2050. While concentrations in OECD countries are expected to slowly decline, concentrations in the BRIICS, in total, are projected to rise until 2030 before declining slightly by 2050. Within the BRIICS, Brazil, Russia and China are likely to see a slight decrease by 2030. Concentrations in the large cities in the rest of the world are expected to continue to increase over this period. It should be noted that the concentrations presented here are weighted averages and that for several countries within a region (*e.g.* Canada and New Zealand for the OECD region) concentrations are below the WHO Air Quality Guideline.

Today, only 2% of the global urban population are living with acceptable PM_{10} concentrations (*i.e. below* the WHO Air Quality Guideline of 20 µg/m^3; Figure 6.3). Approximately 70% of the urban population in the BRIICS and RoW countries are exposed to concentrations *above* the highest interim standard (above 70 µg/m^3). In 2050, the *Baseline* projects that the percentage of people living in cities with concentrations above the highest

Figure 6.2. **PM_{10} concentrations for major cities: *Baseline*, 2010-2050**

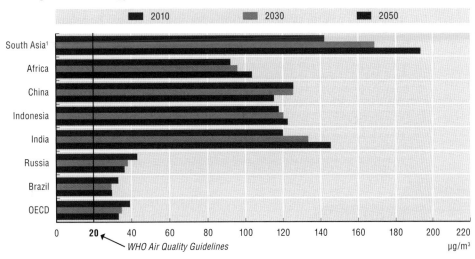

1. The region South Asia excludes India.

Source: OECD Environmental Outlook Baseline; output from IMAGE.

StatLink ᵃᵐˢᵖ *http://dx.doi.org/10.1787/888932571532*

Figure 6.3. **Urban population and annual mean PM_{10} concentrations: *Baseline*, 2010-2050**

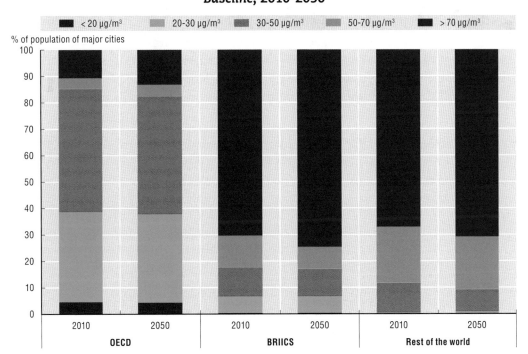

Source: OECD Environmental Outlook Baseline; output from IMAGE.

StatLink ᵃᵐˢᵖ *http://dx.doi.org/10.1787/888932571551*

WHO target of 70 µg/m^3 will be even higher in all regions. This is despite the air quality improvements projected to 2050 in OECD countries and the BRIICS, as these improvements are expected to be eclipsed by population growth in urban areas.

Similarly, the *Baseline* scenario projects concentrations of ground-level ozone in cities with populations over 100 000 to continue to rise significantly to 2050 globally; by 35% in OECD, about 90% in Russia and 39% in China (Figure 6.4) when compared to 2010 levels.

Figure 6.4. **Ground-level ozone concentrations for major cities: *Baseline*, 2010-2050**

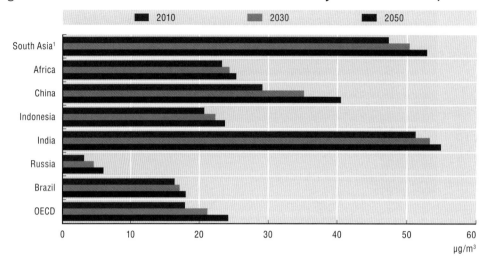

1. The region South Asia excludes India.

Source: OECD Environmental Outlook Baseline; output from IMAGE.

StatLink ⓘ *http://dx.doi.org/10.1787/888932571570*

Projected health impacts from PM and ozone pollution

The *OECD Environmental Outlook Baseline* projects the number of premature deaths associated with exposure to PM$_{10}$ and PM$_{2.5}$ to increase from just over 1 million worldwide in 2000 to over 3.5 million in 2050 (Figure 6.5, Panel A). Most of this increase is expected to be in the BRIICS. This represents a significant portion of the world's urban population

---

Box 6.2. Factors behind the increase in premature deaths from exposure to urban PM air pollution

Estimating the health impacts of air pollution is complex. Various factors – such as population growth, population ageing, urbanisation, declining air quality and overall health improvements – influence the burden of disease associated with air pollution, both mortality and morbidity (see Box 6.1). As part of the modeling for the *Baseline* scenario, an analysis was conducted to determine the degree to which each factor influences the mortality component of the burden of disease over the next 40 years.

This found that expected improvements in health services driven by rising income levels over this period would halve the number of deaths caused by air pollution – all else being constant – but population growth and greater urbanisation would offset this reduction. The factor which exerted the greatest influence on the increase in premature deaths from air pollution was the ageing of populations in the OECD, BRIICS and the RoW countries.

---

exposed to air pollution – urgent action is needed to reverse this trend. Even after adjusting for its population size, China already has the highest rate of premature deaths linked to PM pollution per million inhabitants; with the future ageing of the population, this rate is expected to more than double by 2050 if no new policies are implemented (Figure 6.5, Panel B). While the estimated premature death rates are lower in India and Indonesia, they are projected to triple by 2050, due to increased PM concentrations and also due to the larger number of people exposed through increasing urbanisation and population ageing (see Box 6.2).

Figure 6.5. **Premature deaths worldwide from exposure to PM:** *Baseline*

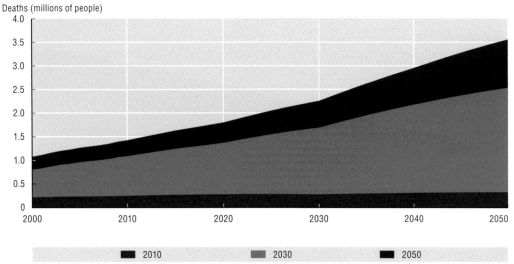

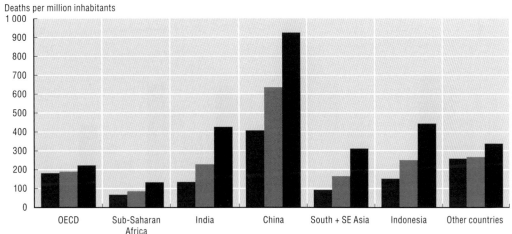

Note: The region South+SE Asia excludes India and Indonesia.

Source: OECD Environmental Outlook Baseline; output from IMAGE.

StatLink ᴬᴵˢᴾ http://dx.doi.org/10.1787/888932571589

The *Baseline* scenario projects the absolute number of premature deaths from exposure to ground-level ozone to more than double worldwide (from 385 000 to nearly 800 000) between 2010 and 2050 (Figure 6.6, Panel A). Most of these deaths are expected to occur in Asia, where the ground-level ozone concentrations as well as the size of the exposed population are likely to be highest. More than 40% of the world's ozone-linked premature deaths in 2050 are expected to occur in China and India. However, once adjusted for the size of the population, ozone-related deaths in OECD countries from 2010 to 2050 are projected to be one of the highest, only after India (Figure 6.6, Panel B).

Figure 6.6. **Premature deaths linked to ground-level ozone worldwide: *Baseline***

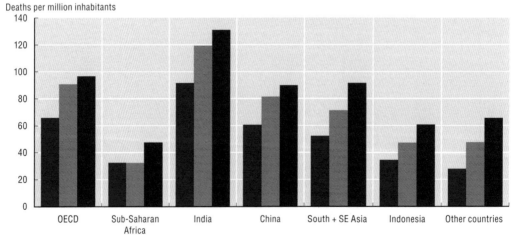

Note: The region South+SE Asia excludes India and Indonesia.

Source: OECD Environmental Outlook Baseline; output from IMAGE.

StatLink  *http://dx.doi.org/10.1787/888932571627*

Air pollution: The state of policy today

There is a range of policy approaches to limit outdoor air pollution.[3] Selected examples of different policy approaches to address air pollution are summarised in Table 6.3. In many countries, so-called "command-and-control" approaches using regulatory standards are complemented by various economic instruments such as taxes and tradable permit schemes. Voluntary programmes aimed at replacing ovens and heaters and retiring old vehicles that are highly polluting have also been introduced in recent years in several countries. Each of these types of approach is discussed below in more detail.

In most OECD countries, air pollution policy interventions have become increasingly integrated over the last 10-15 years, helping to increase cost efficiency. Examples include the US Clean Air Act, the Canada-US Air Quality Agreement, Clean Air for Europe, and the National Environment Protection Measure for Ambient Air Quality (Australia), all of which have set standards for air quality, focusing on target-setting for a range of air pollutants from stationary sources. These overall frameworks include legislative programmes which target specific sectors, such as power generation, transport, industrial and households. In non-OECD countries, there are fewer examples of cohesive programmes for controlling air pollution. Currently, much of the focus is on specific policies for controlling emissions from transport, both through standards and economic instruments.

Table 6.3. **Selected policy approaches for air pollution management**

Regulatory (command and control) approaches	Economic instruments	Others

■ Ambient air quality standards.
■ Industrial emission standards, technology standards.
■ Reporting requirements for stationary sources (*e.g.* pollutant release and transfer registers).
■ Automobile emission standards (see Figure 6.7).
■ Fuel quality standards.
■ Vehicle inspection and maintenance programmes.
	■ Tradable permits schemes for air emissions from stationary sources (*e.g.* SO_2 allowance trading system under the US Clean Air Act).
	■ Fuel taxes (see Figure 6.9).
	■ Congestion charges.
	■ Taxes on emissions (see Figure 6.8).
	■ Financial incentives for the development of alternative and renewable fuels and advanced transportation technologies (*e.g.* California's DRIVE programme).
		■ Information collection:
		  – emission and air quality monitoring;
		  – cost-benefit analyses to support policy evaluation (with valuation of health impacts);
		  – public education (*e.g.* Canada's Air Quality Health Index).
		■ Voluntary car-scrapping schemes.
		■ International conventions (*e.g.* The Convention on Long-range Transboundary Air Pollution).
		■ Telework initiatives (*e.g.* the US Telework Enhancement Act of 2010).

Regulatory approaches

Most countries have regulatory standards for *ambient air quality* to limit health impacts on populations. These are often based on WHO guidelines (Table 6.2). Standards for particulate matter are generally based on daily and annual averages and, in some cases, hourly averages. Standards for the more serious $PM_{2.5}$ are lower (*i.e.* stricter) than for PM_{10} and annual standards are lower than daily standards.

Countries also regulate specific *point-source air emissions* using standards, monitoring and reporting. An example is the US Clean Air Act. The European Environment Agency notes that industrial combustion (comprising emissions from power plants, refineries and the manufacturing sector) is a key contributor to emissions of particulate matter and acidifying pollutants in Europe (EEA, 2010). Among the most important instruments that have been put in place in the European Union are the Large Combustion Plant Directive

(EC, 2001) and the Integrated Pollution Prevention and Control Directive (EC, 1996), which, among other things, require the use of the "best available technologies" for pollution abatement.

Emissions from motor vehicles are also regulated by standards in most countries. Figure 6.7 shows trends in emission standards for hydrocarbons (HC)[4] and nitrogen oxides (NO_x) from petrol-driven passenger cars in the United States, Japan and the European Union, respectively, between 1970 and 2010. It is evident that much stricter emission standards have been established over time in these regions. And while for many years the standards for these pollutants were more lenient in the European Union than in Japan and the United States, they are now of similar stringency. Similar trends can be observed for emissions standards for diesel-driven passenger vehicles in these countries.

Figure 6.7. **Standards for HC and NO_x emissions from petrol-driven vehicles in the US, Japan and the EU, 1970-2010**

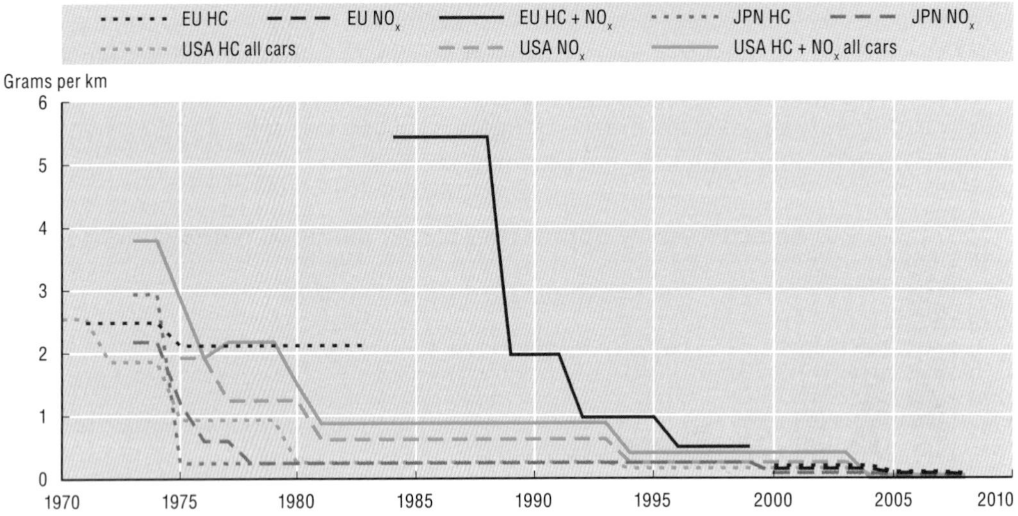

Notes: HC = hydrocarbon; NO_x = nitrous oxides.
Source: OECD (2010c), *Fuel Taxes, Motor Vehicle Emission Standards and Patents related to the Fuel-Efficiency and Emissions of Motor Vehicles*, OECD, Paris.

StatLink http://dx.doi.org/10.1787/888932571665

Economic instruments

Emission cap-and-trade programmes (see Chapter 3) can give greater flexibility to industrial plants to decide how to reduce their emissions. For example, the 1990 Clean Air Act Amendments in the United States not only tightened regulations for a number of emission sources, they also introduced a cap-and-trade programme for SO_2 emissions from coal-fired power plants. This allowed a great proportion of the emission reductions to be achieved by cheaper means (such as switching to low-sulphur coal) than with scrubbers, which plants had previously been required to install (Burtraw *et al.*, 2005).

Since 1999, a cap-and-trade system has also been used to reduce NO_x emissions in the northeastern United States, stretching from Maryland to Maine, as well as covering the District of Columbia and some counties of Virginia. The objective is to address the regional transport of ozone and help meet the National Ambient Air Quality Standards for ground-level ozone set under the Clean Air Act. A regional NO_x trading programme, RECLAIM, is also in place in Southern California (see Burtraw et al., 2005).

In Korea, a trading programme addressing both SO_x and NO_x emissions has been established in order to reduce these emissions from large point sources in the Seoul metropolitan area (OECD, 2010a). In Canada, the Province of Ontario has been operating a NO_x and SO_2 trading programme since 2001 to reduce these emissions from the electricity sector (Ontario, 2001).

A number of OECD countries apply taxes on measured or estimated NO_x emissions from major sources (Figure 6.8). The tax rates vary significantly, with the highest tax rates being applied in the Nordic countries,[5] Estonia and in the state of New South Wales in Australia. The tax rates that are applied in some of the other jurisdictions are so low that they are unlikely to have an impact on the level of emissions.

Figure 6.8. **Tax rates on NO_x emissions in selected OECD countries, 2010**

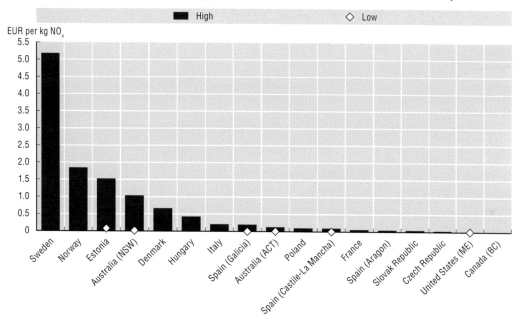

Note: "High" rates represent the highest rate applicable in a country (typically the standard rate) and "low" rates represent the lowest rate applicable in a jurisdiction (generally based on when, where and how emissions are brought about). For Australia, NSW indicates the state of New South Wales and ACT indicates the Australia Capital Territory; for Spain, Castile-La Mancha indicates the autonomous community of Castile-La Mancha; for the United States, ME indicates the State of Maine; and for Canada, BC indicates the Province of British Columbia.

Source: OECD/EEA Database on Environmentally Related Taxes, available at www.oecd.org/env/policies/database.

StatLink ⎯⎯ http://dx.doi.org/10.1787/888932571684

Sufficiently high fuel taxes can influence the size, number and fuel efficiency of vehicles purchased and affect emissions per kilometre travelled. Moderate levels of taxes on motor vehicle fuels generally have only a modest impact on the number of vehicles and how much they are driven. There are large differences in the motor vehicle fuel taxes applied in OECD countries (Figure 6.9).

As NO_x emissions from diesel-driven vehicles are considerably higher than from petrol-driven vehicles,[6] the relative shares of these two engine categories in the vehicle stock is of great importance for local air quality. The tax preference given to diesel fuel

Figure 6.9. **Taxes on petrol and diesel in OECD countries, 2000 and 2011**

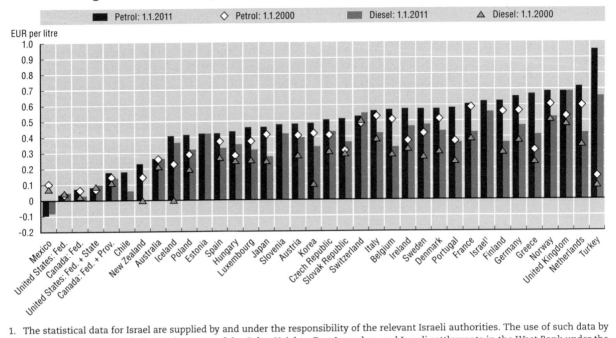

1. The statistical data for Israel are supplied by and under the responsibility of the relevant Israeli authorities. The use of such data by the OECD is without prejudice to the status of the Golan Heights, East Jerusalem and Israeli settlements in the West Bank under the terms of international law.

Source: OECD/EEA Database on Environmentally Related Taxes, available at *www.oecd.org/env/policies/database.*

StatLink http://dx.doi.org/10.1787/888932571703

(compared to petrol) in most countries is one of the factors behind the increase in the share of diesel-driven cars.

An important factor behind this favouring of diesel cars is the increasing focus on taxing vehicle carbon dioxide (CO_2) emissions through CO_2-related tax rate differentiation. Diesel cars tend to emit less CO_2 per kilometre than petrol-driven vehicles due to the higher fuel-efficiency of the diesel engine. However, this advantage regarding CO_2 emissions is fully "internalised", *i.e.* the drivers benefit directly from the savings. From this point of view, no tax preference for diesel is called for. On the other hand, *each litre* of diesel leads to larger CO_2 emissions than a litre of petrol. Also, the disadvantages of diesel vehicles in terms of their NO_x emissions are not internalised, as their negative health impacts are not borne by the driver, but by the general public. Drivers have no economic incentive to take these into account when choosing what type of vehicle to buy.

The shift towards diesel vehicles stimulated by the focus on CO_2 emissions in motor vehicle taxes could be "corrected". Israel has recently done this by introducing in their vehicle purchase tax a graded bonus system that *also* takes emissions of carbon monoxide (CO), HC, NO_x and PM_{10} into account.[7] This could have significant impacts on the composition of the car fleet in Israel, especially as the vehicle tax is already relatively high.

In considering policy options to address motor vehicle emissions, it should be noted that emission standards (and one-off registration taxes) only affect emissions from new vehicles, while a very large share of air pollutant emissions stem from old vehicles. On the other hand, fuel taxes can affect emissions from older vehicles, by influencing how much they are used. Further, while motor vehicles are becoming more fuel efficient, these gains are being eroded as automobiles are being driven longer distances. Policy mixes to address motor vehicle emissions therefore need to also include options to reduce km travelled via modal shifts (*e.g.* promoting public transport to reduce private vehicle use). Behavioural changes in business models and lifestyle (*e.g.* through car sharing, the use of teleconferencing, teleworking) should also be encouraged.

How do the costs of air pollution legislation compare to the benefits?

There have been a number of studies done to quantify the economic value of health benefits of air pollution legislation – the premature deaths avoided often dominate these estimates. For example, the US Environmental Protection Agency studied the benefits and costs of all the abatement policies under the 1990 Clean Air Act Amendments (CAAA). The study estimated that by 2020, total life years gained will be 1.9 million and that the benefits of the CAAA outweigh the costs by a ratio of 28 to 1 (US EPA, 2010).

A UK study by the Inter-departmental Group on Costs and Benefits found that a number of policy measures for controlling emissions from transport had positive benefit values (DEFRA, 2007). According to this analysis, measures for phasing out older vehicles were less preferable as policy options. On the other hand, the net benefits of measures to reduce PM emissions were consistently positive across all policy variants. However, the net benefits of measures to reduce ozone emissions were negative in many, if not most, policy variants.

The European Environment Agency (EEA, 2010) found that significant emission reductions have been achieved following the introduction in the early 1990s of the European vehicle emission standards (known as the "Euro standards") in the road transport sector, especially for CO and non-methane volatile organic compounds (NMVOC). By 2005, emissions of CO were 80% below those projected in a no-policy scenario, and NMVOC emissions were 68% lower. Emissions of NO_x were 40% below the no-policy scenario, and $PM_{2.5}$ emissions were 60% lower, with the decrease commencing in the mid-1990s. However, Carslaw *et al.* (2011) indicate that the EEA estimates for NO_x emissions from motor vehicles could be rather optimistic.

EEA also noted that industrial NO_x emissions decreased from 1990 to 2005 following the EU directives on integrated pollution prevention and control and large combustion plants. However, they have since remained more or less constant. SO_2 emissions were reduced more significantly. The reduction in PM emissions from industrial combustion was estimated to have been more significant than that of the road transport sector, and greatest in major industrialised areas such as Germany, Italy's Po Valley, the Netherlands and Poland. The health benefits of this decrease in $PM_{2.5}$ emissions would equate to a reduction of about 60% in Years of Life Lost (YLL) compared to a no-policy scenario.

Need for further action

Making the most of policy synergies

Policies that address several goals (environmental, social or economic) can help maximise benefits effectively. Such opportunities exist for tackling climate change mitigation and improving human health, as some of the damaging air pollutants are also greenhouse gases (GHGs) (Box 6.3). GHG emission reductions affect climate change in the long run, whereas the benefits of reducing local air pollution are likely to be felt more quickly. This works the other way around as well, in that targets to reduce local air pollution are likely to have positive long-term impacts on climate change.

Box 6.3. **Air pollutants and global warming gases**

Air pollution and climate change are closely linked environmental problems. Energy use and transportation are important causes of both, and measures to combat climate change are likely to have considerable ancillary benefits in reducing air pollution and its adverse effects on health and ecosystems.

Common pollutants play a role in climate change and air pollution. Ground-level ozone is a significant GHG. The reduction of the ozone precursor gases methane (CH_4) and carbon monoxide (CO) – which are both direct and indirect GHGs (via formation of CO_2) – would reduce ozone concentrations and climate change. Methane is considered a "short-lived climate forcer" similar to black carbon, because it remains in the atmosphere for approximately 12 years, much shorter than longer-lived carbon dioxide. Methane is also the second largest contributor to human-induced warming after carbon dioxide (Forster *et al.*, 2007).

Black carbon particles absorb solar radiation, and can contribute to atmospheric warming by reflecting infrared light. This effect continues after deposition of the black carbon particles on snow or ice surfaces, as darkening of the snow and ice will absorb more sunlight, leading to further melting (see Chapter 3).

The particles formed from SO_2 and NO_x may also influence the climate, directly through reflection or absorption of sunlight and indirectly through acting as condensation nuclei for cloud formation. In general, this type of aerosol has a net cooling effect on the atmosphere.

For example, regulating methane, a highly potent GHG and also a precursor for ozone formation, could offer double dividends for both human health and climate change. As the concentrations of ground-level ozone vary from region to region, abatement policies would have global climate benefits as well as different regional benefits, not only in terms of reducing asthma and mortality rates, but also increased crop yields (see Chapter 3, on climate change).

There are many examples of methane reduction policies. Methane reduction measures include changing agricultural practices, sealing leaks from natural gas pipelines and storage facilities, and capturing methane from landfill sites. Such policies are often cost-saving and in some cases profitable because methane has a commodity value as the main component of natural gas (US EPA, 2006). Methane is listed as a Kyoto Protocol gas and is therefore part of the Clean Development Mechanism (CDM) under the Protocol (see Chapter 3). Many CDM projects have proven that methane reduction can be cost-effective and a source of revenue for developing countries and project developers (Clapp *et al.*, 2010).

However, while there are several possibilities for creating "win-win" policy options to tackle both climate change and health impacts of air pollution, in some areas there are also possible trade-offs (Box 6.4).

Box 6.4. **Ensuring coherence between climate change and air pollution policies:
The case of indoor air pollution**

In 2000, about 2.9 billion people relied on traditional fuels (such as firewood and cow dung) for cooking, mainly in Asia and Sub-Saharan Africa (IEA, 2010). The *OECD Environmental Outlook Baseline* scenario suggests that the use of solid fuels in Sub-Saharan Africa will continue to rise until 2030 (Figure 6.10, Panel A). However, the emerging economies of Brazil, India, Indonesia, China and South Africa began to

Figure 6.10. **Solid fuel use and associated premature deaths:** *Baseline,* **2010-2050**

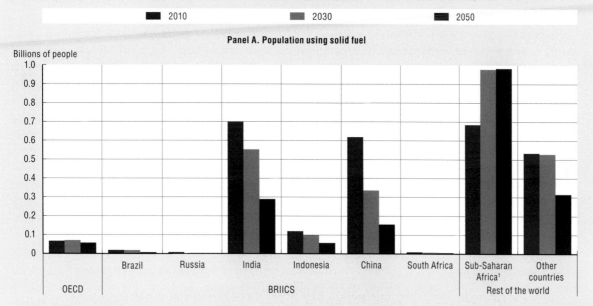

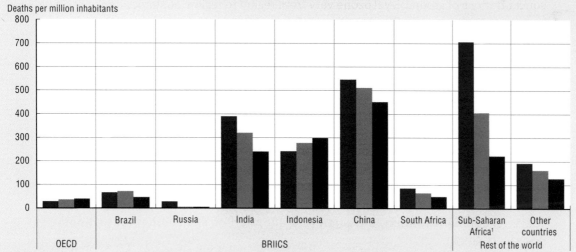

Note: There are uncertainties associated with the methodology used to model the impacts of exposure to indoor air pollution, particularly with regard to translating domestic energy use to levels of exposure from solid fuel use. The underlying data sources (from the WHO and the International Energy Agency – IEA) use different definitions. For example, the WHO uses main source of energy while the IEA uses total solid fuel use. Further, while exposure levels can be influenced to a significant degree by the use of improved stoves and/or basic ventilation, such as opening a window while cooking, these factors have not been considered due to lack of data.

1. The region Sub-Saharan Africa does not include the Republic of South Africa.

Source: OECD Environmental Outlook Baseline; output from IMAGE.   *StatLink* ⟪ms⟫ http://dx.doi.org/10.1787/888932571722

Box 6.4. **Ensuring coherence between climate change and air pollution policies: The case of indoor air pollution** *(cont.)*

reduce their reliance on traditional solid fuels for cooking and heating in the 1990s, and this downward trend is likely to continue over the next 40 years. The *Baseline* scenario projects that globally the number of deaths caused by solid fuel use will gradually decline in the coming decades (Figure 6.10, Panel B). This will be due to higher incomes (and hence a greater ability to purchase cleaner fuels) and better health services. While the number of deaths due to respiratory infections is expected to decrease in South Asia and Sub-Saharan Africa, the number of deaths related to COPD is expected to increase in Southeast and South Asia, mainly due to ageing of the population.

It is possible that climate mitigation policies could result in higher global prices of fossil-fuel based energy sources such as kerosene and liquefied petroleum gas. If this happens, poorer households could find that these cleaner-burning fuels become too expensive, making the move away from traditional energy sources more difficult. In that event, the projected number of premature deaths might increase. As an illustration, the impacts on premature death linked to indoor air pollution were assessed for the policy simulation for climate stabilisation via a global carbon tax applied to all energy users including households (see Chapter 3 on climate change). This stylised simulation suggests that increased energy costs would lead to an additional 300 million people lacking access to modern energy sources in 2050. This would in turn imply 300 000 more premature deaths by 2050 than under the *Baseline* scenario projections. To prevent this incompatible outcome, targeted policies would be needed to provide alternative clean energy for poor households. These might include public-private partnerships to facilitate the use of new model stoves which burn hotter and more efficiently (*e.g.* the Global Alliance for Clean Cookstoves) and education policies aimed at ensuring proper ventilation indoors.

Other sources of indoor air pollution more relevant to OECD countries include dampness and mould growth, combustion by-products released from heating or cooking appliances, and releases of chemicals from products. Climate change also has the potential to affect indoor air due to the alterations made in buildings to protect against outdoor conditions (*e.g.* tightly-sealed buildings) which may increase exposure of inhabitants to indoor pollutants.

Getting the policy mix right

In addition to the direct health benefits of reducing air pollution, there are also economic benefits, such as increased productivity for those affected and their caregivers, reduced expenditures for medicines and medical services, and reduced expenditures on averting behaviour (*e.g.* avoiding polluted areas, purchasing filtration devices). As a consequence, "pricing" these pollutants will not only yield health benefits, but may also have positive economic consequences. Market-based instruments, such as taxes and tradable permits, are the most direct mean of pricing pollution. The great advantage of market-based instruments compared to most other policies is that they operate on all levels, inducing invention, diffusion and adoption of environmental technologies (see OECD, 2010a).

One difficulty with tackling air pollution is that many of the main source sectors (electricity supply and transport) possess features which necessitate broader policy reforms (OECD, 2011b). The long-lived nature of the physical infrastructure, the interdependence of different elements of service delivery, and the complex regulatory background mean that shifting onto a greener trajectory may take some time and come at relatively greater cost if the burden rests entirely on the pricing of pollution, rather than a broader mix of policy incentives. For instance, targeted support for R&D in mitigation technologies can be an effective complementary policy. While very unlikely to be economically efficient when used alone, such support can reduce mitigation costs when used in conjunction with policies which price pollution directly (Popp, 2006; OECD, 2009b). Co-ordination among a number of policy spheres is required, as well as a forward-looking policy regime which does not favour those market incumbents at the expense of new entrants.

Encouraging innovation in pollution abatement technologies is key to bringing about this transition. A flexible policy regime will encourage innovators to devote resources to identifying least-cost solutions, and give firms and households the option to adopt the most appropriate technologies for their situation. In addition, a predictable policy framework will reduce some of the uncertainty associated with undertaking the risky investments required to develop innovative solutions (OECD, 2011b; Johnstone et al., 2010). Organisational and behavioural innovations also have an important role to play.

What if… air pollution emissions were reduced by up to 25%?

A policy simulation was run of a hypothetical air pollution abatement approach which would reduce emissions of NO_x, SO_2 and black carbon by up to 25%. This 25% Air Pollution Reduction scenario estimates the number of avoided premature deaths compared to the Baseline of no new policies up to the year 2050 (for more details of the analysis see Annex 6.A).[8]

This scenario suggests that about half of the total emission reductions are projected to come from end-of-pipe measures, such as scrubbers on smokestacks and catalytic converters on automobile tailpipes (Table 6.4). This is somewhat higher in the BRIICS and in the rest of the world (RoW) as many of the OECD countries have already implemented end-of-pipe measures and are focusing on other approaches (e.g. energy efficiency). This distinction is important as structural measures tend to have more co-benefits for climate change related emissions, resulting in 5% less global emissions of CO_2 compared to the Baseline in 2030 and 2050.

The health benefits, in terms of avoided deaths, are projected to be greatest in the BRIICS in both 2030 and 2050 compared to the Baseline. These health gains could be even greater if additional policies in other sectors were included in the analysis (e.g. those that address forest burning and transport). However, despite relatively significant reductions in emissions projected under this simulation, the number of avoided deaths when compared to the Baseline would be relatively modest. This may be due to the fact that in some cities, especially in Asia, concentration levels projected in the Baseline are far above the maximum threshold level and thus huge reduction efforts would be needed before positive health impacts are seen. In addition, greater urbanisation expected during the next 40 years, and the large increase in the number of elderly people (the most susceptible group) is likely to lead to more premature deaths, all else being equal. Overall, this suggests that even greater reductions would be needed to have any significant impact on the growing number of premature deaths.

A rough approximation of the benefit/cost for each region (see Annex 6.A) suggests that the benefit/cost ratio would be highest in the BRIICS, followed by OECD countries and the rest of the world, and that the benefits would be higher in 2050 than in 2030. However, it is important to note the benefit values are *highly dependent* on the value of statistical life (VSL) used in the estimation[9] and that they do not account for reduction in morbidity (for more details, see Annex 6.A).

Table 6.4. **Impacts of the 25% Air Pollution Reduction scenario, 2030 and 2050**[1]

			OECD	BRIICS	RoW	World
2030	Policy mix	End-of-pipe[3]	47%	51%	56%	51%
		Structural[3]	53%	49%	44%	49%
	CO_2 reduction[2]		−5.4%	−6.4%	−1.4%	−5.1%
	Number of avoided deaths[2]		11 246	64 566	14 446	90 258
	Benefits/cost ratio		~1	1.8	0.7	1.5
2050	Policy mix	End-of-pipe[3]	48%	60%	54%	56%
		Structural[3]	52%	40%	46%	44%
	CO_2 reduction[2]		−7.9%	−7.4%	−1.8%	−5.1%
	Number of avoided deaths[2]		17 754	119 238	40 302	177 294
	Benefits/cost ratio		1.5	10	0.75	4.1

1. Pollutants covered = NO_x, SO_2 and black carbon.
2. Compared to *Baseline*.
3. Percentage of measures assumed in policy mix.
Source: OECD Environmental Outlook projections; output from IMAGE.

3. Unsafe water supply and poor sanitation

Impacts on human health

In 2004, unsafe water supply and poor sanitation and the associated exposure to pathogenic micro-organisms were responsible for around 1.6 million deaths and 6.3% of worldwide disability adjusted life-years (DALYs), mainly due to diarrhoea (WHO, 2009a). Children are most affected, with 20% of DALYs in children under 14, and 30% of deaths of children under 5 (Prüss-Üstün *et al.*, 2008). Approximately 88% of diarrhoeal deaths globally are caused by unsafe water, poor sanitation and hygiene, and 99% of these are in developing countries (WHO, 2009a). In addition to the personal tragedy involved, these losses exert a significant financial cost on developing countries. In Africa alone, the economic loss due to the lack of access to safe drinking water (*i.e.* water for human consumption) and sanitation is about 5% of GDP per year (UN WWAP, 2009). This section discusses the *health impact* of unsafe water and poor sanitation. Data in this section also appear in Chapter 5 of this *Outlook*, where the focus is more on *access* to an improved water source and basic sanitation.

Key trends and projections in water supply and sanitation
Current data and past trends

Water supply and sanitation can be categorised into three levels of service: no coverage; "improved" services (such as public standpipes or boreholes); and household connections. Each has a particular risk potential for incidence of diarrhoea (Cairncross and Valdmanis, 2006). These levels of risk depend on the level of urbanisation, income and population density. It is also important to emphasise the *safety* of the water provided (Box 6.5) – improved services through household connections may not necessarily provide

---

Box 6.5. **A word about the OECD Environmental Outlook water analysis**

The OECD Environmental Outlook Baseline projections of connection rates for water supply and sanitation are based on a regression model using country data from the WHO/UNICEF Joint Monitoring Programme (JMP; see the Annex to Chapter 5). The health impacts are based on relative risks as reported in the literature, taking into account greater risks due to increasing atmospheric temperature as well as the size of the child population which is underweight, while less risk due to possible interventions such as use of oral rehydration therapy.

The category "improved" water supply and sanitation encompasses a broad range of possible types of connection for which each is assumed to lead to the same health risk potential. The analysis considers only two classes of urbanisation – urban and rural. This may not reflect all situations within urban areas (which can include slums and more affluent areas). While increasing water and sanitation connections may be easier in urban areas, it is not always the case that greater urbanisation will result in greater connections and may instead lead to increased health risks, as in less favourable urban conditions. Overall, empirical data on the combination of water supply and sanitation categories are lacking, though the health risks are specifically related to combinations of the two. Therefore, the assumption is that there is no dependency between the two, which may affect the estimation of health risks.

It is also important to note that data on access to water and sanitation services as monitored by the JMP do not measure access to safe water. The JMP measures access to specific water supply and sanitation technologies, rather than the actual quality of service to which people have access. The projections which have been made in this OECD Environmental Outlook are based on the JMP data and therefore also overestimate these coverage rates. The number of people without access to safe water is uncertain, but exceeds the number of people without access to an improved water source by one order of magnitude.

---

safer water. Today, almost 900 million people lack access to improved water supplies and 2.6 billion people do not have access to basic sanitation (see Chapter 5). Over 80% of the sewage in developing countries is discharged untreated into water bodies (UN WWAP, 2009). Around 70% of all people without improved sanitation live in Asia (WHO/UNICEF, 2010). Of the world's regions, Sub-Saharan Africa has been moving the most slowly towards improved sanitation: only 31% of residents had access to improved sanitation in 2006.

The share of OECD populations connected to public wastewater treatment plants rose from 50% in the early 1980s to almost 70% in 2010 (see Chapter 5). However, the situation varies across countries, especially in terms of the sophistication of wastewater treatment: some countries have installed secondary and tertiary treatment[10] while others are still completing sewerage networks or the installation of first generation treatment plants. Several countries have found alternative environmentally effective and economically efficient ways of treating wastewater from small, isolated settlements.

Future projections

The Millennium Development Goals (MDGs) set targets for human development. One such target is to "halve, by 2015, the proportion of people without sustainable access to safe drinking-water and basic sanitation" (Target 7.C).

The *OECD Environmental Outlook Baseline* projects that if current trends continue, the world as a whole might meet the MDG drinking water target by 2015, though this will mainly be because of rapid progress in large emerging economies such as China and India. Other regions, such as Sub-Saharan Africa, are unlikely to meet the water supply target. The number of city dwellers without access to an improved water source has actually increased between 1990 and 2008, as urbanisation outpaces progress in access. Access to improved water supply is expected to be universal in OECD and BRIICS countries before 2050 under the *Baseline*.

Progress is slower for sanitation – the *OECD Environmental Outlook Baseline* projects that on current trends, the MDG sanitation target will not be met. It projects that by 2030 more than 2 billion people will still lack basic sanitation facilities, and this figure would only drop to 1.4 billion by 2050. In 2030, the majority of those who lack basic sanitation would live outside the OECD and BRIICS countries (*i.e.* mainly in developing countries), and this proportion will continue to grow over the following two decades. As can be seen in Figures 5.12 and 5.13 in Chapter 5, today the vast majority of those without access to an improved water supply and basic sanitation live in rural areas. This is projected to continue to 2050, when the number of people in rural areas who lack access to sanitation would drop significantly to become comparable with that in urban areas.

With greater access to improved water supply and basic sanitation facilities, the *Baseline* projects that the coming decades will see a reduction in child mortality from diarrhoea (Figure 6.11). This assumes that increasing urbanisation will *in general* (see Box 6.5) make it

Figure 6.11. **Child premature mortality due to unsafe water supply and sanitation: Baseline, 2010-2050**

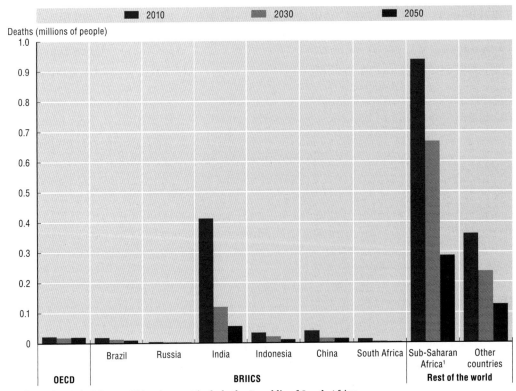

1. The region Sub-Saharan Africa does not include the Republic of South Africa.

Source: OECD Environmental Outlook Baseline; output from IMAGE.

StatLink ⬛⬛ *http://dx.doi.org/10.1787/888932571760*

easier and cheaper to connect residents to water supplies and sanitation facilities; that greater economic growth will increase the basic standard of living (including access to medical treatment); and that the number of people most susceptible to unsafe water and sanitation (*i.e.* children under the age of five) will decrease due to the continuing ageing of the population in most countries, including developing countries. Despite these assumptions, it is important to note that greater urbanisation can in some cases magnify water challenges – such as the management of waste and water in slums – with serious consequences for human health.

It is assumed that in the future, improvements in access to drinking water supplies will be implemented ahead of improvements in sanitation, as water supply levels are higher today than sanitation levels for almost all countries. Average water supply and sanitation coverage levels are expected to improve continually over the next two decades and, as a result, childhood deaths due to diarrhoea should also decline.

Need for further action

Investing in water supply and sanitation

Access to clean drinking water and sanitation provides economic, environmental and social benefits. Benefit-to-cost ratios have been reported to be as high as 7 to 1 in developing countries (WHO figure, cited in OECD, 2011c). Three-quarters of these benefits stem from time gains, *i.e.* less time spent having to walk long distances to collect water or to queue at the water source. To a large degree the other benefits are linked to a reduction of water-borne diseases such as reduced incidence of diarrhoea, malaria or dengue fever. An empirical study by Whittington *et al.* (2009) estimates that the avoided cost of illness would amount to USD 1 per month per household, which is much less than the costs of improved water and sanitation services, estimated at approximately USD 4 per month (Pattanayak *et al.*, 2005). Other non-health benefits must therefore be taken into consideration when adding up the full benefits stemming from improved access to water and sanitation. The benefits mean more time available for education and a more productive labour force.

Health experts have debated whether it is water quantity or quality that matters most in terms of driving health benefits. Cairncross and Valdmanis (2006) estimate that most of the benefits from water supply are attributable to improved convenience of access to water in terms of quantity. Other experts argue that water quality is a critical determinant driving health benefits. Waddington *et al.* (2009) points out that while water supply interventions appear ineffective – with a negligible or insignificant impact on diarrhoea morbidity on average – water quality interventions can reduce the incidence of diarrhoea in children by about 40%. Prüss *et al.* (2002) state that point-of-use treatment solutions (*e.g.* boiling) can significantly improve the impact of water supply interventions, with an estimated 45% reduction in diarrhoea rates. Such analysts argue that treatment at point of use is more efficient than treatment at the point of source.

In most OECD countries, large benefits were reaped in the late 19th or early 20th centuries when basic water and sanitation infrastructure was extended to much larger parts of the population. For instance, the introduction of water chlorination and filtration in 13 major US cities during the early 20th century led to significant reductions in mortality, with a calculated ratio of benefits to costs to society of 23 to 1 and a saving of about

USD 500 per person in 2003 (OECD, 2011c). OECD experience shows, however, that the rate of return of water and sanitation interventions diminishes with the increasing sophistication of measures.

The benefits from wastewater treatment are not obvious to the public and are more difficult to assess in monetary terms. However, anecdotal evidence can be derived from case studies. For instance, the health benefits of quality improvements of recreational waters in south-west Scotland have been calculated at GBP 1.3 million per year (Hanley *et al.*, 2003).

Uncertainty related to the economic valuation of health impacts of unsafe water and poor sanitation remains an issue. Data are scarce, and where they do exist, for instance on health benefits, experts question the reliability of the information. Further, health concerns vary depending on the type of infrastructure developed and how the water will be used (Box 6.6). Better information is needed to build a strong political case for action. Finally, the benefits of additional investments in water services vary among countries, so local assessments are needed.

Box 6.6. **Overcoming health concerns surrounding water reuse and recycling**

Reused water (either reclaimed water or grey water[*]) is increasingly seen as a sustainable source for some uses of water, essentially for irrigation, groundwater recharge, and possibly for non-potable domestic uses. It is regarded as one option to address the increasing mismatch between rising demand and available water resources in both OECD and developing countries. Reused water can be supplied from either centralised or decentralised distributed systems.

Markets for water reuse are booming. In addition, emerging economies and rural areas are gaining experience with distributed water infrastructure for water supply and sanitation services, but this is less the case in urban areas in OECD countries. Australia, Israel, Spain and some states in the United States are pioneering these new technologies, spurred by serious constraints to water resources.

However, health-related issues are a major constraint in the development of such systems. First, these systems can generate public health risks (*e.g.* possible water contamination during domestic use, or salinisation of irrigated soils). Second, the payback period of the additional investment costs required by such systems (due to additional equipment, or in-house dual plumbing, for instance) depends on the standards set by the regulatory agencies (environment and/or health authorities) for reused water. These standards govern what water can be harvested, quality standards of reused water for specific applications, building standards, agricultural standards, etc. The National Water Quality Management Strategy in Australia, for example, addresses such risks by including quality guidelines and monitoring for the safe use of recycled water, and includes an easy-to-use Decision Support Tool to help users to create a draft management plan for their water recycling scheme.

[*] Wastewater from domestic uses such as laundry, dishwashing, or bathing.

Source: for more detailed information, see OECD (2009a), *Alternative Ways of Providing Water: Emerging Options and their Policy Implications*, OECD, Paris.

What if… there was universal access to improved water supply and basic sanitation in 2050?

Chapter 5 has already presented the *Accelerated Access* scenario, a hypothetical policy simulation to estimate the expected additional annual costs and health benefits of achieving universal access to improved water supply and basic sanitation by 2050. In comparison with the *Baseline* of no new policies, this simulation includes: *i)* halving, by 2030, the population without access to an improved water source and basic sanitation from a 2005 base year; and then *ii)* moving to universal access in 2050. This scenario does not assume access to safe water. This chapter outlines the health impacts of these additional connections to improved water supply and basic sanitation facilities.

This simulation projects that compared to the *Baseline,* by 2030 almost 100 million additional people would have access to an improved source of water and around 472 million more would have access to basic sanitation facilities. Almost all of the additional people with access to an improved water source would be living outside the OECD and BRIICS countries (Table 6.5). By 2050, universal access would mean that 242 million more people than in the *Baseline* scenario would have access to an improved water source, with the RoW accounting for most of this gain. An additional 1.36 billion people would have access to sanitation facilities (795 million in the RoW, and 562 million in the BRIICS). In terms of health impacts, over the next 40 years, the highest number of avoided deaths under this policy would be in the RoW group of countries. Morbidity levels would also be expected to improve, although only mortality results were obtained from this particular simulation. It is important to note that while access to improved water sources will increase significantly, there will not be a commensurate reduction in mortality, as access to improved water sources does not necessarily mean access to "safe" water.

The policy simulation indicates that an additional USD 1.9 billion globally would need to be invested each year between 2010 and 2030 (beyond that invested under the *Baseline*) to achieve the 2030 target; and an additional USD 7.6 billion would be needed annually between 2031 and 2050 to achieve the 2050 target.[11]

Table 6.5. **Impacts of accelerated access to water supply and sanitation, 2030 and 2050**

Compared to the *Baseline*

		OECD	BRIICS	RoW	World
2030	Additional people served (water supply)	–	–	97 000 000	97 000 000
	Additional people served (sanitation)	3 000 000	152 000 000	317 000 000	472 000 000
	Avoided deaths per year	< 100	3 000	73 000	76 000
	Additional costs per year	Approximately USD 1.9 billion per year (2010 to 2030)			
2050	Additional people served (water supply)	–	2 000 000	240 000 000	242 000 000
	Additional people served (sanitation)	4 000 000	562 000 000	795 000 000	1 361 000 000
	Avoided deaths per year	< 100	6 000	75 000	81 000
	Additional costs per year	Approximately USD 7.6 billion per year (2031 to 2050)			

Source: OECD Environmental Outlook projections: output from IMAGE.

4. Chemicals

The chemicals industry is one of the world's largest industrial sectors – it makes a significant contribution to the global economy and to the living standards and health of people throughout the world. However, the production and use of chemicals can also have a negative impact on human health and the environment.

This section examines the current and projected negative impacts of chemicals on human health, and government and industry approaches to addressing these impacts. Although the focus is on health impacts, this does not imply that there are no environmental effects of concern from chemicals but their assessment is beyond the scope of this current *Outlook*. Substances of particular ecotoxicological concern such as persistent, bioaccumulative, toxic (PBT) substances; very persistent very bioaccumulative (vPvB) substances; or persistent organic pollutants (POPs) are discussed in this section, but only in the context of their impacts on human health (due to their persistence, accumulation and widespread exposure potential).

Impacts on human health

The chemicals industry is very diverse, comprising basic or commodity chemicals (*e.g.* inorganic chemicals, petrochemicals, petrochemical derivatives); speciality chemicals derived from basic chemicals (*e.g.* adhesives and sealants, catalysts, coatings, electronic chemicals, plastic additives); products derived from life sciences (*e.g.* pharmaceuticals, pesticides and products of modern biotechnology); and consumer care products (*e.g.* soap, detergents, bleaches, hair and skin care products, and fragrances).

Products developed by the chemicals industry can improve people's health and well-being. Pharmaceuticals have played a major role in increasing life expectancy, agrochemicals can improve crop yields and new modified crops can resist drought and salinity, allowing farmers to better adapt to changes in climatic conditions. Some products help in preventing water borne and vector borne diseases, and others, such as insulation material and low-temperature detergents, can improve energy efficiency.

While not all chemicals are hazardous, exposure to some chemicals can cause serious human health and/or environmental effects. Of particular concern for human health from environmental exposure are persistent and bio-accumulative substances, endocrine-disrupting chemicals (Box 6.8) and heavy metals (EEA, 2011).

Human health effects from exposure to chemicals depend on the inherent toxic properties of chemicals; the level, frequency and duration of exposure; and individual susceptibility. Table 6.6 summarises the health effects associated with some chemicals. This table also lists sensitive population groups who can be particularly vulnerable due to physiological factors (EEA, 1999). Early human life stages, especially the embryonic, foetal and infant stages, are known to be particularly sensitive to chemicals – toxic exposure at these stages can lead to disease and disability throughout a lifespan, including reproductive effects (Gee, 2008; Grandjean *et al.*, 2007).

Although the specific health impacts of chemicals are complex and sometimes open to debate, some deleterious effects are well documented, such as cancer from exposure to asbestos and leukaemia from exposure to benzene. Others, such as adverse reproductive effects from exposure to endocrine disrupting substances, are currently the subject of extensive research (Box 6.8).

Table 6.6. **Examples of health effects associated with exposure to some chemicals**

Health effect	Sensitive group	Some associated chemicals
Cancer	All	Asbestos – polycyclic aromatic hydrocarbons (PAHs) – benzene – some metals – some pesticides – some solvents – natural toxins
Cardiovascular diseases	Especially elderly	Carbon monoxide – arsenic – lead – cadmium – cobalt – calcium – magnesium
Respiratory diseases	Children, especially asthmatics	Inhalable particles – sulphur dioxide – nitrogen dioxide – ozone – hydrocarbons – some solvents
Allergies and hypersensitivities	All, especially children	Particles – ozone – nickel – chromium
Reproduction	Adults of reproductive age, foetuses	Polychlorinated biphenyls (PCBs) – DDT – phthalates
Developmental	Foetuses, children	PCBs – lead – mercury – other endocrine disruptors
Nervous system disorders	Foetuses, children	PCBs – methyl mercury – lead – manganese – aluminium – arsenic – organic solvents

Source: Adapted from EEA (European Environment Agency) (1999), *Chemicals in the European Environment: Low Doses, High Stakes?* The EEA and UNEP Annual Message 2 on the State of Europe's Environment, EEA, Copenhagen.

Based on data gathered in 2004, the WHO has estimated the global disease burden attributable to *i)* chemicals in acute poisoning episodes (including drugs but excluding self inflicted injuries); *ii)* selected chemicals in occupational exposures; and *iii)* lead. In total it estimates these three categories caused around one million deaths globally in 2004, and 21 million disability adjusted life years (DALYs). This represents 1.7% of total deaths and 1.4% total DALYs worldwide (Prüss-Ustün *et al.*, 2011). While this section focuses mainly on human exposure to chemicals in the environment, it is important to note that the portion of the disease burden attributed to *occupational* exposure is significant: 581 000 deaths and 6 763 000 DALYs in 2004.

However, the real burden of disease associated with chemicals is likely to be higher than the figures presented above. This is because, at a minimum, the WHO estimate does not include most chronic consumer exposure to chemicals, or chronic exposure to pesticides and heavy metals such as cadmium and mercury, for which incomplete data are available.

For all three categories of chemicals studied by the WHO, the global burden of disease falls more heavily on non-OECD countries. The United Nations Environment Programme (UNEP) also found a link between poverty and increased risks of exposure to hazardous chemicals and waste. People in developing countries are primarily affected by hazardous chemicals because of their occupation, living situation and lack of knowledge about the detrimental impacts of exposure to these chemicals and wastes (UNEP, 2009).

Exposure

Given the ubiquitous nature of chemicals, humans can be exposed through many daily activities and multiple routes. Exposure can occur from consuming water or food contaminated with chemicals from agricultural and industrial processes (*e.g.* pesticides, heavy metals, dioxins); from ingestion, inhalation or skin contact with chemicals emitted from construction materials or indoor products, or chemicals contained in toys, jewellery, textiles, food containers, or consumer products (*e.g.* heavy metals, phthalates, formaldehyde, dyes, fungicides or pesticides); and from foetal exposure during pregnancy. Ingestion of paints (particularly by children), and ingestion or inhalation of soil contaminated by industrial and agricultural processes and household waste (*e.g.* heavy metals, pesticides, and persistent organic pollutants) are other possible routes of exposure (Prüss-Ustün *et al.*, 2011).

Biomonitoring studies assessing human exposure to chemicals in the environment have shown that numerous chemicals are found in the human body at various levels (CDC, 2009). These studies have contributed to a growing recognition that risk assessments need to i) consider potential exposure throughout the whole life cycle of the chemical (Box 6.7); and ii) account for the potential additive and synergistic effects of human exposure to multiple chemicals (Box 6.8) (EEA, 2011).

To better characterise chemical exposure and provide the public with data on chemical releases, most OECD countries and some non-OECD economies have established Pollutant Release and Transfer Registers (PRTRs)[12] that document the quantities of potentially harmful chemicals reported by facilities which are routinely released to air, water, soil and/or transferred off-site. PRTRs are an important tool for providing the public with environmental data and promoting improvements in the management of chemical substances. In Japan, for example, the total amount of chemicals released or transferred from facilities was reduced by one-third between 2001 and 2009 as a result of voluntary actions taken by business operators, regulations set by local authorities or agreements between local authorities and industries based on numerical targets using PRTR data. While a considerable amount of PRTR data on environmental releases are available, data gaps still remain: PRTRs may not be comprehensive (*e.g.* they may only cover a limited number of chemicals) and they have some limitations (*e.g.* small facilities may not be required to report, and very few PRTRs provide data on diffuse sources of releases) (EEA, 2011).

In addition to PRTRs, governments and industry apply calculations and methodologies described in Emission Scenario Documents (ESDs) to estimate the releases of chemicals following their production and use, as well as the concentration of chemicals in the environment. Governments, working through the OECD, have developed a number of ESDs which can be applied to industrial sectors and chemical uses.[13]

Industrial installations are not the only source of chemical releases to the environment; chemicals can also be emitted from agricultural processes (*e.g.* spraying of pesticides) and from products during use (Box 6.7); or from waste, although data on such releases are limited. Gathering accurate data is further complicated by the fact that chemicals in products and waste are shipped around the globe, and thus difficult to track. Chemical waste is of particular concern in non-OECD countries, where inadequate monitoring capacities and institutional mechanisms to manage it may lead to serious air, water and soil pollution (UNEP, 2007).

Box 6.7. **Assessing chemical releases: The example of phthalates**

Quantifying releases of chemicals from products and assessing related health effects are difficult and such data are not often included in chemical risk assessments. One exception is phthalates used in plastics – a subject of recent studies due to concerns over their possible endocrine-disrupting effects (Box 6.8). Phthalates are mainly used as plasticisers (substances added to plastics to increase their flexibility, transparency, durability, and longevity). They are used in products ranging from adhesives and glues, electronics to packaging, children's toys, modelling clay, waxes, paints, printing inks and coatings, pharmaceuticals, medical devices, food products, and textiles.

Box 6.7. **Assessing chemical releases: The example of phthalates** *(cont.)*

Although PRTRs provide information on releases from production sites, major use sites and landfills, it is unlikely that all material containing phthalates will be disposed of through monitored routes. Ascertaining the difference (or mass balance) between what went into a plastic and what is present on disposal is difficult, but methods do exist to estimate their release from plastic (and other materials). These methods are outlined in the OECD ESDs. Substances can be released to the air through volatilisation from the surface of the material, into water or indirectly into the soil through leaching. How they are released depends on the properties of the substance and the circumstances in which the material is used. As an example, plastics used in outdoor materials are exposed to air and to the water flowing over them and hence releases to both media are possible. Plastic items used indoors are also exposed to air but are probably less likely to come into contact with water; an exception would be vinyl flooring, which is washed. There is also the possibility of loss of the material itself to air and water through abrasion and wear. So, the use pattern for plastics containing phthalates has a significant impact on the potential for release to the environment.

As an illustration of the potential importance of these releases, the values below are taken from the risk assessment for diethylhexyl phthalate (DEHP) carried out for the Existing Substances Regulation in the EU (EC, 2008). The overall release was about one quarter of the amount of substance produced per year; the rest is assumed to be destroyed on disposal (through incineration or degradation in landfill) or as part of the emission control measures at formulation and use. Other phthalates or other plastic additives could have a different distribution of releases depending on their properties and their use patterns. While realistic estimates are now available for exposure to phthalates in products, much less is known about the many other chemical products on the market.

Table 6.7. **Releases from different life cycle stages of diethylhexyl phthalate**

Life cycle stage	Proportion of releases (%)
Production, formulation and use	5.1
Service life – indoor use	6.2
Service life – outdoor use	26.1
Waste in the environment[1]	62.3
Disposal	0.3

1. The releases of waste in the environment estimated here are not releases of the substance as such, but of particles of material containing the substance. Hence there is the potential for the substance to be released over time to the environment as the plastic material breaks down.

Source: EC (2008), "European Union Risk Assessment Report: Bis(2-ethylhexyl) phthalate (DEHP)", *Existing Substances Second Priority List,* Vol. 80, EUR 23384 EN, Joint Research Centre, European Commission Joint Research Centre, Brussels.

Assessing chemical hazards

OECD governments have established programmes for collecting data, assessing and then managing the risks posed by chemicals using both regulatory and non-regulatory approaches. The testing of chemicals can be labour intensive, time consuming and expensive. Because of the need to relieve some of this burden and to speed up the process, the OECD Council adopted in 1981 a Decision on the Mutual Acceptance of Data (MAD), which requires that a safety test carried out in accordance with the OECD Test Guidelines and Principles of Good Laboratory Practice in one OECD country must be accepted by other OECD countries for assessment purposes. MAD increases the efficiency and effectiveness of chemical notification and registration procedures for both governments and industry, enabling them to save around EUR 150 million per year by avoiding duplicative testing and sharing data (OECD, 2010b). Since 1997 an OECD Council Decision has allowed non-OECD economies to also take part in this system. Argentina, Brazil, India, South Africa and Singapore have implemented this system via the appropriate legislative and administrative procedures and are full adherents to MAD; and Malaysia and Thailand are provisional adherents.

To date, much of the information needed to determine the hazard of a chemical has been generated from laboratory tests through *in vivo* dosing of experimental animals, and *in vitro* tests. While this approach has supported regulatory decision making over the past several decades, new advances in science (*e.g.* in biology, biotechnology and bioinformatics) are leading to a greater understanding of how cells and cell systems work. This may lead to new toxicity testing approaches that rely mainly on understanding cellular response pathways or "toxicity pathways" at the cellular level (National Research Council, 2007). In addition, other approaches, such as computer simulations called (quantitative) structure-activity relationships or (Q)SARs, are more and more used to provide information on the hazards of chemicals.

Governments in OECD countries are working together to collect and assess toxicity and exposure data using harmonised formats, to share data collection strategies, to develop assessment methodologies, and to co-ordinate actions on chemicals internationally. Governments are also working through the OECD to develop new and innovative alternative methods and computer models for testing and assessment and to facilitate access to these tools through the Internet.

Nevertheless, challenges remain in assessing the effects of chemicals on human health (see Box 6.8) and collecting sufficient data to complete risk assessments on the thousands of chemicals on the market. As a result, a high priority for the OECD and its member countries will be to continue to work towards i) developing harmonised new or updated test methods that can be used for regulatory decision-making and allow industry and governments to benefit from MAD; and ii) harmonising integrated approaches to testing and assessment used by member countries in their regulatory framework. These could include the use of (Q)SARs, toxicogenomics (the study of the response of a genome to hazardous chemicals) and high-throughput screening *in vitro* assays (that can be applied rapidly to thousands of chemicals).

To supplement the information generated by chemical testing and predictive models, in recent years governments have embarked on large-scale epidemiological studies of the patterns of illness in the population which might be associated with chemical exposure. Recent work has focused in particular on early life stages, including two large-scale birth cohort studies launched in Japan and the United States.

Box 6.8. **Addressing certain chemical assessment challenges**

Endocrine disrupters

A recent priority area for governments is to investigate chemicals or mixtures of chemicals which may have endocrine-disrupting properties. These substances "alter the function(s) of the endocrine system and consequently cause adverse health effects in an intact organism, or its progeny, or (sub) populations" (Damstra *et al.*, 2002). A number of observations of health effects have been made in which endocrine disrupters (ED) could play a role, including: declining sperm counts, congenital malformations in children, cancer, retarded sexual development, retarded neurobehavioural development, impaired immune functions and effects on metabolism. However, certain lifestyle factors are also known to be important elements of these problems, and the part attributable to ED needs to be better evaluated. New OECD validated and standardised screens or assays have been developed to test chemicals for their possible endocrine-disrupting effects. Many OECD member countries are actively involved in gathering information on endocrine disrupters to help support regulatory actions.[1]

Manufactured nanomaterials

Nanomaterials can be metals, ceramics, polymeric materials, or composite materials. Their defining characteristic is their very small size – in the range of 1-100 nanometers (nm) in at least one dimension. Over the past decade, nanomaterials have been the subject of enormous interest. These materials have the potential for wide-ranging industrial, biomedical, and electronic applications and are likely to offer many economic benefits. However, unlocking this potential will require a responsible and co-ordinated approach to ensure that potential safety issues are being addressed at the same time as the technology is developing.

Manufactured nanomaterials (MNs) present unique challenges as a class of substances. Other than their size, they may not have much in common with each other. While some are nano-scale counterparts of existing chemicals, other substances have novel chemical structures. As governments contemplate how to define and distinguish MNs under their respective regulatory and statutory regimes, they have come together globally in the OECD to address the human health and environmental implications of nanomaterials. The OECD Programme on the Safety of Manufactured Nanomaterials includes testing commercially relevant representative nanomaterial categories for 59 human health and environment relevant end-points (including physical-chemical properties, fate, and effects). This effort, which requires scientists to modify dozens of tests and involves nearly 20 OECD and non-OECD governments as well as industry, will feed into ongoing work to develop more specific guidance for testing broader sets of materials. As the sheer numbers of different materials proliferate, the OECD is also fostering co-operation to rapidly assess these substances using alternative methods, such as *in vitro* approaches; develop techniques to assess exposure of workers, consumers, the general population and the environment; and measure the broader positive and negative environmental impacts that could result from these new technologies. While the future needs in the environment, health and safety area for this rapidly evolving field are difficult to predict, this initial co-operation should provide a firm basis for future efforts in addressing the safety of emerging technologies.

Box 6.8. **Addressing certain chemical assessment challenges** (cont.)

Assessment of combined exposure to multiple chemicals or "mixtures"

Chemical risk assessments generally consider the effects of single substances in isolation. However, humans are exposed to mixtures of chemicals, which together may have additive or synergistic effects in the human body. The current risk-assessment approach (which assesses the effects of individual chemicals only) may therefore underestimate the risk to human health and to the environment. For example, Acceptable Daily Intakes are set as estimates of the acceptable amount of certain substances in food or drinking water. As they are currently derived from individual chemical risk assessments, they might not provide sufficient protection from combined exposures to multiple chemicals or mixtures. There is a growing trend both at the national and international level towards considering the assessment of combined exposure to multiple chemicals.[2]

1. This work includes i) screening of EDs, *e.g.* the US Endocrine Disrupter Screening Program and the Japanese Further Actions on Endocrine Disrupting Effects of Chemical Substances (EXTEND 2010); ii) research into the mechanisms of EDs and the effects of mixtures of EDs, *e.g.* the work done by the Danish National Center on Endocrine Disrupters (*www.cend.dk/index-filer/Page319.htm*); iii) epidemiology studies on specific health effects associated with exposure to EDs, *e.g.* Swiss male fertility study, the results of which are expected by the end of 2012 or the Danish prenatal pesticide exposure study which started in 2011; and iv) OECD work on the assessment of ED activity (*www.oecd.org/env/testguidelines*).

2. Meek *et al.* (2011) describe a framework for the risk assessment of combined exposure to multiple chemicals based on the 2007 World Health Organization/International Programme on Chemical Safety *Workshop on Aggregate/Cumulative Risk Assessment*. The framework is designed to aid risk assessors in identifying priorities for risk management for a wide range of applications where co-exposures to multiple chemicals are expected. In 2011 the WHO and OECD also co-hosted an international workshop on risk assessment of combined exposures to multiple chemicals, which identified areas for further work, such as the development of exposure models (OECD, 2011f).

Key trends and projections in chemical safety

Current trends

The global chemicals industry has grown significantly over the past 50 years. Annual global sales of products from the chemicals sector doubled just between 2000 and 2009 (Figure 6.12). Over this same period, the OECD's share of the global market dropped from 77% to 63%, while the BRIICS increased their share from 13% to 28%. Some of this increase is due to the lower costs associated with production in the BRIICS, but also the need for facilities to be closer to growing markets and feedstock sources. In addition, technology transfer from companies in developed countries to emerging economies (due to, among other things, joint ventures and mergers and acquisitions) has helped emerging economies innovate and play a larger role in the global market (Kiriyama, 2010). Chinese companies in particular are active in gaining access to advanced technologies in partnership with multinationals, alongside in-house research and development (Kiriyama, 2010).

In addition to this shift in production, there has been a shift in the types of chemicals produced. Non-OECD countries, especially the BRIICS (which traditionally produced more low value, high-volume basic chemicals), now also produce high value, specialty and life science chemicals, including pharmaceuticals and agrochemicals. In the past these were typically produced only in OECD countries. Some companies in China, India and the Middle East are turning to specialty and fine chemicals for their sources of profit in response to increasing competitive pressure in the basic industrial chemicals sector (Kiriyama, 2010). Since specialty and fine chemicals are characterised by continuous product innovation and differentiation, this means that more new chemicals will be developed in non-member

Figure 6.12. **Growth in chemical sales, 2000-2009**

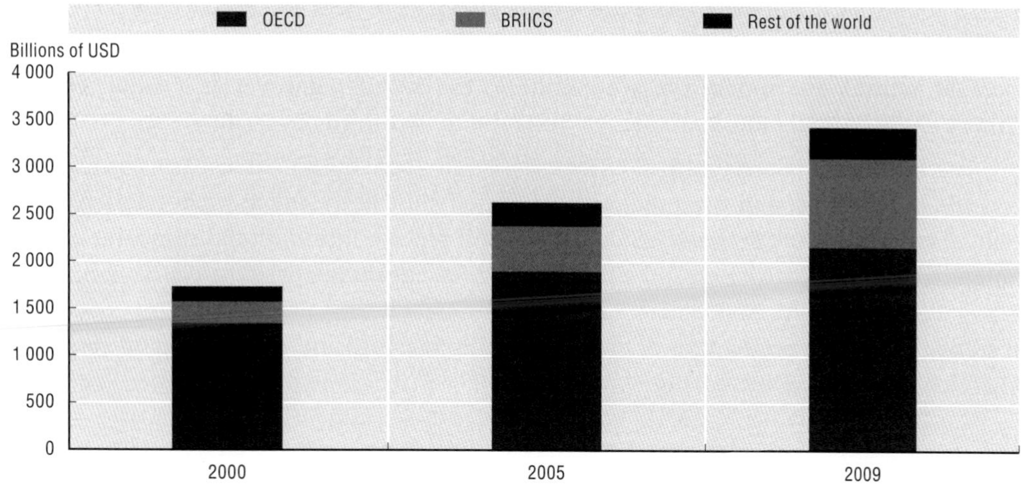

■ OECD   ■ BRIICS   ■ Rest of the world

Billions of USD

Source: American Chemistry Council.

StatLink ⬚ *http://dx.doi.org/10.1787/888932571779*

economies. It is important to note that while high-volume commodity chemicals have traditionally been the focus of risk assessments at the national and international level (*i.e.* OECD), risks are less likely to have been characterised for other chemicals, such as the lower volume and specialty chemicals.

Future trends in production

The *OECD Environmental Outlook Baseline* projects the world chemicals industry to grow (in terms of sales) by approximately 3% annually to 2050. As shown in recent years, annual growth for the BRIICS is expected to continue to outpace that in OECD countries (4% compared to 1.7%), and total production in the BRIICS will surpass OECD production

Figure 6.13. **Projected chemicals production by region (in sales): Baseline, 2010-2050**

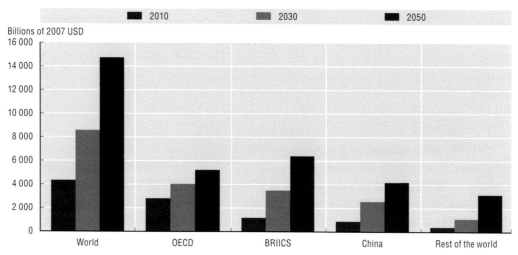

■ 2010   ■ 2030   ■ 2050

Note: China is included in the BRIICS data, but has also been singled out to show its share in the BRIICS projected chemical production.

Source: OECD Environmental Outlook Baseline, output from ENV-Linkages.

StatLink ⬚ *http://dx.doi.org/10.1787/888932571798*

by 2050 (Figure 6.13). While total production in the rest of the world will still trail OECD and BRIICS countries, it will experience the largest growth rate between 2010 and 2050 (4.9%).

China is the main contributor to BRIICS chemicals production and currently represents three-quarters of the production in the BRIICS. However, it is expected that China's share of total BRIICS production will drop to two-thirds by 2050.

The significant contribution of chemicals to the global burden of disease, especially in non-OECD countries, and the predicted continued shift in chemical production over the next 40 years from OECD to BRIICS countries, will require international co-operation and capacity building for the sound management of chemicals in non-OECD countries, especially through SAICM (Box 6.9). This international effort is needed both for economies in transition where production of chemicals is increasing, and for developing countries where chemical use is increasing.

Box 6.9. **SAICM: Managing chemicals strategically**

The **S**trategic **A**pproach to International **C**hemicals **M**anagement (**SAICM**) was adopted by the International Conference on Chemicals Management (ICCM) on 6 February 2006 in Dubai. It is a policy framework to foster the sound management of chemicals. **SAICM** was developed by a multi-stakeholder and multi-sectoral Preparatory Committee. It supports the achievement of the goal agreed at the 2002 Johannesburg World Summit on Sustainable Development of ensuring that, by the year 2020, chemicals are produced and used in ways that minimise significant adverse impacts on the environment and human health. In 2012, world leaders will assemble at the Third International Conference on Chemicals Management (ICCM3) to review progress on SAICM implementation.

Chemicals: The state of policy today

With the growth of the global chemicals industry, governments are looking for ways to manage chemicals as efficiently as possible. The management of risks posed by chemicals can take many forms (Table 6.8). Governments ensure the safety of chemicals through the assessment and regulation of new and existing chemicals, as well as the use of economic instruments such as taxes. In addition, governments also ensure chemical safety through the use of non-regulatory approaches, such as voluntary initiatives aimed at the removal of harmful chemical products from the market, and through the promotion of the development of greener chemicals. Each type of approach is described in more detail below.

Policy evaluations

Cost-benefit analyses of policy interventions may help risk-management decision makers by describing the implications of choosing one approach over another. However, to date, although many studies have estimated the impacts of chemicals policies, few include estimates of the monetary valuation of the benefits. Recently, the European Chemicals Agency's Socio-Economic Analysis Committee has begun preparing opinions about proposals for restriction or requests for authorisation under the new Registration, Evaluation, Authorisation and Restriction of Chemical substances (REACH) regulation (see below). These opinions are prepared taking into account the envisaged costs to society and benefits to human health and the environment. At the global level, the WHO initiative

Table 6.8. **Examples of policy instruments for managing chemical substances**

Regulatory (command and control) approaches	Economic instruments	Information and other instruments
■ Notification of new and existing substances. ■ Testing and assessment of chemical substances. ■ Risk reduction (bans or limitations on production, use and disposal; *e.g.* US Pollution Prevention Act 1990). ■ Food quality standards. ■ Product quality standards (lead in paint, toys, gasoline, etc.).	■ Taxes/charges (*e.g.* leaded petrol). ■ Grants and tax preferences for R&D expenditures related to green chemistry. ■ Green procurement by the public sector.	■ Information campaigns (*e.g.* product warnings, awareness-raising campaigns). ■ Voluntary agreements between industry and governments to reduce production and use of harmful chemicals (*e.g.* brominated flame retardants). ■ International framework for the safe management of chemicals (*i.e.* SAICM). ■ International conventions on specific chemicals (*e.g.* Stockholm Convention on Persistent Organic Pollutants). ■ Globally Harmonized System (GHS) of Chemical Classification and Labelling. ■ Work sharing, through the OECD on chemicals prioritised by member countries. ■ Internet data access, tools and IT systems. ■ Reporting for Pollutant Release and Transfer Registers. ■ Alternatives assessments for priority chemicals to inform substitution to safer alternatives. ■ Green chemistry promotion where safer alternatives do not exist.

CHOICE (CHOosing Interventions that are Cost-Effective) has developed a methodology to provide policy makers with the evidence for deciding on interventions and programmes which maximise health benefits within available resources (WHO, 2003). Greater co-operation in the development of this kind of methodologies would both ensure that state-of-the-art methods are used in policy evaluation and allow more cross-border use of methodologies and results.

National regulatory frameworks

Recent years have seen significant changes in national chemicals management programmes, both in OECD and non-OECD countries (although enforcement is still incomplete). Many of these new initiatives aim to enhance data collection efforts, extend regulatory coverage to include chemicals already on the market and increase incentives for the development of safer and more environmentally friendly chemicals. A few examples are given below.

European legislation on chemicals changed significantly in 2007 when the EU REACH Regulation came into force. REACH places the responsibility on industry to provide and assess data and manage the risks that chemicals may pose to human health and the environment. In addition, a major driver for this regulation was the need to establish a level playing field for the regulation of existing and new chemicals. Previously in the European Union, new chemicals were subject to a significantly stricter regulatory regime than those already in use. REACH was designed to solve this anomaly by requiring all chemicals to be assessed (EC, 2007).

In the United States, the Obama Administration announced *Essential Principles for Reform of Chemicals Management Legislation* in September 2009, setting out the Administration's goals for updating the current chemical legislation – the Toxic Substances

Control Act (TSCA). The emphasis is on the review of chemicals against a safety standard based on sound science and risk-based criteria; submission of sufficient information to demonstrate that chemicals are safe; and greater authority for the Environmental Protection Agency (EPA) to quickly and efficiently require testing or obtain other information and to set priorities for conducting safety reviews.

The Canadian Chemicals Management Plan was announced by the government in 2006. This national programme focuses on protecting the health of Canadians and their environment from the potential risks posed by legacy chemicals that have not previously been assessed.

Japan amended its Chemical Substances Control Law (*Kashinho*) in 2009 to introduce an annual notification of production and import for quantities of above one ton per year for all chemical substances.[14] On receiving the notification, the government chooses chemical substances (known as Priority Assessment Chemical Substances or PACSs) for further assessment using available exposure and hazard information. Following the designation of PACSs, the government of Japan conducts detailed risk assessments. In parallel, since 2005, there has been an effort by industry to collect safety information on priority existing chemicals under the "Japan Challenge" programme.

In 2010, China expanded its Measures on Environmental Management of New Chemical Substances which continues the approach of the current law, but expands the data requirement and risk-management obligations by industry (Freshfields Bruckhaus Deringer, 2009).

Economic instruments

The use of taxes on hazardous chemicals can be an effective way of reducing their use, in some cases. For example, the European Union Nordic countries use taxes as part of their policy package for regulating pesticides. However, although in many instances economic incentives such as input taxes work well in isolation, a mix of quantitative regulations and economic incentives tend to be the best way to control chemical use (Söderholm, 2009).

Another non-regulatory approach is "green procurement" in the public sector. The government is a significant purchaser of goods and services and therefore its procurement preferences can act as an incentive to industry to develop more environmentally friendly products. Also, if there is sufficient government demand this can send a signal to private purchasers, giving the greener technology a competitive advantage and encouraging innovation. For example, the Canadian Policy on Green Procurement requires that environmental performance considerations be incorporated into federal procurement decision-making processes. The US Environmentally Preferable Purchasing (EPP) programme helps the federal government "buy green", using the federal government's buying power to stimulate market demand for green products and services.

Voluntary agreements

Voluntary agreements can be an important complement to market instruments. In many cases, voluntary agreements are proposed by industries when government is likely to impose requirements for the control of a chemical. For instance, Responsible Care, an initiative of the International Council of Chemical Association (ICCA), is a key part of the global industry's contribution to SAICM (Box 6.9). Responsible Care has also fostered the development of the ICCA Global Product Strategy which seeks to improve the industry's management of chemicals, including the communication of chemical risks throughout the supply chain.

International regulatory framework and international co-ordination

There are a number of multinational and legally binding agreements to control specific chemicals for various purposes. These include the:

■ Basel Convention (transboundary movements of hazardous waste);

■ Montreal Protocol (CFCs and other ozone depleting substances);

■ Rotterdam Convention (export of hazardous chemicals);

■ Stockholm Convention (persistent organic pollutants);

■ United Nations Convention Against Illicit Traffic in Narcotic Drugs and Psychotropic Substances (drug control);

■ Chemical Weapons Convention (arms control).

To strengthen the links and increase synergies between three of these conventions, the Basel and Stockholm Convention Secretariats and the UNEP part of the Rotterdam Convention are now led by a Joint Head.

In addition, UNITAR's (United Nations Institute for Training and Research) Global Capacity Building Programme plays a significant role in the safe management of chemicals in non-OECD countries, by providing institutional, technical, and legal support to governments and stakeholders to develop sustainable capacity for managing dangerous chemicals and wastes. Project activities take place within the framework of implementing international agreements (e.g. SAICM, Stockholm Convention, Rotterdam Convention, United Nations Globally Harmonised System of Classification and Labelling of Chemicals).

The OECD is one of the leading international organisations in the field of chemicals management – its products are used widely by member and non-member countries.[15] Many activities are undertaken (together with UN organisations, via the Inter-Organization Programme for the Sound Management of Chemicals[16]) to help non-member countries establish and improve their chemicals management systems and to introduce them to the principles and tools used in OECD countries. In 2008, the OECD Council adopted a Resolution on the Implementation of the SAICM (Box 6.9) that calls for countries to work together through the OECD to ensure that as chemicals management programmes are established or upgraded, OECD products will be accessible, relevant and useful to non-members to help them develop their capacities for managing chemicals.

Need for further action

The impacts of chemicals on human health are still not well understood. While progress has been made over the years in both collecting and assessing data, new and more sophisticated tools will be needed to assess more chemicals more quickly, as well as new types of chemicals (such as those developed from manufactured nanomaterials), and specific effects (such as endocrine disrupters, see Box 6.8). In addition, more remains to be done at all levels to ensure the sound management of chemicals over their life cycle – from production to use and disposal – to minimise the negative impacts on human health and the environment. There is a need to move towards an integrated approach to the assessment and management of chemicals, and this will include the factors described below.

Co-operate and share in chemical assessment

Greater co-operation through work sharing and improved assessment tools are needed. Non-OECD countries, particularly the BRIICs, will need to do more to meet the growing challenge of safely managing existing chemicals and new chemicals. Where not already in place, a first step will be to establish chemical inventories. By becoming members of the MAD system, these countries will be able to work with OECD members to share the burden of assessing existing chemicals. Greater international co-operation will be needed to build capacity, share expertise and promote effective chemical management globally. Co-operation will also be needed to ensure that new national chemical management systems do not lead to duplicative testing and assessments or to new trade barriers.

Improve data on chemical hazards and population exposure

Greater efforts will also be needed to identify and describe how individuals and populations are exposed to harmful chemicals, and to quantify sources of exposure. This is likely to involve wider use of environmental public health surveillance, biomonitoring, environmental monitoring and other evolving public health information research techniques, as well as sharing such data across countries.

With the growing number of current and planned epidemiology studies, and the considerable volume of data being collected, it may be more efficient for countries to co-ordinate their efforts. To this end, in 2009 the WHO published a guide on the design of birth cohort studies (Golding *et al.*, 2009). Another international initiative (STROBE, or Strengthening the Reporting of Observational Studies in Epidemiology) provides guidance on reporting results for any kind of epidemiology study. In addition to these principles, other areas of co-ordination could be developed. For example, creating an international database of epidemiological studies listing the main features of studies (*e.g.* cohort size, criteria for inclusion/exclusion, biological samples collected) would make existing work and data more accessible and thus help in the design of future epidemiological studies.

Improve emphasis on prevention, in particular at early life stages

Based on the recognition that foetuses and children are more vulnerable to harmful chemicals than adults, there is a need to refocus risk assessments on the effects of chemicals following prenatal and early life exposures. First, these are the most vulnerable life stages and chemical exposure during this period may lead to significant disease in children and adults. Second, they are the stages where preventive action may be the most effective in terms of health and well-being, as well as in terms of economic benefits, such as reduced health and education costs and increased national productivity.

Promote sustainable use of chemicals and green chemistry

Green or "sustainable chemistry" concerns the design, manufacture and use of more environmentally friendly chemicals throughout their life cycle. It contributes to sustainable development through the manufacture of products that are less harmful to human health and the environment: i) through the use of less hazardous and harmful feedstocks and reagents; ii) by improving the energy and material efficiency of chemical processes; iii) by using renewable feedstocks or wastes in preference to fossil fuels or mined resources; and iv) by designing chemical products for better reuse or recycling. A recent report based on patent data shows that some green chemistry technologies, such as biochemical fuel cells and green plastics, have grown at least seven times faster than the rate of patents in the chemicals industry overall (OECD, 2011d).

Significant gains can be made by providing positive support to help industry adopt greener technologies. A number of governments provide financial support (grants and tax preferences) for R&D expenditure on green chemistry. In the United States, grants are provided under the EPA/National Science Foundation programme on "Technology for a Sustainable Environment".[17] In Japan, the National Institute of Advanced Industrial Science and Technology undertakes a considerable amount of research on green and sustainable chemistry, particularly in the areas of catalysis, membranes, supercritical fluids and renewable resources. Awards have also proven to be a successful means of inducing innovation in a number of areas, including health and energy technologies (e.g. see Newell and Wilson, 2005).

More can also be done to find safer substitutes for priority chemicals. Known as alternatives assessments, this involves evaluating a broad range of health and environmental effects to ensure that safer alternatives are selected and to minimise the potential for unintended consequences. By identifying and evaluating the safety of alternative chemicals, this approach can encourage industry to move to safer alternatives, it can complement regulatory action by showing that safer and higher functioning alternatives are available, or it can point out the limitations to chemical substitution for a particular use. The US EPA's Design for the Environment programme has developed a methodology for chemical alternatives assessments (Lavoie et al., 2010).

Improving the public's right to know

OECD governments have developed information systems and other tools to enhance public access to chemical hazard data and risk information prepared by government chemical review programmes. These tools, including the OECD's eChemPortal,[18] support long-standing international commitments (e.g. under SAICM) to improve the public availability of data on chemicals. They also make these efforts more transparent. However, more information on the constituents and effects of chemicals, for example in articles, food or cosmetics, should be made available to comply with the public's right to know about chemical exposures and health and environmental risk factors.

5. Climate change

The Intergovernmental Panel on Climate Change's Fourth Assessment report concluded, with a very high degree of confidence,[19] that climate change is contributing to the global burden of disease and causing premature deaths, and that while currently these effects are small, they are "projected to progressively increase in all countries and regions" (Confalonieri et al., 2007; Chapter 3). Climate change affects human health adversely through extremes in temperature, weather disasters, photochemical air pollutants, vector-borne and rodent-borne diseases, and food-related and waterborne infections (Box 6.10). The impacts may be direct – such as temperature-related mortality (i.e. heat and cold stress) – or indirect by increasing the incidence of flooding, malnutrition, diarrhoea and malaria (Campbell-Lendrum et al., 2003). The WHO estimates that in 2004, around 3% of all deaths globally from diarrhoea, malaria and dengue fever were caused by climate change (McMichael et al., 2004; WHO, 2009b). In many cases, those regions which will be most affected will be the poorest and least able to respond to such impacts.

Box 6.10. **Climate change, health determinants and health impacts: Facts and figures**

Air. Extreme high air temperatures can kill directly; it has been estimated that more than 70 000 excess deaths were recorded in the extreme heat of summer 2003 in Europe (Robine *et al.*, 2008). By the second half of this century, such extreme temperatures will be the norm (Beniston and Diaz, 2004). In addition, rising air temperatures will increase levels of important air pollutants such as ground-level ozone, particularly in areas that are already polluted. Urban air pollution currently causes about 1.2 million deaths each year (WHO, 2008, 2009a) mainly by increasing mortality from cardiovascular and respiratory diseases.

Water. Shifting rainfall patterns, increased rates of evaporation and melting of glaciers, combined with population and economic growth, are expected to increase the number of people living in water-stressed water basins from about 1.5 billion in 1990 to 3-6 billion by 2050 (Arnell, 2004). By the 2090s, climate change may bring a doubling in the frequency of extreme drought events, a sixfold increase in mean duration, and a tenfold to thirtyfold increase in the land area in extreme drought (Burke *et al.*, 2006). Almost 90% of the burden of diarrhoeal disease is attributable to lack of access to safe water and sanitation (Prüss-Üstün and Corvalán, 2006; Prüss-Üstün *et al.*, 2004; WHO, 2009a) and reductions in the availability and reliability of freshwater supplies are expected to amplify this hazard.

Food. Increasing temperatures and more variable precipitation are expected to reduce crop yields in many tropical developing regions. In some African countries, yields from rain-fed agriculture could be reduced by up to 50% by 2020 (IPCC, 2007). This is likely to aggravate the burden of undernutrition in developing countries, which currently causes 3.5 million deaths each year, both directly through nutritional deficiencies and indirectly by intensifying vulnerability to diseases such as malaria and diarrhoeal and respiratory infections (Black *et al.*, 2008; WHO, 2009a).

Shelter. By the second half of this century, climate change is projected to cause a several-fold increase in the frequency of extreme storms, heavy rainfall and heatwaves. In the absence of improvements to protection, by 2080 sea level rise could also multiply the number of people exposed to coastal flooding more than tenfold, to more than 100 million people a year (IPCC, 2007). These trends will also increase the hazards of weather-related natural disasters, which killed approximately 600 000 people during the 1990s (Hales *et al.*, 2003). Repeated floods and droughts may force population displacement – which, in turn, is associated with heightened risks of a range of health effects, from mental disorders such as depression to communicable diseases and, potentially, civil conflict.

Freedom from disease. Rising temperatures, shifting rainfall patterns and increasing humidity affect the transmission of diseases by vectors and through water and food. Vector-borne diseases currently kill approximately 1.1 million people a year, and diarrhoeal diseases 2.2 million (WHO, 2008). Studies suggest that climate change may swell the population at risk of malaria in Africa by 170 million by 2030 (Hay *et al.*, 2006) and the global population at risk of dengue by 2 billion by the 2080s (Hales *et al.*, 2002).

Health equity. Climate change and associated development patterns threaten to widen existing health inequalities between and within populations. A WHO assessment of the burden of disease caused by climate change suggested that the modest warming that has occurred since the 1970s was already causing over 140 000 excess deaths annually by the year 2004 (McMichael *et al.*, 2004; WHO, 2009a). The estimated per-capita impacts were many times greater in regions that already had the greatest disease burden (McMichael *et al.*, 2004; Patz *et al.*, 2007). Health benefits of climate change – mainly decreased mortality from cold winters – are less strongly supported by evidence; to the extent that they do occur, they are expected to benefit mainly populations in high-latitude developed countries (Confalonieri *et al.*, 2007; McMichael *et al.*, 2004). The ongoing process of climate change is therefore likely to widen the existing health disparities between the richest and the poorest populations.

Source: WHO (World Health Organization) (2009b), *Protecting Health From Climate Change: Connecting Science, Policy and People*, WHO, Geneva.

Climate change and malaria: A case study

The *OECD Environmental Outlook Baseline* focuses on malaria as the most important infectious disease that is exacerbated by climate change. Some other health-related impacts of climate change are covered elsewhere in this *Outlook* (*e.g.* for diarrhoea, see Section 3 of this chapter; for flooding, see Chapter 5; and for agricultural yields, see Chapter 2). While climate change has other types of health impacts, such as heat and cold stress, they are not modelled for this *Outlook*.

Currently, more than half of the world's population, around 3.7 billion, lives in areas where there is a potential risk of malaria (*i.e.* areas which are a suitable habitat for the malaria mosquito), and this number is expected to grow to 5.7 billion people by 2050.[20] By 2050, the bulk of the population living in potential malaria risk areas will be in Asia (3.2 billion) and Africa (1.6 billion) (Figure 6.14). However, in many areas these risks have been greatly reduced by vector control programmes, with the exception of Africa, where more than 90% of all malaria deaths occurred in 2004.

Figure 6.14. **Potential population at risk from malaria: *Baseline*, 2010-2050**

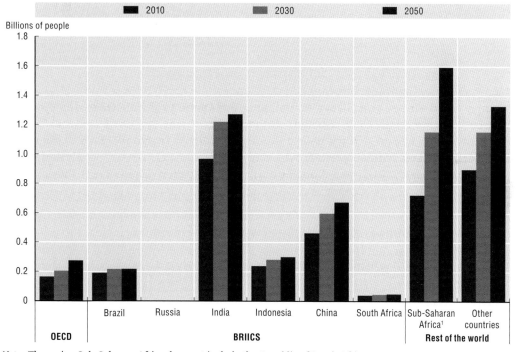

Note: The region Sub-Saharan Africa does not include the Republic of South Africa.

Source: *OECD Environmental Outlook Baseline*; output from IMAGE.

StatLink http://dx.doi.org/10.1787/888932571817

Despite the greater number of people living in malaria risk areas, the *OECD Environmental Outlook Baseline* projects that from 2010 to 2050 global premature mortality from malaria will actually fall significantly (Figure 6.15).[21] This is due to the projected greater urbanisation, increased per-capita income (which supports adaptation approaches and health treatments) and the ageing of the population (children are the most vulnerable to malaria). Climate change only plays a limited role in future projections of changes in the disease burden due to malaria. However, even with this significant reduction in premature

Figure 6.15. **Malaria deaths:** *Baseline,* **2010-2050**

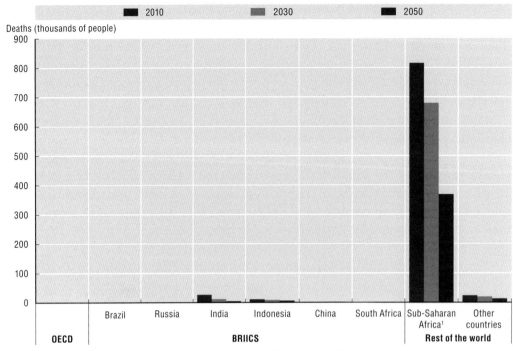

Note: The region *Sub-Saharan Africa* does not include the Republic of South Africa.

Source: *OECD Environmental Outlook Baseline;* output from IMAGE.

StatLink *∎∎∎* *http://dx.doi.org/10.1787/888932571836*

global mortality, in 2050 it is estimated that there will still be almost 400 000 premature deaths from malaria, with almost all occurring in Africa.

To understand whether alternative climate policy scenarios would make a difference to malaria incidence, the *450 Core* scenario described in Chapter 3 was extended to assess the impact of this policy scenario on malaria incidence. The *450 Core* scenario models a climate change mitigation pathway that limits the global average temperature increase to below 2 °C by the end of the 21st century. This is compared to the *Baseline,* which being a no-new-policy scenario, projects that global mean temperature would increase by between 3 and 6 °C by the end of the century. The extended *450 Core* simulation implies that there would be only a small reduction in the number of people at risk of malaria compared to the *Baseline.* Some areas would become more prone to the malarial mosquito (such as the Ethiopian highlands), while other areas would not. Overall, the differences in the size of the malaria-suitable areas (*i.e.,* areas with suitable climatic conditions) between the *Baseline* and policy scenario are small, and thus the change in impact on human health would be minimal.

Considerable knowledge exists on ways to prevent and counteract outbreaks of malaria – this knowledge must be used to prevent the potential spread of malaria. Adaptation options include better surveillance and development of early warning systems for potential outbreaks, clearing susceptible habitats, vector control programmes such as distribution of mosquito nets, R&D on vector control, vaccines and disease eradication, and better design of buildings and housing structures. Governments and relevant international organisations should work together to systematically map potential new areas for malaria and design appropriate policy instruments. These could include incentives for R&D as well as regulatory incentives (*e.g.* building codes and insurance).

Notes

1. Particulate matter discussed in this section includes PM_{10} (particulate matter with a diameter of less than or equal to 10 micrometres) and $PM_{2.5}$ (particulate matter with a diameter of less than or equal to 2.5 micrometres).

2. Although the World Bank data were compiled in 2001, they still represent the best global and consistent data which are necessary for modelling.

3. Information on a large number of economic instruments and voluntary approaches for air pollution can be found in the OECD/EEA database on instruments used for environmental policy, at *www.oecd.org/env/policies/database*.

4. When in a gaseous form, HCs are called volatile organic compounds (VOCs).

5. OECD (2010a) gives an in-depth discussion of the NO_x tax in Sweden, including its impacts on the environment and on innovation.

6. The upper limit on new vehicles' emissions of NO_x in the European Union were, in 2008, 0.06 grams per km for petrol-driven vehicles and 0.2 grams per km for diesel-driven ones – more than three times higher. There are also indications that the tightening of the emission standards over the years in practice have had modest impact on real-world NO_x emissions from diesel-driven vehicles, (Carslaw *et al.*, 2011).

7. As an illustration, under current tax rates and assuming everything else is unchanged, the tax on a car that emits 0.75 grams of CO, 0.05 grams HC and 0.03 grams NO_x per km driven would have been EUR 977 lower if the tax had only taken CO_2 emissions into account and ignored the other emission categories.

8. For purposes of this simulation, it is recognised that reducing emissions relatively uniformly across the globe will lead to variations in mortality rates across countries due to differences in existing concentrations in countries and the degree to which they are above or below health threshold levels.

9. Under the approach used for these calculations, the VSL values vary with income; *i.e.*, they are lower in countries with lower per-capita GDP. This allows for local preferences to be more accurately represented in decision making; however, it also means that a global view of the scale of a particular environmental action, and the case for concerted international finance, is less clear.

10. Secondary treatment refers to treatment of (urban) wastewater by a process generally involving biological treatment with a secondary settlement or other process, resulting in a BOD (organic content) removal of at least 70% and a COD (chemical content) removal of at least 75%. Tertiary treatment refers to treatment (additional to secondary treatment) of nitrogen and/or phosphorous and/or any other pollutant affecting the quality or a specific use of water (microbiological pollution, colour, etc.).

11. The associated costs for these connection rates are based on Hutton and Haller (2004) who made estimates of annual costs of the various levels of connection rates. Their annual cost assumptions are based on investment and recurrent costs, using values from the literature. For example, the annual costs for in-house piped water are USD 10-15 per person, while other improved water supply connections range from USD 1-4 per person. It is important to note that the costs in the OECD *Outlook* simulation are approximate since the categories and regions do not fully match those of Hutton and Haller. In addition, translating initial investment costs to annual costs might underestimate the costs when using them over time. See Annex 5.A at the end of Chapter 5 for more details on the assumptions behind this scenario.

12. Currently 39 countries have an operational PRTR system: all 27 EU countries, 3 European Economic Area (EEA) countries (Iceland, Liechtenstein and Norway) and 9 other countries: 8 OECD countries (Australia, Canada, Chile, Japan, Korea, Mexico, Switzerland and the United States), and Croatia. New Zealand does not have a single integrated PRTR but each of the 16 New Zealand regional authorities is responsible for implementing national environmental standards and independently manages and maintains information on resource consent, including pollutant discharges. Turkey and Israel have each completed a PRTR Pilot Project.

13. For more information see the OECD web page on ESDs: *www.oecd.org/env/exposure/esd*.

14. See Naiki (2010) for a comparative analysis of Japanese chemicals regulation and REACH.

15. For more information see the brochure, *The Environment, Health and Safety Programme – Managing Chemicals through OECD*, available at *www.oecd.org/dataoecd/18/0/1900785.pdf*.

16. See *www.who.int/iomc/en/*.

17. See *www.epa.gov/greenchemistry/pubs/grants.html#TSE*.

18. See *www.echemportal.org*.

19. Very high confidence means "at least 9 out of 10 chance of being correct".

20. For more discussion of the modelling approach used for projecting malaria risk, see Annex 6.A.

21. The modelling for malaria risk areas is based on a simple relationship between climatic conditions and the suitability for the malaria mosquito. In practice, however, other factors such as the amount and types of vegetation and the presence of still water are also of relevance. In addition, due to the lack of global data, future vector control programmes have not been considered.

References

Aardenne, J. van *et al.* (2010), *Climate and Air Quality Impacts of Combined Climate Change and Air Pollution Policy Scenarios*, Report EUR 24572, Joint Research Centre Scientific and Technical Reports, Publications Office of the European Union.

Arnell, N.W. (2004), "Climate Change and Global Water Resources: SRES Emissions and Socio-Economic Scenarios", *Global Environmental Change-Human and Policy Dimensions*, 14(1): 31-52.

Beniston, M. and H.F. Diaz (2004), "The 2003 Heat Wave as an Example of Summers in a Greenhouse Climate? Observations and Climate Model Simulations for Basel, Switzerland", *Global and Planetary Change*, 44(1-4): 73-81.

Black, R.E. *et al.* (2008), "Maternal and child undernutrition: global and regional exposures and health consequences", *Lancet*, 371(9608): 243-260.

Bollen, J. and C. Brink (2011), "The Economic Impacts of Air Pollution Policies in the EU" (unpublished), *www.cpb.nl/sites/default/files/publicaties/download/achtergronddocument-economic-impacts-air-pollution-policies-eu.pdf*.

Bouwman, A.F., T. Kram and K. Klein Goldewijk (eds.) (2006), *Integrated Modelling of Global Environmental Change: An Overview of IMAGE 2.4*, PBL Netherlands Environmental Assessment Agency, The Hague/Bilthoven.

Burke, E.J., S.J. Brown and N. Christidis (2006), "Modeling the Recent Evolution of Global Drought and Projections for the Twenty-First Century with the Hadley Centre Climate Model", *Journal of Hydrometeorology*, 7(5): 1113-1125.

Burtraw, D. *et al.* (2005), "Economics of Pollution Trading for SO_2 and NO_x", *Annual Review of Environment and Resources*, 30: 253-289.

Cairncross, S. and V. Valdmanis (2006), "Water Supply, Sanitation and Hygiene Promotion", in D.T. Jamison, J.G. Breman, A.R. Measham, G. Alleyne, M. Claeson, D.B. Evans, P. Jha, A. Mills and P. Musgrove (eds.), *Disease Control Priorities in Developing Countries*, 2nd Edition, Oxford University Press and the World Bank, Washington, DC.

Campbell-Lendrum, D., A. Prüss-Üstün and C. Corvalán (2003), "How Much Disease could Climate Change Cause?", in A. McMichael, D. Campbell-Lendrum, C. Corvalán, K. Ebi, A. Githeko, J. Scheraga and A. Woodward (eds.), *Climate Change and Human Health: Risks and Responses*, WHO (World Health Organization), Geneva.

Carslaw, B.C. *et al.* (2011), "Recent Evidence Concerning Higher NO_x Emissions from Passenger Cars and Light Duty Vehicles", *Atmospheric Environment*, 45 (39): 7053-7063.

CDC (Centers for Disease Control and Prevention) (2009), *Fourth National Report on Human Exposure to Environmental Chemicals*, CDC, Atlanta, GA, *www.cdc.gov/exposurereport*.

Clapp, C. *et al.* (2010), "Cities and Carbon Market Finance: Taking Stock of Cities' Experience With Clean Development Mechanism (CDM) and Joint Implementation (JI)", *OECD Environment Working Papers*, No. 29, OECD Publishing, doi: *10.1787/5km4hv5p1vr7-en*.

Confalonieri, U. *et al.* (2007), "Human Health", in M.L. Parry, O.F. Canziani, J.P. Palutikof, P.J. van der Linden and C.E. Hanson (eds.), *Climate Change 2007: Impacts, Adaptation and Vulnerability. Contribution of Working Group II to the Fourth Assessment Report of the Intergovernmental Panel on Climate Change*, Cambridge University Press, Cambridge, UK.

Craig, M.H. *et al.* (1999), "A Climate-Based Distribution Model of Malaria Transmission in Africa", *Parasitology Today*, 15(3): 105-111.

Damstra, T. et al. (eds.) (2002), *Global Assessment of the State of the Science of Endocrine Disruptors*, International Programme on Chemical Safety, WHO, Geneva.

DEFRA (Department for Environment, Food and Rural Affairs) (2007), *An Economic Analysis to Inform the Air Quality Strategy. Updated Third Report of the Interdepartmental Group on Costs and Benefits*, DEFRA, London.

Desai, M.A., S. Mehta and K.R. Smith (2004), *Indoor Smoke from Solid Fuels: Assessing the Environmental Burden of Disease*, Environmental Burden of Disease Series No. 4, WHO, Geneva.

EC (European Commission) (1996), "Council Directive 96/61/EC of 24 September 1996 Concerning Integrated Pollution Prevention and Control", *Official Journal of the European Communities*, L 257, 10/10/1996, pp. 26-40.

EC (2001), "Directive 2001/80/EC of the European Parliament and of the Council of 23 October 2001 on the Limitation of Emissions of Certain Pollutants into the Air from Large Combustion Plants", *Official Journal of the European Communities*, L 309/1, 27/11/2001.

EC (2007), *REACH in Brief*, Environment Directorate General, EC, Brussels, *http://ec.europa.eu/environment/chemicals/reach/pdf/2007_02_reach_in_brief.pdf*.

EC (2008), "European Union Risk Assessment Report: Bis(2-ethylhexyl) phthalate (DEHP)", *Existing Substances Second Priority List*, Vol. 80, EUR 23384 EN, Joint Research Centre, European Commission Joint Research Centre, Brussels.

Edejer, T. et al. (2005), "Cost Effectiveness Analysis of Strategies for Child Health in Developing Countries", *BMJ*, 19 (331 Nov. 10).

EEA (European Environment Agency) (1999), *Chemicals in the European Environment: Low Doses, High Stakes?* The EEA and UNEP Annual Message 2 on the State of Europe's Environment, EEA, Copenhagen.

EEA (2010), *The European Environment – State and Outlook 2010: Synthesis*, State of the Environment Report 1/2010, EEA, Copenhagen.

EEA (2011), *Hazardous Substances in Europe's Fresh and Marine Waters – An Overview*, Technical Report No. 8/2011, EEA, Copenhagen.

Fiore, A.M. et al. (2002), "Linking Ozone Pollution and Climate Change: The Case for Controlling Methane", *Geophysical Research Letters*, 29, doi: 10.1029/2002GL015601.

Forster, P. et al. (2007), "Changes in Atmospheric Constituents and in Radiative Forcing", in S. Solomon, D. Qin, M. Manning, Z. Chen, M. Marquis, K.B. Averyt, M. Tignor and H.L. Miller (eds.), *Climate Change 2007: The Physical Science Basis. Contribution of Working Group I to the Fourth Assessment Report of the Intergovernmental Panel on Climate Change*, Cambridge University Press, Cambridge.

Freshfields Bruckhaus Deringer (2009), *China REACH: The PRC's Revised Regime for "New" Chemicals*, Briefing, June 2009, Freshfields Bruckhaus Deringer, *www.freshfields.com/publications/pdfs/2009/jun09/26182.pdf*.

Gee, D. (2008), "Establishing Evidence for Early Action: The Prevention of Reproductive and Developmental Harm", *Basic and Clinical Pharmacology and Toxicology*, (102) pp. 257-266.

Golding, J., K. Birmingham and R. Jones (2009), "Special Issue: A Guide to Undertaking a Birth Cohort Study: Purposes, Pitfalls and Practicalities", *Pediatric and Perinatal Epidemiology*, 23(s1):1-236.

Grandjean, P. et al. (2007), "The Faroes Statement: Human Health Effects of Developmental Exposure to Chemicals in our Environment", *Basic and Clinical Pharmacology and Toxicology*, (102) pp. 73-75.

Hales, S., N. de Wet, J. Maindonald and A. Woodward (2002), "Potential Effect of Population and Climate Changes on Global Distribution of Dengue Fever: an Empirical Model", *The Lancet*, 360(9336): 830-834.

Hales, S., S. Edwards and R. Kovats (2003), "Impacts on Health of Climate Extremes", in A.J. McMichael, D. Campbell-Lendrum, C. Corvalán, K. Ebi, A. Githeko, J. Scheraga and A. Woodward (eds.), *Climate Change and Human Health: Risks and Responses*, WHO, Geneva.

Hanley, N., D. Bell and B. Alvarez-Farizo (2003), "Valuing the Benefits of Coastal Water Quality Improvements Using Contingent and Real Behaviour", *Environmental and Resources Economics*, Vol. 24, No. 3, pp. 273-285.

Hay, S.I., A.J. Tatem, C.A. Guerra and R.W. Snow (2006), *Foresight on Population at Malaria Risk in Africa: 2005, 2015 and 2030*, Scenario review paper prepared for the Foresight Project, Detection and Identification of Infectious Diseases Project (DIID), Office of Science and Innovation, London, UK.

Hilderink, H.B.M. and P.L. Lucas (eds.) (2008), *Towards a Global Integrated Sustainability Model: GISMO 1.0 Status Report*, PBL Netherlands Environmental Assessment Agency, The Hague/Bilthoven.

Holland, M. *et al.* (2005), *Final Methodology Paper (Volume 1) for Service Contract for Carrying Out Cost-Benefit Analysis of Air Quality Related Issues, in Particular in the Clean Air for Europe (CAFE) Programme*, AEAT/ED51014/Methodology Paper, Issue 4, EC-DG Environment, Brussels.

Hutton, G. and L. Haller (2004), *Evaluation of Costs and Benefits of Water and Sanitation Improvements at the Global Level*, WHO, Geneva.

IIASA (2001), The Greenhouse Gas and Air Pollution Interactions and Synergies (GAINS)-Model *http://gains.iiasa.ac.at/index.php/home-page*.

International Energy Agency (2010), *World Energy Outlook 2010*, OECD Publishing, doi: *10.1787/weo-2010-en*.

IPCC (Intergovernmental Panel on Climate Change) (2007), *Climate Change 2007:Climate Change Impacts, Adaptation and Vulnerability, Contribution of Working Group II to the Fourth Assessment Report of the Intergovernmental Panel on Climate Change*, M.L. Parry, O.F. Canziani, J.P. Palutikof, P.J. van der Linden and C.E. Hanson (eds.), Cambridge University Press, Cambridge.

Johnstone, N., I. Haščič and M. Kalamova (2010), "Environmental Policy Design Characteristics and Technological Innovation: Evidence from Patent Data", *OECD Environment Working Papers*, No. 16, OECD Publishing, doi: *10.1787/5kmjstwtqwhd-en*.

Kiriyama, N. (2010), "Trade and Innovation: Report on the Chemicals Sector", *OECD Trade Policy Working Papers*, No. 103, OECD Publishing, doi: *10.1787/5km69t4hmr6c-en*.

Lavoie, E.T. *et al.* (2010), "Chemical Alternatives Assessment: Enabling Substitution to Safer Chemicals", *Environmental Science and Technology*, 44 (24): 9244-9249.

Lejour, A.M., P. Veenendaal, G. Verweij and N. van Leeuwen (2006), *WorldScan: A Model for International Economic Policy Analysis*, CPB Document 111, The Hague.

Mathers, C.D. and D. Loncar (2006), "Projections of Global Mortality and Burden of Disease from 2002 to 2030", *PLoS Medicine*, 3(11): 2011-2030.

McMichael, A. *et al.* (2004), "Global Climate Change", in M. Ezzati, A. Lopez, A. Rodgers and C. Murray (eds.), *Comparative Quantification of Health Risks: Global and Regional Burden of Disease Attributable to Selected Major Risk Factors*, WHO, Geneva.

Meek, M.E. *et al.* (2011), "Risk Assessment of Combined Exposure to Multiple Chemicals: A WHO/IPCS Framework", *Regulatory Toxicology and Pharmacology*, 60 S1-S14.

Mol, W.J.A., P.R. van Hooydonk and F.A.A.M. de Leeuw (2011), *The State of the Air Quality in 2008 and the European Exchange of Monitoring Information in 2010*, ETC/ACC Technical Paper 2011/1, The European Topic Centre on Air and Climate Change, Bilthoven.

Morel, C., J. Lauer and D.B Evans (2005), "Cost Effectiveness Analysis of Strategies to Combat Malaria in Developing Countries?", *BMJ*, 3(331).

Naiki, Y. (2010), "Assessing Policy Reach: Japan's Chemical Policy Reform in Response to the EU's REACH Regulation", *Journal of Environmental Law*, 22 (2): 171-196.

Narayanan B.G. and T.L. Walmsley (eds.) (2008), *Global Trade, Assistance, and Production: The GTAP 7 Data Base*, Center for Global Trade Analysis, Purdue University, West Lafayette.

National Research Council (2007), *Toxicity Testing in the Twenty-first Century: A Vision and a Strategy*, The National Academies Press, Washington, DC.

Newell, R.G. and N.E. Wilson (2005), *Technology Prizes for Climate Change Mitigation*, Discussion Paper 05-33, Resources for the Future, *www.rff.org/documents/RFF-DP-05-33.pdf*.

OECD (2007), *OECD Environmental Data Compendium 2006/2007*, OECD, Paris.

OECD (2009a), *Alternative Ways of Providing Water: Emerging Options and their Policy Implications*, OECD, Paris.

OECD (2009b), *The Economics of Climate Change Mitigation: Policies and Options for Global Action beyond 2012*, OECD Publishing, doi: *10.1787/9789264073616-en*.

OECD (2010a), *Taxation, Innovation and the Environment*, OECD Publishing, doi: *10.1787/9789264087637-en*.

OECD (2010b), *Cutting Costs in Chemicals Management: How OECD Helps Governments and Industry*, OECD Publishing, doi: *10.1787/9789264085930-en*.

OECD (2010c), *Fuel Taxes, Motor Vehicle Emission Standards and Patents related to the Fuel-Efficiency and Emissions of Motor Vehicles*, OECD, Paris.

OECD (2011a), OECD Health Data 2011, online, OECD Publishing, *http://stats.oecd.org/index.aspx* (Health).

OECD (2011b), *Towards Green Growth*, OECD Green Growth Studies, OECD Publishing, doi: 10.1787/9789264111318-en.

OECD (2011c), *Benefits of Investing in Water and Sanitation: An OECD Perspective*, OECD Publishing. doi: 10.1787/9789264100817-en.

OECD (2011d), "Sustainable Chemistry: Evidence on Innovation from Patent Data", *Series on Risk Management*, No. 25, OECD, Paris.

OECD (2011e), *Valuing Mortality Risk Reductions in Regulatory Analysis of Environmental, Health and Transport Policies: Policy Implications*, OECD, Paris. *www.oecd.org/env/policies/vsl*.

OECD (2011f), "WHO OECD ILSI/HESI International Workshop on Risk Assessment of Combined Exposures to Multiple Chemicals", *Series on Testing and Assessment*, No. 140, OECD, Paris.

Ontario (2001), *Ontario Regulation 397/01, made under the Environmental Protection Act*, Ontario, Canada.

Pandey, K.D. et al. (2006), *Ambient Particulate Matter Concentrations in Residential and Pollution Hotspot Areas of World Cities: New Estimates based on the Global Model of Ambient Particulates (GMAPS)*, The World Bank Development Economics Research Group and the *Environment Department Working Paper*, The World Bank, Washington, DC.

Pattanayak, S.K., J.-C. Yang, D. Whittington and K.C. Bal Kumar (2005), "Coping with Unreliable Public Water Supplies: Averting Expenditures by Households in Kathmandu, Nepal", *Water Resources Research*, 41, W02012.

Patz, J. et al. (2007), "Climate Change and Global Health: Quantifying a Growing Ethical Crisis", *Ecohealth*, 4: 397-405.

Popp, D. (2006), "Entice-BR: The Effects of Backstop Technology and R&D on Climate Policy Models", *Energy Economics*, Vol. 28: 188-222.

Prüss, A., D. Kay, L. Fewtrell and J. Bartram (2002), "Estimating the Burden of Disease from Water, Sanitation, and Hygiene at a Global Level", *Environmental Health Perspectives*, 110:537-542.

Prüss-Üstün, A., D. Kay, F. Fewtrell and J. Bartram (2004), "Unsafe Water, Sanitation and Hygiene", in M. Ezzati, A. Lopez, A. Rodgers and C. Murray (eds.), *Comparative Quantification of Health Risks: Global and Regional Burden of Disease Attributable to Selected Major Risk Factors*, WHO, Geneva.

Prüss-Üstün, A. and C. Corvalán (2006), *Preventing Disease through Healthy Environments: Towards an Estimate of the Environmental Burden of Disease*, WHO, Geneva.

Prüss-Üstün, A., R. Bos, F. Gore and J. Bartram (2008), *Safer Water, Better Health: Cost, Benefits and Sustainability of Interventions to Protect and Promote Health*, WHO, Geneva.

Prüss-Ustün, A., C. Vickers, P. Haefliger and R. Bertollini (2011), "Knowns and Unknowns on the Burden of Disease Due to Chemicals: a Systematic Review", *Environmental Health*, 10:9.

Robine, J.M. et al. (2008), "Death Toll Exceeded 70,000 in Europe During the Summer of 2003", *Comptes Rendus Biologies*, 331(2): 171-178.

Ruijven, B. van (2008), *Energy and Development – A Modelling Approach*, Utrecht University, Utrecht.

Schoeters G.E.R. et al. (2011), "Biomonitoring and Biomarkers to Unravel the Risks from Prenatal Environmental Exposures for Later Health Outcomes", *American Journal of Clinical Nutrition*, June 2001.

Söderholm, P. (2009), *Economic Instruments in Chemicals Policy: Past Experiences and Prospects for Future Use*, Report to the Nordic Council of Ministers, TemaNord, Copenhagen.

Royal Society, The (2008), *Ground-Level Ozone in the 21st Century: Air Future Trends, Impacts and Policy Implications*, Science Policy Report 15/08, The Royal Society, London.

UNECE (United Nations Economic Commission for Europe) (2010), *Hemispheric Transport of Air Pollution 2010: Executive Summary*, Informal Document No. 10, Executive Body for the Convention on Long-range Transboundary Air Pollution, Geneva.

UNEP (United Nations Environment Programme) (2007), *Global Environment Outlook 4: Summary for Decision Makers*, UNEP, Geneva.

UNEP (2009), "Desk Study on Financing Options for Chemicals and Wastes", Report of the Second consultative meeting of UNEP-led Consultative Process on Financing Options for Chemicals and Wastes, Bangkok, 25-26 October 2009.

US EPA (United States Environmental Protection Agency) (2006), *Air Quality Criteria for Ozone and Related Photochemical Oxidants (2006 Final)*, US EPA, Washington, DC.

US EPA (2010), *The Benefits and Costs of the Clean Air Act: 1990-2020*, Office of Air and Radiation, US EPA, Washington, DC, *www.epa.gov/oar/sect812/aug10/fullreport.pdf*.

UN WWAP (United Nations World Water Assessment Programme) (2009), *The Third United Nations World Water Development Report: Water in a Changing World*, UNESCO, Paris and Earthscan, London.

Waddington, H., B. Snilstveit, H. White and L. Fewtrell (2009), *Water, Sanitation and Hygiene Interventions to Combat Childhood Diarrhoea in Developing Countries. International Initiative for Impact Evaluation*, Synthetic Review 001, International Initiative for Impact Evaluation (3ie), London, *www.3ieimpact.org/admin/pdfs2/17.pdf*.

Whittington, D., W.M. Hanemann, C. Sadoff and M. Jeuland (2009), "Chapter 7: Sanitation and Water", in B. Lomborg (ed.), *Global Crises, Global Solutions*, 2nd ed., Cambridge University Press, Cambridge, UK.

WHO (World Health Organization) (2002a), *The World Health Report 2002, Reducing Risks, Promoting Healthy Life*, WHO, Geneva.

WHO (2002b), Global Burden of Disease Estimates, WHO website, *www.who.int/healthinfo/global_burden_disease/estimates_regional_2002/en/index.html#*.

WHO (2003), *Making Choices in Health: WHO Guide to Cost Effectiveness Analysis*, WHO, Geneva.

WHO (2005), *WHO Launches Project to Minimize Risks of Radon*, WHO website, *www.who.int/mediacentre/news/notes/2005/np15/en/index.html*.

WHO (2006), *Air Quality Guidelines for Particulate Matter, Ozone, Nitrogen Dioxide and Sulfur Dioxide: Global Update 2005*, WHO, Geneva.

WHO (2008), *The Global Burden of Disease: 2004 Update*, WHO, Geneva.

WHO (2009a), *Global Health Risks: Mortality and Burden of Disease Attributable to Selected Major Risks*, WHO, Geneva.

WHO (2009b), *Protecting Health From Climate Change: Connecting Science, Policy and People*, WHO, Geneva.

WHO (2009c), *Country Profile of Environmental Burden of Disease: China*, WHO, Geneva, *www.who.int/quantifying_ehimpacts/national/countryprofile/china.pdf*.

WHO (2009d), *Country Profile of Environmental Burden of Disease: India*, WHO, Geneva, *www.who.int/quantifying_ehimpacts/national/countryprofile/india.pdf*.

WHO/UNICEF (United Nations Children's Fund) (2010), *Progress on Drinking Water and Sanitation: 2010 Update*, WHO/UNICEF Joint Monitoring Programme for Water Supply and Sanitation, New York/Geneva.

World Bank (2001), "Development Economics Research Group Estimates", The World Bank, *http://siteresources.worldbank.org/INTRES/Resources/AirPollutionConcentrationData2.xls*.

ANNEX 6.A

Modelling Background Information on Health and Environment

This annex describes the most important aspects of the Global Integrated Sustainability Model (GISMO), which is a part of the IMAGE suite (see Chapter 1 and Annex on the Modelling Framework), and which was used for modelling the health impacts in this chapter (see Hilderink and Lukas, 2008).

Health impact modelling

The main purpose of the health model is to describe the burden of disease by gender and age. The methodology used for communicable (infectious) diseases – such as malaria, diarrhoea, lower respiratory infections, protein deficiency and AIDS (Figure 6.A1) is a multi-state modelling approach which largely follows the approach as described in the *World Health Report 2002* (WHO, 2002a) and the Disease Control Priorities Project (DCPP) (Cairncross and Valdmanis, 2006). The states distinguished are exposure, disease and death. This implies that for various health risk factors, incidence and case fatality rates (*i.e.* the ratio of the number of deaths caused by a specified disease over the number of diagnosed cases of that disease) are taken into account. Some risk factors (such as children who are underweight) can also enhance other risk factors (*e.g.* lack of improved water supply). The level of health services can also modify these rates. The method for projecting the other causes of death – *i.e.* non-communicable (chronic) diseases, remainder of communicable and injuries – is based on Mathers and Loncar (2006) who developed a method to link changes in mortality rates for the most important causes of death to factors such as GDP, smoking behaviour and human capital. This method was used for the global burden of disease projections (WHO, 2002b) and has also been included in the health model. The projections of cause-specific mortality are used to determine the attributable (and avoidable) relative risks on mortality, as reported in literature.

Valuing health impacts

The modelling of the health impacts results in cause-specific deaths by sex and age for the various regions distinguished in the model. These impacts are expressed in monetary terms by using the value of statistical life (VSL) (see Holland *et al.*, 2005). The estimate used for the VSL is based on OECD and values USD 3.5 million (2005 USD) for OECD regions (OECD, 2011e). The value for the other regions has been derived based on their per-capita GDP on purchasing power parity assuming an elasticity of 0.8. The future value of VSL is directly calculated based on changes in GDP per capita.

Figure 6.A1. **Health modelling overview**

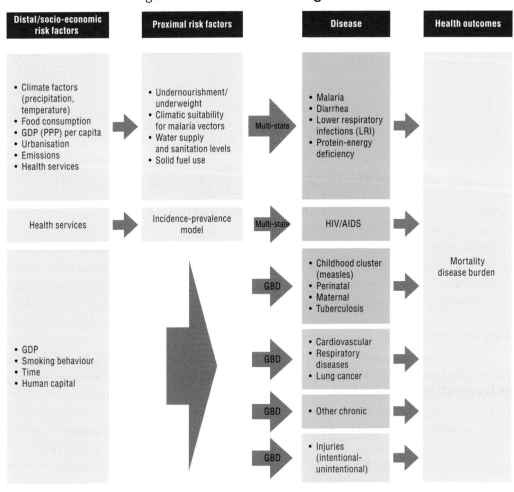

Source: Hilderink, H.B.M. and P.L. Lucas (eds.) (2008), Towards a Global Integrated Sustainability Model: GISMO 1.0 Status Report, PBL Netherlands Environmental Assessment Agency, The Hague/Bilthoven.

Indoor air pollution

The main risk factor for lower respiratory infections (LRI), or pneumonia, is indoor air pollution, caused by cooking and/or heating with solid fuels. The effect is increased in children who are underweight. The exposure to indoor air pollution modelling is based on the Residential Energy Model Global (REMG, van Ruijven, 2008). Indoor air pollution not only increases the risk of pneumonia mortality, but also of chronic obstructive pulmonary disease (COPD) and lung cancer. Other diseases are suspected to be related to this risk factor, but evidence for these diseases is limited and they are not included. The health effects of exposure to this risk factor can, however, be lowered by proper ventilation when cooking and heating. The methodology to describe the burden of disease attributable to this risk factor is adopted from the WHO (Desai *et al.*, 2004).

Water supply and sanitation

Model projections concerning levels of water supply and sanitation are mostly described in the Annex to Chapter 5 of this *Outlook*. Note that for the analysis in this chapter, separate levels of connection rates to water supplies and sanitation facilities are calculated for urban and rural populations. This makes it possible to determine the urban and rural diarrhoeal burden of disease. Given the different levels of connection to water supply and sanitation facilities in the regions, relative risks are used to calculate incidence levels, based on the so-called "realistic scenario" used in the DCPP (Cairncross and Valdmanis, 2006). The incidence is modified by the level to which a child is underweight (distinguished by mild, moderate and severe underweight; see Edejer et al., 2005) and temperature levels (McMichael, 2004). The case fatality rates are modified by underweight levels and the use of oral rehydration therapy (ORT). Underweight levels are derived from the average levels of food consumption.

Malaria

The methodology for estimating malaria risk is based on the MARA/ARMA malaria suitability model (Craig et al., 1999) which maps areas which are suitable for the malaria mosquito based on climatic factors. Mosquitoes which spread the infection can only survive in climates with high average temperatures, no frost and sufficient precipitation. For each climatic factor, a suitability index is calculated which indicates the conditions under which the malaria mosquito is able to survive. The climatic levels required for the maximum suitability of 1, and for the minimum suitability of 0, are shown in Table 6.A1. For indicators with levels between those required for 0 and 1 suitability, a level is calculated by using a simple function (Craig et al., 1999). All these factors are calculated at half-by-half degree geographic grid level, making use of the output from the IMAGE model (Bouwman et al., 2006). Total climatic malaria suitability for each grid cell is determined by the lowest of these three indices.

Table 6.A1. **Malaria suitability indices for climatic determinants**

	Suitability = 0	Suitability = 1
Monthly temperature (degrees Celsius)	< 18	> 22
	> 40	< 32
Annual minimum monthly temperature (degrees Celsius)	< 0	> 4
Precipitation (mm/month)	0	> 80

Source: Craig et al., 1999.

This model was originally developed for Africa, where most malaria cases and deaths occur, but for GISMO, this model is applied worldwide. Based on climatic malaria suitability, the potential population at risk of malaria is estimated. Malaria control has reduced or eliminated malaria vectors in most regions outside Africa and, therefore, needs to be considered. Future vector control programmes are assumed not to change. Insecticide treated bed nets and indoor residual spraying are modelled separately as potential policy options, which modify incidence rates. Case fatality of malaria is modified by the level to which a child is underweight and case management (i.e. diagnosis and treatment) (Morel et al., 2005).

Outdoor air pollution

The modelling of air pollution presented in this chapter involved several aspects, namely health impacts related to particulate matter (PM), ground-level ozone, the policy simulations performed by WorldScan, and a simulation of a 25% Air Pollution Reduction Scenario. Each is discussed in turn below.

Particulate matter

The Global Urban Air quality Model (GUAM) has been developed to estimate PM_{10} concentrations and their attributable effects on human health for more than 3 200 "major" cities in the world (*i.e.* cities with populations over 100 000 or national capitals). GUAM originates from the GMAPS model (Pandey *et al*, 2006) and links observed PM_{10} concentrations to a set of variables of economic activity, population, urbanisation and meteorological information.

Based on these concentration levels, the health effects (acute respiratory diseases, lung cancer, and cardiopulmonary diseases) of the population being exposed are determined. Health impacts are based on the assumption "one population – one average exposure level". This means that the exposure of the urban population is estimated as the modelled average urban concentration. Concentration gradients within the city (*e.g.* hot-spots), different exposures for different population classes and indoor pollution have not been considered. The assessment does not incorporate the effects of ambient air pollution on the population living in cities with less than 100 000 inhabitants or on rural populations. Other assumptions and uncertainties are outlined in Box 6.A1.

Box 6.A1. **Assumptions and uncertainties in the models**

i) Most of the empirical data on PM_{10} concentrations comes from developed countries, where concentrations tend to be lower than in developing countries. These data are used to estimate concentrations in all 3 245 cities, which leads to uncertainties when extrapolating to cities with high concentrations.

ii) Since data on $PM_{2.5}$ concentrations are scarce (compared to PM_{10} concentrations), it is assumed that $PM_{2.5}$ concentrations can be derived by applying a PM_{10}-$PM_{2.5}$ ratio which is based on relatively few observations. The ratios vary from 0.4 in Brazil to 0.65 in most OECD countries. Concentrations are modelled following the World Bank Global Model of Ambient Particulates (GMAPS; Pandey *et al.*, 2006) approach using local and national data on emissions, wind speed, urban density and precipitation, with emissions weighted the highest of all these factors.

iii) Health impacts are based on exposure-response relationships (described in the literature), and it is assumed that these relationships are the same across the globe and stay constant over time.

iv) It is assumed that no *additional* human health effects will occur beyond 150 $\mu g/m^3$ concentrations of PM_{10} (*i.e.* health impacts at PM_{10} concentrations above 150 $\mu g/m^3$ will be no more severe than at 150 $\mu g/m^3$).

v) The modelling only includes deaths caused by PM pollution, and thus underestimates the true impacts on human health (*i.e.* it does not consider non-lethal effects such as chronic and acute bronchitis, asthma, etc.). As described in Box 6.2, the ageing of the population has a strong influence on the number of premature deaths from air pollution in all country groupings.

Ground-level ozone

Global mean ozone concentrations in the troposphere (*i.e.* ground level) are modelled in an atmospheric chemical "box model". In a box model, the difference between the sources and sinks of a component is calculated and converted to an increase or decrease in the atmospheric concentration. The sources taken into account here are *i)* the direct anthropogenic and natural emissions of ozone precursors – CO, NO_x and VOCs including methane (CH_4); and *ii)* the *in situ* production or losses in atmospheric photochemical processes and other losses like deposition or transport to the stratosphere. The chemistry is described in a number of parameterised relations. Of crucial importance is the fate of the hydroxyl radical (OH), the chemical species that initiates most of the atmospheric oxidation processes. Changes in the production of OH depend on changes in tropospheric ozone, water vapour, NO_x emissions, stratospheric ozone and temperature. The loss of OH is governed by the levels of CH_4, CO and VOC. As the life-time of the other gases depends on the OH concentrations, the system becomes non-linear. The model used here is an updated and extended version of the chemical module in the IMAGE model using the global atmospheric chemistry transport model TM5. van Aardenne *et al.* (2010) have modelled global ozone concentration fields for nine different scenarios for the period 2000-2050. Using these results, a relation – as a function of CH_4 and CO emissions – between the global mean ozone concentration and the ozone concentration in the IMAGE regions has been established. Using empirical relations (based on an analysis of the AirBase data, Mol *et al.*, 2011) the annual mean and standard deviation of the maximum daily 8-hour mean are estimated. These two parameters are sufficient to calculate the SOMO35 (*i.e.* the Sum of Ozone Means Over 35 ppb) in each region.

Policy simulation with WorldScan

The macroeconomic consequences of specific air policy simulations are assessed using the global applied general equilibrium model WorldScan. A detailed description of the model is given in Lejour *et al.* (2006). Bollen and Brink (2011) extended WorldScan to also include emissions of air pollutants and the possibility to invest in emission control by modelling abatement supply curves (*i.e.* marginal abatement cost curves) for emissions in each sector. These abatement supply curves represent the potential and cost of technical abatement measures. These are mainly "end-of-pipe" abatement options, removing emissions largely without affecting the emission-producing activity itself. WorldScan data for the base year are to a large extent taken from the GTAP-7 database (Narayanan and Walmsley, 2008) that provides integrated data on bilateral trade flows and input-output accounts. The version used here features 25 regions and 13 sectors. WorldScan is set up to simulate deviations from a "business as usual" (BAU) path by imposing specific additional policy measures such as taxes or restrictions on emissions. The BAU used here is calibrated on the time series for population and GDP by region, energy use by region and energy carrier, and world fossil fuel prices by energy carrier as assumed in the *Baseline*. Data on emissions of air pollutants are taken from IMAGE, whereas the technical abatement potential and cost was based on data for 2030 in the GAINS model (IIASA, 2011). Beyond 2030, an autonomous reduction in marginal abatement costs is assumed within each sector of 0.5% per year. This autonomous cost reduction is apart from changes in the prices of inputs that are required to produce the emission abatement (such as labour and capital) which is endogenous in the model. Moreover, to reflect a certain rate of technological improvement, the maximum feasible reduction potential (as a percentage of unabated emissions) is assumed to increase by 0.5%.

Environmental policies are implemented in the model by introducing a price on emissions (Lejour *et al.*, 2006). This emission price makes polluting activities more expensive and will provide an incentive to reduce these emissions. For emissions directly related to the use of a specific input, such as fossil fuels, the emission price will in fact cause a rise in the user price of this input. Consequently, this will lead to a fall in the demand for it (either by using less energy or by substituting more carbon emitting fuels for less emitting ones) and hence a reduction in emissions. For emissions related to sectoral output levels, the emission price will cause a rise in the output price of the associated product. Again, this will lead to a fall in demand for this product and hence in a reduction in emissions. Moreover, if emission control options are available, these will be implemented up to the level where the marginal cost of emission control equals the emission price. The emission price can be introduced exogenously, but in the policy scenario presented here, a restriction is put on the weighted sum of emissions of different air polluting substances, leading to a reduction in emissions of 25% compared to the *Baseline*. Weights are based on the relative contribution of these substances to PM exposure. In this case the emission price is endogenously determined in the model at the level needed to reduce emissions to the predetermined emission target, which represents the shadow price of this restriction. As in some regions (in particular those with a small share of anthropogenic emissions in the total emissions of air pollutants) a reduction in emissions by 25% requires a very high emission price, an upper bound on the emission price was introduced, which is related to the VSL in a region. Consequently, the actual emission reduction is not equal to 25%, as in some regions the emission price would have to exceed this upper bound in order to achieve a 25% emission reduction.

The 25% Air Pollution Reduction scenario

The goal of this simulation was to reduce particulate matter concentrations; however, to achieve a reduction in PM concentrations, one has to reduce the emissions which are contributing to PM (*i.e.* NO_x, SO_2 and black carbon). The health impacts were estimated based on exposure to both particulate matter and ozone formed from NO_x, SO_2 and black carbon. Emission taxes were used as a proxy for policies triggering the reduction in air emissions (*i.e.* to increase the cost of polluting activities) and therefore reduce emissions through: i) structural changes (*e.g.* shifts to less polluting energy sources, energy efficiency improvements, shifts in demand, changes in location of economic activities); and ii) installing end-of-pipe measures to remove PM-related emissions (*e.g.* using scrubbers/ filters). The reduction in mortality was translated into economic benefits by applying a value of statistical life (VSL), and these results were then compared to the costs of the policies to provide a rough approximation of the benefit/cost for each region. Under the approach used for these calculations, the VSL values vary with income: *i.e.* they are lower in countries with lower per-capita GDP. This allows for local preferences to be more accurately represented in decision making; however, it also means that a global view of the scale of a particular environmental action, and the case for concerted international finance, is less clear.

For purposes of this simulation, it is recognised that reducing emissions relatively uniformly across the globe will lead to variations in mortality rates across countries due to differences in existing concentrations and the degree to which they are above or below health threshold levels.

ANNEX A

Modelling Framework

Introduction

The analysis for the *OECD Environmental Outlook* is supported by two modelling frameworks that have been coupled: *i)* the ENV-Linkages economic model; and *ii)* a set of environmental models linked to the Integrated Model to Assess the Global Environment (IMAGE) framework created by the PBL Netherlands Environmental Assessment Agency (PBL for short). This annex summarises the models and provides web-links to more in-depth descriptions. The methods of analysis and tools used in the *OECD Environmental Outlook* are more fully described in background documentation available at *www.oecd.org/environment/outlookto2050*.

A short overview of the ENV-Linkages model[1]

The OECD's ENV-Linkages general equilibrium (GE) model is an economic model that describes how economic activities are linked to each other across sectors and regions. It also links economic activity to environmental pressures, specifically to emissions of greenhouse gases (GHGs). The model projects these links between economic activities and emissions several decades into the future to shed light on the medium- and long-term impacts of environmental policies. The advantages of multi-sectoral, multi-regional dynamic GE models like ENV-Linkages are numerous, and include their global dimension, their overall consistency and the fact that they build on rigorous microeconomic foundations. These models are best suited for analysing the medium- and long-term implications of large policy shifts requiring significant reallocation across sectors and countries/regions, as well as the associated spill-over effects. In that sense, these models are the tools of choice for assessing a wide range of climate change policies.

ENV-Linkages is the successor to the OECD GREEN model, initially developed by the OECD's Economics Department (Burniaux, *et al.,* 1992) and is now hosted by the OECD Environment Directorate. Much of the applied work carried out with the model has been reported in various chapters of the *OECD Environmental Outlook to 2030* (OECD, 2008). An updated version of the model was used extensively in the joint project between the OECD Economics Department and the OECD Environment Directorate on the economics of climate change mitigation (OECD, 2009). Most recently, the model has been used to study the impacts of phasing out fossil fuels subsidies (IEA, OPEC, OECD, World Bank, 2010; Burniaux and Chateau, 2011); the impacts of border-tax adjustments (Burniaux *et al.*, 2010);

direct and indirect linking of carbon markets (Dellink *et al.*, 2010a); and the costs and effectiveness of the Copenhagen pledges (Dellink *et al.*, 2010b). A more detailed overview of the ENV-Linkages version 3, as used for this *OECD Environmental Outlook to 2050*, is provided in Chateau *et al.* (2012).

How does it work?

ENV-Linkages is built primarily on a database of national economies. In the version of the model used here, the world economy is divided into 15 countries/regions (see Chapter 1, Table 1.3), each with 26 economic sectors, including 5 electricity sectors (see Table A.1 below). Each of the regions is underpinned by an economic input-output table (usually published by a national statistical agency). These tables identify all the inputs into an industry (rather than individual firms) and identify all the industries that buy specific products. Some industries explicitly use land, while others, such as fisheries and forestry, also have a "natural resource" input – *e.g.* fish and trees.

Table A.1. **ENV-Linkages model sectors and products**

SECTORS	DESCRIPTION
Rice	Paddy rice: rice, husked and in the husk.
Other crops	Wheat: wheat and meslin
	Other grains: maize (corn), barley, rye, oats, other cereals
	Vegetables and fruits: vegetables, fruits, fruit and nuts, potatoes, cassava, truffles
	Oil seeds: oil seeds and oleaginous fruits; soy beans, copra
	Cane and beet: sugar cane and sugar beet
	Plant fibers: cotton, flax, hemp, sisal and other raw vegetable materials used in textiles
	Other crops
Livestock	Cattle: cattle, sheep, goats, horses, asses, mules, and hinnies; and semen thereof
	Other animal products: swine, poultry and other live animals; eggs, in shell, natural honey, snails
	Raw milk
	Wool: wool, silk, and other raw animal materials used in textile
Forestry	Forestry, logging and related service activities
Fisheries	Fishing: hunting, trapping and game propagation including related service activities, fishing, fish farms; service activities incidental to fishing
Crude Oil	Parts of extraction of crude petroleum and service activities incidental to oil extraction excl. surveying
Coal	Mining and agglomeration of hard coal, lignite and peat
Gas extraction and distribution	Parts of extraction of natural gas and service activities incidental to gas extraction excl. surveying
	Distribution of gaseous fuels through mains; steam and hot water supply
Electricity	Production, collection and distribution
Petroleum and coal products	Petroleum and coke: coke oven products, refined petroleum products, processing of nuclear fuel
Food products	Cattle meat: fresh or chilled meat and edible offal of cattle, sheep, goats, horses, asses, mules
	Other meat: Pig meat and offal. Preserves and preparations of meat, meat offal or blood, flours
	Vegetable oils: crude and refined oils of soya-bean, maize, olive, sesame, groundnut, olive seeds
	Milk: dairy products
	Processed rice: rice, semi- or wholly milled
	Sugar
	Other food: prepared and preserved fish or vegetables, fruit and vegetable juices, prepared fruits, all cereal flours
	Beverages and tobacco products
Other mining	Mining of metal ores, uranium, gems. other mining and quarrying
Non-ferrous metals	Production and casting of copper, aluminum, zinc, lead, gold, and silver

Table A.1. **ENV-Linkages model sectors and products** (*cont.*)

SECTORS	DESCRIPTION
Iron and steel	Basic production and casting
Chemicals	Basic chemicals, other chemical products, rubber and plastics products
Fabricated metal products	Sheet metal products, but not machinery and equipment
Paper and paper products	Includes publishing, printing and reproduction of recorded media
Non-metallic minerals	Cement, plaster, lime, gravel, concrete
Other manufacturing	Textiles: textiles and man-made fibers
	Wearing apparel: clothing, dressing and dyeing of fur
	Leather: tanning and dressing of leather; luggage, handbags, saddlery, harness and footwear
	Other transport equipment: manufacture of other transport equipment
	Electronic equipment: office, accounting and computing, radio, television and communication equipment
	Other machinery and equipment: electrical machinery, medical, precision and optical, watches
	Other manufacturing: includes recycling
	Motor vehicles: cars, lorries, trailers and semi-trailers
	Lumber: wood and products of wood and cork, except furniture; articles of straw and plaiting materials
Transport services	Water transport
	Air transport
	Other transport: road, rail ; pipelines, auxiliary transport activities; travel agencies
Services	Trade: all retail sales; wholesale trade and commission trade; hotels and restaurants; repairs of motor vehicles and personal and household goods
	Water: collection, purification and distribution
	Retail sale of automotive fuel
	Communications: post and telecommunications
	Other financial intermediation: includes auxiliary activities but not insurance and pension funding
	Insurance: includes pension funding, except compulsory social security
	Other business services: real estate, renting and business activities
	Recreation and other services: recreational, cultural and sporting activities, other service activities; private households with employed persons
	Other services (government): public administration and defense; compulsory social security, education, health and social work, sewage and refuse disposal, sanitation and similar activities, activities of membership organisations n.e.c., extra-territorial organisations and bodies
Construction and dwellings	Construction: building houses factories offices and roads
	Dwellings: ownership of dwellings (imputed rents of houses occupied by owners)

Since it is an economic model, ENV-Linkages does not represent physical processes. Instead, physical processes are summarised from empirically derived relationships between inputs and outputs. That is, industries are observed over time to be able to vary the use of inputs such as labour, capital, energy and materials (see below – *production*).

The core of the model for the base year is formed by a set of Social Account Matrices (SAMs) that describe how economic sectors are linked; these are based on the GTAP database.[2] Many key parameters are based on information drawn from various empirical studies and data sources (see Chateau *et al.*, 2011).

Income generated by economic activity ultimately reflects expenditures on goods and services by consumers (such as households and government). The ENV-Linkages model assumes a representative household that reflects the average household of the region and that allocates their disposable income among consumer goods and savings. They are assumed to base their decisions on static expectations about prices and quantities in the current time period, rather than to have forward-looking behaviour. This means that consumers are saving a proportion of their income and not adjusting that to reflect future events that may affect income. Household consumption, demand and savings are implemented through an "Extended Linear Expenditure System". Since consumers are assumed not to have forward-looking behaviour, some care needs to be exercised in studying policies that consumers may reasonably be expected to anticipate – either the policy itself or its consequences. Investment – net-of-economic depreciation – is equal to the sum of government savings, consumer savings and net capital flows from abroad.

Production in the model is represented using a nested sequence of constant elasticity of substitution (CES) functions (see Figure A.1 for a stylised representation of this structure). Four types of input factors are specified: labour, capital, energy and a sector-specific natural resource (*e.g.* land). Production is assumed to operate under cost minimisation, perfect markets and constant returns to scale technology. The substitutability between inputs means that the intensity of using capital, energy, labour and land changes when their relative price changes: for example, as labour becomes more expensive, less of it is used relative to capital, energy and land. The possibilities to shift away from expensive inputs is however limited. Specific sectors, such as in agriculture or energy production, have an adjusted production function to reflect the specifics of that sector (*e.g.* fertiliser use is linked to land use for crop production).

World trade in ENV-Linkages is based on a set of regional bilateral flows. In each region, total import demand for each good is allocated across trading partners according to the relationship between their export prices. Allocation of trade between partners responds to changes in relative prices between regions. This specification of imports – commonly referred to as the Armington specification – formally implies that each region faces a reduction in demand for its exports if domestic prices increase. Exchange rates between regions adjust to ensure that trade balances are not affected by the policies.

The government in each region collects various kinds of taxes in order to finance government expenditures. For simplicity it is assumed in the *Baseline* that these expenditures grow at the same rate as the real GDP. Assuming a given stream of public savings (or deficits), the government budget is balanced through the adjustment of a lump-sum transfer (tax) to the household.

Market goods equilibrium implies that, on the one side, the total production of any good or service is equal to the demand addressed to domestic producers plus exports; and, on the other side, the total demand is allocated between the demands (both final and intermediary) addressed to domestic producers and the import demand. The general equilibrium framework ensures that a unique set of relative prices emerges such that demand equals supply in all markets simultaneously (*i.e.* across all regions, commodities, and factors of production). All prices are expressed relatively to the *numéraire* of the price system that is chosen as the index of OECD manufacturing exports prices. Implementation of a policy in the model leads to a new equilibration process and thus a new set of equilibrium prices and quantities to compare with the original equilibrium.

The land-based sectors, including three agricultural sectors and forestry, provide direct links to indicators for climate change (*e.g.* emissions from deforestation), biodiversity (*e.g.* land under forest cover) and water. The recently improved **land-use module** of ENV-Linkages is calibrated to mimic land-use relations in the coupled IMAGE-LEITAP models described below. The underlying complexities of the land model in IMAGE, and its detailed links with the agricultural model LEITAP (see below), are approximated in

Figure A.1. **Stylised structure of production in ENV-Linkages**

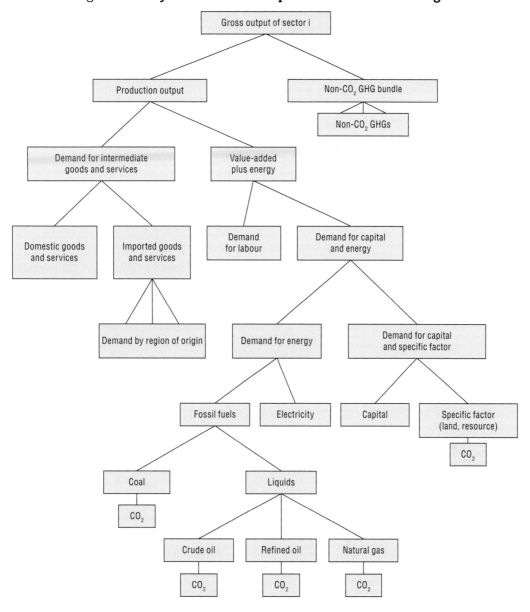

ENV-Linkages in a stylised and aggregated manner where region- and sector-specific elasticities are used to represent the possibilities to change between different land uses, such as transforming grazing land into cropland.

The structure of **energy** inputs in production is of particular interest for analysing climate change and health impacts of local air pollution. In the model, energy is a composite of fossil fuels and electricity. In turn, fossil fuel is a composite of coal and the other fossil fuels (crude oil, refined oil products and gas products). A higher degree of substitution is assumed among the other fuels than with electricity and coal.

CO_2 emissions from the combustion of energy in the model are directly linked to the use of different fuels in production. Other GHG emissions are linked to output. The following non-CO_2 emission sources are considered: *i)* methane from rice cultivation, livestock production (enteric fermentation and manure management), coal mining, crude oil extraction, natural gas and services (landfills); *ii)* nitrous oxide from crops (nitrogenous fertilisers), livestock (manure management), chemicals (non-combustion industrial processes) and services (landfills); *iii)* industrial gases (SF_6, PFCs and HFCs) from chemicals industry (foams, adipic acid, solvents), aluminium, magnesium and semi-conductors production. These emissions are calibrated with historical data collected by the International Energy Agency (IEA, 2010a). For non-CO_2 GHGs data the IEA relies on the EDGAR 4.1 database developed by PBL. For projections of future non-CO_2 emissions and for allocation of different sources to activities by the different economic sectors the model uses information provided by the United States Environmental Protection Agency.

How is the model used to make projections?

ENV-Linkages uses a complex approach for its projections. Unlike models which assume that the economy is on a steady-state growth path, it is able to produce more realistic patterns of the major variables over the model horizon.

The process of calibrating the ENV-Linkages model is broken down into three stages (*cf.* Chateau *et al.*, 2012):

i)   A number of parameters are calibrated to represent the data for 2004 as an initial economic equilibrium. This process is referred to as the static calibration.

ii) The 2004 database is updated to 2007 by simulating the model dynamically to match historical trends over this period. Price levels are further adjusted such that all values in the model reflect 2010 real USD using purchasing power parities provided by the IMF.

iii) The *Baseline* projection for the model horizon 2008-2050 is based on conditional convergence assumptions about labour productivity and other socio-economic drivers (demographic trends, future trends in energy prices and energy efficiency improvements; see Duval and de la Maissonneuve, 2009). These convergence assumptions are used to identify the evolution of key economic and environmental variables.

iv) The *Baseline* projection is then obtained by running the model dynamically over the period 2007-2050, keeping these key variables exogenous but letting the model parameters adjust endogenously. Thus, the model parameters are calibrated using the structural relations of the model (production functions, household preferences, etc.) to mimic the evolution of the key variables over time. It should be emphasised that when the policy simulations are performed on this calibrated baseline, the model parameters are exogenously fixed, while the model variables are fully endogenous. For instance, while GDP is exogenous in the *Baseline* projection, it becomes fully endogenous in policy simulations.

The *Baseline* has been adjusted to incorporate the effects of the economic crisis of 2008-2009 and medium-term projections made by the World Bank (2010), IMF (2010) and OECD (2010). Note that while the *Baseline* assumes no new policies for the environmental issues addressed in the *Outlook*, it does include the energy policies listed in the reference (current policies) energy projections of the IEA (2009a&b; 2010b). It also assumes that the EU Emission Trading System (EU-ETS) is implemented between 2006 and 2012, with a permit price that would rise gradually from 5 to 25 constant USD by 2012 and is not extended thereafter.[3]

The IMAGE model suite[4]

The scenarios and projections for the *OECD Environmental Outlook* are the result of an integrated analysis of the economy-environment interface. The previous section has described the economic modelling (ENV-Linkages). IMAGE is the central tool for the environmental analysis. Data on economic activities described by ENV-Linkages steer the IMAGE framework, which is a suite of related models connected through harmonised dataflows (Figure A.2).

IMAGE is a dynamic integrated assessment framework to model global change. It was developed at the National Institute for Public Health and the Environment (RIVM) in the Netherlands initially to assess the impact of anthropogenic climate change (Rotmans, 1990). Later it was extended to include a more comprehensive coverage of global change issues (IMAGE team, 2001). The main objectives of IMAGE today are to contribute to scientific understanding and support decision making by quantifying the relative importance of major processes and interactions in the society-biosphere-climate system.

The IMAGE framework operates at a resolution of 24/26 world regions (see Table 1.3 in Chapter 1) for most socio-economic parameters, and a geographical 0.5 × 0.5 degree[5] grid for land use and environmental parameters. This medium level of complexity allows analyses to take into account key characteristics of the physical world (*e.g.* local soil and climate characteristics of technology detail) without excessive calculation times. The central box in Figure A.2 contains the core IMAGE model framework used for this *OECD Environmental Outlook*. The current version is IMAGE 2.5, a further development of IMAGE version 2.4, documented in Bouwman *et al.* (2006).

In addition to the simple one-dimensional relationship between economic driving forces and changes in the environment, the physical flows of energy and the availability of land are important drivers and sometimes limiting factors to developments in the environment. In this *Outlook,* the latter have been taken explicitly into account and these two groups of variables have a central position in the modelling framework: next to the link from the economic modelling in ENV-Linkages to IMAGE, energy use is modelled in detail in the TIMER model (Targets IMage Energy Regional Model), which looks at regional energy consumption, energy efficiency improvements, fuel substitution, supply and trade of fossil fuels and renewable energy technologies. It also computes emissions of GHGs, ozone precursors and acidifying compounds (see below). Land-use factors (agricultural demand, production and trade) are processed through the LEITAP model (discussed further below).

Some of the models in Figure A.2 are described elsewhere in the *Outlook,* for example see Annex 6.A in Chapter 6 on Health and Environment for more on the GISMO model for health aspects of quality-of-life, and the GUAM and REMG models for outdoor and indoor air quality.

Land and climate

An important aspect of the IMAGE model is the geographically explicit description of land use and land-cover change. The model distinguishes 14 natural and forest land-cover types and 6 man-made land-cover types. IMAGE's land and climate module computes land-use changes based on regional production of food, animal feed, fodder, grass and timber, and changes in natural vegetation due to climate change. This also allows emissions and carbon exchange from land-use changes, natural ecosystems and agricultural production systems to be calculated. The Atmospheric Ocean System then

Figure A.2. **Overview of the IMAGE model suite**

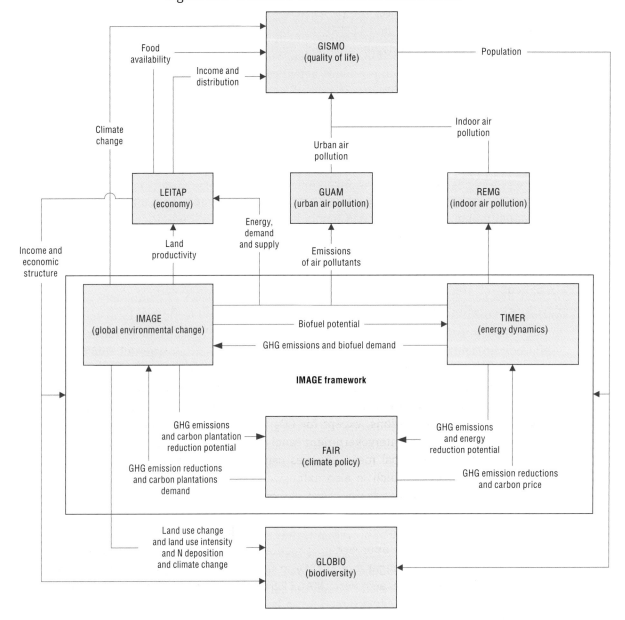

computes changes in atmospheric composition and climate using these emissions, and the emissions from the TIMER model.

The land-use model describes both crop and livestock systems on the basis of agricultural demand, demand for food and feed crops, animal products, energy crops and forestry products. A crop module based on the FAO agro-ecological zones approach (FAO, 1978-1981) computes the spatially explicit yields of the different crop groups and pasture, and the areas used for their production, as determined by climate and soil quality. Where expansion of agricultural land is required, a rule-based "suitability map" determines the order by which grid cells get selected on the basis of the grid cell's potential crop yield, its proximity to other agricultural areas, to water bodies and to human settlements. An initial land-use map for 1970 is incorporated on the basis of satellite observations combined with statistical information. For the period 1970-2000, the model is calibrated to be fully consistent with FAO statistics. For the period 2001-2050 the simulations are driven by the input from the TIMER model and LEITAP, and by additional scenario assumptions, for example on technology development, yield improvements and efficiency of animal production systems.

Changes in natural vegetation cover are simulated in IMAGE 2.5 on the basis of a modified version of the BIOME natural vegetation model (Prentice *et al.*, 1992). This model computes changes in potential vegetation for 14 biome types on the basis of climate characteristics. The potential vegetation is the equilibrium vegetation that should eventually develop under a given climate.

The consequences of land use and land-cover changes for the carbon cycle are simulated by a geographically explicit terrestrial carbon cycle model. This simulates global and regional carbon pools and fluxes (pools include the living vegetation, and several stocks of carbon stored in soils). The model accounts for important feedback mechanisms related to changing climate (*e.g.* different growth characteristics), carbon dioxide concentrations (carbon fertilisation) and land use (*e.g.* conversion of natural vegetation into agricultural land or *vice versa*). In addition, it allows for an evaluation of the potential for carbon sequestration by natural vegetation and carbon plantations.

The carbon cycle model also describes the carbon included in the atmospheric and ocean systems, the fluxes between these systems, and their subsequent effect on atmospheric GHG concentrations and thus climate change (van Minnen *et al.*, 2000).

The emissions of GHGs and air pollutants are used in IMAGE to calculate changes in the concentrations of GHGs, ozone precursors and species involved in aerosol formation at a global scale. These calculations, except for CO_2 (see carbon cycle), are based on the 4th Assessment Report of the Intergovernment Panel on Climate Change (IPCC). Changes in climate are calculated as global mean changes using a slightly adapted version of the MAGICC 6.0 climate model which is also extensively used by the IPCC (Schaeffer and Stehfest, 2010). Climatic changes do not manifest themselves uniformly over the globe, and patterns of temperature and precipitation change differ between different climate models. Hence changes in temperature and precipitation in each 0.5×0.5 degree grid cell are differentiated using the IPCC approach to produce global patterns. This includes the approach proposed by Schlesinger *et al.*, (2000) to account for the regional temperature effect of short-lived sulphate aerosols. IMAGE 2.5 uses temperature and precipitation projections from the HadCM2 climate model run by the UK's Meteorological Office (data obtained from the IPCC Data Distribution Centre).

Water stress

Recently, the IMAGE land and climate model has been extended by coupling with the LPJmL (Lund--Potsdam-Jena managed Land) model to better simulate the global terrestrial carbon cycle and natural vegetation distribution. It also includes a global hydrological model and improved crop modelling (Bouwman *et al.*, 2006). The LPJmL model, having started life as a dynamic global vegetation model (Sitch *et al.*, 2003), has since been extended to include managed land (Bondeau *et al.*, 2007) and the hydrological cycle (Gerten *et al.*, 2004). For this *Outlook*, IMAGE 2.5 was used without the coupled LPJmL model. However, for the water stress analysis (Chapter 5) LPJmL was used as a stand-alone model.

LPJmL's hydrological model has been validated against discharge observations for 300 river basins worldwide (Biemans *et al.*, 2009) and against irrigation water use and consumption (Rost *et al.*, 2008). By linking with the LPJmL hydrological model, IMAGE scenarios now also model future changes in water availability, agricultural water use and an indicator for water stress. Water availability in the form of renewable water supply is computed by the hydrology module of the LPJmL model, although water in deep aquifers is not considered. LPJmL also estimates the water demand for irrigation, starting from the gap between precipitation surplus and potential evapotranspiration for the crop type(s) grown on irrigated land (for more information, see the Annex 5.A to Chapter 5). Current demand for other sectors (households, manufacturing, electricity and livestock) is adopted from the WaterGAP model calculations for the *OECD Environmental Outlook to 2030* (OECD, 2008). The 2008 WaterGAP projection was only adjusted for differences in development of key drivers from the 2008 Outlook, such as industrial value added and (thermal) electricity production by fuel as projected with IMAGE-TIMER.

Agricultural land supply and use[6]

Land-use factors in IMAGE are processed through the LEITAP model to give sectoral production growth rates, land-use change and the degree of intensification resulting from endogenous technological improvement estimated by FAO (Bruinsma, 2003) and other endogenous factors.

The LEITAP model is a multi-regional, multi-sectoral, static, applied general equilibrium model based on neo-classical microeconomic theory (Nowicki *et al.*, 2006 and van Meijl *et al.*, 2006). It allows for the substitution of different primary production factors (land, labour, capital and natural resources) and intermediate production factors (*e.g.* energy and animal feed components). It also allows for substitution between different energy sources, including biofuels (Banse *et al.*, 2008) and their by-products. Regional land supply curves in LEITAP represent the total area available for agriculture, in the order of the degree of suitability according to the IMAGE allocation rules. IMAGE also makes scenario-specific assumptions about the breakdown of livestock production over different systems, with consequences for feed composition, land conversion and overall productivity.

To model biofuels use in the fuel production, the GTAP-E model (Burniaux and Truong, 2002) was adopted and applied to the petrol sector, which allows for substitution between crude oil, ethanol and biodiesel. The nested CES structure of GTAP-E implies that biofuel demand is determined by the relative price of crude oil *versus* ethanol and biodiesel, including taxes and subsidies. Substitution between the different fuels is assumed to be almost perfect.

Regional endowments of labour, capital and natural resources are fixed and fully employed and land supply is modelled by land supply curves (Eickhout *et al.*, 2008), which specify the relationship between land supply and a land rental rate. The regional land-supply curves determine how additional outputs are met by a combination of land expansion and intensity of land use. Labour is divided into two categories: skilled and unskilled. These categories are considered imperfect substitutes in the production process. Land and natural resources are heterogeneous production factors, and this heterogeneity is introduced by a constant elasticity of transformation (CET) function which allocates these production factors among the agricultural sectors. Capital and labour markets are segmented between agriculture and non-agriculture. Labour and capital are assumed to be fully mobile within each of these two groups of sectors, but imperfectly mobile across them.

Energy[7]

The global energy system model TIMER (Targets IMage Energy Regional Model) has been developed to simulate long-term energy baseline and climate mitigation scenarios. The model describes the investments in, and the use of, different types of energy options influenced by technology development and resource depletion. Inputs to the model are macroeconomic scenarios and assumptions about technology development, preference levels and restrictions to fuel trade from ENV-Linkages. The output of the model demonstrates how energy intensity, fuel costs and competing non-fossil supply technologies develop over time. It generates primary and final energy consumption by energy type, sector and region; capacity build-up and use; cost indicators; and GHG and other emissions.

In TIMER, implementation of mitigation is generally modeled on the basis of price signals (a tax on carbon dioxide). A carbon tax (used as a generic measure of climate policy) induces additional investments in energy efficiency, fossil fuel substitution, and investments in bioenergy, nuclear power, solar power, wind power and carbon capture and storage. Selection of options throughout the model is based on a multinomial logic model that assigns market shares on the basis of production costs and preferences (cheaper, more attractive options get a larger market share; but there is no full optimisation) (de Vries *et al.*, 2001).

The TIMER model describes the chain from demand for energy services (useful energy) to the supply of energy by different primary energy sources and related emissions. The steps are connected by demand for energy (from left to right) and by feedbacks, mainly in the form of energy prices (from right to left). The TIMER model has three types of submodels: *i)* the energy demand model; *ii)* models for energy conversion (electricity and hydrogen production), and *iii)* models for primary energy supply.

International climate policy regimes[8]

The policy decision-support tool Framework to Assess International Regimes for the differentiation of commitments (FAIR) has been developed to explore the environmental and abatement cost implications of various international regimes and commitments for meeting long-term climate targets, such as stabilisation of the atmospheric GHG concentrations (den Elzen *et al.*, 2005).

The FAIR model consists of three linked models:

- A climate model: calculates the climate impacts of global emission profiles and emission scenarios, and determines the global emission reduction objective as the difference between the baseline emissions scenario and a global emission profile for a given climate policy.

- An emission allocation model: calculates the regional GHG emission allowances for different regimes to differentiate future commitments within the context of the global reduction objective from the climate model.

- An abatement costs model: calculates the regional abatement costs and emission levels after trading, on the basis of the emission allowances coming from the emission allocation model following a least-cost approach. The model makes full use of the flexible Kyoto mechanisms as emissions trading and substitution of reductions between the different gases and sources.

The model calculations are done at the level of 24/26 IMAGE world regions. The GHG emissions of the six GHGs specified in the Kyoto Protocol are converted to carbon dioxide equivalent (see Chapter 3), *i.e.* the sum of the global warming potential weighted emissions. Various data sets of historical emissions, baseline scenarios, emission profiles and marginal abatement cost curves are included in the model framework to assess the sensitivity of the outcomes to variation in these key inputs.

In recent years a range of extensions and enhancements have been implemented in FAIR in accord with new proposals for global architectures for post-Kyoto agreements. In particular the so-called Copenhagen pledges are implemented and analysed for their expected outcome, recognising the uncertainties contained within the commitments made by parties in their pledges (den Elzen *et al.*, 2010).

Biodiversity

Terrestrial biodiversity[9]

The GLOBIO model,[10] including GLOBIO-aquatic, was used to calculate changes in MSA (mean species abundance). The MSA indicator maps the compound effect of drivers of biodiversity loss, and uses a suite of direct and indirect drivers provided by IMAGE in conjunction with an economic model LEITAP (see Chapter 4). The compound effect on biodiversity is computed with the GLOBIO3 model for terrestrial ecosystems (Alkemade *et al.*, 2009) (and recently also for freshwater systems; see below). In addition, the future pathway of direct and indirect drivers depends on a variety of socio-economic assumptions, technological developments and policy assumptions, which are represented in the IMAGE and GTAP. As the IMAGE and the GLOBIO3 are spatially explicit, the impacts on MSA can be analysed by region, main biome and pressure factor.

GLOBIO3 takes into account the impacts of climate and land-use change, ecosystem fragmentation, expansion of infrastructure such as roads and built-up areas, deposition of acidity and reactive nitrogen.

For projections into the future, the underlying assumption is that higher pressures on biodiversity lead to lower MSA. The GLOBIO3 model contains global cause-effect relationships between each of the pressure factors considered and mean species abundance, based on more than 700 publications. These are applied in a spatially explicit fashion, namely grid cells of 0.5×0.5 degree longitude × latitude, with a frequency distribution representing the occurrence of various biomes within each cell. The effects of the considered pressure values are calculated and combined per grid cell to obtain an overall MSA score. The MSA per region or for the world is the uniformly weighted sum over the underlying grid cells. In other words, each square kilometre of every biome is weighted as equal (ten Brink, 2000).

Aquatic (freshwater) biodiversity

The driving forces of pressures on inland aquatic ecosystems included in the current version of GLOBIO are land-use changes in the catchment, eutrophication by phosphorus and nitrogen, and flow changes due to water abstraction or river damming.

Like the terrestrial model, the cause-effect relationships are based on a review of existing data in the literature on species composition as a function of different degrees of pressure (Weijters et al., 2009; Alkemade et al., 2011). Biodiversity was again expressed as the abundance of the original species relative to the pristine state, or a proxy for that. Separate analyses were made for shallow and deep lakes (as a function of phosphorus and nitrogen concentrations), wetlands (dependent on human land use) and rivers (dependent on both human land use and deviation from the natural flow regime). The effects of different pressures (if applicable) are assumed to be independent and hence multiplied. For lakes, the probability of the occurrence of harmful algal blooms is also calculated.

Nutrients

The Global Nutrient Model describes the fate of nitrogen (N) and phosphorus (P) emerging from more concentrated or point sources such as human settlements, and from dispersed or non-point sources such as agricultural and natural land. Through rivers and lakes, the remaining nutrient load eventually enters into coastal water bodies. Below, the main steps involved with N are presented (and see Chapter 5 for more).

Point sources

A conceptual relationship of per capita N emission and per-capita income was used to calculate urban wastewater N discharge (modified from van Drecht et al., 2003; Bouwman et al., 2005). The N emission is calculated as an annual mean per capita and country as a function of food intake. Low-income countries have per capita N emissions of about 10g per day and industrialised countries are between 15 g and 18 g per day.

The amount of N that is actually discharged to surface water is calculated as a function of the N emission, the rate of removal in wastewater treatment plants (expressed as a fraction of the N emission in raw wastewater), and the fraction of the total population connected to public sewerage systems. In this approach, wastewater N emissions from rural populations are excluded and coastal areas with direct discharge to the sea are not accounted for.

Different types of wastewater treatment with varying removal rates are distinguished for the removal of nitrogen: no treatment, mechanical, biological and advanced treatment; see also the Annex to the Freshwater Chapter.

Non-point sources

Each IMAGE agricultural grid cell is divided into four aggregate agricultural land uses: grassland, wetland rice, leguminous crops (pulses, soybeans) and other upland crops. The annual surface nitrogen balance includes the nitrogen inputs and outputs for each land-use type. Nitrogen inputs include biological nitrogen fixation, atmospheric nitrogen deposition, application of synthetic nitrogen fertiliser and animal manure. Outputs in the surface nitrogen balance include nitrogen removal from the field by crop harvesting, hay and grass-cutting, and grass consumption by grazing animals. The surplus of the surface nitrogen balance is calculated from these components. The different input and output terms of the surface balance are discussed in detail in various publications (Bouwman et al., 2005, Bouwman et al., 2006 and Bouwman et al., 2011).

The groundwater flowing into draining surface water is a mixture of water flows with varying residence times in the groundwater system. The nitrate concentration in groundwater depends on the residence time of water infiltration into the saturated zone and the denitrification loss during its transport. Two groundwater subsystems are distinguished in the model: *i)* rapid transport of nitrate in surface run-off and flow through shallow groundwater to local water courses; and *ii)* slow transport through deep groundwater towards larger streams and rivers.

River nitrogen transport

The total nitrogen from point sources, direct atmospheric deposition and nitrate flows from shallow and deep groundwater act as the input to the surface water within each grid cell. In-stream metabolic processes remove nitrogen from the stream water by transferring it to the biota, the atmosphere or stream sediments. A global river-export coefficient of 0.7 (implying retention and loss of 30% of the nitrogen discharged to streams and rivers) is used, which represents a mean of a wide variety of river basins in Europe and the United States (van Drecht *et al.*, 2003).

Notes

1. A technical description of the OECD ENV-Linkages model, as well as other recent publications based on the model, can be found on *www.oecd.org/environment/modelling*.

2. The GTAP (Global Trade Analysis Project) global economic database describes bilateral trade patterns, production, consumption and intermediate use of commodities and services. There are satellite databases for such things as GHG emissions, and land use. GTAP version 7.1 (GTAP, 2008) is used for this *Outlook's Baseline* scenario.

3. Note that all policy simulations carried out for the *Environmental Outlook* assume continuation of the EU-ETS until 2020. This way, the costs of the policies are explicitly represented in the simulations.

4. See *http://themasites.pbl.nl/en/themasites/image/index.html*.

5. Degrees in terms of latitude and longitude on the Earth's surface.

6. For more detail in LEITAP, see Kram and Stehfest (2012).

7. The TIMER model has been described in various documents (de Vries *et al.*, 2001; van Vuuren, 2007). See: *http://themasites.pbl.nl/en/themasites/image/model_details/energy_supply_demand/index.html*.

8. For more see *http://themasites.pbl.nl/en/themasites/fair/index.html*.

9. For more on the GLOBIO model, the MSA indicator and the relationship with environmental pressures, see Alkemade *et al.* (2009) and *www.globio.info*.

10. The GLOBIO model is a joint venture between the Netherlands Environmental Assessment Agency, the UNEP World Conservation Monitoring Centre in Cambridge (UK) and the UNEP GRID-Arendal Centre.

References

Alkemade, R., M.van Oorschot, L. Miles, C. Nellemann, M. Bakkenes, B. ten Brink (2009), "GLOBIO 3: A Framework to Investigate Options for Reducing Global Terrestrial Biodiversity Loss", *Ecosystems, Volume 12, Number 3*, 374-390, doi: *http://dx.doi.org/10.1007/s10021-009-9229-5*.

Alkemade, R., J. Janse, W. van Rooij, Y. Trisurat (2011), "Applying GLOBIO at different geographical levels" in: Trisurat, Y., R. Shrestha, R. Alkemade (eds.), *Land use, climate change and biodiversity modelling*, IGI Global, Hershey PA, USA.

Banse, M., H. van Meijl, A. Tabeau, and G. Woltjer (2008), "Will EU Biofuel Policies Affect Global Agricultural Markets?", *European Review of Agricultural Economics*, 35(2):117-141.

Biemans, H., R. Hutjes, P. Kabat, B. Strengers, D. Gerten, S. Rost (2009), "Effects of Precipitation Uncertainty on Discharge Calculations for Main River Basins", *J. Hydrometeor*, 10, 1011-1025, doi: *http://dx.doi.org/10.1175/2008JHM1067.1*.

Bondeau, A., P.C. Smith, S. Zaehle, S. Schaphoff, W. Lucht, W. Cramer, D. Gerten, H. Lotze-Campen, C. Müller, M. Reichstein and B. Smith (2007), "Modelling the role of agriculture for the 20th century global terrestrial carbon balance", *Global Change Biology*, 13: 679-706, doi: *http://dx.doi.org/10.1111/j.1365-2486.2006.01305.x*.

Bouwman, A.F., K. Klein Goldewijk, K.W. van der Hoek, A.H.W. Beusen, D.P. van Vuuren, W. J. Willems, M. C. Rufino, E. Stehfest (2011), "Exploring global changes in nitrogen and phosphorus cycles in agriculture induced by livestock production over the 1900-2050 period", Proceedings of the National Academy of Sciences of the United States of America, *http://dx.doi.org/10.1073/pnas.1012878108*.

Bouwman, A.F., T. Kram and K. Klein Goldewijk (eds.) (2006), *Integrated Modelling of Global Environmental Change. An Overview of IMAGE 2.4*, PBL Netherlands Environmental Assessment Agency, The Hague/Bilthoven.

Bouwman, A.F., G. van Drecht, K.W. van der Hoek (2005), "Surface N balances and reactive N loss to the environment from intensive agricultural production systems for the period 1970-2030", *Science in China Series C. Life Sciences*, 48(Suppl): 1-13.

Brink, B.J.E. ten (2000), "Biodiversity Indicators for the OECD Environmental Outlook and Strategy, a Feasibility Study", RIVM National Institute for Public Health and the Environment, in co-operation with WCMC, Cambridge/Bilthoven.

Bruinsma, J.E. (2003), *World agriculture: towards 2015/2030. An FAO perspective*, Earthscan, London.

Burniaux, J., G. Nicoletti, and J. Oliveira Martins (1992), "GREEN: A Global Model for Quantifying the Costs of Policies to Curb CO2 Emissions", *OECD Economic Studies*, 19 (Winter).

Burniaux, J., T.P. Truong (2002), "GTAP-E: an Energy–Environmental Version of the GTAP model,"*GTAP Technical Paper*, No. 16. Revised Version, Center for Global Trade Analysis, Purdue University.

Burniaux, J., J. Chateau, and R. Duval (2010), "Is there a Case for Carbon-Based Border Tax Adjustment?: An Applied General Equilibrium Analysis", *OECD Economics Department Working Papers*, No. 794, OECD Publishing, doi: *10.1787/5kmbjhcqqk0r-en*.

Burniaux, J. and J. Chateau (2011), "Mitigation Potential of Removing Fossil Fuel Subsidies: A General Equilibrium Assessment", *OECD Economics Department Working Papers*, No. 853, OECD Publishing, doi: *10.1787/5kgdx1jr2plp-en*.

Chateau, J., C. Rebolledo, R. Dellink (2011), "The ENV-Linkages economic baseline projections to 2050", *OECD Environment Working Papers*, No. 41, OECD Publishing.

Chateau, J., R. Dellink, E. Lanzi, and B. Magne (2012), "An overview of the ENV-Linkages Model, version 3", *OECD Environment Working Paper,* No. 2, OECD Publishing.

Dellink, R., S, Jamet, J. Chateau, R. Duval (2010a), "Towards Global Carbon Pricing: Direct and Indirect Linking of Carbon Markets", *OECD Environment Working Papers*, No. 20, OECD Publishing. doi: *10.1787/5km975t0cfr8-en*.

Dellink, R., G. Briner and C. Clapp (2010b), "Costs, Revenues, and Effectiveness of the Copenhagen Accord Emission Pledges for 2020", *OECD Environment Working Papers*, No. 22, OECD Publishing. doi: *10.1787/5km975plmzg6-en*.

Drecht, G. van, A. F. Bouwman, J.M. Knoop, A.H. W. Beusen, and C.R. Meinardi (2003), "Global modeling of the fate of nitrogen from point and nonpoint sources in soils, groundwater and surface water", *Global Biogeochemical Cycles*, 17(4): 26-1 to 26-20 (1115, doi: 10.1029/2003GB002060).

Duval, R. and C. de la Maisonneuve (2009), "Long-Run GDP Growth Scenarios for the World Economy", *OECD Economics Department Working Papers,* No. 663, February 2009, doi: *10.1787/227205684023*.

Eickhout, B., G.J. van den Born, J. Notenboom, M. van Oorschot, J.P. M Ros, D.P. van Vuuren and H. J. Westhoek (2008), *Local and Global Consequences of the EU Renewable Directive for Biofuels: Testing the Sustainability Criteria*, MNP Report 500143001/2008.

Elzen, M. den and P.L. Lucas (2005), "The FAIR model: A tool to analyse environmental and costs implications of regimes of future commitments", *Environmental Modeling and Assessment*, Volume 10, Number 2, 115-134, doi: *http://dx.doi.org/10.1007/s10666-005-4647-z*

Elzen, M. den and N. Höhne (2010), "Sharing the reduction effort to limit global warming to 2 °C", *Climate Policy*, Volume 10, Number 3, 2010 , pp. 247-260(14).

FAO (1978-81), "Report on the agro-ecological zones project", *World Soil Resources Report 48*, FAO, Rome.

GTAP (2008), "Global Trade, Assistance, and Production: The GTAP 7 Data Base", Narayanan, B. and T. Walmsey (ed.), Center for Global Trade Analysis, Dpt. of Agricultural Economics, Purdue University.

Gerten, D., S. Schaphoff, U. Haberlandt, W. Lucht, S. Sitch (2004), "Terrestrial vegetation and water balance: hydrological evaluation of a dynamic global vegetation model", *Journal of Hydrology 286*: 249-270.

Hertel, T.W. (ed.) (1997), *Global Trade Analysis: Modeling and Applications*, Cambridge University Press.

International Energy Agency (2009a), *World Energy Outlook 2009*, OECD Publishing, doi: *10.1787/weo-2009-en*.

International Energy Agency (2009b), *Energy Technology Perspectives 2010: Scenarios and Strategies to 2050*, OECD Publishing, doi: *10.1787/energy_tech-2010-en*.

International Energy Agency (2010a), CO_2 *Emissions from Fuel Combustion 2010*, OECD Publishing, doi: *10.1787/9789264096134-en*.

International Energy Agency (2010b), *World Energy Outlook 2010*, OECD Publishing, doi: *10.1787/weo-2010-en*.

IEA, OPEC, OECD, World Bank (2010), "Analysis of the Scope of Energy Subsidies and Suggestions for the G-2) initiative", Joint Report prepared for submission to the G-20 Meeting of the Finance Ministers and Central Bank Governors, Busan (Korea), 5 June 2010, 26 May 2010.

IMAGE Team (2001), *The IMAGE 2.2 Implementation of the SRES Scenarios. A Comprehensive Analysis of Emissions, Climate Change and Impacts in the 21st Century* (RIVM CD-ROM publication 481508018), National Institute for Public Health and the Environment, Bilthoven

IMF (2010), "World Economic Outlook Database", *www.imf.org/external/pubs/ft/weo/2010/02/weodata/index.aspx*.

Kram, T. and E.E. Stehfest (2012), "The IMAGE Model Suite used for the OECD Environmental Outlook to 2050", PBL Netherlands Environmental Assessment Agency report 500113002, The Hague/ Bilthoven, the Netherlands.

Meijl, H. van, T. van Rheenen, A. Tabeau, B. Eickhout (2006), "The Impact of Different Policy Environments on Agricultural Land Use in Europe", *Agriculture, Ecosystems and Environment* 114:21-38

Minnen, J. van and R. Leemans (2000), "Defining the Importance of Including Transient Ecosystem Responses to Simulate C-cycle Dynamics in a Global Change Model", *Global Change Biology*, 6:595-612.

Nowicki, P., H. van Meijl, A. Knierim, M. Banse, J. Helming, O. Margraf, B. Matzdorf, R. Mnatsakanian, M. Reutter, I. Terluin, K. Overmars, C. Verhoog, C. Weeger, H. Westhoek (2006), "Scenar 2020 – Scenario study on agriculture and the rural world", European Commission, Directorate-General Agriculture and Rural Development, Brussels.

OECD (2008), *OECD Environmental Outlook to 2030*, OECD Publishing, doi: *10.1787/9789264040519-en*.

OECD (2009), *The Economics of Climate Change Mitigation: Policies and Options for Global Action beyond 2012*, OECD Publishing, doi: *10.1787/9789264073616-en*.

OECD (2010), "OECD Economic Outlook No. 88", *OECD Economic Outlook: Statistics and Projections* (database), doi: *10.1787/data-00533-en*.

Prentice, I.C. *et al.* (1992), "A global biome model based on plant physiology and dominance, soil properties and climate", *Journal of Biogeography*, 19:117-134.

Rost, S., D. Gerten, U. Heyder (2008), "Human alterations of the terrestrial water cycle through land management", *Advances in Geosciences*, 18, 43-50.

Rotmans, J. (1990), *IMAGE. An Integrated Model to Assess the Greenhouse Effect*, Kluwer Academic Publishers, Dordrecht.

Schaeffer, M. and E. Stehfest (2010), *The climate subsystem in IMAGE updated to MAGICC 6.0*, PBL report 500110005, PBL Netherlands Environmental Assessment Agency, The Hague/Bilthoven, June 2010.

Schlesinger, M.E. *et al.* (2000), "Geographical Distributions of Temperature Change for Scenarios of Greenhouse Gas and Sulphur Dioxide Emissions", *Technological Forecasting and Social Change* 65, 167-193.

Shiklomanov, I. (2000), "Appraisal and Assessment of World Water Resources", *Water International*, 25(1), pp. 11-32.

Sitch, S., B. Smith, I.C. Prentice, A. Arneth, A. Bondeau, W. Cramer, J.O. Kaplan, S. Levis, W. Lucht, M.T. Sykes, K. Thonicke, S. Venevsky (2003), "Evaluation of ecosystem dynamics, plant geography and terrestrial carbon cycling in the LPJ dynamic global vegetation model", *Global Change Biology, Volume 9, Issue 2,* pages 161-185, February 2003, doi: *http://dx.doi.org/10.1046/j.1365-2486.2003.00569.x*

Vries, H.J.M. de *et al.* (2001), *The Timer IMage Energy Regional (TIMER) Model*, National Institute for Public Health and the Environment (RIVM), Bilthoven.

Vuuren, D.P. van (2007), "Energy Systems and Climate Policy", PhD thesis, Utrecht University.

Weijters, M.J., J.H. Janse, R. Alkemade and J.T.A. Verhoeven (2009), "Quantifying the effect of catchment land-use and water nutrient concentrations on freshwater river and stream biodiversity", Aquat. Cons.: Mar. Freshw. *Ecosyst.* 19: 104-112.

World Bank (2010), "World Development Indicators", *http://data.worldbank.org/data-catalog/world-development-indicators.*

ORGANISATION FOR ECONOMIC CO-OPERATION AND DEVELOPMENT

The OECD is a unique forum where governments work together to address the economic, social and environmental challenges of globalisation. The OECD is also at the forefront of efforts to understand and to help governments respond to new developments and concerns, such as corporate governance, the information economy and the challenges of an ageing population. The Organisation provides a setting where governments can compare policy experiences, seek answers to common problems, identify good practice and work to co-ordinate domestic and international policies.

The OECD member countries are: Australia, Austria, Belgium, Canada, Chile, the Czech Republic, Denmark, Estonia, Finland, France, Germany, Greece, Hungary, Iceland, Ireland, Israel, Italy, Japan, Korea, Luxembourg, Mexico, the Netherlands, New Zealand, Norway, Poland, Portugal, the Slovak Republic, Slovenia, Spain, Sweden, Switzerland, Turkey, the United Kingdom and the United States. The European Union takes part in the work of the OECD.

OECD Publishing disseminates widely the results of the Organisation's statistics gathering and research on economic, social and environmental issues, as well as the conventions, guidelines and standards agreed by its members.

OECD PUBLISHING, 2, rue André-Pascal, 75775 PARIS CEDEX 16
(97 2012 01 1P) ISBN 978-92-64-12216-1 – No. 59031 2012-08